NOW TAKING THE FIELD

Baseball's All-Time Dream Teams
for All 30 Franchises

Tom Stone

Now Taking the Field
Baseball's All-Time Dream Teams for All 30 Franchises

Copyright © 2019 by Thomas Stone

Published by ACTA Sports, a division of ACTA Publications
4848 N. Clark Street, Chicago, IL 60077 (800) 397-2282
www.actasports.com

Typeset by Courter & Company

Library of Congress Catalog Number: 2018912321
ISBN: 978-0-87946-666-4
Printed in the USA by Total Printing Systems
Year 30 29 28 27 26 25 24 23 22 21 20 19
Printing 15 14 13 12 11 10 9 8 7 6 5 4

"Baseball fans will find Tom Stone's book among the most interesting they have read. His exhaustive research brings to us a treasure chest of information, allowing us to see how the use of modern metrics can facilitate the comparison of each team's best players across the decades. ... This volume joins Bill James' Historical Baseball Abstract and a few other books of its genre on an accessible bookshelf."

—Bill Brown, Broadcaster for Cincinnati and Houston for 37 years

"Mantle or DiMaggio? Campanella or Piazza? Cedeno or Wynn? Tom Stone ends every old baseball argument—and starts new ones—in a guide that is as breezy to read as it is meticulously researched. You will lose yourself in pages that bring the histories of 30 franchises to life, and go willingly. This is the joy of *Now Taking the Field*, a massive undertaking executed with style and substance. Mantle or DiMaggio? Hmm. Both?"

—Tim Brown, National baseball writer for Yahoo Sports and *New York Times* bestseller author

"Tom Stone did incredible research with this book which provides a wondrous history and ranking of the top players and managers on each major league team over the past many years and decades. They aren't just recent players—some go back more than 100 years—which makes the book all that more interesting. I was very impressed with his picks, all of whom deserve their spots. You'll love reading his list for your favorite team—as well as those of others (even the rival teams you may hate.)"

—Jim Caple, Former longtime writer for ESPN who has covered baseball for more than 30 years

"Stone takes a look at each franchise's history through a unique lens, spanning the generations by using modern-day metrics. This takes the classic baseball bar room debate to the next level."

—Mark Feinsand, MLB.com Executive Reporter

"As a broadcaster and baseball fan for nearly 40 years, it's my great pleasure to endorse this wonderful book, *Now Taking the Field*. I was actually the Orioles batboy when many players from the great Oriole teams in the 70's, Brooks and Frank Robinson, Jim Palmer, Boog Powell and many others were dominating the sport. I had also great professional relationships with Cal Ripken Jr., Eddie Murray and Earl Weaver. ... I found this book fascinating and compelling and a must for any baseball fan. 5 stars!!"

—Roy Firestone, 7-Time Emmy Award Winner with ESPN

"The only thing that dedicated baseball fans like more than a good argument is having 30 good arguments. Tom Stone presents his studious case for every franchise's all-time team, which no doubt will spark many lively conversations and inspire a lot of interesting thought."

—Mark Herrmann, *Newsday* columnist

"What a great concept. A book that is guaranteed to generate arguments from fans of every major-league team! That is what Tom Stone has done in his new book *Now Taking the Field*. Stone picks the all-time, all-star team for each franchise, which would stir debates on its own merit. But add in his use of modern-day sabermetrics like WAR to complement traditional Triple Crown statistics and you've got an old school-new school war of words. ... You can't argue with Stone's research, though, nor the fact that this book is a fun to read and fun to talk about when you are done. That's a pretty good double-play combination.

—Bob Herzog, Veteran sports writer and editor for *Newsday*

"View your favorite team in a new light thanks to Tom Stone's exhaustively researched and immensely enjoyable *Now Taking the Field*. This book is sure to spark debates and bring back treasured memories for any baseball fan."

—Bryan Hoch, MLB.com reporter

"Tom Stone's dream team lineup for every team is a joyful read even if your team is out of contention. It's all about the glory days and what makes your team special. Every fan can appreciate putting that one of a kind time-machine team on the field together at last, the ultimate fantasy team for each franchise."

—Kevin Kernan, *New York Post* columnist

"Tom Stone's *Now Taking the Field* is a great reminder that there is nothing more fun than a good baseball argument. This book is filled with them. For instance, Thurman Munson. Really? Thurman Munson? I have very strong feelings about Thurman Munson's place in Tom's all-Yankees team and I would very much like to argue with him about it for the next three days. This book is filled with countless Thurman Munson-like arguments, which will make it endlessly fun for baseball fans everywhere."

—Joe Posnanski, Columnist for MLB.com and
New York Times bestseller author

"Tom Stone delivers his ingenious version of baseball history in *Now Taking the Field*, a book guaranteed to entertain, enlighten and at times even exasperate you. In selecting his all-time dream teams for each MLB franchise, Stone cuts across eras and infuses modern-day sabermetrics to assemble starting lineups that will provoke debate and evoke awe. Whether he's writing about Babe Ruth or Barry Bonds, Honus Wagner or Derek Jeter, the vintage Yankees or the expansion Marlins, Stone's knowledge and love for the game carry the reader along like a ballpark organ melody. It's the ultimate fantasy league."

—Linda Robertson, *Miami Herald* columnist

"Here's a book that actually answers Abbott & Costello's questions. Using modern analytics and a sense of history, Tom Stone has thoughtfully constructed all-time lineups for every franchise. And in the process, he tells you who's on first, why that guy is the left fielder and the reason for today's catcher. He also makes difficult decisions that will lead to both arguments and epiphanies."

—Steve Wulf, ESPN Senior Writer

Contents

Introduction

Backstory

I started writing this book around 1983. I was 10 years old at the time. I knew that one day I would write a book about baseball All-Time teams—I didn't know when exactly, or what format such a book would ultimately take. But it was around that age that I started thinking about the questions of who the best players at each position are for each team.

I grew up in Western New York, out in the country, near a town about 20 minutes from Rochester. My street had only a few children close to my age, so there wasn't a wide variety of things to do. A small group of us spent most of our summers playing versions of baseball and at times other sports. Often the games were played with only four or five players—total. Nonetheless, we spent countless happy sun-filled days playing ball—the kind of pure baseball joy that grown men think of when they become emotional over movies like *Field of Dreams* or *The Natural*.

When it was raining, or during the winter (Rochester is well known for its lake-effect snowfall), we didn't let baseball completely leave our minds. We'd sometimes play All-Star Baseball, a game by Cadaco, that provided spinner discs representing the greats of the game, allowing you to statistically simulate realistic games on paper (we even went so far as to create our own player discs out of construction paper and cardboard). I was also fortunate enough to have an early Atari computer, so we played early baseball simulation games such as MicroLeague Baseball, a game that was statistics-based instead of action- or joystick-based.

It is here that the connection with this book is made. In order to choose teams for such endeavors, we would spend long hours discussing the greatest players in baseball history. We would compare contemporary greats like Mike Schmidt and Tom Seaver with stars from our dads' eras like Mickey Mantle and Warren Spahn, not to mention the mythical players from long ago like Babe Ruth and Walter Johnson. We would discuss and argue over the greatest at each position, the greatest for each team, the best single teams and seasons, and just about every question you could think of. We'd stump each other with trivia, trade baseball cards, and do everything else that baseball-loving kids did in the late '70s and early '80s.

The Perennial Topic

The topic of baseball All-Time dream teams has been discussed amongst baseball fans for many decades. Once baseball had enough history, it was natural for even the casual fan to ponder who the best of the game had been up to that point. Since baseball has well-defined positions, creating a mythical roster of greats is often more appealing than trying to create an overall top-10 or top-100 players listing. The most common form of this question is to ask for an overall dream team covering the entire history of the sport. However, with over 100 years of stars to choose from, this is now an extremely difficult and argumentative question.

Another approach to All-Time dream teams is that taken by this book: to create a dream team roster for each franchise. I am of course not the first to attempt such a thing; numerous authors have done so in the past, are doing so in the present, and will no doubt do so in the future. Fan surveys have at times asked this question in various cities with MLB teams, producing a similar (if more popularity-driven) dream team result. Sometimes these efforts produced just a starting nine, and sometimes a few backups were chosen. On some occasions a full roster was chosen, and with reasons given for each selection.

While not unique, this book will attempt to differentiate itself in a few ways. First, my selections will be informed by one of the current and popular statistical techniques for comparing players across teams and eras that has arisen in recent years. This is called Wins Above Replacement, or WAR for short, and I'll say more about it shortly. I don't use this statistic as the sole factor in my selections, though one could use the data in this book to do exactly that. Instead, I use WAR-based numbers as a starting point, and then also consider more traditional statistics such as home runs, stolen bases, batting average, earned run average, etc., as well as postseason accomplishments and key awards such as MVP, Cy Young, Gold Glove, and Rookie of the Year.

Another unique aspect of this book is that after making and explaining my selections, I compare these picks with those of past writers, as well as whatever fan surveys or other published attempts at answering this All-Time dream team question I could find.

Along the way, each chapter has some fun additional features, including separate starting lineups against right-handed and left-handed pitchers, a depth chart of the players chosen, lists of the single seasons with a WAR score of 8 or higher (7 or higher for expansion-era teams), and a selection of a single franchise player for each team at the end (represented by the silhouette image that begins each chapter).

Format and Ground Rules

It is a well-known fact that no one cares more about the sanctity of rules than 10-year-olds. Not scientists, not judges, not the police. In fact, politicians would do well to think back to their childhood when justice and rules were held to be inviolate. To a 10-year-old, setting the rules of the game and making sure they are fair is just as important as the game itself. With this in mind, here are the ground rules for this book:

1. Each of the 30 chapters represents a currently existing team franchise, a long-standing entity that survives intact through such things as moves from city to city, changes in team nickname, or the demolition of a stadium. So, for example, the Dodgers chapter will cover the Los Angeles and Brooklyn Dodgers—as well as the earlier clubs with various nicknames (Robins, Superbas, Bridegrooms, Grooms, Grays, and Atlantics) that stretched back to 1884. Similarly, the Nationals chapter will somewhat awkwardly cover the history of the franchise, which for a few decades was the Montreal Expos.

2. Only a player's accomplishments for the particular franchise will be considered when picking players for that team's All-Time dream team. A player may have had a great career, but if he played for a team for only a short while, he likely won't make the cut. However, players can be chosen (and many are) for more than one All-Time dream team.

3. Attempts will be made to choose a player at the position he played most often, but this is flexible. A sense of "reasonableness" will be used to determine, in each particular case, what would be best for the roster. Playing only a few games at a position doesn't qualify the player to make the squad at that position, but playing dozens or over a hundred games at a secondary position definitely does.

4. Two players at each infield position will be selected, a starter and a backup. Six outfielders will be chosen, with some attention paid to RF/CF/LF balance. However, this will not be a strict rule: a team with five LF and one RF would not be acceptable, but a team with one LF, three CF, and two RF would be. Two additional "extra spots" will be awarded to position players not otherwise chosen, and these can be from any position (e.g., a 3B and a 1B, two additional catchers, etc.).

5. Twelve pitchers will be chosen, with a minimum of two required to be relief pitchers (which can include pitchers who logged significant time as both starter and reliever). In this way, starting pitchers are emphasized for these dream team rosters, because for most of the history of the game relief pitching was not the focused specialty that it is today.

Statistics and Other Considerations

As noted earlier, in considering players for each All-Time dream team, several different statistics and accomplishments were taken into account. Most notably:

- Wins Above Replacement (WAR)
- Traditional statistics (batting average, home runs, stolen bases, wins, strikeouts, etc.)
- Awards (Most Valuable Player Awards, Cy Young Awards, Gold Glove Awards, and Rookie of the Year Awards)
- Postseason performance (both statistics and awards)

Some readers might be unfamiliar with WAR. In short, WAR is the latest in a series of statistics developed in the past several decades that attempt to indicate a player's overall value, his total contribution to his team. Such statistics are examples of what are sometimes referred to as "sabermetrics," a term derived from SABR, the Society for American Baseball Research (founded in 1971). Such statistics provide a means to compare players across time when traditional statistics, such as batting average or earned run average, have proved notoriously inconsistent and problematic.

Wins Above Replacement gets its name because a player's WAR value approximates the wins his team achieved above what it would have had if that player had been replaced by a typical replacement-level player (think AAA minor league player on the verge of making the majors). WAR brings together value from batting, base running, fielding, and pitching. There is also a position factor included, with higher value given to weak-hitting positions like catcher, and lower value given to strong-hitting positions like first base. For example, if a player in a particular season had a WAR score of 5, then this indicates that his team won 5 more games than they would have if a replacement-level player had played the same number of games (or innings pitched for pitchers) in his place. A WAR score of 5 or more is generally considered All-Star quality, and a WAR score of 8 or more is MVP level.

While WAR has recently become popular enough to be regularly mentioned on ESPN, MLB TV, and other broadcasts, no such statistic is yet universally agreed upon to be perfect in judging player value today, let alone comparing players across the long history of baseball. There are many proponents of WAR but also many great baseball minds who find fault with it and argue for other approaches (e.g., Bill James' Win Shares, and others). Even for those who accept the basic approach that WAR takes, there are currently several different equations for calculating WAR, and while they produce generally similar results, they are not identical.

That said, because WAR has gained solid popularity and familiarity amongst even casual fans, I decided I'd use it as a starting point in evaluating players for the All-Time dream teams in this book. As for which version of WAR, I elected to use the WAR results that are provided by the primary baseball statistics website, Baseball-Reference.com. To learn more about their approach to WAR, and for links to the debate about WAR, see this page at their site: https://www.baseball-reference.com/about/war_explained.shtml.

In the tables throughout this book you can easily see who had the highest career WAR score at each position for each team. While such players are often the logical choices for the top spots on their respective dream team rosters, there are reasons to not just stop there. First, the total WAR for a player favors longevity over peak performance. Consider two players: one with a total WAR of 40 accumulated from 15 seasons, and another with a total WAR of 38 accumulated from 6 seasons. If I went strictly by total WAR, then the first player would win out, 40–38. But the reality is that the first player, while a long-time veteran of that team, probably had only a couple of truly good seasons, with the vast majority being rather mediocre. The second player was a great player for most or all of his six seasons, so most fans would agree he is the more deserving selection in this case.

To handle such considerations, I included two additional stats in the tables in each chapter. The first, W3, is simply the player's top three seasons (or fewer, if he didn't play three seasons for that team). This allows us to quickly compare players' peak performances. I could have chosen the top four or top five seasons, but I went with the top three because in many instances players didn't play four or more seasons for the particular franchise.

The second additional statistic is W/G, which stands for WAR per Game. This gives us a sense for the player's value (according to WAR) on a per-game basis, which again helps indicate players who were great for shorter periods of time vs. those who were mediocre for long periods of time. I didn't include W/G for pitchers, because some pitchers split their time as starters and relievers, making "game" an inconsistent denominator for the formula, and the resulting W/G numbers very misleading in such cases.

So how much should WAR, W3, and W/G be weighted in considering players? I tried to weigh them fairly equally, but baseball fans can reasonably disagree on this, variously choosing to favor longevity, peak performance, or average value. That is what makes the topic of All-Time dream teams—even informed by such modern statistics—one that will continue to be debated.

Beyond WAR, I also considered traditional statistics, for a couple of reasons. As noted, WAR is not considered perfect (by me or any fans that I know) in determining a player's overall value. All fans continue to track, discuss, and generally care about the traditional statistics, and many potential readers are familiar only with them and not with newer metrics like WAR. For this book I assumed that most readers would be familiar enough with all of the following: batting average, runs, RBI (runs batted in), doubles, triples, home runs, stolen bases, walks, strikeouts, OBP (on-base percentage), slugging percentage, assists, putouts, fielding percentage, earned run average, wins, losses, innings pitched, saves, and WHIP (Walks and Hits per Inning Pitched).

Two others might be less familiar. OPS+ is derived from OPS, which is a hitter's on-base percentage plus slugging percentage. Rather than being a number like .894, OPS+ relativizes the combined stat to the average OBP and average slugging percentage for the player's league that year, and also adjusts for the player's ballparks. An OPS+ of 100 is therefore average for that league for that year; anything over 100 is above average and anything under 100 is below average. While it excludes base running, fielding, and other aspects of value, it does make OPS+ more useful than OPS for comparing players across time periods.

Similar to OPS+ but for pitchers, ERA+ is derived from ERA, and relativizes the standard ERA statistic to the average ERA for the league that year, and also adjusts for the player's ballparks. An ERA+ of 100 is average for that league for that year; anything over 100 is above average and anything under 100 is below average.

As many baseball fans know, traditional statistics have varied a lot over the years. There have been time periods where pitching dominated or hitting dominated, and this is easily seen by the trends in the traditional statistics. Home runs were not very frequent until Babe Ruth came along and changed the game. Players stole a lot of bases in the early days of baseball, but far fewer during the 1930s–1950s. Pitchers' earned run averages were far lower from 1900 through 1919 than in subsequent years.

There are also individual seasons that are outliers, usually with well-known reasons. Some seasons, such as 1893–1895, 1929–1930, and 1999–2000 produced very high offensive numbers, while others, such as 1900–1919 (the "Deadball Era") and 1967–1968 produced very good pitching numbers. Throughout this book, I did my best to note such outlier considerations when describing individual player accomplishments in these types of seasons.

Another issue is that baseball statistics have developed over time, not only in their sophistication as described earlier, but simply in their being tracked at all. For instance, stolen base statistics are not available for the National League from 1876 to 1885, so for some old-timers their SB totals are incomplete.

Some statistics, such as earned run average, on-base percentage, and others did not exist during the early days of baseball, so when I say that a player led the league in such stats during such early years, it needs to be understood that no fan, reporter, or player back then would have spoken that way.

The situation with relief pitching saves is even more problematic. The term "save" was used as far back as 1952, but it didn't become an official statistic until 1969. The way saves were awarded was amended in 1974 and 1975, and has stayed consistent since then. I've used the save numbers provided by Baseball-Reference.com, which notes that "for games played before 1969, saves have been figured retroactively using the 1969 definition." So this means such pre-1969 saves are not calculated according to the current rules, an important caveat in considering the numbers (specifically, for some games, pitchers were awarded a save that would not qualify as such by the current rules).

I did my best to fairly consider the players from the earliest years of baseball, the old-timers from the late 1800s. The game was very different back then in many ways. The seasons were shorter, so players had less opportunity to accumulate statistics per year. The rules changed more often than in the modern game, and it even took a while for players to start using gloves on the field and for catchers to crouch and wear protective gear. Teams also used far fewer pitchers than they do today—they had two- and three-man rotations rather than the five-man rotation that is standard today, and they also used far fewer relief pitchers than the modern game does. Because of this, starting pitchers often would pitch 350+ innings per year, sometimes even topping 500 innings in a season. They would also frequently win (or lose!) 30–40+ games per season. This amount of involvement in their team's success naturally led to some very high WAR scores for some pitchers, making comparing their seasons with those of pitchers that came later very difficult. As a result, I often heavily discounted the statistics of such early pitchers, excluding many of them from the dream teams in this book. There are exceptions, as in some cases a dominant pitcher played for a team for many years during that era, and that of course deserves recognition.

The PED (performance-enhancing drugs) era, aka the Steroids era, was roughly from the late 1980s through the early 2000s, with its peak being from 1998 through 2003. In considering players for All-Time dream teams, I used their statistics as they are, and relied on WAR, OPS+, and so on to help even out the analysis. That said, I did mention in many instances where players were known or suspected of being PED users, and baseball fans will of course vary in how much they discount the statistics of such individual players. I respect the strong opinions that exist on this issue, but because it is so complicated, for this book I didn't exclude players who used or were suspected of using such substances. (Nor for that matter did I follow MLB and the Baseball Hall of Fame in excluding players banned from the game for other rule violations, such as Pete Rose or Shoeless Joe Jackson.)

Lastly, this book's statistics and text include the 2018 regular season, but not the 2018 postseason or awards, both of which happened after the book went to print.

Acknowledgements

I am grateful to so many people, where should I start? As I did at the outset, I'll start at the beginning. The fun times I had as a child were because of the great kids in my neighborhood. I won't mention them all, but two deserve a brief shout out. Steve Grattan was a year older and a far better athlete than I was. It was in his front yard where we played baseball most often. And my brother David (two years younger) was even more important because he was my constant companion while growing up. While other kids would play ball with us, it was these two who most often participated in discussions of who the greatest players were for each team, each era, and so on.

Related to this, I'd like to thank my parents, Paul and Cathy Stone, who have always been supportive in everything I do. Of most relevance to this book, they must be thanked for letting me spend so much of my childhood playing, watching, and reading about baseball. Even when my brother and I were late for supper (time and time again), they always let us go back out to play until we could no longer see the ball coming towards us.

The actual writing of this book started in 1999, and I've worked on it off and on for nearly 20 years. Over these many years I have received encouragement and support from many friends and family members, but I wanted to single out Mike Lynch, baseball book author and creator of the Seamheads.com website, for always being enthusiastic about my project and for being willing to read drafts, provide feedback, and more.

Although my thinking on this topic for years relied on print baseball encyclopedias and other books, as the Internet grew, baseball fans were blessed with the creation of the incredible website Baseball-Reference.com. It quickly became the standard for baseball statistics sites, and I am indebted to Sean Forman and the team involved in maintaining and growing the site over the years. This book would have been much more difficult to produce if not for this outstanding resource.

I also want to acknowledge another website, The Baseball Gauge (thebaseballgauge.com), by Dan Hirsch, which provides a wealth of data presented in useful interesting formats. This site was helpful when initially researching the WAR numbers for each franchise.

As this book got closer to being ready for publication, I found myself surrounded by a dream team of my own. Gabriel Schechter first edited a partial draft back in 2012, giving me good feedback on that version. But his editing of this final version of the book really was above and beyond, as he not only provided a copy edit but also used his extensive baseball knowledge (he worked for years as a researcher at the Baseball Hall of Fame) to give me loads of substantive feedback that made the book better in many ways. In fact, I made so many changes based on his feedback that I then hired another editor, Joe McElveney, to do one final copy edit, as I was quite certain I had introduced several errors in making so many changes. Thank you both for your flexibility and attention to detail.

Next on my dream team is Tim Lewis, who worked with me over the years on various potential cover designs, including the one we finally settled on. He also helped with the final depth charts used in the book. I also want to thank Ian Courter for his efforts in laying out the final typesetting for the book.

When it came to publishing, I had planned to self-publish this book directly with Amazon, but through a series of fortunate events I was introduced to Greg Pierce and his company ACTA Sports. I appreciate his advice and flexibility, and I am glad to be partnered with him in publishing this book.

In some ways it is easier than ever to write a book and get the word out about it all by yourself. But that doesn't mean that is always the best approach to take, as a good publicist can be an important partner in helping any author—but particularly an author new to a genre as I am—reach far more potential readers. I looked around, and it quickly became clear that Press Box Publicity, headed up by Adam Rifenberick, and now a part of Smith Publicity (led by Dan Smith), would be the ideal publicity partner for me. Adam and Dan guided me through the various possibilities and approaches, and I appreciate their and their team's efforts and expertise in helping me reach a broader audience.

And finally, I want to thank my wonderful wife, Kassy LaBorie, for her support, enthusiasm, and patience with me as I spent countless hours working on this project. She isn't a big baseball fan, but she enjoys learning more about the game, and she has always encouraged me to reach my goals.

Join the Discussion!

The topic of All-Time dream teams generates a lot of fun discussion and debate. I wrote this book in the hopes that it would become part of that discussion, and perhaps foster more such debate. I welcome your comments, feedback, and suggestions or edits for future editions.

I encourage you to visit the website **www.nowtakingthefield.com** to contact me directly, connect via social media, keep up with the latest related content at the blog, and interact with other fans interested in this fun topic.

CHAPTER 1

The Yankees Franchise All-Time Dream Team

Without doubt, the Yankees are the most successful and well-known team in all of American professional sports, having won 27 championships and 40 American League pennants. The franchise actually started as the Baltimore Orioles (believe it or not) with the birth of the AL in 1901. For the 1903 season they moved to New York and went by the name of the Highlanders until 1913, when they became the Yankees. They didn't win any pennants until 1921, the year after Babe Ruth joined the club. They took the AL pennant in six of the next eight years, winning the World Series three times.

Their next big streak was from 1936 through 1943, when they led the AL in seven out of eight seasons, and won the World Series in six of those years. They were no better than third for the next three years, but then their longest dynasty was launched in 1947 and ran for 18 years through 1964. They won the AL pennant an amazing 15 times, and won the World Series 10 times.

After a decade-long slump, the Yankees came alive again and made the playoffs five out of the six years from 1976 through 1981, winning the championship in 1977–78. Another lengthy slump followed, but now—given the economics of the game and the Yankees' willingness to spend big money on star players—the Yankees have returned to greatness by making the playoffs in 19 of the past 23 seasons, winning the World Series another five times.

Naturally, their All-Time team is loaded with talent, and some hard decisions had to be made that kept very deserving players off the roster. They are stronger at some positions than others, but up and down, this squad is a powerhouse.

1st Base

Name	YR	WAR	W3	W/G	AVG	HR	SB	OPS+
Lou Gehrig	17	112.4	31.8	.0519	.340	493	102	179
Don Mattingly	14	42.2	19.9	.0236	.307	222	14	127
Wally Pipp	11	29.0	12.1	.0195	.282	80	114	107
Bill Skowron	9	23.6	12.0	.0217	.294	165	14	129
Jason Giambi	7	22.0	16.5	.0245	.260	209	9	143
Mark Teixeira	8	20.6	13.2	.0215	.248	206	13	118
Tino Martinez	7	16.7	10.6	.0158	.276	192	17	113
Chris Chambliss	7	15.4	10.6	.0174	.282	79	10	108
Hal Chase	9	9.4	7.4	.0089	.284	20	248	101
Joe Pepitone	8	7.4	6.7	.0070	.252	166	31	105

Still arguably the greatest 1B of all time, **Lou Gehrig** (1923–39) played his entire career with the Yankees. He was The Iron Horse, until ALS weakened him and ultimately took his life. Virtually every baseball fan knows he played in 2,130 consecutive games, the longest streak of its kind until Cal Ripken surpassed it in 1995. He batted cleanup behind the Babe, providing protection which no doubt aided The Bambino's HR numbers. Batting fourth for Murderers' Row also boosted Gehrig's RBI numbers: he *averaged* 153 RBI for 11 seasons from 1927 to 1937. It is hard to say which of his seasons was his best—perhaps 1927, when he hit .373 with 47 HR and 175 RBI (producing a career-high 11.8 WAR), or his Triple Crown year in 1934, when he hit .363 with 49 HR and 165 RBI (10.4 WAR). He led the AL in HR three times, runs four times, and RBI five times, and ended his career with a .340 average, .447 OBP, and .632 SLG. To top it off, Gehrig also batted .361 with 10 HR in 119 at-bats across seven World Series.

The backup to Gehrig really can't be contested either. **Don Mattingly** (1982–95) played the second-most games at 1B for the Yankees, and was MVP in 1985 with a .324 average, 35 HR, 145 RBI, and 48 doubles. The following year he set Yankee records for hits (238) and doubles (53). Like Gehrig, he played his entire career with the Yankees, during which time he nabbed nine Gold Glove Awards and had five 100+-RBI seasons. Although a back injury led in part to an early retirement, Donnie Baseball still ranks tenth in games played for NY.

Who ranks after Gehrig and Mattingly here is debatable, so I'll present four players in chronological order. Wally Pipp (1915–25) led the AL in HR twice during the Deadball Era, with 12 in 1916 and 9 the following year—all it took in those days. He three times posted 100+ RBI, and he hit 10+ triples for the Yankees seven times, including a league-leading 19 in 1924. The next year, he lost his starting job to Lou Gehrig, and after that season was sold to the Reds, where he finished out his career.

Bill "Moose" Skowron (1954–62) played over half of his career, and certainly had his best seasons, with the Yankees. During that time, he batted .294, was an All-Star from 1957 through 1961, and four times had over 20 homers.

Jason Giambi (2002–08) signed with the Yankees as a free agent after having several big years for Oakland. He hit 41 HR in each of his first two seasons in NY, and he hit 30+ HR five times for the Yankees.

Mark Teixeira (2009–16) also signed with the Yankees as a free agent, and immediately led the AL in HR with 39 and RBI with 122 in 2009. In all, he hit 30+ HR four times for New York. He also provided great defense, taking home three Gold Glove Awards with the Yankees.

Beyond those four, another four deserve brief mention (in chronological order):

- Hal Chase (1905–13) was a consistent 1B for this franchise and provided some speed, including 248 stolen bases.

- Joe Pepitone (1962–69) took over for Skowron in 1963, hit for a lower average, but managed 20+ HR four times and was an All-Star three times.

- Chris Chambliss (1974–79) was the 1B for the Yanks during their strong 1970s campaigns, and his production was solid but not spectacular. He never hit 20+ HR during those years, but three times had 90+ RBI.

- Tino Martinez (1996–01, '05) took over for Mattingly in 1996 after being acquired by trade from the Mariners. He provided five seasons of good defense and 100+-RBI production, and he had his best year in 1997, when he hit .296 with 44 HR and 141 RBI and came in second in the AL MVP vote.

2nd Base

Name	YR	WAR	W3	W/G	AVG	HR	SB	OPS+
Willie Randolph	13	53.7	17.6	.0317	.275	48	251	105
Tony Lazzeri	12	48.3	19.3	.0291	.293	169	147	120
Robinson Canó	9	45.3	24.3	.0330	.307	204	38	127
Gil McDougald	10	40.7	16.1	.0305	.276	112	45	111
Joe Gordon	7	37.5	21.2	.0375	.271	153	68	120
Snuffy Stirnweiss	8	27.6	20.6	.0312	.274	27	130	108
Jimmy Williams	7	20.7	12.4	.0220	.277	31	94	116
Horace Clarke	10	16.0	10.5	.0130	.257	27	151	84
Bobby Richardson	12	8.2	7.9	.0058	.266	34	73	77

This is a very difficult position to choose a starter and backup for on this All-Time dream team. There were several good candidates already, and then **Robinson Canó** (2005–13) came along and made the decision even harder. He hit an impressive .342 in his second season in the majors, and he went on to develop home run power as well, smacking 25+ in five consecutive seasons for the Yankees. Great defensively (two Gold Gloves), he was an All-Star five times for NY.

Murderers' Row wasn't all Ruth and Gehrig, as **Tony Lazzeri** (1926–37) was a slugging 2B not only for the famous '27 club, but well into the 1930s as well. He had good power for a middle infielder and was a regular RBI threat, providing 100+ RBI seven times. He also regularly posted double-digit HR and SB in the same season. Poosh 'Em Up Tony hit for a pretty high average too, with .332 in 1928 and .354 in 1929 as his best.

Playing in more games at 2B than any other Yankee, **Willie Randolph** (1976–1988) was consistent but not particularly durable, as he only once topped 150 games in 13 seasons for New York. He was a five-time All-Star for the Yankees, with a keen eye at the plate and some speed on the bases, stealing 30+ bases four times early in his career.

I think the peak performance of Canó makes him worthy of the top spot here, and I give a slight edge to Lazzeri for the backup spot. But Randolph proponents need not worry, as there is room on this roster for him as one of the two position player "extra spots."

Beyond those three, there were three other strong candidates I considered, starting with Joe Gordon (1938–43, '46). His career with the Yanks was not a long one, though we must acknowledge the two years he missed due to World War II. An All-Star in six of his seven seasons in NY, Flash Gordon was good defensively and put up some great numbers for a middle infielder, such as 18 HR, 103 RBI, and a .322 average in 1942. He won the MVP Award that year, although surely Ted Williams was more deserving statistically, since he took home the Triple Crown.

Gil McDougald (1951–60) split time at 2B, 3B, and SS. He made five All-Star teams and was AL Rookie of the Year in 1951, but he doesn't have quite enough credentials to make the team at any of these positions. He'd make a nice utility bench player on such a dream team roster, but given that this is the Yankees we are talking about, there is a lot of competition for the two "extra spots" as well.

Snuffy Stirnweiss (1943–50) had two strong seasons for the Yankees: in 1944 he led the AL in four categories (125 runs, 205 hits, 16 triples, and 55 SB), and then in 1945 he did the same and added a fifth (107 runs, 195 hits, 22 triples, 33 SB, and a .309 average).

Three others worth a brief mention include (in chronological order):

- Jimmy Williams (1901–07) was the franchise's first regular 2B, and he led the AL in triples with 21 in both 1901 and 1902.

- Many readers will also think of Bobby Richardson (1955–66) as a good Yankees second baseman, as he was a seven-time All-Star and won five Gold Glove Awards. But he played nearly 300 fewer games than Randolph, retired at the age of 31 in 1966, and his overall numbers just don't compare with the other candidates very well.

- Horace Clarke (1965–73) took over where Richardson left off, but relatively speaking didn't have a very impressive career (.257 average and 151 SB).

3rd Base

Name	YR	WAR	W3	W/G	AVG	HR	SB	OPS+
Álex Rodríguez	12	54.2	26.4	.0359	.283	351	152	136
Graig Nettles	11	44.3	19.2	.0289	.253	250	18	114
Red Rolfe	10	23.5	14.5	.0200	.289	69	44	99
Frank Baker	6	20.5	13.5	.0303	.288	48	63	113
Clete Boyer	8	19.6	12.4	.0184	.241	95	27	86
Wade Boggs	5	18.3	12.9	.0304	.313	24	4	112

Unlike 2B, the top two at 3B are easier to see. Although the PED issue clouds the analysis, based on numbers alone **Álex Rodríguez** (2004–13, '15–16) deserves the nod as the starting 3B for this All-Time team. He had 30+ HR and

100+ RBI in his first seven years as a Yankee, including leading the league with 48 HR in 2005 and 54 HR and 156 RBI in 2007, winning the AL MVP Award both years.

Graig Nettles (1973–83) is an obvious choice as backup, and one could make a case for him as starter too. He was an All-Star five times for the Yanks and was well known for his solid glove at the hot corner (two Gold Glove Awards). He regularly hit 20+ homers, topping a light league with 32 in 1976 and finishing as runner-up the next year with 37.

Four other Yankees 3B were considered, starting with Red Rolfe (1934–42), who had a short career but was an All-Star four times. He was a .289 hitter and scored 100+ runs in seven consecutive seasons, with highs of 143, 132, and 139 from 1937 through 1939.

John Franklin "Home Run" Baker (1916–19, '21–22) played out his declining years in NY, hitting .288 but no longer leading the league in HR each year as he did for the Athletics.

Wade Boggs (1993–97) also joined the Yankees late in his career, and while his batting titles and 200+-hit seasons were a thing of the past, he continued to provide a solid average (.313) and OBP (.396). He won two Gold Gloves at the hot corner and continued to be a popular player, as he was an All-Star in NY four times even though he played in 140+ games only once.

Lastly, Clete Boyer (1959–66) provided great defense and some pop in the 1960s, but he hit only .241 with a .298 OBP and 86 OPS+.

Shortstop

Name	YR	WAR	W3	W/G	AVG	HR	SB	OPS+
Derek Jeter	20	71.8	22.0	.0261	.310	260	358	115
Phil Rizzuto	13	40.8	17.7	.0246	.273	38	149	93
Roger Peckinpaugh	9	31.9	14.7	.0262	.257	36	143	93
Frankie Crosetti	17	23.9	10.5	.0142	.245	98	113	83
Kid Elberfeld	7	18.8	12.0	.0282	.268	4	117	106
Tony Kubek	9	18.3	9.9	.0168	.266	57	29	85

The rise of **Derek Jeter** (1995–2014) in recent years kept SS from being a weak spot on this roster. Jeter started out strong by winning the Rookie of the Year Award in 1996 after hitting .314 with 104 runs. A high-average hitter (.310), he scored 100+ runs an impressive 13 times. He also provided a good combo of speed and power, with double-digit SB and HR every year (until turning age 37 in 2011). A 14-time All-Star, there is debate about how good Jeter was defensively, so I'll just note for the record that he won five Gold Glove Awards in the second half of his career. He has the distinction of having by far the most games played, at-bats, and hits of anyone for this storied franchise, and also leads in doubles and stolen bases. Mr. November essentially played an entire additional season by participating in 33 postseason series (16 ALDS, 10 ALCS, and 7 World Series). He was MVP of the 2000 World Series against the Mets, and overall batted .308 (200-for-650 in 158 games), with 111 runs, 20 HR, and 18 SB in the postseason.

Until Jeter came along, the starter here would have been **Phil Rizzuto** (1941–42, '46–56). He was an All-Star five times (while losing three prime years to WWII) and won the MVP Award in 1950. Scooter was a good fielder, a superb bunter, but a light hitter overall. And although he regularly appeared amongst the league leaders in stolen bases, this was a notoriously slow era, as Rizzuto never had more than 22 SB in a season.

Several other Yankees deserve brief mention, starting with Deadball-Era shortstop Roger Peckinpaugh (1913–21). He stole 15+ bases five times, including a high of 38 in 1914, and then later scored 109 runs in 1920 and 128 runs in 1921.

Frankie Crosetti (1932–48) played his entire career with the Yankees, and actually played in almost as many games at SS as Rizzuto. He scored 100+ runs four times, including a high of 137 in 1936. But he was only a .245 hitter, so overall his résumé for this All-Time team came up short.

Old-timer Kid Elberfeld (1903–09) had some speed and was fairly productive on a per-game basis, but the problem was that he played 120+ games only twice for New York.

Lastly, Tony Kubek (1957–65) won the Rookie of the Year Award in 1957 after batting .297, and he was a three-time All-Star. But like his double-play partner Richardson, he had a short career, retiring in 1965 due to a back injury.

Catcher

Name	YR	WAR	W3	W/G	AVG	HR	SB	OPS+
Yogi Berra	18	59.6	17.5	.0282	.285	358	30	125
Bill Dickey	17	55.8	16.4	.0312	.313	202	36	127
Thurman Munson	11	45.9	19.3	.0323	.292	113	48	116
Jorge Posada	17	42.7	16.8	.0233	.273	275	20	121
Elston Howard	13	27.7	16.0	.0186	.279	161	8	110

The Yankees are without a doubt the most loaded All-Time team at the catcher position. For starters, they have two players whose names are often mentioned in discussions of the best catcher of all time. **Yogi Berra** (1946–63) had 25+ HR six times and 100+ RBI five times. He won three MVP Awards (1951, '54, '55) and was an All-Star for an amazing 15 consecutive seasons from 1948 through 1962. One striking thing about his career: he never led the league in any major offensive category—partially because as a catcher he needed the occasional day off (he played 140+ games in a season only six times). That said, he certainly remains the all-time leader in puzzling, accidentally humorous quotations.

Berra got the starting nod, but that's not to take anything away from the man who taught him the ropes, **Bill Dickey** (1928–43, '46). Dickey regularly batted over .300 (with a high of .362 in 1936) and provided great defense for the powerhouse Yankees clubs of the 1930s, but he never played more than 140 games in a season. Nonetheless, each year from 1936 through 1939 he had 20+ HR and 100+ RBI. Until recently, his name always surfaced along with Bench, Berra, Gibson, and Cochrane when the greatest catchers of all time were being discussed.

Next on this impressive list was **Thurman Munson** (1969–79), whose life was tragically ended by a plane crash in 1979. While his numbers were starting to slip by then, he had already provided 100+ RBI three times. He took home lots of trophies too: seven-time All-Star, 1970 Rookie of the Year, 1976 MVP, and the Gold Glove from 1973 through 1975. Although one could make a case for a few others, I gave Thurman the other "extra spot" on this roster.

But the quality didn't end there, as lifetime Yankee Jorge Posada (1996–2011) also had an outstanding career. The five-time All-Star regularly hit 20+ HR and had 275 in total. He was a key part of many championship clubs, so you could certainly argue that he deserves the other "extra spot" on this All-Time team roster.

One more catcher deserved a close look, and that was Elston Howard (1955–67), who for a while formed a LF/C tandem with Berra, doing more catching as Berra grew older. Few might remember that Howard was an All-Star in nine consecutive seasons, won two Gold Glove Awards, was the AL MVP in 1963, and batted .348 for the juggernaut 1961 champions. He'd be a capable backup for most All-Time teams, but only managed to rank fifth for the Yankees.

Left Field

Name	YR	WAR	W3	W/G	AVG	HR	SB	OPS+
Roy White	15	46.7	19.0	.0248	.271	160	233	121
Charlie Keller	11	41.8	20.0	.0392	.286	184	45	152
Brett Gardner	11	37.5	16.6	.0276	.261	96	257	99

Bob Meusel	10	27.6	11.9	.0213	.311	146	134	121
Ben Chapman	7	25.3	15.0	.0278	.305	60	184	119
Tom Tresh	9	21.4	13.8	.0195	.247	140	43	115
Hideki Matsui	7	20.4	13.6	.0222	.292	140	12	123

The Yankees outfield is loaded with talent and includes some of the best players of all time. But none of them primarily played LF, so this list is relatively unimpressive for this dream team roster. **Charlie "King Kong" Keller** (1939–43, '45–49, '52) was a five-time All-Star and had three 30+-HR seasons. His best season was arguably 1941, when he hit .298 with 33 HR and 122 RBI. A .286 hitter for the Yankees, he had a good eye and so carried a .410 OBP.

Roy White (1965–79) spent his entire career with the Yankees and managed a higher career WAR for the Yankees than Keller. A two-time All-Star, he had some speed and some power, and provided good defense in LF. But White's peak performance numbers, relatively speaking, were not very impressive: his best season was probably 1970, when he hit .296 with 22 HR, 94 RBI, 109 runs, and 24 SB. So I think it is hard to make a case for him to make this All-Time Yankees dream team roster—I'm going to select extra center fielders (who played some left or right field) instead of a second player here.

Similarly, Brett Gardner (2008–18) is a fine player, and thus far has played his entire career for the Yankees. He provides good defense (he won his first Gold Glove in 2016) and some speed on the bases, with highs of 47 SB in 2010 and a league-leading 49 in 2011. But as a .261 hitter with only moderate power, I doubt he'll build a résumé strong enough to crack this All-Time team roster.

A few others I considered who deserve brief mention include (in chronological order):

- Bob Meusel (1920–29) was part of the powerhouse Yankees of the 1920s. He had five seasons with 100+ RBI, five with 40+ doubles, and five with 10+ triples. He consistently batted between .290 and .340. And the year his average dipped to .290 was 1925, when he led the AL in homers with 33 and RBI with 138.

- Ben Chapman (1930–36) had six fine seasons for the Yanks, hitting .305 and leading the league in stolen bases three times. His 1931 season stood out to me: .315, 17 HR, 122 RBI, 120 runs, and 61 SB.

- Tom Tresh (1961–69) won the Rookie of the Year Award in 1962 after hitting .286 with 20 HR and 93 RBI, while playing more at SS than LF. He was an All-Star that year and the following, and provided good defense, earning a Gold Glove in 1965. He played mostly LF, but he did return to the infield (both SS and 3B) in the late '60s. A switch-hitter, he hit 20+ HR four times, but from 1967 forward couldn't manage a batting average over .219. He was traded in 1969 to the Tigers, who released him before the 1970 season, leading to his retirement from the game at age 31.

- Hideki Matsui (2003–09) brought new excitement to New York from Japan at age 29 in 2003. Godzilla provided the team with 100+ RBI four times and 100+ runs three times. He ended his Yankees career as a postseason hero, hitting three HR in the 2009 World Series.

Center Field

Name	YR	WAR	W3	W/G	AVG	HR	SB	OPS+
Mickey Mantle	18	109.7	33.0	.0457	.298	536	153	172
Joe DiMaggio	13	78.1	25.4	.0450	.325	361	30	155
Bernie Williams	16	49.4	17.3	.0238	.297	287	147	125
Earle Combs	12	42.5	16.9	.0292	.325	58	98	125
Rickey Henderson	5	30.8	22.5	.0517	.288	78	326	135
Bobby Murcer	13	27.6	19.7	.0220	.278	175	74	129

As was the case at catcher, the Yankees have historically been loaded at the center field position. The list starts with the great **Mickey Mantle** (1951–68), who was a 16-time All-Star, won three MVP Awards (1956, '57, '62), and won the Triple Crown in 1956 with 52 HR, 130 RBI, and a .353 BA. He struck out a lot, but he also walked a lot—leading to a career .420 OBP. The Mick led the league in HR four times, and he led the league in runs six times during a stretch of nine consecutive years with 100+ from 1953 through 1961. In 12 World Series, Mantle batted only .257 but made up for it by belting 18 HR in 230 at-bats.

Famous for his 56-game hitting streak, **Joe DiMaggio** (1936–42, '46–51) is also well remembered for his persona and celebrity status in America. Like Berra and Mantle, he too took home three MVP Awards (1939, '41, '47)—though one could argue that Ted Williams deserved the award in 1941 (when he batted .406) and in 1947 (when he won the Triple Crown). Regardless, Joltin' Joe's numbers are undeniable: two batting titles and a .325 lifetime average, eight seasons with 100+ runs, nine seasons with 100+ RBI, and never more than 39 strikeouts in a season. All of that while losing three prime years to World War

II. Perhaps it's enough just to note that he was named an All-Star in all of his 13 seasons in the majors.

Although not at the level of Mantle or DiMaggio, **Earle Combs** (1924–35), yet another lifetime Yankee, was a key part of the famed Murderers' Row teams. The Kentucky Colonel had eight consecutive seasons with at least 113 runs (he had Ruth and Gehrig driving him in), and his lowest average in a full season was .299, leading to a career .325 mark. And he was also a phenomenal triples hitter, three times leading the league by slicing 20 or more.

And a fourth center fielder who played his entire career in New York was **Bernie Williams** (1991–2006). Although his potential took a few years to actualize, starting in 1996 he could generally be counted on to produce 100 runs, 100 RBI, 25 HR, and a .300+ BA (he led the AL with a .339 average in 1998). In the contemporary game, such numbers won't blow you away, but he does rank third in doubles, fifth in hits, sixth in total bases, and seventh in home runs for the Yankees. The five-time All-Star was also great defensively, winning four Gold Glove Awards.

Two other Yankees center fielders deserve mention, starting with Rickey Henderson (1985–89), who had four strong years for the Yankees (though one was shortened by injuries) before being traded back to Oakland nearly midway through the 1989 campaign. He was the definition of a leadoff hitter in 1985, '86, and '88, with run totals of 146, 130, and 118, and SB totals of 80, 87, and 93 (the top three single-season SB totals for the Yankees).

And Bobby Murcer (1965–66, '69–74, '79–83) had two significant stints with the Yankees: several fine seasons to start his career, as well as several years at the end. A four-time All-Star for the Yanks, he had five consecutive seasons of 20+ homers, took home one Gold Glove Award, and batted .331 in 1971.

Right Field

Name	YR	WAR	W3	W/G	AVG	HR	SB	OPS+
Babe Ruth	15	142.4	39.4	.0683	.349	659	110	209
Tommy Henrich	11	35.7	14.6	.0278	.282	183	37	132
Hank Bauer	12	28.6	14.3	.0203	.277	158	48	115
Dave Winfield	9	26.9	14.2	.0230	.290	205	76	134
Paul O'Neill	9	26.6	13.9	.0212	.303	185	80	125
Roger Maris	7	26.3	18.3	.0309	.265	203	7	139
George Selkirk	9	22.1	13.6	.0261	.290	108	49	127
Reggie Jackson	5	17.1	12.7	.0262	.281	144	41	148

Babe Ruth (1920–34) single-handedly ushered in a new era in baseball. Paired with Lou Gehrig, they anchored some of the best teams of all time. A few sentences just don't do Ruth justice, so I suggest that you take the time now to look up his stats and consider them anew. Of course, his first several years for the Red Sox don't count here, nor does his final partial year for the Boston Braves. But his numbers from his prime Yankees seasons are mind-boggling. During that span he led the league in batting only once (.378 in 1924) but finished in the top five seven other times. The Sultan of Swat led the league in slugging 11 times, runs 7 times, RBI 5 times, HR 10 times, and walks 11 times. Overall for the Yankees he had a .349 average, .474 OBP, and a ridiculous .711 slugging percentage.

Tommy Henrich (1937–42, '46–50) came into his own as a star for the Yankees in the 1940s but missed three prime years to World War II. A five-time All-Star, his 1948 season was outstanding, as he led the league in runs with 138 and triples with 14, and also had 42 doubles, 25 HR, 100 RBI, and a .308 average.

There were many other Yankees right fielders who deserve brief mention, including (in chronological order):

- George Selkirk (1934–42) had a short career (all with the Yankees), and played 100+ games in only four seasons. He split his time between RF and LF, was an All-Star twice, and hit a respectable .290.

- Hank Bauer (1948–59) provided some pop (15+ HR five times) and was an All-Star three times, but was far from spectacular enough to make this All-Time team roster.

- Roger Maris (1960–66) is of course a famous New York Yankee, and while he had three outstanding seasons, including two MVP years in 1960 and 1961, his other Yankees seasons were far from impressive. His 1961 statistics are very interesting: what is well known was his breaking of Babe Ruth's single-season record with 61 HR, and also leading the AL with 141 RBI and 132 runs. But it was a high-offense year, so his OPS was 167 and his WAR was only 6.9, actually lower than the 7.5 he had the previous year. He really swung for the fences that year, as he had only 16 doubles to go along with the 61 homers.

- Reggie Jackson (1977–81) had four solid years in NY, including a league-leading 41 home runs in 1980. He earned the nickname Mr. October for his outstanding postseason hitting in

1977–78, but his strike-shortened 1981 season was poor, so he was granted free agency and in 1982 moved his show out west.

- Dave Winfield (1981–90) is sometimes remembered for his abysmal pinstripes performance in the 1981 World Series, but he also had many of his finest seasons for the Yankees. He had six seasons of 100+ RBI, and surprised with a .340 average in 1984. Eight times an All-Star with the Yanks, he also took home five Gold Glove Awards.

- Paul O'Neill (1993–01) was good defensively in RF and posted some impressive and consistent numbers. In his nine years with the Yankees he regularly provided 20 HR, 90+ RBI, and a .300+ average. The strike-shortened 1994 season was shaping up to be his best: .359 (led the league), 21 HR, and 83 RBI in 103 games.

Starting Pitching

Name	YR	WAR	W3	W-L	ERA	WHIP	ERA+
Red Ruffing	15	58.7	20.7	231-124	3.47	1.282	119
Whitey Ford	16	57.3	17.4	236-106	2.75	1.215	133
Andy Pettitte	15	51.6	20.2	219-127	3.94	1.373	115
Ron Guidry	14	48.1	21.4	170-91	3.29	1.184	119
Bob Shawkey	13	43.3	21.1	168-131	3.12	1.269	117
Mel Stottlemyre	11	43.1	18.6	164-139	2.97	1.219	112
Lefty Gomez	13	38.6	22.2	189-101	3.34	1.351	125
Waite Hoyt	10	35.5	16.2	157-98	3.48	1.336	115
Mike Mussina	8	35.2	18.9	123-72	3.88	1.212	114
Ray Caldwell	9	35.1	18.8	96-99	3.00	1.219	101
Herb Pennock	11	33.2	19.9	162-90	3.54	1.335	114
CC Sabathia	10	29.4	17.4	129-84	3.74	1.264	115
Jack Chesbro	7	29.2	21.1	128-93	2.58	1.120	109
Russ Ford	5	26.8	23.4	73-56	2.54	1.166	126
Spud Chandler	11	24.4	15.8	109-43	2.84	1.205	132
Al Orth	6	21.4	17.1	72-73	2.72	1.131	104
Roger Clemens	6	21.3	14.3	83-42	4.01	1.307	114
Fritz Peterson	9	21.1	12.1	109-106	3.10	1.146	106
Allie Reynolds	8	20.7	12.2	131-60	3.30	1.364	115
David Cone	6	20.4	15.9	64-40	3.91	1.331	118

Given the strength of the Yankees' lineup, the uneducated reader might be disappointed by their pitching staff. That isn't to say it is poor, because it certainly is not. But there is a reason the Yankees are so often referred to as the Bronx

Bombers—their hitting is what has led the way more often than not.

Choosing a top starter for this All-Time dream team is not clear-cut, as I think there are four candidates you could reasonably argue for. For most readers I'm sure the Yankees' All-Time pitching staff would start with **Whitey Ford** (1950, '53–67). He had only two 20+-win seasons, but they were strong ones: 25-4 in 1961 and 24-7 in 1963. He won the Cy Young Award in 1961 and captured ERA titles in 1956 and 1958. The Chairman of the Board had more wins than any other Yankee in history, and his .690 career winning percentage is phenomenal—though like many (though not all) on the list above, he had plenty of run support.

You could also make a strong argument that **Red Ruffing** (1930–42, '45–46) should be listed as the first pitcher on this team. Indeed, his career W-L numbers with the Yankees were actually quite close to Ford's. He had four 20+-win seasons and eight others with 15 or more. His career started horribly with Boston, where he went 39-96 over five-plus seasons. But he improved greatly in early 1930 when he joined the Yanks and was coached to change his delivery. It should also be noted that Ruffing could swing a pretty good bat too, as he hit .270, six times finished the season over .300, and ended up with 31 HR in 1,475 at-bats for the Yankees. He just couldn't run well, owing to the loss of four toes on his left foot due to a mining accident as a teenager.

The pitcher with the third-highest career WAR with the Yankees is **Andy Pettitte** (1995–2003, '07–10, '12), who pitched all but three of his seasons for New York. He had two 21-8 seasons, was an All-Star three times, and his 3.95 ERA is not bad given the era he pitched in (115 ERA+). The all-time leader in strikeouts amongst Yankee pitchers, Pettitte also made 40 postseason starts for the Yankees, compiling an impressive 18-10 record.

The fourth starter I considered to be in the top group for the Yankees was southpaw **Ron Guidry** (1975–88). Louisiana Lightning won 20+ games three times, and captured two ERA titles and five Gold Glove Awards. His famous 1978 season was one of the best performances ever: 25-3, 1.74 ERA, 6.15 H/9 IP, and 248 strikeouts while winning the AL Cy Young Award in a unanimous vote. While his peak seasons were strong, he pitched a bit less than Ford, Ruffing, and Pettitte, so that is why I rank him fourth on this list.

After those four, the choosing gets a bit difficult, though I think the next three on the career WAR list deserve spots on this roster. **Bob Shawkey** (1915–27) won 20+ games four times, including an impressive 1916 campaign in which he went 24-14, starting 27 games but also relieving in 26 games. And it wasn't only that season that Shawkey did double-duty like that: overall, he started 274 games for the Yankees and came out of the bullpen 141 times.

Lifetime Yankees hurler **Mel Stottlemyre** (1964–74) pitched for the club during a particularly lean period. For example, did you know that the 1968 Yankees recorded the lowest team batting average since the Deadball Era, a paltry .214? This contributed to his respectable-but-less-than-stellar .541 winning percentage (note his 12-20 record in 1966). But he still managed to win 20+ games three times and was an All-Star five times. After being released by the Yankees before the 1975 season, he retired early at the age of 33.

Vernon "Lefty" Gomez (1930–42) played all but his final game for the Yankees. He won 20+ games four times, including records of 24-7 in 1932 and 26-5 in 1934. He twice won ERA titles with a 2.33 mark in both 1934 and 1937. In fact, in 1934 he captured the pitching Triple Crown by leading the league in strikeouts (158 is all it took), only to win the Crown in 1937 as well, when he went 21-11 with a 2.33 ERA and 194 strikeouts. Gomez was undefeated (6-0) in seven starts across five different World Series while posting a 2.86 postseason ERA.

Choosing more starting pitchers to round out this All-Time team pitching staff is not easy. After my analysis I gave a slight edge to **Mike Mussina** (2001–08), who pitched the latter half of his career in New York, and finally capped it off with his only 20-win season in his final year. His 123-72 record is a .631 winning percentage, and he also fielded his position well, as noted by the three Gold Glove Awards he took home while with the Yankees.

If you wanted to go with one or two more additional starters, and fewer relievers on this roster, then I think the two choices would be two Hall of Fame teammates from the 1920s, Waite Hoyt (1921–30) and Herb Pennock (1923–33). Pennock had great control, three times leading the league in fewest walks per nine innings. He won 20+ games twice and won 19 twice also. It would be hard to choose him over Hoyt, though, as Hoyt also won 20+ games twice, and 19 twice too.

There were several others whom I considered and who deserve brief mention, including (in chronological order):

- Jack Chesbro (1903–1909) in 1904 went 41-12 with a 1.82 ERA while completing 48 of the 51 games he started. Beyond that amazing season, he won 19+ games for the Yankees in three of his other five seasons.

- Al Orth (1904–09) was a 204-game winner who finished his career with the New York Highlanders. He had one outstanding season for New York, in 1906, when he led the AL in wins with a 27-17 record to go with a 2.36 ERA and 36 complete games in 39 starts.

- Russ Ford (1909–13) had a short career that started with four full seasons for New York. The first two were winning seasons; the latter two were losing seasons (including a league-leading 21 losses in 1912). His rookie season of 1910 was his best year, going 26-6, posting a 1.65 ERA, and completing 29 of 33 starts.

- Ray Caldwell (1910–18) was mostly a starting pitcher for the Yankees and had his best season in 1914, when he posted an 18-9 record and 1.94 ERA.

- Spud Chandler (1937–47) pitched his entire career for the Yankees, and for pitchers with 100+ decisions after 1901, he still has the highest career winning percentage (.717). Chandler had two 20+-win seasons, including a 20-4 mark in 1943 to go with a league-leading 1.64 ERA.

- Allie Reynolds (1947–54) pitched for eight years in NY. He won 16 to 20 games for the first six of those seasons, and then was used increasingly in relief during the last two. He led the league in ERA once and strikeouts twice, and backed by the powerful Yankees lineup, posted a 131-60 record (.686). A fun fact is that in 1951 Reynolds became the first AL pitcher to toss two no-hitters in the same season.

- Fritz Peterson (1966–74) was Stottlemyre's teammate during the lean years, but managed one 20-win season, going 20-11 in 1970.

- David Cone (1995–2000) pitched four full seasons for the Yankees, was an All-Star twice, and had the most success for them in 1998, when he posted a 20-7 record.

- Roger Clemens (1999–2003, '07) pitched five full seasons for the Yankees late in his career, and then after three years in Houston returned for one final partial season before retiring. His most impressive season in New York came in 2001, when he posted a 20-3 record with 213 strikeouts and took home the AL Cy Young Award.

- CC Sabathia (2009–18) has been an All-Star three times for the Yankees, and he led the AL wins with 19 in 2009 and 21 in 2010. Now in his mid-thirties, his numbers have definitely slipped, so it would take quite a revival for him to make a run at a spot on this All-Time Yankees roster.

Relief Pitching

Name	YR	WAR	W3	SV	W-L	ERA	WHIP	ERA+
Mariano Rivera	19	57.1	13.5	652	82-60	2.21	1.000	205
Dave Righetti	11	23.3	10.9	224	74-61	3.11	1.295	127
Rich Gossage	7	19.0	11.5	151	42-28	2.14	1.079	179
Sparky Lyle	7	15.3	10.7	141	57-40	2.41	1.207	148
Johnny Murphy	12	12.8	8.3	104	93-53	3.54	1.373	116

As if this team needs more positions of strength, this Yankees roster has arguably the greatest one-inning closer of all time. After one year as a dominating setup man for John Wetteland, **Mariano Rivera** (1995–2013) established himself as the top ninth-inning man in the game in 1997. He had two 50+-save seasons, and seven others with 40+, including his final season in 2013, when at age 43 he notched 44 saves. A 13-time All-Star, The Sandman had 11 seasons with an ERA under 2.00. And he only seemed to kick it up a notch in the postseason, posting a microscopic 0.70 ERA, an 8-1 record, and 42 saves from 141 innings of work in 32 series.

Dave Righetti (1979, '81–90) was a top-notch reliever for many years in NY, seven times posting 25+ saves, but we sometimes forget that he began his career as a starter. He even pitched a no-hitter against Boston on the 4th of July in 1983. He was AL Rookie of the Year in the strike-shortened 1981 season and led the league in saves in 1986 with 46.

Rich "Goose" Gossage (1978–83, '89) was more than dominating: he was at times downright feared by hitters around the league. He pitched six masterful seasons in pinstripes from 1978 through 1983. His ERA was never over 2.62 during that stretch, and in the strike-shortened 1981 season it was an amazing 0.77.

Sparky Lyle (1972–78) was also often dominating, starting with his first year in New York in 1972, when he led the AL with 35 saves while posting a 1.92 ERA. A three-time All-Star for the Yankees, he led the league in saves again in 1976 with 23, and then in 1977 won the Cy Young Award with a 13-5 record, 26 saves, and a 2.17 ERA.

The other serious candidate I considered was Johnny Murphy (1932, '34–43, '46), a pioneer as a short reliever in the 1930s and 1940s. If the save stat had existed back then, he would have led the league four times with totals of 11,

11, 15, and a high of 19 in 1939. He was an All-Star three times—a rarity for relievers in those days. And he also had several nicknames, including Fireman, Fordham Johnny, and Grandma.

Managers

Name	YR	From-To	W-L	PCT	PS	WS
Joe McCarthy	16	1931–46	1460-867	.627	8	7
Casey Stengel	12	1949–60	1149-696	.623	10	7
Joe Torre	12	1996–2007	1173-767	.605	12	4
Miller Huggins	12	1918–29	1067-719	.597	6	3
Billy Martin	8	1975–88	556-385	.591	3	2
Joe Girardi	10	2008–17	910-710	.562	6	1
Ralph Houk	11	1961–73	944-806	.539	3	2

The Yankees' success over the years can be attributed mostly to their outstanding players on the field, but they've also had some very good managers too. You could make a case for any of the top four above as the best by getting into details such as the talent they had to work with, the relative competition they faced, and other factors. **Joe McCarthy** and **Casey Stengel** have slightly higher winning percentages than **Joe Torre** and **Miller Huggins**, and they each led the Yankees to seven World Series championships. Torre led the Yankees to the postseason in all 12 of his seasons, and Huggins was at the helm of the famous Murderers' Row teams of the late 1920s. Any way you rank them, having one at the helm and the other three as coaches would make for an outstanding brain trust in the dugout.

Starting Lineup

What would mythical starting lineups look like for this All-Time roster?

Against RHP:
Derek Jeter SS (R)
Joe DiMaggio CF (R)
Babe Ruth RF (L)
Lou Gehrig 1B (L)
Mickey Mantle DH (S)
Álex Rodríguez 3B (R)
Charlie Keller LF (L)
Yogi Berra/Bill Dickey C (L)
Robinson Canó 2B (L)

Against LHP:
Derek Jeter SS (R)
Joe DiMaggio CF (R)
Babe Ruth RF (L)
Mickey Mantle LF (S)
Lou Gehrig 1B (L)
Álex Rodríguez 3B (R)
Thurman Munson DH (R)
Yogi Berra/Bill Dickey C (L)
Tony Lazzeri 2B (R)

These lineups are Murderers' Row no matter how you arrange them. The first thing you'll notice is that with both Mantle and DiMaggio as center fielders, I elected to shift Mantle to LF against lefties (he did play there one season) and use him as the DH against righties. The only obvious natural platoon was at 2B, where Canó is a lefty and Lazzeri is a righty (as is Randolph).

Berra and Dickey were both lefties, so they would need to just split time according to whose knees needed rest. You could use Munson behind the dish against the toughest lefties, but I actually went with Munson as a DH (Williams as a switch-hitter was another option).

The only thing missing from these lineups is a significant stolen-base threat (since Henderson didn't play for the Yankees long enough to crack this roster). But wow… otherwise these lineups are downright scary.

Depth Chart

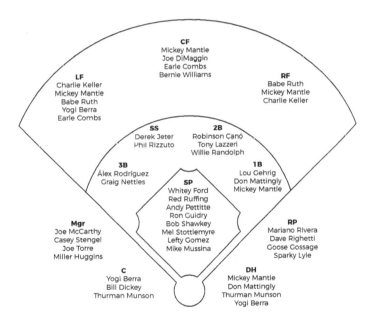

CF
Mickey Mantle
Joe DiMaggio
Earle Combs
Bernie Williams

LF
Charlie Keller
Mickey Mantle
Babe Ruth
Yogi Berra
Earle Combs

RF
Babe Ruth
Mickey Mantle
Charlie Keller

SS
Derek Jeter
Phil Rizzuto

2B
Robinson Canó
Tony Lazzeri
Willie Randolph

3B
Álex Rodríguez
Graig Nettles

1B
Lou Gehrig
Don Mattingly
Mickey Mantle

SP
Whitey Ford
Red Ruffing
Andy Pettitte
Ron Guidry
Bob Shawkey
Mel Stottlemyre
Lefty Gomez
Mike Mussina

Mgr
Joe McCarthy
Casey Stengel
Joe Torre
Miller Huggins

RP
Mariano Rivera
Dave Righetti
Goose Gossage
Sparky Lyle

C
Yogi Berra
Bill Dickey
Thurman Munson

DH
Mickey Mantle
Don Mattingly
Thurman Munson
Yogi Berra

Prospects for Current Players

What are the prospects of current Yankees players making this All-Time team? Not very good, but not because they don't have talent on their roster. Players trying to crack this All-Time dream team roster have arguably the most difficult task of any franchise. As noted above, I don't think Brett Gardner is likely going to do enough to supplant Keller, Williams, or Combs for an outfield spot. CC Sabathia is still pitching well, but is clearly nearing the end of his career. While Masahiro Tanaka is only 30, he'll need to up his game and play for the Yankees for a long time to earn one of the spots on this pitching staff. And youngsters like Aaron Judge, Gary Sánchez, and Didi Gregorius are impressive, but they have a long way to go to amass a worthy résumé. We'll see...

Retired Player Numbers

Billy Martin (1, manager), Babe Ruth (3), Lou Gehrig (4), Joe DiMaggio (5), Joe Torre (6, manager), Mickey Mantle (7), Yogi Berra (8), Bill Dickey (8), Roger Maris (9), Phil Rizzuto (10), Thurman Munson (15), Whitey Ford (16), Jorge Posada (20), Don Mattingly (23), Elston Howard (32), Casey Stengel (37, manager), Mariano Rivera (42), Reggie Jackson (44), Andy Pettitte (46), Ron Guidry (49), Bernie Williams (51)

Selections from Other Authors and Fan Surveys

1949: *The Yankees: A Pictorial History of Baseball's Greatest Club*, by John Durant

On pg. 121 of this book an "All-Time, All-Star Yankee Team" was provided, said to have been "selected by a consensus of experts" (whatever that meant exactly). The results were: 1B Gehrig, 2B Lazzeri, 3B Rolfe, SS Crosetti, C Dickey, RF Ruth, CF DiMaggio, LF Keeler, SP Chesbro, Shawkey, Pennock, Ruffing.

Not a bad team, but before I comment I should note that the book listed the lifetime statistics for each player—perhaps implying that more than just their Yankees accomplishments were considered. That could explain the choice of Keeler, who had a great career, but with few of his good seasons as a Yankee. I also don't understand leaving Lefty Gomez off this team, especially since his feats should have been fresh on the minds of the experts (he retired in 1943).

1953: 50th Yankee Anniversary All-Time Yankee Team, as provided in *The Yankee Encyclopedia*, 4th edition, 2000, by Mark Gallagher and Walter LeConte

This All-Time team was "selected by a poll of 48 veteran sportswriters, baseball officials and other experts." The results were (number of votes in parentheses):

1B: Lou Gehrig (46), Hal Chase (2)

2B: Tony Lazzeri (36), Joe Gordon (12)

3B: Red Rolfe (38), Joe Dugan (10)

SS: Phil Rizzuto (42), Frank Crosetti (3), Roger Peckinpaugh (1), Everett Scott (1), Tony Lazzeri (1)

C: Bill Dickey (unanimous)

Utility Infield: Frank Crosetti (23), Joe Gordon (11), Tony Lazzeri (3), Joe Dugan (2), nine others (1)

OF: Babe Ruth (unanimous), Joe DiMaggio (unanimous), Bob Meusel (24), Earle Combs (14), Tommy Henrich (8), Willie Keeler (2)

RHP: Red Ruffing (28), Waite Hoyt (11), Jack Chesbro (4), Vic Raschi (2), Bob Shawkey (2), Spud Chandler (1)

LHP: Lefty Gomez (24), Herb Pennock (24)

RP: Johnny Murphy (25), Wilcy Moore (11), Joe Page (10), Waite Hoyt (1), Lefty Gomez (1)

I think Hal Chase was a fine player, but how could Gehrig not have joined Ruth, DiMaggio, and Dickey as unanimous choices? The other infield vote totals were reasonable, and the pitching vote totals were sensible too, though I find it interesting that just two guys split the LHP vote while it was a bit more complicated for RHP.

1959: *Sport* magazine, February issue

As part of a running series, *Sport* magazine reported on all-time all-star teams picked by "big league publicity departments and the writers covering the clubs." Here is what they had to say:

First Base: Lou Gehrig, the immortal "Iron Man," took over first base one day in 1925 and played in 2,130 consecutive games before the crippling disease that was to kill him forced him to quit in 1939. He still holds the major-league record for grand-slam home runs, with 23, and is fourth on the all-time home run listing, with 494. He was elected to the Hall of Fame in 1939.

Second Base: Tony Lazzeri, one of the most popular Yankees during his playing days between 1926 and 1937, was an excellent fielder and an underrated hitter. With Ruth and Gehrig around, nobody noticed "Poosh 'Em Up's" bat, but he was always a spray-hitting threat and his .354 led the team in 1929.

Shortstop: Phil "Scooter" Rizzuto, one of the finest fielding shortstops ever to play in the American League, performed from 1941 to 1955 and still holds the league record for consecutive games without an error, 58, and the major-league record for fewest errors in a season, 14 in 1950. His best years were 1950, when he set his fielding record and was Most Valuable Player; and 1951, when he won the Babe Ruth Award as the top World Series player.

Third Base: Robert "Red" Rolfe, a reliable, hard-hitting Yankee from 1934 to 1942, was a key factor in six Yankee pennants in that stretch. Five of those teams also won the World Series. His best years were 1939, when he hit .329, and 1936, when he hit .319.

Left Field: Bob Meusel, a hard-hitting outfielder who played the outfield in the shadow of Ruth from 1920 to 1929, was a consistent .300 hitter and would have been the top star on any other team of his era. In 1925, a year in which he hit only .295, he got 33 home runs and drove in 138 runs to lead the league in both departments.

Center Field: Joe DiMaggio, the great "Yankee Clipper" and idol of Yankee Stadium from 1936 to 1951, finished up with a fine .325 lifetime average and a long list of distinguished hitting and fielding achievements. His .381 in 1939 and .352 in 1940 were both good for batting titles and he led in home runs three times and in runs-batted-in twice. Named Most Valuable Player in 1939, 1941, and 1947, he was elected to the Hall of Fame in 1955. His hitting streak of 56 straight games, set in 1941, is still the longest in major-league history.

Right Field: Babe Ruth, the one and only Bambino, was the greatest hitter baseball ever has known. From 1920 to 1934, he was only twice under .300 and his Yankee lifetime average was .349. His 60 home runs in 1927 remains an unmatched major-league record. So is his slugging average of .847 in 1920, his 177 runs scored in '21, 170 walks in '23, and his 714 lifetime home runs. Although he was a home-run champion for 12 years and runs-batted-in leader for five years, Babe won only one batting championship, with .378 in 1924. He was the Most Valuable Player in 1923 and was named to the Hall of Fame in 1936.

Catcher: Bill Dickey, whose career stretched from 1928 to 1946, still holds a longevity record for catching 100 or more games in 13 consecutive seasons. A consistent .300 hitter, he is best remembered for his fine defensive work and his brilliant handling of a generation of Yankee pitchers. He was named to the Hall of Fame in 1954.

Righthanded Pitcher: Charles "Red" Ruffing, the workhorse of the Yankee pitching staff between 1930 and 1946, won 20 or more games in four seasons and holds the Yankee record of 231 career victories. In one three-year stretch, from 1937 to 1939, he compiled consecutive records of 20-7, 21-7, and 21-7.

Lefthanded Pitcher: Vernon "Lefty" Gomez gets the berth by a whisker over Herb Pennock of an earlier vintage. Occasionally erratic, Gomez often pitched brilliantly from 1930 to 1942 with the Yankees. He was a 20-game winner on four occasions and his 26-5 record of 1934, for an .839 percentage, is a Yankee record. He twice led the league in low earned-run average.

Back in 1959 this was an entirely reasonable roster. What interested me in reading the write-ups for each player was the almost quaint reference to records, such as Gehrig ranking fourth in all-time home runs, and also Ruth's 60 homers—a record that would be broken just two years later. It also makes you appreciate again DiMaggio's incredible hitting streak, which still stands as a record today.

1963: The All-Yankee Team: The First 60 Years: 1903–1963, as provided in *The New York Yankees 1982 Official Yearbook*

Only one 1B is listed, Lou Gehrig. 2B has Lazzeri, Gordon, Martin, and Richardson. SS has Crosetti, Kubek, and Rizzuto, which I think is not listing Rizzuto high enough. But for reasons that will become clear in a moment, perhaps the order they are listed in does not have significance in this book. 3B is Joe Sewell (who played for the Yankees for only three years, 1931–33), Baker, Dugan, and Boyer, which seriously ignores Rolfe. There are seven outfielders: Ruth, DiMaggio, Mantle, Maris, Combs, Meusel, and Keeler. I think Keller is more deserving than Keeler, but don't try to say that really fast too many times or you'll get confused. And like SS, the catcher list seems out of order with Dickey, Howard, and then Berra. But the biggest ordering problem is for pitchers: Chesbro, Pennock, Gomez, Ruffing, Chandler, Reynolds, and Ford. A good group, but obviously Ford should not be last, so likely the order was not significant.

1969: *The Sporting News* Fan Poll

The July 5, 1969, issue reported the results of a fan poll for the long-standing franchises of the day. The results for New York were: 1B Gehrig, 2B Lazzeri, 3B Rolfe, SS Rizzuto, C Dickey, LF Mantle, CF DiMaggio, RF Ruth, RHP Ruffing, and LHP Ford.

For 1969, all of these were good choices (allowing for Mantle to be chosen largely out of position). *The Yankees: An Illustrated History*, by George Sullivan and John Powers, included in an Appendix a 1969 fan survey whose results are identical, so I assume it was the same survey. However, they also report a "second team" from that survey, as follows: 1B Pepitone, 2B Richardson, SS Crosetti, 3B Boyer, LF Keller, CF Mantle, RF Mantle, C Berra, RHP Reynolds, and LHP Gomez. I would have preferred at least Skowron, and perhaps others, over Pepitone at 1B. The rest of the infield is fine, as is Berra as the extra backstop since he wasn't chosen as the starter. Ruffing and Hoyt were both righties, so I prefer them over Reynolds. And the fans apparently liked Mantle so much they found a way to get him listed at all three OF spots!

1990: "All-Time All-Star Teams," in *The Baseball Research Journal*

In an interesting article, Robert C. Berlo used John Thorn and Pete Palmer's TPR (Total Player Rating) system to choose all-time teams. He selected players based on their best 800 consecutive games for the franchise, with a minimum of five years played. His results: 1B Gehrig, 2B Gordon, SS Peckinpaugh, 3B McDougald, RF Ruth, CF DiMaggio, LF Mantle, C Berra, SP Chandler, SP Ruffing, SP Ford, SP Gomez, RP Gossage.

No surprises at 1B, C, and OF. Gordon wasn't surprising at 2B, since the approach used here rewarded peak performance. But Peckinpaugh? He was a Yankee from 1913 to 1921, batted over .300 once, and had 38 SB one season, but had no other statistics that caught my eye. I would have thought that Rizzuto's peak consecutive stretch would have come out ahead of Peckinpaugh's. Seeing Chandler as the top pitcher is understandable, since he didn't join the Yankees until he was 29 and had a relatively short (but strong) career.

1991: *Louisville Slugger Presents: The New York Yankees*, by Dick Lally

In the Yankees installment of this series of books in 1991, the author chose an All-Time all-star team that consisted of Gehrig, Lazzeri, Rizzuto, Nettles, and Berra in the infield, Mantle in LF, DiMaggio in CF, and Ruth in LF. The top LHP was Ford, the top RHP was Hoyt, and Gossage was chosen as relief pitcher.

1992: *The All-Time All-Star Baseball Book*, by Nick Acocella and Donald Dewey

These authors went with the same starting nine that I would have in 1992 except Dickey over Berra at catcher. They also listed as honorable mention Bobby Richardson, Red Rolfe, Bob Meusel, Earle Combs, Reggie Jackson, Yogi Berra, Red Ruffing, Herb Pennock, Lefty Gomez, and Ron Guidry.

1995: *Baseball Ratings*, by Charles F. Faber

The Faber system as applied in 1995 created a reasonable all-time team. Identical to my choices were Gehrig, Berra, and the outfielders. Nettles and Rizzuto were the best choices at 3B and SS in 1995, which left just 2B, where Randolph came out on top of Lazzeri. The pitching staff was also reasonable: Ford, Guidry, Ruffing, Gomez, and Pennock, with Righetti listed as the top reliever.

2001: *Few and Chosen: Defining Yankee Greatness Across the Eras*, by Whitey Ford with Phil Pepe

As with each book in this fun series, the authors chose a top-five list at each position. For the Yankees, their lists in order were:

Catcher: Berra, Dickey, Munson, Howard, Posada

First Base: Gehrig, Mattingly, Skowron, Chambliss, Martinez

Second Base: Lazzeri, Gordon, Richardson, Randolph, Jerry Coleman

Shortstop: Jeter, Rizzuto, Kubek, Crosetti, Mark Koenig

Third Base: Nettles, Rolfe, Boyer, Boggs, Dugan

(*Note: McDougald was chosen as a "utility" selection, indicating that he could be chosen at any of three positions.*)

Left Field: Winfield, Meusel, Keller, White, Bauer/Woodling (tie)

Center Field: DiMaggio, Mantle, Williams, Combs, Rivers

Right Field: Ruth, Jackson, Maris, O'Neill, Henrich

Right-Handed Pitcher: Ruffing, Reynolds, Raschi, Stottlemyre, Hoyt

Left-Handed Pitcher: Gomez, Guidry, Pennock, Eddie Lopat, Pettitte

Relief Pitcher: Rivera, Gossage, Lyle, Righetti, Page

Manager: Stengel, McCarthy, Torre, Houk/Martin (tie), Huggins

I have no major issues with the choices at C and 1B. At 2B, Mr. Ford clearly went with peak performance by rating Gordon second and Randolph fourth. Ford admitted that at this point Jeter didn't have a long résumé, but he nonetheless felt he was deserving of the top spot at this relatively weak all-time Yankees position (Mark Koenig was a .285 hitter over six seasons in the late 1920s). Winfield played more games in RF than in LF, but listing him under LF gets him a top spot (something he wasn't going to get at RF). Ford chose to rate DiMaggio over Mantle—going, in his words, with his "head" over his "heart." I have no issues with his RF choices, as Ruth is the obvious top selection and the other four can be reasonably debated as to order.

I won't presume to argue over Ford's ordering of his right-handed pitcher list. For left-handed hurlers, Mr. Ford clearly has omitted himself from consideration, and he admitted that at that time Pettitte was still racking up accolades. For relief pitchers, Ford considered Rivera's dominance to already deserve the top spot. He then noted that you could reorder Gossage, Lyle, and Righetti any way you like and he wouldn't argue. Although he spoke highly of Murphy, he nonetheless listed Joe Page as his fifth reliever, noting that he "may have been the first high-profile relief pitcher in baseball because of his flamboyance." That might be true, but Page really only had two strong seasons: 1947, when he went 14-8 with a 2.48 ERA and led the league with 17 saves, and 1949, when he went 13-8 with a 2.59 ERA and led the league with 27 saves.

2002: *Yankees Century: 100 Years of New York Yankees Baseball*, by Glenn Stout

In Appendix A, Mr. Stout provided two All-Time Yankees rosters, one for pre–World War II (1903–1944), and one for post–World War II (1945–2001). He also included a brief write-up for each player, giving some indication of why they were chosen.

For the earlier squad, he listed Gehrig and Chase at 1B, Lazzeri and Gordon at 2B, Crosetti and Elberfeld at SS, and Rolfe, Baker, and Dugan at 3B. About Elberfeld, Stout wrote: "The 'Tabasco Kid' was one of the toughest players of the Dead Ball Era and a fan favorite at Hilltop Park." He might have been tough while on the field, but he never played more than 122 games in a season. Only one catcher was chosen, Bill Dickey, described as one of the greatest catchers of his generation, "along with Mickey Cochrane and Josh Gibson."

The OF for this roster was loaded with Ruth, DiMaggio, Combs, Meusel, Henrich, Keeler, William "Birdie" Cree, and George Selkirk. Cree's New York career lasted from 1908 to 1915 but included only four seasons of 100+ games played. His only standout season was 1911, when he had 22 triples, 48 SB, and batted .348.

The starting staff was solid with Ruffing, Chesbro, Shawkey, Hoyt, Gomez, and Pennock. And the two relievers were good choices too, Wilcy Moore and Johnny Murphy. Moore had a very impressive rookie campaign in 1927, when he went 19-7 as a combined starter and reliever, leading the league with a 2.28 ERA and 13 saves. But then he didn't do much for the Yankees in four seasons after that.

For the post-WWII club, I can't object to any of the infield selections: Mattingly and Martinez at 1B, Randolph and Martin at 2B, McDougald as a utility infielder, Nettles and Boyer at 3B, Jeter and Rizzuto at SS, and Berra, Howard, and Munson behind the plate. The OF was also sensible and included DiMaggio, Mantle, Williams, Henderson, White, Jackson, Maris, O'Neill, and Winfield.

His selections for starting pitchers were pretty good ones, with a RHP list of Reynolds, Stottlemyre, and Catfish Hunter, who was an All-Star for the Yankees twice, including in 1975, when he led the AL in wins with a 23-14 record. The LHP list was Ford, Eddie Lopat (who posted a 3.19 ERA and .657 winning percentage across eight seasons), and Guidry. For relievers, he went with LHP Page and Lyle and RHP Gossage and Rivera.

2003: *Rob Neyer's Big Book of Baseball Lineups*, by Rob Neyer

Neyer's choices were solid, with his starting and backup infield exactly the same as mine would have been in 2003. He went with a strict two players per OF position, and so reasonably listed Ruth and Jackson in RF, Mantle and DiMaggio in CF, and Keller and White in LF.

His starting pitchers list included Ford, Ruffing, Guidry, Gomez, Reynolds, Lopat, Shawkey, and Stottlemyre. His choices of Rivera and Gossage as the two relievers were good picks, as were his top five managers: Stengel, McCarthy, Huggins, Torre, and Martin.

2016: *101 All-Time Fantasy Baseball Teams*, by Jack Sweeney

Sweeney's book had mostly the same infield I do, though he chose Lazzeri over Canó at 2B. He listed Ruth as DH, and then chose Mantle, DiMaggio, and Winfield as the three outfielders. His first three starting pitching choices of Ford, Gomez, and Ruffing are solid, but then choosing Hoyt as the fourth I think is a disservice to at least Pettitte and Guidry. Rivera was the obvious choice as top reliever.

Top WAR Single Seasons – Hitters (8+)

Name	Year	WAR	AVG	HR	R	RBI	SB	OPS+
Babe Ruth	1923	14.1	.393	41	151	130	17	239
Babe Ruth	1921	12.6	.378	59	177	168	17	238
Babe Ruth	1927	12.4	.356	60	158	165	7	225
Lou Gehrig	1927	11.8	.373	47	149	173	10	220
Babe Ruth	1920	11.8	.376	54	158	135	14	255
Babe Ruth	1924	11.7	.378	46	143	124	9	220
Babe Ruth	1926	11.5	.372	47	139	153	11	225
Mickey Mantle	1957	11.3	.365	34	121	94	16	221
Mickey Mantle	1956	11.2	.353	52	132	130	10	210
Babe Ruth	1930	10.5	.359	49	150	153	10	211
Mickey Mantle	1961	10.5	.317	54	131	128	12	206
Lou Gehrig	1934	10.4	.363	49	128	166	9	206
Babe Ruth	1931	10.3	.373	46	149	162	5	218
Babe Ruth	1928	10.1	.323	54	163	146	4	206
R. Henderson	1985	9.9	.314	24	146	72	80	157
Lou Gehrig	1930	9.6	.379	41	143	173	12	203
Mickey Mantle	1955	9.5	.306	37	121	99	8	180
Álex Rodríguez	2007	9.4	.314	54	143	156	24	176
Lou Gehrig	1928	9.4	.374	27	139	147	4	193
Álex Rodríguez	2005	9.4	.321	48	124	130	21	173

Lou Gehrig	1936	9.1	.354	49	167	152	3	190
Joe DiMaggio	1941	9.1	.357	30	122	125	4	184
Lou Gehrig	1931	8.8	.341	46	163	185	17	194
Snuffy Stirnweiss	1945	8.7	.309	10	107	64	33	145
Mickey Mantle	1958	8.7	.304	42	127	97	18	188
Lou Gehrig	1935	8.7	.329	30	125	120	8	176
Snuffy Stirnweiss	1944	8.5	.319	8	125	43	55	139
Robinson Canó	2012	8.5	.313	33	105	94	3	148
Babe Ruth	1932	8.3	.341	41	120	137	2	201
Joe Gordon	1942	8.2	.322	18	88	103	12	154
Joe DiMaggio	1937	8.2	.346	46	151	167	3	166
Aaron Judge	2017	8.1	.284	52	128	114	9	171
Bobby Murcer	1972	8.1	.292	33	102	96	11	169
Robinson Canó	2010	8.1	.319	29	103	109	3	141
Joe DiMaggio	1939	8.1	.381	30	108	126	3	184
Babe Ruth	1929	8.0	.345	46	121	154	5	193
Graig Nettles	1976	8.0	.254	32	88	93	11	135
Derek Jeter	1999	8.0	.349	24	134	102	19	153

Not surprising to see Babe Ruth's domination of this list: he had 11 seasons with a WAR of 8.0 or higher, including six of the top seven for the Yankees all-time. The top 14 WAR scores here belong to just three players: Ruth, Gehrig, and Mantle. At the 15th spot is Rickey Henderson's 1985 season with his 80 stolen bases. The great DiMaggio doesn't appear until 22nd on this list, and Jeter doesn't appear until the very end of the list. I found it interesting that both of Stirnweiss' great years made this list, as did Nettles' 1976 campaign, when he managed to pace the AL with just 32 home runs. And lastly, Aaron Judge's breakout Rookie of the Year 2017 campaign rated 8.1 WAR after leading the AL in HR, runs, and walks (though also strikeouts with 208).

Top WAR Single Seasons – Pitchers 8+)

Name	Year	WAR	W-L	ERA	IP	SO	ERA+
Russ Ford	1910	11.5	26-6	1.65	299.2	209	160
Jack Chesbro	1904	11.0	41-12	1.82	454.2	239	150
Ron Guidry	1978	9.6	25-3	1.74	273.2	248	208
Lefty Gomez	1937	9.2	21-11	2.33	278.1	194	193
Al Orth	1906	8.7	27-17	2.34	338.2	133	127
Andy Pettitte	1997	8.4	18-7	2.88	240.1	166	156
Catfish Hunter	1975	8.1	23-14	2.58	328.0	177	144

I found a couple of things interesting about this list. First, it isn't very long. Second, there is a Ford at the top of the list, but it is not the one you might think. In fact, the "other" Ford, Whitey, never had a season with a WAR rating of 7.0 or higher. His best was actually not his Cy Young Award season in 1961, but rather a 6.8 WAR in 1964, when he went 17-6 with a 2.13 ERA, a 170 ERA+, and a career-high 8 shutouts. If you discount the two old-timers at the top of this list, then Ron Guidry's 1978 season is not surprisingly the best ever for the Yankees.

Franchise Player

With apologies to Gehrig, Mantle, DiMaggio, and others, this honor surely must be given to Babe Ruth. With only a potential argument in favor of Ted Williams or Barry Bonds, Ruth's per-at-bat numbers just tower above every other hitter ever.

CHAPTER 2

The Giants Franchise All-Time Dream Team

This franchise began as the New York Gothams in 1883, becoming the Giants in 1885. After various ups and downs during their early years, they managed a .600+ winning percentage in 14 of the 21 seasons from 1904 through 1924. This stretch produced nine pennants, though only three World Series titles. They slipped only slightly for the next decade, before capturing three pennants and one World Series from 1933 through 1937.

The club then entered a dry spell until the Willie Mays era began, during which the team was regularly above .500, and won three pennants and one World Series—in 1954, which was their last while in New York. They moved to San Francisco for the 1958 season and continued to be a generally strong contender until the 1970s, when they slipped to the bottom half of their division. They took the division title twice in the late 1980s and went to the World Series in 1989, only to be swept in four games.

The Giants finished first or second in their division every year from 1997 to 2004, and then finally had ultimate success again by winning the World Series in 2010, 2012, and 2014.

The New York/San Francisco Giants All-Time team is full of outstanding players, including some of the best ever to play the game. Their top outfielders and starting pitchers are superb, though they are a bit weaker, relatively speaking, at some other positions.

1st Base

Name	YR	WAR	W3	W/G	AVG	HR	SB	OPS+
Willie McCovey	19	59.3	21.7	.0263	.274	469	24	149
Bill Terry	14	54.2	20.9	.0315	.341	154	56	136
Roger Connor	10	52.9	22.7	.0472	.319	76	161	161
Will Clark	8	35.5	20.4	.0306	.299	176	52	145
Orlando Cepeda	9	30.4	15.8	.0273	.308	226	92	140
Johnny Mize	5	28.3	20.0	.0432	.299	157	13	155
Brandon Belt	8	22.7	12.5	.0245	.266	112	39	124
George Kelly	11	22.6	12.3	.0199	.301	123	54	117
Fred Merkle	10	13.9	9.2	.0126	.272	49	212	110
J.T. Snow	10	12.4	8.2	.0105	.273	124	14	112

The Giants are loaded with great candidates at 1B, and the choice for the top spot is not obvious. **Willie McCovey** (1959–73, '77–80) played all of his best years for the Giants, leaving for only three years to play for San Diego and Oakland. Not the most durable of players (he played 150+ games in a season only four times, and 140+ only seven times), he was still a leading power hitter of his day, smashing 30+ HR and 90+ RBI seven times. He led the NL in HR three times and RBI twice. Though he played in only 52 games in 1959, his 13 HR and .354 BA were enough to take home top rookie honors. His career year was 1969, as he batted .320 with 45 HR, 126 RBI, and 121 BB to win the NL MVP Award. His propensity to strike out decreased as he gained more experience, and eventually he became patient enough to be amongst the league leaders in walks each year. He wasn't quick on the bases or in the field, but his lanky 6'4" frame made Stretch an adequate fielder at 1B.

You could make a case for **Bill Terry** (1923–36) as the starter over McCovey, and he certainly deserves a spot on this All-Time team. He played his entire Hall of Fame career with the Giants and had the team's highest career batting average (.341). He never won an MVP Award, but he was amongst the top ten in voting six times. And that doesn't include 1930, when no MVP Award was given, a year that saw Terry lead the league with a .401 average and a whopping 254 hits. Aside from that, Terry rarely led the league in any offensive categories, but he was regularly amongst the leaders in BA, OBP, hits, doubles, triples, runs, RBI, and more. He also was a successful manager for the Giants for ten seasons, the first five of which he was a player-manager. Under his leadership the team won 90+ games five years in a row, took home three pennants, and won the World Series in 1933.

Old-timer **Roger Connor** (1883–89, '91, '93–94) was one of the leading power hitters of his day, regularly hitting double-digit HR and triples in the same season. He paced the NL in batting in 1885 with a .371 mark and was regularly amongst the league leaders in just about every offensive category. Did you know that he was major league baseball's career HR leader until Babe Ruth came along? His WAR total was accomplished during shorter seasons too, so on a per-game basis you could make a case for him over McCovey or Terry. But as the game was so different back in those early days, I consider it hard to trust the numbers. So I'll just include Connor on this All-Time Giants roster by giving him one of the two "extra spots."

In terms of peak WAR and WAR per game, **Will "The Thrill" Clark** (1986–93) rates up there with McCovey and Terry—he just didn't play for the Giants for as long. Clark spent his first eight seasons in San Francisco and was an All-Star in five of them. His best year was 1989, when he led the league with 104 runs and was runner-up with a .333 average and 196 hits, earning him second place in the MVP balloting behind teammate Kevin Mitchell. In fact, Clark finished in the top five in NL MVP votes four times during his short tenure with the Giants, and also took home one Gold Glove Award (1991). Although it meant loading up on 1B, and it was a close call with several good OF candidates, I gave Clark the second "extra spot" on this All-Time team roster.

There was no room for Orlando Cepeda here at 1B (his primary position), so I considered him later for an OF spot. And Johnny Mize (1942, '46–49) had two good seasons and two great seasons for the Giants, including his impressive 1947 numbers: .302, 51 HR, 138 RBI, 137 runs. But three years of military service in World War II interrupted his Giants tenure and kept him from accumulating enough numbers to crack this roster.

Four other Giants 1B deserve brief mention. During the early 1920s, while Babe Ruth was redefining the game, George "High Pockets" Kelly (1915–17, '19–26) twice led the NL in RBI and once in HR. A .301 hitter, he was a good RBI man (with six consecutive 90+-RBI seasons) and was a good fielder as well. Fred Merkle (1907–16) stole a lot of bases—20 to 49 per year during his six full seasons with the Giants. J.T. Snow (1997–2005, '08) hit 20+ HR twice and took home four of his six Gold Glove Awards as a Giant. And lastly, current Giants 1B Brandon Belt was an All-Star in 2016 when he hit 41 doubles and 17 HR with a .394 OBP.

2nd Base

Name	YR	WAR	W3	W/G	AVG	HR	SB	OPS+
Larry Doyle	13	42.8	14.8	.0264	.292	67	291	127
Frankie Frisch	8	37.8	21.4	.0378	.321	54	224	116
Robby Thompson	11	33.6	17.5	.0258	.257	119	103	105
Jeff Kent	6	31.4	19.4	.0349	.297	175	57	136

Compared to 1B, the Giants have rarely had star players at 2B. After considering several candidates, I decided to give the starting spot here to **Jeff Kent** (1997–2002). His six seasons in San Francisco provided between 22 and 37 HR and over 100 RBI every year. His best year was in 2000, when he hit .334 with 33 HR, 114 runs, and 125 RBI, enough to capture the NL MVP Award (beating out teammate Barry Bonds).

Frankie Frisch played more games at 2B than 3B for the Giants, but after considering all the candidates at both positions, I decided to give him a spot at the hot corner. So that meant the backup 2B was **Larry Doyle** (1907–16, '18–20), a Deadball-Era star who played most of his career for the Giants. He paced the NL with 25 triples in 1911, and in 1912 earned MVP honors (Chalmers Award), with his .330 average, 36 SB, and 10 HR edging out Honus Wagner's résumé. He went on to win the batting title in 1915, though with a rather mediocre .320 average. He had some speed too, compiling five consecutive seasons with 30+ SB.

The only other Giants 2B deserving brief mention was Robby Thompson (1986–96), who played his entire 11-year career for the Giants. He had moderate power for a 2B (double-digit HR in six seasons) and was a good fielder (Gold Glove Award in 1993). But he was fragile, playing the most games (149) in his rookie season, and ending his career early due to injury as well.

3rd Base

Name	YR	WAR	W3	W/G	AVG	HR	SB	OPS+
Frankie Frisch	8	37.8	21.4	.0378	.321	54	224	116
Art Devlin	8	34.5	17.4	.0309	.268	10	266	112
Matt Williams	10	33.9	16.1	.0303	.264	247	29	122
Jim Ray Hart	11	25.1	17.7	.0251	.282	157	17	130
Hank Thompson	8	24.7	14.5	.0273	.267	129	31	119
Freddie Lindstrom	9	23.2	15.6	.0213	.318	91	80	112
Darrell Evans	8	21.3	11.8	.0195	.255	142	55	119
Jim Davenport	13	18.2	11.3	.0121	.258	77	16	90
Sid Gordon	8	17.8	13.9	.0234	.278	90	14	123

As noted earlier, **Frankie Frisch** (1919–26) played more games at 2B (622) than at 3B (347) for the Giants, but he spent enough time at the hot corner to qualify here. The switch-hitting Frisch had seven solid seasons in New York before joining the Cardinals (in a big trade for Rogers Hornsby after the 1926 season). He had 20+ steals each full year as a Giant and batted over .300 in all but one, ending up with a .321 mark. He scored 100+ runs in four consecutive years and provided solid defense at both positions. He was a key player for the pennant-winning Giants from 1921 through 1924 and performed very well in all four World Series (of which they won the first two).

You could make a case for **Matt Williams** (1987–96) as the starter here, based on his combination of power and defense. It did take him a while to find his major league swing: in his first three partial seasons he batted .188, .205, and .202. But then in 1990 he belted 33 HR and led the league in RBI with 122. His 43 dingers in the strike-shortened 1994 season led the NL, and the talk that year was of Williams, Griffey Jr., and others making a run at Roger Maris' HR record. He was the runner-up in the MVP balloting that season and took home his third Gold Glove for the Giants.

I considered several others, starting with old-timer Art Devlin (1904–11), who played for the Giants for most of his career and was a good fielder and base runner: he had 266 SB and a league-leading 59 in 1905. But he was a mediocre hitter (.268) with virtually no power: he hit a total of 10 HR in eight seasons and never even topped 23 doubles or 8 triples in a season. By shifting Frisch over to 2B, you could make a case for Devlin over his teammate Doyle for this All-Time team, and I wouldn't really argue with you either way.

Hall of Famer Freddie Lindstrom (1924–32) hit .318 for the Giants and had several fine offensive seasons, including 1928, when he batted .358 with 231 hits, 39 doubles, 14 HR, and 107 RBI, and 1930, when he batted .379 with 231 hits, 39 doubles, 22 HR, 127 runs, and 106 RBI.

Several others deserve brief mention, including Jim Ray Hart (1963–73), who hit 20+ HR each year from 1964 through 1968, but had only five full seasons with the franchise and was weak defensively. Darrell Evans (1976–83) had seven full seasons with the Giants during the middle of his long career. He hit 20+ homers three times and was patient at the plate. Another power source for the Giants was Hank Thompson (1949–56), who played for the Giants about as long as Evans and Hart, and like them displayed some power at the plate, with three seasons of 20+ HR.

Just before Thompson there was Sid Gordon (1941–43, '46–49, '55), who played a mix of 3B and LF for the Giants. He was an All-Star in 1948, when he hit 30 HR with 107 RBI, and again in 1949, when he hit 26 HR with 90 RBI. And lastly, Jim Davenport (1958–70) played his entire career in San Francisco and was a good fielder (Gold Glove Award in 1962), but not much of a hitter (.258).

Shortstop

Name	YR	WAR	W3	W/G	AVG	HR	SB	OPS+
George Davis	10	44.5	18.0	.0405	.332	53	357	132
Travis Jackson	15	44.0	16.5	.0266	.291	135	71	102
Art Fletcher	12	42.2	19.0	.0319	.275	21	153	100
Dick Bartell	8	27.3	17.0	.0327	.279	60	35	108
Al Dark	7	26.8	16.9	.0287	.292	98	41	103
Monte Ward	9	25.8	11.6	.0241	.279	17	332	89
Brandon Crawford	8	23.3	13.7	.0211	.252	87	28	97
Dave Bancroft	5	22.5	19.1	.0421	.310	11	48	111
Chris Speier	10	20.2	13.0	.0181	.248	70	33	93
Rich Aurilia	12	14.8	11.1	.0115	.275	143	17	98

Old-timer **George Davis** (1893–1901, '03) was both a solid fielder, splitting his time between SS and 3B, and a good hitter. He posted a .300+ average in all nine of his full seasons as a Giant, and in five of those seasons managed both 90+ runs and 90+ RBI. He also stole between 25 and 65 bases per season. His three best seasons were 1893 (.355, 27 triples), 1894 (.352, 125 runs), and 1897 (.353, and a league-leading 135 RBI).

I went with **Travis Jackson** (1922–36) as the backup SS. Jackson played his entire career for the Giants and was elected to the Hall of Fame by the Veterans Committee in 1982 (one of their more questionable selections in my opinion). He had six .300+ seasons, but 20+ HR and 100+ RBI only once each. Jackson often missed games due to illness or injuries, and so played 140+ games only four times. He also wasn't much of a base stealer, but he was a good fielder (he played about 80 percent of his games at SS, and the remainder at 3B). He did not hit well in four World Series: he batted only .149 with one extra-base hit in 67 at-bats.

Between Davis and Jackson was Art Fletcher (1909–20), who played nearly his entire career for the Giants. He was apparently a typical player of the 1910s: no power, moderate speed, etc. He was also a good fielder, as he led the NL in defensive WAR four times. The only remarkable statistic I found was that he led the league in being hit by pitches five times and finished in at least the top four in that category every year from 1911 through 1920. You could make a case for Fletcher over Jackson as the backup SS on this roster, and I wouldn't argue.

John "Monte" Ward (1883–89) was an extremely versatile 19th century star, playing mostly SS but also seeing time at OF, 2B, and even as a pitcher (he had been a star pitcher earlier in his career for Providence, an early National League team, once tossing a perfect game). He played nine seasons for New York and was a good contact hitter, rarely striking out. He was also a good base runner, leading the league with 111 SB in 1887 (his SB totals from the first half of his career are unavailable, including three seasons for New York).

Several others deserve brief mention, starting with Hall of Famer Dave Bancroft (1920–23, '30). He played for the Giants for only parts of five seasons but was a .310 hitter for them, scoring 121 runs in 1921 and 117 the next year. Dick Bartell (1935–38, '41–43, '46) had two primary stints with the Giants, hitting .278 with moderate power. His best season was an All-Star campaign in 1937, when he batted .306 with 38 doubles and 14 HR. Alvin Dark (1950–56) was a .292 hitter and an All-Star three times for the Giants. He had double-digit HR in five consecutive seasons, scored 90+ runs four times, and batted 17-for-41 (.415) in his two New York World Series (1951, 1954). He also managed the team from 1961 to 1964, leading them to a pennant in 1962 with a 103-62 record.

Rich Aurilia (1995–2003, '07–09) had two stints with the Giants, at both the beginning and end of his career. His one All-Star campaign was his 2001 career year, when he ended up batting .324 with 37 HR, 97 RBI, 114 runs, and a league-leading 206 hits. Chris Speier (1971–77, '87–89) played his first six seasons in San Francisco, as well as his last three, finally retiring in 1989. He had a little pop in his bat (double-digit HR four times) and was an All-Star each year from 1972 to 1974. And lastly, current Giants SS Brandon Crawford (2011–18) is only a .252 hitter with moderate power, including a career-high 21 HR in 2015. But his main value comes from his defense, where he has earned the Gold Glove Award three times.

Catcher

Name	YR	WAR	W3	W/G	AVG	HR	SB	OPS+
Buster Posey	10	41.3	19.0	.0361	.306	133	23	132
Buck Ewing	9	33.2	14.2	.0453	.306	47	178	146
Roger Bresnahan	7	27.2	15.1	.0362	.293	15	118	140
Chief Meyers	7	21.4	11.9	.0255	.301	14	38	122
Tom Haller	7	19.0	10.6	.0250	.248	107	10	114
Harry Danning	10	15.5	10.7	.0174	.285	57	13	104
Bob Brenly	9	13.3	10.2	.0161	.250	90	44	108
Wes Westrum	11	12.1	9.5	.0132	.217	96	10	94
Shanty Hogan	5	11.8	9.3	.0191	.311	48	4	107

Until recently, the history of Giants who have donned the tools of ignorance is not a pretty sight. But at this point, **Buster Posey** (2009–18) has accomplished enough and is a true star deserving of the starting spot on this roster. In 2010 he took home NL Rookie of the Year honors after hitting .305 with 18 HR in 108 games. Two years later, at age 25, he was the NL MVP after he hit 24 HR with 103 RBI and a league-leading .336 batting average. A six-time All-Star, Posey is also a good defender (Gold Glove Award in 2016) and has been a key part of three Giants World Champion teams.

Hall of Famer **Buck Ewing** (1883–89, '91–92) played more than half his games as a catcher but also played OF, 1B, 2B, and 3B. He batted over .300 in eight of his nine full seasons for NY, though it should be noted that he played in over 100 games in a season only twice (somewhat typical for catchers of that era). He was a superb run scorer, though, crossing the plate 643 times in 734 games. As with many 19th century stars, he had triples power and stole a lot of bases (though like Ward, the available statistics for the latter are incomplete).

Before Posey came along, Hall of Famer Roger Bresnahan (1902–08) would have made this All-Time team. He played six full seasons for New York, catching most of the time but also playing some OF. He was regularly amongst the league leaders in OBP, and he ran quite well for a catcher too. He was good behind the plate and is perhaps most famous for introducing shin guards to the major leagues in 1908. If you preferred Bresnahan over Clark for the second "extra spot" on this roster, I'd certainly understand.

I considered a few other catchers, starting with the Deadball Era's Chief Meyers (1909–15). A .301 hitter while with New York, he led the NL in 1912 with a .441 OBP and was second with a .358 batting average. Shanty Hogan (1928–32) was the Giants' catcher for five seasons, providing a solid .311 average and three times hitting 10+ HR. Harry Danning (1933–42) played his entire career as a Giant and was an All-Star in four consecutive seasons. He had two double-digit HR seasons, and three with a .300+ average.

Two-time All-Star Wes Westrum (1947–57) played his entire 11-year career for the Giants, hit 20+ HR twice and was good defensively, but he was only a .217 hitter and played in 125+ games only once. Tom Haller (1961–67) was also an All-Star twice for the Giants, and he produced six double-digit HR seasons while always batting around .250. And lastly, many readers will remember Bob Brenly (1981–89), who had four 15+-HR seasons in the 1980s and was an All-Star in 1984, when he hit .291 with 20 HR and 80 RBI.

Left Field

Name	YR	WAR	W3	W/G	AVG	HR	SB	OPS+
Barry Bonds	15	112.3	34.3	.0568	.312	586	263	199
George Burns	11	36.1	17.5	.0265	.290	34	334	124
Orlando Cepeda	9	30.4	15.8	.0273	.308	226	92	140

Whitey Lockman	13	19.3	12.5	.0130	.281	113	41	97
Kevin Mitchell	5	19.1	13.9	.0306	.278	143	23	151
Monte Irvin	7	18.9	14.8	.0289	.296	84	27	127
Jim O'Rourke	8	18.0	10.0	.0223	.299	21	153	126
Jo-Jo Moore	12	17.0	9.5	.0127	.298	79	46	104
Irish Meusel	6	12.7	8.8	.0166	.314	70	46	117

After seven seasons with the Pirates, **Barry Bonds** (1993–2007) played the rest of his incredible career in San Francisco. Bonds won five MVP Awards as a Giant and of course set the single-season HR record with 73 in 2001 and the walks record with 198 in 2002, only to surpass the latter in 2004 with 232. In San Francisco he had ten seasons of 100+ runs and nine with 100+ RBI. And he won two batting titles, hitting .370 in 2002 and .362 in 2004. Though knee problems slowed him down over time, he did have six 25+-SB seasons when he first came to the Bay Area, including a 40/40 season in 1996. Also an outstanding fielder, he won five Gold Glove Awards as a Giant. For many, the steroid situation taints all of those accomplishments, but unless you are going to rule him out on that ground, he pretty obviously deserves a starting spot on this All-Time team roster.

I mentioned **Orlando Cepeda** (1958–66) when discussing 1B, but there was no room for him to make this roster at that position. Cepeda played roughly the first half of his Hall of Fame career alongside Mays and McCovey with the Giants. His 1958 campaign of 25 HR, 96 RBI, 15 SB, and a .312 average earned him Rookie of the Year honors. In his seven full seasons with the Giants, Baby Bull had 100+ runs three times, 100+ RBI three times, 30+ HR four times, and he never batted below .297, resulting in a .308 overall average for the Giants. His best year was surely 1961, when he led the NL with 46 HR and 142 RBI, earning him a distant second-place finish (behind Frank Robinson) in the MVP vote.

George Joseph Burns (1911–21), not to be confused with his contemporary in the AL, George Henry Burns, led the NL in runs five times and stolen bases twice, including a high of 62 in 1914. An even earlier old-timer was Hall of Famer Jim O'Rourke (1885–89, '91–92), who played for the Giants late in his career. He played mostly in the outfield, but he was versatile, also playing C, 3B, and 1B. He could steal bases, posting a high of 46 in 1887. Hi best season for the Giants came in 1885, when he scored 119 runs and led the NL with 16 triples.

Jo-Jo Moore (1930–41) was a six-time All-Star who played his entire career with the Giants. He had only moderate power but batted .298 and had three 100+-run seasons. He was also good defensively, a master at playing the tricky left field at the Polo Grounds, and he led the NL in LF assists four times.

A few others deserve brief mention, starting with Kevin Mitchell (1987–91), who was only in San Fran for parts of five seasons but provided significant power, most notably during his 1989 NL MVP campaign, when he hit .291 and led the league with 47 HR and 125 RBI. Monte Irvin (1949–55) starred for many years in the Negro Leagues and joined the Giants at age 30. He had a few fine offensive seasons in the majors, including 1951, when he batted .312 with 24 HR and a league-leading 121 RBI.

Emil "Irish" Meusel (1921–26) was a .314 hitter, had moderate power, and was a reliable RBI man with four consecutive seasons of 100+ and highs of 132 in 1922 and a league-leading 125 in 1923. And lastly, Whitey Lockman (1945, '47–57), who played nine full seasons for the Giants, split his time between 1B and LF, and provided a .281 average with moderate power.

Center Field

Name	YR	WAR	W3	W/G	AVG	HR	SB	OPS+
Willie Mays	21	154.6	32.8	.0541	.304	646	336	157
Bobby Thomson	9	25.8	15.9	.0227	.277	189	31	116
George Van Haltren	10	25.1	11.5	.0205	.321	29	320	118
Cy Seymour	10	21.2	13.9	.0291	.285	22	96	109
Chili Davis	7	16.9	12.0	.0193	.267	101	95	113
Benny Kauff	5	14.4	11.6	.0255	.287	29	103	136

The man who many have said is the greatest all-around player of all time, **Willie Mays** (1951–52, '54–72), played all but his last one-and-a-half seasons for the Giants. He took home Rookie of the Year honors at age 20 in 1951, and after losing most of the next two seasons to the Korean War, he won his only batting title with a .345 mark in 1954. He took home MVP honors in 1954 and 1965, 12 times was in the top six in MVP balloting, and was an All-Star 19 times for the Giants. The Say Hey Kid scored 100+ runs in 12 consecutive seasons, had 100+ RBI 10 times, 30+ HR 11 times (four times led the league), and batted over .300 10 times. Plus, he was a legendary center fielder (12 Gold Glove Awards) and led the league in SB four times.

Comparing anyone else to Mays seems unfair, but even leaving that aside, I didn't find that any of the other players who primarily played CF did quite enough to earn a spot on this All-Time team roster. Old-timer George Van Haltren (1894–03) perhaps came the closest, as he was a great run-scorer. As a Giant he had seven consecutive 100+-run seasons, including a high of 136 in 1896. He was a .321 hitter, and like many of his era, he could run well (seven seasons of 30+ steals). Bobby Thomson (1946–53, '57) had six 20+-HR seasons and four 100+-RBI seasons for the Giants. A three-time All-Star, he played 176 games at 3B but spent most of his time in CF.

Cy Seymour (1896–1900, '06–10) was an interesting case, as he started out primarily as a pitcher, played a bit in the field as well, and then returned to New York at the end of his career as an outfielder only. As a pitcher he had three full seasons (1897–99), going 18-14, 25-19, and 14-18. His weakness was his lack of control, as he paced the NL in walks each year. As a hitter his best seasons were during his time in Cincinnati, between his two stints in New York.

Benny Kauff (1916–20) had two fantastic seasons in the short-lived Federal League and then played parts of five seasons for the Giants, providing some offense and speed. But Kauff lived a wild life in many ways and was implicated in a car-theft ring. Although a jury acquitted him, Commissioner Landis was unconvinced of his innocence and so banned Kauff from the game for life.

And lastly, Chili Davis (1981–87) started his career with the Giants and was a two-time All-Star for San Francisco. He provided only mediocre HR numbers, with his biggest power seasons coming later in his career.

Right Field

Name	YR	WAR	W3	W/G	AVG	HR	SB	OPS+
Mel Ott	22	107.8	24.6	.0395	.304	511	89	155
Mike Tiernan	13	41.5	15.8	.0281	.311	106	428	138
Bobby Bonds	7	38.0	20.7	.0375	.273	186	263	131
Ross Youngs	10	32.2	16.2	.0266	.322	42	153	130
Jack Clark	10	30.6	14.6	.0293	.277	163	60	134
Felipe Alou	6	17.2	13.4	.0239	.286	85	51	116

Mel Ott (1926–47) played his entire Hall of Fame career for the New York Giants, starting at 17 years old and busting out at age 20 in 1929 with 42 HR, 151 RBI, 138 runs, a .328 average, and a .449 OBP. He had nine seasons with 100+ runs, nine with 100+ RBI, eight with 30+ HR, ten with 100+ walks, and ten with a .300+ average. He took home six HR crowns, though he never placed higher than third in the MVP voting. He is the franchise's all-time RBI leader (1,860), which is one more than Willie Mays. He had far less success as a manager of the Giants, where he had a .467 winning percentage over six-and-a-half seasons.

Bobby Bonds (1968–74), Barry's father, started his career in San Francisco, playing his first seven seasons there. After a mediocre half-season as a rookie, he put together six consecutive 20+-HR seasons and had 40+ steals in five of them. Easily possessing the best power/speed combination of his day, he also had an infamous strikeout problem, posting six 100+-K seasons, including two embarrassing totals of 189 and 187—not a quality you want in a leadoff man. Nonetheless, he scored 100+ runs five times (first or second in the league each year) and was also an excellent defender, as he won three Gold Glove Awards in right field.

Old-timer **Mike Tiernan** (1887–1899) played his entire career for New York and earned a spot on this All-Time team as he twice led the league in HR, with 13 in 1890 and 16 in 1891, but also had a franchise-leading 162 triples over his career (including 21 in both 1890 and 1895). He scored 100+ runs seven times, with his best being 147 in only 122 games in 1889. In fact, his runs-scored-per-game ratio is very impressive: 1,316 runs in only 1,478 games played. He had 50+ steals three times and is the franchise's all-time SB leader.

Ross Youngs (1917–26) played his entire Hall of Fame career as a Giant, overlapping some with Burns' tenure. He scored 100+ runs three times, leading the league with 121 in 1923. He was a solid .322 hitter and likely would have had a truly fine career, but a kidney disorder led to his premature death at the age of 30. I really wouldn't argue much if you preferred Youngs over Clark or Bresnahan for the second "extra spot" on this roster.

Another Clark, Jack Clark (1975–84), played roughly the first half of his career in San Francisco. He had five 20+-HR seasons there, with his best perhaps being 1978, when he hit .306 with 25 HR, 98 RBI, 46 doubles, and 15 SB. Felipe Alou also started his career for the Giants, and he hit 20+ HR twice, with his best season coming in 1962, when he hit 25 HR with 98 RBI and a .316 average.

Starting Pitching

Name	YR	WAR	W3	W-L	ERA	WHIP	ERA+
Christy Mathewson	17	101.8	31.6	372-188	2.12	1.057	136
Amos Rusie	8	71.0	35.1	234-163	2.89	1.327	137
Carl Hubbell	16	67.5	26.1	253-154	2.98	1.166	130
Juan Marichal	14	63.7	28.4	238-140	2.84	1.095	125
Mickey Welch	10	52.3	30.8	238-146	2.69	1.225	119
Tim Keefe	6	34.7	26.1	174-82	2.54	1.101	129
Gaylord Perry	10	34.5	18.7	134-109	2.96	1.152	119
Madison Bumgarner	10	34.1	16.9	110-83	3.03	1.108	123
Joe McGinnity	7	32.1	23.4	151-88	2.38	1.116	118
Johnny Antonelli	7	31.5	18.7	108-84	3.13	1.228	124
Matt Cain	13	30.5	15.4	14-118	3.68	1.228	108
Hal Schumacher	13	29.9	14.2	158-121	3.36	1.340	111

Jim Barr	10	28.7	18.4	90-96	3.41	1.252	109
Hooks Wiltse	11	28.3	14.2	136-85	2.48	1.137	112
Jouett Meekin	6	26.4	21.9	116-74	4.01	1.467	108
Sal Maglie	7	24.5	14.7	95-42	3.13	1.272	128
Freddie Fitzsimmons	13	24.5	8.7	170-114	3.54	1.303	110
Jeff Tesreau	7	22.9	16.4	119-72	2.43	1.145	115
Tim Lincecum	9	22.7	19.6	108-83	3.61	1.268	107
Jason Schmidt	6	22.0	17.0	78-37	3.36	1.183	126
Larry Jansen	8	21.4	15.1	120-86	3.55	1.221	113
Rube Marquard	8	15.6	17.3	103-76	2.85	1.197	106
Red Ames	11	15.0	7.1	108-77	2.45	1.199	117
Dummy Taylor	9	13.5	7.9	115-103	2.77	1.266	106

There was lots of great pitching talent to consider for this team, but the staff ace was clearly **Christy Mathewson** (1900–16). He pitched all but his final game for the Giants, yet the striking thing is that his career was only 15 full seasons long. During that time, he *averaged* over 24 wins a season and topped 30 wins four times. His minuscule 2.12 ERA for the Giants has to be seen in light of his era (when the average ERA was relatively low), but he often beat the league average by a full run (such as in 1909, when he posted his lowest, a 1.14 mark, compared to a 2.54 league average). Indeed, he had the NL's best ERA five times, led the league in wins four times, and led in strikeouts five times. He twice won the pitching Triple Crown: in 1905 he went 31-9 with a 1.28 ERA and 206 K, while in 1908 he posted a 37-11 record with a 1.43 ERA and 259 K. A control master, Matty led the league in fewest walks per nine innings seven times, and in 1913 pitched 68 consecutive innings without issuing a walk. His 5-5 record in the postseason seems unfair, since he posted a 1.06 ERA in 11 starts (including three shutouts in the 1905 Series, the only one of the four Series his Giants won).

I found it tremendously difficult to choose who should be the second and third pitcher on this roster, as **Carl "Meal Ticket" Hubbell** (1928–43) and **Juan Marichal** (1960–73) were both superb and had very similar career and peak statistics. Hubbell played his entire career with the Giants, using his screwball to win 20+ games five times (consecutive). He led the league in wins three times and ERA three times. Most notably, he won two MVP Awards: in 1933 with a 23-12 record and a 1.66 ERA, and again in 1936 with a 26-6 record and a 2.31 ERA. Like many pitchers of his time, he helped from the bullpen on the days he wasn't starting, pitching 102 games in relief and saving 33 games. King Carl was an All-Star nine times, a midsummer tradition that didn't start until Carl's sixth season in the majors. In the 1934 All-Star game, Hubbell allowed two base runners, but then famously struck out five potent hitters in a row: Babe Ruth, Lou Gehrig, Jimmie Foxx, Al Simmons, and Joe Cronin.

Marichal pitched nearly his entire career for the Giants, winning 20+ games six times. The Dominican Dandy led the league in ERA once and wins twice, and was an All-Star nine times. Very durable, he completed 244 of his 446 starts for the Giants, with five seasons of 20+ and a high of 30 complete games in 1968. Hubbell and Marichal also each pitched a no-hitter for the Giants (Mathewson pitched two). In the end, I gave the slight edge to Hubbell over Marichal, due to his two MVP Awards and my assumption that he would have been an All-Star more times had the All-Star game existed for his entire career.

Next up is **Joe "Iron Man" McGinnity** (1902–08), who joined New York during the 1902 season after three 25+-win seasons for other teams. He won 25+ games three times for the Giants too, leading the league each time. His best season was 1904: 35-8 with a 1.61 ERA, which paired nicely with Mathewson's 33 wins (the highest win total in the modern era for a pair of teammates).

Gaylord Perry (1962–71) started his long career for the Giants as a mixed starter/reliever and then had six seasons as a full-time starter. He had two 20+-win seasons for the Giants and was regularly amongst the league leaders in ERA and strikeouts, though some of his best seasons (including his two Cy Young Awards) came later with other clubs. A bit earlier, **Johnny Antonelli** (1954–60) also had two 20+-win seasons, led the league with a 2.30 ERA in 1954, and was an All-Star in five of his six full seasons as a Giant.

At this point, **Madison Bumgarner** (2009–18) has accomplished enough to earn a spot on this All-Time team's pitching staff. Until a shoulder injury in 2017, Bumgarner had been very durable for the Giants, starting 31 to 34 games and throwing 200+ innings each year from 2011 through 2016. During that time, he has won 13 to 18 games per year, and he increased his strikeout totals to highs of 234 in 2015 and 251 in 2016. Mad Bum also swings the bat quite well for a pitcher: although only a .183 hitter, he has 18 doubles and 17 HR in 531 at-bats. He has also been generally good in the postseason, going 8-3 with a 2.11 ERA in 14 starts, highlighted by his performance in the 2014 World Series, when he allowed only nine hits and one earned run over 21 innings pitched.

As with other long-standing clubs, it was tough to compare pitchers from the 1800s (with its three-man rotations and 40-win seasons) to modern-era stars. That said, a good case could be made that three such old-timers deserve spots on this All-Time team: Hall of Famers **Amos Rusie** (1890–95, '97–98), **Mickey Welch** (1883–92), and **Tim Keefe** (1885–89, '91). Rusie pitched eight full seasons for New York and had his best season in 1894 with a 36-13 record and a 2.78 ERA (compared to a very high 5.26 league ERA). He won the pitching Triple Crown that year and regularly led the league in strikeouts (though he also led the league in walks every year from 1890 through 1894). Welch also pitched eight full seasons for New York, with his best being 1885, when he went 44-11 with a 1.66 ERA (compared to a low league ERA of 2.68). He was always amongst the league leaders in most pitching categories but never led the league in anything significant. And Keefe was a teammate of Welch but pitched only five full years for the Giants. During those years, he led the league in ERA twice and wins twice, and had records of 32-13, 42-20, 35-19, 35-12, and 28-13, ending with a .680 winning percentage for the Giants.

This means several good starting pitchers didn't have quite enough to make it onto this All-Time dream team, starting with Sal Maglie (1945, '50–55). After pitching in 13 games in 1945, his first season in the majors, Maglie jumped over to the Mexican League and was banned from the major leagues by commissioner Happy Chandler. He reemerged for the Giants in 1950, at the age of 33, and posted an 18-4 record while capturing the NL ERA title with a 2.71 mark. A master of the brushback pitch, he led the NL in wins the following year with a 23-6 record. In 1952 he went 18-8, but never won that many games in a season again.

Readers will be familiar with three more recent Giants starting pitchers, starting with Tim Lincecum (2007–15), who won the NL Cy Young Award in his second and third major league seasons and led the league in strikeouts for three consecutive seasons. A four-time All-Star, he lost his effectiveness in 2012 and beyond. Matt Cain (2005–17) pitched well early in his career but was a hard- luck loser with records of 7-16 and 8-14. He later was an All-Star three times and was quite durable, starting between 30 and 34 games every year from 2006 to 2013. A career highlight came in 2012, when he pitched a perfect game on June 13 against the Houston Astros. But injuries and ineffectiveness have become the new normal for Cain the past four years, so it appears unlikely he'll work his way onto this roster. And before either Lincecum or Cain there was Jason Schmidt (2001–06), who pitched five complete seasons for the Giants and was an All-Star in three of them. His best season came in 2003, when he went 17-5 and led the NL with a 2.34 ERA, good enough for second in the Cy Young Award voting.

The others I looked at briefly were (in chronological order):

- Jouett Meekin (1894–99) went 33-9 in his first season in New York and also posted seasons with 26-14 and 20-11 records. But his 4.01 ERA and 1.467 WHIP were much higher than fellow old-timers Rusie, Welch, and Keefe.

- Luther "Dummy" Taylor (1900–08) played almost his entire career for the Giants, going 18-27 in his first full season, but then having better success later, including seasons with 21-15, 16-9, and 17-9 records. A deaf mute, he and manager John McGraw hold the distinction of having been thrown out of a game for arguing the umpire's calls and using profanity... in sign language.

- Red Ames (1903–13) was a teammate of Taylor, went 22-8 in his first full season, and compiled a 2.45 ERA during an era of relatively low ERAs.

- Hooks Wiltse (1904–14) pitched almost his entire career in New York and was a teammate of McGinnity and Mathewson. He had two 20+-win seasons, and six others where he won between 12 and 16 games.

- Rube Marquard (1908–15), a very marginal Hall of Famer in my opinion, had three strong seasons for the Giants, posting records of 24-7, 26-11, and 23-10 from 1911 through 1913. In 1912 he tied fellow Giant Tim Keefe's major league record of 19 consecutive games won.

- Jeff Tesreau (1912–18) pitched his entire, short career for the Giants. He started strong, capturing the ERA crown in his rookie season (1.96) and winning 20+ games the next two years. But he slowly faded after that, and eventually disagreements with manager John McGraw led to his early retirement (at age 31).

- Freddie Fitzsimmons (1925–37) pitched most of his career for the Giants, posting a 20-9 record in 1928 and 19-7 in 1930, and having four other seasons with 16+ wins. Overall, he ended up with a 170-114 record for New York, which amounts to a .599 winning percentage.

- Hal Schumacher (1931–42, '46) pitched his entire career with the Giants, starting off great from 1933 through 1935, going 19-12, 23-10, and 19-9, but never again earning more than 13 wins in a season.

- Larry Jansen (1947–54) pitched most of his career for the Giants, was 21-5 as rookie, and later led the NL in wins with a 23-11 record in 1951.

- Jim Barr (1971–78, '82–83) played most of his career for the Giants but never won more than 15 games in a season, and ended up with a losing 90-96 record.

Relief Pitching

Name	YR	WAR	W3	SV	W-L	ERA	WHIP	ERA+
Gary Lavelle	11	19.0	9.6	127	73-67	2.82	1.318	128
Marv Grissom	7	13.1	10.2	57	31-25	2.88	1.274	139
Stu Miller	6	12.9	10.5	47	47-44	3.16	1.240	120
Greg Minton	13	12.7	9.9	125	45-52	3.23	1.417	110
Hoyt Wilhelm	5	11.0	9.4	41	42-25	2.98	1.317	135
Robb Nen	5	10.6	8.4	206	24-25	2.43	1.084	169
Frank Linzy	7	10.5	9.2	77	48-39	2.71	1.292	128
Sergio Romo	9	9.7	5.8	84	32-26	2.58	0.955	146
Santiago Casilla	7	8.9	5.1	123	32-22	2.42	1.160	153
Rod Beck	7	7.2	6.3	199	21-28	2.97	1.073	129
Brian Wilson	7	5.4	5.2	171	20-20	3.21	1.338	129

I decided to go with ten starting pitchers only after I considered the relief pitching candidates. Here too, there are many who are deserving of recognition. In the end, I decided to just go with two of the more recent dominant closers, starting with **Robb Nen** (1998–02), who admittedly pitched only five seasons for the Giants. Nen's "Terminator" slider helped him notch between 37 and 45 saves each year—leading the league in 2001 with 45. In 1998 he had 40 SV and a 1.52 ERA, with 110 K and only 25 BB in 88.6 IP. In 2000 he was even more dominating: 41 SV and a 1.50 ERA, with 92 K and only 19 BB in 66 IP. After spending a lot of time rehabilitating from three surgeries for a torn rotator cuff injury, Nen formally retired during the winter of 2005.

Rod Beck (1991–97) was the closer for the Giants immediately before Nen's tenure began. He had 30+ saves four times, plus 28 in the strike-shortened 1994 season. His best year was 1993, when he had 48 SV, a 2.16 ERA, 86 K, and only 13 BB in 79.1 IP.

More recently, Giants fans had Brian Wilson (2006–12) and his beard coming out of the bullpen to shut down opponents. Wilson had 41 saves in 2008, but with a 4.62 ERA. That dropped to 2.74 the next year, and an impressive 1.81 in 2010 to go with a league-leading 48 saves. Unfortunately, Tommy

John surgery shut him down for the 2012 season, and his career ended after two seasons for the Dodgers. In 2010 and 2011, Wilson had two outstanding setup men in Sergio Romo (2008–16) and Santiago Casilla (2010–16). They shared the closer duties for several years after that, with Romo notching 38 saves in 2013, and Casilla posting 38 in 2015 and 31 in 2016.

Before all of these contemporary short relievers, the Giants had two long-time relief specialists in Gary Lavelle (1974–84) and Greg Minton (1975–87), who seemed to alternate as primary closers. Minton had 19 or more saves in five consecutive seasons as the closer from 1980 through 1984, with 1982 clearly his career year: 10-4, 30 SV, and a 1.83 ERA over 123 IP. That was good enough for sixth in the Cy Young Award voting and eighth in the MVP Award voting. Lavelle was a two-time All-Star, had three 20-save seasons, and had three others with 10+. They both pitched nearly twice as many innings as Beck or Nen, over twice as many seasons. If you think they had a greater positive impact on the Giants, then you could go with them instead—the tough thing would be trying to mix and match, taking Nen or Beck with Minton or Lavelle. If you wanted all four on the team, then you would need to choose two fewer starting pitchers for this roster—not easy decisions!

Four other earlier relief pitchers also deserve brief mention, starting with Hoyt Wilhelm (1952–56), who started his Hall of Fame career at the age of 28 with the Giants. In his first season in the majors, he became the only ERA champ (2.43) who was exclusively a reliever. He also posted a 15-3 record that year and was fourth in the MVP Award voting. A fun fact: he hit a homer in his first major league at-bat, but then never hit another in his 21 years in the big leagues.

A teammate of Wilhelm in the 1950s was Marv Grissom (1953–58), who posted an impressive 1.56 ERA in 1956. Stu Miller (1957–62) followed Wilhelm and Grissom, and actually led the NL in ERA (2.47) in 1958 as a mixed starter and reliever, and then had a fine 1961 campaign with a 14-5 record, 2.66 ERA, and a league-leading 17 saves. And lastly, Frank Linzy (1963, '65–70) came along after Miller and was the Giants' bullpen ace during the late '60s. He posted double-digit save totals five years in a row, and had some impressive ERA numbers during that span, such as 1.43, 1.51, and 2.08.

Managers

Name	YR	From-To	W-L	PCT	PS	WS
John McGraw	31	1902-32	2,583-1,790	.591	11	3
Bruce Bochy	12	2007-18	975-969	.502	4	3

Bill Terry	10	1932–41	823-661	.555	3	1
Dusty Baker	10	1993–02	840-715	.540	3	0
Leo Durocher	8	1948–55	637-523	.549	2	1
Roger Craig	8	1985–92	586-566	.509	2	0

The obvious top manager in Giants history was the great **John McGraw**. Over 31 seasons he led the Giants to 11 pennants, though ultimate success in the World Series was harder to come by, as they won only three championships. But a .591 winning percentage and 2,583 career wins is an amazing managerial career.

Current Giants skipper **Bruce Bochy** has actually matched McGraw in one aspect, as he too has led them to three World Series championships. He's done so in only 11 seasons at the helm, making him the clear number two on this list.

As mentioned earlier, **Bill Terry** was a very successful manager for the Giants for ten seasons, the first five of which he was a player-manager. Under his leadership the team won 90+ games five years in a row, took home three pennants, and won the World Series in 1933.

In choosing a fourth manager for this All-Time team, I went with **Dusty Baker**, who ended his tenure in San Francisco with a .540 winning percentage and three postseason appearances. Honorable mention goes to Leo Durocher, who had a .549 winning percentage over eight seasons, including two pennants and one championship, and Roger Craig, who led the Giants to two postseason appearances in his eight years at the helm.

Starting Lineup

What would mythical starting lineups look like for this All-Time roster?

Against RHP:
George Davis SS (S)
Willie Mays CF (R)
Barry Bonds LF (L)
Willie McCovey 1B (L)
Mel Ott RF (R)
Bill Terry DH (L)
Frankie Frisch 3B (S)
Buster Posey C (R)
Larry Doyle 2B (L)

Against LHP:
George Davis SS (S)
Willie Mays CF (R)
Mel Ott RF (R)
Barry Bonds LF (L)
Orlando Cepeda DH (R)
Matt Williams 3B (R)
Roger Connor 1B (S)
Jeff Kent 2B (R)
Buster Posey C (R)

Clearly these are very powerful lineups. I listed platoons at three of the four infield positions and went with a mix of Terry and Cepeda at DH. Frisch could certainly be swapped with Davis and lead off against right-handers, and the power in the middle of each lineup could be reordered in various ways.

Depth Chart

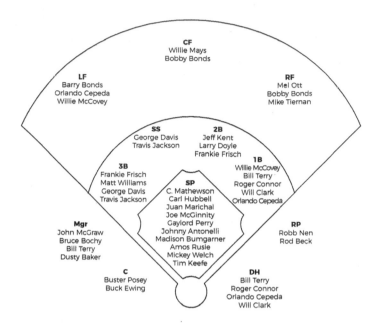

CF
Willie Mays
Bobby Bonds

LF
Barry Bonds
Orlando Cepeda
Willie McCovey

RF
Mel Ott
Bobby Bonds
Mike Tiernan

SS
George Davis
Travis Jackson

2B
Jeff Kent
Larry Doyle
Frankie Frisch

3B
Frankie Frisch
Matt Williams
George Davis
Travis Jackson

1B
Willie McCovey
Bill Terry
Roger Connor
Will Clark
Orlando Cepeda

SP
C. Mathewson
Carl Hubbell
Juan Marichal
Joe McGinnity
Gaylord Perry
Johnny Antonelli
Madison Bumgarner
Amos Rusie
Mickey Welch
Tim Keefe

Mgr
John McGraw
Bruce Bochy
Bill Terry
Dusty Baker

RP
Robb Nen
Rod Beck

C
Buster Posey
Buck Ewing

DH
Bill Terry
Roger Connor
Orlando Cepeda
Will Clark

Prospects for Current Players

What are the prospects of current Giants players making this All-Time team? Posey and Bumgarner are already on this roster. No one else is even close really, so I don't see any changes to this All-Time team anytime soon. We'll see…

Retired Player Numbers

Christy Mathewson (no number), John McGraw (no number), Bill Terry (3), Mel Ott (4), Carl Hubbell (11), Monte Irvin (20), Willie Mays (24), Juan Marichal (27), Orlando Cepeda (30), Gaylord Perry (36), Willie McCovey (44)

Selections from Other Authors and Fan Surveys

1959: *Sport* magazine, January issue

As part of a running series, *Sport* magazine reported on all-time all-star teams picked by "big league publicity departments and the writers covering the clubs."

In the case of the Giants, a roster was selected one year after the team was "transplanted from New York to San Francisco." Here is what they had to say:

First Base: Bill Terry was the last of the National League's .400 hitters and was a brilliant fielder as well as an exceptional hitter. He spent his entire career with the Giants, from 1923 to 1936, and was player-manager for his last five seasons.

Second Base: Frank Frisch, the old Fordham Flash, perhaps is best remembered as a St. Louis Cardinal star, but he played eight seasons for the Giants, from 1919 to 1926, during which he did some of his best hitting and helped the team to four pennants.

Shortstop: Travis Jackson, "Stonewall" to old Polo Grounds fans, held the position for most of his 14 years with the Giants, from 1923 to 1936. He gets the nod over Dave Bancroft, Dick Bartell and Alvin Dark because he combined powerful hitting with exceptional range in the field and a throwing arm that was the best of its time.

Third Base: Freddy Lindstrom, who played from 1924 to 1932, gets a close vote over Art Devlin of an earlier era, chiefly because of his fine hitting. In 1930, Freddy hit .379 only to have teammate Terry outdo him with .401.

Right Field: Mel Ott, the outstanding Giant of them all, played 20 years and set home-run records that still stand. He played from 1926 to 1947, the last six years as player-manager, and was a great fielder and thrower in addition to being one of the league's top all-time hitters.

Center Field: Willie Mays, a brilliant hitter, fielder, base-runner and inspirational player since he joined the team in 1951, has to be included even in mid-career. He sparked a makeshift team to pennants in 1951 and 1954 and was named the National League's Most Valuable Player in 1954.

Left Field: Ross Youngs never actually played left field during his career with the Giants, from 1917 to 1926, but he was too good to leave off the team. He was the right-fielder just before Ott and was noted as an aggressive player and a fine hitter. He dropped under .300 only once and his best marks were .355 in 1924 and .351 in 1920.

Catcher: Roger Bresnahan, the Duke of Tralee, was in a class by himself from 1902 to 1908, when he was both an outfielder and a catcher for the Giants. His best hitting year was 1903, when he hit .350, but it was his remarkable ability behind the plate that stamps Bresnahan as outstanding.

Righthanded Pitcher: Christy Mathewson is matched only by Grover Cleveland Alexander among all-time National League pitchers. He played for the Giants from 1900 to 1916 and won 20 games or more for 12 straight years. He won 37 games in 1908 and 33 in 1904, his two best years. He won 371 games for the Giants.

Lefthanded Pitcher: Carl Hubbell, the King of the Screwball, pitched from 1928 to 1943 and won 263 games. He won 20 games or more for five straight seasons, his best mark being a 26-6 record in 1936.

Back in 1959 this was a reasonable lineup. I thought not even giving honorable mention to Davis at SS was a mistake. And it was a little odd that they admitted to choosing a non-LF for LF, as at that point they might as well just select three generic outfielders.

1969: *The Sporting News* Fan Poll

The July 5, 1969, issue reported the results of a fan poll for the long-standing franchises of the day. The results for the Giants were more complicated than for other teams. The fans in San Francisco selected separate all-time teams for the Giants of SF and the Giants of NY, but the fans of the Mets also selected an all-time New York Giants team.

In 1969 a San Francisco Giants roster was drawing on only a little over a decade of history, and was composed of 1B McCovey, 2B Ron Hunt, 3B Davenport, SS Hal Lanier, C Tom Haller, LF Harvey Kuenn, CF Mays, RF Alou, RHP Marichal, and LHP Antonelli. Lanier was a very weak hitter, but at that point had played the most at SS. I might have gone with José Pagán at SS and voted for Lanier at 2B, since Ron Hunt had played only one-and-a-half years for the Giants. Kuenn had only four mediocre seasons as a Giant, and choosing him left Cepeda out of the lineup.

The San Francisco fans chose the following for the NY Giants lineup: 1B Terry, 2B Frisch, 3B Lindstrom, SS Dark, C Westrum, LF Thomson, CF Mays, RF Ott, RHP Mathewson, and LHP Hubbell. And the Mets fans chose mostly the same as the San Francisco fans for the NY Giants lineup, though they more sensibly selected Jackson at SS and Bresnahan at C. They also swapped Youngs in for Thomson in LF, which was a bit of a cheat since Youngs played almost entirely in RF (and only one game in LF).

1981: Fan Poll as reported in *The Giants Encyclopedia*, by Tom Schott and Nick Peters, 1999

At the end of the 1981 season fans selected the following all-time team for the first 25 years of the San Francisco Giants: 1B McCovey, 2B Tito Fuentes, SS Johnnie LeMaster, 3B Davenport, C Tom Haller, LF Gary Matthews, CF Mays, RF Clark, "Utility" Cepeda, RHP Marichal, LHP Vida Blue, RHRP Miller, and LHRP Al Holland.

Perhaps the pain of the 1981 strike rattled some fans' brains, because I don't understand how they could vote for LeMaster as the SS over three-time All-Star Chris Speier. Matthews is someone I didn't look at much, but through 1981 he was a sensible selection for LF—given that Cepeda was on the roster as a 1B/OF "utility" player. Fans in 1981 likely had Vida Blue on their minds, but he was only 54-40 for them over four seasons, whereas southpaw Mike McCormick went 104-89, and had a 22-10 season. And I'm not sure how they could choose Al Holland over Gary Lavelle. Holland had just finished his second full season for them, and while he had only 7 saves in each, he did have fine ERAs of 1.75 and 2.41. But Lavelle also had many fine ERA seasons and by then had 87 saves.

1990: "All-Time All-Star Teams," in *The Baseball Research Journal*

In an interesting article, Robert C. Berlo used Thorn and Palmer's TPR (Total Player Rating) system to choose all-time teams. He selected players based on their best 800 consecutive games for the franchise, with a minimum of five years played. His results: 1B McCovey, 2B Frisch, SS Davis, 3B Devlin, RF Ott, CF Mays, LF Bonds, C Ewing, SP Mathewson, SP Hubbell, SP Marichal, SP Rusie, RP Linzy.

Interesting results, and no real surprises. As this approach favors peak performance over longevity, I was a little surprised that Devlin beat out Lindstrom for 3B. Bonds listed as LF was troubling because he never played a single game as left fielder for the Giants (he played mostly in RF, with some games in CF).

1991: *Louisville Slugger Presents: The San Francisco Giants*, by Bill Shannon

In the Giants installment of this series of books in 1991, the author chose an All-Time all-star team that consisted of Terry, Frisch, Jackson, Lindstrom, and

Ewing in the infield, Moore in LF, Mays in CF, and Ott in RF. The choice of Lindstrom was at least debatable, and I think Cepeda, Burns, or Irvin would have been better picks than Moore in LF. Hubbell as the top LHP, Mathewson as the top RHP, and Lavelle as the top reliever were all solid choices.

1992: *The All-Time All-Star Baseball Book*, by Nick Acocella and Donald Dewey

These authors split it up and had separate lineups for NY and SF. For NY they first noted, "This is the only franchise that can boast a Hall of Famer at every position," and then gave a lineup of Terry, Frisch, Lindstrom, Jackson, Ott, Mays, Youngs, Bresnahan, and Mathewson. As a means of honorable mention, they wrote, "Among the Cooperstown residents not making the team are Tim Keefe, Mickey Welch, Monte Ward, Buck Ewing, Roger Connor, George Kelly, Amos Rusie, Carl Hubbell, Monte Irvin, Rube Marquard, and Dave Bancroft."

For the San Francisco list, they begin by writing, "The West Coast Giants have always had slugging outfielders and rarely had catchers who lasted more than a couple of seasons." They chose Cepeda, Thompson, Davenport, Speier, McCovey, Mays, Bonds, Haller, and Marichal. Interesting that they listed Cepeda at 1B and McCovey in the OF—could go either way I suppose.

1995: *Baseball Ratings*, by Charles F. Faber

The Faber system as applied in 1995 created two reasonable lineups. For NY he listed the same players that Acocella, et al., did except for George Burns in the OF in place of Youngs. For SF, McCovey, Thompson, and Speier again make it, and Matt Williams by then had done enough to join them. Haller was again the backstop. Mays and Bonds (the elder) were in the OF, with Jack Clark joining them—leaving Cepeda out. The combined rotation was Mathewson, Marichal, Hubbell, Fitzsimmons, and Schumacher, and Lavelle was the top reliever.

1999: Fan Poll as reported in *The Giants Encyclopedia*, by Tom Schott and Nick Peters, 1999

Eighteen years after the 1981 fan poll, Bay Area faithful selected another all-time SF Giants team. This time they wisely chose Speier at SS, and by then Robby Thompson and Matt Williams had done enough to replace Fuentes and Davenport. And the updated outfield not only had Barry Bonds in LF, but sensibly also had his dad in RF. Cepeda again cracked the lineup as the "Utility" man. They smartly chose McCormick as LHP and Beck as the reliever.

2003: *Rob Neyer's Big Book of Baseball Lineups,* by Rob Neyer

Neyer first chose a starter and backup for only the San Francisco Giants, and then later in his book chose a starting lineup for the combined NY and SF franchise. So, focusing on just the latter, he listed Bresnahan as the C and McCovey at 1B, both good selections. He started Kent at 2B, but then wrote, "The best of the Giants' old-time second basement was Frankie Frisch, but I'm partial to Larry Doyle, who said 'Gee, it's great to be young and a Giant.'"

At SS he favored Travis Jackson, writing, "Have to go with the Hall of Famer who spent his entire career as a Giant, but Dick Bartell (1935-38) was better than Jackson at his best." I made that sort of "peak performance" case as the reason for going with George Davis over Jackson. That said, I agreed with Neyer's choice of Williams at 3B.

The OF of Mays, Bonds, and Ott was obvious. His first three starting pitchers were solid (Mathewson, Hubbell, Marichal), but then he included Fitzsimmons as the fourth, writing that Freddie was "pushed here by Hal Schumacher and Joe McGinnity." Nen was a good choice as closer, and his top five managers were McGraw, Durocher, Baker, Terry, and Dark.

2007: *Few and Chosen: Defining Giants Greatness Across the Eras,* by Bobby Thomson with Phil Pepe

As with each book in this fun series, the authors chose the top five players at each position. For the Giants, their lists in order were:

C: Bresnahan, Walker Cooper, Hogan, Ernie Lombardi, Westrum

1B: McCovey, Terry, Cepeda, Mize, Lockman

2B: Frisch, Kent, Doyle, Burgess Whitehead, Eddie Stanky

SS: Jackson, Dark, Bancroft, Bartell, Buddy Kerr

3B: Lindstrom, Williams, Gordon, Davenport, Hart

LF: Barry Bonds, Irvin, Moore, Meusel, Mitchell

CF: Mays, Davis, Hank Leiber, Kauff, Garry Maddox

RF: Ott, Bobby Bonds, Youngs, Don Mueller, Alou

RHP: Mathewson, Marichal, Perry, Maglie, Jansen

LHP: Hubbell, Marquard, Art Nehf, Antonelli, Billy Pierce

RP: Wilhelm, Miller, Grissom, Nen, Beck

Manager: McGraw, Durocher, Terry, Baker, Craig

These selections routinely skipped the old-timers, at several positions. At catcher, for instance, Walker Cooper (1946–49) played only a few seasons for the Giants and had one great year in 1947, when he hit .305 with 35 HR and 122 RBI. And just before Cooper, Ernie Lombardi (1943–47) finished his Hall of Fame career with five seasons in New York.

Burgess Whitehead (1936–37, '39–41) played only five seasons for New York and didn't do much to merit inclusion at second base, even fourth in the list. And Stanky (1950–51) played only two seasons for the Giants, though Thomson noted that he was a key player for those clubs. At shortstop, Buddy Kerr (1943–49) played most of his career for the Giants and was a good fielder but only a .256 hitter with minimal power or speed.

In the outfield, Thompson omitted himself from consideration in CF. Hank Leiber (1933–38, '42) played parts of seven seasons for the Giants but only had one full season, in 1935, when he hit .331 with 22 HR, 107 RBI, and 110 runs. Garry Maddox (1972–75) started his fine career with the Giants, providing them with a .287 average, 20+ SB twice, and the early days of his legendary defense. And in RF, Don Mueller (1948–57) played most of his career for the Giants, was an All-Star twice, and hit .298, though with little power or speed.

For the pitchers, the choice of Pierce (1962–64) was particularly odd, as he won only 22 games with the Giants at the end of his career, but Thomson defended the selection based on Pierce's key role for the pennant-winning 1962 team. For relievers, he clearly preferred quality bullpen guys from the era before the extreme specialization we have today, arguing that Wilhelm, Miller, or Grissom would have posted equal or better numbers than Nen or Beck if they pitched during the same time period.

2016: *101 All-Time Fantasy Baseball Teams*, by Jack Sweeney

Sweeney's lineup is generally solid with Terry, Kent, Lindstrom, Jackson, Bonds, Mays, Ott, Posey, and McCovey (listed at DH). The only one I would argue with is Lindstrom over Williams or Frisch at 3B. His four starting pitchers are solid in Mathewson, Hubbell, Marichal, and Perry, but then his selection of Bumgarner as the relief pitcher is a bit odd, though a nice acknowledgement of Mad Bum's value to the Giants.

Top WAR Single Seasons – Hitters (8+)

Name	Year	WAR	AVG	HR	R	RBI	SB	OPS+
Barry Bonds	2001	11.9	.328	73	129	137	13	259
Barry Bonds	2002	11.8	.370	46	117	110	9	268
Willie Mays	1965	11.2	.317	52	118	112	9	185
Willie Mays	1964	11.0	.296	47	121	111	19	172
Barry Bonds	2004	10.6	.362	45	129	101	6	263
Willie Mays	1954	10.6	.345	41	119	110	8	175
Willie Mays	1963	10.6	.314	38	115	103	8	175
Willie Mays	1962	10.5	.304	49	130	141	18	165
Willie Mays	1958	10.2	.347	29	121	96	31	165
Rogers Hornsby	1927	10.1	.361	26	133	125	9	175
Barry Bonds	1993	9.9	.336	46	129	123	29	206
Barry Bonds	1996	9.6	.308	42	122	129	40	188
Willie Mays	1960	9.5	.319	29	107	103	25	160
Barry Bonds	2003	9.2	.341	45	111	90	7	231
Willie Mays	1955	9.0	.319	51	123	127	24	174
Willie Mays	1966	9.0	.288	37	99	103	5	149
Mel Ott	1938	8.9	.311	36	116	116	2	178
Willie Mays	1961	8.7	.308	40	129	123	18	160
Will Clark	1989	8.6	.333	23	104	111	8	175
Willie Mays	1957	8.3	.333	35	112	97	38	173
Barry Bonds	1997	8.2	.291	40	123	101	37	170
Roger Connor	1885	8.1	.371	1	102	65	NA	200
Barry Bonds	1998	8.1	.303	37	120	122	28	178
Willie McCovey	1969	8.1	.320	45	101	126	0	209
Eddie Stanky	1950	8.0	.300	8	115	51	9	130
Art Devlin	1906	8.0	.299	2	76	65	54	143

This list is dominated by two players, Willie Mays who appears 11 times, and Barry Bonds who appears 8 times. Of the seven other hitters who have had seasons with 8+ WAR for this franchise, none did so more than once.

Regarding Mays, there is a reason many still consider him the best all-around player ever. From 1954 to 1966 he had a WAR of 7.6 or higher every season, and was in the top six in the NL MVP vote in all but one of those years.

As for Bonds, his early seasons with the Giants were already impressive enough, but when you look at his 2001–2004 years, the numbers look unreal (and some would say, they were unreal). No longer a great base-stealer, he took home four consecutive MVP Awards due to a combination of HR power and insanely high OBP. His RBI totals were limited in part because of the number of intentional walks he was given, with a record-setting peak of 232 walks, 120 intentional walks, and a .609 OBP in 2004.

Of the other seven players listed above, I'll comment on the two seasons from players not described earlier. After many outstanding years for the Cardinals, Rogers Hornsby had an off year in 1926. Negotiations for a new contract with St. Louis broke down, so he was traded to the Giants in a swap of infield stars—Frankie Frisch (and pitcher Jimmy Ring) went from the Giants to the Cardinals. Hornsby rebounded in New York in 1927, posting the highest WAR for a Giants batter not named Mays or Bonds. But between his racetrack gambling and distrust of Giants management, he was immediately dealt after that one season to the Boston Braves.

Fellow second baseman Eddie Stanky also makes an appearance on the above list, as in 1950 he led the league with 144 walks, 12 HBP, and a .460 OBP, which—coupled with strong defense, 115 runs, and a .300 average—was good enough to come in third in the NL MVP voting. He played for five clubs over 11 seasons but spent only two years with the Giants.

Top WAR Single Seasons – Pitchers (8+)

Name	Year	WAR	W-L	ERA	IP	SO	ERA+
Joe McGinnity	1903	11.3	31-20	2.43	434.0	171	139
Christy Mathewson	1908	11.2	37-11	1.43	390.2	259	168
Juan Marichal	1965	10.5	22-13	2.13	295.1	240	169
Christy Mathewson	1903	10.2	30-13	2.26	366.1	267	149
Christy Mathewson	1909	10.2	25-6	1.14	275.1	149	222
Christy Mathewson	1905	10.1	31-9	1.28	338.2	206	230
Carl Hubbell	1936	9.9	26-6	2.31	304.0	123	169
Juan Marichal	1966	9.8	25-6	2.23	307.1	222	167
Joe McGinnity	1904	9.5	35-8	1.61	408.0	144	168
Christy Mathewson	1901	9.0	20-17	2.41	336.0	221	138
Carl Hubbell	1933	8.9	23-12	1.66	308.2	156	193
Juan Marichal	1963	8.1	25-8	2.41	321.1	248	133
Christy Mathewson	1910	8.1	27-9	1.89	318.1	184	157
Tim Lincecum	2008	8.1	18-5	2.62	227.0	265	168

I omitted the many seasons of 8+ WAR from the old-timers Rusie, Welch, Keefe, and Meekin. But even if I had included them, Christy Mathewson would still have had the most seasons (six) on this list. I was surprised to see McGinnity's 1903 season rate at the top of this list, especially compared to his seemingly superior 1904 season, which comes in only ninth. Two possible explanations are that he pitched a higher percentage of the team's games and innings in 1903 (34.5 percent of games started) than in 1904 (only 28.8 percent), and the team's defense was a bit worse in 1904 than in 1903.

Franchise Player

This honor had to go to Willie Mays. The other two starting outfielders, Barry Bonds and Mel Ott, were honorable mentions, along with SP Christy Mathewson.

CHAPTER 3

The Dodgers Franchise All-Time Dream Team

The Dodgers franchise has a long history, dating all the way back to 1884 in the American Association. One of the more interesting facts about their first 50 years is the number of names they played under. For their first season they were known as the Brooklyn Atlantics, and through 1898 they went by the nicknames Grays, Grooms, and Bridegrooms. Their only real success during this period was in winning the league championship in 1889, and then joining the National League the following year and winning another title. They changed their name to the Brooklyn Superbas in 1899, when Ned Hanlon came on board as manager. He was not related to the vaudevillian acrobats the Hanlon Brothers, whose second show was named Superba!; nonetheless, a connection was made, leading to the team adopting the name through 1910. At that time the Brooklyn borough's primary form of transportation led to a new nickname—the Trolley Dodgers, or just Dodgers for short. This name lasted only a few years, as they went by the name Brooklyn Robins from 1914–31.

Finally named the Dodgers permanently starting in 1932, they didn't have much success until 1941, when they won the NL pennant, only to lose to the cross-town rival Yankees in the World Series. This soon became a pattern, as the Dodgers were good enough to win the NL pennant seven times from 1941 through 1956, but they lost to the powerful Yankees in the World Series every time except 1955, when they took the championship in seven games.

The big move from Brooklyn to Los Angeles occurred before the 1958 season, and the team initially slumped to seventh place in the National League. But they bounced right back and won the World Series (over the White Sox this time) in 1959, and went on to win three NL pennants and two World Series titles from 1963 through '66.

Led by a consistent and strong infield, the Dodgers were a good team throughout the 1970s, though again they lost in all three World Series appearances they made. They took home the championship in the strike-shortened 1981 season, and won it again in 1988. Since then they have made the playoffs 12 times, taking home the NL pennant again finally in 2017.

Overall, I found this franchise's All-Time team to be remarkably balanced, with starting pitching arguably being the greatest position of strength.

1st Base

Name	YR	WAR	W3	W/G	AVG	HR	SB	OPS+
Gil Hodges	16	44.4	17.4	.0221	.274	361	63	120
Steve Garvey	14	36.4	14.5	.0211	.301	211	77	122
Dolph Camilli	6	29.1	18.2	.0347	.270	139	31	143
Jake Daubert	9	27.5	11.8	.0227	.305	33	187	123
Wes Parker	9	22.9	12.1	.0178	.267	64	60	111
Jack Fournier	4	18.7	17.4	.0360	.337	82	22	157
Eric Karros	12	11.9	9.7	.0074	.268	270	57	109

There were two top candidates at 1B for this All-Time team, but to me the clear starter was **Gil Hodges** (1943, '47–61). An eight-time All-Star, Hodges hit 20+ HR for 11 consecutive seasons, including 30+ HR six times. He also provided 100+ RBI in seven consecutive seasons, with his best statistical season being 1954, when he batted .304 with 42 HR and 130 RBI. Also a good fielder, he earned Gold Glove Awards from 1957 through '59.

The popular **Steve Garvey** (1969–82) played most of his career for the Dodgers, starting out slowly as a third baseman before making the shift to 1B. He hit 20+ HR with 100+ RBI five times, including his NL MVP season in 1974, when he hit .312 with 21 HR and 111 RBI. A .301 career hitter, Garvey didn't walk a lot, so his OBP was only .337. A ten-time All-Star, he provided good defense at 1B and won four Gold Glove Awards from 1974 through '77.

Dolph Camilli (1938–43) played the second half of his career for Brooklyn, hit 20+ HR five times and had 100+ RBI four times. Only a .270 hitter, he led the league in walks twice, resulting in a .392 OBP during his time with the Dodgers. His best season came in 1941, when he won the NL MVP Award after leading the league with 34 HR and 120 RBI. There were many candidates for the two "extra spots" on this roster, but ultimately, I decided to give one of them to Camilli.

Jake Daubert (1910–18) played most of a decade for Brooklyn and led the league with a .350 average in 1913 and a .329 average in 1914. Like most hitters in the Deadball Era, he provided little power but some speed, stealing 20+ bases six times. Wes Parker (1964–72) played his entire brief career for the Dodgers and was most valuable for his defense at 1B, where he took home six consecutive Gold Glove Awards. He was a generally light hitter, although in 1970 he hit .319 with 10 HR, 111 RBI, and a league-leading 47 doubles. Jack Fournier (1923–27) played four seasons for Brooklyn near the end of his career, but he managed to hit .337 for the club and had three seasons with 20+ HR and 100+ RBI.

And lastly, Eric Karros (1991–2002) played all but his final two seasons with the Dodgers. He started out strong, taking home the NL Rookie of the Year Award in 1992 after hitting 20 HR with 88 RBI. Overall, he hit 20+ HR eight times, including five seasons with 30+ HR and 100+ RBI. Only a .268 hitter, he also didn't walk much, so his OBP was an unimpressive .325.

2nd Base

Name	YR	WAR	W3	W/G	AVG	HR	SB	OPS+
Jackie Robinson	10	61.5	27.8	.0445	.311	137	197	132
Jim Gilliam	14	40.7	15.7	.0208	.265	65	203	93
Davey Lopes	10	32.1	14.8	.0266	.262	99	418	105
Tom Daly	11	25.1	10.8	.0229	.294	44	298	119
Steve Sax	8	15.9	10.2	.0146	.282	30	290	97

The starter for this roster at 2B was obviously **Jackie Robinson** (1947–56). A versatile player, Robinson played more games at 2B than elsewhere, but also logged time at 3B, 1B, and the OF. In his history-making 1947 season he won Rookie of the Year honors at age 28 after hitting .297, scoring 125 runs, and leading the league with 29 SB. He never had more than 19 HR in a season, but he was a .311 hitter, scored 100+ runs six times, and stole 20+ bases five times. A six-time All-Star, his most impressive numbers came in 1949, when he hit 16 HR with 122 runs and 124 RBI, and led the league with both a .342 average and 37 SB.

Jim Gilliam (1953–66) was a teammate of Robinson, similarly played his entire career for the Dodgers, and was also versatile on the diamond, splitting his time between 2B (1,046 games) and 3B (761). After evaluating the talent at both positions, I decided to select him as the backup at 3B, so I'll say more about him there. This allowed the speedy **Davey Lopes** (1972–81) to make this All-Time team as the backup at 2B. Lopes played a little more than half of his career for Los Angeles, making the All-Star team four times and earning one Gold Glove Award in 1978. While he did manage to hit 28 HR in 1979, he was best known for his efficient thievery on the bases, racking up 418 SB against only 85 CS. This involved six consecutive seasons with 40+ SB, including leading the league with 77 in 1975 and 63 the following year.

There were two other 2B candidates I considered and who deserve brief mention. Old-timer Tom Daly (1890–96, 1898–1901) played a variety of positions, was a .294 hitter, and stole 20+ bases eight times for Brooklyn, including a high of 51 SB in 1894. And more recently, Steve Sax (1981–88) played just over half of his career for the Dodgers, winning the Rookie of the Year Award in 1982 after batting .282 with 49 SB. He was an All-Star three times for Los Angeles and stole between 27 and 56 bases in each of his seven full seasons with the club.

3rd Base

Name	YR	WAR	W3	W/G	AVG	HR	SB	OPS+
Ron Cey	12	47.5	17.8	.0321	.264	228	20	125
Jim Gilliam	14	40.7	15.7	.0208	.265	65	203	93
Adrián Beltré	7	23.3	17.0	.0241	.274	147	62	108
Justin Turner	5	23.3	15.0	.0376	.305	85	24	141
George Pinkney	7	20.3	12.3	.0218	.271	20	280	111
Jimmy Johnston	10	17.5	9.8	.0138	.297	20	164	102
Cookie Lavagetto	7	12.1	8.6	.0148	.275	35	56	105

The starter for this dream team at 3B was **Ron Cey** (1971–82). He played all but his last five seasons for Los Angeles and hit 20+ HR seven times, with 100+ RBI twice. He wasn't a fast runner—and was even nicknamed The Penguin for his running gait early in his career. He was nonetheless a good defensive 3B and was named an All-Star six times.

As mentioned earlier, **Jim "Junior" Gilliam** (1953–66) split his time between 2B and 3B, but made this All-Time team roster as the backup 3B. He took home the NL Rookie of the Year Award in 1953 after scoring 125 runs and leading the league with 17 triples. A light hitter (.265 with little power), Gilliam stole 15+ bases eight times.

Adrián Beltré (1998–2004) started his career with the Dodgers at the age of 19 and had several mediocre seasons until 2004, when he was the MVP Award runner-up after hitting .334 with 121 RBI and a league-leading 48 HR.

Unfortunately, after that great season he left LA for Seattle via free agency.

Current Dodgers star Justin Turner (2014–18) is the definition of a late bloomer. It was always pretty clear he could hit minor league pitching, but in various organizations he just didn't get the opportunity to play every day in the big leagues until the Dodgers acquired him at age 29 as a free agent in 2014. Since then he has not only hit .305 but also developed some power, increasing his power with a high of 27 HR in 2016.

A few others deserve brief mention, starting with Jimmy Johnston (1916–25), who played many positions in addition to 3B, was a .297 hitter, scored 100+ runs three times, and stole 15+ bases seven times. Old-timer George Pinkney (1885–91) stole 30+ bases six times and scored 100+ runs five times, including 133 in 1887 and a league-leading 134 the following year. And lastly, Cookie Lavagetto (1937–41, '46–47) was a .275 hitter with a little speed. His career, like so many others, was disrupted by World War II, as he missed four entire seasons due to military service.

Shortstop

Name	YR	WAR	W3	W/G	AVG	HR	SB	OPS+
Pee Wee Reese	16	66.4	19.2	.0307	.269	126	232	99
Maury Wills	12	31.9	15.3	.0200	.281	17	490	87
Bill Russell	18	31.2	10.9	.0143	.263	46	167	83
Bill Dahlen	7	20.6	13.9	.0310	.266	12	137	103

The clear starter at SS for this roster was **Harold "Pee Wee" Reese** (1940–58), who played his entire Hall of Fame career for the Dodgers. He missed three seasons early on due to World War II, yet was an All-Star 11 times and had eight seasons with 15+ SB. Although he never did better than fifth in the MVP vote, he was in the top ten a total of eight times, in part because of his excellent defense. His best season was arguably 1949, when he hit 16 HR, stole 26 bases, posted a .396 OBP, and scored 132 runs.

Maury Wills (1959–66, '69–72) had two stints with the Dodgers, at the beginning and the end of his career. He provided good defense at SS early in his career, taking home Gold Glove Awards in 1961 and 1962. A demon on the basepaths, he led the league in SB every year from 1960 through '65. A five-time All-Star, his best season was his NL MVP year in 1962, when he batted .299, scored 130 runs, and led the league with an impressive 104 SB, surpassing Ty Cobb's record of 96, which had stood for nearly a half-century. More than any other player, Wills revived the SB as a major offensive weapon.

Based on consistency and longevity, you could make a case to include Bill Russell (1969–86) on this All-Time team. He played his entire career for the Dodgers, most of which was spent anchoring the infield at shortstop. He batted only .263 with an unimpressive .310 OBP, and had virtually no power (only 46 HR in 2,181 games). A three-time All-Star, Russell provided only a little speed, stealing 10+ bases nine times.

The only other SS worth brief mention here was old-timer Bill Dahlen (1899–1903, 1910–11), who stole 20+ bases in his five seasons for Brooklyn after many years starring for Chicago.

Catcher

Name	YR	WAR	W3	W/G	AVG	HR	SB	OPS+
Roy Campanella	10	34.2	19.0	.0281	.276	242	25	123
Mike Piazza	7	31.9	21.9	.0439	.331	177	10	160
Mike Scioscia	13	26.0	12.1	.0180	.259	68	29	99
John Roseboro	11	21.8	10.3	.0169	.251	92	59	97
Steve Yeager	14	18.0	8.1	.0148	.228	100	14	84

I decided to give the spot at catcher to **Roy Campanella** (1948–57), who starred for the Dodgers for a decade before a car accident left him paralyzed and ended his career. He hit 20+ HR seven times, was an All-Star eight times, and took home three NL MVP Awards. His first came in 1951, after he batted .325 with 33 HR and 108 RBI; the second came in 1953, after he hit .312 with 41 HR and a league-leading 142 RBI; and the third came in 1955, when he batted .318 with 32 HR and 107 RBI.

You could make a case for another great hitting catcher, **Mike Piazza** (1992–98), to be the starter here rather than the backup. He started his career for Los Angeles and won the Rookie of the Year Award in 1993, after hitting .318 with 35 HR and 112 RBI. That was the first of six consecutive All-Star seasons for the Dodgers, years in which he hit 24 to 40 HR with 92 to 124 RBI. He wasn't great defensively, but in addition to his homers he also batted .331 with a .394 OBP. In the end, I just couldn't get past Campanella earning three MVP Awards, but if you preferred Piazza's stats, I wouldn't argue with you.

There were three other catchers whom I considered and who deserve mention. Mike Scioscia (1980–92) played his entire career for the Dodgers and was best known for his defense, particularly his plate-blocking capability. A two-time All-Star, Scioscia was only a .259 hitter with little power or speed. But he was a good contact hitter, never striking out more than 32 times in a season.

A generation earlier, John Roseboro (1957–67) also provided good defense behind the plate, while hitting only .251 with limited power. A three-time All-Star, he took home two Gold Glove Awards. And lastly, Steve Yeager (1972–85) played all but his final season for the Dodgers. Good defensively with a strong arm, he was a very light hitter with only a .228 average, although he did hit double-digit HR six times even while playing 120+ games only twice.

Left Field

Name	YR	WAR	W3	W/G	AVG	HR	SB	OPS+
Zack Wheat	18	59.7	17.7	.0257	.317	131	203	130
Pedro Guerrero	11	32.6	20.2	.0315	.309	171	86	149
Jimmy Sheckard	8	27.0	17.4	.0310	.295	36	212	136
Augie Galan	6	20.5	16.8	.0327	.301	33	33	143
Dusty Baker	8	19.9	10.8	.0178	.281	144	73	117
Gary Sheffield	4	17.0	13.9	.0323	.312	129	43	160
Tommy Davis	8	16.2	12.9	.0197	.304	86	65	117

Hall of Famer **Zack Wheat** (1909–26) played all but his final season for Brooklyn, and as a result is the franchise's all-time leader in games played, at-bats, hits, total bases, doubles, and triples. He was a .317 hitter and had double-digit triples in 11 seasons. His batting average climbed late in his career, as he hit .375 in both 1923 and 1924, and then at age 37 had a phenomenal campaign in 1925, when he batted .359 with 221 hits, 123 runs, 32 doubles, 14 triples, 14 HR, and 103 RBI.

Pedro Guerrero (1978–88) tried a variety of positions on the field, with substantial time spent at 3B, RF, LF, CF, and 1B, but wasn't strong defensively at any of them. He made up for that by being a solid hitter, batting .309 and hitting 25+ HR four times. He even stole 20+ bases twice, and he was an All-Star four times for the Dodgers.

Jimmy Sheckard (1897–98, 1900–05) had six seasons with 20+ SB for Brooklyn, including leading the league with 67 in 1903. A .295 hitter, he had his best season in 1901, when he batted .354 with 116 runs, 35 SB, 11 HR, 104 RBI, and a league-leading 19 triples.

Augie Galan (1941–46) was a .301 hitter with little power or speed. He was an All-Star in 1943 and 1944, led the league in walks both years, and as a result ended up with an impressive .416 OBP during his time in Brooklyn.

Dusty Baker (1976–83) hit 20+ HR four times for the Dodgers and stole 10+ bases five times too. A two-time All-Star, he provided good defense in LF and took home the Gold Glove Award in 1981.

Gary Sheffield (1998–2001) played for the Dodgers during parts of only four seasons, but he hit .312 overall and had 30+ HR with 100+ RBI three times.

And lastly, Tommy Davis (1959–66) started his long career with the Dodgers, played all three OF positions and some at 3B, and provided a .304 average with moderate power and speed. He was an All-Star in the two seasons when he led the NL in batting average, including his phenomenal 1962 season, when he had 27 HR, 18 SB, and 120 runs, and led the NL with 230 hits, 153 RBI (franchise record), and a .346 average.

Center Field

Name	YR	WAR	W3	W/G	AVG	HR	SB	OPS+
Duke Snider	16	65.8	26.3	.0342	.300	389	99	142
Willie Davis	14	54.4	19.7	.0279	.279	154	335	107
Mike Griffin	8	31.2	14.4	.0316	.305	29	264	125
Matt Kemp	10	22.8	16.8	.0181	.292	203	170	127
Pete Reiser	6	19.7	15.4	.0320	.306	44	78	132

Hall of Famer **Duke Snider** (1947–62) played all but his final two seasons for the Dodgers. He hit 20+ HR nine times, including five consecutive seasons with 40+. He had 100+ RBI six times and scored 100+ runs six times, including leading the league from 1953 through '55 with totals of 132, 120, and 126. A .300 hitter with only moderate stolen base capabilities, he was chosen as an All-Star eight times while with the Dodgers.

The obvious backup to Snider here was **Willie Davis** (1960–73), a fine center fielder who was an All-Star twice and took home three Gold Glove Awards. A .279 hitter with only moderate power, he stole 20+ bases in 11 consecutive seasons and had a high of 42 in 1964.

Old-timer Mike Griffin (1891–98) was a .305 hitter for Brooklyn, scored 100+ runs six times, and provided good speed with six seasons of 20+ SB, including highs of 65 and 49.

Matt Kemp (2006–18) provided a strong combination of power and speed for the Dodgers for several years, with his most impressive season coming in 2011, when he finished second in the MVP vote after hitting .324 with 40 SB and a league-leading 39 HR, 115 runs, and 126 RBI. Kemp was also outstanding defensively, taking home Gold Glove Awards in 2009 and 2011. After playing for the Padres and Braves for a few seasons, he made what some thought was an improbable comeback with the Dodgers in 2018, making the All-Star team for the third time while hitting .290 with 21 HR.

Pete Reiser (1940–42, '46–48) was MVP runner-up in his first full season in 1941, as he led the league with a .343 average, 117 runs, 39 doubles, and 17 triples. A .306 hitter for Brooklyn, Pistol Pete led the league with 20 SB in 1942 and 34 SB in 1946, but lost three prime years to World War II. Between that and numerous injuries, he never achieved his lofty 1941 numbers again.

Right Field

Name	YR	WAR	W3	W/G	AVG	HR	SB	OPS+
Carl Furillo	15	35.2	14.6	.0195	.299	192	48	112
Dixie Walker	9	33.5	16.1	.0278	.311	67	44	129
Babe Herman	7	23.1	15.0	.0260	.339	112	69	144
Andre Ethier	11	21.8	9.5	.0152	.285	160	29	122
Raúl Mondesi	7	21.5	15.1	.0235	.288	163	140	122
Shawn Green	5	20.8	16.8	.0261	.280	162	63	130
Yasiel Puig	6	18.6	13.5	.0261	.279	108	60	127
Oyster Burns	8	17.8	11.0	.0217	.300	40	172	130

Dixie Walker (1939–47) played most of the second half of his career for Brooklyn and was selected as an All-Star four times. He was a .311 hitter with little power, but nonetheless provided 90+ RBI four times, including a league-leading 124 in 1945. He also won the batting title in 1944, with a .357 mark.

You could make a case for **Carl Furillo** (1946–60) for the top spot over Walker, as he played his entire career for the Dodgers, had a .299 average, and had moderate power, hitting 15+ HR eight times. An All-Star only twice, he led the NL with a .344 average in 1953. Defensively, Furillo had a very strong arm and great skill at playing the wall at Ebbets Field.

I decided to give the other "extra spot" on this roster to **Babe Herman** (1926–31), even though admittedly he played for Brooklyn for only his first six seasons. Herman was a .339 hitter and had a lot of extra-base hits: 35+ doubles five times, double-digit triples four times, and double-digit HR all six seasons, with a high of 35 in 1930. He essentially had four good or very good seasons, and two truly exceptional ones. In 1929 he batted .381 with 105 runs, 42 doubles, 13 triples, 21 HR, 113 RBI, and 21 SB. Then in 1930 he did even better and batted .393 with 143 runs, 48 doubles, 11 triples, 35 HR, 130 RBI, and 18 SB.

Old-timer Thomas "Oyster" Burns (1888–95) batted .300 for Brooklyn and had three seasons with both 100+ runs and 100+ RBI. Nicknamed Oyster because he sold shellfish in the off-season, he led the NL in 1890 with 13 HR and 128 RBI.

Four more recent players also deserve mention here, starting with Shawn Green (2000–04), who had three good seasons and two outstanding ones for the Dodgers. In 2001 he batted .297 with 49 HR (franchise record), 125 RBI, and 121 runs, and in 2002 he batted .285 with 42 HR, 114 RBI, and 110 runs. A highlight worth noting was that on May 23, 2002, Green went 6-for-6, with four HR, 7 RBI, and a record-setting 19 total bases.

Raúl Mondesi (1993–99) took home Rookie of the Year honors in 1994, when he hit .306 with 16 HR and 11 SB. He went on to hit 20+ HR for the Dodgers five times, and stole 25+ bases three times. He was actually a 30/30 club member twice, and also provided good defense in RF, winning the Gold Glove Award twice.

Andre Ethier (2006–17) hit 20+ HR four times, including a high of 31 HR and 106 RBI in 2009. He also provided solid defense in RF, winning the Gold Glove Award in 2011.

And lastly, current Dodgers outfielder Yasiel Puig (2013-18) had a strong rookie campaign in 2013 when he hit .319 with 19 HR in 104 games. He had a solid sophomore season, but then injury and inconsistent behavior limited his playing time and productiveness in 2015-16. He seems to have righted the ship hitting 28 HR in 2017 and 23 HR in 2018. The one thing that has been consistent about Puig is his very strong throwing arm in right field.

Starting Pitching

Name	YR	WAR	W3	W-L	ERA	WHIP	ERA+
Don Drysdale	14	67.2	21.8	209-166	2.95	1.148	121
Clayton Kershaw	11	64.6	24.3	153-69	2.39	1.005	159
Dazzy Vance	12	58.9	27.9	190-131	3.17	1.212	129
Don Sutton	16	49.2	17.2	233-181	3.09	1.123	110
Sandy Koufax	12	49.0	28.2	165-87	2.76	1.106	131
Nap Rucker	10	48.1	24.6	134-134	2.42	1.175	119
Orel Hershiser	13	45.1	21.7	135-107	3.12	1.212	116
Fernando Valenzuela	11	37.3	17.5	141-116	3.31	1.283	107
Brickyard Kennedy	10	33.6	16.6	177-149	3.98	1.479	102
Jeff Pfeffer	9	33.4	21.0	113-80	2.31	1.134	125
Bob Welch	10	33.3	16.0	115-86	3.14	1.206	114
Burleigh Grimes	9	33.0	20.9	158-121	3.46	1.357	105
Claude Osteen	9	30.4	16.7	147-126	3.09	1.217	106
Johnny Podres	13	29.5	14.9	136-104	3.66	1.320	107
Van Mungo	11	28.9	16.1	102-99	3.41	1.331	114
Don Newcombe	8	28.6	15.0	123-66	3.51	1.191	116
Watty Clark	11	27.8	16.0	106-88	3.55	1.285	117
Burt Hooton	10	26.2	14.5	112-84	3.14	1.181	113
Ramón Martínez	11	26.2	11.7	123-77	3.45	1.283	109
Bob Caruthers	4	23.7	19.6	110-51	2.92	1.219	113
Preacher Roe	7	21.9	14.9	93-37	3.26	1.222	124
Adonis Terry	8	18.8	13.1	126-139	3.42	1.273	102
Carl Erskine	12	16.6	10.6	122-78	4.00	1.328	101
Tommy John	6	14.2	9.3	87-42	2.97	1.223	118

Choosing the top starting pitcher for this All-Time team was an interesting endeavor. I considered there to be four candidates, and in the end, it came down to the two lefties: Koufax and Kershaw. There is almost a mythology that surrounds the greatness that was Sandy Koufax, or at least the final five seasons of his abruptly ended career. But at this point, I think Kershaw's increasingly strong résumé has at least equaled those accomplishments, and has arguably surpassed them.

Clayton Kershaw (2008–18) joined the Dodgers at age 20 in 2008, and in his second season was already dominating the league, as indicated by leading in fewest hits per nine innings. In 2011 at age 23, he won the pitching Triple Crown with a 21-5 record, 2.28 ERA, and 248 strikeouts. That was the first of four consecutive ERA titles for Kershaw, and the first of three seasons he has thus far led the NL in strikeouts (his high mark has been 301 in 2015). An All-Star each year from 2011 through '17, he has captured three NL Cy Young Awards, finished in the top five another four times, and actually took home NL MVP honors in 2014 after posting a 21-3 record, 1.77 ERA, and 0.857 WHIP. Speaking of which, Kershaw thus far ranks fourth all-time in WHIP, behind only old-timers Addie Joss and Ed Walsh, and reliever Mariano Rivera. Even more impressive, Kershaw ranks number one all-time for ERA+ amongst all starting pitchers.

When people talk about the greatest pitcher ever, the name **Sandy Koufax** (1955–66) is usually included in the conversation at some point. When considering an entire career, Koufax of course doesn't come close—he retired at age 30 due to severe arthritis in his pitching elbow (ironic, as he had been given the nickname The Left Arm of God). But if the focus is peak performance, then Koufax's final five seasons are clearly at or near the top. In his early years, from 1955 through '61, Sandy was difficult to hit but was also quite wild, leading to a 1.368 WHIP, 54-53 record, 3.94 ERA, and 105 ERA+. But then from 1962 through '66 he went 111-34 with a 1.95 ERA, 0.926 WHIP, and 167 ERA+. If he'd had that kind of success a bit sooner, or if it could have continued a bit longer, then I'd rate him as the top pitcher on this roster. Like Kershaw (so far), Koufax was a six-time All-Star, winning three Cy Young Awards and one MVP Award. Some of his numbers look stronger than Kershaw's, but that is partly because of the different era in which he pitched—he three times started 40+ games, enabling him to post records of 25-5, 26-8, and 27-9 (levels not reachable these days). In the end, if you still wanted to rate Koufax before Kershaw, I wouldn't argue with you much—though if Kershaw continues to pitch so well for the Dodgers for another few years, the argument in his favor will surely become conclusive.

Dazzy Vance (1922–32) had an interesting career, in that he spent much of his 20s bouncing around the minor leagues, only making very brief appearances for the Pirates at age 24 and the Yankees at age 27. Finally, at age 31 in 1922, Vance went 18-12 for the Brooklyn Robins, leading the league in strikeouts. That was the first of seven consecutive seasons he would lead the NL in strikeouts, with his best two years coming in 1924, when he won the pitching Triple Crown with a 28-6 record, 2.16 ERA, and 262 strikeouts, and then 1928, when he posted a 22-10 record and again led the NL with a 2.09 ERA.

The fourth contender I considered here was **Don Drysdale** (1956–69), who played his entire Hall of Fame career for the Dodgers, earning 15+ wins seven times. He led the NL with 242 strikeouts in 1959 and 246 the following year, before having his best numbers in 1962, when he won the Cy Young Award after leading the National League in wins with a 25-9 record and again in strikeouts with 232. Big D posted a 23-12 record in 1965 and was an All-Star eight times. He was also a relatively good hitter with a .186 average and 29 HR in his career. Unfortunately, shoulder woes led him to retire early at age 33.

Another Donald was next on this list, **Don Sutton** (1966–80, '88). A reliable workhorse pitcher, Sutton pitched 200+ innings in all 15 of his seasons for Los Angeles (not counting his swan song in 1988). He won 15+ games in nine of those years, but topped 20 only when he went 21-10 in 1976. A four-time All-Star, he is the all-time leader in wins for this franchise (233), as well as games started, innings pitched, strikeouts, and shutouts.

After considering the options for relief pitchers, I decided to go with nine starting pitchers for this staff, so I needed to pick four more to go with the five discussed above. Not an easy task, as there were many good candidates to consider. **Orel Hershiser** (1983–94, 2000) pitched most of his career for the Dodgers, was an All-Star three times, and had several very strong seasons. In 1985 he posted a 19-3 record with a 2.03 ERA, and then in 1988 he won the Cy Young Award, after posting a 2.26 ERA and leading the league in wins with a 23-8 record, as well as complete games with 15 and shutouts with 8. Late that season, The Bulldog also broke the all-time record for consecutive scoreless innings with 59, which was one-third of an inning more than fellow Dodgers hurler Don Drysdale had managed in 1968. Hershiser was also outstanding that year in the postseason, winning the MVP Awards in both the NLCS and World Series, posting a 1.07 ERA and allowing only 25 hits in 42.2 IP.

Fernando Valenzuela (1980–90) was one of the best pitchers of the 1980s, starting out strong during the strike-shortened 1981 season, when he went 13-7 with a 2.48 ERA, led the league with 180 strikeouts, 11 complete games, and 8 shutouts, and took home the league Rookie of the Year and Cy Young Awards.

"Fernandomania" continued as he went 19-13 the following year and then had a high of 21 wins in 1985. He used his devastating screwball to record 200+ strikeouts three times, threw a no-hitter in 1990, and was an All-Star for six consecutive seasons.

Don Newcombe (1949–51, '54–58) won the NL Rookie of the Year Award in 1949, after going 17-8 with a 3.17 ERA. He followed that up with seasons of 19-11 and 20-9 before missing two years due to the Korean War. He managed to go 20-5 in 1955 and then busted out with a 27-7 season in 1956, which was good enough to take home both the Cy Young and MVP Awards. A four-time All-Star, Newcombe was also a relatively capable hitter, posting a .265 average for the Dodgers, and hitting especially well in 1955, when he batted .359 with 9 doubles and 7 HR in 117 at-bats.

For the final spot I went with **Jeff Pfeffer** (1913–21), who in his first three full seasons went 23-12 with a 1.97 ERA, 19-14 with a 2.10 ERA, and 25-11 with a 1.92 ERA. He won 15+ games two more times for Brooklyn, and ended up with a nice 2.31 ERA and 125 ERA+ for the club.

You could make a case for a few others instead of Pfeffer, starting with Hall of Famer Burleigh Grimes (1918–26), who was a teammate of Vance and won 20+ games for Brooklyn four times. His best two seasons were arguably in 1920, when he went 23-11 with a 2.22 ERA, and 1921, when he led the NL in wins with a 22-13 record and strikeouts with a modest 136. Claude Osteen (1965–73) won 15+ games for the Dodgers seven times. A three-time All-Star, his best two seasons came in 1969, when he went 20-15 with a 2.66 ERA, and 1972, when he posted a 20-11 record and 2.64 ERA. And George Napoleon Rucker (1907–16) had the highest career WAR outside of the top five candidates, but I found it hard to include him because of his .500 winning percentage. Nap pitched his entire career for Brooklyn and posted 15+ wins five times, with a tidy 2.42 ERA, which was quite good even for those early years.

As I did for several other teams in this book, I discounted to some extent the numbers and accomplishments of the 19th century pitchers for this franchise. William "Brickyard" Kennedy (1892–1901) pitched most of his career for Brooklyn, winning 20+ games four times, but also losing 20+ games five times. Overall, he had a 177-149 record for the club, but his 3.98 ERA failed to impress me. Adonis Terry (1884–1891) pitched 476 innings in his rookie season, but all of that work earned him a poor 19-35 record that year. He later posted winning seasons, including a 22-15 record in 1889 and a 26-16 record in 1890, but overall had a 126-139 record for this franchise. And Bob Caruthers (1888–91) pitched for Brooklyn for only four years, though he had impressive seasons in 1888, when he went 29-15 with a 2.39 ERA, and 1889, when he led the league in wins with a 40-11 mark.

Several others deserve brief mention, including (in chronological order):

- Watty Clark (1927–37) pitched most of his career for Brooklyn, winning 12+ games six times, including a 20-12 record in 1932.

- Van Mungo (1931–41) also pitched most of his career for Brooklyn, winning 16+ games four times. A three-time All-Star, he was a bit wild, leading the league in walks three times.

- Preacher Roe (1948–54) was an All-Star from 1949 through '52 and had his best season in 1951, when he went 22-3 with a 3.04 ERA. He posted an impressive .715 winning percentage during his time in Brooklyn.

- Carl Erskine (1948–59) pitched his entire career for the Dodgers and had his highest win total in 1953, when he posted a 20-6 mark. He also pitched no-hitters in 1952 and 1956.

- Johnny Podres (1953–55, '57–66) was a three-time All-Star and led the league with a 2.66 ERA in 1957, but never won more than 18 games in a season.

- Tommy John (1972–74, '76–78) won 15+ games for the Dodgers three times and posted a 20-7 record in 1977. He missed the entire 1975 season due to an arm injury that required a revolutionary new surgery—"Tommy John surgery" as it is now commonly known.

- Burt Hooton (1975–84) went 18-7 with a 2.82 ERA for the Dodgers in 1975, and then went 19-10 with a 2.71 ERA in 1978.

- Bob Welch (1978–87) won 13 to 16 games for the Dodgers six times before getting traded to the Athletics as part of a three-team deal.

- Ramón Martínez (1988–98) went 20-6 with a 2.92 ERA and 223 strikeouts in his first full season. He never reached those levels again, but he did manage to have three more 15+-win seasons and throw a no-hitter for the Dodgers in 1995.

Relief Pitching

Name	YR	WAR	W3	SV	W-L	ERA	WHIP	ERA+
Kenley Jansen	9	15.9	8.5	268	25-18	2.20	0.888	173
Jim Brewer	12	15.9	8.8	126	61-51	2.62	1.129	127
Ron Perranoski	8	14.9	10.8	100	54-41	2.56	1.302	132
Eric Gagne	8	11.1	8.8	161	25-21	3.27	1.111	125
Clem Labine	11	10.6	6.5	81	70-52	3.63	1.317	113
Jay Howell	5	10.4	7.8	85	22-19	2.07	1.086	170
Takashi Saito	3	8.1	8.1	81	12-7	1.95	0.912	227
Steve Howe	5	6.6	7.0	59	24-25	2.35	1.156	150
Jonathan Broxton	7	6.2	5.8	84	25-20	3.19	1.232	132
Jeff Shaw	4	3.6	3.4	129	9-17	3.37	1.186	124
Mike Marshall	3	1.9	1.9	42	28-29	3.01	1.244	114
Todd Worrell	5	1.7	3.4	127	17-19	3.93	1.280	99

The Dodgers have had many good relievers over the years, but with many good starting pitchers to consider as well, in the end, I decided to pick just three to make this All-Time team roster. Whom to rank first could be debated, but at this point I think current closer **Kenley Jansen** (2010–18) deserves the honor. After two years as a setup man, he took over ninth-inning duties in 2012 and has thus far had save totals of 25, 28, 44, 36, 47, and then a league-leading 41 in 2017. His overall ERA is a tidy 2.20, with his best coming in 2017, when he posted a 1.32 mark. He also has provided the Dodgers with an impressive 13.5 K/9 ratio and 0.888 WHIP.

After struggling as a starter, **Eric Gagne** (1999–2006) took over the closer role in 2002 and saved 52 games with a 1.97 ERA. He did even better in 2003, leading the league with 55 saves and providing a 1.20 ERA en route to winning the NL Cy Young Award. He was an All-Star for a third time the following year, when he saved 45 games and had a 2.19 ERA. Interestingly, he pitched exactly 82.1 innings in all three of these seasons, striking out an impressive 114, 137, and 114 batters, respectively. He also set the record for consecutive saves with 84, although his achievements are somewhat tainted by his being listed in the Mitchell Report as a user of HGH.

The third reliever spot is a close call, but I decided to go with **Ron Perranoski** (1961–67, '72), who pitched the first half of his career for the Dodgers and posted double-digit saves five times. His best season came in 1963, when he came in fourth in the NL MVP vote after saving 21 games, with a 16-3 record and impressive 1.67 ERA.

You could make a case for **Jim Brewer** (1964–75), who had mixed results as a reliever and spot starter until he took over the short-relief duties in 1968.

He then saved 14 to 24 games for the Dodgers for six consecutive seasons and posted a 1.88 ERA in 1971 and 1.26 ERA in 1972, with a 2.62 overall ERA for Los Angeles. If you preferred him over Perranoski or Gagne, or even Pfeffer instead of a ninth starter, I wouldn't argue with you much.

Todd Worrell (1993–1997) finished his career with the Dodgers, and posted 32 saves with a 2.02 ERA in 1995, and then managed to lead the league with 44 saves in 1996. Although he had 35 saves in 1997, he struggled with a 5.28 ERA. The Dodgers traded away Paul Konerko to acquire closer Jeff Shaw (1998–2001) from the Reds during the 1998 season. Although the price was high, Shaw did manage to pitch 3+ seasons and remains third in all-time Dodgers saves with 129. His high actually came in his final season, when he saved 43 games at age 34.

The others I considered who deserve brief mention include (in chronological order):

- Clem Labine (1950–60) was a reliever and spot starter for several years before taking over the short-relief duties and posting 19 saves in 1956 and 17 saves in 1957.

- Mike Marshall (1974–76) pitched for the Dodgers for only two-and-a-half years, but his 1974 NL Cy Young Award season was amazing. He led the league with 106 games pitched, 83 games finished, and 21 saves. He had a 15-12 record and pitched 208.1 innings—all in relief.

- Steve Howe (1980–83, '85) won the NL Rookie of the Year Award in 1980 after posting 17 saves and a 2.66 ERA. He pitched 4+ years for the Dodgers and had a 2.35 ERA, but his career got derailed by drug and alcohol abuse problems.

- Jay Howell (1988–92) served as the Dodgers closer for four years, provided a low 2.07 ERA, and had his best year in 1989, when he saved 28 games with a 1.58 ERA.

- Takashi Saito (2006–08) still had a lot left when he came over from Japan at age 36, saving 24 games with a 2.07 ERA in 2006, and then saving 39 games with a 1.40 ERA the following year.

- Jonathan Broxton (2005–11) was a strong setup man for Saito for a couple of years, split closer duties with him in 2008, and then had two All-Star campaigns in which he saved 36 and 22 games.

Managers

Name	YR	From-To	W-L	PCT	PS	WS
Walter Alston	23	1954–76	2,040-1,613	.558	7	4
Tommy Lasorda	21	1976–96	1,599-1,439	.526	8	2
Wilbert Robinson	18	1914–31	1,375-1,341	.506	2	0
Leo Durocher	9	1939–48	738-565	.566	1	0
Ned Hanlon	7	1899–1905	511-488	.512	2	0
Don Mattingly	5	2011–15	446-363	.551	3	0
Jim Tracy	5	2001–05	427-383	.527	1	0

I think the top three managers here are the ones who combined to lead this franchise for 62 years, and their rank should correspond to their years at the helm. **Walter Alston** leads them all in wins, winning percentage, and World Series championships, so he deserves the top spot. **Tommy Lasorda** clearly comes next and deserves high honors for leading the Dodgers to the postseason in 8 of his 21 seasons. **Wilbert Robinson** and his 18 seasons comes next, followed by **Leo Durocher**'s 9 years and .566 winning percentage, which seems clearly stronger than Don Mattingly's 5 years and .551 winning percentage.

Starting Lineup

What would mythical starting lineups look like for this All-Time roster?

Against RHP:
Jackie Robinson 2B (R)
Zack Wheat LF (L)
Duke Snider RF (L)
Roy Campanella C (R)
Mike Piazza DH (R)
Gil Hodges 1B (R)
Willie Davis CF (L)
Jim Gilliam 3B (S)
Pee Wee Reese SS (R)

Against LHP:
Pee Wee Reese SS (R)
Jackie Robinson 2B (R)
Duke Snider CF (L)
Roy Campanella C (R)
Mike Piazza DH (R)
Gil Hodges 1B (R)
Ron Cey 3B (R)
Carl Furillo RF (R)
Zack Wheat LF (L)

In the lineups above I leveraged two natural platoons, with Gilliam and Cey splitting the time at 3B and Davis and Furillo splitting time in the OF, with Snider switching between RF and CF accordingly (though you could also just play Snider in CF all the time and platoon Dixie Walker and Furillo in RF). Hodges and Garvey were both right-handed, as was Piazza, so that left Garvey out of these lineups, unfortunately.

Depth Chart

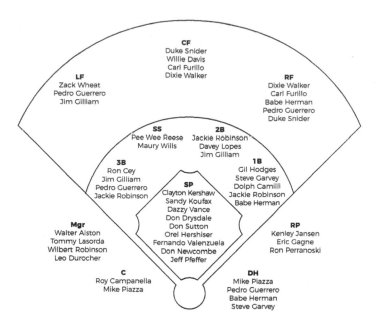

CF
Duke Snider
Willie Davis
Carl Furillo
Dixie Walker

LF
Zack Wheat
Pedro Guerrero
Jim Gilliam

RF
Dixie Walker
Carl Furillo
Babe Herman
Pedro Guerrero
Duke Snider

SS
Pee Wee Reese
Maury Wills

2B
Jackie Robinson
Davey Lopes
Jim Gilliam

3B
Ron Cey
Jim Gilliam
Pedro Guerrero
Jackie Robinson

SP
Clayton Kershaw
Sandy Koufax
Dazzy Vance
Don Drysdale
Don Sutton
Orel Hershiser
Fernando Valenzuela
Don Newcombe
Jeff Pfeffer

1B
Gil Hodges
Steve Garvey
Dolph Camilli
Jackie Robinson
Babe Herman

Mgr
Walter Alston
Tommy Lasorda
Wilbert Robinson
Leo Durocher

RP
Kenley Jansen
Eric Gagne
Ron Perranoski

C
Roy Campanella
Mike Piazza

DH
Mike Piazza
Pedro Guerrero
Babe Herman
Steve Garvey

Prospects for Current Players

What are the prospects of current Dodgers players making this All-Time team? Kershaw and Jansen are already on this roster. Justin Turner is hitting well but is already 33 years old. Yasiel Puig is only 27 and has loads of talent, but he has been infamously inconsistent so far. Youngsters Corey Seager and Cody Bellinger are off to good starts. We'll see...

Retired Player Numbers

Pee Wee Reese (1), Tommy Lasorda (2), Duke Snider (4), Jim Gilliam (19), Don Sutton (20), Walter Alston (24), Sandy Koufax (32), Roy Campanella (39), Jackie Robinson (42), Don Drysdale (53)

Selections from Other Authors and Fan Surveys

1958: *Sport* magazine, December issue

As part of a running series, *Sport* magazine reported on all-time all-star teams picked by "big league publicity departments and the writers covering the clubs." Here is what they had to say:

First Base: Gil Hodges, the easy-going, hard-hitting incumbent, wins a close battle with Dolph Camilli, and Jake Daubert for the honor. The big slugger has a fine lifetime average of nearly .280 and more than 300 home runs to his credit while developing into an accomplished fielder.

Second Base: Jackie Robinson, the first and certainly one of the greatest Negro players in the major leagues, overcame football injuries and a comparatively late start to sparkplug the Dodgers from a perennial second-division team to a pennant winner. His consistently fine hitting, fielding and hustle gave him the position over Billy Herman, another Dodger great.

Shortstop: Pee Wee Reese, often overlooked as a hitter because of his many years of superb fielding, sports a surprisingly good lifetime average of nearly .270 and easily beats out his immediate predecessor, Leo Durocher, as the top Dodger at the position.

Third Base: Harry Lavagetto is probably one of the most underrated players ever to make an all-time, all-star team. Overlooked as a hitter because there were always better hitters on the team, and overlooked as a fielder because the Dodgers had a low-hitting fielding wizard named Billy Cox at third base, Cookie's combined talents certainly deserve more than the single recognition as the man who broke up Bill Bevens' World Series no-hitter with two out in the ninth back in 1947.

Left Field: Zach Wheat came up from Mobile in 1909 and played 18 seasons for the Dodgers, during which he compiled a .317 lifetime average and was one of the greatest lefthanded hitters in the league. It has been 22 years since he last wore a Dodger uniform, but there hasn't been anyone to challenge him since those days of Dodger daffiness.

Center Field: Duke Snider may not have enjoyed one of his best years in 1958, but you can't overlook his fine record in the past. Up to this season he was one of the few veterans in either league to boast a lifetime average of better than .300. He has demolished virtually all the Dodger home-run records and, until hampered by injuries, was one of the outstanding defensive outfielders in the league.

Right Field: Dixie Walker, the old "Peepul's Cherce" at Ebbets Field, was almost 29 when he was waived out of the American League and into a Dodger uniform in 1939. He proceeded to put together a completely new career as one of the most consistent clutch hitters in baseball and became a darling of the fans. He held many of the club hitting records that Snider has broken.

Catcher: Roy Campanella, whose career was prematurely ended by his paralyzing auto accident last winter, is still entitled to ranking as one of the hardest-hitting catchers of all time. He holds both the home run and RBI records for major-league catchers and was named as the National League's Most Valuable Player in both 1951 and 1953 [sic].

Pitcher: Dazzy Vance, the first Dodger to be named to the Hall of Fame, had worked for 13 different teams and was 31 years old when he joined the Dodgers in 1922. He had never won a major-league game but he amazed the baseball world by winning 18 games in each of his first two seasons and then, in 1924, rolling up a 28-6 record, striking out 262 men and posting an earned run average of 2.16. He was easily the league's Most Valuable Player that year. In all, he had 11 great seasons at Brooklyn, returning for a 12th season in 1935. He holds the Dodger career record of 197 victories.

These were all really good, in most cases obvious, selections—at most the choice of Lavagetto at 3B could have been debated with regard to Jimmy Johnston.

1969: *The Sporting News* Fan Poll

The July 5, 1969, issue reported the results of a fan poll for the long-standing franchises of the day. The results for the Dodgers were: 1B Hodges, 2B Robinson, 3B Gilliam, SS Reese, C Campanella, LF Wheat, CF Snider, RF Walker, RHP Drysdale, LHP Koufax.

A good lineup, with the only close calls being RF (Walker vs. Furillo) and RHP (Drysdale vs. Vance).

1980: "Roger Kahn's All-Time Dodger Team" in *Sport* magazine, June 1980

In the June 1980 issue, Roger Kahn wrote an article titled "Hurry, Hurry, Hurry, The Dodgers Are In Town!" A sidebar to this article was titled "Roger Kahn's All-Time Dodger Team," and included the following all-time lineup and commentary:

Pee Wee Reese, Shortstop: As much for his team leadership as for his skills. Wins Most Courteous to Reporters Award.

Jackie Robinson, Second Base: The most exciting ballplayer I've seen. Most exciting play: Jack in a rundown.

Duke Snider, Centerfield: He *could* hit lefthanders when he had to. Ask Whitey Ford.

Roy Campanella, Catcher: Hit for average and power; superb defensively. Funniest storyteller on club.

Babe Herman, Leftfield: Magic bat. Defense? Reese, Snider and Billy Cox could cover a lot of left.

Steve Garvey, First Base: Easy, there, Hodges fans. We're giving up reach for a better, steadier righthanded hitter.

Carl Furillo, Rightfield: The way he played the rightfield wall (and threw) was art.

Billy Cox, Third Base: Best of all gloves, and in the big series, he'd get big hits.

Sandy Koufax, Pitcher: Overpowering speed, perfect control and a curve that would make you take up tennis.

Kahn also indicated Don Drysdale as RHP, Clem Labine as right-handed relief, Ron Perranoski as left-handed relief, and Pete Reiser as "super-sub." He noted that the pitching staff could be fleshed out with Don Newcombe, Preacher Roe, Carl Erskine, and Don Sutton.

Importantly, Kahn noted that he had "limited the team to ballplayers I have watched work." So that explained why Zack Wheat was not taken as the left fielder, and presumably why Dazzy Vance was not mentioned either.

1990: "All-Time All-Star Teams," in *The Baseball Research Journal*

In an interesting article, Robert C. Berlo used Thorn and Palmer's TPR (Total Player Rating) system to choose all-time teams. He selected players based on their best 800 consecutive games for the franchise, with a minimum of five years played. His results: 1B Hodges, 2B Robinson, SS Reese, 3B Guerrero, RF Snider, CF Griffin, LF Sheckard, C Campanella, SP Vance, SP Koufax, SP Drysdale, SP Newcombe, RP Perranoski.

Interesting results, and not surprising given the method used, which favored players with stronger peak performances. This explains why Griffin and Sheckard could rate higher than Davis and Wheat (though why list Snider as a RF?). It also explains why Newcombe could rate higher than Sutton for the fourth starting pitcher spot.

1991: *Louisville Slugger Presents: The Los Angeles Dodgers*, by Bill Shannon

In the Dodgers installment of this series of books in 1991, the author chose an All-Time all-star team that consisted of Hodges, Robinson, Reese, Cey, and Campanella in the infield, Wheat in LF, Snider in CF, and Furillo in RF. Koufax was the top LHP, Drysdale the top RHP, and Brewer the top reliever.

1992: *The All-Time All-Star Baseball Book*, by Nick Acocella and Donald Dewey

The authors provided separate lineups for the Brooklyn and Los Angeles franchises. For the earlier team they selected Hodges, Robinson, Cox, Reese, Wheat, Snider, Furillo, Campanella, and Vance. All reasonable picks, as were the honorable mentions of Grimes, Reiser, Walker, Herman, and Camilli.

The Los Angeles lineup was Garvey, Lopes, Cey, Wills, T. Davis, Baker, Guerrero, Roseboro, and Koufax. Here I think they made a mistake by not choosing Willie Davis, one made worse when they didn't even include him in the list of those getting honorable mention: Drysdale, Sutton, Frank Howard, Sax, and Scioscia.

1995: *Baseball Ratings*, by Charles F. Faber

Faber also provided separate lineups for Brooklyn and Los Angeles. For Brooklyn, his system resulted in a very reasonable lineup of Hodges, Robinson, Reese, Johnston, Campanella, Snider, Wheat, and Furillo. For Los Angeles, his system again produced a reasonable lineup of Garvey, Lopes, Wills, Cey, Roseboro, W.

Davis, Guerrero, and Baker. A list of the top five pitchers was given for the combined Brooklyn/Los Angeles franchise: Vance, Sutton, Koufax, Drysdale, and Grimes. And the top reliever was Perranoski.

2003: *Rob Neyer's Big Book of Baseball Lineups*, by Rob Neyer

Neyer covered this franchise twice, first providing lists of starters and backups for only the Los Angeles era. His infield picks were sensible and composed of 1B Garvey and Karros, 2B Lopes and Sax, 3B Cey and Gilliam, SS Wills and Russell, and C Piazza and Roseboro. For the outfield he selected LF Sheffield and Baker, CF W. Davis and Brett Butler, and RF Mondesi and Reggie Smith. About Smith he wrote, "Played only 542 games with Dodgers, but many of his teammates considered him their MVP in 1977 and '78; benefited from the promotion of Tommy Lasorda."

His starting pitchers were Koufax, Sutton, Drysdale, Hershiser, Andy Messersmith, Valenzuela, Osteen, and Martínez. About Messersmith he wrote, "Pitched only three full seasons for Dodgers, but went 53-30 with 2.51 ERA; fastballer was never the same after throwing league-most 322 innings in '75." His two relief pitching picks were Brewer and Perranoski.

Later in his book, Neyer provided a starting lineup for the combined Brooklyn/Los Angeles franchise: Campanella, Garvey, Robinson, Reese, Cey, Wheat, Snider, and Walker. He admitted the choice of Garvey was a close call, writing, "There's certainly an argument for Gil Hodges here, but Hodges was *not* widely considered a great player while active; and never finished higher than seventh in MVP vote." And regarding Walker at RF, he wrote, "No Hall of Famers, but a strong position over the years, with players like Harry Lumley, Babe Herman, Carl Furillo, Reggie Smith, and now Shawn Green." The four starting pitchers Neyer chose were solid: Koufax, Vance, Drysdale, and Sutton. Interestingly, he went with Clem Labine as the top reliever, noting, "Supposedly retired Stan Musial 49 straight times; that's a myth, but lefty with the great sinker and curve did hold Musial to 10 hits, 1 homer in 42 at-bats." Lastly, his top five managers were Alston, Lasorda, Robinson, Durocher, and Charlie Dressen, who led the Dodgers from 1951 through '53 and had a .642 winning percentage.

2006: *Few and Chosen: Defining Dodgers Greatness Across the Eras*, by Duke Snider with Phil Pepe

As with each book in this fun series, the authors chose five players at each position. For the Dodgers, the lists in order were:

1B: Hodges, Camilli, Garvey, Parker, Eddie Murray

2B: Robinson, Gilliam, Lopes, Herman, Eddie Stanky

3B: Arky Vaughan, Billy Cox, Cey, Lavagetto, Gilliam

SS: Reese, Russell, Wills, Leo Durocher, Lonny Frey

C: Campanella, Roseboro, Yeager, Piazza, Al López

LF: Joe Medwick, T. Davis, Wheat, Galan, Lou Johnson

CF: Reiser, W. Davis, Brett Butler, Rick Monday, Max Carey

RF: Furillo, Reggie Smith, Walker, Herman, Frank Howard

RHP: Drysdale, Newcombe, Vance, Grimes, Erskine

LHP: Koufax, Roe, Podres, Valenzuela, John

RP: Gagne, Labine, Perranoski, Hugh Casey, Ed Roebuck

With all due respect to Mr. Snider, I found many of these selections to be strange to say the least. In some cases, it seemed he was evaluating a player's entire career, not just the time he spent with the Dodgers franchise. But then in other cases this didn't seem to be true, so I was a bit confused overall.

At 1B I thought rating Camilli ahead of Garvey was a mistake, and Eddie Murray played only three full seasons for the Dodgers. He gave honorable mention to Ron Fairly, but surely Eric Karros (or even Jake Daubert) should have been listed over Murray. Similarly at 2B, where the first three players were great picks, but then Hall of Famer Billy Herman was given the fourth spot even though he also played for the Dodgers for three full seasons (admittedly missing two seasons for military service). Ditto Eddie Stanky, who led the NL in walks twice and runs once while with the Dodgers, but played just three full seasons for the team.

The strangest choice by Snider had to be ranking Arky Vaughan first on his 3B list. A great Hall of Famer, Vaughan played almost all of his career for the Pirates. He came to Brooklyn at age 30, had one good season, one mediocre one, lost three seasons during the war years, and then came back for two more partial seasons. How those accomplishments compared favorably to Ron Cey's is a mystery to me, and nothing Snider said in his descriptions of the players made it clear either. On the other hand, I was pleased to see Snider give Gilliam double credit by listing him amongst his top five at both 2B and 3B.

At catcher, Snider clearly gave preference to defensive capabilities, listing Piazza fourth behind Roseboro and even Yeager. Al López (1928, '30–35) played six full seasons for Brooklyn, but was a light hitter, so I think Scioscia (due to his longevity if nothing else) would have been the better pick here.

Almost as confusing as the choice of Vaughan was Snider's listing of Joe Medwick as the top left fielder. A great Hall of Famer, Medwick played for Brooklyn for only three full seasons. Although he hit .303 for the club, his highs of 18 HR and 96 RBI were good but not incredible. Surely Zack Wheat deserved to be listed first here, not third.

Regarding Rick Monday (1977–84), by the time he joined the Dodgers he was only a part-time player, hitting .254 with moderate power. And while I could agree with Mr. Snider that if Max Carey (1926–29) had played his entire career with the Dodgers, then he would be at the top of the list of center fielders, the fact is that he didn't; he played only one full season and parts of three others for the Dodgers at the end of his Hall of Fame career.

There were a lot of good candidates for a top-five list of RHP for this franchise, but surely Sutton deserved to be somewhere on the list. At least Snider included Sutton in the list of nine others that he considered.

Listing Gagne as the top reliever based on his strong peak performances was fine by me. And the last two relievers Snider chose were interesting, as I didn't discuss them earlier. Hugh Casey (1939–42, '46–48) spent time initially as both a starter and reliever, but eventually became just a short-relief pitcher. He had a 2.25 ERA and saved 13 games in 1942, but then like so many others he lost several prime playing years to World War II. When he came back he posted a 1.99 ERA in 1946 and saved 18 games the following year. And Snider described his teammate Ed Roebuck (1955–58, '60–63) as a valuable setup man for Clem Labine and a pitcher capable of earning saves when necessary (43 in six full seasons). The top managers listed were Dressen, Alston, Durocher, Lasorda, and Robinson, with Dressen getting the top spot because for Snider he was the "best manager I ever played for."

2016: *101 All-Time Fantasy Baseball Teams*, by Jack Sxweeney

Sweeney chose a mostly solid group consisting of 1B Hodges, 2B Robinson, 3B Wills, SS Reese, OF Wheat, Snider, and Kemp, C Campanella, DH Babe Herman, and then starting pitchers Koufax, Kershaw, Drysdale, and Sutton, with Gagne as the reliever. Listing Wills at 3B is a little sneaky, as he played only 77 games at the hot corner. Kemp was a fine player, and his 2011 season was outstanding, but overall, I think W. Davis, Walker, and Furillo are better choices as a third OF.

Top WAR Single Seasons – Hitters (8+)

Name	Year	WAR	AVG	HR	R	RBI	SB	OPS+
Jackie Robinson	1951	9.7	.338	19	106	88	25	154
Jackie Robinson	1949	9.6	.342	16	122	124	37	152
Adrián Beltré	2004	9.5	.334	48	104	121	7	163
Duke Snider	1953	9.3	.336	42	132	126	16	165
Dan Brouthers	1892	8.8	.335	5	121	124	31	179
Mike Piazza	1997	8.7	.362	40	104	124	5	185
Duke Snider	1955	8.6	.309	42	126	136	9	169
Jackie Robinson	1952	8.5	.308	19	104	75	24	149
Duke Snider	1954	8.4	.341	40	120	130	6	171
Willie Davis	1964	8.3	.294	12	91	77	42	110
Matt Kemp	2011	8.2	.324	39	115	126	40	172

I was a bit surprised that Jackie Robinson had the top two seasons on this list, and that amongst them his 1951 season rated slightly higher than his MVP season of 1949, when he led the NL in batting average and stolen bases, and had far more runs and RBI (the difference came from the defensive component of WAR, which rated higher in 1951 than 1949). But I was not surprised that he, and Duke Snider, were the only two players with three seasons each on this list.

I would have guessed that the career years for Adrián Beltré and Matt Kemp would have made it on this list. I would not have guessed that we'd see Dan Brouthers on this list—a Hall of Famer from the old days to be sure, but he played only two full seasons for this franchise.

Top WAR Single Seasons – Pitchers (8+)

Name	Year	WAR	W-L	ERA	IP	SO	ERA+
Dazzy Vance	1924	10.3	28-6	2.16	308.1	262	174
Dazzy Vance	1928	10.1	22-10	2.09	280.1	200	190
Sandy Koufax	1963	9.9	25-5	1.88	311.0	306	159
Zack Greinke	2015	9.9	19-3	1.66	222.2	200	222
Sandy Koufax	1966	9.8	27-9	1.73	323.0	317	190
Nap Rucker	1911	8.9	22-18	2.71	315.2	190	122
Bob Caruthers	1889	8.7	40-11	3.13	445.0	118	110
Sandy Koufax	1965	8.6	26-8	2.04	335.2	382	160
Don Drysdale	1964	8.4	18-16	2.18	321.1	237	147
Nap Rucker	1912	8.4	18-21	2.21	297.2	151	151
Clayton Kershaw	2013	8.4	16-9	1.83	236.0	232	194
Burleigh Grimes	1920	8.2	23-11	2.22	303.2	131	144
Jay Hughes	1899	8.0	28-6	2.68	291.2	99	145
Burleigh Grimes	1921	8.0	22-13	2.83	302.1	136	139
Clayton Kershaw	2014	8.0	21-3	1.77	198.1	239	197

First off, it is interesting that for this franchise there have been more pitchers with 8+ WAR seasons than hitters with 8+ WAR seasons. Then next, the top two seasons are not from a pitcher whose last name starts with "K"? I figured a few of Vance's seasons would make this list, but I wouldn't have guessed he'd have the top two. Zack Greinke's outstanding 2015 season ranked very highly here, and of course old-timer Bob Caruthers' 1889 season is hard to compare with anything from the past 100 years.

The only complete surprise on this list is the one from a pitcher I wasn't at all familiar with: Jay Hughes' impressive 1899 campaign. He pitched only four seasons in the majors, one with the Baltimore and three with Brooklyn. He had a winning record each year and ended his short career in the majors with an 83-40 record and .675 winning percentage, at which point he chose to return home to California and continued to pitch for a few more years in the minor leagues.

Franchise Player

There was no obvious choice for the title of franchise player. You could make a case for Robinson, Reese, Snider, Wheat, Drysdale, Vance, Koufax, or Kershaw. I chose Robinson due to his WAR totals, his peak WAR value, and the clear impact he had on the game. That said, if Kershaw continues his dominance and plays for the Dodgers for several more years, then his statistical résumé could earn him this top honor eventually.

CHAPTER 4

The Cardinals Franchise All-Time Dream Team

Existing as the St. Louis Browns for most of the 19th century, this franchise had a lot of success when part of the American Association but were downright awful in their first seven years in the National League. They were renamed the Perfectos for one year in 1899, but since then have gone by the Cardinals.

The modern franchise didn't start to win consistently until the mid-1920s, but at that point they were a dominant club, winning three of the five World Series they appeared in from 1926 to 1934. They remained a contender every year until they found ultimate success again in 1942, and that started a five-year stretch in which they won three of the four World Series they appeared in.

After that they were generally a contender more years than not, but they didn't have another spurt of World Series appearances until the mid-1960s, when they won two of three World Series from 1964 to 1968. A generation later, the running Redbirds won the championship in 1982 and appeared again in both 1985 and 1987. And finally, from 2000 to 2018 the Cardinals have been consistently good, making the playoffs in 12 of those 19 seasons, winning the World Series two of the four times they reached it during that time span.

Overall, in the modern era (since 1901) they have won 11 World Series and 19 pennants, and have made the postseason 28 times. They are truly one of the elite franchises in the game, and as such their All-Time team was very strong at many positions, though not as strong in starting pitching as you might expect.

1st Base

Name	YR	WAR	W3	W/G	AVG	HR	SB	OPS+
Albert Pujols	11	86.4	27.6	.0507	.328	445	84	170
Johnny Mize	6	39.0	22.1	.0457	.336	158	14	171
Keith Hernandez	10	34.3	18.8	.0294	.299	81	81	130
Jim Bottomley	11	33.5	15.2	.0241	.325	181	50	136
Bill White	8	28.1	16.8	.0252	.298	140	65	119
Ed Konetchy	7	27.5	15.0	.0280	.283	36	151	131
Mark McGwire	5	19.3	16.9	.0354	.270	220	4	180
Charlie Comiskey	9	11.8	7.0	.0114	.273	25	333	92

Simply stated, **Albert Pujols** (2001–11) was consistently spectacular during his time with the Cardinals. He was Rookie of the Year in 2001, hitting .329 with 37 HR, 47 doubles, and 130 RBI. His "sophomore slump" provided a .314 BA, 34 HR, and 127 RBI. He had 100+ RBI in his first ten seasons, slipping to a mere 99 in 2011. Prince Albert also led the league in runs five times, and similar to RBI, he had 100+ every year except one (2007, when he had 99). He led the league in HR twice and won the batting title in 2003 with a .359 mark. Pujols played a strong 1B defensively too, earning two Gold Glove Awards. He won three MVP Awards, but would have won more if not for Barry Bonds and his now-often-questioned accomplishments. Amazingly, he was in the top five in the NL MVP vote in 10 of his 11 seasons in St. Louis.

Prince Albert was far from the only great 1B in Cardinals history. Relatively speaking, this might be the deepest position for the Cardinals, so it created difficulties for picking just two for this roster. Stan Musial played over a thousand games at 1B, but he was included at his primary position (OF). After some thought, I went with Hall of Famer **Johnny Mize** as the backup (1936–41.) Although he played for St. Louis for only his first six seasons, The Big Cat put up some big numbers. Overall, he batted .336 with a .600 slugging percentage. This included two MVP runner-up seasons in 1939 (.349 and 28 HR, both leading the league) and 1940 (.314, with his 43 HR again leading the league). He was also runner-up for the batting title in 1937 when teammate Joe Medwick edged him out, .374 to .364.

Who would rate third here was a close call, with WAR numbers giving a slight edge to Keith Hernandez (1974–83). Perhaps best known for his outstanding defense, he took home 6 of his 11 Gold Glove Awards while in St. Louis. No slouch at the plate, Hernandez led the league in runs twice, including 116 in his co-MVP season in 1979, when he also led the NL with 48 doubles and a .344 batting average.

Hall of Famer Jim Bottomley (1922–32) played most of his career for the Cardinals, hitting .325 with six consecutive seasons of 100+ RBI. Sunny Jim batted .367 and led the NL with 227 hits and 44 doubles in 1925, and then was the league's MVP in 1928, when he hit .325 with 123 runs and a league-leading 20 triples, 31 HR, and 136 RBI.

Bill White (1959–65, '69) played most of his career with the Cardinals and was an All-Star five times. Like Hernandez, he was great defensively, taking home six Gold Glove Awards. White could hit too, batting .298 with 20+ HR five times and 100+ RBI three times.

A few others deserve brief mention, starting with Ed Konetchy (1907–13), who started his career for the Cardinals and hit double-digit triples in all six of his full seasons, while also stealing 25+ bases four times. An even earlier player, Charlie Comiskey (1882–89, '91) stole even more bases, though some of his statistics are incomplete. He had 117 SB in 1887, then managed 72 and 65 the next two years. He also had 103 and 102 RBI in 1887 and 1889, even with HR totals of only 4 and 3 in those seasons. He was also manager for the team during most of his time in St. Louis, leading them to four pennants and an impressive .673 winning percentage.

What about Mark McGwire (1997–2001), you ask? His numbers in 1998 and 1999 were stellar, as he belted a combined 135 HR (leaving aside the issue of PEDs). But largely due to injuries, Big Mac managed only three other partial seasons for the Cards.

2nd Base

Name	YR	WAR	W3	W/G	AVG	HR	SB	OPS+
Rogers Hornsby	13	91.4	33.1	.0578	.359	193	118	177
Red Schoendienst	15	33.1	16.4	.0184	.289	65	80	93
Frankie Frisch	11	32.6	18.0	.0249	.312	51	195	105
Miller Huggins	7	19.0	11.1	.0237	.270	5	174	110
Tom Herr	10	18.9	11.9	.0184	.274	19	152	96
José Oquendo	10	14.9	9.8	.0151	.264	13	17	93
Julián Javier	12	14.0	8.3	.0089	.258	76	134	78

Rogers Hornsby (1915–26, '33) was the clear starter at 2B, as all but three of his best years were with the Cardinals. The Rajah remains the greatest hitting 2B of all time, and is arguably the greatest right-handed hitter of all time. His five-year stretch from 1921 to 1925 was a well-known statistical marvel, as he averaged .402 during that period! He won the NL BA, OBP, and SLG titles every year from 1920 through 1925. Two of those seasons, 1922 and 1925, were

Triple Crown years, as he led the league with 42 and 39 HR, and 152 and 143 RBI. Although early on he played more SS and 3B, he eventually settled in at 2B, so this was the right spot for him on this roster.

Frankie Frisch (1927–37) played the first half of his career for the Giants but had many of his best seasons in St. Louis. He beat out Chuck Klein and Bill Terry for the NL MVP Award in 1931, although statistically this was surely not his best season: his 1931 numbers were .311 BA, 4 HR, 82 RBI, 96 runs, and 28 SB, whereas the previous year he managed .346, 10 HR, 114 RBI, 121 runs, and 46 doubles (in both seasons he missed over 20 games). The Fordham Flash led the NL with 48 SB in 1927 and again in 1931 with 28. And his fielding was solid, playing mostly 2B, with some time at 3B.

Fellow Hall of Famer **Red Schoendienst** (1945–56, '61–63) was not a major offensive force, as in 11 full seasons, the switch-hitter batted over .300 three times, had double-digit home runs and stolen bases only twice each, and scored 100+ runs only twice. His nine All-Star appearances were more a result of his excellent fielding than his hitting. It perhaps also indicated the lack of talent at the position at that time in the NL: Jackie Robinson was the other perennial All-Star, but until Bill Mazeroski came onto the scene, there were generally better 2B in the AL (e.g., Joe Gordon, Nellie Fox, and Bobby Doerr). A fixture in St. Louis, Red also managed the team for parts of 14 seasons, leading them to two pennants and one World Series championship. His longevity and overall productivity for the club earned him one of the two "extra spots" on this All-Time team roster.

Relative to these top three, other candidates deserve only the briefest mention. Miller Huggins (1910–16) led the NL in walks twice while with the Cardinals and stole 174 bases over his six full seasons. Tom Herr (1979–88) hit over .300 twice, stole 152 bases for the Cardinals, and was an All-Star in 1985 when he had 110 RBI even while hitting only 8 HR. Julián Javier (1960–71) actually played in more Cardinals games at 2B than anyone, had moderate speed, and was an All-Star twice. And the versatile José Oquendo (1986–95) literally played every position on the field, but played in 130+ games in a season only three times.

3rd Base

Name	YR	WAR	W3	W/G	AVG	HR	SB	OPS+
Ken Boyer	11	58.1	22.1	.0349	.293	255	97	119
Scott Rolen	6	25.9	19.7	.0392	.286	111	33	127

Matt Carpenter	8	25.9	15.4	.0254	.274	133	19	130
Whitey Kurowski	9	24.0	15.6	.0262	.286	106	19	125
Joe Torre	6	22.4	14.5	.0244	.308	98	12	133
Arlie Latham	8	16.8	11.8	.0198	.266	11	369	94

Ken Boyer (1955–65) was a solid hitter, amassing 20+ HR and 90+ RBI in 8 of his 11 seasons in St. Louis. The seven-time All-Star was extremely consistent from season to season, and in 1964 he took home NL MVP honors, when he had 24 HR, 119 RBI, 100 runs, and a .295 average. His fielding was superb (five Gold Glove Awards), though his brief stint as manager for the Redbirds in the '70s was less impressive (.466 over 357 games).

There were two candidates for the backup at 3B, but I decided to go with **Scott Rolen** (2002–07). On a per-game basis his offensive and defensive contributions were the equal of Boyer, he just played for the Cardinals for a much shorter time. An All-Star four times, he won four Gold Glove Awards while in St. Louis. He had some injuries, but when on the field he put up strong numbers, including in 2004, when he came in fourth in the MVP vote after hitting .314 with 34 HR and 124 RBI.

You could make a good case for Joe Torre (1969–74) as the backup instead of Rolen, as he had six solid years for the Cardinals and was an All-Star in four of them. This included a 1971 MVP season in which he hit 24 HR and led the league with a .363 average, 230 hits, and 137 RBI. He was versatile, playing 427 games at 3B, 425 at 1B, and 107 at C, but his defense at the hot corner wasn't nearly as good as Rolen's or Boyer's. He did later manage the Cardinals, but he had a winning percentage just under .500 in 706 games.

Several others deserved consideration, starting with Whitey Kurowski (1941–49), who had a relatively short career, entirely with the Cardinals. He provided 20+ HR three times, 80+ RBI four times, was good defensively at 3B, and was an All-Star four times. His best season came in 1947, when he batted .310 with 27 HR, 104 RBI, and 108 runs, but then arm and elbow injuries struck and abruptly ended his career two years later.

Like Torre, current Cardinals star Matt Carpenter (2011–18) has played several positions for the Redbirds, primarily 3B (528 games), 1B (309), and 2B (212). In his first full season he batted .318 and led the league with 55 doubles, 199 hits, and 126 runs. The three-time All-Star's power has increased more recently, with 20+ HR the past four seasons and a high of 36 in 2018. If he is productive for the Cardinals for just one or two more years, he could surpass both Torre and Rolen and claim a spot on this roster.

Lastly, Arlie Latham (1883–89, '96) played for the franchise when they were the St. Louis Browns and a part of the American Association in the 1880s. It is hard to grasp some statistics from that era, and Latham's are a prime case. Two things are certain: he was a good run scorer (five out of seven seasons he scored 100 or more, including two with 150+) and a demon on the basepaths, as he twice stole over 100 bases in a season. He has the record for most errors at 3B, but that is due as much to his longevity during the no-gloves, and therefore poor-fielding, 19th century as anything else.

Shortstop

Name	YR	WAR	W3	W/G	AVG	HR	SB	OPS+
Ozzie Smith	15	65.6	20.3	.0330	.272	27	433	93
Marty Marion	11	31.6	13.3	.0210	.264	34	35	82
Solly Hemus	9	21.6	16.5	.0305	.275	38	16	116
Garry Templeton	6	18.7	12.4	.0263	.305	25	138	104
Edgar Rentería	6	16.5	12.0	.0183	.290	71	148	98

Ozzie Smith (1982–96) was the obvious starter at SS on this All-Time team. The Wizard of Oz is widely considered the gold standard for defense at shortstop, and his back flips and one-handed plays dazzled fans for years. He never had any pop in his bat (one postseason miracle HR notwithstanding), but once he was traded to St. Louis from San Diego he worked very hard to raise his average and on-base percentage to respectable levels. His only support for MVP was ironically in 1987—a year of increased offense—but his votes were split with teammate Jack Clark, so he took second place to Andre Dawson of the cellar-dwelling Cubs. In addition to his defense, his other primary positive was his speed on the basepaths, as he stole 433 bases during his time in St. Louis. He was an All-Star in 14 of his 15 Cardinals seasons and won 11 Gold Glove Awards during that time.

Marty Marion (1940–50) was also an obvious choice as the backup. Similar to Smith, his strength was his defense, not his offense. He had as little power as Smith, but unlike Ozzie had no speed on the basepaths. He actually won an MVP Award, during the war-depleted 1944 season, even though he had only 6 HR and a .267 average. There was no consensus choice, demonstrated by eight players getting first-place votes. Marion edged out Bill Nicholson by one point in the balloting. In 11 seasons, he was an All-Star an impressive 7 times.

Not the outstanding fielder that Marion was, Solly Hemus (1949–56, '59) also provided little power or speed. His one standout attribute appears to have been a good batting eye, as he had a .392 OBP and even led the NL in HBP with 20 in 1952 and 12 the following year, helping him to score 100+ runs in both seasons.

Garry Templeton (1976–81) was the other side of the Smith trade, the offense-focused side. He led the league in triples three times for the Cardinals, and hits once. While in St. Louis he batted .305, stole 138 bases, and made two All-Star squads.

And it seemed that Edgar Rentería (2000–04) was well on his way to making this All-Time team until he left St. Louis by signing as a free agent with Boston before the 2005 season. He hit double-digit HR and stole between 17 and 37 bases every year in St. Louis. His 2003 season was his best: .330, 13 HR, 100 RBI, 47 doubles, and 34 SB. He took home two Gold Glove Awards and was an All-Star three times.

Catcher

Name	YR	WAR	W3	W/G	AVG	HR	SB	OPS+
Ted Simmons	13	44.8	16.2	.0286	.298	172	11	127
Yadier Molina	15	38.9	16.5	.0208	.282	146	60	99
Tim McCarver	12	20.5	12.8	.0174	.272	66	39	100
Walker Cooper	8	9.2	9.1	.0175	.296	35	11	116
Darrell Porter	5	11.7	8.6	.0218	.237	54	14	109
Del Rice	12	6.0	4.0	.0058	.241	60	2	79

The starting catcher for this team was **Ted Simmons** (1968–80). While in St. Louis, he managed six seasons with a .300 or better average, five with 20+ HR, and six with 90+ RBI. Best known for his hitting, his defense was underrated though not stellar. Simmons was an All-Star for St. Louis six times.

The backup here was also pretty obvious. **Yadier Molina** (2004–18) has so far played his entire career for the Cardinals, and in some ways has been the inverse of Simmons in that he has provided some value via offense, but is mostly known for his defensive prowess. A .284 hitter, his best offensive year came in 2012, when he hit .315 with career highs of 22 HR and 12 SB. But Yadi has been an All-Star eight times more so because of his defense, which thus far has earned him eight Gold Glove Awards.

Before Molina came to town, the backup catcher on this All-Time team would have been Tim McCarver (1959–61, '63–69, '73–74). He was a good receiver, and the two-time All-Star also provided some offense. He was MVP runner-up in 1967, when teammate Orlando Cepeda was the unanimous winner. And he went 11-for-23 as the Cards' offensive star in their 1964 World Series win over the Yankees.

A few others deserve brief mention, starting with Walker Cooper (1940–45, '56–57), who played only three full seasons for the Cardinals but was an All-Star each year. Darrell Porter (1981–85) had his best seasons earlier for Milwaukee and Kansas City, and was only a .237 hitter with moderate power for St. Louis. And lastly, Del Rice (1945–55, '60) was good defensively but hit .241 with little power in his decade playing for the Cardinals.

Left Field

Name	YR	WAR	W3	W/G	AVG	HR	SB	OPS+
Stan Musial	22	128.1	29.8	.0423	.331	475	78	159
Lou Brock	16	41.6	17.1	.0182	.297	129	888	112
Joe Medwick	11	39.8	21.7	.0327	.335	152	28	142
Tip O'Neill	7	25.5	15.9	.0326	.344	47	118	159
Matt Holliday	8	23.1	13.8	.0235	.293	156	29	138
Chick Hafey	8	20.6	13.6	.0254	.326	127	56	137
Vince Coleman	6	12.2	8.3	.0139	.265	15	549	85

Stan "The Man" Musial (1941–44, '46–63) is often neglected in short lists of the greatest players of all time, but his career was very impressive—and all of it was played in St. Louis. He had 11 straight 100+-run seasons and 16 straight .300+ years. He racked up ten 100+-RBI seasons and nine with 40+ doubles. He was a power hitter, capturing six slugging titles, though he never led the league in HR. But he did lead the NL in plenty of other categories: runs five times, hits six times, doubles eight times, triples five times, and RBI twice. He also won seven batting titles and six OBP titles. He won three MVP Awards (1943, '46, and '48), and came in second in the MVP voting another four times. Musial was an All-Star an amazing 20 times. He wasn't a base thief (never had double-digit SB in a season), but he did everything else.

Joe Medwick (1932–40, '47–48) played his best years in St. Louis before bouncing around with other teams and winding up in St. Louis again for two partial seasons before retiring. Ducky's best season was 1937, when he took home the MVP with a Triple Crown season: .374, 31 HR, 154 RBI (leading the league also with 237 hits, 56 doubles, and 111 runs). The year before, he posted 64 doubles, which still ranks as the second most in a season. He had five consecutive 100+-run seasons, six consecutive with 100+ RBI, and led the league in doubles and RBI in three consecutive seasons.

Left field is such a loaded position for the Cardinals that a third player must be included on this All-Time team roster. After a few unimpressive years with the Cubs, **Lou Brock** (1964–79) joined the Cardinals in a very lopsided trade and quickly started his reign of terror on the basepaths. He set a new standard for thievery, surpassed since only by Rickey Henderson. He led the NL in SB 8 times, stole 50+ 12 times, and really ran wild in 1974, when he swiped 118. A six-time All-Star, Brock had some pop in his bat, but his defense was surprisingly poor for someone with so much speed. He had superb postseason numbers, batting .391 and slugging .655 in 21 games. He did strike out a lot, one reason that he had a less-than-stellar .347 OBP. Just think, how many more runs could he have scored, given his prowess on the basepaths, if he had just managed to get on base a bit more often?

A few others were considered, starting with old-timer Tip O'Neill (1884–1889, '91), some of whose numbers just didn't look right. In particular, his 1887 season was inhuman: .435 BA, .490 OBP, .691 SLG, 225 hits, 167 runs, 52 doubles, 19 triples, 14 HR, 123 RBI—leading the league in all of those categories. He had three other good seasons, but that was not enough to qualify for this dream team.

A few decades later, Chick Hafey (1924–31) started out slowly but then became a solid hitter for St. Louis for four years, hitting .330+ with 20+ HR and 100+ RBI in three seasons, and then hitting .349 to win the batting title in 1931. He was elected to the Hall of Fame in 1971 by the Veterans Committee, but this was a very questionable decision, as his relatively short career just doesn't measure up and he never garnered more than 10.8 percent of the vote from the BBWAA (the normal route to the HOF, where 75 percent of the vote is required).

Much more recently, Matt Holliday (2009–16) provided consistent power in the Cardinals lineup. A four-time All-Star while in St. Louis, he hit 20+ HR six times, and twice provided 100+ RBI.

And lastly, many fans will likely remember speedster Vince Coleman (1985–90), who had 100+ SB in each of his first three seasons and led the league in SB in all six of his years in St. Louis. Unlike Brock before him, Coleman had very little power, but similar to Brock, he struck out too much and had a very low OBP (.326). I'll ask a similar question here: how many stolen bases would he have had if he had just gotten on base more often?

Center Field

Name	YR	WAR	W3	W/G	AVG	HR	SB	OPS+
Curt Flood	12	42.2	15.8	.0243	.293	84	88	100
Jim Edmonds	8	37.8	20.2	.0342	.285	241	37	143
Ray Lankford	13	37.5	16.4	.0237	.273	228	250	124
Willie McGee	13	25.5	16.7	.0154	.294	63	301	99
Terry Moore	11	19.0	10.6	.0146	.280	80	82	99
Pepper Martin	13	17.5	10.1	.0147	.298	59	146	113

There are three candidates for the top CF spot on this roster, but after some consideration the top choice seemed to pretty clearly be **Jim Edmonds** (2000–07), a power hitter who also provided superb defense (six consecutive Gold Glove Awards). In his first six seasons after coming over from the Angels, he hit between 28 and 42 HR and had 100+ RBIs three times. A three-time All-Star, his most impressive numbers came in 2000, when he hit .295 with 42 HR, 129 runs, and 108 RBI, and even added 10 SB.

Curt Flood (1958–69) also played superb defense in CF, winning seven Gold Glove Awards, and was a consistent if not star batsman. He didn't strike out a lot, but he didn't have much power either. A three-time All-Star, he batted over .300 six times, and led the NL in hits in 1964 with 211. His greatest legacy of course came in refusing to report to the Phillies after being traded by the Cardinals, and then launching a lawsuit against MLB and its commissioner Bowie Kuhn that went all the way to the Supreme Court. Although he lost the suit, it did lead to changes that eventually ushered in the modern era of free agency in baseball and indeed professional sports more generally.

Another CF deserved to be included on this All-Time team, by using one of the two "extra spots." **Ray Lankford** (1990–01, '04) played most of his career in St. Louis and provided a great combination of power and speed. In fact, he was a 20/20 man five times, with 40+ SB twice early in his career and 30+ HR twice later in his career. His best all-around season was perhaps 1998, when he hit .293 with 31 HR, 105 RBI, and 26 SB. One negative was that he struck out often, with 12 consecutive 100+ seasons. This, along with his lack of durability (he played 140+ games in four of his ten full seasons), helped explain why he was an All-Star only once.

Willie McGee (1982–90, '96–99) spent most of his career with the Cardinals as well, split into two stints at the beginning and end of his career. Like Lankford, McGee wasn't particularly durable—in fact he looked fragile just running the bases! But he was a good hitter, had good speed early in his career, and even won an MVP Award in the Cardinals' pennant-winning 1985 campaign. That year he won the batting crown with a .353 average, scored 114 runs, stole 56 bases, and paced the NL with 216 hits and 18 triples. Oddly, like Brock, McGee had a low OBP, which reduced his base-stealing opportunities. He was an All-Star four times, and was outstanding defensively, taking home three Gold Glove Awards.

Four-time All-Star Terry Moore (1935–42, '46–48) played his entire career for the Cardinals, was an excellent center fielder defensively, and a solid if not spectacular hitter. He lost three prime years to World War II, but assuming similar numbers to what he produced right before that, his résumé would still have come up short for this All-Time team roster.

Lastly, Johnny Leonard Roosevelt "Pepper" Martin (1928, '30–40, '44) also played his entire career for St. Louis, and was a key part of the Gas House Gang club from the 1930s. He scored 100+ runs three times and led the league in stolen bases three times. He batted .298 overall and excelled at the plate in the 1931 and 1934 World Series, batting .418 with 7 SB in 14 games. He split his time when on the field (613 OF, 429 3B), but managed to play in 130+ games in only three seasons.

Right Field

Name	YR	WAR	W3	W/G	AVG	HR	SB	OPS+
Enos Slaughter	13	50.3	17.8	.0276	.305	146	64	126
Brian Jordan	7	20.0	17.6	.0311	.291	84	86	115
J.D. Drew	6	18.0	11.9	.0302	.282	96	59	124
George Hendrick	7	17.8	9.8	.0199	.294	122	19	125
Joe Cunningham	7	16.0	11.2	.0217	.304	52	12	124

Unlike LF and CF, only one player who primarily played RF for the Cardinals was worthy of this roster, and that was **Enos Slaughter** (1938–42, '46–53), who played all of his best seasons for the Cardinals, before winding down his career with the Yankees and other clubs. He was a consistently good hitter, batting over .300 in 8 of his 13 seasons in St. Louis, and managing double-digit HR ten times and double-digit triples seven times. Country Enos led the NL with 52 doubles in 1939, 130 RBI in 1946, and twice led the league in triples. He missed three prime years during World War II, so his numbers as a Cardinal—.305 BA, 2,064 hits, 146 HR, 135 triples, 1,148 RBI, 1,071 runs—should have been even stronger than they were.

A few others deserved consideration, starting with Brian Jordan (1992–98), an outstanding athlete who for a brief period played both professional baseball and professional football. He played for the Atlanta Falcons for a few seasons as he rose through the baseball minor league system, but once he joined the Cardinals in the majors he signed a deal that kept him from further playing pro football. His athleticism gave him both power and speed, as he twice hit 20+ HR and twice had 20+ SB during his time in St Louis, while also playing good defense in RF.

Another great athlete, David Jonathan "J.D." Drew (1998–2003) had an outstanding collegiate career, as he hit .455 in 1997 and was the first player in college history to hit 30 HR and have 30 SB in a season. He batted .350 with 16 HR in 260 at-bats in the minors in 1998, and then hit .417 with 5 HR in

36 at-bats in his brief Cardinals debut that year. But his time in St. Louis, and throughout his career, was marked by frequent injuries. Drew's best numbers for the Cardinals came in 2001, when he batted .323 with 27 HR and 13 SB in only 109 games. He never played in more than 135 games in a season while in St. Louis, and had better seasons later for the Braves, Dodgers, and Red Sox.

George Hendrick (1978–84) spent the middle part of his career with the Cardinals, providing both some power (two 100+-RBI seasons) and a solid batting average (.294). A two-time All-Star, he hit 16 to 25 HR in six of his seven seasons in St. Louis.

Lastly, Joe Cunningham (1954, '56–61) started his career with the Cardinals and played a mix of RF and 1B. Lacking in power or speed, he batted .301 while in St. Louis and walked a lot, leading to an impressive .413 OBP. He was an All-Star in 1959, a year in which he batted .345 and led the NL with a .453 OBP.

Starting Pitching

Name	YR	WAR	W3	W-L	ERA	WHIP	ERA+
Bob Gibson	17	89.9	33.3	251-174	2.91	1.188	127
Dizzy Dean	7	40.8	23.3	134-75	2.99	1.204	132
Harry Brecheen	11	39.6	18.6	128-79	2.91	1.181	133
Adam Wainwright	13	38.2	19.5	148-85	3.32	1.213	120
Bob Caruthers	5	36.6	32.9	108-48	2.75	1.095	133
Ted Breitenstein	7	32.7	27.6	94-125	4.28	1.480	108
Jesse Haines	18	32.4	13.1	210-158	3.64	1.350	109
Silver King	3	30.1	30.1	112-48	2.70	1.122	143
Bill Sherdel	14	29.2	14.8	153-131	3.64	1.353	105
Mort Cooper	8	29.0	19.5	105-50	2.77	1.206	133
Max Lanier	12	29.0	13.3	101-69	2.84	1.275	133
Howie Pollet	9	28.1	17.5	97-65	3.06	1.297	127
Larry Jackson	8	27.7	16.4	101-86	3.67	1.296	113
Bob Forsch	15	27.4	12.6	163-127	3.67	1.272	101
Chris Carpenter	9	26.8	17.1	95-44	3.07	1.125	133
Dave Foutz	4	22.2	20.7	114-48	2.67	1.144	135
Steve Carlton	7	22.2	15.9	77-62	3.10	1.279	114
Bill Doak	13	18.7	12.7	144-136	2.93	1.267	105
John Tudor	5	12.3	10.6	62-26	2.52	1.080	146

Bob Gibson (1959–75) spent his entire Hall of Fame career in St. Louis. A five-time 20-game winner, he was a dominating strikeout ace and an excellent fielder (nine Gold Glove Awards). He posted an incredible 1.12 ERA in 1968—an admittedly pitcher-friendly year, but his ERA+ was still an amazing 258. Gibson won the MVP and Cy Young Awards that year, and captured the latter again in

1970. He ended up with a 251-174 record with 3,117 strikeouts in 3,884.1 IP. He also starred in the postseason, going 7-2 with a 1.89 ERA in 9 games, winning the World Series MVP Award twice.

Jay Hanna "Dizzy" Dean (1930, '32–37) also had strong peak performances, but unlike Gibson had an unfortunately short career. He too won an MVP Award, in 1934, posting a 30-7 record and a 2.66 ERA (the league average was 4.22). He was MVP runner-up in the next two seasons, posting records of 28-12 and 24-13. He led the league in strikeouts four times, and his overall Cardinals record was 134-75 (.641). Like other star pitchers of that era, when he wasn't the starter he often was used in relief, saving 31 games for the Cardinals. An Earl Averill line drive in the 1937 All-Star Game broke Dean's left big toe, leading him to change his mechanics going forward. This change quickly hurt his arm, leading to the Cardinals letting him be signed by the Cubs, where he quickly declined and played for just a few partial seasons.

By now **Adam Wainwright** (2005–18) has done enough to have earned the third spot on this All-Time team's pitching staff. After one year in relief in 2006, he has been an important part of the Cardinals' rotation each year except 2011 and 2015, when major injuries kept him away from the game. He won 20 games in both 2010 and 2014, but actually led the NL in wins with 19 in 2009 and 2013. In those four seasons he came in second twice and third twice in the NL Cy Young Award voting.

Harry Brecheen (1940, '43–52) played almost his entire career for the Cardinals, posting a solid record of 128-79. Twice an All-Star, he won 20 games only once, in 1948, when he also took the ERA title with a 2.24 mark.

Jesse Haines (1920–37) had a long and productive career, playing all but his first game for the Cardinals. He managed three 20+-win campaigns, but beyond that only once had over 14. He was a good pitcher in the postseason (3-1, 1.67), but surely was one of the worst Hall of Fame selections ever.

Mort Cooper (1938–45) had several mediocre seasons before posting seasons of 22-7, 21-8, and 22-7 during the war-depleted seasons of 1942–44. In 1942 he was good enough to capture the MVP Award, leading the league in both wins and ERA (1.78). Overall, he ended up with a 105-50 record (.677) for the Cardinals.

Chris Carpenter (2004–12) won the Cy Young Award in 2005 after posting a 21-5 record and 2.83 ERA. His 2007 and 2008 seasons were basically wiped out by injury, but then he came back very strong, at age 34, to go 17-4 and lead the NL with a 2.24 ERA. A three-time All-Star for the Cardinals, his .683 winning percentage makes him worthy of a spot on this All-Time team.

Howie Pollet (1941–43, '46–51) was a teammate of Cooper, and won 20+ games twice, including in 1946, when he led the league with 21 wins and a 2.10 ERA. An All-Star three times, he lost two baseball years to World War II military service.

For the ninth and final starting pitcher spot, I considered several candidates, but in the end, I went with **Max Lanier** (1938–46, '49–51), whose ERA+ of 133 was as good as anyone above. He was a two-time All-Star who had his best season in 1943, when he went 15-7 and won the ERA title with a 1.90 mark. He went 17-12 the following season, but never posted more wins than that in a season. He was a key part of the pennant-winning teams of 1942–44, and had a 1.71 ERA with 25 K in 31.2 IP in World Series play.

You could make a case for several others, starting with two teammates from the 1920s named Bill. One was Bill Sherdel (1918–30, '32), who won 21 games once and 15 or more five times (he also pitched almost half his games in relief). The other was Bill Doak (1913–24, '29), who won 20 games once and 19 games once, and led the league in ERA twice.

Bob Forsch (1974–88) won 20 games in a year only once, going 20-7 in 1977, but won as many as 15 in just two other seasons. He never led the league in any significant categories, but he started 401 games for St. Louis, second only to Gibson. He also pitched two no-hitters for the Cards, in 1978 and 1983.

Larry Jackson (1955–62) played the first half of his career in St. Louis and was consistent by winning between 13 and 18 games from 1957 through '62, but had his one standout year with a 24-11 record in 1964 for the Cubs. The great Steve Carlton (1965–71) was a three-time All-Star for the Cardinals, but his best years came later for the Phillies. And John Tudor (1985–88, '90) had one great year, 1985, when he went 21-8 with a 1.93 ERA and an amazing 10 shutouts.

Lastly, I considered several of the primary pitchers for this franchise from the 1800s, but as with most long-standing franchises decided not to include any of them on this All-Time team. I have trouble relating to the statistics and accomplishments from this era, so I only seriously considered the very best of the best—usually those who played significantly longer than these guys did. Dave Foutz (1884–87) and Bob Caruthers (1884–87, '92) were teammates for four years, with Silver King (1887–89) joining them in 1887, and then Ted Breitenstein (1891–96) pitching for the club a few years later. Their statistics were the typically bizarre 25–40-win (or loss) seasons common for pitchers of that time. Highlights include Caruthers going 40-13 and leading the American Association with a 2.07 ERA in 1885, then Foutz doing almost the same with a 41-16 mark and a league-leading 2.11 ERA in 1886, followed by King posting a 45-20 record and a league leading 1.63 ERA in 1988 (that year King started and *completed* 64 games, racking up 584.2 IP in the process). Breitenstein wasn't nearly as successful, posting a losing 94-125 record for St. Louis, including 19 wins and a league-leading 30 losses in 1895. Caruthers was the only one of them to provide much offense, as he often played outfield when not pitching and managed to hit .300 with a .401 OBP, with 35 triples and 18 HR in 1,498 at-bats, and an impressive high of 49 SB in 1887.

Relief Pitching

Name	YR	WAR	W3	SV	W-L	ERA	WHIP	ERA+
Ted Wilks	8	13.1	11.1	29	51-20	3.25	1.216	118
Lindy McDaniel	8	10.9	11.1	66	66-54	3.88	1.332	106
Todd Worrell	6	9.6	7.7	129	33-33	2.56	1.203	145
Al Hrabosky	8	7.6	7.0	59	40-20	2.93	1.256	127
Jason Isringhausen	7	7.1	5.0	217	17-20	2.98	1.191	143
Joe Hoerner	4	6.4	6.0	59	19-10	2.10	1.019	161
Bruce Sutter	4	6.3	7.0	127	26-30	2.72	1.165	132
Lee Smith	4	4.4	4.5	160	15-20	2.90	1.151	128

By choosing nine starting pitchers, I had three spots left for relievers. **Jason Isringhausen** (2002–2008) is the all-time leader in saves for the Cardinals with 217. He posted five seasons with 30+ saves, led the NL with 47 saves in 2004, but was only an All-Star once, the following year when he posted 39 saves and a 2.14 ERA.

Hard-throwing **Todd Worrell** (1985–89, '92) had three 30+-save seasons, including his league-leading 36 in his 1986 Rookie of the Year campaign. He performed well in the postseason in both 1985 and 1987. But an injury at the end of the 1989 season, followed by an extended rehab, forced him to miss all of the 1990–91 seasons.

The third and final spot was a close call, but I went with the strong peak performances of Hall of Famer **Bruce Sutter** (1981–84), who joined the Cardinals in a trade with the Cubs after the 1980 season. He led the NL in saves in three of his four seasons in St. Louis, including 45 in 1984, when he also posted an impressive 1.54 ERA. He also was important to the Cardinals' 1982 World Series championship season, including recording two wins and three saves in the postseason.

You could make a case for a few others, starting with Lee Smith (1990–93), who posted 40+ saves in three All-Star seasons in St. Louis, including leading the NL with 47 in 1991 and 43 in 1992. Joe Hoerner (1966–69) had four solid years out of the St. Louis bullpen, and compiled a minuscule 2.10 ERA. Al Hrabosky, "The Mad Hungarian" (1970–77), had several good years and one outstanding one in 1975, when he went 13-3 with a 1.66 ERA and a league-leading 22 saves.

Lastly, two others deserve mention, and they both split their time for the Cardinals between starting and relief pitching. After many successful seasons in the minors, at the age of 28 Ted Wilks (1944–51) had an outstanding rookie campaign, completing 16 of 21 starts, but also pitching 15 games in relief, ending the season with a 17-4 record and 2.64 ERA. Arm difficulties eventually led him to shift entirely to the bullpen, where he led the NL in saves with modest totals of 9 in 1949 and 13 in 1951. Lindy McDaniel (1955–62) started his long career with the Cardinals at age 19, and had mixed success as a starter before becoming a reliever. In an era before the closer's role was turned into a science, McDaniel managed double-digit saves three times, including an excellent 1960 season with a 12-4 record, 2.09 ERA, and a league-leading 27 saves. You could make a case for McDaniel as a sort of swingman for this All-Time team, taking Lanier's ninth starting pitcher spot or Sutter's third reliever spot, and I wouldn't really argue.

Managers

Name	YR	From-To	W-L	PCT	PS	WS
Tony LaRussa	16	1996–2011	1,408-1,182	.544	9	2
Whitey Herzog	11	1980–90	822-728	.530	3	1
Red Schoendienst	14	1965–90	1,041-955	.522	2	1
Billy Southworth	7	1929–45	620-346	.642	3	2
Charles Comiskey	8	1883–91	563-273	.673	4	0
Mike Matheny	7	2012–18	591-474	.555	4	0
Eddie Dyer	5	1946–50	446-325	.578	1	1
Frankie Frisch	6	1933–38	458-354	.564	1	1
Gabby Street	5	1929–33	312-242	.563	2	1

The top choice here seemed pretty obvious, as **Tony LaRussa** had by far the most career wins, a respectable .544 winning percentage, and an impressive nine postseasons and two World Championships. After him, there was room for debate, but I decided to favor longevity over stronger winning percentages and so went with **Whitey Herzog** and **Red Schoendienst** for the second and third spots on this list. That is not a typo for Red either, as he managed for 12 full seasons and then served briefly as an interim manager in both 1980 and 1990. After serving as manager in his final playing season in 1929, **Billy Southworth** later led the Cardinals to two World Series championships. You could make a case for old-timer Charles Comiskey (who later was founding owner of the

Chicago White Sox) based on his outstanding .673 winning percentage, but I favored the similarly successful Southworth in part because he had that success during the modern era.

Starting Lineup

What would mythical starting lineups look like for this All-Time roster?

Against RHP:
2B Rogers Hornsby (R)
RF Enos Slaughter (L)
LF Stan Musial (L)
DH Johnny Mize (L)
1B Albert Pujols (R)
CF Jim Edmonds (L)
C Ted Simmons (S)
3B Ken Boyer (R)
SS Ozzie Smith (S)

Against LHP:
2B Rogers Hornsby (R)
DH Joe Medwick (R)
LF Stan Musial (L)
1B Albert Pujols (R)
3B Ken Boyer (R)
RF Enos Slaughter (L)
C Yadier Molina (R)
CF Curt Flood (R)
SS Ozzie Smith (S)

I went with a few platoons—for C, CF and DH—to take advantage of L/R hitting balance. Perhaps the most conspicuous by his absence in either lineup was Lou Brock. But with his fairly low OBP (.347), and the desire to have true center fielders in the lineup, Brock is left as a strong player off the bench.

Depth Chart

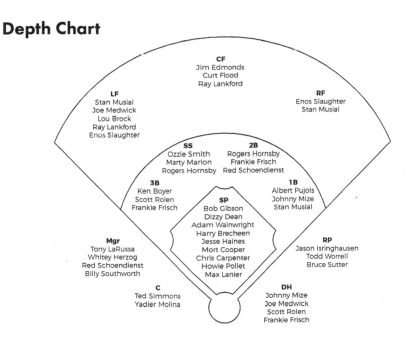

123

Prospects for Current Players

What are the prospects of current Cardinals players making this All-Time team? Molina and Wainwright are already on this roster. Matt Carpenter has been an All-Star three times so far and could crack this roster with just one or two more good seasons. We'll see...

Retired Player Numbers

Rogers Hornsby (no number), Ozzie Smith (1), Red Schoendienst (2), Stan Musial (6), Enos Slaughter (9), Tony LaRussa (10), Ken Boyer (14), Dizzy Dean (17), Lou Brock (20), Whitey Herzog (24), Bruce Sutter (42), Bob Gibson (45)

Selections from Other Authors and Fan Surveys

1957: Sport magazine, October issue

As part of a running series, *Sport* magazine reported on all-time all-star teams picked by "big league publicity departments and the writers covering the clubs." Here is what they had to say:

First Base: Jim Bottomley, who played with the Cards from 1922 until 1933. His lifetime batting mark was .309.

Second Base: Rogers Hornsby, one of the greatest players of all time. He played for the Cardinals from 1915 through 1926 and then returned briefly in 1932 [*sic*]. He became the Cards' manager in 1925 and led the team to its first pennant and world championship the following year. His batting average for 23 big-league seasons was a fantastic .358 and he is now in baseball's Hall of Fame.

Shortstop: Marty Marion, rated by some as the finest defensive shortstop they have ever seen. He was with the Cards from 1940 through 1950, and his lifetime average was .263. But what a shortstop!

Third Base: Frankie Frisch, the Old Flash himself! While Frank spent most of his career at second base, he could play anywhere in the infield and this way we get both Frisch and Hornsby in the same infield. Frankie came to St. Louis from the Giants in 1927 (in exchange for Hornsby) and remained there through 1937. He served as manager of the Gas House Gang from 1933 until '37. He batted .316 as a National Leaguer and he, too, is in the Hall of Fame.

Left Field: Chick Hafey, a deadly hitter who made life miserable for NL pitchers while playing in St. Louis from 1924 through '31. His lifetime average was .317.

Center Field: Terry Moore, who is always mentioned with Tris Speaker, the DiMaggio brothers and Willie Mays when the talk swings to defensive outfielders. He spent all of his big-league career with the Cardinals (1935-48), with time out for World War II, and he batted .281.

Right Field: A fellow by the name of Musial who has batted at a .340 clip since arriving in St. Louis in 1941. Stan can't get in the Hall of Fame until he quits as an active player – after that, they won't be able to keep him out.

Catcher: Bob O'Farrell, who played 21 seasons in the big leagues and was with the Cardinals three different times – 1925-28; 1933 and 1935. His big-league average was .273, and he managed St. Louis in 1927.

Righthanded Pitcher: Dizzy Dean, who first came to the Cards in 1930, then returned there to become the most colorful of Modern pitchers from 1932 through 1937. He won 150 National League games and pitched and talked his way into the Hall of Fame.

Lefthanded Pitcher: Harry Brecheen, the great little clutch pitcher who won 128 big-league games, plus four more in the World Series. "The Cat" was with the Cardinals briefly in 1940, and then from 1943 through 1952.

Back in 1957 this was a reasonable lineup. They used Frisch as the 3B for the same reason I would have back then. Moore in CF was a good choice, as he was superb with the glove. But I'd rather see Medwick in LF in place of Hafey. Chick had only four strong seasons in St. Louis, while Ducky had seven. O'Farrell had one full season for the Cardinals, in 1926, when he won the MVP Award while batting a modest .293 with 7 HR (he was a leader on the pennant- and World Series–winning team). Given this limited résumé, I think Walker Cooper was more deserving.

1969: *The Sporting News* Fan Poll

The July 5, 1969, issue reported the results of a fan poll for the long-standing franchises of the day. The results for the Cardinals were: George Sisler, Rogers Hornsby, Ken Boyer, Marty Marion, Walker Cooper, Joe Medwick, Curt Flood, Stan Musial, Bob Gibson, and Dizzy Dean.

All of these were good choices, with just one very confusing one: Sisler at 1B. He was a great hitter, and played most of his career in St. Louis—just not for the Cardinals! He played for the AL club, the St. Louis Browns. In the article it was noted that Baltimore picked a team covering the Orioles' short modern history, leaving the St. Louis Browns, the Orioles' predecessor club, out in the cold. However, the Cardinals crossed the league lines and included the Browns in the St. Louis fans' voting. Just one such player made it, George Sisler.

1990: "All-Time All-Star Teams," in *The Baseball Research Journal*

In an interesting article, Robert C. Berlo used Thorn and Palmer's TPR (Total Player Rating) system to choose all-time teams. He selected players based on their best 800 consecutive games for the franchise, with a minimum of five years played. His results: 1B Mize, 2B Hornsby, SS Smith, 3B Boyer, RF Musial, CF Hendrick, LF Medwick, C Simmons, SP Gibson, Brecheen, Caruthers, Dean, RP Brazle.

Hendrick over Flood or Moore was a curious result, especially since Hendrick played far more in RF than CF for the Cardinals. Bruce Sutter and Todd Worrell didn't qualify because they didn't pitch the minimum required for relievers (350 games), whereas Al Brazle was a mixed starter and reliever who pitched his entire career (1943, '46–54) for the Cardinals, ended up with a 97-64 record, and led the NL in saves with 16 in 1952 and 18 in 1953.

1992: *The All-Time All-Star Baseball Book*, by Nick Acocella and Donald Dewey

In their brief write-up on the Cardinals, the authors selected a pretty reasonable lineup of Mize, Hornsby, Boyer, Smith, Cooper, Musial, Medwick, Brock, and Gibson. They concluded by writing: "Honorable mentions to Frankie Frisch, Enos Slaughter, Dizzy Dean, Mort Cooper, Chick Hafey, Marty Marion, Terry Moore, Ted Simmons, Bill White, Orlando Cepeda, Joe Torre, and Keith Hernandez." A good list, but I think Jim Bottomley should also have been mentioned.

1992: Fan Survey

Selected by fans in 1992, and reported in *The Cardinals Encyclopedia*, by Mike Eisenbath, there were two separate all-time teams: one pre–World War II, and one post–World War II. They were both excellent. For the first team, the fans picked Mize, Hornsby, Marion, Kurowski, Medwick, Moore, Martin, Cooper, and Dean. For the post-WWII team, they went with Musial, Schoendienst, Smith, Boyer, Brock, McGee, Slaughter, McCarver, Gibson, and Sutter. For 1992 this was a great Cardinals lineup. Using Musial at 1B is fine, because then McGee (or Flood?) could play CF (though it meant Hernandez and White were left off).

1995: *Baseball Ratings*, by Charles F. Faber

The Faber system as applied in 1995 created a reasonable all-time team. The hitting lineup was the same as mine would have been then, except Bottomley beat out Mize at 1B. The top five starters are not as well aligned with my choices, though: Gibson, Haines, Forsch, Doak, and Sherdel. No reliever was listed, because at that time none had completed five or more years of eligibility for Faber's system.

2003: *Rob Neyer's Big Book of Baseball Lineups*, by Rob Neyer

Neyer's choices were similar to mine, but there were some notable differences. He went with Mize and McGwire at 1B (Pujols had only played two seasons at that time). He sensibly went with Simmons and McCarver at C, Hornsby and Frisch at 2B, and Smith and Marion at SS. At 3B he listed Boyer as the starter, and then chose Kurowski as the backup, perhaps favoring him over Torre since the latter split his time between various positions.

In the outfield he started Musial in LF, Flood in CF, and Slaughter in RF. The backups were Medwick in LF, Lankford in CF, and Hendrick in RF. Going strictly by separate OF positions, I can't argue with these choices, though it is unfortunate Brock has to be left out in favor of Hendrick. His first two starters were Gibson and Dean, but next were Larry Jackson and Lon Warneke. About the latter he wrote, "He's primarily remembered for his long service with the Cubs, but Warneke went 83-49 in five-plus seasons and never had anything close to a losing record." All true, as he completed 18 of 33 starts with an 18-11 record in 1937, and later had solid records of 16-10 in 1940 and 17-9 in 1941, a season in which he tossed a no-hitter. He accomplished all of this while never striking out more than 89 batters in a season for the Cardinals and ending up with only 434 strikeouts in 1,157.2 IP. Neyer rated Tudor, Haines, Brecheen, and Cooper next; his two relievers were Sutter and Worrell; and his top five managers were Southworth, Herzog, Schoendienst, Frisch, and Dyer.

2003: *Few and Chosen: Defining Cardinal Greatness Across the Eras*, by Tim McCarver with Phil Pepe

As with each book in this fun series, the authors chose five players at each position. For the Cardinals, their lists in order were:

C: Simmons, Cooper, Hal Smith, Tom Pagnozzi, Rice

1B: McGwire, Hernandez, Bottomley, Mize, White

2B: Hornsby, Schoendienst, Frisch, Javier, Herr

SS: Smith, Marion, Dal Maxvill, Dick Groat, Leo Durocher

3B: Boyer, Kurowski, Terry Pendleton, Torre, Martin

LF: Musial, Brock, Medwick, Hafey, Lankford

CF: Moore, Flood, McGee, Edmonds, Martin

RF: Musial, Slaughter, Roger Maris, Wally Moon, Hendrick

RHP: Gibson, Haines, Dean, Cooper, Forsch

LHP: Carlton, Brecheen, Howie Pollet, Lanier, Tudor

RP: Sutter, Worrell, Smith, McDaniel, Hrabosky

Manager: Herzog, LaRussa, Schoendienst, Southworth, Johnny Keane
As was typical in this book series, McCarver omitted himself from consideration, hence the catcher list without his name included. He included Hal Smith (1956–61), a two-time All-Star, admitting that Smith wasn't much of an offensive player, but noting his great defensive skills and ability to handle pitchers. And Tom Pagnozzi (1987–98) played his entire career for the Cardinals, and was a fine defensive catcher, taking home three Gold Glove Awards. He only played in 100+ games three times though, and was a light hitter with a .250 average and no power or speed.

At 1B McCarver praised McGwire's incredible power numbers, but I wonder if he'd still rank him first now given all of the steroid headlines that have since come out. He ranked Hernandez over Bottomley and Mize because of the former's great defensive ability, even suggesting that Hernandez might be the best defensive first baseman ever.

I found it interesting that he listed Pepper Martin as fifth on both his 3B and CF lists, and similarly listed Stan Musial on two lists—though in that case he rated first at LF and RF. McCarver's nostalgia for Maris' role in two Cardinals pennants was what got him listed third on the RF list, even though those 1967–68 seasons were the only ones he played for St. Louis. And right after Maris he listed Wally Moon (1954–58), a player who won the Rookie of the Year Award in 1954 and overall provided the Cardinals with a .291 average and moderate power and speed.

2016: *101 All-Time Fantasy Baseball Teams*, by Jack Sweeney

Sweeney's lineup was very solid with Pujols, Frisch, Boyer, Smith, Medwick, Brock, Musial (all three just listed as OF), Molina, and Hornsby (listed as DH). He chose four starting pitchers: Gibson, Dean, Carpenter, and Haines, which I think elevates Carpenter above the more deserving Wainwright at least. He went with McDaniel as the reliever, which although not one of my three top choices, is by no means a bad pick.

Top WAR Single Seasons – Hitters (8+)

Name	Year	WAR	AVG	HR	R	RBI	SB	OPS+
Rogers Hornsby	1924	12.1	.424	25	121	94	5	222
Stan Musial	1948	11.1	.376	39	135	131	7	200
Rogers Hornsby	1921	10.8	.397	21	131	126	13	191
Rogers Hornsby	1925	10.2	.403	39	133	143	5	210
Rogers Hornsby	1922	10.0	.401	42	141	152	17	207
Rogers Hornsby	1917	9.9	.327	8	86	66	17	169
Albert Pujols	2009	9.7	.327	47	124	135	16	189
Rogers Hornsby	1920	9.6	.370	9	96	94	12	185
Stan Musial	1943	9.4	.357	13	108	81	9	177
Stan Musial	1949	9.3	.338	36	128	123	3	177
Frankie Frisch	1927	9.2	.337	10	112	78	48	124
Albert Pujols	2008	9.2	.357	37	100	116	7	192
Scott Rolen	2004	9.1	.314	34	109	124	4	158
Stan Musial	1951	9.1	.355	32	124	108	4	183
Stan Musial	1944	8.8	.347	12	112	94	7	174
Albert Pujols	2007	8.7	.327	32	99	103	2	157
Stan Musial	1946	8.6	.365	16	124	103	7	183
Albert Pujols	2003	8.6	.359	43	137	124	5	187
Joe Medwick	1937	8.5	.374	31	111	154	4	182
Albert Pujols	2004	8.5	.331	46	133	123	5	173
Albert Pujols	2006	8.5	.331	49	119	137	7	178
Albert Pujols	2005	8.4	.330	41	129	117	16	168
Willie McGee	1985	8.1	.353	10	114	82	56	147
Stan Musial	1952	8.0	.336	21	105	91	7	167

This list is dominated by Pujols (seven), Musial (seven), and Hornsby (six)—that is 20 out of 24 seasons of 8+ WAR for this franchise. And while Pujols and Musial appear on the list one more time than Hornsby does, the six seasons from Hornsby are amazingly six of the top eight ever for a Cardinals position player.

Top WAR Single Seasons – Pitchers (8+)

Name	Year	WAR	W-L	ERA	IP	SO	ERA+
Bob Gibson	1968	11.9	22-9	1.12	304.2	268	258
Bob Gibson	1969	11.3	20-13	2.18	314.0	269	164
Bob Gibson	1970	10.1	23-7	3.12	294.0	274	133
Dizzy Dean	1934	9.1	30-7	2.66	311.2	195	159
Harry Brecheen	1948	8.6	20-7	2.24	233.1	149	182
Cy Young	1899	8.4	26-16	2.58	369.1	111	154
Mort Cooper	1942	8.4	22-7	1.78	278.2	152	192
John Tudor	1985	8.3	21-8	1.93	275.0	169	185

This list is much shorter, though I should note that I've excluded several seasons from pitchers from the 1800s when they often had well over 350 IP. Of the eight seasons listed, Bob Gibson of course has the very best years—his peak from 1968 through 1970. I decided to list the one and only Cy Young, who pitched two years for St. Louis in the middle of his career. His 1899 season rated an 8.4 WAR, while in 1900 he had a down year, going 19-19 with a 3.00 ERA—though he did complete 32 of the 35 games he started and led the league in fewest BB/IP, something he did 14 times in his career.

Franchise Player

Clearly the honor here had to go to Stan Musial. His career totals speak for themselves, as he is the all-time franchise leader in games played, at-bats, hits, runs, RBI, singles, doubles, triples, HR, and walks. Honorable mention went to Pujols, Hornsby, and Gibson.

CHAPTER 5

The Red Sox Franchise All-Time Dream Team

The Red Sox history is rich with talent: Young, Williams, Yastrzemski, Boggs, Clemens, and many more. The franchise began in 1901, the year the American League was born. The team didn't always carry the nickname Red Sox, variously using Americans, Somersets, and Pilgrims during their first few seasons.

They won five World Series titles in their first 18 campaigns, but then the "Curse" set in, and the team had a losing record for 15 consecutive seasons. They managed some American League success over the years, capturing four pennants from 1946 to 1986, but couldn't take home the World Series title.

That finally changed in 2004, when the Sox captured the World Series crown in dramatic fashion, and followed that up with titles in 2007 and 2013. Overall, Boston has taken home eight World Series titles and an additional five American League pennants.

As longtime Fenway hopefuls would expect, this team is loaded with power and high-average hitters, but pretty thin on speed. The pitching staff has some great stars, and between them they have pitched some of the best single seasons ever, but then the bullpen is less impressive than most long-time franchises.

1st Base

Name	YR	WAR	W3	W/G	AVG	HR	SB	OPS+
Carl Yastrzemski	23	96.1	32.4	.0291	.285	452	168	130
David Ortiz	14	52.9	17.4	.0271	.290	483	13	148
Jimmie Foxx	7	34.6	20.3	.0390	.320	222	38	156
Kevin Youkilis	9	31.4	18.3	.0329	.287	133	26	126
Mo Vaughn	8	24.7	15.5	.0236	.304	230	28	140
Pete Runnels	5	20.3	15.5	.0212	.320	29	20	125
George Scott	9	13.8	10.7	.0116	.257	154	27	103

Carl Yastrzemski (1961–83) needed to be considered here, even though he logged more games in the outfield (2,076 OF, 765 1B), because the outfield was even more crowded (like many All-Time teams). Yaz not only had a great career (entirely in Boston), he also had some outstanding peak performances, including an MVP and Triple Crown year in 1967. He was an All-Star 18 times and took home seven Gold Glove Awards. He even excelled in the postseason, batting .369 with 4 HR and 15 runs in 17 games. His longevity with Boston also means he is the team's all-time leader in games played, at-bats, hits, runs, doubles, and RBI.

The next name listed above, **David Ortiz** (2003–16) played most of his career with the Red Sox, and most of that time as a DH (1,750) rather than on the field at 1B (146). But that didn't stop him from ranking in the top five in the AL MVP vote in his first five seasons in Boston, a period in which he hit 30+ HR and 100 RBI each year, with highs of 47 and then 54 HR in 2005–06 (and 54 is the franchise record). A ten-time All-Star, Big Papi retired at the age of 40 still very much on top of his game as a hitter: .315 BA, .401 OBP, 38 HR, and amazingly he led the league with 48 doubles and 127 RBI. He is second all-time for the Red Sox in HR, third in doubles, and third in RBI.

Since Ortiz earns a spot on this All-Time team roster at DH rather than 1B, there is still space for a backup 1B. I considered a few candidates, but in the end, the choice seemed pretty clear: **Jimmie Foxx** (1936–42). He played most of his games at 1B (807), while catching a few dozen as well. He had a near–Triple Crown in 1938: he led the league with a .349 average and 175 RBI, and his 50 home runs were 16 more than the next guy, but unfortunately Hank Greenberg chose that year to crank out 58.

Kevin Youkilis (2004–12) was a three-time All-Star for the Red Sox, splitting his time between 1B and 3B, winning a Gold Glove at 1B in 2007. He hit 15+ HR six times, with highs of 29 and 27 in 2008–09.

Mo Vaughn (1991–98) also misses out. A three-time All-Star, he won the

1995 AL MVP Award with 39 HR, a .300 average, and a league-leading 126 RBI. He was a strong slugger for the Red Sox, as he *averaged* 36 HR and 111 RBI from 1993 through 1998 (which included two strike-shortened seasons).

Pete Runnels (1958–62) played five years with Boston, mostly at 1B (407) and 2B (343). A three-time All-Star, he hit .300+ every season, leading the league with a .320 average in 1960 and .326 in 1962.

George Scott (1966–71, '77–79) had two stints in Boston and actually played more games at 1B than anyone else. He had some power, was an All-Star for Boston twice, and won three Gold Glove Awards, but his other numbers didn't measure up.

2nd Base

Name	YR	WAR	W3	W/G	AVG	HR	SB	OPS+
Dustin Pedroia	13	52.1	21.2	.0346	.300	140	138	114
Bobby Doerr	14	51.2	16.6	.0275	.288	223	54	115
Billy Goodman	11	21.9	10.6	.0186	.306	14	33	101

Here there were two players who were the clear choices to make this All-Time team roster, so the only question was who should be chosen as the starter. **Dustin Pedroia** (2006–18) started his career well by winning the Rookie of the Year Award in 2007 after hitting .317 with 39 doubles. He followed that up by winning the AL MVP Award with a .326 average, 118 runs, 54 doubles, 213 hits, 17 HR, and 20 SB. He hasn't quite matched that level of output since, but he has been an All-Star four times and has four Gold Glove Awards too.

A standout second baseman of the 1940s, Hall of Famer **Bobby Doerr** (1937–51) was until recently the obvious starter here. He was a power hitter at a position that rarely showcased power: he provided 100 RBI six times—which amazingly is once more than Yastrzemski did. Also a very good defender, Doerr was named an All-Star nine times. That said, I think at this point Pedroia is deserving of the top spot, as his peak performance numbers are stronger than Doerr's, and in 2017 he surpassed him in career WAR as well.

The only other player I considered here was Billy Goodman (1947–57), a utility man who played most of his games at 2B but also played some 1B, OF, and 3B. He led the league in batting in 1950 with a .354 mark, the only player in history (as far as I could determine) to do so while not having a regular position: OF (45), 3B (27), 1B (21), 2B (5), SS (1).

3rd Base

Name	YR	WAR	W3	W/G	AVG	HR	SB	OPS+
Wade Boggs	11	71.6	25.8	.0441	.338	85	16	142
Larry Gardner	10	30.5	14.5	.0272	.282	16	134	115
Jimmy Collins	7	28.0	17.3	.0378	.296	25	102	124
Frank Malzone	11	16.9	9.7	.0124	.276	131	14	93

One of the two best high-average hitters of the 1980s, **Wade Boggs** (1982–92) was the clear first choice at 3B for this All-Time team. He had 200+ hits seven times, 100+ runs eight times, 40+ doubles eight times, and won five batting titles. An eight-time All-Star, after the 1992 season he left Boston for New York and eventually Tampa Bay. But he did so having hit an impressive .338 with a .428 OBP over 11 seasons—I guess all those chickens he ate paid off.

The backup spot was a tougher call, because there were several players who split their time between 3B and SS. But I decided to go with Hall of Famer **Jimmy Collins** (1901–07). He was the first 3B for this franchise and managed the club for their first six seasons as well, which included winning the first World Series ever. He provided great defense, was often amongst the league leaders in several offensive categories, and until the 1970s was regarded as one of the best 3B ever.

We'll get to the 3B/SS players in a moment, but I also considered two other 3B candidates briefly, starting with Larry Gardner (1908–17), who was a .282 hitter and a fairly typical offensive player for his era—hitting triples and stealing some bases. And lastly, Frank Malzone (1955–65) was a six-time All-Star in part because he was good defensively, taking home three Gold Glove Awards. He was steady with the bat as well, consistently providing 15 home runs and 80 to 100 RBI a year.

Shortstop

Name	YR	WAR	W3	W/G	AVG	HR	SB	OPS+
Nomar Garciaparra	9	41.1	21.3	.0425	.323	178	84	133
Rico Petrocelli	13	39.1	19.7	.0252	.251	210	10	108
John Valentin	10	32.1	18.2	.0324	.281	121	47	110
Johnny Pesky	8	30.5	16.3	.0296	.313	13	48	110
Joe Cronin	11	29.4	15.4	.0259	.300	119	31	122
Freddy Parent	7	27.5	17.6	.0279	.273	19	129	103
Vern Stephens	5	19.4	15.1	.0294	.283	122	7	118
Rick Burleson	7	18.2	10.1	.0177	.274	38	67	85
Heinie Wagner	11	17.4	10.5	.0180	.251	10	141	96

Although **Nomar Garciaparra** (1996–2004) was traded as part of a four-team exchange in the middle of the 2004 season, he was the superstar in town for enough years to warrant making this All-Time team—and arguably as the SS starter. He was Rookie of the Year in 1997, after batting .306 with 30 HR, 98 RBI, 44 doubles, 122 runs, and leading the AL with 209 hits and 11 triples. In each of his six full seasons he hit over .300 with 20+ HR, 100+ runs, and 95+ RBI. A five-time All-Star for Boston, he led the league in batting in both 1999 at .357 and 2000 at .372.

As I said earlier, there are many candidates for the backup SS spot (and backup 3B spot too). In the end, I decided to give a spot on this All-Time dream team roster to Boston favorite **Johnny Pesky** (1942, '46–52), who split his time between SS (549) and 3B (457). He had an outstanding rookie campaign in 1942, then returned to the Sox after WWII and was a high-average hitter for Boston for more than seven seasons. He led the AL in hits three times, and six times scored over 100 runs. If he hadn't lost several years to the war, his résumé would be even stronger, and you could also give him bonus points for additional contributions to the Red Sox as a coach, announcer, and general manager.

Like Doerr at 2B, **Rico Petrocelli** (1963–76) provided Boston with power at a position that rarely demonstrated it during that time period. He regularly hit double-digit home runs and cranked out 40 in 1969 after the leagues once again expanded. Like Pesky before him, Petrocelli split his time evenly between SS (774) and 3B (727). After considering several candidates, I decided to give him the second "extra spot" on this roster.

Another candidate was John Valentin (1992–2001), who had several fine seasons in the late '90s, splitting time at SS, 3B, and a little 2B as well. He led the AL in doubles in 1997 with 47, but his best season was two years earlier when he hit 27 HR, stole 20 bases, and had 108 runs and 102 RBI.

You could also make a case for Joe Cronin (1935–45) to make this roster at SS. Although his best seasons were with Washington, he provided Boston with a .300 average and had 90+ RBI six times for the Sox. Like Jimmy Collins before him, Cronin was a member of that rare fraternity of player-managers, and he was a five-time All-Star for the Red Sox.

As if that weren't enough, I did briefly consider four other Boston short-stops. Vern Stephens (1948–52) had three incredible seasons in Boston from 1948 through 1950, with HR totals of 29, 39, and 30, and even more impressive RBI totals of 137, 159, and 144. But then he played only parts of the 1951–52 seasons. He was named an All-Star four times during those years, but just didn't play long enough to qualify for this squad.

Rick Burleson (1974–80) was a light hitter but a good fielder (Gold Glove in 1979) and was an All-Star three times. Between them, Freddy Parent (1901–07) and Heinie Wagner (1906–13, '15–16, '18) essentially manned SS for Boston during the franchise's first dozen seasons, and as was typical of the era both were capable of stealing some bases.

Catcher

Name	YR	WAR	W3	W/G	AVG	HR	SB	OPS+
Carlton Fisk	11	39.5	20.2	.0366	.284	162	61	126
Jason Varitek	15	24.3	10.9	.0157	.256	193	25	99
Bill Carrigan	10	12.0	6.7	.0169	.257	6	37	94
Rick Ferrell	5	11.1	8.0	.0212	.302	16	7	103
Rich Gedman	11	11.8	12.0	.0130	.259	83	3	95

Starting for this team at catcher would be **Carlton Fisk** (1969, '71–80), who had some key seasons in Bean Town before taking off for The Windy City. He is perhaps most remembered for postseason heroics, but he also hit 20+ HR four times. Pudge was named an All-Star seven times and won both the Rookie of the Year and Gold Glove Awards in 1972.

Jason Varitek (1997–2011) took over the bulk of the catching duties in 1999 and was a key part of the team's success for a decade. A three-time All-Star, he was only a .256 hitter but provided 20+ HR three times. He also deserves credit for playing a leadership role as team captain for their recent championship teams.

The Red Sox don't have a history of strength at catcher, as no other candidates came close to Fisk and Varitek. Bill Carrigan (1906–16) was their primary backstop during the early years, but he played over 90 games in a season only twice and was not much of a hitter. That said, he gets bonus credit for being a player-manager for Boston from 1913 through 1916, leading them to back-to-back World Series championships in 1915 and 1916. (His return as manager from 1927 through 1929 was not successful, as he couldn't muster a win-loss percentage above .377.)

Rick Ferrell (1933–37) had a long career, but played for the Red Sox for only parts of five seasons. He was not a home run threat, but his .302 average and good defense got him included as an All-Star all five seasons. Lastly, Rich Gedman (1980–90) had a lower batting average but a little more pop (three times hitting 15+ HR), and was an All-Star twice.

Left Field

Name	YR	WAR	W3	W/G	AVG	HR	SB	OPS+
Ted Williams	19	123.2	32.1	.0537	.344	521	24	190
Carl Yastrzemski	23	96.1	32.4	.0291	.285	452	168	130
Jim Rice	16	47.4	19.4	.0227	.298	382	58	128
Manny Ramírez	8	33.2	16.6	.0307	.312	274	7	155
Mike Greenwell	12	25.7	14.7	.0203	.303	130	80	120
Duffy Lewis	8	22.5	11.6	.0190	.289	27	102	117

Some good players have already been left out, and the same was true here in the outfield—even after shifting Yaz over to 1B (included above for reference). Words don't do justice to the greatness of **Ted Williams** (1939–42, '46–60). He had two Triple Crown seasons ('42 and '47) and won two MVP Awards ('46 and '49)—but note that he didn't win the MVP in either of his Triple Crown seasons! Joe Gordon took the award in 1942 and Joe DiMaggio in 1947 (by just one vote). And then there was 1941, when Williams batted .406 but also failed to win the MVP, as DiMaggio took it by riding on his 56-game hitting streak. The Splendid Splinter won six batting titles and led the AL in HR 4 times, RBI 4 times, runs 6 times, and OBP an insane 12 times. On the downside, he managed to go only 5-for-25 with no home runs in seven postseason games. But a career OPS+ of 190? Enough said.

Just as Williams is the clear starter in LF for this All-Time team, so too is **Jim Rice** (1974–89) obviously deserving for the backup spot. He had one of the most impressive offensive Red Sox seasons ever in 1978, when he took home the AL MVP after hitting .315 with 46 HR, 121 runs, 139 RBI, and 15 triples, giving him 406 total bases (the Red Sox record). Spending his entire career in Boston, Rice was an All-Star eight times, led the league in HR three times, and had eight 100+-RBI seasons.

Unlike Williams and Rice, another fearsome Red Sox slugger didn't spend his entire career in Boston. **Manny Ramírez** (2001–2008) played most of eight seasons for the Red Sox and made the All-Star squad every year. In 2002 he paced the AL with a .349 average, and in 2004 led the league with 43 HR. He hit 30+ HR and 100+ RBI in seven of those eight seasons, with a robust .312 average and .411 OBP. And he didn't slow down during the postseason either: in 43 games he hit .321 with 11 HR and 36 RBI.

Two other Red Sox left fielders deserve mention, starting with Mike Greenwell (1985–1996). A two-time All-Star, he played his entire MLB career for the Red Sox, only leaving for Japan briefly before a foot injury caused his early retirement. His best season came in 1988, when he batted .325 with 39 doubles,

22 HR, 119 RBI, and 16 SB—good enough for second in the AL MVP vote (behind only the now-controversial 40/40 season of Jose Canseco).

Lastly, Duffy Lewis (1910–17) was part of a great trio of outfielders the Red Sox had in the early part of the 20th century. He was outstanding defensively and a solid hitter, providing 109 RBI in 1912 even though he hit only 6 HR.

Center Field

Name	YR	WAR	W3	W/G	AVG	HR	SB	OPS+
Tris Speaker	9	55.4	28.3	.0520	.337	39	267	166
Reggie Smith	8	34.2	17.5	.0337	.281	149	84	129
Dom DiMaggio	11	32.0	13.3	.0229	.298	87	100	110
Fred Lynn	7	31.9	20.9	.0385	.308	124	43	141
Jacoby Ellsbury	7	21.1	16.8	.0295	.297	65	241	108
Jim Piersall	8	19.4	12.2	.0208	.273	66	58	93

As with left field, there is a clear top choice for the Red Sox in center field: Hall of Famer **Tris Speaker** (1907–15), who split most of his career between Boston and Cleveland. He had his best year in 1912, when he hit .383 with 222 hits, 136 runs, 52 SB, and 53 doubles. He brings speed to this rather slow All-Time team, as he stole 25+ bases in all seven of his full seasons for the Sox. While Speaker hit for a .337 average, he never won a batting title while in Boston, largely due to playing during the Ty Cobb era. The Grey Eagle was also a great defender in center field, often considered one of the all-time best.

The backup spot here was a tougher selection, as there were three strong candidates. In the end, I went with **Fred Lynn** (1974–80) even though he had a slightly lower career WAR in Boston. After proving himself with a .419 average in a brief stint in 1974, Lynn burst onto the scene with a famous rookie season, becoming the first player to win both the Rookie of the Year and league MVP Awards in the same season). That year he hit .331 with 21 HR, 105 RBI, and a league-leading 103 runs and 47 doubles. In 1979 he hit .333 with 39 HR and 122 RBI. He was a great defender at Fenway, taking home four Gold Glove Awards, and he was an AL All-Star in all six of his full seasons in Boston.

If you were to go strictly by career WAR for the Red Sox, then the backup CF would be Reggie Smith (1966–73). Like Speaker and Lynn, he started his career in Boston before moving on to other clubs. Smith regularly hit 20+ HR, was an All-Star for the Sox twice, and won a Gold Glove Award in 1968.

The third candidate was lifetime Red Sox center fielder Dom DiMaggio (1940–42, '46–53). He had little power and only moderate speed (he was a good center fielder and led the league in SB once, but with only 15). But The Little Professor had many productive seasons, scored 100+ runs six times, and was an All-Star seven times. And like Williams and many others, he missed three of his prime years for WWII.

Two other Red Sox center fielders deserve at least brief mention, starting with Jacoby Ellsbury (2007–13). Known more for his speed than his power, he three times paced the AL in stolen bases with totals of 50, 70, and 52 (70 is Boston's record). That said, in 2011 he was the AL MVP runner-up after he uncharacteristically swatted 32 HR to go with 46 doubles, 119 runs, 105 RBI, 39 SB, a .321 average, a Gold Glove Award, and his one All-Star appearance.

Lastly, Jimmy Piersall (1950, '52–58) provided only moderate power and speed, but was a good fielder (one Gold Glove Award with the Sox) and led the AL with 40 doubles in 1956.

Right Field

Name	YR	WAR	W3	W/G	AVG	HR	SB	OPS+
Dwight Evans	19	66.2	18.5	.0264	.272	379	76	127
Harry Hooper	12	38.4	14.1	.0233	.272	30	300	114
Mookie Betts	5	35.2	27.0	.0547	.303	110	110	134
Jackie Jensen	7	22.4	13.2	.0216	.282	170	95	123
Trot Nixon	10	22.4	12.2	.0228	.278	133	29	116
Buck Freeman	7	18.2	12.7	.0222	.286	48	59	130
Tony Conigliaro	7	12.1	9.7	.0151	.267	162	17	122

As with LF and CF, the top choice here was easy: **Dwight Evans** (1972–90). An outstanding defender, Evans took home eight Gold Glove Awards. While he lacked the slugging power that his teammate Rice provided, he was a consistent threat who hit 20+ HR 11 times and had 4 100+-RBI seasons.

Deadball-Era Hall of Famer **Harry Hooper** (1909–20) could run well and is this franchise's all-time leader in SB with 300. This speed made him a consistent, if not a flashy, run scorer with 75–100 runs in each of 11 full seasons with the Red Sox. And for many years he was a part of an outstanding outfield trio (with Speaker and Lewis) who for some time after were considered by many to be the best outfield assembled on one team.

You could make a case that Mookie Betts (2014–18), after only four full seasons, is deserving of a spot on this All-Time team—either in place of Lynn or Hooper in the OF, or Petrocelli for the second "extra spot." He showed a lot of promise in his first two seasons and then busted out in 2016 with 31 HR, 113 RBI, 122 runs, 26 SB, and a .318 average, coming in second in the AL MVP vote. His numbers dipped in 2017, but then he came back strong in 2018 with 32 HR, 47 doubles, and a league-leading .346 average and 129 runs. A three-time All-Star, Betts has also taken home two Gold Glove Awards.

The top two were pretty obvious choices for RF, but I did consider three other candidates:

- Jackie Jensen (1954–59, '61) had seven good seasons with Boston, including six with 20+ HR and five with 100+ RBI (three times leading the league). He won one Gold Glove Award, was an All-Star twice, and was AL MVP in 1958, when he batted .286 with 35 HR and a league-leading 122 RBI. A fear of flying and a desire to spend more time with his family led to his early retirement, at age 34, after the 1961 season.

- Trot Nixon (1996, 1998–2006) played most of his career for Boston, but played in 140 or more games only twice. He was a very good fielder and managed 20+ HR in three consecutive seasons.

- Old-timer Buck Freeman (1901–07) was an early "power hitter" in the American League. He led the league in RBI twice with 121 in 1902 and 104 in 1903, and was regularly amongst the league leaders in HR, pacing the junior circuit with 13 in 1903.

Lastly, some readers might also remember the popular Tony Conigliaro (1964–70, '75), who had a strong rookie campaign with a .290 average and 24 HR before breaking his arm and toes in August. The following season, he paced the AL with 32 HR, in what was clearly a light offensive season. In 1967 he was hit in the face by a pitch and suffered a severe eye injury, but still managed to come back and hit 36 HR with 116 RBI in 1970. He played for the Angels in 1971, but his deteriorating eyesight forced his retirement after a brief comeback attempt in Boston in 1975.

Starting Pitching

Name	YR	WAR	W3	W-L	ERA	WHIP	ERA+
Roger Clemens	13	81.6	28.9	192-111	3.06	1.158	145
Cy Young	8	68.5	32.6	192-112	2.00	0.970	147
Pedro Martínez	7	53.6	29.4	117-37	2.52	0.978	190
Lefty Grove	8	41.9	28.6	105-62	3.34	1.321	143

Babe Ruth	6	41.0	29.2	89-46	2.19	1.142	125
Luis Tiant	8	36.1	20.4	122-81	3.36	1.201	118
Joe Wood	8	33.8	21.0	117-56	1.99	1.080	149
Tim Wakefield	17	32.7	13.5	186-168	4.43	1.339	106
Jon Lester	9	30.3	17.4	110-63	3.64	1.287	120
Mel Parnell	10	27.6	19.0	123-75	3.50	1.411	125
Dutch Leonard	6	27.5	18.8	90-64	2.13	1.136	129
Ray Collins	7	23.8	16.8	84-62	2.51	1.134	115
Wes Ferrell	4	23.7	24.0	62-40	4.11	1.472	120
Tex Hughson	8	23.5	17.6	96-54	2.94	1.194	125
Josh Beckett	7	22.9	17.5	89-58	4.17	1.223	109
Dennis Eckersley	8	22.3	19.1	88-71	3.92	1.254	109
Joe Dobson	9	21.0	12.4	106-72	3.57	1.339	115
Frank Sullivan	8	20.7	14.4	90-80	3.47	1.282	120

This dream team's pitching staff started out with two all-time greats: one whose name is on the top award for the position, and another who has won that award more than anyone else. **Roger Clemens** (1984–96) started his career and had many of his best years in Boston, including a 24-4 record in 1986. He took home three of his seven Cy Young Awards and four of his seven ERA titles while in Boston. The Rocket was also very durable, posting 17+ wins and 200+ strikeouts in seven consecutive seasons.

Cy Young's (1901–08) almost unbelievable career began in 1890 with the Cleveland Spiders. But many of his best seasons were spent in Boston, where he pitched for eight years, anchoring the first dominant team of the American League. During those years, Denton True Young posted the following ERAs: 1.63, 2.15, 2.08, 1.97, 1.82, 3.19, 1.99, and 1.26. As impressive as those look, note that his ERA+ is only two points higher than Clemens' for the Red Sox—showing the importance of considering a stat like ERA in the context of a player's (ahem) era. Interestingly, the two have almost the same W-L record for the Red Sox. That said, Young's *average* W-L record was 25-15, and he completed 275 of his 297 starts. No wonder the award was named after him.

The quality hurlers on this All-Time team don't end with Clemens and Young, as next up is **Pedro Martínez** (1998–2004), who was electric during his seven seasons in Boston. He won four ERA titles and led the AL in strikeouts three times. His 1999 and 2000 seasons, for which he won Cy Young Awards, were arguably two of the very best pitching seasons in the history of the game, especially if you consider his numbers relative to the rest of the league:

- 23-4, 2.07 (vs. 5.07 league average), 213.1 IP, 160 H, 313 K, 37 BB
- 18-6, 1.74 (vs. 4.97 league average), 217.0 IP, 128 H, 284 K, 32 BB

Next up was Hall of Famer **Lefty Grove** (1934–41). He had a simply awesome career, though his most dominating seasons were with the Athletics. After he was traded to the Red Sox, an arm injury limited his success in 1934. Having lost his blazing fastball, Grove was no longer the league-leading strikeout pitcher he had been. But he quickly adjusted and was a five-time All-Star, capturing four ERA titles and ending up with a .629 winning percentage for the Red Sox.

Another player who put up some outstanding numbers for Boston was none other than **Babe Ruth** (1914–19). His combined pitching and hitting numbers during his short time in Boston earned him this roster spot. Ruth was a dominating pitcher, posting an 89-46 record and a 2.19 ERA, letting batters hit only .207 against him. He had two 20+-win seasons, with ERAs of 2.01 and 1.75 (led league), and a few other good pitching years as well. Further, each year he batted more and more, being used on some off days in the field at 1B or OF. In 1919, his last year in Boston, he exploded for 29 home runs, which was only the tip of the iceberg of course.

Luis Tiant (1971–78) had his most dominating years earlier in his career (with Cleveland), but also had many fine seasons for Boston. These included three 20+-win seasons and a 15-6 campaign in 1972 in which he posted a league-leading 1.91 ERA.

Smokey Joe Wood (1908–15), at the young age of 22 in 1912, posted an incredible 34-5 record in the regular season and won three games in the World Series, leading the Red Sox to victory over the Giants. Arm problems soon cut his career short, but he compiled a 116-56 record (.676), completing 121 of his 157 starts, and posting a 1.99 ERA while in Boston.

After those seven, the choices become a bit harder, as there are several candidates for only two remaining spots. **Jon Lester** (2006–14) posted five seasons with 15+-wins for the Red Sox and had a very strong .636 winning percentage along the way. His best season was perhaps 2010, when he tallied a 19-9 mark with 225 strikeouts in 208 innings.

Mel Parnell (1947–56) twice won 20+ games, and two other times had 18. The highlights of his career were going 25-7 with a 2.77 ERA in 1949 and tossing a no-hitter in 1956.

Ending the starting pitcher selections there leaves out two interesting cases, starting with Dutch Leonard (1913–18). He played for Boston only a short while but compiled a fine 90-63 record with a 2.13 ERA. In 1914 he went 19-5 with a microscopic 0.96 ERA, and he was versatile in that he was effective coming in from the bullpen as well as starting games. He threw no-hitters in both 1916 and 1918.

Quite different from Leonard was Tim Wakefield (1995–2011), who some might argue deserves a spot on this All-Time dream team roster based on longevity. After all, he has a higher career WAR for Boston than Lester, Parnell, or Leonard, ranks first in Red Sox history in innings pitched and games started, and is second in strikeouts and third in wins. But he is also first in losses, hits allowed, base on balls allowed, earned runs allowed, wild pitches, hit batters, and HR allowed (401, more than twice that of second-place Clemens' 194). Wakefield was often part of the Sox rotation but also spent some time as a long-relief man. In terms of single-season accomplishments, he won 17 games twice and 16 games twice, but never led the league in any (positive) pitching statistics.

Seven other starting pitchers were also considered, including (in chronological order):

- Ray Collins (1909–15) played all of his short major league career with the Red Sox, going 19-8 in 1913 and 20-13 in 1914. Then in 1915 the team had an abundance of quality hurlers and he was mostly relegated to the bullpen, where he didn't perform as well, so he abruptly retired at age 29.

- Wes Ferrell (1934–37) had many fine years in Cleveland before being traded to Boston. He pitched parts of four seasons there and went 25-14 in 1935 and 20-15 in 1936. In addition, he was one of the best hitting pitchers of all time. For Boston he batted .308 with 17 HR and 82 RBI in only 396 at-bats.

- Tex Hughson (1941–44, '46–49), a lifetime Red Sox pitcher, ended his short career with a fine 96-54 record and 2.94 ERA. A three-time All-Star, his best season was his first full one in 1942, when he went 22-6 with a 2.59 ERA and led the AL with an admittedly low 113 strikeouts.

- Joe Dobson (1941–43, '46–50, '54) pitched the majority of his career for the Red Sox and had his best season in 1947, when he posted an 18-8 record and 2.95 ERA.

- Frank Sullivan (1953–60) also pitched the majority of his career for the Red Sox and led the AL in wins in 1955 with an 18-13 record and 2.91 ERA.

- Dennis Eckersley (1978–84) mostly pitched for Boston as a starter early in his career, and posted 20-8 and 17-7 records with a 2.99 ERA in both 1978 and 1979. He returned to Boston for his final season in 1998, but at age 43 didn't have anything left.

- Josh Beckett (2006–12) established himself with the Florida Marlins and then was traded to the Red Sox. A three-time All-Star in Boston, he at first stumbled with a 5.01 ERA in 2006 before posting a 20-7 record and 3.27 ERA in 2007 as runner-up for the AL Cy Young Award.

Relief Pitching

Name	YR	WAR	W3	SV	W-L	ERA	WHIP	ERA+
Ellis Kinder	8	25.7	14.0	93	86-52	3.28	1.303	135
Bob Stanley	13	24.3	12.6	132	115-97	3.64	1.364	119
Derek Lowe	8	19.6	14.0	85	70-55	3.72	1.288	127
Dick Radatz	5	17.8	16.7	102	49-34	2.65	1.136	147
Jonathan Papelbon	7	16.4	11.6	219	23-19	2.33	1.018	197

Relief pitcher was not the deepest position for this All-Time team, and I'd respect various choices here. After seriously looking at five candidates, I decided to select three. First up is **Jonathan Papelbon** (2005–11), who in 2006 took over the closer duties, and in his next six Red Sox seasons posted save totals of 35, 37, 41, 38, 37, and 31, making him their all-time leader in the category. A four-time All Star while in Boston, he averaged more than a strikeout per inning in all six years, and had impressive ERAs in the first four: 0.92, 1.85, 2.23, and 1.85.

I was also impressed enough with the dominating **Dick Radatz** (1962–66) to include him on this All-Time team. Dubbed The Monster by Mickey Mantle, Radatz stood 6⊠6⊠ tall at a time when pitchers were on average a few inches shorter than today's hurlers. Weighing in at 230+ pounds during his career, Radatz threw with sidearm motion that was unfamiliar and intimidating to many batters. As a result, he put up some very impressive numbers, including these from his first three seasons:

- 9-6, 24 SV, 2.24 ERA, 124.2 IP, 144 K

- 15-6, 25 SV, 1.97 ERA, 132.1 IP, 162 K

- 16-9, 29 SV, 2.29 ERA, 157 IP, 181 K (a record for most strikeouts in a season by a reliever)

Lastly, I thought **Ellis Kinder** (1948–55) was deserving of a spot on this roster, as he went 23-6 in 1949 before becoming a short reliever for the Sox. He led the league in saves with 16 in 1951, and then did so again in 1953, when he posted 27 saves and a 1.85 ERA.

This leaves out Bob Stanley (1977–89), who pitched his entire 13-year career for the Red Sox. He spent a few seasons as a starter and others as a middle reliever or setup man. But he was also the closer for a few years, providing 33 saves in 1983 and 22 the following year. And until recently, he had accumulated more saves than any other Red Sox reliever.

Like Kinder, Derek Lowe (1997–2004) was an interesting case to consider. He pitched his first five seasons in Boston as a reliever (three as closer) and his last three as a starter. In 2000 he tied for the league lead in saves with 42, and then in 2002 he tossed a no-hitter and went 21-8 with a 2.58 ERA for the season. I wouldn't argue if you preferred him or Stanley to any of the other relief pitchers I've included.

Managers

Name	YR	From-To	W-L	PCT	PS	WS
Terry Francona	8	2004–11	744-552	.574	5	2
Joe Cronin	13	1935–47	1,071-916	.539	1	0
Jimmy Collins	6	1901–06	455-376	.548	2	1
John Farrell	5	2013–17	432-378	.533	3	1
Bill Carrigan	7	1913–29	489-500	.494	2	2
John McNamara	4	1985–88	297-273	.521	2	0
Jimy Williams	5	1997–2001	414-352	.540	2	0
Don Zimmer	5	1976–80	411-304	.575	0	0
Pinky Higgins	8	1955–62	560-556	.502	0	0

Terry Francona piloted Boston to five postseasons and importantly two World Series championships after such a long and painful drought. **Joe Cronin** managed the Red Sox longer than anyone else, and in so doing racked up over 1,000 wins. I'd rank those two first and second, followed by **Jimmy Collins** and then recent skipper **John Farrell**.

Starting Lineup

What would mythical starting lineups look like for this All-Time roster?

Against RHP:
Tris Speaker CF (L)
Wade Boggs 3B (L)
Carl Yastrzemski 1B (L)
Ted Williams LF (L)
David Ortiz DH (L)
Nomar Garciaparra SS (R)
Dustin Pedroia/Bobby Doerr 2B (R)
Carlton Fisk C (R)
Harry Hooper RF (L)

Against LHP:
Tris Speaker CF (L)
Wade Boggs 3B (L)
Jimmie Foxx 1B (R)
Jim Rice DH (R)
Ted Williams LF (L)
Nomar Garciaparra SS (R)
Dustin Pedroia/Bobby Doerr 2B (R)
Dwight Evans RF (R)
Jason Varitek C (S)

The DH spot worked out perfectly since Rice and Ortiz could trade off based on who is pitching. Although Varitek was a switch-hitter, he seemed to hit better against LHP, so you could use him either as a platoon with Fisk or at least to give him an occasional rest. On this roster, Yastrzemski could play every day of course, or you could use Jimmie Foxx's right-handed power against tough southpaws. Similarly, lefty-hitting Hooper could start in place of Evans against the better RHPs, thereby providing some speed at the bottom of the order (something that is rare in these two lineups outside of Speaker at the top).

Depth Chart

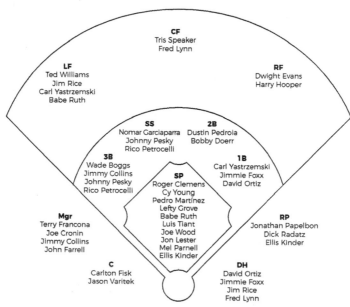

146

Prospects for Current Players

What are the prospects of current Red Sox players making this All-Time team? Dustin Pedroia is already on the roster. As noted, you could make a case that Mookie Betts should be as well. And other current stars like Chris Sale, David Price, Craig Kimbrel, Xander Bogaerts, and J.D. Martinez might soon at least deserve consideration. We'll see…

Retired Player Numbers

Bobby Doerr (1), Joe Cronin (4, player/manager), Johnny Pesky (6), Carl Yastrzemski (8), Ted Williams (9), Jim Rice (14), Carlton Fisk (27), Pedro Martinez (45)

Selections from Other Authors and Fan Surveys

1958: *Sport* magazine, February issue

As part of a running series, *Sport* magazine reported on all-time all-star teams picked by "big league publicity departments and the writers covering the clubs." Here is what they had to say:

First Base: Jimmy Foxx, old "Double X," who played in Boston from 1936 through 1942. He is in Baseball's Hall of Fame.

Second Base: Bobby Doerr, one of the most popular players Boston has ever had. Bobby played there from 1937 through 1951.

Shortstop: Joe Cronin, who came to the Red Sox from Washington for $250,000 in 1935 and played there until he retired in 1945. He was the team's manager during that time, too, and he held the job until he moved into the front office after the 1947 season.

Third Base: Jimmy Collins, called by many fans the best third-baseman of all time, arrived in Boston in 1895, and remained there until 1907. He is a member of the Hall of Fame. Collins managed Boston for six years, 1901-1906.

Left Field: Ted Williams. Even the Boston writers (well, anyway, most of them) put Ted on the team.

Center Field: Tris Speaker, possibility the greatest of all time and a member of the Hall of Fame. Tris began his big-league career with the Red Sox in 1907 and was traded to Cleveland in the winter of 1915-1916.

Right Field: Harry Hooper, who played with the Sox from 1909 to 1920.

Catcher: Bill Carrigan, who played with the Sox from 1906 through 1916 and managed them in his last four active seasons. He returned to Boston as a manager in 1927-1929.

Righthanded Pitcher: Cy Young, another Hall of Famer, who played in Boston from 1901 through 1908. Cy won 510 big league games, a record that no one else has come close to.

Lefthanded Pitcher: Lefty Grove, the great fireballer who came to Boston from the A's in 1934 and retired in 1941. Lefty is in the Hall of Fame, too.

Back in 1958 this was an entirely reasonable roster. A case could have been made for Pesky at SS or 3B, but Cronin and Collins were good choices. And Carrigan is a reasonable choice as catcher, as there weren't many options to choose from.

1969: *The Sporting News* Fan Poll

The July 5, 1969, issue reported the results of a fan poll for the long-standing franchises of the day. The results for Boston were: 1B Jimmie Foxx, 2B Bobby Doerr, 3B Frank Malzone, SS Joe Cronin, C Birdie Tebbetts, LF Ted Williams, CF Tris Speaker, RF Carl Yastrzemski, RHP Cy Young, and LHP Lefty Grove.

For 1969, most of these were good choices. One exception was at the weakest position of catcher, where I think Carrigan was more deserving than Tebbetts. Birdie played parts of only four seasons for the Sox, although he was an All-Star for them twice. I think Collins, Pesky, or even Gardner would have been better choices than Malzone at 3B, so perhaps the fans had a bit of bias towards the more recent player. And lastly, I must note that while it could have been argued that Yastrzemski already deserved in 1969 to be one of the three outfielders, to list him as the right fielder was rather strange. In his entire career, his OF games played broke down as follows: LF = 1,913, CF = 166, RF = 8.

1982: Fan Vote, as reported in *The Boston Red Sox Fan Book*, by David S. Neft, Michael L. Neft, Bob Carroll, and Richard M. Cohen

The fans in 1982 chose Jimmie Foxx and George Scott at 1B, Bobby Doerr and Jerry Remy at 2B, Rico Petrocelli and Frank Malzone at 3B, and Rick Burleson and Johnny Pesky at SS. I seriously question giving spots to contemporaries Remy and Burleson. Carlton Fisk and Birdie Tebbetts were chosen as the catchers. The starting OF was Ted Williams, Carl Yastrzemski, and Dwight Evans, and the backups were Jim Rice, Dom DiMaggio, and Fred Lynn. The right-handed pitchers were Cy Young and Luis Tiant, and the lefties were Babe Ruth and Lefty Grove. The relievers were Dick Radatz and Sparky Lyle, who started his fine career as a reliever with five years in Boston.

1990: "All-Time All-Star Teams," in *The Baseball Research Journal*

In an interesting article, Robert C. Berlo used Thorn and Palmer's TPR (Total Player Rating) system to choose all-time teams. He selected players based on their best 800 consecutive games for the franchise, with a minimum of five years played. His results: 1B Jimmie Foxx, 2B Bobby Doerr, SS Joe Cronin, 3B Wade Boggs, RF Ted Williams, CF Tris Speaker, LF Carl Yastrzemski, C Carlton Fisk, SP Cy Young, SP Lefty Grove, SP Joe Wood, SP Mel Parnell, RP Bob Stanley.

Listing Ted Williams as a RF wasn't as bad as listing Yaz there, but it is a little odd, as he played only 169 games in RF compared with 1,984 in LF. And I suppose Roger Clemens hadn't done quite enough for the Sox at the time this analysis was done.

1991: *Louisville Slugger Presents: The Boston Red Sox*, by Dick Lally

In the Red Sox installment of this series of books in 1991, the author chose an All-Time all-star team that consisted of Foxx, Doerr, Cronin, Boggs, and Fisk in the infield, Williams in LF, Speaker in CF, and Evans in RF. The author noted that this leaves Yastrzemski the odd man out. Clemens was the top RHP, Ruth was an interesting choice over Grove as the top LHP, and Radatz was the top reliever.

1992: *The All-Time All-Star Baseball Book*, by Nick Acocella and Donald Dewey

Their lineup was a solid one for 1992: C Fisk, 1B Foxx, 2B Doerr, 3B Boggs, SS Cronin, OF Williams, Yastrzemski, Speaker, SP Clemens. Their honorable mentions were Collins, Stephens, Hooper, Rice, Wood, and Parnell. My only minor beef here is why they would mention Stephens, but not the likes of Evans, Young, or Grove.

1995: *Baseball Ratings*, by Charles F. Faber

The Faber system as applied in 1995 created a reasonable all-time team. The Faber system understandably listed Yastrzemski in the OF, which thereby left Evans out of the lineup and meant Foxx was the starting 1B. The only odd result was Burleson at SS, instead of Petrocelli or Cronin. His five starting pitchers were solid: Young, Clemens, Tiant, Grove, and Parnell. And the top reliever was deemed to be Stanley.

2000: *Red Sox Century*, by Glenn Stout and Richard A. Johnson

These authors chose two separate rosters: one for pre–World War II and one for post–World War II. And since they didn't seem to have a strict limit per position, their combined rosters were much larger than mine.

For the pre-WWII squad, Foxx and Doerr were the only 1B and 2B included. Three shortstops were mentioned: Cronin, Scott, and Wagner (who they noted played for four World Series champions). At 3B they had Collins, who they wrote was "acknowledged as the greatest third baseman of his era." They also chose Gardner as a backup, calling him a "steady performer for a decade."

Their outfield was split up by position: the starters presumably would have been Williams, Speaker, and Hooper. The backups would then have been Lewis, Chick Stahl (a .290 hitter from 1901–06), and Freeman. At catcher they mentioned Lou Criger, an extremely weak-hitting defensive whiz (.208 average from 1901–08), along with Ferrell.

The pitching staff included many obvious selections: Young, Wood, Grove, Ruth, and Leonard. The authors also included Carl Mays, whom I didn't discuss earlier but who had a few good seasons with Boston to start his career, with his best being 1917, when he went 22-9 with a 1.74 ERA. Lastly, they included Bill Dinneen, who had three consecutive 20+-win seasons from 1902 through '04, but ended up with an 85-86 lifetime record for the Sox.

For their post-WWII roster, most of their infield choices were fairly sensible: Vaughn, Remy, Pesky, Stephens, Garciaparra, Boggs, and Malone. Remy had some speed and hit for a pretty good average, but he had only three full-time seasons in Boston.

They included Williams again here, and rightfully so. The rest of the OF were all good choices: Yastrzemski, Rice, DiMaggio, Lynn, Evans, and Conigliaro. The same was true at catcher, where Fisk and Gedman were recognized. The starting pitchers list of course included Clemens, Parnell, Tiant, and Martínez. Jim Lonborg was listed too, as he won the 1967 AL Cy Young Award with a 22-9 campaign, though he was a mediocre starter in Boston otherwise. And Bill

Lee made their team, due in part to him "mastering the New York Yankees." The relievers were fine choices: Kinder, Radatz, and Stanley.

2001: Fan Ballots in *Boston Globe* Vote, as reported in *The Boston Red Sox Fan Book*, by David S. Neft, Michael L. Neft, Bob Carroll, and Richard M. Cohen

This time around the fans chose only a starting lineup: Fisk, Foxx, Doerr, Boggs, Garciaparra, Williams, Yastrzemski, and Rice. The four starters were Young, Martínez, Clemens, and Wood, and the reliever was Radatz.

2003: *Rob Neyer's Big Book of Baseball Lineups*, by Rob Neyer

Neyer went with Foxx and Vaughn at 1B. He liked Runnels as the backup to Doerr at 2B, noting that he was "not great with the glove, but hit for average and walked." Garciaparra and Pesky were rightly listed at SS, as were Boggs and Collins at 3B, noting that Collins was "universally regarded as the top fielder of his time." Neyer choose Wally Schang as the backup catcher, even though he played only three years for the Sox. Through 2002, Varitek hadn't yet done enough, so I won't argue here given the lack of strong candidates. In Schang's defense, he wrote, "Stalwart with the A's and Yankees, too, but his two best seasons were with Sox; best catcher of his time, and should be in the Hall of Fame rather than Ray Schalk."

Carl Yastrzemski was the LF backup to Williams, and Yaz was also listed as the second DH behind Jim Rice. Speaker and Lynn were the CF choices, with Evans and Hooper in RF.

Neyer's list of eight starters was solid: Clemens, Martínez, Young, Wood, Grove, Parnell, Ruth, and Tiant. He then listed Radatz and Kinder as his two relief choices. And lastly, his top five managers were Carrigan, Cronin, Collins, Williams, and Joe Morgan, who led the Red Sox to winning seasons from 1988 through 1991.

2004: *The Red Sox Century*, by Alan Ross

Ross selected a fine starting lineup composed of Foxx, Doerr, Boggs, Garciaparra, Fisk, Williams, Yastrzemski, and Speaker, with Parnell as LHP and Clemens as RHP. Interestingly, the author noted the OF difficulty as he wrote, "I hear the fire coming from the camps of Evans, Rice, Hooper, Jensen, DiMaggio, and Greenwell, in what is without doubt the toughest all-time Bosox position to fill, Ted and Yaz being givens."

2004: *Few and Chosen: Defining Red Sox Greatness Across the Eras*, by Johnny Pesky with Phil Pepe

As with each book in this fun series, the authors chose the top five players at each position. For the Red Sox, their lists in order were:

C: Fisk, Sammy White, Tebbetts, Gedman, Varitek

1B: Foxx, Yastrzemski, Vaughn, Cecil Cooper, Walt Dropo

2B: Doerr, Remy, Runnels, Goodman, Chuck Schilling

SS: Cronin, Garciaparra, Petrocelli, Luis Aparicio, Stephens

3B: Boggs, Malzone, Shea Hillenbrand, Carney Lansford, George Kell

LF: Williams, Yastrzemski, Ramirez, Rice, Greenwell

CF: DiMaggio, Speaker, Lynn, Ellis Burks, Piersall

RF: Yastrzemski, Evans, Conigliaro, Smith, Jensen

RHP: Clemens, Young, Martínez, Tiant, Hughson

LHP: Ruth, Grove, Parnell, Bruce Hurst, Lee

RP: Radatz, Stanley, Kinder, Lyle, Gordon

Manager: Joe McCarthy, Cronin, Williams, Zimmer, Ed Barrow

I didn't discuss catcher Sammy White earlier, because although he was an All-Star in 1953, he accumulated a WAR of only 1.6 over eight full seasons for Boston. He did set one record though, as on June 18, 1953, he became the only 20th century player to score three runs in one inning, when the Red Sox scored a modern major league record 17 runs in one inning against the Tigers.

They decided to list Yastrzemski at three different positions, which was a little confusing, but they wanted to list him #1 somewhere I guess. At 1B, I didn't understand the inclusion of Cooper, as they seemed to emphasize Cecil's entire career, not just his few, early seasons with Boston. And the selection of Dropo was based largely on his incredible rookie year of 1950, when he hit .322 with 34 HR and 144 RBI.

Regarding the choice of Remy as the second 2B, Pesky told a nostalgic story, described Remy's recurring knee problems, and then noted, "Because of what he could have done, and what he did, Remy is my choice for number two on my all time list of Red Sox second basemen."

Pesky gave Petrocelli plenty of praise, even going so far as to say "Petrocelli was as good a ballplayer as we've ever had in Boston." What I didn't understand was the inclusion of Hall of Famer Luis Aparicio as the fourth in the list, since he played only three seasons in Boston, at the very end of his career.

Boggs and even Malzone were fine choices atop his 3B list. But by not including himself, Mr. Pesky then listed "three players who were in Boston just a short time but still made their mark." Hillenbrand started his career with Boston, but played only two full seasons there, including 2002, when he was an All-Star and hit .293 with 18 HR and 83 RBI. Lansford played only two seasons for the Red Sox, winning the batting title in strike-shortened 1981 with a .336 mark. And George Kell played parts of three seasons in Boston, with his best coming in 1953, when he was an All-Star and hit .307 with 41 doubles.

For CF, Pesky admitted to a bit of bias in choosing his teammate and personal friend DiMaggio ahead of Speaker. The RF list omitted Hooper, which Pesky addressed by noting that because Hooper played "long before my time," he knew little about him and so would abstain from selecting him.

I mostly liked the pitching selections, but the manager list was a bit odd, starting with Joe McCarthy at the top. An all-time great manager to be sure, he mostly managed the Yankees and was only at the helm of the Red Sox for two-and-a-half seasons at the end of his career. They had an impressive 223-145 (.606) record during that time, but the write-up by Pesky makes clear that he gave this honor based on his personal experience, as McCarthy was "the best manager I ever played for."

2009: *Jerry Remy's Red Sox Heroes*, by Jerry Remy with Corey Sandler

This book discussed Red Sox players throughout history grouped into four eras based on the author's own timeline: The Golden Red Sox, Heroes of My Youth, Days of My Baseball Life, and Modern Times. He also provided a handy full roster, though he didn't list the players in a ranking order by position.

His infield selections sensibly included 1B Foxx, Scott, Vaughn, 2B Doerr, Pesky, 3B Boggs, Collins, SS Burleson, Cronin, Garciaparra, Petrocelli, and catchers Ferrell, Fisk, Varitek. He also included Ortiz as DH.

For LF he had Lewis, Ramirez, Rice, Williams, and Yaz; for CF Johnny Damon, DiMaggio, Lynn, and Speaker; and for RF Conigliaro, Evans, Hooper, Jensen, and Nixon. The one not mentioned previously in this chapter was Damon, who played for Boston for only four years, but was a .295 hitter overall and scored 100+ runs each year.

His list of pitchers included Clemens, Eckersley, Keith Foulke, Grove, Lonborg, Lowe, Martínez, Radatz, Ruth, Curt Schilling, Stanley, Tiant, Wakefield,

Wood, and Young. In my view Keith Foulke wasn't deserving of inclusion alongside these other greats, but Remy did so based on his fine 2004 season and postseason performance. And of course, ditto for Curt Schilling, whose 2004 campaign was his only great one for Boston. I admit it is hard to talk about all-time great Red Sox players and not mention the man who made "bloody sock" a phrase amongst baseball fans.

2016: *101 All-Time Fantasy Baseball Teams*, by Jack Sweeney

Sweeney's book doesn't allow players to be on more than one all-time lineup, so this means Speaker makes it on the Indians team but not the Red Sox. His lineup is generally solid, with Yastrzemski, Doerr, Boggs, Cronin, Williams, Hooper, Rice, Fisk, and Ortiz. His four starting pitchers are solid in Clemens, Martínez, Young, and Tiant (given that Lefty Grove couldn't make this list since he clearly had to be included for the Athletics), and Radatz was his relief pitcher.

Top WAR Single Seasons – Hitters (8+)

Name	Year	WAR	AVG	HR	R	RBI	SB	OPS+
Carl Yastrzemski	1967	12.4	.326	44	112	121	10	193
Ted Williams	1946	10.9	.342	38	142	123	0	215
Mookie Betts	2018	10.9	.346	32	129	80	30	186
Ted Williams	1942	10.6	.356	36	141	137	3	216
Ted Williams	1941	10.6	.406	37	135	120	2	235
Carl Yastrzemski	1968	10.5	.301	23	90	74	13	171
Tris Speaker	1912	10.1	.383	10	136	90	52	189
Rico Petrocelli	1969	10.0	.297	40	92	97	3	168
Ted Williams	1947	9.9	.343	32	125	114	0	205
Ted Williams	1957	9.7	.388	38	96	87	0	233
Mookie Betts	2016	9.6	.318	31	122	113	26	131
Carl Yastrzemski	1970	9.5	.329	40	125	102	23	177
Ted Williams	1949	9.2	.343	43	150	159	1	191
Wade Boggs	1985	9.1	.368	8	107	78	2	151
Fred Lynn	1979	8.8	.333	39	116	122	2	176
Ted Williams	1948	8.5	.369	25	124	127	4	189
Wade Boggs	1989	8.4	.330	3	113	54	2	142
Wade Boggs	1987	8.3	.363	24	108	89	1	174
Tris Speaker	1913	8.3	.363	3	94	71	46	182
John Valentin	1995	8.3	.298	27	108	102	20	138
Wade Boggs	1988	8.3	.366	5	128	58	2	168
Jacoby Ellsbury	2011	8.1	.321	32	119	105	39	146
Wade Boggs	1986	8.0	.357	8	107	71	0	157

I wasn't surprised that Williams had the most seasons on this list with seven, though Yastrzemski's 1967 Triple Crown campaign takes the top spot. Boggs had the second-most seasons on the list—his five consecutive prime years. Petrocelli's career year in 1969 ranks high, as does Lynn's 1979 campaign. And Mookie Betts' 2016 and 2018 seasons have made clear that he is a superstar.

Top WAR Single Seasons – Pitchers (8+)

Name	Year	WAR	W-L	ERA	IP	SO	ERA+
Cy Young	1901	12.6	33-10	1.62	371.1	158	219
Pedro Martínez	2000	11.7	18-6	1.74	217.0	284	291
Smoky Joe Wood	1912	11.7	34-5	1.91	344.0	258	177
Wes Ferrell	1935	11.0	25-14	3.52	322.1	110	134
Roger Clemens	1990	10.6	21-6	1.93	228.1	209	211
Lefty Grove	1936	10.5	17-12	2.81	253.1	130	189
Babe Ruth	1916	10.4	23-12	1.75	323.2	170	158
Babe Ruth	1919	10.2	9-5	2.97	133.1	30	102
Cy Young	1902	10.1	32-11	2.15	384.2	160	164
Cy Young	1908	10.0	21-11	1.26	299.0	150	193
Cy Young	1904	9.8	26-16	1.97	380.0	200	136
Pedro Martínez	1999	9.7	23-4	2.07	213.1	313	243
Roger Clemens	1987	9.5	20-9	2.97	281.2	256	154
Dutch Leonard	1914	9.2	19-5	0.96	224.2	176	279
Lefty Grove	1937	9.2	17-9	3.02	262.0	153	159
Roger Clemens	1986	8.9	24-4	2.48	254.0	238	169
Roger Clemens	1992	8.9	18-11	2.41	246.2	208	174
Lefty Grove	1935	8.8	20-12	2.70	273.0	121	175
Babe Ruth	1917	8.7	24-13	2.01	326.1	128	128
Cy Young	1903	8.6	28-9	2.08	341.2	176	145
Mel Parnell	1949	8.2	25-7	2.77	295.1	122	158
Howard Ehmke	1924	8.2	19-17	3.46	315.0	119	126
Wes Ferrell	1936	8.1	20-15	4.19	301.0	106	126
Pedro Martínez	2003	8.0	14-4	2.22	186.2	206	211
Roger Clemens	1991	8.0	18-10	2.62	271.1	241	165

Cy Young's 1901 season tops the list, and not surprisingly both Young and Clemens appear the most on this list at five times each. Next up are Martínez and Grove, with three seasons each. Not surprisingly, Wood's incredible 34-5 season ranked highly, coming in third overall. Both Wes Ferrell and Babe Ruth have seasons on this list in part because of their hitting contributions. This is especially true for Ruth of course, where by 1919 he was more of a hitter than a pitcher, leading the league in HR, runs, RBI, OBP, and SLG. The only name that surprised me on this list was Howard Ehmke, a right-hander who pitched for Boston from 1923 through '26. His 1924 season produced an 8.1 WAR score, as he led the league in innings pitched while also leading the league with 17 losses.

Franchise Player

With honorable mention going to Yastrzemski, Boggs, Clemens, and Young, this honor obviously had to go to Ted Williams. Though Yaz played longer, his average season performance was nowhere near that of Williams, and neither were his peak performances. Ted was arguably the greatest hitter of all time, while Yaz would be, at best, in the 20–40th spots in such a ranking. And Young and Clemens had comparably great careers, but they spent significant amounts of time for teams other than Boston.

CHAPTER 6

The Cubs Franchise All-Time Dream Team

The Chicago Cubs are famous for their devoted fans, who year in and year out "root for the Cubbies" as the song goes, even though championships have been few and far between. The team actually got its start as a charter member of the National League way back in 1876, ironically going by the name Chicago White Stockings for their first 14 seasons. They played under the name Chicago Colts and then Chicago Orphans before finally settling on Cubs starting in 1903. That year began a string of ten consecutive seasons where the Cubs finished with a .590+ winning percentage, including four NL pennants and two consecutive World Series crowns in 1907 and 1908.

The next period of consistent success started in 1926, with the Cubs proceeding to post winning seasons every year through 1939. This included four NL pennants but sadly did not include any World Series championships. The same was true in 1945—the last time the Cubs won the NL pennant—until 2016 when a very strong pitching rotation backed by some maturing star hitters finally led them to a World Series crown.

Not surprisingly given this franchise's combination of long history but limited ultimate success, their All-Time team, relatively speaking, has several stars but few really strong positions.

1st Base

Name	YR	WAR	W3	W/G	AVG	HR	SB	OPS+
Cap Anson	22	84.3	20.2	.0370	.331	97	247	142
Frank Chance	15	45.5	18.9	.0357	.297	20	402	136
Mark Grace	13	43.9	13.9	.0230	.308	148	67	122
Phil Cavarretta	20	34.0	14.7	.0174	.292	92	61	118
Anthony Rizzo	7	29.2	17.1	.0289	.275	190	50	131
Derrek Lee	7	22.5	16.6	.0244	.298	179	51	129
Vic Saier	7	15.2	11.7	.0188	.265	53	116	123
Leon Durham	8	15.1	10.9	.0164	.279	138	98	128
Charlie Grimm	12	11.4	7.6	.0085	.296	61	26	97
Bill Buckner	8	8.6	6.7	.0088	.300	81	56	107

For the starter at 1B I had to go all the way back to the start of this franchise in 1876. Arguably the first bona fide star of major league baseball, **Cap Anson** (1876–97) played most of his professional career for the Chicago White Stockings, Colts, and Orphans. A .331 hitter, he tallied 3,012 hits for the franchise, scored 1,722 runs, and provided 1,880 RBI. He won two batting titles, with a .399 average in 1881 and a .344 average in 1888, and came in second four times. He could steal bases, and his total of 247 includes only 12 of his 22 seasons, as SB data doesn't exist for his 1876–85 seasons. But relative to his peers his best statistic was RBI, as he led the league eight times, including a high of 147 in only 125 games in 1888.

The backup was another early 1B for this franchise, **Frank Chance** (1898–1912), who started his career as a catcher but quickly switched to 1B and became part of the famed Tinker-to-Evers-to-Chance double-play infield. He played most of his career for Chicago, hitting .297 but playing in 100+ games only six times. He had little power but ran the bases well, stealing 25+ bases nine times, leading the league with 67 in 1903 and 57 in 1906 (and also amassing the most all-time SB for this franchise). He was also a good fielder at 1B, and more importantly did all of this while serving as the team's player-manager from 1905 through '12, during which time he led them to four NL pennants and the franchise's first two World Series championships.

You could make a case for a much more recent 1B for the Cubs, Mark Grace (1988–2000), who was a .308 hitter in 13 seasons for the Cubs. He didn't provide much power at a position that usually provides a lot of it; he hit double-digit HR seven times, but never more than 17 in a season. More a doubles hitter, he smacked 35+ doubles seven times, leading the league with 51 in 1995. A three-time All-Star, Grace was very good defensively, winning four Gold Glove Awards.

Phil Cavarretta (1934–54) played for this franchise nearly as long as Anson did, logging most of his time at 1B but also playing all three outfield positions. A three-time All-Star, he hit .292 but provided very little power or speed. He had a fine rookie campaign in 1935 when, at the young age of 18, he scored 85 runs and had 82 RBI. His best season was clearly 1945, when he helped lead the Cubs to the World Series by leading the NL with a .355 average and .449 OBP en route to winning the league MVP Award.

Current Cubs star 1B Anthony Rizzo (2012–18) is on his way to making this All-Time team, but he hasn't done enough quite yet. Already a three-time All-Star, he has hit between 25-32 HR each year from 2014 through 2018. Rizzo is a good defender as well, taking home the Gold Glove Award in 2016.

Between Grace and Rizzo there was Derrek Lee (2004–10), a .298 hitter with 20+ HR five times for the Cubs. He was a good fielder, taking home two Gold Glove Awards while in Chicago, and had his best overall season in 2005, when he had 46 HR, 107 RBI, 120 runs, and 15 SB, while leading the NL with 199 hits, 50 doubles, and a .335 average.

Several other 1B for this franchise deserve brief mention, including (in chronological order):

- Vic Saier (1911–17) played most of his short career for the Cubs, stole 20+ bases three times, and led the league with 21 triples in 1913.

- Charlie Grimm (1925–36) batted .296 for the Cubs, but he provided little power or speed. He was well known, however, for his banjo-playing abilities.

- Bill Buckner (1977–84) played for Chicago during the middle of his career, hitting .300 for them four times, with a league-leading .324 in 1980.

- Leon "Bull" Durham (1981–88) played most of his career for the Cubs, hit 20+ HR five times, stole 20+ bases twice, and was an All-Star twice.

2nd Base

Name	YR	WAR	W3	W/G	AVG	HR	SB	OPS+
Ryne Sandberg	15	67.7	23.4	.0315	.285	282	344	115
Billy Herman	11	39.7	19.4	.0295	.309	37	53	112
Johnny Evers	12	39.5	16.8	.0280	.276	9	291	108
Fred Pfeffer	10	21.2	12.6	.0194	.254	78	263	95
Glenn Beckert	9	16.3	12.8	.0131	.283	22	49	83
Rogers Hornsby	4	16.0	15.9	.0505	.350	58	3	161

As with 1B, I had a similar situation at 2B where there was a clear starter for this All-Time team, but then a tougher decision for the backup spot. **Ryne Sandberg** (1982–94, '96–97) came to the Cubs with Larry Bowa in a trade for Iván de Jesus. Chicago definitely got the better of that deal, as Sandberg went on to play the rest of his Hall of Fame career for the Cubs, including ten consecutive seasons as an All-Star. He was great defensively, winning an impressive nine Gold Glove Awards. Ryno was a solid .285 hitter over his career and provided a good combination of power and speed, hitting 25+ HR five times and stealing 25+ bases seven times. He had exactly 100 RBI twice, but scored 100+ runs six times, leading the league three times. He won the NL MVP Award in 1984 after hitting .314 with 32 SB, 19 HR, 84 RBI, and a league-leading 19 triples and 114 runs.

Billy Herman (1931–41) played over half of his Hall of Fame career with the Cubs, was a good fielder, and represented them as an All-Star in seven consecutive seasons. A .309 hitter, he didn't provide much power or speed. But he scored 100+ runs five times and hit .341 in 1935 while leading the league with 227 hits and 57 doubles. He followed that up with another 57 doubles in 1936, while batting .334 with 211 hits.

A third Hall of Fame 2B who played most of his career for the Cubs, **Johnny Evers** (1902–13) comes up just short of Herman, but I thought he deserved one of the two "extra spots" on this roster. Evers was a good fielder and provided solid speed with 25+ SB in seven seasons. He hit 20+ doubles only three times, and provided 9 HR in 4,858 at-bats for the Cubs. But Evers did have a 108 OPS+, so it's not like he was a below-average hitter for his era.

Three others deserve brief mention, starting with old-timer Fred Pfeffer (1883–89, '91, 96–97) who regularly stole 40+ bases a year, and even managed to hit 25 HR with 101 RBI in 112 games way back in 1884. Glenn Beckert (1965–73) played most of his career with the Cubs, earning a Gold Glove Award in 1968. A .283 hitter for Chicago, he hit .342 in 1971 and was an All-Star from 1969 through 1972. And lastly, all-time great Rogers Hornsby (1929–32) played one full season and three partial seasons for the Cubs late in his career. His 1929 season was one of the best ever for any Cubs player, as he won the NL MVP Award after hitting .380 with 39 HR, 149 RBI, and a league-leading 156 runs.

3rd Base

Name	YR	WAR	W3	W/G	AVG	HR	SB	OPS+
Ron Santo	14	72.0	27.6	.0339	.279	337	35	128
Stan Hack	16	52.5	17.1	.0271	.301	57	165	119
Ned Williamson	11	36.0	14.8	.0338	.260	61	85	119

Heinie Zimmerman	10	23.9	15.1	.0234	.304	48	131	128
Aramis Ramírez	9	23.8	13.2	.0212	.294	239	8	126
Tom Burns	12	22.5	9.3	.0182	.266	39	161	97
Kris Bryant	4	21.6	19.7	.0386	.285	107	30	137
Harry Steinfeldt	5	19.4	15.6	.0265	.268	9	92	107

Ron Santo (1960–73) was finally inducted into the Hall of Fame in 2012 via the Veterans Committee. He played all but his final season for the Cubs, but stayed with the team much longer than that, primarily as a radio broadcaster for 20 years. As a player, Santo was outstanding: he was chosen as an All-Star nine times, earned five consecutive Gold Glove Awards, and had a good eye at the plate, leading the league in walks four times. A .279 hitter for the Cubs, he provided consistent power, hitting 25+ HR with 90+ RBI in eight consecutive seasons. And he did all of this while battling diabetes, a disease less well understood at the time, and one factor in his early retirement at age 34.

Stan Hack (1932–47) played his entire career for the Cubs and was an All-Star four times. He was a .301 hitter with a solid .394 OBP. He had very little power, but enough speed to lead the league in SB twice (albeit with totals of only 16 in 1938 and 17 in 1939). Smiling Stan also led the league in hits twice and scored 100+ runs seven times.

Besides Santo and Hack, this franchise had a few other 3B worth mentioning, including (in chronological order):

- Ned Williamson (1879–89) was a good fielder and a .260 hitter with some speed, as incomplete records mean his 85 SB "total" is from only 4 of his 11 seasons. He never hit more than 9 HR in a season except in 1884, when he busted out with 27 (the record until 1919 when Babe Ruth hit 29). That sudden surge in power was not because he suddenly got stronger. His home field, Chicago's Lakeshore Park, had very short outfield dimensions of 186 feet in left field, 300 feet in center field, and 190 feet in right field. Prior to 1884, balls hit over the fence were counted as doubles, not home runs. This changed in 1884, and Williamson took advantage with 25 of his 27 home runs coming at home. The team moved to West Side Park the next year, and without the short fence distances, Williamson's HR total plummeted.

- Tom Burns (1880–91) was a teammate of Williamson, played a mix of 3B and SS, and similarly hit .266 with little power but some speed on the bases (records indicate 161 SB in 6 of his 12 seasons).

- Harry Steinfeldt (1906–10) played for the Cubs for only five seasons, but had a fine 1906 campaign in which he batted .327 and led the league with modest totals of 176 hits and 83 RBI.

- Heinie Zimmerman (1907–16) played most of his career for the Cubs and had by far his best season in 1912, when he led the NL with a .372 average, 207 hits, 41 doubles, and 14 HR.

- Aramis Ramírez (2003–11) batted .294 for the Cubs and was an All-Star twice. He provided good power numbers, including 25+ HR seven times and 100+ RBI four times.

- Kris Bryant (2015–18) is a current superstar and is off to a great start in his Cubs career, taking home the Rookie of the Year Award and then the MVP Award in 2016 after hitting 39 HR with 121 runs and 102 RBI. His patience has improved each year at the plate as well, as he led the NL in strikeouts with 199 as a rookie but saw that number drop to 154 and then 128 in the following two seasons.

Shortstop

Name	YR	WAR	W3	W/G	AVG	HR	SB	OPS+
Ernie Banks	19	67.4	27.7	.0267	.274	512	50	122
Joe Tinker	12	45.3	17.1	.0294	.259	28	304	93
Bill Dahlen	8	33.9	18.9	.0343	.299	57	286	123
Woody English	10	24.5	13.1	.0223	.291	31	51	97
Charlie Hollocher	7	23.2	14.1	.0305	.304	14	99	110
Billy Jurges	10	17.3	9.6	.0161	.254	20	22	77
Shawon Dunston	12	9.7	5.6	.0077	.267	107	175	88
Don Kessinger	12	9.4	8.4	.0057	.255	11	92	73

The situation at SS was like that at 1B and 2B, where the pick for starter was obvious, but the backup decision was a close call. **Ernie Banks** (1953–71) played his entire career for Chicago, splitting his time almost in half between SS (1,125 games) and 1B (1,259). An All-Star an impressive 11 times, he did win one Gold Glove Award at shortstop in 1960 before transitioning over to first base. Mr. Cub was a .274 hitter who belted 512 HR in his career, including five seasons with 40+ HR, and another five with 25 or more. His best two statistical seasons were his back-to-back NL MVP years in 1958 and '59. He first hit .313 and led the NL with 47 HR and 129 RBI, and then hit .304 with 45 HR and a league-leading 143 RBI.

Bill Dahlen (1891–98) started his career with the Cubs and was a .299 hitter with a .384 OBP for them. He scored 100+ runs in his first six seasons, including 150 in only 122 games in 1894. Dahlen provided good defense and also stole a lot of bases, with a high of 60 in 1892 and 30+ in five seasons for the Cubs overall.

Hall of Famer **Joe Tinker** (1902–12, '16) provided excellent defense and stole 25+ bases in eight seasons. He hit double-digit triples in five seasons, but was otherwise a very light hitter, with only a .259 average and .303 OBP. With apologies to Mark Grace, I decided to give the other "extra spot" on this dream team roster to Tinker, thereby including all three parts of the Tinker-to-Evers-to-Chance double-play combo. This also means that at least for now, Evers and Tinker are together again, even though they didn't get along well, starting with a fistfight in 1905. That led to a 33-year feud during which they didn't speak with each other (not even on the field!), one that only ended when they were reunited on a radio broadcast of the 1938 World Series.

There were five other shortstops for this franchise that deserve brief mention, including (in chronological order):

- Charlie Hollocher (1918–24) played his entire, short career for the Cubs. He was a .304 hitter and stole 15+ bases four times, but he had very little power (14 HR in 2,936 at-bats).

- Woody English (1927–36) was a .291 hitter and scored 100+ runs in three consecutive seasons, including his impressive campaign in 1930, when he batted .335 with a .430 OBP and scored 152 runs.

- Billy Jurges (1931–38, '46–47) was a good defensive shortstop but a light hitter with only a .254 average and little power or speed on the bases.

- Don Kessinger (1964–75) played most of his career with the Cubs. He also was a light hitter with only a .255 average and .315 OBP, but he was named an All-Star six times largely due to his good defense (Gold Glove Awards in 1969 and '70).

- Shawon Dunston (1985–95, '97) played over half of his career for the Cubs and was an All-Star for them twice. He was only a .267 hitter and had an abysmal .295 OBP, but he had enough speed to steal 20+ bases three times, and enough power to hit 17 HR twice. He is perhaps most remembered for his very strong throwing arm, especially early in his career.

Catcher

Name	YR	WAR	W3	W/G	AVG	HR	SB	OPS+
Gabby Hartnett	19	52.3	15.2	.0271	.297	231	28	126
King Kelly	7	23.8	16.7	.0349	.316	33	NA	149
Johnny Kling	11	22.4	11.4	.0219	.272	16	119	103
Jody Davis	8	17.1	9.8	.0173	.251	122	7	97
Bob O'Farrell	12	12.3	10.1	.0185	.279	27	23	106
Rick Wilkins	5	12.2	10.0	.0268	.254	57	9	109
Randy Hundley	10	11.8	9.9	.0125	.240	80	12	80

The starting catcher for this squad was another obvious pick, Hall of Famer **Charles "Gabby" Hartnett** (1922–40), who played all but his final season for the Cubs. A .297 hitter with a .370 OBP, Hartnett provided decent power for a catcher, with his best statistical season coming in 1930, when he hit .339 with 37 HR and 122 RBI. He won the NL MVP Award in 1935, when he hit .344 with 13 HR and 91 RBI. He was also a good catcher defensively, and once the All-Star game got going late in his career, Gabby was of course chosen in six consecutive seasons (1933 through '38).

For the backup spot I went with another Hall of Famer, old-timer **Mike "King" Kelly** (1880–86), who mostly split his time for this franchise between C and RF (while also playing other positions some too). While in Chicago, he led the league in batting twice (.354 in 1884 and .388 in 1886) and runs three times, including a high of 155 in only 118 games in 1886. He also stole a lot of bases, though we don't know exactly how many. SB record keeping started during his last year in Chicago, when at age 28 he stole 53—so odds are he stole quite a lot during his other six seasons too.

I considered several other catchers, starting with Johnny Kling (1900–08, '10–11), who was a good defender and managed double-digit SB five times, but was only a typical Deadball-Era hitter, batting .272 with very little power. Jody Davis (1981–88) played most of his career with the Cubs and hit 17 to 24 HR in five consecutive seasons. He batted only .251, but was an All-Star twice and took home the Gold Glove Award in 1986. Randy Hundley (1966–73, '76–77) also played most of his career for the Cubs, and similarly had a low average (.240) with some home run power. He also was good defensively, winning the

Gold Glove Award in 1967, and was selected as an All-Star two years later.

Bob O'Farrell (1915–25, '34) started his long career with the Cubs, playing in six games spread over three seasons when only 18 to 20 years old. He then started to play a bit more, but played 100+ games for the Cubs in only two seasons, in 1922, when he batted .324, and in 1923, when he batted .319 with 12 HR and 84 RBI. And lastly, Rick Wilkins (1991–95) started his career with the Cubs, playing parts of five seasons in Chicago. He had his career year in 1993, when he batted .303 with 30 HR (he never hit more than 14 in any other season).

Left Field

Name	YR	WAR	W3	W/G	AVG	HR	SB	OPS+
Billy Williams	16	61.7	20.8	.0279	.296	392	86	135
Riggs Stephenson	9	23.9	13.3	.0244	.336	49	39	129
Hank Sauer	7	19.3	12.7	.0224	.269	198	6	126
Jimmy Sheckard	7	19.2	11.3	.0192	.257	17	163	113
Abner Dalrymple	8	16.2	10.2	.0228	.295	40	NA	130
Augie Galan	8	15.3	10.7	.0169	.277	59	90	107

Billy Williams (1959–74) played all but his final two years with the Cubs, starting with a fine Rookie of the Year campaign in 1961, when he hit .278 with 25 HR and 86 RBI. That was the first of 13 consecutive 20+-HR seasons, including 5 with 30+ HR. A five-time All-Star, Williams hit .296 for the Cubs, and had his best seasons in 1965, when he hit .315 with 34 HR; 1970, when he hit .322 with 42 HR, 129 RBI, and a league-leading 137 runs and 205 hits; and then in 1972, when he hit 37 HR with 122 RBI and a league-leading .333 average.

Riggs Stephenson (1926–34) was a high-average (.336) hitter with little power. Due to injuries and platoon time, he played 130 or more games only four times for the Cubs. His best all-around season came in 1929, when he batted .362 with 17 HR and 110 RBI. You could make a case for him to make this All-Time team, but in the end, I elected to go with some other outfielders.

Hank Sauer (1949–55) was a two-time All-Star who provided solid power for the Cubs, including four seasons with 30+ HR. His best year was his 1952 NL MVP campaign, when he hit .270 and led the NL with 37 HR and 121 RBI. Jimmy Sheckard (1906–12) played for Chicago during the second half of his career and had a fine 1911 campaign, when he led the league with 147 walks, 121 runs, and a .434 OBP.

Old-timer Abner Dalrymple (1879–86) hit .295, scored 100+ runs twice (even while playing only 111 and 113 games in those seasons), and led the league in hits and home runs once each. And lastly, Augie Galan (1934–41) was a switch-hitter who started his career with the Cubs and led the NL in stolen bases with modest totals of 22 in 1935 and 23 in 1937. That 1935 season was his first full year in the majors and his best statistically too, as he hit .314 with 203 hits and a league-leading 133 runs scored.

Center Field

Name	YR	WAR	W3	W/G	AVG	HR	SB	OPS+
Jimmy Ryan	15	36.1	15.0	.0217	.308	99	370	125
Hack Wilson	6	31.1	19.5	.0366	.322	190	34	155
George Gore	8	28.4	14.0	.0395	.315	24	NA	151
Andy Pafko	9	27.2	16.8	.0283	.294	126	28	126
Bill Lange	7	22.9	13.4	.0282	.330	39	400	123

Hack Wilson (1926–31) joined the Cubs after a couple of unimpressive seasons with the Giants. He made an immediate impact, leading the NL in HR in four of the next five seasons and providing 100+ RBI in all five seasons. In 1929 he batted .345 with a .425 OBP, and slugged 39 HR with 135 runs and a league-leading 159 RBI. Then in 1930 his numbers were just crazy: a .356 average, .454 OBP, 146 runs, and a league-leading 56 HR and 191 RBI (still a major league record). And he did all of that despite being only 5⬛6⬛ tall and drinking to excess.

Old-timer **Jimmy Ryan** (1885–89, 1891–1900) played for this franchise a long time, mostly in CF but also logged a lot of time in RF and LF. He led the NL in 1888 with 16 HR, 33 doubles, and 182 hits in only 129 games. The following year he scored 140 runs, one of eight times he scored 100+ runs. He also ran well, stealing 25+ bases eight times, with highs of 50 in 1887 and 60 in '88.

An even older old-timer, **George Gore** (1879–86), led the NL with a .360 average in 1880 and overall batted .315 for this franchise. Based on his regularly stealing 25+ a year later in his career, we can assume he stole plenty of bases during his earlier years for Chicago. Like many players back then, he didn't hit many homers, but he did score 100+ runs four times, including an impressive high of 150 in only 118 games in 1886. Based on the numbers he put up during these short early seasons, I gave him one of the OF spots on this roster over Stephenson and others.

You also could make a case for Andy Pafko (1943–51), as he was a four-time All-Star with a .294 average for the Cubs. He provided decent power with 26 HR and 101 RBI in 1948, and 36 HR and 92 RBI in 1950.

And lastly, old-timer Bill Lange (1893–99) played all of his short but impressive career for Chicago. He batted .330, including a .389 average in 1895. He also stole 400 bases in seven seasons, including four seasons of 60 or more, with highs of 84 in 1896, and a league-leading 73 in 1897. He retired early at age 28, as his future father-in-law forbid his daughter from marrying a ballplayer.

Right Field

Name	YR	WAR	W3	W/G	AVG	HR	SB	OPS+
Sammy Sosa	13	58.5	22.4	.0323	.284	545	181	139
Bill Nicholson	10	38.3	18.7	.0284	.272	205	26	136
Kiki Cuyler	8	25.5	15.1	.0269	.325	79	161	126
Frank Schulte	13	21.9	12.1	.0140	.272	91	214	116
Andre Dawson	6	18.6	11.7	.0215	.285	174	57	125

Sammy Sosa (1992–2004) played most of his career in Chicago, a few years early on with the White Sox and then all of his best seasons with the Cubs. Although the PED issue taints his accomplishments, his raw numbers were of course very impressive: 11 seasons of 30+ HR, with 7 seasons of 40+ and 3 with 60+. A seven-time All-Star, Slammin' Sammy was most famous for his 1998 MVP season, when he and McGwire staged the HR race to break Roger Maris' record. That year Sosa hit .308 with 66 HR, 18 SB, and a league-leading 134 runs and 158 RBI (though he also led the league with 171 strikeouts). He ran well early in his career, stealing 20+ bases for the Cubs four times. And he led the NL in runs three times, HR twice, and RBI twice.

Bill Nicholson (1939–48) also clearly deserved a spot on this All-Time team roster. He played all of his best years with the Cubs, including four seasons as an All-Star. He hit 20+ HR six times and led the league in both HR and RBI in 1943–44, when he provided 29 and 128, and then 33 and 122.

You could make a case for Kiki Cuyler (1928–35), a Hall of Famer who played more for the Cubs than any other team. While in Chicago he was very good defensively, led the league in SB three times, and his 1930 season was very impressive: .355 average, 13 HR, 17 triples, 50 doubles, 228 hits, 37 SB, 134 RBI, and 155 runs. And regarding the name Kiki, you'd gladly adopt that name too if your real full name was Hazen Shirley Cuyler.

Frank "Wildfire" Schulte (1904–16) played most of his fine career for the Cubs. He stole 20+ bases five times, hit double-digit triples six times, and led the league with a modest 10 HR in 1910 and then 21 HR and 107 RBI in 1911. That year he became the first of only a handful of players to post 20 doubles, triples, and home runs in one season.

And lastly, Andre Dawson (1987–92) signed with the Cubs as a free agent after a decade of stardom with the Expos. He immediately paid off, having his career year in 1987, when he led the league with 49 HR and 137 RBI, taking home the NL MVP Award even though the Cubs came in last in their division. Dawson hit 20+ HR in all six of his seasons with the team, was an All-Star five times, and took home two Gold Glove Awards for his work in RF.

Starting Pitching

Name	YR	WAR	W3	W-L	ERA	WHIP	ERA+
Fergie Jenkins	10	55.2	26.0	167-132	3.20	1.123	119
Rick Reuschel	12	49.5	21.0	135-127	3.50	1.312	113
Clark Griffith	8	46.5	25.6	152-96	3.40	1.353	129
Mordecai Brown	10	45.6	24.1	188-86	1.80	0.998	153
Carlos Zambrano	11	44.2	20.0	125-81	3.60	1.319	122
Pete Alexander	9	43.8	25.6	128-83	2.84	1.161	131
Hippo Vaughn	9	41.1	22.4	151-105	2.33	1.169	125
Bill Hutchinson	7	38.6	25.9	180-158	3.56	1.378	113
Charlie Root	16	38.4	13.2	201-156	3.55	1.292	112
John Clarkson	4	36.5	34.7	137-57	2.39	1.053	151
Greg Maddux	10	35.0	20.5	133-112	3.61	1.245	112
Claude Passeau	9	33.7	17.1	124-94	2.96	1.250	120
Bob Rush	10	32.0	16.9	110-140	3.71	1.298	109
Lon Warneke	10	30.8	19.8	109-72	2.84	1.208	131
Bill Lee	11	27.6	16.4	139-123	3.51	1.330	108
Ed Reulbach	9	26.9	18.2	136-65	2.24	1.131	124
Kerry Wood	12	26.5	15.1	80-68	3.67	1.258	118
Larry Corcoran	6	26.4	18.7	175-85	2.26	1.089	127
Bill Hands	7	24.6	14.1	92-86	3.18	1.198	121
Rick Sutcliffe	8	24.1	14.9	82-65	3.74	1.315	105

The top spot for this pitching staff went to Hall of Famer **Fergie Jenkins** (1966–73, '82–83). One of the best pitchers of the late '60s and early '70s, Jenkins won 20+ games in six consecutive seasons. He was a workhorse, leading the league in complete games three times and had 200+ strikeouts five times, including leading the league with 273 in 1969. Leveraging a rare combination of power and control, Jenkins was an All-Star three times, including in 1971, when he won the NL Cy Young Award after posting a 2.77 ERA and leading the league in wins with a 24-13 record.

You could make a case for Hall of Famer **Mordecai "Three Finger" Brown** (1904–12, '16) as the top starter instead of Jenkins, but I went with the order dictated by the WAR numbers. His nickname came from a farm-machinery accident in his youth, where he lost parts of two fingers on his right hand. He overcame this injury and actually turned it to his advantage by developing a devastating curveball as his primary pitching weapon. He threw during the Deadball Era, but even so his numbers for the Cubs were impressive: a 1.80 ERA and 188-86 record for a .686 winning percentage. He was stingy with both walks and hits, leading to a 0.998 WHIP. He won 20+ games in six consecutive seasons, including a 26-6 record and 1.04 ERA in 1906, a 29-9 record and 1.47 ERA in 1908, and a 27-9 record and 1.31 ERA in 1909. In addition to completing 20+ games as a starter for eight consecutive seasons, he was also useful out of the bullpen, and would have led the league in saves from 1908 through '11 if that stat had existed then.

Hall of Famer **Pete Alexander** (1918–26), a.k.a., Grover Cleveland Alexander, had most of his best years for the Philadelphia Phillies but also put in some strong seasons for the Cubs. He led the NL with a 1.71 ERA in 1919, and then earned the pitching Triple Crown the following year with a 1.91 ERA, 173 strikeouts, and a 27-14 record. His numbers declined a bit after that, but he did manage four more 15+-win seasons, including a 22-12 record in 1923.

Lefty **James "Hippo" Vaughn** (1913–21) played most of his career for the Cubs and won 20+ games for them five times. He compiled a 2.33 ERA and had his best season in 1918, when he won the pitching Triple Crown with a 1.74 ERA, a 22-10 record, and a modest 148 strikeouts.

Rick Reuschel (1972–81, '83–84) started and pitched over half of his long career with the Cubs. He was an All-Star for Chicago only once, in 1977, when he posted a 2.79 ERA with a 20-10 record, but he was a workhorse who started 35 to 38 games and threw 230+ innings in eight consecutive seasons in the 1970s.

Carlos Zambrano (2001–11) was an All-Star three times for the Cubs. A durable pitcher in the sense that he rarely missed a start, he also pitched just nine complete games in 282 games started—surely one reason he won 16 or more games in a season only three times (although his 16 wins in 2006 was enough to lead the NL). A very capable hitter, Big Z batted .241 for the Cubs, with 23 HR in 659 at-bats.

Greg Maddux (1986–92, 2004–06) had two stints with the Cubs, starting his great career in Chicago and then returning later at age 38. Although his best years were of course with the Braves, he won 15+ games for the Cubs six times, including his first Cy Young Award season in 1992, when he went 20-11 with a 2.18 ERA. He also took home 5 of his 18 Gold Glove Awards while with the Cubs.

You could make a case that **Charlie Root** (1926–41) should rate higher on this list, as he pitched all but his first season for the Cubs and is the franchise's all-time leader in wins (201). He won 15+ games eight times, but topped 20 wins only once, in 1927, when he led the league in wins with a 26-15 record.

After looking at the relief pitching candidates, I decided to go with ten starting pitchers for this roster. So that meant there was room for two more starters, and for one spot I decided to go with an old-timer, but one from late in the 19th century whose numbers are not that far removed from what good pitchers produced in the decades that followed. Hall of Famer **Clark Griffith** (1894–1900) pitched most of his best years for this franchise, including six consecutive seasons with 20+ wins. He led the NL with a 1.88 ERA in 1898, and ended up with an impressive 152-96 record for the club.

There are several candidates for the last spot, and I wouldn't argue with you if you preferred someone else, but in the end, I selected **Ed Reulbach** (1905–13). He was a teammate of Brown's, and like him posted a very low 2.24 ERA during his time with the Cubs. In fact, his ERAs during his first five seasons were quite impressive: 1.42, 1.65, 1.69, 2.03, and 1.78. He won 15+ games for them six times, but topped 20 wins only once, in 1908, when he went 24-7. Interestingly, on September 26 of that season he pitched both games of a doubleheader, pitching a shutout in each while allowing a combined eight hits.

You could make a case for Lon Warneke (1930–36, '42–43, '45) over Reulbach, as he had three 20+-win seasons for Chicago. His best year was in 1932, his first full season, when he led the NL in wins with a 22-6 record, and in ERA with a 2.37 mark. Another option was Claude Passeau (1939–47), who was a four-time All-Star and won 15+ games for the Cubs five times. His best two seasons came in 1940, when he went 20-13 with a 2.50 ERA, and in 1942, when he went 19-14 with a 2.68 ERA. He also pitched a one-hitter against the Tigers in the 1945 World Series.

Other contenders were a trio of old-timers, starting with Hall of Famer John Clarkson (1884–87), who admittedly pitched only three full seasons for Chicago, but produced numbers that are baffling to the modern eye. In 1885 he pitched 623 innings, completed 68 of the 70 games he started, and led the league in wins with an impressive 53-16 record. He went 36-17 the following year, and then led the NL again 1887 with 523 innings pitched, 56 complete games, and 38 wins.

You could make a case for Bill Hutchinson (1889–95), who pitched seven full seasons for the club, with three of them being outstanding and the other four mediocre at best. He led the NL in wins for three consecutive seasons, going 41-25 in 1890, 44-19 in 1891, and 36-36 in 1892. He was good those seasons to be sure, but he also got so many decisions in part because he pitched more than anyone else those years, leading the league each year in games, games started, complete games (65, 56, 67), and innings pitched (603, 561, 622). Unfortunately, he didn't adjust well to the pitcher's area being moved back for the 1893 season, and so he never came close to this level of greatness again.

One more old-timer of note was Larry Corcoran (1880–85), who had five seasons with 25+ wins. He posted a 27-12 record and led the league with a 1.95 ERA in 1882. He had a 175-85 record (.673) for Chicago, with his rookie campaign of 1880 being his best, when he went 43-14 with a 1.95 ERA and a league-leading 268 strikeouts.

I also considered a much more recent Cubs star, Kerry Wood (1998, 2000–08, '11–12), who burst onto the major league scene as a 20-year-old in 1998, striking out 233 batters in only 166.2 IP, and notching a 13-6 record and 3.40 ERA on his way to winning the NL Rookie of the Year Award. In only his fifth start that season, he tied Roger Clemens' major league record by striking out 20 batters. He missed the next season due to Tommy John surgery, before coming back and striking out 200+ in three consecutive seasons, including a league-leading 266 in 2003. Injuries continued to hamper his career, so he eventually converted to a relief role and was an All-Star while posting 34 saves for the Cubs in 2008.

A few others deserve brief mention, including (in chronological order):

- Bill Lee (1934–43, '47) won 20+ games for the Cubs twice, and had his best season in 1938, when he led the league with a 2.66 ERA and wins with a 22-9 record.

- Bob Rush (1948–57) pitched most of his career for the Cubs, was an All-Star twice, but won more than 13 games only once, in 1952, when he went 17-13 with a 2.70 ERA.

- Bill Hands (1966–72) also pitched most of his career for the Cubs and had his best success in 1968, when he went 16-10 with a 2.89 ERA, and then in 1969, when he went 20-14 with a 2.49 ERA.

- Rick Sutcliffe (1984–91) was an outstanding acquisition by the Cubs in June of 1984, as he went 16-1 with a 2.69 in 20 starts the rest of the season, earning him the NL Cy Young Award. He had mixed success during the rest of his career for the Cubs, winning 15 or more games only two more times.

Relief Pitching

Name	YR	WAR	W3	SV	W-L	ERA	WHIP	ERA+
Lee Smith	8	19.0	11.2	180	40-51	2.92	1.255	134
Ryan Dempster	9	18.8	13.6	87	67-66	3.74	1.318	116
Bruce Sutter	5	18.6	14.9	133	32-30	2.39	1.055	171
Carlos Mármol	8	10.5	8.4	117	23-32	3.50	1.329	124
Don Elston	9	9.3	7.5	64	49-54	3.70	1.362	106
Randy Myers	3	2.2	2.2	112	4-11	3.52	1.307	115

There were really only two relief pitchers who deserved spots on this All-Time team roster. **Bruce Sutter** (1976–80) pitched the first five years of his Hall of Fame career for the Cubs. A four-time All-Star, he provided 25+ saves in those four seasons, including a league-leading 37 in 1979 and 28 in 1980. He also had a 2.39 ERA for the team, including a 1.34 mark in 1977 and a 2.22 mark in 1979, when he took home the NL Cy Young Award.

Lee Smith (1980–87) also started his career with the Cubs, taking over the closer duties soon after Sutter left. Smith had a 1.65 ERA with a league-leading 29 saves in 1983, and then posted 30+ saves in the four seasons that followed, and he remains the franchise's all-time leader with 180.

A few others deserve brief mention, starting with Randy Myers (1993–95), who pitched for the Cubs for only three seasons but led the NL with 53 saves in 1993 (the franchise record) and 38 saves in 1995.

Don Elston (1953, '57–64) pitched most of his career for the Cubs, had a sub-2.00 ERA in three seasons, and was an All-Star in 1959.

Carlos Mármol (2006–13) was an outstanding setup man in 2007, when he posted a 1.43 ERA with 96 K in 69.1 IP. He was effective mostly as a setup man again the next two seasons before taking over as the team's closer for three years, with highs of 38 saves in 2010 and 34 in 2011.

And lastly, Ryan Dempster (2004–12) logged time for the Cubs first as a reliever and later as a starter. He had 24 to 33 saves in his three years as Chicago's closer, and then was an All-Star in 2008, when he posted a 17-6 record and 2.96 ERA.

Managers

Name	YR	From-To	W-L	PCT	PS	WS
Cap Anson	19	1879–1897	1,283-932	.579	5	NA
Frank Chance	8	1905–1912	768-389	.664	4	2
Charlie Grimm	14	1932–1960	946-782	.547	4	0

Joe Maddon	4	2015–2018	387-261	.597	4	1
Joe McCarthy	5	1926–1930	443-321	.579	1	0
Leo Durocher	7	1966–1972	535-526	.504	0	0

The top manager here had to be old-timer player-manager **Cap Anson**. He not only managed the team for 19 years, but also did so with great success in terms of both winning percentage (.579) and championships (five). Next up was **Frank Chance**, who managed the club to an impressive .664 winning percentage and two World Series championships. Third here was **Charlie Grimm**, who managed the team for 14 seasons and had a fine .547 winning percentage with four NL pennants.

For a fourth spot, I considered three candidates, but liked **Joe Maddon** over the two who had more success elsewhere, Joe McCarthy and Leo Durocher. Maddon has managed for only four seasons—a blink of an eye relative to the long Cubs history—but a .597 winning percentage and especially the 103-58, World Series championship year of 2016 deserve recognition.

Starting Lineup

What would mythical starting lineups look like for this All-Time roster?

Against RHP:
Cap Anson 1B (R)
Ryne Sandberg 2B (R)
Billy Williams LF (L)
Sammy Sosa RF (R)
Ernie Banks SS (R)
Bill Nicholson DH (L)
Hack Wilson CF (R)
Ron Santo 3B (R)
Gabby Hartnett C (R)

Against LHP:
Cap Anson 1B (R)
Ryne Sandberg 2B (R)
Ernie Banks SS (R)
Sammy Sosa RF (R)
Hack Wilson CF (R)
Ron Santo 3B (R)
Billy Williams LF (L)
Gabby Hartnett C (R)
Jimmy Ryan DH (R)

This roster was definitely weighted towards righties, with Billy Williams being the only starter who batted left-handed. You could platoon Hack and Santo at 3B, but I elected to list Santo in both lineups. For the DH spot, I went with Nicholson and Ryan, though there are other fine candidates like Chance, Herman, and others. Against lefties another lineup configuration would be to bat Ryan leadoff and shift Anson down to the three-hole, in order to make better use of his significant RBI talents. But then that would mean the power bats would all be shifted back a slot—Wilson, Banks, or Sosa batting sixth? With Santo seventh and Williams eighth? Suffice to say, this team has plenty of power in the middle of the order.

Depth Chart

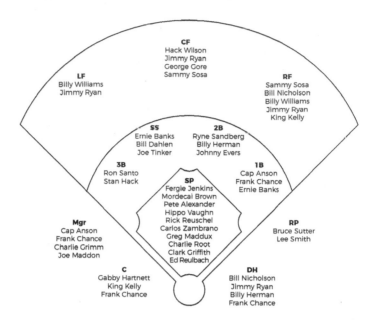

CF
Hack Wilson
Jimmy Ryan
George Gore
Sammy Sosa

LF
Billy Williams
Jimmy Ryan

RF
Sammy Sosa
Bill Nicholson
Billy Williams
Jimmy Ryan
King Kelly

SS
Ernie Banks
Bill Dahlen
Joe Tinker

2B
Ryne Sandberg
Billy Herman
Johnny Evers

3B
Ron Santo
Stan Hack

1B
Cap Anson
Frank Chance
Ernie Banks

SP
Fergie Jenkins
Mordecai Brown
Pete Alexander
Hippo Vaughn
Rick Reuschel
Carlos Zambrano
Greg Maddux
Charlie Root
Clark Griffith
Ed Reulbach

Mgr
Cap Anson
Frank Chance
Charlie Grimm
Joe Maddon

RP
Bruce Sutter
Lee Smith

C
Gabby Hartnett
King Kelly
Frank Chance

DH
Bill Nicholson
Jimmy Ryan
Billy Herman
Frank Chance

Prospects for Current Players

What are the prospects of current Cubs players making this All-Time team? The Cubs have a strong team right now, so if their best young players like Anthony Rizzo, Kris Bryant, Javier Báez, Wilson Contreras, and others stay with the team long enough, they could one day crack this roster. Pitchers Jon Lester and Kyle Hendricks could deserve consideration soon too. We'll see...

Retired Player Numbers

Ron Santo (10), Ernie Banks (14), Ryne Sandberg (23), Billy Williams (26), Ferguson Jenkins (31), Greg Maddux (31)

Selections from Other Authors and Fan Surveys

1946: *The Chicago Cubs*, by Warren Brown

Chapter 37 of this book provided a very early "all time list of Cubs" as chosen by the author. Included were:

C: Mike Kelly, John Kling, Jimmy Archer, Gabby Hartnett

1B: Adrian Anson, Frank Chance, Charlie Grimm, Phil Cavarretta

2B: Johnny Evers, Billy Herman, Rogers Hornsby

3B: Harry Steinfeldt, Stanley Hack, Heinie Zimmerman

SS: Joe Tinker, Billy Jurges

OF: Bill Lange, Frank Schulte, Riggs Stephenson, Hack Wilson, Kiki Cuyler

P: Larry Corcoran, John Clarkson, Clark Griffith, Ed Reulbach, Mordecai Brown, Jim Vaughn, Grover Cleveland Alexander, Charley Root, Lon Warneke, Claude Passeau

The players at each position appeared to be listed in more or less chronological order. After listing the players, Brown playfully wrote, "That's it, folks – the All Time Chicago National League Baseball Squad. Now all you have to do is arrange your own starting line-up and give it to the field announcer."

1958: *Sport* magazine, May issue

As part of a running series, *Sport* magazine reported on all-time all-star teams picked by "big league publicity departments and the writers covering the clubs." Here is what they had to say:

First Base: Charley Grimm, the celebrated banjo player and itinerant manager who played with the Cubs from 1925 through 1936.

Second Base: Billy Herman, who worked his hit-and-run magic there from 1931 until 1941.

Shortstop: Billy Jurges, a brilliant defensive man who sparked the Cubs to three pennants during his years (1931-1938) at Wrigley Field.

Third Base: Stan Hack, who spent his entire big-league career (1932-1947) with the Cubs and was one of the most underrated players of his time.

Left Field: Riggs Stephenson, who came to the Cubs from Cleveland in 1926. When he had finished his career there in 1934 he had a lifetime batting average of .336.

Center Field: Hack Wilson, who played at Wrigley Field from 1926 through 1931 and hit 56 homers in 1929 [*sic*].

Right Field: Kiki Cuyler, who starred for the Cubs from 1928 through 1935. He had a lifetime average of .321.

Catcher: Gabby Hartnett, "Old Tomato Face," who began his career in Chicago way back in 1922 and didn't leave until 1940.

Lefthanded Pitcher: Jim "Hippo" Vaughn, who hurled in Chicago from 1914 through 1921, winning 20 games five times and 19 once.

Righthanded Pitcher: Charlie Root, who won 201 games for the Cubs during the years 1926-1941.

Surely, they must have been excluding 19th century players, otherwise how could they have chosen Grimm over Anson at 1B? Assuming this, I still would have gone with Chance over Grimm at that position—was Grimm really that good of a banjo player, and was this somehow relevant to the Cubs' success on the field? Similarly, at shortstop they must have excluded Dahlen, but then why not choose Tinker over Jurges? Ignoring 19th century players, I liked the picks of Stephenson in LF and Wilson in CF, and I hoped they considered it a close call between Cuyler and Nicholson in RF. Vaughn was then, and would be today, the only candidate for LHP. But Root over Brown as the RHP? As they noted, he won 201 games for the Cubs—still the most in franchise history. But Brown was second in all-time wins and had far better individual seasons than Root provided.

1969: *The Sporting News* Fan Poll

The July 5, 1969, issue reported the results of a fan poll for the long-standing franchises of the day. The results for the Cubs were 1B Grimm, 2B Hornsby, 3B Santo, SS Banks, C Hartnett, LF Williams, CF Wilson, RF Cuyler, RHP Root, and LHP French.

The fans apparently were excluding or ignoring the many 19th century stars, most notably Cap Anson at 1B. But even leaving that aside, I again didn't understand the selection of Grimm over Chance at 1B. At 2B, the selection of Rogers Hornsby also confused me. He was admittedly one of the best three 2B of all time. But he had only two good seasons for the Cubs, one where he batted .331 but played in just 100 games, and one that was truly exceptional when he won the MVP Award after hitting .380 with 39 HR, 149 RBI, and a league-leading 156 runs. But was that enough to warrant his selection over Billy Herman or even Johnny Evers?

Lastly, the fans' pitching selections didn't make any sense to me at all. Again, there was the odd pick of Root over Brown as RHP, but this time there was also the choice of French over Vaughn as LHP. French pitched for the Cubs from 1935 through '41 and managed 15+ wins for them four times. But as noted earlier, Vaughn won 20+ games for the Cubs five times and won the pitching Triple Crown for them in 1918.

1990: "All-Time All-Star Teams," in *The Baseball Research Journal*

In an interesting article, Robert C. Berlo used Thorn and Palmer's TPR (Total Player Rating) system to choose all-time teams. He selected players based on their best 800 consecutive games for the franchise, with a minimum of five years played. His results: 1B Chance, 2B Herman, SS Dahlen, 3B Santo, LF Nicholson, CF Gore, RF Wilson, C Hartnett, SP Brown, Griffith, Alexander, Jenkins, RP Sutter.

The results at 1B and SS were interesting, as while both Chance and Dahlen had good stretches for this franchise, I was surprised that Banks' best 800 consecutive games didn't win for at least one of the two positions. I was glad to see Nicholson rated as the top LF here, but I was confused by the listing of Gore as top CF and Wilson as top RF, since Wilson played a total of only three games in RF for the Cubs, playing almost all of his games in CF instead.

1991: *Louisville Slugger Presents: The Chicago Cubs*, by Dick Lally

In the Cubs installment of this series of books in 1991, the author chose an All-Time all-star team that consisted of Chance, Sandberg, Banks, Santo, and Hartnett in the infield, Williams in LF, Wilson in CF, and Dawson in RF. The history section of this book did discuss the early years led by Cap Anson, so I found it odd that Chance was chosen as the 1B. And Dawson's MVP season notwithstanding, surely Nicholson was the better choice for RF. The pitching selections were solid, with Jenkins as the RHP, Vaughn as the LHP, and Sutter the choice as reliever.

1992: *The All-Time All-Star Baseball Book*, by Nick Acocella and Donald Dewey

The authors chose a starting lineup of Anson, Sandberg, Hack, Banks, Stephenson, Wilson, Cuyler, Kelly, and Brown. It was nice to finally see one of these Cubs all-time teams recognize the early greatness of Cap Anson. It was also interesting that they went with Hack over fan favorite Santo at 3B, and favored Stephenson over Williams in the outfield. Perhaps they felt bad for him, as they wrote, "At .336 for 14 seasons, outfielder Stephenson holds the second highest average for any player not in the Hall of Fame. (The highest is held by Shoeless

Joe Jackson, who was excluded because of the Black Sox scandal.)"

While Kelly was a great player, I didn't understand how they could choose him over Hartnett as the catcher. They at least included Gabby in their list of honorable mentions, along with Herman, Williams, Jenkins, and Santo.

1995: *Baseball Ratings*, by Charles F. Faber

Faber's system produced a fairly reasonable lineup (excluding 19th century players): 1B Grace, 2B Sandberg, 3B Santo, SS Banks, C Hartnett, OF Williams, Schulte, and Nicholson. The top five pitchers were indicated to be Brown, Root, Bush, Jenkins, and Vaughn, with Smith as the top reliever.

2003: *Rob Neyer's Big Book of Baseball Lineups*, by Rob Neyer

Neyer's book didn't include 19th century players, so with that caveat in mind his picks at 1B of Grace and Chance made sense. The rest of his infield selections were all solid as well: Sandberg and Herman, Santo and Hack, Banks and Tinker, Hartnett and Kling.

In the outfield he went with Williams and Sauer in LF, Wilson and Pafko in CF, and Sosa and Cuyler in RF. He noted that Cuyler edged out Dawson, "who was well past his peak by the time he was a Cub"—true except for his first season with the Cubs of course. His eight starting pitcher selections were solid: Brown, Jenkins, Alexander, Maddux, Vaughn, Root, Warneke, Reulbach, with Sutter and Smith as the obvious relief choices. And his top five managers were Chance, Grimm, McCarthy, Hartnett, and Durocher.

2005: *Few and Chosen: Defining Cubs Greatness Across the Eras*, by Ron Santo with Phil Pepe

As with each book in this fun series, the author chose five top players at each position. For the Cubs, the lists in order were:

C: Hartnett, Hundley, Davis, Kling, Bob Scheffing

1B: Banks, Anson, Cavarretta, Grace, Buckner

2B: Sandberg, Herman, Beckert, Evers, Hornsby

3B: Hack, Bill Madlock, Ramírez, Williamson, English

SS: Banks, Jurges, Kessinger, Tinker, Dunston

LF: Williams, Sauer, Moises Alou, Gary Matthews, Stephenson

CF: Wilson, Pafko, Rick Monday, Cy Williams, Schulte

RF: Sosa, Dawson, Nicholson, Cuyler, Kelly

RHP: Jenkins, Brown, Maddux, Wood, Sutcliffe

LHP: Ken Holtzman, Vaughn, Dick Ellsworth, French, Jack Pfiester

RP: Sutter, Smith, Myers, Phil Regan, Don Elston

Manager: Durocher, Don Zimmer, Anson, Dusty Baker, Grimm

Santo honored Banks by listing him as the top player at both 1B and SS, so that explains why Anson was dropped down a spot. At 3B he listed Bill Madlock higher than I think was warranted, liking Madlock's swing and the fact that he won two batting titles in his three seasons for the Cubs. And in line with the other books in this "Few and Chosen" series, modesty kept Santo from including himself in the 3B list.

In left field, I didn't understand the listing of Alou and Matthews over Stephenson. In the case of Alou, I think the pick was based on his liking for the Alou baseball family, and reasonably based on the big season Moises had just provided in 2004: .293 average, 39 HR, 106 RBI. But that turned out to be his third and final season with the Cubs. And in the case of Matthews, Santo's description of The Sarge made clear his admiration for Matthews as a player, especially the leadership he displayed with younger players when he joined the Cubs late in his career. Interestingly, Santo stated that Stephenson was perhaps the most underrated hitter in Cubs history.

For CF, two omissions were Jimmy Ryan and George Gore (neither of whom was even mentioned in the book). Either of them, but especially Ryan, would have been better picks than Cy Williams, as Williams played for the Cubs for only three full seasons. He led the NL with a modest total of 12 HR in 1916 and went on to become a legitimate slugger for the Phillies.

With all due respect, I thought some of Santo's pitching selections were based more on sentimentality and personal friendships than on the players' actual, full résumés while playing for the Cubs. The best example of this was Kerry Wood as the fourth RHP. His fifth RHP selection was Rick Sutcliffe, and his first sentence about him told it all: "Rick Sutcliffe is a very dear friend."

Even more strange to me was the selection of Ken Holtzman over Hippo Vaughn as the top LHP. The Cubs did not have many candidates here, so I had no problem with Holtzman being in a top-five list, but he won 17 games for the Cubs only twice and never won more than 11 in any other season. As Santo noted, he did toss two no-hitters for the Cubs, one in 1969 and one in 1971. But in terms of overall accomplishments while playing for Chicago, Vaughn's résumé was clearly the better of the two lefties.

2016: *101 All-Time Fantasy Baseball Teams,* by Jack Sweeney

Sweeney's lineup was very solid (assuming no 19th century players were considered) with Chance, Sandberg, Santo, Banks, Williams, Wilson, Cuyler, Hartnett, and Sosa (listed as DH). He chose four starting pitchers: Jenkins, Brown, Root, and Holtzman, which clearly elevates Holtzman over Alexander, Vaughn, and several others. No argument with his choice of Sutter as the top reliever.

Top WAR Single Seasons – Hitters (8+)

Name	Year	WAR	AVG	HR	R	RBI	SB	OPS+
Rogers Hornsby	1929	10.4	.380	39	156	149	2	178
Sammy Sosa	2001	10.3	.328	64	146	160	0	203
Ernie Banks	1959	10.2	.304	45	97	143	2	156
Ron Santo	1967	9.8	.300	31	107	98	1	153
Ernie Banks	1958	9.4	.313	47	119	129	4	155
Ron Santo	1964	8.9	.313	30	94	114	3	164
Ron Santo	1966	8.9	.312	30	93	94	4	161
Ryne Sandberg	1984	8.5	.314	19	114	84	32	140
Ernie Banks	1955	8.1	.295	44	98	117	9	144

It was interesting to see Rogers Hornsby's only full season for the Cubs at the top of this list. And that only one of Sosa's impressive seasons makes the list, and it wasn't his 1998 MVP year (that had a 6.4 score). To me this demonstrates the power of WAR to compare players across decades, etc. Sandberg's MVP season makes the list, and he had others with scores of 7+. Aside from those three years, fan favorites Banks and Santo dominate the list with three seasons each.

Top WAR Single Seasons – Pitchers (8+)

Name	Year	WAR	W-L	ERA	IP	SO	ERA+
Pete Alexander	1920	12.8	27-14	1.91	363.1	173	166
Fergie Jenkins	1971	12.0	24-13	2.77	325.0	263	141
Clark Griffith	1898	10.5	24-10	1.88	325.2	97	192
Jack Taylor	1902	10.2	23-11	1.29	333.2	88	206
Dick Ellsworth	1963	9.9	22-10	2.11	290.2	185	167
Rick Reuschel	1977	9.6	20-10	2.79	252.0	166	158
Greg Maddux	1992	9.4	20-11	2.18	268.0	199	166
Jake Arrieta	2015	9.0	22-6	1.77	229.0	236	215
Clark Griffith	1895	8.8	26-14	3.93	353.0	79	130
Mordecai Brown	1909	8.8	27-9	1.31	342.2	172	193
Hippo Vaughn	1918	8.3	22-10	1.74	290.1	148	159
Orval Overall	1909	8.1	20-11	1.42	285.0	205	179
Mordecai Brown	1908	8.1	29-9	1.47	312.1	123	160
Mark Prior	2003	8.0	18-6	2.43	211.1	245	179

I included the two seasons by Clark Griffith, but excluded several from before 1895, when the innings pitched by starters were often significantly over 350, making comparison with the seasons since then difficult and unfair. Very interesting to see that, aside from Griffith, only Mordecai Brown appears on this list twice.

Franchise Player

Some will immediately think of Ernie Banks here, after all he is Mr. Cub. But with all due respect to Banks, as well as to Sandberg, Santo, and Williams, I decided to go with the original star of this franchise, Cap Anson. Leading the league in RBI eight times and being a .330+ hitter well into his 40s, all while managing the team too, impressed me enough to give him this franchise player honor.

CHAPTER 7

The Indians Franchise All-Time Dream Team

The Cleveland Indians franchise started with the birth of the American League in 1901. They went by the name Blues that year, then Bronchos the next, and became the Cleveland Naps from 1903 to 1914, named after their star player, Napoleon Lajoie. They finally took the nickname Indians starting in 1915.

This team didn't win any AL pennants until 1920, when they went on to win the World Series against Brooklyn. They had another long dry spell from 1921 through 1947, finishing in second place in the AL only three times. They won the World Series against the Boston Braves in 1948 and made it again in 1954, losing to the New York Giants.

Their longest gap in postseason appearances was a full 40 years, from 1955 through 1994, a period during which they managed to be above .500 only 12 times. In 1995 they not only made the playoffs but also made it to the World Series, losing to the Braves in six games. This was the first of five consecutive AL Central Division titles. A period of mixed success followed until 2016, when they won the AL Central Division and went all the way to the World Series, ultimately losing in Game 7 to the Cubs.

This franchise's All-Time team has a few positions that are weaker than others, most notably catching and relief pitching. But it also includes a few legitimate All-Time superstars as well.

1st Base

Name	YR	WAR	W3	W/G	AVG	HR	SB	OPS+
Jim Thome	13	47.9	20.8	.0342	.287	337	18	152
Hal Trosky	9	29.8	15.1	.0265	.313	216	21	135
Travis Hafner	10	25.0	16.3	.0232	.278	200	9	138
Andre Thornton	10	19.0	13.1	.0155	.254	214	39	122
Mike Hargrove	7	14.0	9.3	.0158	.292	33	14	116

Jim Thome (1991–2002, '11) started his career as the Indians' 3B and was a part-time player for his first four seasons. He later switched to 1B and had seven consecutive seasons with 30+ HR, with highs of 49 in 2001 and 52 in 2003 (his 337 HR for the Indians are the most all-time for the franchise). He also had both 100+ runs and 100+ RBI in six seasons. A three-time All-Star for the Indians, he did strike out a lot, but he also walked a lot, which led to an impressive .414 OBP.

An earlier power hitter is the backup 1B on this roster, **Hal Trosky** (1933–41). He played nearly all of his career for the Indians, hit 25+ HR six times, and had 100+ RBI six times and 100+ runs four times. A .313 hitter for the Tribe, his most impressive numbers came in 1936, when he batted .343 with 41 HR, 162 RBI, and 124 runs.

You could make a case for Travis Hafner (2003–12) to make this All-Time team, though it would need to be primarily as a DH, as that is what he did in 1,043 games, compared to only 72 on the field at 1B. From 2004 through '06 Hafner was one of the best power hitters in the AL, as he hit .300+ with 28 to 42 HR and 100+ RBI each year. The following year, he still hit 24 HR with 100 RBI, but his average dipped to .266. After that, injuries limited his playing time and reduced his hitting production. Never a good base runner, he was nicknamed Pronk by a teammate as a combination of "project" and "donkey" for the way he ran the bases.

Another power-hitting Indians 1B who played more games for them as their DH was Andre Thornton (1977–79, '81–87). Only a .254 hitter, he clubbed 25+ HR five times. A two-time All-Star, he had his best offensive numbers in 1982, when he hit .273 with 32 HR and 116 RBI.

And lastly, Mike Hargrove (1979–85) played the second half of his career with the Indians and hit .292 but with little power or speed. He later was the Indians manager for nine seasons and led them to AL pennants in 1995 and 1997.

2nd Base

Name	YR	WAR	W3	W/G	AVG	HR	SB	OPS+
Nap Lajoie	13	80.0	28.4	.0496	.339	33	240	155
Bobby Avila	10	27.9	16.5	.0231	.284	74	75	106
Jason Kipnis	8	21.8	14.5	.0218	.263	106	128	105
Roberto Alomar	3	20.3	20.3	.0431	.323	63	106	124
Joe Gordon	4	19.6	17.7	.0346	.262	100	21	120
Carlos Baerga	8	19.6	14.6	.0208	.299	104	49	109
Odell Hale	9	16.1	11.6	.0160	.293	72	56	102

After several outstanding seasons for the Philadelphia Phillies and Athletics, **Napoleon Lajoie** (1902–14) signed with Cleveland and quickly became so central to the team that their official nickname was changed to the Naps. A Hall of Famer, he led the AL in hitting with a .344 average in 1903 and again with a .384 mark in 1910. He didn't hit for home-run or triples power, but he did smack 30+ doubles in nine seasons and led the league with 49 in 1904, 48 in 1906, and 51 in 1910. A .339 hitter for Cleveland, Nap also stole 20+ bases five times and provided outstanding defense.

There were several candidates to consider for the backup spot, and it was hard to compare them, as it was a case of longevity vs. peak performances. In the end, for now, I selected **Bobby Avila** (1949–58). He played all but his final three seasons for the Indians and was an All-Star for them three times. He led the AL with a .341 average in 1954, and overall was a .284 hitter with some power and speed.

You could almost make a case for Jason Kipnis (2011–18), who has been an All-Star twice for the Indians so far. He stole 30+ bases in his first two full seasons, though fewer since then. He has shown some power too, with a high of 23 HR in 2016. Assuming he continues to be productive for the Indians for another few years, I think he'll soon take the spot away from Avila.

Another strong candidate was Carlos Baerga (1990–96, '99), a .299 hitter and three-time All-Star for the Indians. He hit 20+ HR with 100+ RBI in both 1992 and 1993. And Odell Hale (1931, '33–40) played most of his career with the Indians, splitting his time between 2B and 3B. He was a .293 hitter, and provided 101 RBI in both 1934 and 1935, with 126 runs scored in 1936.

There were also two 2B who had short careers for the Indians but provided strong peak performances, starting with Hall of Famer Roberto Alomar (1999–2001). He had three All-Star, Gold Glove seasons for the Indians in the second half of his career. His 1999 season was arguably the best, as he hit .323 with 24 HR, 120 RBI, 37 SB, and a league-leading 138 runs. Lastly, Hall of Famer Joe

Gordon (1947–50) ended his career with four seasons in Cleveland, three as an All-Star in which he hit 20 to 32 HR with a high of 124 RBI in 1948.

3rd Base

Name	YR	WAR	W3	W/G	AVG	HR	SB	OPS+
Bill Bradley	10	34.9	20.4	.0284	.272	27	157	111
Ken Keltner	12	33.8	16.4	.0223	.276	163	39	112
Al Rosen	10	32.6	22.0	.0312	.285	192	39	137
Buddy Bell	7	24.4	12.4	.0247	.274	64	24	103
José Ramírez	6	22.0	18.9	.0343	.285	87	93	122
Toby Harrah	5	18.6	14.3	.0261	.281	70	82	120
Graig Nettles	3	17.5	17.5	.0376	.250	71	12	108
Brook Jacoby	9	15.9	10.9	.0128	.273	120	14	107
Max Alvis	8	9.2	7.4	.0097	.249	108	42	99

Unlike 1B and 2B, there wasn't a clear-cut first choice at 3B. After some consideration, I went with power hitter **Al Rosen** (1947–56), who played his entire, relatively short career for the Tribe. He didn't play much in the majors until 1950, when he led the AL in HR with 37 to go along with a .287 average, 116 RBI, and 100 runs. He paced the AL with 105 RBI in 1952 and then had his best season in 1953, when he earned the MVP Award after hitting .336 with a league-leading 43 HR, 145 RBI, and 115 runs. Overall, he hit 20+ HR six times and was a four-time All-Star.

Ken Keltner (1937–44, '46–49) was not as prolific a HR producer as Rosen, but he did hit 20+ three times, including 26 HR with 113 RBI in his rookie season and 31 HR with 119 RBI in his final full year. A seven-time All-Star and excellent fielder, he also lost one full season to World War II military service.

Based on his peak and career WAR numbers, you could also make a case for Bill Bradley (1901–10), this franchise's first regular 3B. A typical Deadball-Era hitter, he batted .272, hit plenty of doubles and triples, and stole 20+ bases four times.

Current star José Ramírez (2013-18) took a few years to make his mark, but in 2016 he hit .312 with 46 doubles and 22 SB. His power then increased as he hit 29 HR with a league-leading 56 doubles in 2017 and then had his best season thus far in 2018 when he posted 39 HR, 110 runs, 105 RBI, and 34 SB. A two-time All-Star, he also provides the Indians with position versatility as he can play 3B, 2B, SS, and LF.

A few others deserve brief mention, essentially the five 3B for the Indians from the early '60s through the late '80s:

- Max Alvis (1962–69), who played all but his final season for the Indians, was only a .249 hitter but provided 17 to 22 HR in five consecutive seasons.

- Graig Nettles (1970–72) played three seasons for the Indians early in his career. He provided outstanding defense and some power, including 26 HR in 1970 and 28 HR in 1971.

- Buddy Bell (1972–78) started his fine career for Cleveland, providing them with good defense and a .274 average.

- Toby Harrah (1979–83) took over for Bell at the hot corner, hit 20+ HR for the Indians twice, and stole 15+ bases four times.

- Brook Jacoby (1984–91, '93) played most of his career for Cleveland, providing them with some power, including 32 HR in 1987.

Shortstop

Name	YR	WAR	W3	W/G	AVG	HR	SB	OPS+
Lou Boudreau	13	61.7	26.3	.0396	.296	63	50	122
Joe Sewell	11	45.6	18.8	.0301	.320	30	71	111
Terry Turner	15	39.0	17.2	.0241	.254	8	254	91
Omar Vizquel	11	30.0	13.5	.0203	.283	60	279	90
Ray Chapman	9	29.0	15.9	.0276	.278	17	238	111
Francisco Lindor	4	23.9	19.3	.0416	.288	98	71	119
Asdrúbal Cabrera	8	20.7	12.5	.0226	.270	82	69	105
Woodie Held	7	18.8	11.5	.0220	.249	130	10	113
Julio Franco	8	17.2	9.4	.0158	.297	62	147	103

Hall of Famer **Lou Boudreau** (1938–50) played almost his entire career for the Indians, including nine years from 1942 through 1950 as their player-manager. A seven-time All-Star and a very good fielder, Boudreau was a .296 hitter and led the league with a .327 average in 1944. Handsome Lou didn't have much power or speed, but he did lead the AL with 45 doubles three times. His best year came in 1948, when he won the MVP award after piloting the team to the World Series championship and batting .355 with 18 HR, 106 RBI, and 116 runs. On top of that, in the one-game pennant playoff against the Red Sox he went 4-for-4 with two homers to lead his team into the World Series.

Another Hall of Famer, **Joe Sewell** (1920–30), played all but his final three seasons for the Indians. He was a .320 hitter with a .398 OBP and was extremely difficult to strikeout. In fact, for the Indians he had only 99 strikeouts in 5,621 at-bats. He didn't provide much power or speed, but he did score 90+ runs five times and also managed 90+ RBI five times.

You could make a case for Omar Vizquel (1994–2004), who played the middle portion of his long career for the Indians, providing outstanding defense that earned him eight Gold Glove Awards while in Cleveland. He batted .283 for the Tribe and was a consistent run scorer, crossing the plate 80+ times in nine seasons. A three-time All-Star, he also stole 25+ bases five times for the Indians.

Ray Chapman (1912–20) played his entire, tragically short career for the Indians. He was a .278 hitter who ran well, stealing 20+ bases six times with a high of 52 in 1917. A very good fielder and an excellent bunter, Chapman led the AL in sacrifice hits three times and in 1917 set the record with 67. On August 16, 1920, Chapman was hit in the head by a pitch from Carl Mays, had to be assisted off the field, and died in a hospital 12 hours later.

Terry Turner (1904–18) played most of his career for Cleveland, splitting his time between SS, 3B, and 2B. He was a good fielder, and like many players from his era, he had some speed, stealing 15+ bases nine times. But he was only a .254 hitter with virtually no power; he had only 8 HR in 5,787 at-bats and even had 20+ doubles only twice.

Current star Francisco Lindor (2015-18) has increased his HR production each year, with highs of 33 in 2017 and 38 in 2018. Already a three-time All-Star, he led the league with 129 runs in 2018 and also provides good defense, taking home a Gold Glove award in 2016.

Asdrúbal Cabrera (2007–14) started his career for Cleveland and was an All-Star twice. He provided a moderate power and speed combo for a middle infielder, with his best season coming in 2011, when he hit 25 HR with 17 SB.

Two other Cleveland shortstops deserve brief mention, starting with Woodie Held (1958–64). Although only a .249 hitter, he provided 17 to 29 HR in his six full seasons for the Indians. And lastly, Julio Franco (1983–88, '96–97) had two stints for Cleveland during his long career. He batted .297 for the Indians and stole 25+ bases three times.

Catcher

Name	YR	WAR	W3	W/G	AVG	HR	SB	OPS+
Carlos Santana	8	24.5	12.0	.0220	.249	174	40	121
Steve O'Neill	13	23.2	12.1	.0170	.265	11	30	91
Victor Martinez	8	19.2	13.2	.0234	.297	103	1	120

John Romano	5	14.6	11.8	.0251	.263	91	6	123
Sandy Alomar Jr.	11	13.3	8.4	.0135	.277	92	24	92
Jim Hegan	14	4.7	3.5	.0031	.230	90	15	76

Catcher has not traditionally been a position of strength in Cleveland. It was not an easy decision as to who the starter or backup should be, but in the end, I gave the top spot to **Victor Martinez** (2002–09), who batted .297 for the Indians and had three seasons with 20+ HR. A three-time All-Star, his best season was 2007, when he hit .301 with 25 HR and 114 RBI.

Carlos Santana (2010–17) has admittedly played more games at 1B than C, but he has hit between 18 and 34 HR in seven full seasons so far. Although only a .249 batter, he makes up for that by having a great eye at the plate that has led to a .365 OBP.

If you prefer stronger defense behind the plate, then you could argue for Steve O'Neill (1911–23), who mostly played during the Deadball Era and was a .265 hitter with very limited power or speed. He did improve as a hitter as his career progressed, and he posted a .300+ average in three consecutive years from 1920 through '22. Jim Hegan (1941–42, '46–57) lost three early seasons to World War II, but he went on to provide excellent defense, which made him an All-Star five times, even though he batted only .230 with limited power.

Two other Indians backstops deserve to be mentioned, starting with Sandy Alomar Jr. (1990–2000), who won the Gold Glove and Rookie of the Year Awards in 1990, after hitting .290 with 9 HR and 66 RBI. A six-time All-Star and the brother of Robert Alomar, he had his best season in 1997, when he hit .324 with 21 HR and 83 RBI. And lastly, John Romano (1960–64) hit 15+ HR for the Indians four times and was an All-Star twice.

Left Field

Name	YR	WAR	W3	W/G	AVG	HR	SB	OPS+
Albert Belle	8	27.3	18.2	.0299	.295	242	61	150
Jeff Heath	10	24.8	13.5	.0259	.298	122	52	137
Charlie Jamieson	14	23.9	11.9	.0161	.316	18	107	104
Michael Brantley	10	22.7	13.7	.0216	.295	87	118	114
Dale Mitchell	11	19.3	9.9	.0174	.312	41	45	114
Joe Vosmik	7	16.6	12.4	.0202	.313	44	17	111
Jack Graney	14	14.4	6.5	.0103	.250	18	148	101
Joe Carter	6	14.3	10.6	.0170	.269	151	126	112

In terms of overall candidates for this All-Time team, LF is the weakest of the three OF positions. After considering all the options, I ended up choosing only one here, slugger **Albert Belle** (1989–96). He was a four-time All-Star for the Indians and hit 25+ HR for them six times. He hit 38 HR and led the league with 129 RBI in 1993 (and stole a career-high 23 bases too), and then batted .357 in 106 games in 1994. His best season was 1995, when he was the MVP runner-up after batting .317 and leading the AL with 50 HR, 126 RBI, 121 runs, and 52 doubles. He followed that up in 1996 with a .311 average, 48 HR, 124 runs, and a league-leading 148 RBI.

Jeff Heath (1936–45) had several good and two outstanding seasons for Cleveland. In 1938 he batted .343 with 21 HR, 112 RBI, 104 runs, and a league-leading 18 triples, and then in 1941 he hit .340 with 24 HR, 123 RBI, 18 SB, and a league-leading 20 triples (one of only eight hitters ever to have 20 doubles, triples, and homers in a single season.) You could make a case for him to make this All-Time team, but as you will see there were many outfield candidates to consider.

Charlie Jamieson (1919–32) played parts of 14 seasons for the Indians and was a .316 hitter with a .388 OBP. He had little power and only moderate speed, but he had impressive batting averages of .345 in 1923 and .359 in 1924.

Michael Brantley (2009–18) has shown flashes of excellence thus far for the Indians, with his best season coming in 2014, when he batted .327 with 20 HR and 23 SB. A three-time All-Star, he'll need to stay healthy and keep producing for several more seasons before he could be a real candidate for this All-Time team.

Joe Vosmik (1930–36) was a good fielder and provided the Indians with a .313 average over six full seasons, including his one All-Star campaign in 1935, when he batted .348 with 10 HR, 110 RBI, and a league-leading 216 hits, 47 doubles, and 20 triples.

Dale Mitchell (1946–56) played all but his final two seasons for Cleveland and was a .312 hitter and two-time All-Star. He didn't provide much power or speed, but he did lead the league in 1949 with 203 hits and 23 triples.

Joe Carter (1984–89) played 1B and all three outfield positions and provided solid power numbers for the Indians early in his career. He hit 25+ HR for four consecutive seasons, with a high of 35 HR in 1989, and had a league-leading 121 RBI in 1986. He also stole 24 to 31 bases in four consecutive seasons, though he didn't take many walks and so had a pitiful .309 OBP.

And lastly, Jack Graney (1908, 1910–22) played his entire career for Cleveland and was in many ways a typical Deadball-Era hitter, batting only .250 (albeit with a .354 OBP) with very little power but some speed, as he stole 15+ bases five times. One item of note: Graney went on to become the first former player to make the switch to becoming a baseball broadcaster.

Center Field

Name	YR	WAR	W3	W/G	AVG	HR	SB	OPS+
Tris Speaker	11	74.2	26.2	.0488	.354	73	155	158
Kenny Lofton	10	48.5	21.4	.0380	.300	87	452	109
Earl Averill	11	47.9	19.4	.0317	.322	226	66	136
Larry Doby	10	43.4	20.2	.0351	.286	215	44	140
Grady Sizemore	8	27.5	19.1	.0308	.269	139	134	120

Hall of Famer **Tris Speaker** (1916–26) joined the Indians after having already established himself as a star with the Red Sox. In his first season in Cleveland, he led the AL with 211 hits, 41 doubles, and a .386 average. Overall, he hit an impressive .354 for the Indians, scored 100+ runs four times, and led the league in doubles six times, including three seasons with 50 or more. His most productive offensive season was 1923, when he hit .380 with 17 HR, 130 RBI, 133 runs, and 59 doubles. The Grey Eagle was an outstanding center fielder, one of the best defenders in the history of the game at that position. And from 1919 through 1926 he served as player-manager, leading the team to winning seasons in six of those eight years and a World Series championship in 1920.

The Indians have had many outstanding CF, and how you rank the next three could certainly be debated. Speedy **Kenny Lofton** (1992–96, 1998–2001, '07) led the AL in SB every year from 1992 through 1996. Overall, he stole 50+ bases for the Indians six times, with a high of 75 in 1996 (and his 452 SB for the Indians are by far the most for the franchise). A .300 hitter, he scored 100+ runs six times. Lofton was an All-Star for Cleveland five times and excelled in center field as well, taking home four consecutive Gold Glove Awards.

Hall of Famer **Larry Doby** (1947–55, '58) played the majority of his career for the Indians. He is perhaps most well known for being the first African-American player in the American League, following what Jackie Robinson did in the National League in 1947. Doby was a great power hitter, providing the Indians with 20+ HR in eight consecutive seasons, including leading the AL with modest totals of 32 HR in both 1952 and 1954. A seven-time All-Star, Doby was a .286 hitter with a .389 OBP and had 100+ RBI five times.

Hall of Famer **Earl Averill** (1929–39) was the star center fielder for the Indians in the era that followed Speaker. He played most of his career in Cleveland and hit .322 with a .399 OBP for the club. The Earl of Snohomish hit 20+ HR five times, had 100+ RBI five times, and scored 100+ runs nine times. His two best seasons statistically came in 1931, when he hit .333 with 32 HR, 143 RBI, and 140 runs, and in 1936, when he hit .378 with 28 HR, 126 RBI, 136 runs, and a league-leading 15 triples and 232 hits.

All of these talented center fielders means there is no room on this roster for Grady Sizemore (2004–11). Before back and knee injuries greatly reduced his production and eventually led to him missing two entire seasons, Sizemore had four consecutive seasons of 20+ HR, 20+ SB, and 100+ runs. In 2006 he led the AL with 134 runs and 53 doubles, and in 2008 he joined the 30/30 club by hitting 33 HR and stealing 38 bases. He also provided great defense in center field, taking home Gold Glove Awards in 2007 and 2008.

Right Field

Name	YR	WAR	W3	W/G	AVG	HR	SB	OPS+
Joe Jackson	6	35.0	26.4	.0519	.375	24	138	182
Elmer Flick	9	31.2	18.6	.0334	.299	19	207	145
Manny Ramírez	8	29.9	17.3	.0309	.313	236	28	152
Rocky Colavito	8	23.1	14.7	.0253	.267	190	9	137
Shin-Soo Choo	7	21.7	15.0	.0317	.292	83	85	135

The great **Shoeless Joe Jackson** (1910–15) provided very high batting averages of .408, .395, and .373 from 1911 through 1913. He also led the league with 26 triples in 1912, stole 20+ bases for Cleveland four times, and scored 100+ runs three times. Even though he played for this franchise for only four-and-a-half seasons, he did enough in that short span to earn the top RF spot on this roster.

While at this point I have already chosen six outfielders for this All-Time team, the two "extra spots" for this roster are still open. One should be used for Hall of Famer **Elmer Flick** (1902–10) who was a .299 hitter for Cleveland after batting .338 over four seasons for the Phillies. He hit a lot of triples, leading the AL with between 18 and 22 each year from 1905 through '07. He also stole 20+ bases in six consecutive seasons, leading the league with 38 in 1904 and 39 in 1906.

Manny Ramírez (1993–2000) started his career for the Indians and hit 25+ HR in six consecutive seasons. He was an All-Star for Cleveland four times, and he hit .294 with 45 HR and 145 RBI in 1998, .333 with 44 HR and a league-leading 165 RBI in 1999 (the first player with 160+ in over 60 years), and .351 with 38 HR and 122 RBI in only 118 games in 2000. Although you could argue in favor of Sizemore or various infielders, given some of these impressive numbers, I decided to give Ramírez the second "extra spot" on this roster.

Rocky Colavito (1955–59, '65–67) had two stints with the Indians and slugged 20+ HR for them six times. A three-time All-Star, his power highs for Cleveland were 41 HR and 113 RBI in 1958, and 42 HR and 111 RBI the following season. And lastly, Shin-Soo Choo (2006–12) provided a nice balance of power and speed, with 20+ HR and 20+ SB in both 2009 and 2010.

Starting Pitching

Name	YR	WAR	W3	W-L	ERA	WHIP	ERA+
Bob Feller	18	63.6	29.2	266-162	3.25	1.316	122
Stan Coveleski	9	51.7	25.7	172-123	2.80	1.225	129
Bob Lemon	15	48.8	19.6	207-128	3.23	1.337	119
Mel Harder	20	43.8	19.9	223-186	3.80	1.408	113
Addie Joss	9	43.7	19.9	160-97	1.89	0.968	142
Sam McDowell	11	41.5	22.0	122-109	2.99	1.268	119
Early Wynn	10	39.6	20.1	164-102	3.24	1.274	119
George Uhle	11	37.5	21.8	147-119	3.92	1.432	105
Wes Ferrell	7	36.2	24.4	102-62	3.67	1.437	126
Corey Kluber	8	33.6	22.5	96-55	3.09	1.070	137
Willis Hudlin	15	33.4	18.3	157-151	4.34	1.471	104
Jim Bagby	7	30.6	22.2	122-86	3.03	1.265	112
Mike García	12	30.3	14.6	142-96	3.24	1.309	118
Gaylord Perry	4	29.3	27.3	70-57	2.71	1.104	134
CC Sabathia	8	28.1	14.8	106-71	3.83	1.265	115
Luis Tiant	6	26.1	17.0	75-64	2.84	1.143	120
Charles Nagy	13	25.4	16.9	129-103	4.51	1.419	101
Bartolo Colon	6	22.6	13.9	75-45	3.92	1.363	121
Tom Candiotti	7	22.0	15.3	73-66	3.62	1.291	115
Vean Gregg	4	21.3	20.5	72-36	2.31	1.233	140

The top choice for this All-Time team's pitching staff was pretty clearly **Bob Feller** (1936–1, '45–56). He lost nearly four prime years to World War II but still had an outstanding career, all of which was spent with the Indians. He was already pitching for the Indians at age 17 and was a regular in the rotation by 19. He ended up with a 266-162 record, which is a .621 winning percentage. Like many hard-throwing strikeout kings, he did walk a lot of batters—especially early in his career when he led the league four times, including highs of 208 in 1938 and 194 in 1941. But Rapid Robert led the AL in wins six times, ERA once, complete games three times, and strikeouts an impressive seven times. An eight-time All-Star, it is hard to choose one season as his best. Perhaps it was 1940, when he won the AL pitching Triple Crown with a 27-11 record, 2.61 ERA, and 261 strikeouts. Or perhaps it was his first full season after the war, in 1946, when he had a 2.18 ERA and led the AL in wins with a 26-15 record, complete games with 36, shutouts with 10, and strikeouts with a then-record 348. Considering that the Indians gave him only 19 runs of support in his 15 losses, he really should have been a 30-game winner that year. Lastly, Feller pitched three no-hitters in his career, the first 20th century pitcher to do so.

Next up was **Stan Coveleski** (1916–24) who pitched most of his Hall of Fame career for Cleveland. He won 22 to 24 games for them in four consecutive seasons. In 1917 he had a 1.81 ERA, the following year he had a 1.82 ERA, and in 1923 he led the AL in ERA with a 2.76 mark. He also pitched three complete-game wins to lead the Indians to the 1920 World Series championship.

Addie Joss (1902–10) pitched his entire, tragically short, career for Cleveland. He won 20+ games four times, leading the league with a 27-11 record in 1907. He had an amazing lifetime ERA of 1.89, led the AL in 1904 with a 1.59 mark, and led again in 1908 with a very low 1.16. In 1908 he pitched the fourth-ever major league perfect game, needing only 74 pitches to pull it off (he tossed a second no-hitter in 1910). But his career and his life ended suddenly when he died from tuberculous meningitis in 1911 at age 31.

Bob Lemon (1946–58) also pitched his entire Hall of Fame career for the Indians and was an All-Star in seven consecutive seasons. He won 20+ games six times and led the league in wins three times, ending up with an excellent 207-128 record (.618 percentage). He was a workhorse, leading the league in innings pitched four times and complete games five times. And Lemon wasn't the typical easy out at the plate, as he was an outfielder in the minors and so managed to hit .232 with 37 HR in 1,183 at-bats.

Early Wynn (1949–57, '63) was a teammate of Lemon, pitched for the Indians in the middle of his career, and then returned for a brief final season at age 43. He won 20+ games for Cleveland four times, ending up with a 164-102 record (.617 percentage) for the franchise. While with the Indians he led the league in the Triple Crown categories one time each: a 3.20 ERA in 1950, wins with a 23-11 record in 1954, and 184 strikeouts in 1957.

Those first five pitcher selections were pretty easy and straightforward. After considering the relative weakness of the relief pitching candidates, I decided to go with ten starting pitchers for this squad, so I needed to pick five more. The first was hard-throwing **Sam McDowell** (1961–71), who pitched most of his career, and certainly all of his best seasons, for the Indians. A six-time All-Star, he won 20 games for the team only once, in 1970, when he went 20-12. He didn't have nearly as good of a win-loss record as the five Hall of Famers just described, but he did pace the AL with a 2.18 ERA in 1965 and had a 1.81 mark in the pitching-dominant 1968 season. Sudden Sam was best known as a strikeout artist, leading the league five times, including four seasons with 250+ and highs of 325 in 1965 and 304 in 1970. Like Feller before him, McDowell did also walk a lot of batters, leading the league in that category five times, but his overall résumé is more than enough to make him the first left-hander on this All-Time team's pitching staff.

Mel Harder (1928–47) pitched his entire 20-year career for the Indians, including four consecutive All-Star seasons from 1934 through 1937. He won 20+ games twice and 15+ another six times. The only major statistical category he ever led the AL in was ERA, with a 2.95 mark in 1933.

Wes Ferrell (1927–33) started his career for the Indians and won 20+ games in his first four full seasons. His best season was the second of these, when he posted a 25-13 record with a 3.31 ERA. Sometimes used as a pinch-hitter, he was one of the best-hitting pitchers of all-time, batting .274 for the Indians with an impressive 19 HR, 10 triples, 31 doubles, and 100 RBI in 599 at-bats. (I'll note that his W/G statistic above is a bit inflated, as to be consistent with all other pitchers in this book I divided his total WAR by only his games pitched, not the total games he played in.)

Corey Kluber (2011–2018) is the current ace of the Indians, and his strong 2017 and 2018 campaigns earned him a spot on this roster. After a couple of partial seasons, Kluber took home the AL Cy Young Award in 2014 after leading the league in wins with an 18-9 record to go with 269 strikeouts and a 2.44 ERA. In 2017 he earned a second Cy Young Award after posting an 18-4 record, 265 strikeouts, and league-leading 2.25 ERA and 0.869 WHIP. And then 2018 was his fifth consecutive season with 200+ strikeouts, and his first 20-win season.

After considering several candidates, for the tenth spot, I went with **Mike Garcia** (1948–59), who was a teammate of Feller, Lemon, and Wynn, and provided the Indians with 18+ wins four times, including two 20-win seasons. A three-time All-Star, he led the AL with a 2.36 ERA in 1949 and again with a 2.64 ERA in 1954. He pitched all but his final two seasons with Cleveland, ending up with a solid 142-96 record (.597 percentage).

You could make a case for several others, starting with George Uhle (1919–28), who won 20+ games three times, leading the league with a 26-16 record in 1923 and a 27-11 record in 1926. Like Ferrell, he was also a good hitter, batting .289 for the Indians overall. In 1923 he hit .361 and set the record for hits in a season by a pitcher with 52.

Based on peak performance, you could certainly make a strong case for Gaylord Perry (1972–75) over Uhle or Garcia. He was acquired in a trade with the Giants for Sam McDowell—a great deal for the Indians, as it turned out that McDowell's best years were behind him while the future Hall of Famer Perry was still in his prime. He immediately won the AL Cy Young Award in 1972 after posting a 1.92 ERA and 234 strikeouts, while leading the league with 29 complete games and in wins with a 24-16 record. He again led the league with 29 complete games the following year, although his record was only an even

19-19. In 1974 he posted a solid 21-13 record but was traded to the Rangers in June of 1975.

And there were four others whom I gave strong consideration to, starting with Jim Bagby (1916–22), who was a teammate of Coveleski, won 15+ games five times, and had two very strong seasons. In 1917 he went 23-13 with a 1.99 ERA, and in 1920 he provided a 2.89 ERA while leading the league in wins with an impressive 31-12 record. Only Lefty Grove and Denny McLain have won 30+ games in the AL since.

Luis Tiant (1964–69) started his career with the Indians, winning only 10 to 12 games in his first four seasons. He was an All-Star in 1968, ending the season with a 21-9 record and a league-leading 9 shutouts and 1.60 ERA. He lost his control the following year and saw his walks total climb from 73 to a league-leading 129. He ended that year with a poor 9-20 record and was traded in the off-season to the Minnesota Twins.

CC Sabathia (2001–08) started his fine career with Cleveland and was a good, if not outstanding, pitcher until 2007, when he took home the AL Cy Young Award after going 19-7 with a 3.21 ERA and 209 strikeouts. He didn't start out well the following year and so was dealt to the contending Brewers, where he went on to finish strong with an 11-2 record and 1.65 ERA. The Indians received four players in return, one of whom, outfielder Michael Brantley, made the deal worthwhile for the Indians.

Willis Hudlin (1926–40) pitched a long time for Cleveland and won 15 to 18 games for the Indians five times. He was mostly a starter but also pitched over 150 games in relief and ended up with a less-than-impressive 4.34 ERA for the franchise.

There were a few others who deserve brief mention, including (in chronological order):

- Vean Gregg (1911–14) had a short career, but it started out with four strong seasons for Cleveland. In his rookie year in 1911, he led the AL with a 1.80 ERA to go with a 23-7 record. He posted a 20-13 record the next two years, along with solid ERAs of 2.59 and 2.24. And in case you are wondering, Vean was short for Sylveanus.

- Tom Candiotti (1986–91, '99) pitched early in his long career for the Indians, using his knuckleball to have four seasons of 13 to 16 wins. He led the AL with 17 complete games in his first full season in 1986, though he faltered the next year with a nasty 7-18 record.

- Charles Nagy (1990–2002) pitched all but his last five games for the Indians, including six seasons with 15 to 17 wins. He had a modest 4.51 ERA but was an All-Star three times.

- Bartolo Colon (1997–2002) started his very long career with the Indians, winning 14 to 18 games in each of his first four seasons, and even getting 200+ strikeouts twice. In 2002 he went 10-4 with a 2.55 ERA in the first half of the season before being traded to the Expos for an impressive package of prospects that included future stars Cliff Lee, Brandon Phillips, and Grady Sizemore.

Relief Pitching

Name	YR	WAR	W3	SV	W-L	ERA	WHIP	ERA+
Doug Jones	7	10.9	8.4	129	27-34	3.06	1.227	137
José Mesa	7	10.7	7.5	104	33-36	3.88	1.361	116
Eric Plunk	7	10.2	7.3	26	36-23	3.25	1.320	140
Cody Allen	7	8.9	5.8	149	24-29	2.98	1.189	142
Mike Jackson	3	6.1	6.1	94	6-10	2.99	1.108	161
Bob Wickman	6	5.5	5.3	139	8-16	3.23	1.317	138

As noted in this chapter's introductory remarks, relief pitching has rarely been a position of major strength for the Indians. As a result, I decided to include only my imposed minimum of two relievers on this All-Time team's pitching staff. After nine years as both a starter and reliever in the minors, **Doug Jones** (1986–91, '98) joined the Indians and quickly became their closer. He was an All-Star from 1988 through 1990, notching 37 saves with a 2.27 ERA, 32 saves with a 2.34 ERA, and then 43 saves with a 2.56 ERA.

José Mesa (1992–98) also served as the Tribe's primary closer for three years and was an All-Star in two of them. In fact, his 1995 season was good enough to earn him second place in the AL Cy Young Award vote, after he posted a 1.13 ERA with a league-leading 46 saves.

Bob Wickman (2000–02, '04–06) is actually the all-time leader in saves (139) for this franchise, and he did have two fine seasons: in 2001, he posted 32 saves with a 2.39 ERA, and in his one All-Star season in 2005, he had a 2.47 ERA and led the AL with 45 saves. Michael Jackson (1997–99) was the closer in Cleveland for three years, but he was particularly impressive only in 1998, when he recorded 40 saves with a 1.55 ERA. Eric Plunk (1992–98) was a capable setup man for the Indians for several years, grabbing 15 saves in 1993, his first of four consecutive seasons with a sub-3.00 ERA. And lastly, current

Indians reliever Cody Allen (2012–18) seemed on track to one day make this roster. He has posted between 24 and 34 saves each year from 2014 through '18, but he also had a troubling 4.70 ERA in 2018.

Managers

Name	YR	From-To	W-L	PCT	PS	WS
Tris Speaker	8	1919–26	617-520	.543	1	1
Lou Boudreau	9	1942–50	728-649	.529	1	1
Al López	6	1951–56	570-354	.617	1	0
Mike Hargrove	9	1991–99	721-591	.550	5	0
Terry Francona	6	2013–18	545-425	.562	4	0
Nap Lajoie	5	1905–09	377-309	.550	0	0
Eric Wedge	7	2003–09	561-573	.495	1	0
Roger Peckinpaugh	7	1928–41	490-481	.505	0	0

For top manager, you could make a case for any of four different guys. I decided to rate at the top the two who won World Series championships as players/managers: **Tris Speaker** and **Lou Boudreau**. Next up, **Al López** had an impressive .617 winning percentage, and **Mike Hargrove** is second in all-time wins as a manager for this franchise. And current manager Terry Francona could crack this top four if the Indians keep having success.

Starting Lineup

What would mythical starting lineups look like for this All-Time roster?

Against RHP:	Against LHP:
Tris Speaker CF (L)	Tris Speaker CF (L)
Joe Jackson RF (L)	Joe Jackson RF (L)
Nap Lajoie 2B (R)	Nap Lajoie 2B (R)
Jim Thome 1B (L)	Manny Ramírez DH (R)
Larry Doby DH (L)	Albert Belle LF (R)
Albert Belle LF (R)	Al Rosen 3B (R)
Al Rosen 3B (R)	Jim Thome 1B (L)
Joe Sewell SS (L)	Lou Boudreau SS (R)
Victor Martinez C (S)	Victor Martinez C (S)

There were no natural platoons at 1B, 3B, and C, but you could swap out Thome/Trosky, Rosen/Keltner, and Martinez/Santana as you think best. There was, however, a natural platoon at SS, so I listed both Boudreau and Sewell in the above lineups (even though they both could hit righties and lefties pretty evenly). I found lots of options for how to fill the DH spot—I went with Doby against RHP and Ramírez against LHP. This all leaves Averill as a great bat off the bench, and Lofton as an outstanding pinch-runner. These are impressive lineups when you consider the high-average hitters in spots 1–3, and then the power bats that follow in spots 4–7.

Depth Chart

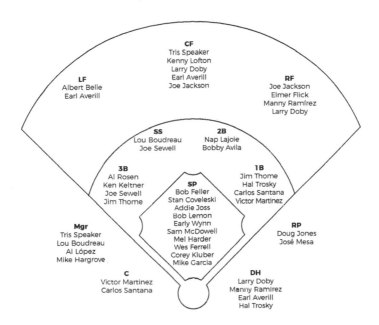

CF
Tris Speaker
Kenny Lofton
Larry Doby
Earl Averill
Joe Jackson

LF
Albert Belle
Earl Averill

RF
Joe Jackson
Elmer Flick
Manny Ramírez
Larry Doby

SS
Lou Boudreau
Joe Sewell

2B
Nap Lajoie
Bobby Avila

3B
Al Rosen
Ken Keltner
Joe Sewell
Jim Thome

SP
Bob Feller
Stan Coveleski
Addie Joss
Bob Lemon
Early Wynn
Sam McDowell
Mel Harder
Wes Ferrell
Corey Kluber
Mike Garcia

1B
Jim Thome
Hal Trosky
Carlos Santana
Victor Martinez

Mgr
Tris Speaker
Lou Boudreau
Al López
Mike Hargrove

RP
Doug Jones
José Mesa

C
Victor Martinez
Carlos Santana

DH
Larry Doby
Manny Ramírez
Earl Averill
Hal Trosky

Prospects for Current Players

What are the prospects of current Indians players making this All-Time team? Kluber is already on the roster. The two young superstars, Lindor and Ramírez, are quickly demanding consideration, and veterans Kipnis, Brantley, and Allen are getting closer too. We'll see...

Indians Retired Player Numbers

Earl Averill (3), Lou Boudreau (5), Larry Doby (14), Mel Harder (18), Bob Feller (19), Frank Robinson (20), Bob Lemon (21), Jim Thome (25)

Selections from Other Authors and Fan Surveys

1958: *Sport* magazine, August issue

As part of a running series, *Sport* magazine reported on all-time all-star teams picked by "big league publicity departments and the writers covering the clubs." Here is what they had to say:

First Base: Hal Trosky, the big slugger who played for the Indians from 1933 through 1941.

Second Base: The great Napoleon Lajoie, a Cleveland star from 1902 through 1914.

Third Base: Ken Keltner, the long-ball hitting, slick-fielding infielder who arrived there in 1937 and stayed through 1949.

Shortstop: Lou Boudreau, an all-time favorite at the Stadium, who played there from 1938 through 1950, and managed the team in the years 1942-50.

Left Field: Earl Averill, a feared slugger there from 1929-39.

Center Field: Tris Speaker, "The Gray Eagle," who is still rated by many as the greatest of all centerfielders. He played with the Indians from 1916 through 1926, and managed them from 1919 to 1926.

Right Field: Shoeless Joe Jackson, the man whom old-timers still call the greatest "natural hitter" they have ever seen. He served in Cleveland from 1910 until 1915, before moving on to Chicago where he was trapped in the Black Sox Scandal of 1919.

Catcher: Steve O'Neill, a Tribe mainstay from 1911 through 1923.

Pitcher: Denton T. "Cy" Young, who pitched for the Indians in the years 1890-98 and 1909-11, and wound up winning more games than any other pitcher who ever lived—511 by the records, 512 by his own count.

Back in 1958 this was a solid all-time team lineup, with two exceptions. The lesser concern is listing Averill as a LF when he mostly played RF. But assuming this was meant to be a Cleveland Indians all-time team, and not a "Cleveland" all-time team, then Cy Young shouldn't have been chosen as the pitcher. As noted, he pitched parts of three seasons for the Indians late in his career, but all of his great seasons from 1890 through 1898 were for the Cleveland Spiders of the National League—a completely different franchise.

1969: *The Sporting News* Fan Poll

The July 5, 1969, issue reported the results of a fan poll for the long-standing franchises of the day. The results for the Indians were: 1B Trosky, 2B Lajoie, 3B Keltner, SS Boudreau, C O'Neill, LF Jamieson, CF Speaker, RF Jackson, RHP Feller, LHP Gregg.

These were pretty good selections overall, although I would have chosen Heath over Jamieson for LF. And while a case could already have been made in July of 1969 for Sam McDowell for the LHP spot, the choice of Vean Gregg was an interesting one.

1990: "All-Time All-Star Teams," in *The Baseball Research Journal*

In an interesting article, Robert C. Berlo used Thorn and Palmer's TPR (Total Player Rating) system to choose all-time teams. He selected players based on their best 800 consecutive games for the franchise, with a minimum of five years played. His results: 1B Thornton, 2B Lajoie, SS Boudreau, 3B Bradley, RF Jackson, CF Speaker, LF Flick, C Romano, with SP Joss, Feller, Lemon, and Ferrell, and Steve Gromek as the reliever.

It was a little odd to see Elmer Flick listed as the top LF, since he played only 9 games as a LF in his entire career. And I didn't mention Steve Gromek earlier, but he pitched for Cleveland from 1941 through '53 as a mixed starter and reliever. He had a fine season in 1945, when he went 19-9 with a 2.55 ERA. He was used in a variety of relief roles but rarely at the end of games, as he saved only 16 games for the Indians.

1992: *The All-Time All-Star Baseball Book*, by Nick Acocella and Donald Dewey

The authors chose an all-time lineup composed of Trosky, Lajoie, Rosen, Boudreau, Doby, Speaker, Jamieson, O'Neill, and Feller. Since they didn't indicate separate OF positions, I think the choice of Jamieson over Averill was definitely a mistake. They didn't even include Averill in their honorable mention list, instead naming only Coveleski, Bagby, Keltner, Lemon, Wynn, Hegan, and Colavito.

1995: *Baseball Ratings*, by Charles F. Faber

The Faber system in 1995 produced a pretty good all-time lineup of Trosky, Lajoie, Boudreau, Keltner, Hegan, Speaker, Averill, and Doby. The top five pitchers were Feller, Lemon, Joss, Harder, and Coveleski, and the top reliever was Jones.

2003: *Rob Neyer's Big Book of Baseball Lineups*, **by Rob Neyer**

Neyer went with Hegan and O'Neill as his two catchers, and of course Thome and Trosky at 1B. I agree with his other infield selections of Boudreau and Sewell at SS and Rosen and Keltner at 3B, and he opted for peak performance over longevity with the club by selecting Alomar over Avila as the backup to Lajoie at 2B.

Neyer's starting outfield was Belle, Speaker, and Jackson and his backups were solid with Heath, Averill, and Ramírez. All ten of his pitching selections were good ones too: Feller, Joss, Coveleski, Lemon, Harder, Wynn, McDowell, and Garcia, with Jones and Mesa as the two relief pitchers. And his top five managers were Hargrove, López, Speaker, Boudreau, and Gordon.

2016: *101 All-Time Fantasy Baseball Teams*, **by Jack Sweeney**

Sweeney's lineup was pretty solid with Thome, Lajoie, Rosen, Boudreau, Doby, Speaker, Colavito, Martinez, and Averill (listed as the DH). He chose four starting pitchers: Feller, Wynn, Lemon, and Coveleski, and then honored the long career of Harder by listing him in the relief pitcher spot.

Top WAR Single Seasons – Hitters (8+)

Name	Year	WAR	AVG	HR	R	RBI	SB	OPS+
Lou Boudreau	1948	10.4	.355	18	116	106	3	165
Al Rosen	1953	10.1	.336	43	115	145	8	180
Nap Lajoie	1906	10.0	.355	0	88	91	20	170
Nap Lajoie	1910	9.8	.384	4	94	76	26	199
Joe Jackson	1912	9.6	.395	3	121	90	35	192
Terry Turner	1906	9.4	.291	2	85	62	27	124
Joe Jackson	1911	9.2	.408	7	126	83	41	193
Tris Speaker	1923	9.0	.380	17	133	130	8	182
Tris Speaker	1916	8.7	.386	2	102	79	35	186
Nap Lajoie	1904	8.6	.376	5	92	102	29	203
Tris Speaker	1920	8.5	.388	8	137	107	10	172
Nap Lajoie	1903	8.0	.344	7	90	93	21	169
Lou Boudreau	1944	8.0	.327	3	91	67	11	145

No surprise to see Lajoie on this list four times, Speaker three times, and Jackson and Boudreau twice. The one that required some investigation was Terry Turner's 1906 season, which although arguably his best offensively, doesn't compare well with the others shown here. The explanation is that he got credit for very strong defense that year, to the tune of a 5.4 dWAR score. And lastly I'll note that the outstanding 2018 seasons by Lindor and Ramírez came very close to making this list, as each had a 7.9 WAR score.

Top WAR Single Seasons – Pitchers (8+)

Name	Year	WAR	W-L	ERA	IP	SO	ERA+
Gaylord Perry	1972	11.2	24-16	1.92	342.2	234	168
Bob Feller	1940	9.8	27-11	2.61	320.1	261	163
Bob Feller	1939	9.8	24-9	2.85	296.2	246	154
Bob Feller	1946	9.6	26-15	2.18	371.1	348	151
Stan Coveleski	1918	9.4	22-13	1.82	311.0	87	164
Wes Ferrell	1930	9.1	25-13	3.31	296.2	143	145
Jim Bagby	1920	8.9	31-12	2.89	339.2	73	133
Vean Gregg	1911	8.8	23-7	1.80	244.2	125	189
George Uhle	1926	8.7	27-11	2.83	318.1	159	144
Stan Coveleski	1920	8.7	24-14	2.49	315.0	133	154
Jim Bagby	1917	8.7	23-13	1.99	320.2	83	142
Gaylord Perry	1974	8.6	21-13	2.51	322.1	216	144
Addie Joss	1908	8.4	24-11	1.16	325.0	130	204
Early Wynn	1956	8.3	20-9	2.72	277.2	158	154
Bob Feller	1941	8.1	25-13	3.15	343.0	260	125
Corey Kluber	2017	8.1	18-4	2.25	203.2	265	202
Wes Ferrell	1931	8.0	22-12	3.75	276.1	123	123

Bob Feller appears four times on this list, including three of the top four with only Gaylord Perry's outstanding 1972 campaign rating higher. Perry's strong 1974 season also made the list, with Coveleski, Ferrell, and Bagby being the others with two appearances here.

Franchise Player

It would be hard to choose between Tris Speaker and Nap Lajoie, who were great offensively and defensively, and who both had success while managing the team too. I instead gave this honor to career-Indians hurler Bob Feller. I was impressed by the fact that he led the league so many times in wins and strikeouts, and no doubt would have a few more times if he hadn't lost most of four prime years to the war.

CHAPTER 8

The Tigers Franchise All-Time Dream Team

The Detroit Tigers were one of the charter clubs of the new American League when it was formed in 1901. That was an exciting time in Detroit, as the new "horseless carriage" was all the rage and would soon propel the city into becoming a manufacturing leader in the United States. Unfortunately, the Tigers didn't find success immediately, failing to place better than 3rd in their first six seasons. Ty Cobb's first full season in 1907 helped to change things, and they won the AL pennant for three consecutive seasons (though failed in the World Series each time).

From 1910 to 1933 they had more winning seasons than losing ones, but never took first place in their league until 1934, when freshly imported catcher and manager Mickey Cochrane led the G-Men (Hank Greenberg, Charlie Gehringer, and Goose Goslin) to a 101-53 record. They lost the World Series to the Cardinals, but then managed to take their first championship the following season by defeating the Cubs four games to two. Greenberg and Gehringer again led the club to a pennant in 1940, and in 1945 a less impressive lineup rode the dominance of pitching ace Hal Newhouser to take the franchise's second World Series title.

After a couple of decades with mixed results, the Tigers again achieved the sport's ultimate success by winning the World Series in 1968, again behind an outstanding ace in Denny McLain (who that year achieved baseball's last 30-win season).

The next positive era for the Tigers began in 1979 when Sparky Anderson became manager. The team steadily built up a good core of players, and this led to an outstanding 104-58 championship-winning club in 1984. They again won their division in 1987, but then entered a stretch with 15 of 18 losing seasons (including an amazingly poor 43-119 record in 2003). They saw success in 2006 when they took the AL Wild Card and ended up going to the World Series—only to lose to the Cardinals in five games—and then again in 2012, when they won the AL Central Division before losing to the Giants in the World Series.

As you will see, the All-Time Tigers team is full of great hitters, while the pitching staff, relatively speaking, isn't quite as strong.

1st Base

Name	YR	WAR	W3	W/G	AVG	HR	SB	OPS+
Hank Greenberg	12	54.1	22.4	.0426	.319	306	58	161
Norm Cash	15	51.7	18.8	.0256	.272	373	42	139
Miguel Cabrera	11	51.2	22.0	.0332	.318	327	21	155
Rudy York	10	31.6	16.2	.0249	.282	239	34	128
Lu Blue	7	20.8	10.6	.0225	.295	19	85	110
Cecil Fielder	7	16.8	12.9	.0171	.258	245	2	126
Tony Clark	7	12.2	9.5	.0158	.277	156	6	121

Hank Greenberg (1930, 1933–41, 1945–47) played all but his final season for Detroit, putting up some monster numbers, starting with leading the league in doubles in 1934 with an amazing 63. He led the league in HR (36) and RBI (170) the next year and topped the AL in RBI three other times: an incredible 183 in 1937, 150 in 1940, and 127 in 1946. He also led the league in HR three additional times, with 58 in 1938, 41 in 1940, and 44 in 1946. He scored 100+ runs six times and ended his 9+ Tigers seasons with a .319 average, 306 HR, 1,200 RBI, a .412 OBP, and a .616 SLG. He took home two MVP awards, in 1935 and 1940. He also lost more than three full seasons to World War II, so just imagine what his numbers could have been!

At this point, I would actually rate Miguel Cabrera as the second-best 1B for the All-Time Tigers. However, as he played a few seasons at 3B, and the candidates for this dream team roster are not nearly as strong at that position, I decided to choose him as the top at that position instead.

So that means that the backup to Greenberg was **Norm Cash** (1960–74). He had a career year that would turn out to be a fluke—a statistical height he'd never reach again (and he later confessed to corking his bat that season). At the age of 26 in 1961, in his first full season in the majors, Cash led the league with 193 hits, a .361 batting average, and a fantastic .487 OBP. He never led the AL in any major offensive category again, though he was a consistent slugger, hitting 20+ HR 11 times. Other than his first two partial seasons, he played his entire career in Detroit, was solid at first base defensively, and was an All-Star four times.

Rudy York (1934, 1937–45) started his career primarily as a catcher but switched to 1B for Detroit in 1940, when Greenberg shifted to the outfield, and then during the war years that followed. Another great slugger, York was a seven-time All-Star who hit 30+ HR four times and had 100+ RBI five times in Detroit. He burst onto the scene in 1937, smacking 35 HR and 103 RBI in only 375 at-bats. In 1943 he paced the AL with 34 HR and 118 RBI, placing third in the MVP balloting. Not a particularly good fielder, he ranked first or second in errors at 1B every year from 1941 through '45. But overall, his résumé was strong enough to earn him one of the two "extra spots" on this All-Time team.

A few others deserve brief mention, starting with Lu Blue (1921–27), who was a .295 hitter during his time in Detroit, walking enough to post a .403 OBP. Cecil Fielder (1990–96) found fame in Detroit after a one-season stint in Japan. He came back to the US and promptly became the first hitter to smash 50+ HR in over a decade when he led the AL with 51 in 1990. He again led with 44 the following year, and managed to lead in RBI both seasons and the next as well. Big Daddy was the archetype of an all-or-nothing swinger, as during his seven seasons he put up 245 dingers, but also struck out 926 times. And lastly, Tony Clark (1995–2001) basically took over for Fielder in both regards, hitting between 27 and 34 HR in four consecutive seasons, but also striking out 125+ times in each.

2nd Base

Name	YR	WAR	W3	W/G	AVG	HR	SB	OPS+
Charlie Gehringer	19	80.6	23.6	.0347	.320	184	181	124
Lou Whitaker	19	74.9	18.8	.0313	.276	244	143	117
Dick McAuliffe	14	37.5	16.7	.0226	.249	192	61	111
Plácido Polanco	5	19.1	14.8	.0302	.311	37	26	103
Ian Kinsler	4	19.9	17.8	.0328	.275	78	53	107
Damion Easley	7	17.7	12.6	.0210	.260	104	81	101

Second base was also a position of strength for this All-Time team, starting with Hall of Famer and lifetime Detroit Tiger **Charlie Gehringer** (1924–42). One of the greatest ever at the position, he hit .320 with a .404 OBP, 2,839 hits, 184 HR, 181 SB, 1,427 RBI, and 1,774 runs. It's hard to determine his best overall season, but in 1929 he hit .339 and led the AL in five categories: 131 runs, 215 hits, 45 doubles, 19 triples, and 27 SB. In 1934 he hit .356 and led the league with 134 runs and 214 hits. Then in 1936 he hit .354 and led the league with 60 doubles. And finally, in 1937, he took home his only batting crown (.371) and won the MVP Award. The Mechanical Man was a great defender too, and surely would have won several Gold Glove Awards had they existed during his era, as he led AL second basemen in fielding percentage six times and ranked second another four times.

Another lifetime Tiger 2B would have been a great choice as the starter for this roster if Gehringer weren't in his way. **Lou Whitaker** (1977–1995) was one half of the double-play tandem, with Alan Trammell, that delighted Tigers fans for years. He had some pop in his bat, hitting 20+ HR four times, although never managing more than 85 RBI. He scored 90+ runs six times. Although his numbers weren't particularly impressive (.285, 3 HR), he was voted the top rookie in the AL in 1978, and then went on to be an All-Star five times and win three Gold Glove Awards.

Dick McAuliffe (1960–73) was almost a lifetime Tiger, but he finished his solid career in Boston. He too had some power for a middle infielder, hitting 20+ HR three times, and managed to lead the AL in runs scored with 95 in their championship 1968 season. Not a high-average hitter (.249), he was an All-Star three times. A good fielder, he played more often at 2B, but he also saw significant action at SS. Overall, his accomplishments were enough to warrant one of the two "extra spots" on this All-Time team roster.

A few others deserve brief mention, starting with Plácido Polanco (2005–09), who had little power or speed but was a solid hitter, providing a .311 batting average. He was also an outstanding fielder, taking home Gold Glove Awards in 2007 and 2009 for the Tigers. Prior to Polanco, Damion Easley (1996–2002) had been playing 2B (and some SS) for the Tigers, providing both some power and speed. He had 22 HR and 28 SB in 1997, and then was an All-Star in 1998, when he hit 38 doubles and 27 HR, with 100 RBI and 15 SB. And finally, Ian Kinsler (2014–17) had four pretty good seasons in Detroit after coming over from the Texas Rangers in a trade for Prince Fielder. Providing both power and speed, Kinsler's best season for the Tigers came in 2016, when he scored 117 runs, with 28 HR and 14 SB, while taking home the Gold Glove Award too. However, after the 2017 season he left the Tigers for the Angels, so it seems he won't add to his résumé for this All-Time team.

3rd Base

Name	YR	WAR	W3	W/G	AVG	HR	SB	OPS+
Miguel Cabrera	11	51.2	22.0	.0332	.318	327	21	155
Travis Fryman	8	27.4	13.9	.0250	.274	149	58	106
George Kell	7	22.8	13.9	.0276	.325	25	34	119
Brandon Inge	12	18.5	11.2	.0131	.234	140	45	83
Ray Boone	6	16.4	12.5	.0240	.291	105	8	130
Pinky Higgins	7	11.3	8.3	.0132	.280	60	25	102
Don Wert	8	10.3	7.9	.0094	.244	77	22	88
Aurelio Rodríguez	9	9.2	6.8	.0074	.239	85	13	76

The weakest position in Tigers history no doubt is third base. That said, as I noted earlier, **Miguel Cabrera** (2008–18) played a few seasons as the Tigers' full-time 3B—including his two MVP seasons—so I elected to include him as the starter here. After having several great seasons for the Marlins, Cabrera led the AL with 37 HR in his first season with the Tigers. He led the AL with a .344 average in 2011, and then became the first player in 45 years to win the Triple Crown, when in 2012 he led the AL with a .330 average, 44 HR, and 139 RBI. Miggy has led the league in batting average four times, and has hit 30+ HR seven times for the Tigers.

The choice for the backup at 3B was a close call, but I went with **George Kell** (1946–52). Playing for five franchises, Kell played about half his career—including several of his best seasons—for the Tigers. In 1949 he led the AL with a .343 average, and then paced the league the following two seasons in both hits and doubles, including 56 two-baggers in 1950. That year was probably his best overall, as he hit .340, scored 114 runs, and provided 101 RBI even while hitting only 8 HR. He ended his time in Detroit with a strong .325 batting average and was an All-Star in five consecutive seasons.

One could make a case for Travis Fryman (1990–97) as the backup over Kell, but in my view he came up a little short. Leaving aside his partial rookie campaign, Fryman hit 15 to 22 HR in his seven other seasons as a Tiger. A four-time All-Star for Detroit, he played some SS in addition to his fine glove work at 3B. According to career WAR for the Tigers, Fryman is ahead of Kell. They are tied for their top three WAR seasons, and Kell is only slightly higher on a WAR-per-game basis. But Kell was an All-Star one more time for the Tigers, and Fryman never led the AL in any major categories.

A handful of others deserve brief mention, starting with Ray Boone (1953–58), who played parts of six seasons for Detroit and hit 20+ HR in four of them. He led the league in RBI with 116 in 1955 and was an All-Star twice.

Brandon Inge (2001–12) showed valuable versatility, playing mostly at 3B but also significant time at catcher and even some outfield too. He hit 27 HR in both 2006 and 2009, though his .237 average and .307 OBP weren't as helpful to the club.

Light-hitting, good-fielding Aurelio Rodríguez (1971–79) actually played more games at 3B than anyone else in Tigers history. Although he provided a little power, his .239 average and anemic .274 OBP never impressed anyone. He won the Gold Glove Award in 1976 and was regularly amongst the leaders in fielding percentage for his position. Michael Franklin "Pinky" Higgins (1939–44) was a solid contributor during the war years, providing 70+ RBI every season he played in Detroit. And lastly, Don Wert (1963–70) played most of his career for the Tigers and provided some pop but a low batting average (.242).

Shortstop

Name	YR	WAR	W3	W/G	AVG	HR	SB	OPS+
Alan Trammell	20	70.4	21.6	.0307	.285	185	236	110
Donie Bush	14	38.5	17.6	.0206	.250	9	402	92
Billy Rogell	10	24.8	15.2	.0205	.274	39	76	89
Harvey Kuenn	8	21.0	12.1	.0200	.314	53	51	112
Carlos Guillén	8	18.7	13.7	.0229	.297	95	59	121

The other half of the long-time double-play tandem, Hall of Famer **Alan Trammell** (1977–96), was the clear starter here. Like Whitaker, he played his entire career for the Tigers. A six-time All-Star and four-time Gold Glove winner, Trammell showed little power until the mid-1980s. In 1987 he batted .343 with 28 HR and 105 RBI en route to a second-place finish in the MVP voting. He also had some speed, swiping 236 bases with a high of 30 in 1983.

For the backup spot, **Donie Bush** (1908–21) was the pretty clear choice, as he played most of his career for the Tigers, showing solid speed by swiping 30 or more bases in eight seasons. He scored 100+ runs four times and had 90+ another four times. He did this in part because of his ability to draw walks, a category in which he led the league five times, which aided his rather low .250 batting average.

I also considered Harvey Kuenn (1952–59) as the backup, as he played the first half of his career with Detroit. He took Rookie of the Year honors in 1953, when he hit .308 with 209 hits. Although he didn't display much speed or power, he led the AL in hits four times, doubles three times, and led the league with a .353 average in 1959. His .314 average for the Tigers earned him an All-Star team selection in all seven of his full seasons, the last two of which he was used in CF and RF, respectively.

Billy Rogell (1930–39) was a good fielder who played most of his career in Detroit. He had his best year in 1934, when he hit .296, scored 114 runs, and provided 100 RBI while hitting just 3 HR. And lastly, in more recent years Carlos Guillén (2004–11) put up some good numbers while playing a variety of positions (but primarily SS). A .297 hitter, he provided moderate power and speed and was an All-Star three times.

Catcher

Name	YR	WAR	W3	W/G	AVG	HR	SB	OPS+
Bill Freehan	15	44.7	18.3	.0252	.262	200	24	112
Lance Parrish	10	29.9	13.7	.0261	.263	212	22	114
Johnny Bassler	7	19.5	10.9	.0254	.308	1	10	106
Mickey Tettleton	4	14.8	13.3	.0260	.249	112	6	135
Iván Rodríguez	5	14.2	10.4	.0232	.298	62	30	103
Mickey Cochrane	4	11.4	10.2	.0362	.313	11	14	126

The top catcher for this roster was **Bill Freehan** (1961, '63–76), the Detroit native who played his entire career for the Tigers. He generally provided 15 to 20 HR each year (solid given the pitching-dominant era he played in), but arguably was even more valuable as a defender. He won five Gold Glove Awards and was an All-Star 11 times. A key part of their 1968 World Championship club, Freehan hit 25 HR with 84 RBI that season, which was good enough for second in the MVP voting (battery-mate McLain took home the honors).

The backup clearly was **Lance Parrish** (1977–86), another outstanding defensive catcher with power. He hit 30+ HR twice for the Tigers and 20+ four other times. In their championship 1984 season, he smashed 33 HR with 98 RBI (though he hit only .237). He took home three Gold Glove Awards and was an All-Star six times as a Tiger.

There were various other Tigers catchers I considered, starting with Mickey Tettleton (1991–94), who had three consecutive 30+ HR seasons for the Tigers as a C/DH/OF/1B. Iván Rodríguez (2004–08) brought his outstanding defense to Detroit, was an All-Star four times, and won three Gold Glove Awards as a Tiger. He hit .334 with 19 HR and 86 RBI in his first season in Detroit, but didn't produce nearly as well after that. And Johnny Bassler (1921–27) was a pretty good hitter back in the day; he managed a .308 average and .420 OBP in his seven years in Detroit, though he had no power (only 1 HR in 2,240 at-bats).

Lastly, Mickey Cochrane (1934–37) played for the Tigers for two full and two partial seasons as a player-manager (and one more as manager only) at the end of his Hall of Fame career. With the Tigers, his power was largely gone, but he could still hit (.313). When he joined the club in 1934, he promptly led them to a 101-53 season and the AL pennant, earning the league's MVP Award (barely besting teammate Gehringer in the vote, in a year when the Yankees' Lou Gehrig won the Triple Crown). The next year Cochrane did even better by guiding the Tigers to the World Series championship.

Left Field

Name	YR	WAR	W3	W/G	AVG	HR	SB	OPS+
Bobby Veach	12	45.8	18.6	.0286	.311	59	189	130
Willie Horton	15	25.9	11.9	.0171	.276	262	14	127
Tony Phillips	5	25.2	15.8	.0349	.281	61	70	120
Bobby Higginson	11	23.0	12.3	.0169	.272	187	91	113
Charlie Maxwell	8	19.2	13.8	.0225	.268	133	15	120
Rocky Colavito	4	17.3	16.2	.0275	.271	139	6	130

LF was the weakest of the three OF positions for this All-Time team, as only **Bobby Veach** (1912–23) was clearly deserving of a roster spot. He batted .310 and like many players of his era had mostly triples power, hitting 10+ triples in ten consecutive seasons. He led the league in triples with 17 in 1919, and led the league in doubles twice and RBI three times. All that and he was outstanding defensively as well.

You could make a case that fan favorite and Detroit native Willie Horton (1963–77) deserves a spot on this dream team. This would be based in part on his longevity with the club, but that's not to say he didn't put up some strong numbers: .276, 262 HR, 886 RBI. A four-time All-Star, he hit 20+ HR in six seasons for the Tigers.

The insanely versatile Tony Phillips (1990–94) started his career with the A's but signed with Detroit as a free agent after the 1989 season. He displayed double-digit HR power and double-digit SB speed, all while spreading his playing time around LF, 3B, 2B, RF, SS, DH, and CF. In fact, in 1991 he became the first player to play at least ten games at five different positions (2B, 3B, SS, OF, DH—and he played all three OF positions: 25 in LF, 23 in RF, and 9 in CF).

Bobby Higginson (1995–2005) played his entire career for the Tigers and showed some good pop, hitting 20+ HR four times, as well as the ability to steal a few bases. His best season statistically was 2000, when he hit .300 with 44 doubles, 30 HR, 104 runs, 102 RBI, and 15 SB.

Charlie Maxwell (1955–62) had his best seasons while with Detroit, including two as an All-Star and four with 20+ HR. And lastly, Rocky Colavito

(1960–63) played four years in Detroit during the middle of his career. An All-Star in two of those seasons, his best numbers came in 1961, when he hit .290 with 45 HR, 140 RBI, and 129 runs.

Center Field

Name	YR	WAR	W3	W/G	AVG	HR	SB	OPS+
Ty Cobb	22	144.8	32.5	.0516	.368	111	869	171
Chet Lemon	9	30.6	16.4	.0254	.263	142	13	117
Curtis Granderson	6	21.2	15.8	.0314	.272	102	67	114
Austin Jackson	5	20.7	15.4	.0309	.277	46	78	105
Mickey Stanley	15	17.3	8.1	.0114	.248	117	44	90
Ron LeFlore	6	14.1	12.4	.0179	.297	51	294	108
Gee Walker	7	11.7	9.1	.0147	.317	61	132	108

Regardless of what you think of Ty Cobb the man, **Ty Cobb** (1905–26) the ballplayer was clearly the top outfielder in Tigers history (and one of the best from any team). Cobb played all but his final two seasons for Detroit, and over that time he accumulated 3,900 hits, 665 doubles, 284 triples, 111 HR, 2,088 runs, 1,805 RBI, 869 SB, and hit .368 with a .433 OBP. In terms of leading his peers, try these on for size: he led the AL in runs five times, hits eight times, doubles three times, triples four times, RBI four times, SB six times, and even HR once with 9 in 1909. Most impressively, The Georgia Peach won 11 batting titles for the Tigers, with his best averages including .420, .409, .401, .390, .384, .383 (twice), and .382. His most impressive single-season numbers came in 1911, when he hit .420 and led the league with all of the following: 248 hits, 147 runs, 47 doubles, 24 triples, 127 RBI, and 83 SB. He didn't produce nearly as well in the three World Series Detroit played in (and lost) from 1907 through 1909, as he hit a mere .262 with only five extra-base hits in 65 at-bats. But aside from that, Cobb's production was simply awesome.

A distant second place amongst outfielders who primarily played CF for the Tigers would be Chet Lemon (1982–90). Traded from the White Sox after the strike-shortened 1981 season, Lemon provided 20+ HR three times. Although he never won a Gold Glove, he covered a lot of ground in center field for the Tigers.

Next up are two center fielders who were traded for each other, Curtis Granderson (2004–09) and Austin Jackson (2010–14). Granderson started his career with the Tigers, providing a good combination of power and speed. He hit 30 HR for them in 2009, but his 2007 season was his most impressive, as he scored 122 runs, hit 23 HR, stole 26 bases, hit .302, and smacked an impressive and league-leading 23 triples. He was traded as part of a three-team deal to the Yankees, and the Tigers got back Jackson, who made an immediate impact as a rookie for the Tigers in 2010 by hitting .293 with 27 SB and 103 runs scored. He then led the AL with 11 triples the following year, and again with 10 the season after that. According to their WAR numbers, it would seem this was just a fairly even swap of center fielders for the Tigers—except Detroit also got pitcher Max Scherzer (from Arizona) as part of the three-way deal.

Ron LeFlore (1974–79) hit .297 and ran a lot for the Tigers for six seasons. He managed 294 stolen bases, including 68 to lead the AL in 1978 and then 78 the next year (and a whopping 97 the year after that for Montreal). He also scored 100+ runs three times, including a league-leading 126 in 1978.

Gee Walker (1931–37) played the first half of his career for the Tigers. He had little power but solid speed, with 20+ SB four times. He was a good hitter, batting .317 for Detroit, including a .353 average with 55 doubles in 1936. He was an All-Star the following season and it was his overall best: .335, 213 hits, 18 HR, 105 runs, 113 RBI, and 23 SB.

Mickey Stanley (1964–78) was a lifetime Tiger but played in 100+ games in only seven seasons. He had little power or speed, and batted only .248, but was a good center fielder, taking home four Gold Glove Awards. He was also quite versatile: he played the vast majority of games in CF, but he played at least a few games at every position on the diamond except catcher and pitcher.

Right Field

Name	YR	WAR	W3	W/G	AVG	HR	SB	OPS+
Al Kaline	22	92.5	24.1	.0326	.297	399	137	134
Harry Heilmann	15	67.6	23.4	.0340	.342	164	111	149
Sam Crawford	15	63.5	17.8	.0300	.309	70	318	145
Kirk Gibson	12	27.6	14.8	.0234	.273	195	194	125
Jim Northrup	11	21.3	13.7	.0167	.267	145	39	115
Vic Wertz	9	16.0	12.1	.0191	.286	109	5	125
Magglio Ordóñez	7	13.5	11.3	.0159	.312	107	12	123
Pete Fox	8	10.6	8.2	.0106	.302	59	107	97

Al Kaline (1953–74) signed out of high school, never spent a day in the minors, and played his entire career for the Tigers. After a mediocre rookie campaign in 1954, at age 20 he took home the AL batting title with a .340 average while leading in hits with 200, also providing 27 HR, 102 RBI, and 121 runs scored. The following year he again hit 27 HR, drove in 128 runs, and batted .314. Mr. Tiger never reached those lofty numbers again, but he had a long and consistently good career. Often overshadowed by the top superstars of his era, Kaline was what might be called a good "gray ink" offensive star, meaning he regularly was amongst the league leaders in major offensive categories, but aside from that early batting title, never led the league in anything. His 399 HR remain the record for the Tigers. He was an All-Star 15 times and was great defensively with an outstanding arm that earned him ten Gold Glove Awards.

Harry Heilmann (1914, '16–29) was an outstanding hitter, leading the AL in batting four times with such lofty results as .403, .398, .394, and .393. Those seasons were also the four in which he had 200+ hits, with an impressive 237 in 1921. He had pretty good power for his era—nothing like Babe Ruth, but double-digit HR in the 1920s was usually good enough to be in the top ten in the league. He scored 100+ runs four times and drove in 100+ in eight seasons. He spent most of his time in the OF, but also played over 20 percent of his games at 1B.

Sam Crawford (1903–17) emerged as a star player first for Cincinnati, and then joined Detroit in his fifth season. He went on to lead the AL in triples five times, en route to being the all-time MLB leader in that category. He also had 100+ RBI five times for the Tigers, leading the league three times. He had solid speed too, stealing 318 bases for Detroit.

Kirk Gibson (1979–87, '93–95) provided a good combination of power (five 20+-HR seasons) and speed (four 20+-SB seasons) for the Tigers. In fact, his career numbers for Detroit ended up very balanced in this regard: 195 HR and 194 SB. Something few people know about Kirk Gibson: he was never an All-Star, even during his 1988 MVP season for the Dodgers. That might be in part because he was often injured: for the Tigers, he only twice played 130+ games in a season. Gibson played all three OF positions, but he spent most of his time in RF. He was good in the postseason for Detroit (.333 average, 4 HR, and 7 SB in 13 games), so while you could make a case for Horton or others, I decided to go with Gibson for the sixth OF spot on this dream team roster.

I considered a few others here, starting with Jim Northrup (1964–74), who played most of his career for Detroit, with moderate power (three seasons with 20+ HR), but was only a .267 hitter with little speed. Vic Wertz (1947–52, '61–63) started his career for Detroit, represented them as an All-Star three times, and provided 133 RBI in 1949 and 123 RBI the following season. Pete Fox (1933–40) played the majority of his career for the Tigers, showing little power but moderate speed. He hit .302 and scored 100+ runs three times. In 1935 he hit .321 with 116 runs, 38 doubles, 15 HR, and 14 SB, and then in 1937 he similarly hit .331 with 116 runs, 39 doubles, 12 HR, and 12 SB.

Lastly, Magglio Ordóñez (2005–11) signed as a free agent after many outstanding seasons for the White Sox. He was a .312 hitter for Detroit and was the MVP runner-up in 2007, when he led the AL with a .363 average and 54 doubles, and also provided 216 hits, 28 HR, 139 RBI, and 117 runs.

Starting Pitching

Name	YR	WAR	W3	W-L	ERA	WHIP	ERA+
Hal Newhouser	15	61.6	30.2	200-148	3.07	1.313	130
Justin Verlander	13	54.7	23.3	183-114	3.49	1.191	123
Tommy Bridges	16	51.1	16.4	194-138	3.57	1.368	126
Dizzy Trout	14	49.8	24.6	161-153	3.20	1.344	125
Mickey Lolich	13	47.8	21.2	207-175	3.45	1.222	105
George Mullin	12	47.1	17.8	209-179	2.76	1.270	102
Hooks Dauss	15	39.2	15.3	223-182	3.30	1.320	102
Jack Morris	14	38.1	16.2	198-150	3.73	1.266	108
Bill Donovan	11	36.6	17.9	140-96	2.49	1.192	109
Jim Bunning	9	30.0	18.7	118-87	3.45	1.208	116
Frank Lary	11	29.5	18.2	123-110	3.46	1.271	116
Schoolboy Rowe	10	28.7	18.2	105-62	4.01	1.331	113
Fred Hutchinson	11	26.6	14.9	95-71	3.73	1.281	113
Ed Killian	7	26.0	20.7	100-74	2.38	1.218	109
Earl Whitehill	10	25.7	12.1	133-119	4.16	1.455	104
Virgil Trucks	12	25.6	13.6	114-96	3.50	1.305	113
Denny McLain	8	21.8	19.2	117-62	3.13	1.112	110
Max Scherzer	5	21.4	16.9	82-35	3.52	1.197	117

The Detroit Tigers' history is stronger in offense than in pitching, though they have had numerous lifetime or nearly lifetime hurlers. That said, the ace of this All-Time team, Hall of Famer **Hal Newhouser** (1939–53), had a three-year span for the ages: 29-9 and a 2.22 ERA in 1944, 25-9 and a 1.81 ERA in 1945, and 26-9 and a 1.94 ERA in 1946. Prince Hal led the AL in wins in all three seasons, strikeouts in the first two, and ERA in latter two. Even as a pitcher, he was the AL MVP in the first two seasons, and runner-up in the third. He slipped to 17-17 in 1947 but rebounded to 21-12 and 18-11 after that. Due to several early losing seasons as a youngster, and hurting his arm at age 30, his lifetime record for the Tigers was "only" 200-148. But his prime years and overall résumé were enough to earn him the top spot on this staff.

Justin Verlander (2005–17) took home Rookie of the Year honors in 2006 after posting a 17-9 record and 3.63 ERA. He improved to 18-6 the next year, before leading the AL in losses in 2008 with an 11-17 record. But then in 2009 his dominance began, as he posted a 19-9 record with 269 strikeouts in 240 innings. He went 18-9 the next year and then captured the pitching Triple Crown in 2011 with a 24-5 record, 2.40 ERA, and 250 strikeouts—good enough to win both the Cy Young and MVP Awards. He led the AL in strikeouts again in 2012 before his numbers dipped dramatically for three years until 2016, when at age 33 he posted a 16-9 record, 3.04 ERA, and league-leading 254 strikeouts to come in second in the AL Cy Young voting. His great career with Detroit seems to have come to an end, as at the end of August 2017 he was traded by the rebuilding Tigers to the contending Astros, for whom he posted a 5-0 record and 1.06 ERA to finish the year and then went 4-1 in their championship postseason.

It is hard to definitively rank the next five pitchers on this staff. The ace of the strong mid-30s Detroit clubs, **Tommy Bridges** (1930–43, '45–46) won 20+ games from 1934 through '36. That included pacing the AL with 23 wins against 11 losses in 1936. Playing his entire career in Detroit, Bridges' strong curveball made him an All-Star six times. His two complete-game wins were also a key factor in the Tigers winning the 1935 World Series.

Newhouser's teammate **Dizzy Trout** (1939–52) played almost his entire career for the Tigers. He led the league with 20 wins in 1943 and then was the other part of the dynamic duo in 1944, when he went 27-14 and led the AL with a 2.12 ERA and 33 complete games.

Sinkerballer **Mickey Lolich** (1963–75) was the hero of the 1968 World Series, pitching and winning three complete games, including topping Bob Gibson in Game 7 on only two days' rest. He later posted consecutive seasons in 1971–72 of 25-14 with a 2.92 ERA and 22-14 with a 2.50 ERA. In that 1971 campaign, he led the league in victories, strikeouts (308), and complete games (29). On the flip side, the durable Lolich also led the AL in losses twice, with a 14-19 record in 1970 and a 16-21 record in 1974.

Another longtime Tigers workhorse, Hall of Famer **Jack Morris** (1977–90) won 20+ games twice for Detroit and led the league in strikeouts with 232 in 1983. He was the 19-11 ace for the 1984 champs, going 3-0 with a 1.80 ERA in the postseason.

And old-timer **George Mullin** (1902–13) pitched most of his career for Detroit, posting five 20+-win seasons and a 2.76 ERA. His best year was in 1909, when he went 29-8 with a 2.22 ERA. A little on the wild side early on, he led the league in walks in four consecutive seasons. But he was outstanding with a 1.86 ERA in seven games in the franchise's first three World Series appearances, and later pitched a no-hitter in 1912.

Next up is **Hooks Dauss** (1912–26), who was a lifetime Tiger, and won 20+ games in three seasons. His best was in 1915, when he tallied a 24-13 record with a 2.50 ERA. George Dauss got the nickname Hooks from his effective curveballs, and he ended his career with 223 wins and 182 losses—both all-time highs for the franchise.

As I decided to go with ten starting pitchers for this roster, at this point I had two spots left. The first was given to old-timer **Wild Bill Donovan** (1903–12, '18), who posted a career record of 140-96 and a 2.49 ERA for the early Tigers. His best season was 1907, when his 25-4 record and 2.19 ERA were an important part of the Tigers' first AL-pennant-winning team.

And lastly, it is hard to deny **Denny McLain** (1963–70) the last spot on this pitching staff. After several fairly productive seasons, McLain led the Tigers to the championship in 1968 and made history by being the last 30-game winner in the majors. That year he went 31-6 with a 1.96 ERA, and he followed it up with a 24-9, 2.80 season (winning the Cy Young Award both years, and the AL MVP in the first). But then a horse-gambling obsession and multiple suspensions resulted in his 1970 record being only 3-5, and he never pitched for the Tigers again.

According to the overall numbers, two teammates from the late '50s and early '60s came very close to making this roster. Jim Bunning (1955–63) pitched the first half of his career for Detroit, with his best season being his first full year in 1957, when he led the AL in wins with a 20-8 record to go with a 2.69 ERA. He went on to win 19 games once, and 17 games twice for the Tigers, making the All-Star team five times. And Frank Lary (1954–64) led the AL in wins with a 21-13 record in his second full season. Later, in 1961, he posted a 23-9 record, coming in third in the AL Cy Young Award vote. A two-time All-Star, he led the AL in complete games three times.

The other pitchers that I considered who deserve brief mention include (in chronological order):

- Ed Killian (1904–10) played most of his short career with the Tigers and posted a 23-14 record and 2.27 ERA in 1905, only to do even better two years later at 25-13 and 1.78. But the rest of his seasons were far less impressive.

- Earl Whitehill (1923–32) was a consistent if not spectacular starter for the Tigers over nine seasons. He won 15 or more games five times, but never more than 17.

- Schoolboy Rowe (1933–42) posted a 24-8 record in his first full season and followed that up with seasons of 19-13 and 19-10. His arm suffered fatigue after the 1936 season, so he pitched very little for a couple of years, and when he later returned to a full-time role, he wasn't the same.

- Fred Hutchinson (1939–40, '46–53) started his professional career at age 18 and had outstanding seasons in the minors in 1938 and 1941, with disappointing stints with the Tigers in 1939 and 1940. He then lost four full years to World War II and as a result didn't start playing regularly again until age 26 in 1946. A lifetime Tiger, he never won more than 18 games in a season, but also never had a losing season as a full-time hurler. He spent his last two playing years as a player-manager.

- Virgil Trucks (1941–43, '45–52, '56) had more than 16 wins in a season only once, in his All-Star season of 1949, when he went 19-11 with a 2.81 ERA. In 1952 the Tigers came in last in the AL with a 50-104 record, and so Trucks had an ugly 5-19 record. Amazingly, he threw two no-hitters that year, winning both games by a 1-0 score.

- Max Scherzer (2010–14) pitched five full seasons for the Tigers and was starting to build up a strong résumé to one day make it onto this All-Time team's staff. His last two years for Detroit were particularly impressive: in 2013 he went 21-3 with a 2.90 ERA and 240 strikeouts, taking home the AL Cy Young Award, followed by an 18-5 record with 252 strikeouts in 2014. But then he was granted free agency and signed with the Washington Nationals.

Relief Pitching

Name	YR	WAR	W3	SV	W–L	ERA	WHIP	ERA+
John Hiller	15	30.9	16.2	125	87-76	2.83	1.268	134
Mike Henneman	9	13.0	7.6	154	57-34	3.05	1.305	136
Aurelio López	7	9.7	9.4	85	53-30	3.41	1.258	119
Willie Hernández	6	8.7	8.1	120	36-31	2.98	1.121	135
Todd Jones	8	3.8	4.1	235	23-32	4.07	1.456	113

Because I chose ten starting pitchers, there were only two spots for relief pitchers on this All-Time team roster. The first was Canadian **John Hiller** (1965–70, '72–80), who played his entire career for the Tigers. Playing in an era before the bullpen positions became as specialized as they are today, Hiller didn't rack up as many saves as modern closers do. After several fairly effective years as a mixed starter and reliever, he suffered a serious stroke and heart attack at the age of only 27. He missed the entire 1971 season and pitched only 44 innings in 1972.

Then he had his career year in 1973, when he set a new record with 38 saves, to go with a 10-5 mark and 1.44 ERA. He never reached those numbers again, but he continued as the Tigers main short reliever for six more seasons and posted an ERA below 3.00 in four of them. He averaged more than two innings per outing, so he often had a lot of decisions too, such as in 1974 when he had 13 saves and an impressive 17-14 record as a reliever (due in part to a rule change for that one year as to when saves were awarded).

For the second relief spot on this roster, I considered several candidates and decided to honor the outstanding peak performance of **Willie Hernández** (1984–89). After a mediocre career in the National League, Hernández was traded by the Phillies to the Tigers before the 1984 season. He was lights out for the Tigers that year, pitching 140 innings, saving 32 games (all of his 32 save chances), and posting a 9-3 record with a 1.92 ERA. He was a key part of their championship team, and so won not only the AL Cy Young Award but the MVP Award as well. He continued to save games in the years that followed, ending up with 120 over six seasons in Detroit, but he was never as good as that one magical season.

Mike Henneman (1987–95) was the next Detroit closer after Hernández, and he was steady if not spectacular. He could be counted on for 20 to 25 saves each year, and ended up with 154 for the Tigers overall, to go with a respectable 3.05 ERA. If you preferred him to Hernández (or even McLain) for this All-Time team, I wouldn't argue too much.

Aurelio López (1979–85) was an effective setup man and sometime-closer for the Tigers. Nicknamed Señor Smoke for his hard-throwing ways, he provided 14 to 21 saves in four seasons, and three times posted double-digit wins as well. He is also the second person named Aurelio who played for the Tigers, and when I checked it seems there have been only three in all of major league history.

And lastly, Todd Jones (1997–2001, 2006–08) was the next regular closer in Detroit after Henneman, and actually had two stints in their bullpen. He has the most career saves for the Tigers with 235, and had 30+ saves in five seasons, including a league-leading 42 in 2000. That year he had an impressive streak of allowing only two runs over a span of 31 appearances. But his work out of the pen could also be headache-inducing, as he'd get into jams and only sometimes escape them, as indicated by his relatively high 4.07 ERA for a closer.

Managers

Name	YR	From-To	W-L	PCT	PS	WS
Sparky Anderson	17	1979–95	1,331-1,248	.516	2	1
Hughie Jennings	14	1907–20	1,131-972	.538	3	0
Jim Leyland	8	2006–13	700-597	.540	4	0
Mickey Cochrane	5	1934–38	348-250	.582	2	1
Steve O'Neill	6	1943–48	509-414	.551	1	1
Mayo Smith	4	1967–70	363-285	.560	1	1
Del Baker	8	1933–42	417-355	.540	1	0
Ty Cobb	6	1921–26	479-444	.519	0	0

Sparky Anderson didn't have as high of an overall winning percentage as the others listed above, but he managed the team the longest, had the most wins, made the postseason twice, and of course led them to the World Series championship in 1984. **Hughie Jennings** was the first long-time manager of the Tigers and led them to three consecutive pennants from 1907 through '09, but they lost in the World Series each year. **Jim Leyland** actually led the Tigers to the most postseasons, and **Mickey Cochrane** was notable for his .582 winning percentage, two pennants, and one World Series championship win.

Starting Lineup

What would mythical starting lineups look like for this All-Time roster?

Against RHP:
Ty Cobb CF (L)
Sam Crawford DH (L)
Charlie Gehringer 2B (L)
Hank Greenberg 1B (R)
Miguel Cabrera 3B (R)
Bobby Veach LF (L)
Al Kaline RF (R)
Bill Freehan C (R)
Alan Trammell SS (R)

Against LHP:
Ty Cobb CF (L)
Harry Heilmann DH (R)
Miguel Cabrera 1B (R)
Hank Greenberg LF (R)
Al Kaline RF (R)
Charlie Gehringer 2B (L)
George Kell 3B (R)
Bill Freehan C (R)
Alan Trammell SS (R)

There were many ways I could have structured these lineups. The only natural platoon was for the DH spot, where Heilmann and Crawford could share the duties (or you could get Cash, York, or Gibson in the mix too). Gehringer and Whitaker were both lefties, and Freehan and Parrish were both righties, so I just went with the first choice in each case in these lineups. If you had chosen Horton for this roster (instead of York, McAuliffe, or Gibson), then you would have a natural platoon with Veach in LF. But without Horton, against lefties

I decided to shift Greenberg to LF (where he played over 200 games) and shifted Cabrera to his main position of 1B, allowing the better fielding Kell to play 3B. The other option would be to keep Cabrera at 3B and play right-handed slugger York at 1B.

Depth Chart

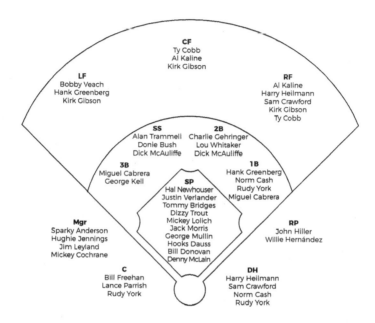

Prospects for Current Players

What are the prospects of current Tigers players making this All-Time team? Cabrera is already included. As the Tigers have just recently unloaded several of their stars (e.g., Verlander, Upton, J.D. Martinez, Kinsler) it appears they are entering a rebuilding mode and so likely won't have many changes to this roster anytime soon. We'll see...

Retired Player Numbers

Ty Cobb (no number), Charlie Gehringer (2), Alan Trammell (3), Hank Greenberg (5), Al Kaline (6), Hal Newhouser (16), Willie Horton (23)), Jack Morris (47)

Selections from Other Authors and Fan Surveys

1957: *Sport* magazine, December issue

As part of a running series, *Sport* magazine reported on all-time all-star teams picked by "big league publicity departments and the writers covering the clubs." Here is what they had to say:

First Base: Hank Greenberg, the all-time home-run great who played in Detroit from 1933 to 1946.

Second Base: Charley Gehringer, a teammate of Hank's on three Tiger pennant winners. Charley spent his entire big-league career in Detroit (1924-42), batted .320, is now in the Hall of Fame.

Shortstop: Donie Bush, a Tiger regular from 1909 until 1921.

Third Base: George Moriarty, who played there from 1909 through 1915 and managed the Tigers in 1927-28.

Outfield: We can wrap these three immortals into one bundle, for they all have one thing in common — they are in baseball's Hall of Fame. Ty Cobb, Sam Crawford, Harry Heilmann are their names.

Catcher: Mickey Cochrane, another Hall of Famer, who played with the Tigers from 1934 through 1937 and managed them from 1934 to 1938.

Lefthanded Pitcher: Hal Newhouser, who pitched for the Tigers from 1939 through 1953, winning exactly 200 games for them.

Righthanded Pitcher: Wild Bill Donovan, who pitched for Detroit from 1903 through 1912 and again in 1918.

Back in 1957 some of these selections were completely obvious: Greenberg, Gehringer, Bush, the outfielders, and Newhouser. The selection of Cochrane was understandable given his importance to the Tigers' success in the 1930s. The selection of Moriarty (1909–15) again underscored the weakness of 3B for the Tigers. Moriarty was a .251 hitter who stole 28 to 34 bases in each of his six seasons in Detroit, so I think Kell would have been a much better choice here. Going with Donovan over Bridges or Trout as top RHP was certainly debatable.

1969: *The Sporting News* Fan Poll

The July 5, 1969, issue reported the results of a fan poll for the long-standing franchises of the day. The results for the Tigers were 1B Greenberg, 2B Gehringer, 3B Kell, SS Rogell, C Cochrane, LF Heilmann, CF Cobb, RF Kaline, RHP McLain, and LHP Newhouser.

Mostly good choices, though Heilmann was really a RF not a LF, so it was misleading to choose him there. And going with McLain was somewhat understandable, since he was just coming off his great 1968 season and in the midst of another fine year, so fans likely assumed he'd have a great career ahead of him.

1981: *The "995" Tigers*, by Fred Smith

This book's title is due to the fact that through that year, there had been 995 men who played for the Tigers. Most of the book is a collection of one-paragraph descriptions of each of these players. But the first section has some special features, including five all-time team lineups: a First, Second, and Third team, plus an All-Time Offensive Team and an All-Time Defense Team. The First team included Greenberg, Gehringer, Kell, Rogell, Kaline, Cobb, Heilmann, and Cochrane. Not bad, but I think this is unfair to Freehan.

The Second team included Cash, McAuliffe, Marv Owen, Bush, Crawford, Heinie Manush, Veach, and of course Freehan. Marv Owen played for Detroit for six seasons in the 1930s and hit .278 with little power or speed. One highlight was providing 105 RBI in 1936 even with only 9 HR. Manush started his Hall of Fame career for the Tigers and during that time won an AL batting title with a .378 average in 1926.

The Third team included Blue, Whitaker, Rodríguez, Trammell, Northrup, Wertz, Hoot Evers, and Ray Hayworth. It was interesting to see Whitaker and Trammell already having accomplished enough by this time to warrant third-team recognition. The selection of Hayworth was based mostly on his defense, as he saw action in parts of nine seasons for the Tigers but played 100+ games only twice, and was only a .268 hitter with virtually no power or speed. I didn't mention Evers earlier, but he was a two-time All-Star for Detroit: in 1948 he hit .314 with 103 RBI, and then in 1950 he did even better with a .323 average, 100 runs, 21 HR, 103 RBI, and a league-leading 11 triples. Not a bad selection here, but this left out long-time Detroit favorite Willie Horton.

For the All-Time Offensive Team, the selections were Greenberg, Gehringer, Kell, Kuenn, Manush, Cobb, Heilmann, and Cochrane. The All-Time Defensive Team was Blue, Gehringer, Kell, Trammell, Kaline, Stanley, Bill Bruton, and Hayworth. After eight seasons with the Milwaukee Braves, Bruton played his last four seasons for the Tigers, and in addition to good defense hit .268 with moderate power and speed.

Lastly, Smith chose a Top 10 list of pitchers, indicated in alphabetical order: Bridges, Dauss, Hiller, Lolich, McLain, Mullin, Newhouser, Rowe, Trout, and

Whitehill. He wrote, "This leaves out Frank Lary, so we will increase the pitching staff to eleven and add Frank who had a record of 123-110."

1990: "All-Time All-Star Teams," in *The Baseball Research Journal*

In an interesting article, Robert C. Berlo used Thorn and Palmer's TPR (Total Player Rating) system to choose all-time teams. He selected players based on their best 800 consecutive games for the franchise, with a minimum of five years played. His results: 1B Greenberg, 2B Gehringer, SS Trammell, 3B Kell, RF Kaline, CF Cobb, LF Heilmann, C Freehan, SP Newhouser, SP Trout, SP Bridges, SP Hutchinson, RP Hiller.

No major surprises here, except seeing Hutchinson rate as the fourth-best starting pitcher, and again seeing Heilmann listed misleadingly as a LF.

1992: *The All-Time All-Star Baseball Book*, by Nick Acocella and Donald Dewey

In their brief write-up on the Tigers, they selected a pretty reasonable lineup of Greenberg, Gehringer, Kell, Trammell, Cobb, Heilmann, Kaline, Cochrane, and Newhouser. The only one I disagreed with here really was Cochrane over Freehan as the catcher. They didn't even mention Freehan as getting honorable mention, including Parrish instead, along with Crawford, Mullin, Bridges, Kuenn, and Morris.

1995: *Baseball Ratings*, by Charles F. Faber

The Faber system as applied in 1995 created an outstanding starting lineup of Greenberg, Gehringer, Trammell, Kell, Freehan, Cobb, Kaline, and Crawford. The five pitchers were solid with Newhouser, Lolich, Mullin, Bridges, and Dauss, with Henneman rated the top reliever.

2000: *They Earned Their Stripes: The Detroit Tigers All-Time Team*

This book provided write-ups about various Tigers all-time greats, and also reported the results of a 25,000-fan survey conducted in 1999 and originally written up in the *Detroit News* on September 27, 1999. The first-team selections were Greenberg, Gehringer, Kell, Trammell, Cobb, Kaline, Gibson, and Freehan, with Hiller as reliever, Morris as the RHP, and a tie between Newhouser and Lolich for the LHP. To me, that elevated Gibson too much. The article noted that aside from the tie, the closest votes were "At second base, Gehringer received 51 percent of the votes and Lou Whitaker received 40 percent. For the third outfielder Gibson received 34 percent and Harry Heilmann, a Hall of Fame outfielder who played from 1914-1929, received 23 percent."

For the runner-up team, the results were Cash at 1B, Whitaker at 2B, Kuenn at SS, no 3B listed, Parrish at C, Heilmann, Stanley, and Horton for the OF, no LHP listed because of the tie, McLain as the RHP, and Hernández as the reliever. Clearly the fans forgot about Crawford and Veach, elevating the more recent Stanley and Horton in their place. And it was interesting that no additional 3B was indicated, again showing this historical weakness for Detroit.

2003: *Rob Neyer's Big Book of Baseball Lineups*, by Rob Neyer

Neyer's starting position players were Greenberg, Gehringer, Trammell, Kell, Freehan, Veach, Cobb, and Kaline. He added Rusty Staub as the starting DH, writing "Made All-Star team as Tigers' RF in '76, but didn't hit much after shifting to DH in '77, notwithstanding his 121 RBI in '78 (thank you, Ron LeFlore)."

His backups were Cash, Whitaker, Bush, Fryman, Parrish, Horton, Lemon, Crawford, and then Gibson as DH. By strictly going with outfielders who primarily played each position, this meant Heilmann was excluded—something Neyer noted by describing RF as a "great spot" for the Tigers.

Neyer's top eight pitchers were Newhouser, Lolich, Bridges, Morris, Trout, Mullin, Dauss, and Donovan, and his two reliever selections were Hiller and Henneman. His top five managers were Jennings, Anderson, O'Neill, Cochrane, and Smith.

2010: *Few and Chosen: Defining Tigers Greatness Across the Eras*, by Lance Parrish with Phil Pepe

As with each book in this fun series, the authors chose a list of the top five players at each position:

C: Freehan, Iván Rodríguez, Cochrane, Tettleton, Matt Nokes

1B: Greenberg, Cash, York, Fielder, Clark

2B: Gehringer, Whitaker, Polanco, McAuliffe, Eddie Mayo

SS: Trammell, Kuenn, Guillen, Rogell, Ed Brinkman

3B: Fryman, Kell, Boone, Higgins, Tom Brookens

LF: Veach, Horton, Colavito, Goose Goslin, Manush

CF: Cobb, Granderson, Lemon, LeFlore, Evers

RF: Kaline, Heilmann, Crawford, Gibson, Ordóñez

RHP: McLain, Bunning, Bridges, Dauss/Rowe (tie)

LHP: Newhouser, Lolich, Harry Coveleski, Frank Tanana, Hank Aguirre

RP: Hiller, Hernández, Jones, Henneman, López

Manager: Anderson, Cochrane, Smith, O'Neill, Jennings

As was typical in this book series, Parrish (as co-author) omitted himself from consideration, hence the catcher list without his name included. Matt Nokes (1986–90) was an All-Star as a rookie in 1987, when he hit .289 with 32 HR and 87 RBI, but never approached those numbers again in his three other partial seasons with the Tigers.

Eddie Mayo (1944–48) played for Detroit for five years, and was a good fielder, but only a .265 hitter with little power or speed. Ed Brinkman (1971–74) was an outstanding shortstop and took home a Gold Glove Award in 1972. He provided an abysmal .222 average and .276 OBP, with very little power except in 1974 when he busted out for a career high 14 HR. Tom Brookens (1979–88) played most of his career for the Tigers, hitting only .246 with minimal power. He stole 10+ bases five times, and had good range at 3B, while also being capable of filling in at 2B or SS when needed. Hall of Famer Goose Goslin (1934–37) played four seasons with Detroit towards the end of his career, including 1936 when he hit .315 with 24 HR, 122 runs, and 125 RBI.

If you went by peak performance, then sure McLain would be a good choice as top RHP. And for the southpaws, after the obvious first two, Harry Coveleski (1914–18) was an interesting choice. He pitched only three full seasons for Detroit, but they were consistently good ones: 22-12 and 2.49 in 1914, 22-13 and 2.45 in 1915, and 21-11 and 1.97 in 1916. Frank Tanana (1985–92) pitched for the Tigers for eight years but never won more than 15 games. Hank Aguirre (1958–67) did lead the AL with a 2.21 ERA in 1962, but he won double-digit games in only three seasons for the Tigers.

2016: *101 All-Time Fantasy Baseball Teams*, by Jack Sweeney

Sweeney's infield was Greenberg, Gehringer, Trammell, Kell, and Parrish. He didn't differentiate between OF positions, so he chose Cobb, Kaline, and Heilmann, and then wisely listed Cabrera as DH. His top reliever was Hernández, and he listed four starting pitchers: Newhouser, Bunning, Morris, and Verlander.

Top WAR Single Seasons – Hitters (8+)

Name	Year	WAR	AVG	HR	R	RBI	SB	OPS+
Ty Cobb	1917	11.3	.383	6	107	106	55	209
Ty Cobb	1911	10.7	.420	8	147	127	83	196
Ty Cobb	1910	10.5	.383	8	106	91	65	206
Ty Cobb	1909	9.8	.377	9	116	107	76	193
Ty Cobb	1915	9.5	.369	3	144	99	96	185
Harry Heilmann	1923	9.3	.403	18	121	115	9	194
Ty Cobb	1912	9.2	.409	7	120	83	61	200
Norm Cash	1961	9.2	.361	41	119	132	11	201
Charlie Gehringer	1934	8.4	.356	11	135	127	11	149
Al Kaline	1961	8.4	.324	19	116	82	14	138
Al Kaline	1955	8.2	.340	27	121	102	6	162
Alan Trammell	1987	8.2	.343	28	109	105	21	155
Ty Cobb	1916	8.0	.371	5	113	68	68	179

It wasn't surprising to see Ty Cobb's name appear so many times on this list, nor really that he'd have the top five spots—he was just that good. Norm Cash's early career year in 1961 was obviously going to make this list. But less obvious was which, if any, of the big seasons would appear here from Heilmann, Gehringer, Kaline, Greenberg, Cabrera, and others.

Top WAR Single Seasons – Pitchers (8+)

Name	Year	WAR	W-L	ERA	IP	SO	ERA+
Hal Newhouser	1945	12.0	25-9	1.81	313.1	212	195
Dizzy Trout	1944	11.1	27-14	2.12	352.1	144	167
Mark Fidrych	1976	9.6	19-9	2.34	250.1	97	159
Hal Newhouser	1946	9.3	26-9	1.94	292.2	275	190
Mickey Lolich	1971	8.7	25-14	2.92	376.0	308	124
Hal Newhouser	1944	8.6	29-9	2.22	312.1	187	159
Justin Verlander	2011	8.4	24-5	2.40	251.0	250	172
Ed Killian	1907	8.1	25-13	1.78	314.0	96	146
John Hiller	1973	8.1	10-5	1.44	125.1	124	283
Denny McLain	1969	8.0	24-9	2.80	325.0	181	134

As with Cobb, I wasn't surprised to see Newhouser appear the most on this list, though I was surprised that no other pitcher appeared more than once. Notably, Denny McLain's 1969 season scored an 8.0 while his other Cy Young Award year in 1968 did not, even though it was superior in most other statistics: 31-6, 1.96 ERA, 280 K in 336 IP, 154 ERA+. It was very interesting to see that John Hiller's outstanding relief season in 1973 rated as the ninth best ever for a Tigers pitcher.

And lastly, Mark "The Bird" Fidrych burst onto the scene as a 21-year-old in 1976 and earned the AL Rookie of the Year award after posting a 19-9 record and leading the league with 24 complete games and a 2.34 ERA. Unfortunately, a shoulder injury struck in 1977, and an attempted comeback spread over several years just never worked out.

Franchise Player

Based on the numbers, this honor had to be given to Ty Cobb. No one else was really close, though honorable mention was deserved by Kaline, Greenberg, Gehringer, and Newhouser.

CHAPTER 9

The Reds Franchise All-Time Dream Team

The early days of baseball in Cincinnati were complicated. The original Cincinnati Red Stockings were baseball's first openly all-professional team (1869). A few franchises came and went in Cincinnati in the years that followed, with a new Cincinnati team joining the American Association starting in 1882, and it was this club that—according to Baseball-Reference.com and other sources—can be said to be the direct ancestor of the current franchise, as the club was granted admission to the NL after the 1889 season.

The Reds had to wait several decades until they won a pennant. It was 1919 when they first won the NL title, and then won the infamous "Black Sox" World Series. They made the postseason again 20 years later, losing the World Series to the Yankees 4-0 in 1939, but then defeating the Tigers in seven games in 1940. They had another two-decade wait until 1961, when they won the NL pennant, only to run into the amazing 1961 Yankees in the World Series (the Reds lost, 4-1).

The best period of this franchise's history of course came in the 1970s, with the Big Red Machine that produced six postseason appearances, two World Series losses (1970 and 1972), and two World Series titles (1975 and 1976). They won the World Series again in 1990, but failed to win their division again (or even grab a Wild Card playoff spot) until 2010.

As you might expect, many members of the Big Red Machine era made this All-Time team roster. But there have also been plenty of other good and great players throughout the franchise's history.

1st Base

Name	YR	WAR	W3	W/G	AVG	HR	SB	OPS+
Joey Votto	12	58.8	22.2	.0373	.311	269	74	155
Tony Pérez	16	45.6	19.1	.0234	.283	287	39	127
Ted Kluszewski	11	30.8	18.1	.0230	.302	251	20	128
Frank McCormick	10	30.4	17.1	.0248	.301	110	23	120
John Reilly	9	24.4	13.4	.0228	.294	69	245	132
Jake Beckley	7	23.5	13.0	.0267	.325	26	114	129
Dan Driessen	12	18.6	7.2	.0126	.271	133	152	115
Sean Casey	8	16.7	11.8	.0155	.305	118	15	114
Lee May	7	15.9	12.7	.0209	.274	147	17	123
Hal Morris	10	13.0	8.7	.0124	.305	74	44	115

Joey Votto (2007–18) has by now earned the top spot at 1B on this All-Time team roster. After a couple of pretty good seasons, he busted out and won the MVP Award in 2010 after hitting .324 with 37 HR, 113 RBI, and a .424 OBP. He took home the Gold Glove Award the next year and also led the NL in doubles, walks, and OBP. In 2012 he was just about on pace to break the single-season record for doubles when an injury took him out of action (he ended the year with 44 doubles in 111 games). Injury shortened his 2014 even more dramatically, but overall Votto has so far been an All-Star six times, batted .311 for his career, hit 20+ HRs seven times, and led the NL in OBP seven times.

According to the table above, Tony Pérez would seem to be the obvious choice as backup at 1B, but as he also played a lot of 3B and the candidates at the hot corner are much weaker, he can actually claim the starting spot at that position. So this means monster home run hitter **Ted Kluszewski** (1947–57) gets the nod as backup 1B on this roster. A .302 hitter, he belted 40+ HR three times and had 100+ RBI five times for the Reds. This included a league-leading 49 HR and 141 RBI in 1954, which earned him second place (to Willie Mays) in the NL MVP balloting. And unlike most power hitters, Big Klu rarely struck out—in fact, in many seasons he had more HR than strikeouts.

After considering all of the position-player candidates, I came back around to 1B and awarded **Frank McCormick** (1934, '37–45) one of the two "extra spots" on this roster. He had four seasons with 100+ RBI, was a good fielder, and was an All-Star eight consecutive years for the Reds. He even won the NL MVP Award in 1940 when he hit .309 with 19 HR and 127 RBI. A .301 hitter, he led the league with 128 RBI in 1939 and led the league in hits three consecutive years (1938 through 1940).

There were others who deserved consideration here, starting with old-timer John Reilly (1883–91). He posted five seasons with 100+ runs and twice led the league in HR, with 11 in 1884 and 13 in 1888. He hit 11 or more triples every season and led the league with 26 in 1890. His earliest SB totals were not available, but he clearly had lots of speed, as shown by 50 SB in 1887 and 82 the following year. Another old-timer, Hall of Famer Jake Beckley (1897–1903), was a high-average hitter (.325) but played only seven seasons with the Reds and never led the league in any significant categories during that time.

The others who deserve brief mention include (in chronological order):

- Lee May (1965–71) started his career with the Reds, was an All-Star for them twice, and had three seasons with 30+ HR.

- Dan Driessen (1973–84) split time between 3B and 1B early in his career and then took over full-time 1B duties in 1977. He provided moderate power and speed, with his best season being 1977, when he hit .300 with 17 HR, 91 RBI, and 31 SB.

- Hal Morris (1990–97, 1999–2000) batted .340 in his partial rookie season and was a .305 hitter for the Reds overall, but he provided minimal power or speed and played 130+ games for them only twice.

- Sean Casey (1998–2005) was a three-time All-Star, had five .300+ seasons, and three seasons with 20+ HR.

2nd Base

Name	YR	WAR	W3	W/G	AVG	HR	SB	OPS+
Joe Morgan	8	57.8	29.9	.0501	.288	152	406	147
Bid McPhee	18	52.4	14.8	.0245	.272	53	568	107
Brandon Phillips	11	30.5	12.6	.0189	.279	191	194	99
Lonny Frey	7	29.9	17.0	.0318	.265	36	68	103
Miller Huggins	6	16.4	11.3	.0209	.260	4	150	104
Johnny Temple	9	15.2	9.2	.0154	.291	15	105	93
Ron Oester	13	11.0	8.6	.0086	.265	42	40	87
Tommy Helms	8	4.4	5.9	.0052	.269	18	23	75

Judging only by career WAR for this franchise, it would appear that the choice for starting 2B was a close call. But once you look at the number of years it took each player to accumulate their totals, the decision became a very easy one. During his time with the Reds, Hall of Famer **Joe Morgan** (1972–79) took home consecutive MVP Awards, sparking the Big Red Machine to World Series championships in both 1975 and 1976. A .288 hitter, The Little General posted a .415 OBP for the Reds, stole 406 bases, and scored 100+ runs in six consecutive seasons. And he was great defensively too, winning five consecutive Gold Glove Awards.

Hall of Famer **Bid McPhee** (1882–1899) started with Cincinnati in their first year in the American Association and played his entire career with the franchise. Ten times he scored 100 or more runs, and that was with a shorter season back then. We lack SB records for his first four seasons, so his total of 568 is incomplete (his highest single-season total was an impressive 95 SB in only 129 games in 1887).

With two such strong candidates, contemporary Brandon Phillips (2006–16) didn't really have much of a shot here. But he nonetheless put in 11 solid years for the Reds, including three as an All-Star. He hit 20+ HR three times and was amazingly consistent by smacking exactly 18 HR each year from 2010 through 2013. He could run well too, stealing 20+ bases five times. And he was an outstanding defender, taking home four Gold Glove Awards.

Lonny Frey (1938–43, '46) was a very good fielder and so ended up with stronger WAR results than his offensive stats alone would have suggested. A .265 hitter with little power, he led the NL in SB with a modest 22 in 1940 and was an All-Star three times.

No one else came close to these four, but several other 2B deserve at least brief mention, including (in chronological order):

- Miller Huggins (1904–09) played the first half of his career in Cincinnati, led the NL in walks twice while with the Reds, and had 25+ SB four times. (His Hall of Fame status comes primarily from his accomplishments as manager of the powerhouse Yankees of the 1920s.)

- Johnny Temple (1952–59, '64) was a .291 hitter and three-time All-Star, stealing between 14 and 21 bases in all six of his full seasons with the Reds.

- Tommy Helms (1964–71) won the NL Rookie of the Year Award in his first full season in 1966. He later was an All-Star twice and earned two Gold Glove Awards, but he didn't provide power or speed and had a low .297 OBP.

- Ron Oester (1978–90) played his entire career with the Reds but was a light hitter (.265) with little power or speed.

3rd Base

Name	YR	WAR	W3	W/G	AVG	HR	SB	OPS+
Tony Pérez	16	45.6	19.1	.0234	.283	287	39	127
Heinie Groh	9	40.6	18.0	.0335	.298	17	158	130
Chris Sabo	7	17.2	14.3	.0210	.270	104	116	111
Todd Frazier	5	15.3	12.2	.0242	.257	108	43	113
Arlie Latham	6	14.5	10.1	.0208	.279	15	340	94
Bobby Adams	10	14.4	6.7	.0132	.272	36	64	91
Grady Hatton	9	14.2	9.1	.0146	.254	81	39	99
Harry Steinfeldt	8	11.7	8.2	.0131	.267	17	109	98
Hick Carpenter	8	6.1	7.4	.0068	.269	16	158	91

As I said earlier, I decided to select **Tony Pérez** (1964–76, '84–86) here, even though he played more games at 1B than 3B (1,092 vs. 760). In addition to allowing Big Klu and McCormick spots at 1B, there just weren't many solid 3B candidates for this roster. Pérez was a seven-time All-Star and the main RBI cog in the Big Red Machine. He had six 100+-RBI seasons for the Reds, plus four others with 90 or more.

You could make a case for him as the starter instead of Pérez, but at the very least **Heinie Groh** (1913–1921) deserved the backup 3B spot. A .298 hitter and a good fielder, he provided a little speed, and he led the league in runs and hits once, and doubles and OBP twice.

Arlie Latham (1890–95) was one of the best early speedsters in baseball, and he had over 340 SB in just over five seasons for Cincinnati near the end of his career. Much more recently, Chris Sabo (1988–93, '96) burst onto the scene in 1988 with 40 doubles and 46 SB, taking home NL Rookie of the Year honors. He was an All-Star that year and two other years as well. And slugger Todd Frazier (2011–15) started his career with the Reds and was an All-Star for them twice, when he hit 29 HR in 2014 and 35 in 2015.

There were various others who deserve brief mention, including (in chronological order):

- Hick Carpenter (1882–1889) was a light hitter, but even without SB numbers for his earliest years, we know he had speed, as he managed 44, 59, and 47 SB in his last three full seasons.

- Harry Steinfeldt (1898–1905) split his time between 3B and 2B for the Reds, stealing between 10 and 19 bases in each of his seven full seasons.

- Grady Hatton (1946–54) was only a .254 hitter but provided moderate power with four seasons with double-digit HR.

- Bobby Adams (1946–55) played ten years for the Reds, but 125+ games only twice. A .272 hitter, he provided little power or speed.

Shortstop

Name	YR	WAR	W3	W/G	AVG	HR	SB	OPS+
Barry Larkin	19	70.2	20.3	.0322	.295	198	379	116
Dave Concepción	19	39.8	14.8	.0160	.267	101	321	88
Roy McMillan	10	18.3	10.4	.0136	.249	42	30	75
Zack Cozart	7	16.5	7.1	.0222	.254	82	21	92
Leo Cardenas	9	14.8	10.4	.0128	.261	72	26	89

Hall of Famer **Barry Larkin** (1986–2004) played his entire career for the Reds. He never led the league in any offensive category, in part because he was not the most durable of players: in 19 seasons he played 140+ games only 7 times. But he nonetheless was an All-Star an impressive 12 times, and was the NL MVP in 1995. He provided speed and moderate power, with nine seasons of 20+ SB (51 was his high), and nine with double-digit HR (with a high of 33 in 1996, when he became the first 30/30 shortstop). He was also an outstanding fielder, taking home three Gold Glove Awards.

Another lifetime Reds SS was the backup for this roster, **Dave Concepción** (1970–88). Though never a tremendous hitter, he was fast (321 SB), won five Gold Glove Awards, and was an All-Star nine times. He also played in the second-most games (Pete Rose is first) in Reds history.

Beyond those two, no one else came close, but a few deserve brief mention, including (in chronological order):

- Roy McMillan (1951–60) was a very good fielder and won three Gold Glove Awards. A two-time All-Star, he was a light hitter (.249) with little power or speed.

- Leo Cardenas (1960–68) was an All-Star four times and also provided good defense, taking the Gold Glove Award in 1965.

A .261 hitter, he managed 20 HR in 1966 but never had more than 11 in any other season in Cincinnati.

- Zack Cozart (2011–17) is a good-fielding but light-hitting shortstop, batting only .254 with moderate power.

Catcher

Name	YR	WAR	W3	W/G	AVG	HR	SB	OPS+
Johnny Bench	17	75.0	23.8	.0348	.267	389	68	126
Ernie Lombardi	10	31.3	13.4	.0260	.311	120	5	127
Ed Bailey	9	18.8	12.2	.0263	.261	94	13	109
Bubbles Hargrave	8	18.5	11.4	.0242	.314	29	27	122
Johnny Edwards	7	8.7	9.1	.0116	.246	53	6	87

Johnny Bench (1967–83), arguably the greatest catcher of all time, played his entire career for the Reds. He was great with the bat, with the glove, and with his pitchers. He won MVP Awards in 1970 (.293, 45 HR, 148 RBI) and 1972 (.270, 40 HR, 125 RBI), leading the league in HR and RBI both years. Amazingly, he was an All-Star every year from 1968 through 1980 and took home lots of other honors, including ten Gold Glove Awards and the NL Rookie of the Year Award in 1968. And Bench is the all-time leader for this franchise in both HR (389) and RBI (1,376).

Like most of the other positions for this team so far, at catcher there was a clear starter and a clear backup. **Ernie Lombardi** (1932–41) was a high-average hitter (.311) who also provided some pop and won the MVP Award in 1938, when he batted .342 (led the league) with 19 HR and 95 RBI. A five-time All-Star for the Reds, he was legendary for his lack of speed, but then again relatively few catchers can truly run well.

A few other catchers deserve brief mention, starting with Eugene Franklin "Bubbles" Hargrave (1921–28), who was a .314 hitter and managed to lead the NL in 1926 with a .353 average (although he played in only 105 games with 366 plate appearances). He acquired his nickname because he stuttered when saying "B" sounds.

Ed Bailey (1953–61) was a three-time All-Star for the Reds and provided them with some pop, hitting 20+ HR twice. And lastly, Johnny Edwards (1961–67) was only a .246 hitter, but he was an All-Star three times and provided good defense, taking home two Gold Glove Awards.

Left Field

Name	YR	WAR	W3	W/G	AVG	HR	SB	OPS+
Pete Rose	19	77.7	21.8	.0285	.307	152	146	124
Frank Robinson	10	63.8	24.3	.0425	.303	324	161	150
George Foster	11	39.3	19.4	.0314	.286	244	46	140
Adam Dunn	8	16.4	9.9	.0151	.247	270	58	130
Bob Bescher	6	14.9	9.3	.0200	.262	11	320	110

Pete Rose (1963–78, '84–86) was very versatile, and played a fair amount of games at several positions: LF (644), 3B (629), 2B (627), RF (556), and 1B (197). Given the relative strengths of the different OF positions here, I decided to include him as the starting RF.

Which means **Frank Robinson** (1956–65) gets the nod as the starting LF on this All-Time dream team. He played the first half of his outstanding career for the Reds and spent time at all three OF positions and 1B. He won the NL MVP Award in 1961 after hitting .323 with 37 HR, 124 RBI, and 22 SB. He followed that up with a statistically superior 1962 season: .342, 39 HR, 136 RBI, 18 SB, and 51 doubles. A .303 hitter while in Cincinnati, he won a Gold Glove Award in 1958 and was an All-Star six times for the Reds.

George Foster (1971–81) won the NL MVP Award in 1977 after hitting .320 with 52 HR and 149 RBI, both of which are all-time highs for this franchise (interestingly, that was the only 50+-HR season by any player in the 1970s or 1980s). Foster led the NL in both HR (40) and RBI (120) the following year, and overall was an All-Star five times for the Reds.

I considered two others, starting with slugger Adam Dunn (2001–08), who provided uncanny power consistency: in 2004 he hit 46 HR, and for the next four years hit exactly 40 HR in each. He batted only .247 but walked a lot and so had a .380 OBP. An All-Star for the Reds only once, he struck out a lot, including leading the league three times with highs of 195 in 2004 and 194 in 2006. And lastly, Bob Bescher (1908–13) was a light-hitting (.262) speedster for the Reds, leading the league in SB in four consecutive seasons with totals of 54, 70, 81, and 67.

Center Field

Name	YR	WAR	W3	W/G	AVG	HR	SB	OPS+
Vada Pinson	11	47.7	20.4	.0305	.297	186	221	119
Edd Roush	12	40.0	15.9	.0286	.331	47	199	135
Eric Davis	9	30.5	17.6	.0310	.271	203	270	137
Cy Seymour	5	19.9	16.6	.0358	.332	26	74	143

Bug Holliday	10	18.1	10.7	.0195	.312	65	252	126
César Gerónimo	9	13.2	11.0	.0110	.261	44	72	95
Gus Bell	9	13.0	10.7	.0105	.288	160	24	105
Ken Griffey Jr.	9	12.8	11.1	.0135	.270	210	17	122

As with LF, there were three candidates in CF who all deserved spots on this All-Time team. **Vada Pinson** (1958–68) had his best seasons for Cincinnati, batting .296 and leading the league in hits, doubles, and triples twice each. He provided a good combination of power and speed, with six 20+-HR and seven 20+-SB seasons. He won a Gold Glove in CF in 1961 but was selected as an All-Star only twice.

Hall of Famer **Edd Roush** (1916–26, '31) played most of his career for the Reds. He was a .331 hitter and won batting titles in both 1917 (.341) and 1919 (.321). He was primarily a singles hitter, but he also had ten seasons with double-digit triples, including a league-leading high of 21 in 1924.

Eric Davis (1984–91, '96) had several of the best power/speed combination seasons of all time, including 27 HR with 80 SB in only 132 G in 1986, and 37 HR with 50 SB in only 129 G in 1987. But these numbers also indicated his downside: Davis was always injury-prone, never playing more than 135 games in a season, for the Reds or any other team. That said, Eric the Red provided excellent defense, taking home three Gold Glove Awards, and he was an All-Star twice.

Several others who primarily played CF deserve to be mentioned, starting with Cy Seymour (1902–06), who was a .332 hitter in his five seasons with the Reds. His best year by far came in 1905, when he led the NL with a .377 average, 219 hits, 40 doubles, 21 triples, and 121 RBI. Old-timer James "Bug" Holliday (1889–98) led the American Association in HR with 19 in his rookie season, and then led the NL with 13 HR in 1892. In 1894 he batted .376 with 126 runs and 123 RBI in only 123 games. He played his entire career with the Reds, was a .312 hitter, and stole 32 to 50 bases in each of his six full seasons.

Many decades later Gus Bell (1953–61) was a four-time All-Star for Cincy. He hit 25+ HR three times and posted 100+ RBI four times for the Reds. César Gerónimo (1972–80) won four consecutive Gold Glove Awards roaming in CF for the Big Red Machine, but he was only a .261 hitter with little power or speed. And lastly, Ken Griffey Jr. (2000–08) came home to Cincinnati with much fanfare and hit 40 HR with 118 RBI in 2000. But sadly, he had only one other season of 140+ games for the Reds. Even so, he hit 20+ HR six times for the Reds, and his enduring popularity led to three All-Star selections.

Right Field

Name	YR	WAR	W3	W/G	AVG	HR	SB	OPS+
Pete Rose	19	77.7	21.8	.0285	.307	152	146	124
Ken Griffey Sr.	12	25.3	12.6	.0207	.303	71	156	123
Reggie Sanders	8	21.4	12.6	.0266	.271	125	158	118
Ival Goodman	8	21.4	14.1	.0222	.279	91	45	118
Curt Walker	7	18.8	11.1	.0197	.303	43	69	114
Jay Bruce	9	16.1	12.0	.0132	.249	233	61	110
Wally Post	12	15.8	11.6	.0175	.266	172	19	113
Mike Mitchell	6	15.5	12.1	.0181	.283	19	165	118

Pete Rose (1963–78, '84–86) was good defensively in the OF, taking home Gold Glove Awards in 1969 and 1970. Charlie Hustle was the most consistent singles and doubles hitter of his time and was an All-Star 13 times for the Reds. During that time, he won three batting titles, six times led the NL in hits, and scored 100+ runs ten times. He was NL MVP in 1973 after hitting .338 with 230 hits and 115 runs. Rose was signed by the Phillies as a free agent after the 1978 season, but he returned to the Reds late in his career as player-manager (a rare occupation in the contemporary game). After retirement, his name has stayed in the news due to his banishment from baseball for gambling on the game, but that punishment didn't extend to this All-Time team roster.

The candidates who primarily played RF were not nearly as strong as those who primarily played LF or CF. That said, I decided to include **Ken Griffey Sr.** (1973–81, 1988–90), who was part of the Big Red Machine era, and overall was a .303 hitter for Cincinnati. A good fielder and three-time All-Star, he had some speed on the bases, with three 20+-SB seasons and a high of 34 in 1976.

Reggie Sanders (1991–98) played the first half of his career in Cincy before becoming a bit of a baseball nomad (appearing for a different team each year from 1999 through 2004). Like Davis, he provided a combination of power and speed and posted his career year in strike-shortened 1995, when he hit .306 with 28 HR, 99 RBI, and 36 SB.

Ival Goodman (1935–42) played most of his short career for the Reds, led the league in triples in his first two seasons with 18 and 14, and hit 30 HR in 1938. He was an All-Star that year and again the following season when he hit a career high .323. In the decade before Goodman, another good triples hitter roamed RF for the Reds, Curt Walker (1924–30). He batted .303 for Cincy and had a high of 20 triples in 1926. And before both Goodman and Walker there was Mike Mitchell (1907–12), who played for the Reds for his first six seasons and led the league in triples with 17 in 1909 and 18 in 1910, and then topped both of those totals with 22 in 1911.

Two HR sluggers also deserve brief mention here, starting with Wally Post (1949, '51–57, '60–63), who hit 20+ HR four times for the Reds, with highs of 40 in 1955 and 36 in 1956. And lastly, Jay Bruce (2008–16) hit 20+ HR in eight of his nine seasons in Cincinnati and had four seasons with 30+ HR. A three-time All-Star, he batted only .249 with a low .319 OBP.

Starting Pitching

Name	YR	WAR	W3	W-L	ERA	WHIP	ERA+
Noodles Hahn	7	44.4	24.4	127-92	2.52	1.134	134
Bucky Walters	11	43.7	23.5	160-107	2.93	1.251	124
Dolf Luque	12	41.9	22.3	154-152	3.09	1.265	121
Tony Mullane	8	39.3	17.2	163-124	3.15	1.276	115
Eppa Rixey	13	39.3	16.4	179-148	3.33	1.286	118
Jim Maloney	11	38.2	21.7	134-81	3.16	1.248	117
José Rijo	10	38.1	22.1	97-61	2.83	1.187	138
Frank Dwyer	8	36.8	19.4	133-100	3.77	1.430	121
Red Lucas	8	34.6	18.4	109-99	3.64	1.226	110
Paul Derringer	10	31.7	14.3	161-150	3.36	1.241	111
Joe Nuxhall	15	29.7	13.4	130-109	3.80	1.325	104
Bob Ewing	8	29.1	18.3	108-103	2.37	1.160	121
Will White	5	27.4	26.0	136-69	2.51	1.096	124
Gary Nolan	10	26.5	14.1	110-67	3.02	1.138	119
Mario Soto	12	26.0	19.3	100-92	3.47	1.186	108
Johnny Vander Meer	11	25.7	13.6	116-116	3.41	1.382	108
Ewell Blackwell	8	25.5	20.1	79-77	3.32	1.288	120
Billy Rhines	6	25.1	20.6	96-79	3.28	1.322	123
Johnny Cueto	8	24.1	15.6	92-63	3.21	1.165	126
Bob Purkey	7	22.2	15.1	103-76	3.49	1.219	112
Tom Seaver	6	19.6	15.1	75-46	3.18	1.177	116
Pete Donohue	10	19.5	12.0	127-110	3.73	1.328	106
Tom Browning	11	19.5	11.0	123-88	3.92	1.268	98
Don Gullett	7	15.7	9.5	91-44	3.03	1.208	114

As I said at the outset, the Reds didn't have a particularly strong corps of starting pitchers for this All-Time team. As you can see from the WAR totals above, you could make a case for several as the ace of the staff, but in the end, I went with **Bucky Walters** (1938–48). He won the MVP Award in 1939, when he captured the pitching Triple Crown with a 27-11 record, 2.29 ERA, and 137 strikeouts (with few exceptions, strikeouts were not plentiful during this era). He then topped the NL in ERA and wins again in 1940 (22-10, 2.48). He also led the league in wins with a 23-8 record in 1944 and was an All-Star five times for the Reds. Not bad for a converted third baseman.

Based on the numbers in the table above, you could make a case for **Frank "Noodles" Hahn** (1899–1905) to be the top starter on this staff. He played most of his brief career for the Reds and had four 20+-win seasons. He led the league in strikeouts three times (including a high of 239 in 375.1 IP in 1901) and was usually amongst the league leaders in wins and ERA.

Hall of Fame lefty **Eppa Rixey** (1921–33) came over from the Phillies and pitched the rest of his career for the Reds. He won 20+ games three times, leading the league with a 25-13 mark in 1922. A control artist, he never struck out more than 100 batters in a season, despite nine seasons with 200+ innings pitched. His 179 wins remain the most of any pitcher for this franchise.

Early Cuban star **Dolf Luque** (1918–1929) was a teammate of Rixey, but he had only a few truly good seasons—most notably 1923, when he led the league in ERA with a 1.93 mark and wins with a 27-8 record. The Pride of Havana also led the league two years later with a 2.63 ERA, but his record that year was only 16-18.

Next up was **Jim Maloney** (1960–70), who pitched all but his final season for the Reds. He was a feared flamethrower, struck out 200+ in four consecutive seasons, and had two 20+-win seasons. He also pitched no-hitters for Cincy in 1965 and 1969.

Paul Derringer (1933–42) struggled when he first joined the Reds, going 7-25 for them in 1933. But he later won 20+ games four times, including a 25-7 record in 1939. He was an All-Star for Cincinnati six times.

José Rijo (1988–95, 2000–01) was still only 18 years old when he made his debut with the Yankees. He floundered a bit with the Yankees and A's before being traded to the Reds for aging slugger Dave Parker. Once in Cincinnati, he never had a losing season and ended up with a 97-61 record and an impressive 2.83 ERA. He was the World Series MVP in 1990 as he won two games and allowed only 1 run in 15.1 IP. Rijo led the league with 227 strikeouts in 1993 but never won more than 15 games in a season. Lastly, he has the rare distinction of mounting a comeback and pitching (albeit briefly) after a five-year absence, meaning he pitched in the majors after having received a vote for the Hall of Fame.

After considering all of the relief-pitching candidates, I decided to go with only those seven starting pitchers for this All-Time team. This meant that Red Lucas (1926–33), who was a teammate of Rixey and Luque, didn't quite make the cut. He had top seasons of 18-11 in 1927 and 19-12 in 1929. Very durable, he led the league three times in complete games, with highs of 28 in 1929 and 1932. He was also a very capable batsman, as he hit .300 with 42 doubles and 132 RBI over 977 at-bats for the Reds.

I also considered Johnny Vander Meer (1937–43, '46–49), who spent most of his career with the Reds and amassed an even 116-116 record while making the All-Star team four times. He led the NL in strikeouts in three years, but his biggest claim to fame of course was throwing consecutive no-hitters in 1938.

Ewell Blackwell (1942, '46–52) was a tall sidearmer who played most of his career for the Reds. In 1947 he almost did what Vander Meer had done nine years earlier, as he threw a no-hitter against the Boston Braves and then in his next start had a no-hitter into the ninth against the Dodgers until Eddie Stanky broke it up. He was considered one of the better pitchers of his era and was an All-Star in six consecutive seasons, even though his numbers didn't end up very impressive in some of those years. His best season came in 1947, when he led the league in wins with a 22-8 record, posted a 2.47 ERA, completed 23 of his 33 starts, led the NL with 193 strikeouts, and came in second in the MVP vote.

Several old-timers were considered as well, starting with Tony Mullane (1886–1893), who is second on the club's all-time win list (behind Rixey). His top-three win totals were 33, 31, and 26. He pitched 400+ innings three times for the Reds, including 529.2 innings in 1886. In that season he started 56 games and completed 55 of them—making it clear why it is so hard to compare these pitchers with those of the early 20th century, let alone the truly modern era.

Will White (1882–86) preceded Mullane, so his numbers were even more bizarre-looking. He pitched 450+ innings three times, including 577 innings in 1883. In those three seasons he posted records of 40-12, 43-22, and 34-18— and completed 204 of the 208 games he started. Billy Rhines (1890–92, '95–97) was a teammate of Mullane and led the NL in ERA twice with 1.95 in 1890 and 2.45 in 1896. And Frank Dwyer (1892–99) pitched seven full seasons for the Reds, posting 16 to 24 wins each year.

The others I considered who deserve brief mention include (in chronological order):

- Bob Ewing (1902–09) managed only a 108-103 record for the Reds but sported a 2.37 ERA, which was good even by the standards of that era.

- Pete Donohue (1921–30) won 20+ games three times for the Reds, with additional fine seasons of 18-9 and 16-9.

- Joe Nuxhall (1944, '52–60, '62–66) infamously pitched 2/3 of an inning at the age of 15, and then returned eight years later to have a good career with the Reds (130-109, 3.80 ERA). He was an All-Star twice, while performing as both a starter and reliever in most seasons.

- Bob Purkey (1958–64) was a three-time All-Star and had an outstanding 1962 season, with a 23-5 record and 2.81 ERA.

- Gary Nolan (1967–73, '75–77) produced well during a brief career, posting a 3.02 ERA and a 110-67 record backed by the Big Red Machine.

- Don Gullett (1970–76) pitched alongside Nolan and posted an even more impressive 91-44 record to go with his 3.03 ERA.

- Tom Seaver (1977–82) was traded by the Mets to the Reds for four players and promptly went 14-3 with a 2.34 ERA for the rest of the year. Also of note was his outstanding work during the strike-shortened 1981 season: 2.54 ERA and a 14-2 record.

- Mario Soto (1977–88) pitched his entire career with the Reds, posting a 100-92 record with a 3.47 ERA. A three-time All-Star, Soto had more strikeouts than any other pitcher from 1980 through '85, with a personal best of 274 in 1982 (which is also the best of any Reds pitcher ever).

- Tom Browning (1984–1994) pitched almost his entire career for the Reds, starting with his NL Rookie of the Year campaign in 1985, when he posted a 20-9 record. He was a workhorse, leading the league in games started four times, and pitched a perfect game for the Reds in 1988.

- Johnny Cueto (2008–15) had a few good seasons for the Reds before being traded to the Royals before the deadline in 2015. His best season came in 2014, when he went 20-9 with a 2.25 ERA and a league-leading 242 strikeouts.

Relief Pitching

Name	YR	WAR	W3	SV	W-L	ERA	WHIP	ERA+
John Franco	6	13.3	8.8	148	42-30	2.49	1.269	153
Clay Carroll	8	12.5	7.0	119	71-43	2.73	1.319	129
Aroldis Chapman	6	10.9	8.3	146	19-20	2.17	1.016	181
Rob Dibble	6	10.2	9.4	88	26-23	2.74	1.127	139
Jeff Brantley	4	6.7	6.6	88	11-11	2.64	1.122	159
Pedro Borbón	10	6.3	5.7	76	62-33	3.32	1.289	107

Danny Graves	9	6.2	6.8	182	39-43	3.94	1.371	112
Rawly Eastwick	4	5.3	5.1	57	18-10	2.40	1.110	151
Francisco Cordero	4	5.2	5.0	150	18-18	2.96	1.296	141
Tom Hume	10	4.9	8.1	88	52-66	3.83	1.358	97

I chose only seven starting pitchers because I wanted to include five relievers for this All-Time team. **Aroldis Chapman** (2010–15) brought his 100+ MPH fastball from Cuba to the Reds and initially served as a setup man while he worked on his control. An All-Star every year from 2012 through '15, he posted consistent saves totals of 38, 38, 36, and 33 to go with ERAs of 1.51, 2.54, 2.00, and 1.63. His most impressive numbers were perhaps his 546 strikeouts in 319 IP, and the fact that he allowed only 169 hits in those 319 IP.

John Franco (1984–89) started his long career with the Reds and had a 12-3 record with 12 saves and a 2.18 ERA in his second year. He then posted 29 or more saves in his next four seasons, including a league-leading 39 with a 1.57 ERA in 1988.

Rob Dibble (1988–93) was one of the Nasty Boys relievers (along with Randy Myers and Norm Charlton), famous for their hard-throwing ways. A two-time All-Star, Dibble posted microscopic ERAs as a setup man of 1.82, 2.09, and 1.74 in his first three seasons. In 1990 he was a key part of their post-season success, as he pitched 9.2 IP over 7 games, with 14 strikeouts, and only 3 hits and 0 runs allowed. He became their primary closer after that and posted 31 saves in 1991 and 25 in 1992.

The powerful Reds teams of the 1970s often split the closer duties between two and sometimes three relievers. **Pedro Borbón** (1970–79) was a key part of this mix and from 1972 through 1977 pitched 120+ innings per year. He saved 18 games once, 14 games twice, and posted a 2.16 ERA in 1973 to go with an 11-4 record. **Clay Carroll** (1968–75) had double-digit saves five times for the Reds, including a league-leading 37 in 1972. Rawly Eastwick (1974–77) was a key third arm during this period, and actually led the league in saves during the Reds two championship years, recording 22 in 1975 and 26 in 1976. But those were his only two full seasons for Cincy, so I decided to go with Borbón and Carroll.

You could make a case for a couple of other Reds relievers to make this All-Time team, starting with their all-time saves leader, Danny Graves (1997–05). He was their closer for five seasons, with a high of 41 saves in 2004. That came a year after the Reds tried Graves as a starter, an experiment that was a failure, as he went 4-15 with a 5.33 ERA.

Next on the Reds' all-time saves list is Francisco Cordero (2008–11), who was their closer for four years and posted consistent save totals of 34, 39, 40, and 37. Jeff Brantley (1994–97) was a closer for the Reds for three seasons, including 1996, when he led the NL with 44 saves (which is still the highest total for any Reds pitcher). And lastly, Tom Hume (1977–85, '87) started as a mixed starter/reliever, but later became a short reliever, posting four seasons with double-digit saves, including 25 in 1980.

Managers

Name	YR	From-To	W-L	PCT	PS	WS
Sparky Anderson	9	1970–78	863-586	.596	5	2
Bill McKechnie	9	1938–46	744-631	.541	2	1
Pat Moran	5	1919–23	425-329	.564	1	1
Fred Hutchinson	6	1959–64	443-372	.544	1	0
Dusty Baker	6	2008–13	509-463	.524	3	0
Buck Ewing	5	1895–99	394-297	.570	0	0
Jack Hendricks	6	1924–29	469-450	.510	0	0
Pete Rose	6	1984–89	412-373	.525	0	0

The clear top spot here goes to **Sparky Anderson**, who was at the helm during the famed Big Red Machine of the 1970s. The next three also seemed pretty clear in **Bill McKechnie**, **Pat Moran**, and **Fred Hutchinson** (though you could make a case for Dusty Baker too). Buck Ewing was a player-manager at the end of his career, as was Pete Rose.

Starting Lineup

What would mythical starting lineups look like for this All-Time roster?

Against RHP:
Pete Rose RF (S)
Joe Morgan 2B (L)
Joey Votto 1B (L)
Ted Kluszewski DH (L)
Frank Robinson LF (R)
Vada Pinson CF (L)
Johnny Bench C (R)
Tony Pérez 3B (R)
Barry Larkin SS (R)

Against LHP:
Pete Rose RF (S)
Barry Larkin SS (R)
Frank Robinson LF (R)
Johnny Bench C (R)
George Foster DH (R)
Tony Pérez 3B (R)
Joe Morgan 2B (L)
Eric Davis CF (R)
Joey Votto 1B (L)

These lineups are very impressive, and you could reasonably rearrange them in a variety of ways. I went with two platoons, Pinson and Davis in CF, and Kluszewski and Foster at DH. And there are some very capable bats on the bench, like Roush, Lombardi, McCormick, and others. Lastly, shifting Joey Votto from third to ninth in the order against lefties doesn't mean to imply he doesn't hit lefties well—he does, at about a .300 clip. These lineups are just loaded with talent, and I rather like the idea Votto's ridiculously high OBP coming up right before the top of the order.

Depth Chart

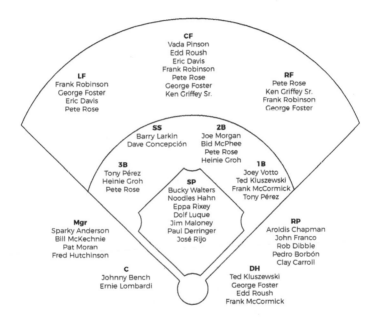

Prospects for Current Players

What are the prospects of current Reds players making this All-Time team roster? Joey Votto is already on the team as the starting 1B. Speedster outfielder Billy Hamilton has stolen 50+ bases four times, but he bats only .245 with an abysmal .298 OBP. The Reds have a few other players with talent (like Scooter Gennett, Adam Duvall, Raisel Iglesias, and others), but they aren't a top team right now, so I don't expect many of these players will stay in Cincinnati long enough to crack this All-Time roster. We'll see...

Retired Player Numbers

Fred Hutchinson (1), Johnny Bench (5), Joe Morgan (8), Sparky Anderson (10, manager), Barry Larkin (11), Dave Concepción (13), Pete Rose (14), Ted Kluszewski (18), Frank Robinson (20), Tony Pérez (24)

Selections from Other Authors and Fan Surveys

1958: *Sport* magazine, January issue

As part of a running series, *Sport* magazine reported on all-time all-star teams picked by "big league publicity departments and the writers covering the clubs." Here is what they had to say:

> **First Base:** Ted Kluszewski, the Redlegs' muscleman who has the fans in Rhineland pulling for him to make a comeback next season.
>
> **Second Base:** Hughie Critz, a great little competitor who held down the position for the Reds from 1924 through 1930.
>
> **Shortstop:** Roy McMillan, one of the most brilliant defensive shortstops anybody has ever had.
>
> **Third Base:** Heinie Groh, a fine fielder and a tough hitter who came to Cincinnati in 1913 and stayed there until 1921.
>
> **Left Field:** Chick Hafey, whose savage line drives are still talked about by Cincy fans. Chick played with the Reds from 1932 to 1937. He finished with a lifetime batting average of .317.
>
> **Center Field:** Edd Roush, who would be an all-time great on anyone's team. He came to the Reds from the Giants in 1916 and played in Cincinnati until 1926. He made a brief comeback in 1931, and finally retired with a lifetime average of .323.
>
> **Right Field:** Gus Bell, who is being moved over from center for this occasion. We figure the readers of SPORT know Gus too well for us to recount his accomplishments here.
>
> **Catcher:** Ernie Lombardi, one of the game's most feared hitters, who played in Cincinnati from 1932 through 1941 and had a lifetime average of .306.
>
> **Lefthanded Pitcher:** Eppa Rixey, whom many fans and writers believe merits a niche in the Hall of Fame. Eppa pitched for the Reds from

1921 through 1933 and, when he finally retired, he had piled up a total of 266 National League victories.

Righthanded Pitcher: Bucky Walters, the converted infielder who arrived in Cincy in 1938, won 27 games in pitching the Reds to the pennant the next year, and was a big name hurler there until 1948. He managed the Reds in his last season at Crosley Field.

Back in 1958 this was a reasonable roster. The only two questionable selections were at 2B and LF. If their project intentionally ignored pre-1900 players, that would explain why McPhee was not chosen. Chick Hafey's best seasons were in St. Louis, and he played only two full years for the Reds. Also, he mostly played CF for the Reds, so assuming any outfielder would have been eligible for the LF spot in their eyes, I would have preferred not only Wally Post, but also Ival Goodman, Curt Walker, or Cy Seymour.

Lastly, regarding the hope expressed in their blurb on Kluszewski, he didn't make a comeback. Instead he was traded to Pittsburgh for fellow first-sacker Dee Fondy, and never had a full, productive season again.

1969: *The Sporting News* Fan Poll

The July 5, 1969, issue reported the results of a fan poll for the long-standing franchises of the day. The results for the Reds were: 1B: Ted Kluszewski, 2B: Hughie Critz, 3B: Heinie Groh, SS: Roy McMillan, C: Ernie Lombardi, OF: Edd Roush, OF: Pete Rose, OF: Frank Robinson, RHP: Bucky Walters, LHP: Eppa Rixey.

I assume that Critz wasn't a runaway winner over Frey at 2B, and obviously fans here weren't remembering McPhee from the old days. It was interesting to see that Rose was already considered good enough to make the club. He won the Rookie of the Year Award in 1963, had four consecutive .300+ seasons, and went on to have a superb 1969 season (a Gold Glove, a .348 average, and a career-high 16 HR and 82 RBI). Fans likely were assuming he would continue to thrive for their club, which he certainly did.

1990: "All-Time All-Star Teams," in *The Baseball Research Journal*

In an interesting article, Robert C. Berlo used Thorn and Palmer's TPR (Total Player Rating) system to choose all-time teams. He selected players based on their best 800 consecutive games for the franchise, with a minimum of five years played. His results: 1B Pérez, 2B Morgan, SS Concepción, 3B Groh, RF Robinson, CF Foster, LF Rose, C Bench, SP Walters, SP Luque, SP Hahn, SP Maloney, RP Franco.

Given the method used, it wasn't surprising to see George Foster rate very highly, over Roush for instance (even though Foster played more LF than CF).

1992: *The All-Time All-Star Baseball Book*, by Nick Acocella and Donald Dewey

In their brief write-up on the Reds, the authors noted as I did the emphasis on hitting over pitching throughout the Reds' history. I thought their choices were very good, starting with Pérez at 1B, as they decided to list Rose at 3B instead of OF. They had Morgan at 2B and Concepción at SS (Larkin was just getting started). The outfield was Robinson, Roush, and Foster. Bench was the catcher and Rixey the pitcher. Honorable mention was given to Ernie Lombardi.

1995: *Baseball Ratings*, by Charles F. Faber

The Faber system resulted in an infield of Pérez, Morgan, Concepción, and Groh, and an outfield of Rose, Robinson, and Pinson. The five starting pitchers were Walters, Rixey, Maloney, Nuxhall, and Derringer, with Carroll as the top reliever.

2003: *Rob Neyer's Big Book of Baseball Lineups*, by Rob Neyer

Neyer's choices didn't differ much from mine. He started Pérez at 1B with Kluszewski as the backup, which meant McCormick was left off. This also meant Groh was promoted to starting at 3B. He had Rose in LF, Roush in CF, and Robinson in RF, and the backups were Foster, Pinson, and Griffey Sr. His eight starting pitchers were Walters, Derringer, Luque, Rixey, Hahn, Maloney, Donohue, and Rijo, with Carroll and Franco as sensible relief choices.

The only two choices I'll comment further on were his backup 3B and backup 2B. At the hot corner he selected Billy Werber to back up Groh. He wrote, "Valuable member of the 'Jungle Club' infield – Werber was 'Tiger' – that helped Reds win pennants in '39 and '40; scored 220 runs in those two seasons." Impressive, but that was all Werber ever did for the Reds. His third and only other season was rather poor. Then again, I wasn't keen on Sabo or others instead, which was the reason I moved Pérez to 3B and bumped Groh to the bench, allowing McCormick to be the backup 1B.

As for backup 2B, he went with Lonnie Frey, about whom he wrote, "Born Linus Reinhard Frey, but nicknamed 'Lonnie,' 'Junior,' and 'Leopard'; easily the best defensive 2B in the National League before he got drafted." Frey wasn't a bad choice, given that Neyer stated in his Introduction that he was only considering players from 1900 forward (so McPhee was not eligible).

Sweeney's lineup was pretty solid with Kluszewski, Morgan, Rose, Larkin, Robinson, Pinson, Roush, Bench, and Pérez (listed as the DH). My only issue here really is that Votto by now is more deserving than Kluszewski. He chose four starting pitchers, with the first three being fine—Rixey, Walters, Maloney—but the fourth, Gullett, being a stretch. The choice of Charlton as the reliever is interesting, as he was only the team's closer for one season, though he was a good setup man for several.

Top WAR Single Seasons – Hitters (8+)

Name	Year	WAR	AVG	HR	R	RBI	SB	OPS+
Joe Morgan	1975	11.0	.327	17	107	94	67	169
Joe Morgan	1976	9.6	.320	27	113	111	60	186
Joe Morgan	1972	9.3	.292	16	122	73	58	149
Joe Morgan	1973	9.2	.290	26	116	82	67	154
Frank Robinson	1962	8.7	.342	39	134	136	18	172
Joe Morgan	1974	8.6	.293	22	107	67	58	159
Johnny Bench	1972	8.6	.270	40	87	125	6	166
George Foster	1977	8.4	.320	52	124	149	6	165
Pete Rose	1973	8.3	.338	5	115	64	10	138
Cy Seymour	1905	8.0	.377	8	95	121	21	182

Just how good was Joe Morgan? Good enough to have the top four seasons in this list, and five of the top six. No one else even appears on this list more than once (Robinson came close with seasons of 7.9 and 7.7, and Bench had a 7.8 season). Any Reds fans would have guessed that the best seasons from Morgan, Robinson, Bench, Foster, and Rose might appear on this list. Less likely to be guessed would have been Seymour's career year in 1905, when he led the NL in batting average, hits, doubles, triples, and RBIs.

Top WAR Single Seasons – Pitchers (8+)

Name	Year	WAR	W-L	ERA	IP	SO	ERA+
Dolf Luque	1923	10.8	27-8	1.93	322.0	151	201
José Rijo	1993	10.2	14-9	2.48	257.1	227	162
Bucky Walters	1939	9.8	27-11	2.29	319.0	137	170
Noodles Hahn	1902	9.0	23-12	1.77	321.0	142	169
Jim Maloney	1965	9.0	20-9	2.54	255.1	244	148
Ewell Blackwell	1947	8.7	22-8	2.47	273.0	193	168
Ted Breitenstein	1897	8.2	23-12	3.62	320.1	98	125

This list intentionally omitted pitching seasons from before 1894, as pitchers back then often threw 400+ IP, making comparison with seasons since then very challenging. Unlike Morgan on the list for hitters, it is interesting to see that no hurlers appear on this list more than once (although Noodles Hahn came close, as his rookie campaign in 1899 scored a 7.9 WAR). And I was a bit surprised to see Rijo's 1993 campaign rate so highly, since he posted only 14 wins.

Franchise Player

There were many reasonable candidates for this honor, but I decided to go with Johnny Bench. I gave some consideration to Pete Rose of course, not only for his numbers but also for his versatility. Frank Robinson, Joe Morgan, and Barry Larkin were also considered, but in the end, I thought Bench was the most deserving because of his combination of offensive and defensive production while playing such a critical position.

CHAPTER 10

The Pirates Franchise All-Time Dream Team

The Pirates franchise began in 1882 as the Pittsburgh Alleghenys of the American Association. They joined the NL in 1887 and switched to their current nickname in 1891. Generally mediocre at best during these early years, they became a blockbuster club during the first decade of the 20th century due in large part to the efforts of superstar Honus Wagner and player-manager Fred Clarke. The decades that followed saw many outstanding players, such as Paul Waner, Arky Vaughan, Ralph Kiner, and Roberto Clemente—but success for the franchise was mixed, with World Series championships not coming until 1960 and 1971.

The Pirates had a very memorable 1979 campaign, winning the World Series with a "We Are Family" mantra and leadership from aging star Willie Stargell. After a period of decline in the 1980s, they briefly flirted with success in the early 1990s. But then a long malaise set in: 20 consecutive losing seasons from 1993 through 2012, largely the result of being a small-market team and ownership's decisions not to pay to retain star players. A strong farm system finally surfaced enough strong talent for the Pirates to develop a core that led them to three playoff appearances from 2013 through 2015.

As noted above, the Pirates have had many great stars over the years. The talent was weighted heavily at certain positions, with pitching and catching not being consistent strengths. As a result, their All-Time team is respectable, but with some relative weak spots.

1st Base

Name	YR	WAR	W3	W/G	AVG	HR	SB	OPS+
Willie Stargell	21	57.5	20.4	.0243	.282	475	17	147
Jake Beckley	8	26.8	12.7	.0288	.300	43	138	122
Elbie Fletcher	7	25.0	15.6	.0273	.279	60	20	128
George Grantham	7	22.0	11.1	.0241	.315	74	58	129
Gus Suhr	10	21.3	12.0	.0156	.278	79	52	112
Donn Clendenon	8	17.6	10.7	.0179	.280	106	81	119

Although I generally tried to select players based on the position they played the most for that particular team, sometimes feast/famine scenarios demanded exceptions. This was one such case, as this Pirates roster was loaded with great OF candidates but was not very strong at 1B. **Willie Stargell** (1962–82) was a lifetime Pirate who played more games as an OF (1,296, mostly LF), but nonetheless played significant time at 1B (848). He smacked 475 HR (by far the most for this franchise) and twice led the league, with 48 in 1971 and 44 in 1973. Pops is perhaps best known for his leadership of the 1979 Pirates when they won the World Series: although physically over the hill, he earned co-MVP honors for the regular season (with batting champion Keith Hernandez of the Cardinals) and then won the World Series MVP Award too.

The backup 1B was a tough choice, as the numbers for WAR, WAR3, W/G, and OPS+ make clear. I went with **Jake Beckley** (1888–89, '91–96), a Hall of Famer who split most of his career between the Pirates and the Reds. He was a productive run producer, often having both 100 runs and 100 RBI. And he had extremely consistent triples numbers: exactly 19 per season for five consecutive years! He played during a time when the number of games per season varied but was generally between 130 and 135 only. That decreased his opportunity to accumulate all counting stats (and also WAR), so I kept that in mind in comparing him with the other candidates here.

You could certainly make a case for Elbie Fletcher (1939–43, '46–47), who missed two seasons due to WWII but was a good hitter and a fine fielder. He had a good eye, walked a lot, led the league in OBP for three consecutive seasons, and made his only All-Star team in 1943.

George Grantham (1925–31) played somewhat more at 1B than 2B for the Pirates. Hitting .315, he had some pop too: in 1930 he hit .324 with 120 runs, 14 triples, 18 HR, and 99 RBI.

Gus Suhr (1930–39) played a bit longer for the Pirates than the other candidates, including an impressive 822 consecutive games played streak. He had three seasons with 100+ RBI and often compiled 30+ doubles, 10+ triples, and

10+ HR. And lastly, Donn Clendenon (1961–68) provided a .280 average with moderate power and speed, with his best year coming in 1966 when he batted .299 and hit 28 HR with 98 RBI.

2nd Base

Name	YR	WAR	W3	W/G	AVG	HR	SB	OPS+
Bill Mazeroski	17	36.2	13.2	.0167	.260	138	27	84
Claude Ritchey	7	25.2	12.7	.0258	.277	5	88	105
Johnny Ray	7	19.1	14.1	.0205	.286	37	68	99
Neil Walker	7	16.4	10.0	.0196	.272	93	26	113
Rennie Stennett	9	14.5	11.1	.0134	.278	38	69	88
Josh Harrison	8	13.9	10.7	.0165	.277	52	75	97
Frankie Gustine	10	8.8	6.8	.0075	.268	34	57	89

Known for his excellent glove, Hall of Famer **Bill Mazeroski** (1957–72) was the clear choice as 2B starter. Mazeroski won eight Gold Glove Awards, was an All-Star seven times, and hit one of the most famous home runs in World Series history in 1960. He also ranks fifth in games played overall for Pirates position players.

George Grantham was considered at 2B as he was at 1B, but in the end, I thought **Claude Ritchey** (1900–06) was deserving of the backup 2B spot, as he has the highest WAR and W/G of the candidates. Overall a .277 hitter, he batted over .290 three times, had moderate speed, and was a good fielder for his era.

Recent fan favorite Neil Walker (2009–15) was well on his way to cracking this roster until he was traded after the 2015 season. Walker provided consistent power, with a high of 23 HR in 2014.

The few others I considered included Rennie Stennett (1971–79), a .278 hitter with minimal power or speed (high of 28 SB in 1977). Johnny Ray (1981–87) followed soon after Stennett and provided a .286 average with 30+ doubles in his five full seasons, including leading the NL with 38 in both 1983 and 1984. Versatile fielder Josh Harrison (2011-18) split his time between 2B and 3B, but also played some SS, LF, and RF. A two-time All-Star, he has provided only moderate power or speed. Lastly, Frankie Gustine (1939–48) was basically a utility infielder for the Pirates for the better part of a decade. Although he was an All-Star in his final three seasons in Pittsburgh, he hit only .268 overall with little power or speed.

3rd Base

Name	YR	WAR	W3	W/G	AVG	HR	SB	OPS+
Tommy Leach	14	36.4	16.1	.0231	.271	43	271	109
Pie Traynor	17	36.2	12.6	.0187	.320	58	158	107
Richie Hebner	11	23.0	12.8	.0201	.277	128	21	121
Bob Elliott	8	22.7	11.7	.0217	.292	50	45	119
Bobby Bonilla	6	20.3	13.8	.0241	.284	114	24	134
Bill Madlock	7	16.2	12.0	.0202	.297	68	82	117

There were two guys who were pretty clearly going to make this roster at 3B: one a well-known Hall of Famer, the other a relatively obscure star from the Deadball Era. **Harold "Pie" Traynor** (1920–37) used to surface regularly in discussions of the greatest third basemen of all time. But today his name is rightly drowned out by more recent stars like Schmidt, Brett, Robinson, Mathews, and Boggs. Playing his entire career with the Pirates, Traynor was a high-average hitter (.320) and didn't have much power, though he did post 100+ RBI seven times. He had only moderate speed, swiping 20+ bases twice, and didn't walk very often (.362 OBP). He was very hard to strikeout, in fact he only struck out 278 times in 7,558 career at-bats. And he was generally regarded as one of the best defensive 3B of his era. Pie played a vital role in the Pirates' 1925 World Series championship over the Senators, as he went 9-26 with two triples and a home run (off the great Walter Johnson). As a final side note, Traynor was a player-manager for the last few years of his playing career, plus a manager for two more seasons after that.

While I gave Traynor the starting spot, you could certainly make a case for **Tommy Leach** (1900–12, '18). He was a good run scorer and hit a lot of triples (he led the NL in triples with 22 in 1902 and runs with 126 in 1909). He ran well, stealing 20+ bases for Pittsburgh seven times, including a high of 43 in 1907. Defensively, he played 850 games at 3B, but also played over 600 games in the OF (mostly in CF), displaying a lot of range at both positions.

The other candidates I considered included Richie Hebner (1968–76, '82–83), who provided some power, hitting 15 to 25 HR for the Pirates five times. Four-time All-Star Bob Elliott (1939–46) managed three seasons with 100+ RBI (especially impressive as he had 10 HR or less each year). Bobby Bonilla (1986–91) was not a good fielder, but he was a five-time All-Star for the Pirates. He collected 100+ RBI three times and played an important role in the team's success in the early 1990s. And lastly, Bill Madlock (1979–85) won two batting titles while with Pittsburgh: .341 in 1981 and .323 in 1983.

Shortstop

Name	YR	WAR	W3	W/G	AVG	HR	SB	OPS+
Honus Wagner	18	120.3	30.9	.0494	.328	82	639	154
Arky Vaughan	10	64.0	25.4	.0454	.324	84	86	141
Jay Bell	8	24.4	13.9	.0213	.269	78	58	102
Gene Alley	11	24.4	15.4	.0204	.254	55	63	88
Dick Groat	9	23.6	14.3	.0177	.290	30	6	89
Jack Wilson	9	21.3	12.6	.0184	.269	60	36	79

The starting shortstop here had to be **Honus Wagner** (1900–17). In fact, he'd get my vote as the greatest ever at the position. He won eight batting titles, and led the NL in doubles seven times, stolen bases five times, RBI four times, and triples three times. Although he only hit 10 HR once, he posted 100+ RBI seven times. Overall, he batted .328 for the Pirates, with 639 SB, 551 doubles, and 232 triples. For many years The Flying Dutchman was considered the best player in the National League, their answer to the AL's Ty Cobb. Wagner was a great fielder too, and the key player in the Pirates' early success as a franchise.

Arky Vaughan (1932–41) would be good enough to start on many all-time teams, so he got the backup spot here. As you can see, his W3, W/G, and OPS+ numbers nearly match Wagner—he just didn't play for the Pirates for nearly as long. He did play most of his career with Pittsburgh, earning an All-Star nomination eight times, before moving on to the Dodgers. He captured a batting title in 1935 with a .385 mark and led the league in runs and triples three times each.

With Wagner and Vaughan, the Pirates arguably have had two of the top ten shortstops of all time. Other candidates are worth brief mention, but pale in comparison. Jay Bell (1989–96) was an All-Star and Gold Glove winner in 1993, when he hit .310 with 102 runs and 16 SB, but overall provided only moderate power and speed. Dick Groat (1952, '55–62) was an All-Star three times for the Pirates and won the NL MVP Award in 1960 after leading the league with a .325 average. Overall, he hit a respectable .290 for the Pirates, but he had virtually no power or speed. Gene Alley (1963–73) played his entire career for Pittsburgh, playing mostly shortstop but also some 2B and 3B. He won two Gold Glove Awards but was only a .254 hitter, with little power or speed. And lastly, Jack Wilson was a good fielder and an All-Star in 2004, when he hit .308 with 41 doubles and a league-leading 12 triples.

Catcher

Name	YR	WAR	W3	W/G	AVG	HR	SB	OPS+
Jason Kendall	9	30.6	14.5	.0244	.306	67	140	108
Manny Sanguillén	12	26.8	13.7	.0207	.299	59	33	105
Tony Peña	7	22.3	13.8	.0278	.286	63	42	104
Fred Carroll	6	16.3	12.0	.0284	.281	19	102	136
George Gibson	12	15.1	8.7	.0129	.238	15	39	82
Doggie Miller	10	14.8	8.8	.0152	.254	19	209	98
Smokey Burgess	6	14.6	9.6	.0249	.296	51	3	116

Going from a position of strength to one of weakness, we can see that the Pirates are not famous for having great catchers. For a team that has been around since the 19th century, it was rather unimpressive to nominate **Jason Kendall** (1996–04) as the starting catcher. A three-time All-Star, he batted .306 and provided some speed, amassing 140 SB during his tenure in Pittsburgh. He also provided a solid .387 OBP, in part due to his knack for getting hit by pitches, something he did 31 times in 1997 and again to lead the league in 1998.

The backup spot is a tough choice, but I went with **Tony Peña** (1980–86), as he was an outstanding defensive backstop (three Gold Glove Awards), was a four-time All-Star, and had a solid batting average (.286) with some pop (five consecutive seasons of 10+ HR).

You could make a case for Manny Sanguillén (1967, '69–76, '78–80), who was a capable backstop and often a .300 hitter. He provided good value to the Pirates after the 1976 season when they traded him to the A's—for manager Chuck Tanner, who led Pittsburgh in their historic 1979 World Championship season. And Manny was part of that success, as he returned to the club for three final seasons in 1978, albeit serving mostly as a pinch-hitter and backup catcher and first baseman.

Old-timer Fred Carroll (1885–89, '91) played almost as many games in the outfield as at catcher and had his best year in 1889, when he hit .330 and led the NL with a .486 OBP (not that people kept track of that stat in those days). The other catcher for the Pirates in those days, George "Doggie" Miller (1884–93) also played some OF and 3B. He had some speed, stealing 25+ bases in six seasons. A bit later came George Gibson (1905–16), a very light hitter (.238) who played in 12 seasons for Pittsburgh, but competed in 120 or more games only three times.

And lastly, Smokey Burgess (1959–64) was a good hitter (.296) and a four-time All-Star for the Pirates, but he wasn't always a full-time catcher, as he was often used as a pinch-hitter (the best of his era).

Left Field

Name	YR	WAR	W3	W/G	AVG	HR	SB	OPS+
Willie Stargell	21	57.5	20.4	.0243	.282	475	17	147
Barry Bonds	7	50.1	26.7	.0496	.275	176	251	147
Fred Clarke	15	46.7	15.4	.0316	.299	33	261	136
Ralph Kiner	8	44.5	24.5	.0406	.280	301	19	157
Starling Marté	7	26.2	15.4	.0319	.286	85	214	114
Brian Giles	5	26.0	18.3	.0364	.308	165	40	158
Mike Smith	7	22.7	15.0	.0296	.325	30	174	136
Jason Bay	6	15.0	12.5	.0209	.281	139	50	131

As I alluded to earlier, the outfield candidates for this All-Time dream team are fairly strong, and that includes LF. I've included Stargell here again as reference, and if you went strictly by highest WAR for players at the position they played the most, then Willie would be your starting LF on this team. As I've chosen him at 1B instead, this means **Barry Bonds** (1986–92) can be the LF starter instead. He was outstanding early in his career for the Pirates but packed his bags for San Francisco before attaining his most impressive numbers. He had MVP seasons for Pittsburgh in 1990 and 1992—also the only two years he represented the club as an All-Star. His pre-controversy numbers certainly deserve recognition, including his 1990 season, which was the first 30/30 Pirates season, and the first .300 average, 30 HR, 100 RBI, and 50 SB season in major league history. He was also a great fielder (three Gold Glove Awards while in Pittsburgh), while admittedly not hitting very well in the postseason for the Bucs.

Next up is **Ralph Kiner** (1946–53), one of the most prolific home run hitters in history if judged by HR per AB over an entire career. Kiner smashed 301 HR in only 3,913 at-bats for Pittsburgh, including a five-year span from 1947 through 1951 with 100+ runs and 100+ RBI per year, and homer totals of 51, 40, 54 (franchise record), 47, and 42. In fact, he actually led the NL in HR in all of his seven full seasons in Pittsburgh—still the record for most consecutive HR crowns.

Technically **Fred Clarke** (1900–15) had a higher WAR total than Kiner, but he did it over many more seasons. During that time, he was also the manager of the team, though in his last three seasons he played very little on the field. Clarke was in many ways a typical Deadball Era star, hitting .299, scoring runs, and stealing bases. Interestingly, he had a higher OPS+ (135) than more well-known Pittsburgh stars Paul Waner (134) or Roberto Clemente (130). And he gets extra points for being a player-manager of one of the greatest dynasties ever, leading the club to four pennants, one World Series championship, and a .595

winning percentage over 16 seasons. I'll use one of my two "extra spots" for this dream team to sneak him on the roster.

Current Pirates outfielder Starling Marté (2012-18) won two Gold Glove Awards playing mostly LF, and then shifted to CF in 2018 when Andrew McCutchen was traded. A consistent hitter with moderate power, he has stolen 30+ bases five times, with a high of 47 in 2016.

There were three other primarily left fielders for the Pirates worth mentioning here, including old-timer Elmer "Mike" Smith (1892–97, 1901), who scored 120+ runs three times and hit .325 for Pittsburgh. Then 100 years later there were two sluggers, starting with Brian Giles (1999–2003), who blossomed after coming to Pittsburgh from Cleveland, batting .308 with a .426 OBP and hitting 35 to 39 HR in each of his four full seasons. Then Jason Bay (2003–2008) was obtained by the Pirates in a trade for Giles and quickly proved to be nearly his equal. He became the first Pirates player ever to win the Rookie of the Year Award (2004), and then hit 30+ HR with 100+ runs and 100+ RBI in both 2005 and 2006.

Center Field

Name	YR	WAR	W3	W/G	AVG	HR	SB	OPS+
Max Carey	17	52.5	15.3	.0241	.287	67	688	111
Andrew McCutchen	9	40.0	21.4	.0297	.291	203	171	136
Andy Van Slyke	8	30.9	17.8	.0292	.283	117	134	124
Al Oliver	10	27.1	12.4	.0208	.296	135	54	119
Lloyd Waner	17	24.0	10.1	.0133	.319	27	65	100
Ginger Beaumont	8	22.2	12.7	.0224	.321	31	200	124

Max Carey (1910–26) was very fast, stealing 688 bases for Pittsburgh, including leading the league an impressive ten times. In 1922 he had an amazing 51 SB while being caught only twice! His speed helped him in the field too, as he is often cited as one of the top defensive center fielders of all time (some put him in company with Speaker, Mays, Ashburn, and the best of today).

You could also certainly argue for recent star **Andrew McCutchen** (2009–17) as the top CF choice. He showed flashes of greatness in his first three seasons, and then finally actualized his potential in 2012 when he hit .327 with 31 HR and 20 SB and took home the Gold Glove Award too. Some of his numbers dropped the next year, when he hit .317 with 21 HR and 27 SB, but that was good enough to earn him MVP honors. A five-time All-Star, Cutch was traded to the Giants after the 2017 season, so it seems his career with the Pirates is over.

There were four other Pittsburgh center fielders I considered. Andy Van Slyke (1987–1994) won five Gold Glove Awards and was an All-Star three times, providing both HR power and speed on the basepaths. Al Oliver (1968–77) played the first half of his impressive career with the Pirates, batting .296 with double-digit HR in all nine of his full seasons. And early 20th century star Ginger Beaumont (1899–1906) hit .321 for the Pirates, stole 200 bases, and scored 757 runs in only 989 games. While in Pittsburgh, he led the league in hits three times and led the league in batting (.357) in 1902.

Lastly, like Pie Traynor, a player I think is in some ways overrated in baseball lore is Lloyd "Little Poison" Waner (1927–41, '44–45). Yes, he did hit for a .319 average, but he was far more one-dimensional than his brother Paul. He hit very few home runs and not even very many doubles, although he did manage to hit double-digit triples five times, including a league-leading 20 in 1929.

Right Field

Name	YR	WAR	W3	W/G	AVG	HR	SB	OPS+
Roberto Clemente	18	94.5	25.2	.0388	.317	240	83	130
Paul Waner	15	68.2	20.6	.0317	.340	109	100	136
Dave Parker	11	34.7	21.0	.0267	.305	166	123	131
Kiki Cuyler	7	17.5	15.9	.0333	.336	38	130	135

For many reasons I needn't retell here, **Roberto Clemente** (1955–72) is considered one of the all-time greats of the game. Interestingly, for a player known for his reckless abandon on the basepaths, he didn't actually collect very many stolen bases (83). But he brought a gun of an arm to right field and provided power while capturing four batting titles and one MVP Award (1966). He was a 12-time All-Star, won 12 Gold Glove Awards, and when his life ended in tragedy he had a .317 average and exactly 3,000 hits—all amassed as a Pittsburgh Pirate.

Paul "Big Poison" Waner (1926–40) hit loads of doubles and triples (highs of 62 and 22, respectively) and is amongst baseball's leaders in lifetime batting average (he hit .340 for the Pirates). He scored 100+ runs nine times and won three batting titles. He even took home MVP honors in only his second season, when he led the NL with a .380 average, 237 hits, 18 triples, and 131 RBI.

I'm awarding the other "extra spot" on this roster to another outfielder, **Dave Parker** (1973–83). He had some great seasons in Pittsburgh, including his 1978 MVP campaign, when he led the NL with a .334 average and added 30 HR, 117 RBI, and 20 SB. A four-time All-Star for the Pirates, he also provided excellent defense in right field (three Gold Glove Awards and a fearsome arm).

The only other right fielder for the Pirates who amassed 15 or more WAR was Kiki Cuyler (1921–27), who started his Hall of Fame career in Pittsburgh. While playing parts of seven seasons there, he had only two full seasons for the Pirates, but they were very impressive. In 1925 he batted .357 with 220 hits, 43 doubles, 18 HR, 102 RBI, 41 SB, and a league-leading 26 triples and 144 runs scored. The following year wasn't quite as stellar but was still solid, as he hit .321 with 15 triples and a league-leading 35 SB and 113 runs.\

Starting Pitching

Name	YR	WAR	W3	W-L	ERA	WHIP	ERA+
Babe Adams	18	52.4	22.9	194-139	2.74	1.090	118
Wilbur Cooper	13	52.4	20.7	202-159	2.74	1.199	120
Bob Friend	15	42.6	16.7	191-218	3.55	1.287	108
Sam Leever	13	41.3	18.3	194-100	2.47	1.141	123
John Candelaria	12	34.2	17.0	124-87	3.17	1.174	117
Vern Law	16	32.7	16.8	162-147	3.77	1.284	102
Jesse Tannehill	6	31.7	21.1	116-58	2.75	1.196	128
Ed Morris	5	30.3	28.4	129-102	2.81	1.125	116
Deacon Phillippe	12	30.0	14.9	168-92	2.50	1.087	119
Rip Sewell	12	27.7	16.7	143-97	3.43	1.338	109
Rick Rhoden	8	24.9	18.9	79-73	3.51	1.313	106
Frank Killen	6	24.2	20.1	112-82	3.97	1.437	110
Ray Kremer	10	23.9	15.9	143-85	3.76	1.326	113
Doug Drabek	6	22.0	14.2	92-62	3.02	1.148	118
Bob Veale	11	21.2	13.4	116-91	3.06	1.321	113
Vic Willis	4	20.8	16.9	89-46	2.08	1.082	119
Howie Camnitz	9	15.8	12.7	116-84	2.63	1.174	110
Dock Ellis	9	12.6	7.6	96-80	3.16	1.254	111

Who the top two stasrting pitchers on this All-Time team should be seems pretty clear—what is not clear is how to rank them. **Babe Adams** (1907, '09–16, '18–26) burst onto the scene in 1909, going 12-3 with a 1.11 ERA and winning three games in the World Series as a rookie. He had great control, leading the league in WHIP five times. **Wilbur Cooper** (1912–24) played most of his career for the Pirates, posting a club-record 202 wins, with four seasons of 20+ wins, leading the league with 22 in 1921. Both Adams and Cooper had a 2.74 ERA for the Pirates, and even their ERA+ is almost the same—so pick who you want as the ace of the staff.

Sam Leever (1898–1910) was a lifetime Pirate and had a nifty Deadball -Era 2.47 ERA with an impressive 194-100 record (a .660 winning percentage). He won 20 games four times, with his best season arguably being 1903, when he went 25-7 with a 2.06 ERA. He is not a well-known name, but he is a quality third arm on the dream-team staff.

Bob Friend (1951–65) played most of his career for Pittsburgh and ended up with a losing record (191-218), in part due to his first four seasons as an unsuccessful spot starter and long reliever (his 1959 season of 8-19 didn't help either). He led the NL in ERA in 1955 with a 2.83 mark and led the league in wins in 1958 when he went 22-14. It is worth noting Friend's great durability in the prime of his career: he led the NL in games started from 1956 through '58 with totals of 42, 38, and 38, and then continued to start 34 to 38 games a year in his next seven seasons.

Jesse Tannehill (1897–1902) had five outstanding seasons at the turn of the century for the Pirates, including four with 20+ wins, and another where he posted 18 wins and a 2.18 ERA to lead the league. Although that is not a long span with Pittsburgh, I argue it is enough to make this team and arguably be ranked as high as fifth on the staff.

John Candelaria (1975–85, '93) pitched the first half of his career in Pittsburgh, posting a solid 3.17 ERA during that time. His best season was easily 1977, when he went 20-5 with a league-leading 2.34 ERA.

Deacon Phillippe (1900–11) had a 2.50 ERA and won 20 games five times for the Pirates during their domination of the early 1900s. He also pitched an impressive five complete games, winning three of them, in the inaugural World Series of 1903.

Vern Law (1950–51, '54–67) was a lifetime Pirate and posted a 20-9 record to win the Cy Young Award in 1960 (when only one was given out for both leagues.) **Rip Sewell** (1938–49) played almost his entire major league career with Pittsburgh, was an All-Star four times, and won 21 games in both 1943 and 1944. And for a tenth starting pitching spot I went with **Ray Kremer** (1924–33), who was a lifetime Pirate and twice won 20 games in a season. He also led the NL in ERA in both 1926 and 1927, with 2.61 and 2.47, respectively.

You could make a case for Rick Rhoden (1979–86), whose best two seasons for the Pirates were in 1984, when he went 14-9 with a 2.72 ERA, and 1986, when he went 15-12 with a 2.84 ERA (the one time he made an NL All-Star team as a Pirate). Rhoden was a relatively good hitter too—he batted .251 with 30 doubles and 5 HR in 506 at-bats for the Pirates.

As noted in this book's introduction, I've set a very high bar for including starting pitchers from the 1800s on these All-Time teams. The game was so different back then, especially regarding pitchers, that it makes rational comparison of statistics and other accomplishments very challenging. Ed "Cannonball" Morris (1885–89) pitched for this franchise for five years in the 1880s, including two strong seasons with 39-24 and 41-20 records. He pitched an amazing 580 and 555 innings in those two years, and had another season with 480. Frank

Killen (1893–98) was on the team a few years after Morris, but his numbers remain mind-boggling by today's standards: he went 36-14 in 1893 and 30-18 in 1896, pitching 415 and 431 innings in those years, respectively.

I did consider five other starting pitchers, starting with two who were key starters during the Pirates' strong run early in the 1900s. Vic Willis (1906–09) is a Hall of Famer who ended his career with the Pirates, with four very consistent seasons: 23-13 with a 1.73 ERA, 21-11 with a 2.34 ERA, 23-11 with a 2.07 ERA, and 22-11 with a 2.24 ERA. Howie Camnitz (1904, 1906–13) won 20+ games for Pittsburgh three times, with his best season being 1909 when he posted a 25-6 record and a 1.62 ERA.

The other three hurlers are ones who, depending on your age, you might remember seeing. Bob Veale (1962–72) pitched most of his career with the Pirates, was an All-Star twice, posted a 3.06 ERA, and recorded 200+ strikeouts four times. The flip side: he also led the NL in walks four times. Dock Ellis (1968–75, '79) posted a 3.16 ERA for the Pirates and had a 19-9 record in 1971. And lastly, Doug Drabek (1987–92) had a 3.02 ERA for the club and won the Cy Young Award in 1990, when he went 22-6.

Relief Pitching

Name	YR	WAR	W3	SV	W-L	ERA	WHIP	ERA+
Roy Face	12	20.2	9.9	186	100-93	3.46	1.239	110
Kent Tekulve	15	19.6	10.4	158	70-61	2.68	1.245	139
Al McBean	9	15.0	9.6	59	65-43	3.08	1.322	113
Dave Giusti	7	8.4	7.0	133	47-28	2.94	1.294	121
Ramón Hernández	6	8.1	5.9	39	23-12	2.51	1.176	139
Mike Williams	6	3.7	4.0	140	15-23	3.78	1.399	119
Mark Melancon	4	8.1	6.5	130	10-10	1.80	0.926	210

As with the top two starting pitchers, the top two relievers (and ultimately the only two I chose for this All-Time team) are hard to rank 1-2. In 1959, **Roy Face** (1953, '55–68) famously posted an 18-1 record in relief, while also saving 10 games. Then in 1962 he had a 1.88 ERA and saved 28 games.

If Face was one of the relief pitching pioneers, then sidearmer **Kent Tekulve** (1974–85) was one of the few in the 1970s who raised the position to specialty status. He twice posted 31 saves, including for the World Champion 1979 team, and had a great ERA of 2.68 during his tenure with the Pirates.

I considered several others who deserve brief mention, starting with Al McBean (1961–68, '70), who pitched with limited success as a starter for two Pirates seasons, but was more successful as a reliever. In 1963 he had a 13-3 record with 11 saves and a 2.57 ERA. The following year, he had a 1.91 ERA with 22 saves, and then had 18 with a 2.29 mark the next year. Dave Giusti (1970–76) was a good reliever for six years for Pittsburgh, after spending several seasons as a mediocre starter for Houston and St. Louis. He led the league with 30 saves in 1971 and followed that up with a 1.93 ERA the next year. Ramón Hernández (1971–76) was a teammate of Giusti and posted a 2.51 ERA while with the Pirates, including a 1.67 mark in 1972, when he had a career-high 14 saves.

Two-time All-Star Mark Melancon (2013–16) had an impressive 1.80 ERA and posted 30+ saves for the Pirates three times, including in 2015, when he led the NL with 51 (and set a new franchise record). And lastly, Mike Williams (1998–2003) posted a 1.94 ERA in 1998 and took over as closer the following year. Also a two-time All-Star, he had five seasons with 20+ saves, with a high of 46 in 2002.

Managers

Name	YR	From-To	W-L	PCT	PS	WS
Fred Clarke	16	1900–15	1,422-969	.595	4	1
Danny Murtaugh	15	1957–76	1,115-950	.540	4	2
Jim Leyland	11	1986–96	851-863	.496	3	0
Chuck Tanner	9	1977–85	711-685	.509	1	1
Frankie Frisch	7	1940–46	539-528	.505	0	0
Clint Hurdle	8	2011–18	666-628	.515	3	0
Pie Traynor	6	1934–39	457-406	.530	0	0
Bill McKechnie	5	1922–26	409-293	.583	1	1
George Gibson	6	1920–34	401-330	.549	0	0

The top manager in Pirates history seems clear—player-manager **Fred Clarke.** He had a lot of talent to work with over his 16 years at the helm, but a .595 winning percentage and four pennants speaks for itself. If I were to choose three others to serve as the coaches with him on this All-Time team, I'd go with those who had the most longevity with the club: **Danny Murtaugh**, **Jim Leyland**, and **Chuck Tanner.**

Starting Lineup

What would mythical starting lineups look like for this All-Time roster?

Against RHP:
Max Carey CF (S)
Paul Waner DH (L)
Honus Wagner SS (R)
Willie Stargell 1B (L)
Barry Bonds LF (L)
Roberto Clemente RF (R)
Pie Traynor 3B (R)
Jason Kendall C (R)
Bill Mazeroski 2B (R)

Against LHP:
Max Carey CF (S)
Roberto Clemente RF (R)
Honus Wagner SS (R)
Ralph Kiner LF (R)
Willie Stargell 1B (L)
Andrew McCutchen (R)
Pie Traynor 3B (R)
Jason Kendall C (R)
Bill Mazeroski 2B (R)

There is a natural platoon in LF between Bonds and Kiner (though Kiner didn't hit lefties better than righties). I also decided to have Waner and McCutchen split the DH duties.

Depth Chart

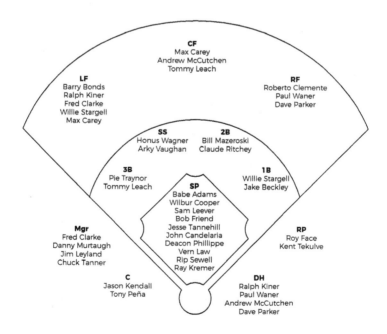

266

Prospects for Current Players

What are the chances of current Pirates players making this All-Time team? The Pirates have a consistently good farm system, and especially seem able to develop good outfielders and starting pitchers. But those are two positions where it would take a long, and consistently good tenure in Pittsburgh for guys like Starling Marte, Gregory Polanco, Jameson Taillon, or others to crack this dream-team roster. We'll see...

Retired Player Numbers

Billy Meyer (1, manager), Ralph Kiner (4), Willie Stargell (8), Bill Mazeroski (9), Paul Waner (11), Pie Traynor (20), Roberto Clemente (21), Honus Wagner (33), Danny Murtaugh (40, player/manager)

Selections from Other Authors and Fan Surveys

1958: *Sport* magazine, March issue

As part of a running series, *Sport* magazine reported on all-time all-star teams picked by "big league publicity departments and the writers covering the clubs." Here is what they had to say:

First Base: Gus Suhr, who played for Pittsburgh from 1930 through 1939.

Second Base: John "Dots" Miller, who played with the Pirates for five seasons, 1909-1913, at the start of a National League career which later took him to St. Louis and Philadelphia.

Shortstop: The immortal Honus Wagner, the greatest any team has ever had at the position. He came to Pittsburgh from Louisville in 1900, compiled a lifetime average of .329, and finally retired after the 1917 season. He is in baseball's Hall of Fame.

Third Base: Harold "Pie" Traynor, possibly the all-time best at his position, too, spent his entire big league career in Pittsburgh (1920-37) and batted .320. He's also in the Hall of Fame.

Left Field: Fred Clarke, who came to the Pirates as player-manager in 1900, played his last game for them in 1915. His lifetime average was .315. He was voted into the Hall of Fame in 1945.

Center Field: Max Carey, one of the greatest base-runners the game has known. He played for the Pirates from 1910 until 1926.

Right Field: Another Hall of Famer, Paul "Big Poison" Waner, who arrived in Pittsburgh in 1926 and stayed there through the 1940 season. His lifetime big-league batting average was .333.

Catcher: Walter Schmidt, the Pirates' backstop from 1916 through 1924.

Lefthanded Pitcher: Wilbur Cooper, a Pirate from 1912 through 1924; he won 216 big-league games.

Righthanded Pitcher: Remy Kremer, who spent his entire big-league career (1924-1933) in Pittsburgh, winning 143 games and losing only 85.

Back in 1958, the 1B and C positions were the weakest, as shown by the lack of accolades listed for Suhr and Schmidt. Dots Miller's numbers for his five seasons in Pittsburgh didn't initially appear impressive, but relative to the era in which he toiled, they weren't too bad (amongst the top five in several offensive categories a few times). I liked seeing the comment about Traynor, because it supported my recollection that until the 1980s Traynor was widely considered one of, if not the, best 3B of all time. I think choosing Ray (Remy) Kremer over Adams, Phillippe, or Leever as the top RHP was a mistake.

1969: *The Sporting News* Fan Poll

The July 5, 1969, issue reported the results of a fan poll for the long-standing franchises of the day. The results for the Pirates were: 1B Suhr, 2B Mazeroski, 3B Traynor, SS Wagner, C Schmidt, OF P. Waner, L. Waner, Clemente, RHP Phillippe, LHP Cooper.

I consider this listing to be very reasonable, with the one mistake being the choice of the younger Waner over Max Carey. And again, I guess Walter Schmidt was an acceptable choice at catcher, though he would be laughed off most other All-Time teams.

1987: Fan Survey

The 1995 Pirates Media Guide had an All-Time lineup based on a fan vote from 1987: 1B Stargell, 2B Mazeroski, 3B Traynor, SS Wagner, C Sanguillén, OF P. Waner, Clemente, Kiner, RHP Law, LHP Harvey Haddix, and RP Face.

This to me is a pretty solid hitting lineup. And I wouldn't argue too much with having Law as the top RHP. But then… Harvey Haddix? He pitched only a few years in Pittsburgh (posting a mediocre 45-38 record) and never had more than 12 wins in a season for the Bucs. I'll grant that Haddix pitched an impressive and famous game in 1959 when he threw 12 perfect innings against the Milwaukee Braves before losing in the 13th. But choosing him over Cooper as top LHP was just wrong.

1990: "All-Time All-Star Teams," in *The Baseball Research Journal*

In an interesting article, Robert C. Berlo used Thorn and Palmer's TPR (Total Player Rating) system to choose all-time teams. He selected players based on their best 800 consecutive games for the franchise, with a minimum of five years played. His results: 1B Stargell, 2B Mazeroski, SS Wagner, 3B Traynor, RF Clemente, CF Carey, LF Kiner, C Sanguillén, SP Tannehill, SP Cooper, SP Adams, SP Leever, RP McBean.

Kiner's few but very powerful seasons earned him big points in the TPR system, resulting in a tie with Roberto Clemente actually. The starting pitchers were all reasonable results, with McBean as the top reliever being a bit of a surprise.

1992: *The All-Time All-Star Baseball Book*, by Nick Acocella and Donald Dewey

The authors provided a lineup of mostly the same hitters I did above, except they started Kiner over Carey in the outfield and had Sanguillén as catcher. However, they inexplicably chose Ray Kremer as the starting pitcher. They noted that catcher and pitcher were the weakest positions for this All-Time team, and wrote, "The most reasonable alternatives to the following battery, for example, would be a pitcher (Bob Friend and Vern Law) who won 20 games only once and a catcher (Smokey Burgess) more noted for pinch hitting than back-stopping." The comment about catching isn't a big deal, but I don't understand how they could not have chosen at least Cooper, Adams, Leever, or some others over Kremer. They concluded by noting, "Honorable mentions to Max Carey, Fred Clarke, Lloyd Waner, Dick Groat, and Dave Parker."

1995: *Baseball Ratings*, by Charles F. Faber

Written in 1995, Faber's system resulted in a lineup of 1B Suhr, 2B Mazeroski, 3B Traynor, SS Wagner, C Sanguillén, OF Clemente, P. Waner, and Clarke. The obvious player missing here was Stargell, apparently coming up short against even Clarke for the third OF spot. His five starting pitchers were pretty good choices in Adams, Cooper, Leever, Law, and Sewell, and Face was the top reliever.

1999: Fan Vote

In 1999, in conjunction with the Pirates organization and the *Pittsburgh Post-Gazette*, fans voted on an All-Time Pirates squad. There were some 14,000 votes, and here were the results:

First Base: Willie Stargell (12,579), Dick Stuart (575), Donn Clendenon (251), Elbie Fletcher (243), Gus Suhr (236)

Second Base: Bill Mazeroski (13,049), Rennie Stennett (364), Chico Lind (314), Johnny Ray (240)

Third Base: Pie Traynor (9,754), Bill Madlock (2,173), Richie Hebner (1,106), Don Hoak (800), Tommy Leach (149)

Shortstop: Honus Wagner (11,106), Dick Groat (951), Jay Bell (937), Arky Vaughan (264), Gene Alley (123)

Catcher: Jason Kendall (5,508), Manny Sanguillén (5,265), Smokey Burgess (1,958), Tony Peña (1,546), George Gibson (225)

Left Field: Ralph Kiner (7,948), Barry Bonds (4,834), Frank Thomas (385), Max Carey (344), Fred Clarke (232)

Center Field: Lloyd Waner (4,726), Andy Van Slyke (4,678), Bill Virdon (2,749), Omar Moreno (1,130), Kiki Cuyler (540)

Right Field: Roberto Clemente (12,791), Paul Waner (890), Dave Parker (497)

Right Handed Pitcher: Vernon Law (4,889), Bob Friend (3,177), Doug Drabek (2,432), Steve Blass (2,293), Babe Adams (673), Deacon Phillippe (656)

Left Handed Pitcher: Harvey Haddix (6,222), John Candelaria (4,249), Wilbur Cooper (1,850), Bob Veale (1,669)

Relief Pitchers: Kent Tekulve (6,366), Roy Face (6,206), Dave Giusti (747), Stan Belinda (597), Grant Jackson (197)

Manager: Danny Murtaugh (7,875), Jim Leyland (2,735), Chuck Tanner (2,369), Fred Clarke (861), Frankie Frisch (196)

As one would expect from such a fan survey, there was a clear bias that favored contemporary players. At SS this was very obvious as Bell and Groat garnered far more support than Vaughan. The OF vote was a little strange, as they had Max Carey listed in left field instead of center field, where he played more games and was fairly well known as one of the all-time great defenders. And again, we see the fans going with Haddix as top LHP.

2003: *Rob Neyer's Big Book of Baseball Lineups*, by Rob Neyer

Like me, Neyer listed Stargell as the top 1B but opted for Fletcher as the backup, noting, "Not exactly a slugger, but he led NL in on-base pct. three straight seasons in the early 1940s; lost two prime seasons to the war, and wasn't the same afterward." Neyer chose Grantham over Ritchey as his backup 2B, though he noted Ritchey's stronger defense. His backup 3B was Madlock, on the basis of his two batting titles (one in strike-shortened 1981), even while he noted Madlock's several deficiencies ("middling power, not many walks, not much defense"). He went with Sanguillén and Peña at catcher, and his outfield had starters Bonds in LF, Carey in CF, and Clemente in RF, all great choices, as were backups LF Kiner and RF P. Waner. His backup CF description was interesting, as he shared his thinking between Beaumont and Van Slyke, noting that both were "finer than Lloyd Waner."

Neyer's first five starting pitchers were Cooper, Adams, Leever, Friend, and Phillippe. He then went with Vic Willis as his sixth, followed by Law and Drabek, with Face and Tekulve being the obvious relief selections.

2016: *101 All-Time Fantasy Baseball Teams*, by Jack Sweeney

Sweeney's book didn't allow players to be on more than one all-time lineup, so this means Bonds made it for the Giants team but not the Pirates. His lineup was generally solid with Stargell, Mazeroski, Traynor, Wagner, and Kiner listed as a DH. His outfield didn't differentiate by position, so P. Waner and Clemente make it, but I think he missed by choosing L. Waner over Carey. And ditto for his choice of Gibson at catcher. He chose four starting pitchers in Sewell, Phillippe, Friend, and Adams, and chose Face as the top reliever.

Top WAR Single Seasons – Hitters (8+)

Name	Year	WAR	AVG	HR	R	RBI	SB	OPS+
Honus Wagner	1908	11.5	.354	10	100	109	53	205
Honus Wagner	1905	10.1	.363	6	114	101	57	175
Barry Bonds	1990	9.7	.301	33	104	114	52	170
Honus Wagner	1906	9.3	.339	2	103	71	53	168
Arky Vaughan	1935	9.2	.385	19	108	99	4	190
Honus Wagner	1909	9.2	.339	5	92	100	35	177
Barry Bonds	1992	9.0	.311	34	109	103	39	204

Honus Wagner	1907	8.9	.350	6	98	82	61	187
Roberto Clemente	1967	8.9	.357	23	103	110	9	171
Arky Vaughan	1938	8.6	.322	7	88	68	14	141
Ralph Kiner	1947	8.3	.313	51	118	127	1	173
Honus Wagner	1904	8.3	.349	4	97	75	53	188
Roberto Clemente	1966	8.2	.317	29	105	119	7	146
Ralph Kiner	1949	8.1	.310	40	116	127	1	186
Andrew McCutchen	2013	8.1	.317	21	97	84	27	157
Honus Wagner	1912	8.1	.324	7	91	101	26	143
Ralph Kiner	1951	8.1	.309	42	124	109	2	185
Roberto Clemente	1968	8.1	.291	18	74	57	2	152
Barry Bonds	1989	8.0	.248	19	96	58	32	126

Not surprising that Wagner dominates the above listing with 7 of these 19 seasons. Roberto Clemente appears three times—his peak consecutive years of 1966–1968. Kiner's reign of terror as NL home run leader also produced three years for this list. And Bonds makes it too, with his two MVP seasons of course, but then surprisingly his 1989 year instead of his 1991 season. His offensive numbers in 1989 were not impressive, but his WAR rating that year was bolstered by a higher than normal defensive score.

Top WAR Single Seasons – Pitchers (8+)

Name	Year	WAR	W–L	ERA	IP	SO	ERA+
Babe Adams	1913	8.8	21-10	2.15	313.2	144	140
Jesse Tannehill	1899	8.4	24-14	2.82	322.0	65	134
Vic Willis	1906	8.1	23-13	1.73	322.0	124	153
John Candelaria	1977	8.0	20-5	2.34	230.2	133	169

This list omits several seasons by pitchers from the 1800s who had over 350 innings pitched, making it hard to compare their numbers with the more modern-era ones listed above. For the record, six of those seasons were produced two each by Ed Morris, Frank Killen, and Pink Hawley, with the highest WAR being 13.0 from Ed Morris' 1885 campaign, when he pitched 585 innings.

Franchise Player

Choosing this honor for the Pirates was a no-brainer. With all due respect to Roberto Clemente, Paul Waner, and Willie Stargell, it seems clear that Honus Wagner remains the best the Pirates have ever had.

CHAPTER 11

The White Sox Franchise All-Time Dream Team

The Chicago White Sox have been an official major league ballclub since 1901, after Charlie Comiskey moved his franchise from St. Paul to help populate the fledgling American League. They won the World Series in 1906 and then saw success again when they took the crown in 1917. They played below .500 the next year, and then poor decisions by several key players led to the infamous Black Sox Scandal, illustrated in the good baseball movie *Eight Men Out*. They 'lost' that 1919 World Series to the Reds, and then as if cursed didn't win another AL pennant until 1959 or another World Series until 2005.

When you compare the White Sox All-Time team with that of the other 15 franchises that have been around since at least 1901, the Sox come up noticeably short. This roster is relatively weak at several positions, including 3B, C, and OF. The middle infield is a highlight, and there are a few other standout stars here and there.

1st Base

Name	YR	WAR	W3	W/G	AVG	HR	SB	OPS+
Frank Thomas	16	68.2	21.3	.0348	.307	448	32	161
Paul Konerko	16	28.8	11.6	.0127	.281	432	9	120
Earl Sheely	7	19.8	11.3	.0209	.305	41	27	110
José Abreu	5	18.7	14.3	.0252	.295	146	8	138
Dick Allen	3	15.3	15.3	.0440	.307	85	33	181
Joe Kuhel	8	10.2	8.0	.0113	.261	75	99	100

From 1901 to 1990, the White Sox didn't have a star first baseman stay with the club for more than a handful of seasons. Consider: Zeke Bonura (1934–37), Eddie Robinson (1950–52), Roy Sievers (1960–61), and Dick Allen (1972–74). These were the only players at 1B who put up impressive offensive numbers for the Sox. Until, of course, The Big Hurt came along. **Frank Thomas** (1990–2005) had some of the most eye-popping all-around slugging numbers since Ted Williams. He was named MVP in both 1993 and 1994, and just missed a third in a huge comeback season in 2000 (after two sub-par years). He had 30+ HR eight times and 100+ RBI ten times. A .307 hitter, he walked a lot too, leading the league in free passes four times while posting a .427 OBP for the Sox.

Another recent White Sox slugger, **Paul Konerko** (1999–2012), was the obvious backup at 1B for this All-Time roster. He had 30+ HR seven times and 100+ RBI six times. Interestingly, Konerko was selected an All-Star six times, while Thomas was selected only five times (perhaps because he played almost as many games at DH as he did at 1B). While their HR totals for the Sox are very close, the comparison ends there, as Konerko never led the league in any major offensive categories, never finished higher than fifth in the MVP vote, had a much lower OBP and OPS+, and so has much lower peak and overall WAR scores.

No one else came close, but I'll briefly mention four others, in chronological order. Earl Sheely (1921–27) didn't reach the majors until age 28, but managed to have two seasons with 100+ RBI and four others with 80+. He also provided a solid .305 average and .391 OBP for the Sox. Joe Kuhel (1938–43, '46–47) had two stints in Chicago, often providing double-digit HR and SB totals. His best year was 1940, when he hit .280 with 27 HR, 94 RBI, and 111 runs.

Dick Allen (1972–74) was an All-Star in all three of his seasons for the White Sox, starting with 1972, when he took home the AL MVP Award after hitting .308 with 19 SB and leading the league with 37 HR, 113 RBI, 99 walks, and a .420 OBP. And current star slugger José Abreu (2014–18) won the AL Rookie of the Year Award in 2014 after hitting .317 with 36 HR and 107 RBI.

A two-time All-Star, he hasn't quite reached that level since, but has been very consistent nonetheless with between 22 and 33 HR each year.

2nd Base

Name	YR	WAR	W3	W/G	AVG	HR	SB	OPS+
Eddie Collins	12	66.6	24.3	.0399	.331	31	368	133
Nellie Fox	14	46.9	19.0	.0222	.291	35	73	95
Ray Durham	8	21.3	12.0	.0186	.278	106	219	102
Don Buford	5	17.0	14.4	.0274	.258	26	115	103
Jorge Orta	8	11.7	9.0	.0118	.281	79	66	112

The two middle infield positions were where this All-Time team truly shined. **Eddie Collins** (1915–26) played about half of his Hall of Fame career for the White Sox. While he had more of his best years earlier with the Philadelphia Athletics, he was a .331 hitter with a .426 OBP for Chicago. He stole 40+ bases five times and was regularly amongst the league leaders in hits, walks, and OBP.

The backup, **Nellie Fox** (1950–63), would easily be the starter for many other All-Time squads. Also a Hall of Famer, he played all of his prime years for Chicago, representing them at the All-Star Game 12 times (that's right: a 12-time All-Star is the *backup*). A key part of the Go-Go White Sox of the 1950s, he provided great defense (three Gold Glove Awards) and was a great contact hitter. He batted .291 for the White Sox and was *very hard* to strike out: amazingly, he never had more than 18 strikeouts in a season. He didn't provide much power or speed on the bases, but he was league MVP in 1959, and four times led the AL in hits.

A few others deserve brief mention, starting with Ray Durham (1995–2002). A two-time All-Star, he provided 10 to 20 HR six times and 30+ SB four times. Don Buford (1963–67) played a mix of 2B and 3B for the Sox at the beginning of his career. Only a .258 hitter with little power, he stole 51 bases in 1966 and 34 the following year. Lastly, Jorge Orta (1972–1979) provided double-digit HR six times and was an All-Star in 1975, when he hit .304 with 11 HR, 10 triples, and 16 SB.

3rd Base

Name	YR	WAR	W3	W/G	AVG	HR	SB	OPS+
Robin Ventura	10	39.3	17.0	.0313	.274	171	15	117
Willie Kamm	9	26.5	13.7	.0226	.279	25	94	99
Lee Tannehill	10	20.9	10.5	.0192	.220	3	63	70
Pete Ward	7	20.0	13.4	.0222	.254	97	20	116
Bill Melton	8	18.7	12.0	.0192	.258	154	20	115

Given the long history of the White Sox franchise, 3B was relatively lacking in strong candidates for this All-Time team. **Robin Ventura** (1989–98) deserves the starting spot, as he provided 90+ RBI six times and also earned five Gold Glove Awards. But he was an All-Star only once for the Sox and never came close to leading the league in any offensive category.

There were four candidates for the backup spot, and **Willie Kamm** (1923–31) emerged as the best of the lot. A .271 hitter with a .370 OBP, he had little power and only moderate speed. But he provided very good defense, leading American League 3B in fielding percentage five times, assists three times, and putouts six times while with the White Sox.

Lee Tannehill (1903–12) played his entire career for Chicago, and was an all-glove, no-hit infielder who played mostly 3B but a lot of SS too. Great defensively, he hit only 3 HR in 3,778 at-bats and had a slash line of .220/.269/.273. Pete Ward (1963–69) was a .254 hitter with moderate power, hitting 22 HR in 1963 and 23 in 1964. And lastly, Bill Melton (1968–75) hit 33 HR in 1970, led the league with 33 in 1971 (obviously a light offensive year), and had three other years with 20+. But his defense wasn't very good, as he led the AL in errors by a 3B twice and was in the top five in four other seasons.

Shortstop

Name	YR	WAR	W3	W/G	AVG	HR	SB	OPS+
Luke Appling	20	74.5	21.2	.0308	.310	45	179	113
Luis Aparicio	10	35.2	15.1	.0233	.269	43	318	83
George Davis	7	33.0	20.7	.0386	.259	6	162	109
Alexei Ramírez	8	22.7	12.2	.0184	.273	109	135	91
Buck Weaver	9	21.1	10.8	.0168	.272	21	173	92
Ozzie Guillén	13	19.5	10.5	.0112	.265	24	163	69
Chico Carrasquel	6	19.2	12.9	.0229	.265	32	29	84

The top two SS candidates were nearly as impressive as the two at 2B. The starter was **Luke Appling** (1930–43, '45–50), a Hall of Famer who played his entire career with the White Sox, representing them as an All-Star seven times. Nicknamed Old Aches and Pains, Appling was a .310 hitter, with his best numbers coming in 1936, when he led the AL with a .388 average, scored 111 runs, and provided 128 RBI, even with only 6 HR. He won another batting title in 1943, when he hit .328, and posted his career-best SB total with 27.

The backup was **Luis Aparicio** (1956–62, '68–70), who had two stints with Chicago. He batted over .300 only once, but he led the league in SB in his first seven seasons in Chicago, including 50+ SB from 1959 through '61. He was Rookie of the Year in 1956, was an All-Star six times, and won seven Gold Glove Awards while playing for the White Sox.

There were four others that I considered, starting with Hall of Famer **George Davis** (1902, 1904–09), who finished his career with the White Sox. He was on the decline by then, but still provided 20+ SB five times. He played well defensively and so overall did enough to earn one of the two "extra spots" on this roster.

Soon after Davis there was Buck Weaver (1912–20), who split his time at two positions, playing about twice as much at SS than 3B. A light hitter at first, he had become a .300+ hitter in his last few years. He was portrayed as a very likeable character in the movie *Eight Men Out*, and he was a fine player, stealing 20+ bases five times and hitting .331 with 102 runs in his final season. Although he wasn't in on the illegal activities in the 1919 World Series, he was banned from the game because he knew about it and didn't speak up.

Chico Carrasquel (1950–55) started his career for the White Sox and was not much of an offensive force, with a highlight being the 106 runs he scored in 1954. But he was very good defensively, and that made him an All-Star four times. Ozzie Guillén (1985–97) played most of his career in Chicago and started out by winning the Rookie of the Year Award in 1985. He stole 20+ bases four times, was an All-Star three times, and took home the Gold Glove Award in 1990. And more recently, Alexei Ramírez (2008–15) was pretty good defensively and was a consistent producer for the White Sox, providing both power and speed with a high of 21 HR in his rookie season and a high of 30 SB in 2013.

Catcher

Name	YR	WAR	W3	W/G	AVG	HR	SB	OPS+
Carlton Fisk	13	28.8	12.5	.0203	.257	214	67	109
Ray Schalk	17	28.6	10.5	.0163	.254	11	177	83
Sherm Lollar	12	26.1	10.8	.0192	.265	124	17	106
Ron Karkovice	12	14.7	7.3	.0157	.221	96	24	81
A.J. Pierzynski	8	12.6	7.5	.0118	.279	118	7	93

Carlton Fisk (1981–93) split his career just about in half between the two Sox clubs, Boston first and then Chicago. Although his famous postseason exploits were for the former, his biggest HR season was for the latter, when he belted 37 with 107 RBI in 1985. Pudge hit between 18 and 26 HR for Chicago in six additional seasons, even though he played in fewer than 140 games each season.

For the backup spot, I went with **Sherm Lollar** (1952–63), who had six seasons with double-digit HR, was an All-Star six times, and was solid defensively, winning three Gold Glove Awards. **Ray Schalk** (1912–28) played nearly his entire career for the White Sox and was eventually elected as a Hall of Famer, though he was clearly one of the weakest selections ever, as he hit only .254 with 11 HR for his entire career. He had some speed, regularly stealing 10+ bases, including a high of 30 in 1916. He was very good defensively but played 140+ games in a season on only three occasions. Due to his longevity and defense, I gave Schalk one of the two "extra spots" on this All-Time team roster.

Two others deserve brief mention, starting with Ron Karkovice (1986–97), who played his entire career for Chicago. A low-average hitter, he developed some power in the second half of his career, with a high of 20 HR in 1993. And lastly, A.J. Pierzynski (2005–12) played for Chicago during the middle portion of his long career. He hit 10+ HR six times and had his best season at age 35 in 2012, when he hit 27 HR with 77 RBI.

Left Field

Name	YR	WAR	W3	W/G	AVG	HR	SB	OPS+
Minnie Miñoso	12	41.3	19.8	.0301	.304	135	171	133
Joe Jackson	6	27.8	20.4	.0429	.340	30	64	159
Bibb Falk	9	18.5	14.5	.0173	.315	50	40	112
Tim Raines	5	16.5	13.1	.0255	.283	50	143	113
Carlos Lee	6	15.7	11.2	.0178	.288	152	64	111
Al Simmons	3	10.9	10.9	.0265	.315	48	12	119
Carlos May	9	10.1	8.0	.0101	.275	85	84	114
Patsy Dougherty	6	9.7	7.6	.0138	.269	4	168	116

For a franchise that has been around since 1901, the outfield for this All-Time team was relatively weak. Two who were primarily LF clearly deserve spots, starting with **Minnie Miñoso** (1951–57, '60–61, '64, '76, '80), who was an often-underrated star. He had *five* stints with Chicago, if you include his ten at-bats in 1976 and 1980 as bona fide stints (he was in his mid-to-late fifties then). The Cuban Comet was a five-tool player who batted .304 with a .397 OBP for the White Sox, won two Gold Glove Awards, hit double-digit HR in each of his full seasons, and led the league in SB three times (1951 through '53). A six-time All-Star, he also led the AL in times hit by pitch an impressive eight times.

"Shoeless" Joe Jackson (1915–20) had only four full seasons with the White Sox, but they were very, very good (though statistically still not as good as some of his earlier years with the Indians). In 1916 he batted .341 and had 40 doubles, 21 triples, and 23 SB. In 1919 he batted .351 and had 96 RBI, and then in his final season he hit .382, with 218 hits, 42 doubles, 20 triples, 12 HR, 104 runs, and 121 RBI. He was only 31 years old at the end of that season, when he was banned from the game because of his connection to the Black Sox scandal.

Several other outfielders who primarily played LF for the White Sox deserve brief mention, including (in chronological order):

- Patsy Dougherty (1906–11) finished his career for the White Sox, providing good speed as he led the AL in SB with 47 in 1908 and had 20+ SB three other times.

- Bibb Falk (1920–28) played most of his career for the White Sox and was a .315 hitter. His best season was in 1926, when he batted .345 with 108 RBI, even with only 8 homers.

- Al Simmons (1933–35) was an All-Star in each of his three seasons in Chicago, hitting .331 with 119 RBI in 1933 and .344 with 104 RBI in 1934.

- Carlos May (1968–76) was a two-time All-Star with moderate power and speed, and hit 20 HR with 96 RBI in 1973.

- Tim Raines (1991–95) came to the White Sox at age 31 and stole 51 and 45 bases in his first two seasons before his speed began to fade.

- Carlos Lee (1999–2004) started his fine career with the White Sox, hit 24 to 31 HR five times, and had double-digit SB four times.

Center Field

Name	YR	WAR	W3	W/G	AVG	HR	SB	OPS+
Fielder Jones	8	31.8	13.8	.0276	.269	10	206	112
Chet Lemon	7	24.9	16.5	.0317	.288	73	45	126
Johnny Mostil	10	24.2	15.1	.0249	.301	23	176	113
Lance Johnson	8	21.2	13.6	.0224	.286	17	226	92
Jim Landis	8	19.8	12.7	.0186	.250	83	127	101
Happy Felsch	6	19.4	14.4	.0259	.293	38	88	123

Fielder Jones (1901–08) was the team's player-manager from 1904 through 1908. He had a good batting eye and some speed, as demonstrated by his regularly being amongst the league leaders in both walks and SB. And yes, his real, full name was in fact Fielder Allison Jones.

There were several candidates to consider for a backup CF on this All-Time team. In the end, I went with **Johnny Mostil** (1918, '21–29), who played his entire career for Chicago, hit .301 with a .386 OBP, and twice led the league in SB with 43 in 1925 and 35 in 1926. He led the league with 135 runs in 1925 and then scored 120 in 1926, coming in second for the AL MVP that year.

Chet Lemon (1975–81) started his career with Chicago, providing good defense and moderate power. He was twice an All-Star for the White Sox, including in 1979, when he batted .318 and led the league with 44 doubles.

Jim Landis (1957–64) provided very strong defense in center field, winning five consecutive Gold Glove Awards, though it didn't translate into very high defensive WAR scores. He provided some speed with 14 to 23 SB in six seasons, and also a little power with double-digit HR five times.

Lance Johnson (1988–95) led the AL in triples each year from 1991 to 1994, including 14 in only 106 games in the strike-shortened 1994 season. He led the league in hits in 1995 and stole between 26 and 41 bases for Chicago for six consecutive seasons.

And finally, Happy Felsch (1915–20) had a short career, played entirely for the White Sox. He was a .293 hitter and his best season was his last, when he hit .338 with 40 doubles, 15 triples, 14 HR, and 115 RBI. But Oscar Emil Felsch was forced out of baseball at that point due to his involvement in the Black Sox scandal.

Right Field

Name	YR	WAR	W3	W/G	AVG	HR	SB	OPS+
Magglio Ordóñez	8	25.2	16.5	.0252	.307	187	82	127
Harold Baines	14	24.5	10.5	.0147	.288	221	32	118
Floyd Robinson	7	18.5	11.9	.0210	.287	65	38	121
Harry Hooper	5	14.7	11.4	.0222	.302	45	75	114
Shano Collins	11	14.6	8.5	.0109	.262	17	193	96

Magglio Ordóñez (1997–2004) played the first half of his career for the White Sox, hitting .307 with good power and some speed. He had four consecutive 30+-HR and 100+-RBI seasons, and barely missed a fifth with 29 HR and 99 RBI in 2003. A four-time All-Star for Chicago, his best numbers came in 2002, when he batted .320 with 38 HR, 135 RBI, 47 doubles, and 116 runs.

Harold Baines (1980–89, '96–97, 2000–01) had three stints for the White Sox, playing mostly RF at first, and then served as a DH in the later years. He hit 20+ HR seven times (but never topped 30) and had 100+ RBI twice. He was an All-Star four times, but he never led the AL in any major hitting category.

Three others who primarily played RF for the White Sox deserve brief mention, including (in chronological order):

- Shano Collins (1910–20) was only a .262 hitter with a .308 OBP, but he still managed 20+ SB four times, with a high of 38 in 1915.

- Harry Hooper (1921–25) played 12 fine years for the Boston Red Sox and then was traded to Chicago for Shano Collins, a swap of aging RF. Hooper didn't steal many bases at that point in his career, but he could still hit (.302 average).

- Floyd Robinson (1960–66) played most of his short career with the White Sox, hitting .287 with five seasons of double-digit HR. His best year was 1962, when he batted .312 with 11 HR, 109 RBI, and a league-leading 45 doubles.

Starting Pitching

Name	YR	WAR	W3	W-L	ERA	WHIP	ERA+
Ted Lyons	21	71.5	19.2	260-230	3.67	1.348	118
Ed Walsh	13	65.6	34.0	195-125	1.81	0.995	146
Red Faber	20	64.8	25.7	254-213	3.15	1.302	119
Wilbur Wood	12	50.3	28.7	163-148	3.18	1.225	116
Eddie Cicotte	9	50.0	28.1	156-101	2.25	1.112	133
Mark Buehrle	12	48.9	15.4	161-119	3.83	1.282	120
Billy Pierce	13	48.7	19.8	186-152	3.19	1.261	123
Doc White	11	39.2	19.1	159-123	2.30	1.106	113
Chris Sale	7	31.1	14.2	74-50	3.00	1.065	135
Thornton Lee	11	30.6	19.6	104-104	3.33	1.316	124
Gary Peters	11	26.6	18.3	91-78	2.92	1.190	115
Jim Scott	9	26.1	17.1	107-114	2.30	1.180	121
Frank Smith	7	24.6	15.2	108-80	2.18	1.079	110
Tommy John	7	24.4	16.4	82-80	2.95	1.220	117
Joe Horlen	11	23.4	14.4	113-113	3.11	1.193	110
Reb Russell	7	22.9	17.1	80-59	2.33	1.080	121
Tommy Thomas	7	22.7	19.7	83-92	3.77	1.344	110
J. McDowell	7	21.8	13.9	91-58	3.50	1.248	117

The top starting pitcher for this All-Time was Hall of Famer **Big Ed Walsh** (1904–16). He pitched nearly his entire career for the White Sox, although he played significantly in only seven seasons. But in those years his ERA was never higher than 2.22, he led the league twice, with a 1.60 mark in 1907 and 1.27 in

1910, and his overall ERA for Chicago was an amazing 1.81. In 1908 he posted a 40-15 record—16 more wins than his closest competitor that year. He used his effective spitball to win 24+ in three other seasons too. He wasn't used just as a starter either: he led the league in saving games five times, in seasons where he was predominantly the ace on the staff (obviously this was well before the invention of the relief specialist).

Ted Lyons (1923–42, '46) is the all-time White Sox wins leader, though it should be noted that he is also the all-time White Sox losses leader (260-230). He pitched his entire career for Chicago, won 20+ games three times, and led the league with a 2.10 ERA in 1942. He was one of the least overpowering, low-strikeout pitchers of all time: he actually ended his career with more walks than strikeouts, even though he led the league in fewest walks per nine innings four times! That's right, he ended with 1,073 Ks and 1,121 walks in 4,161 innings pitched.

You could make a case for **Red Faber** (1914–33) for the number two spot over Lyons, and they were teammates for part of their long, Hall of Fame careers. Like Walsh, Faber had an effective spitball. He won 20+ games four times and regularly posted an ERA below 3.00 during the first half of his career, leading the league in that category in 1921 (2.48) and 1922 (2.81).

After those first three, I found four starters to consider for the next spot. Knuckleball pioneer **Eddie Cicotte** (1912–20) was a central figure in the Black Sox scandal. He was pretty good for the Red Sox early in his career, and only got better when he joined the White Sox. In 1913, in his first full season in Chicago, he went 18-11 with a 1.58 ERA. At age 33 in 1917, he led the league in wins with a 28-12 record and in ERA with a 1.53 mark. After an off year due to injuries in 1918, he was the best pitcher in the AL in 1919, posting a 1.82 ERA and leading the league in wins with a 29-7 record. After participating in the 1919 World Series fix, he managed to go 21-10 in 1920 before being banished from the sport.

Left-hander **Billy Pierce** (1949–61) won 20+ games twice and won 14+ in seven other seasons for the White Sox. He led the league in 1955 with a 1.97 ERA, nearly two runs better than the league average that year. He was a seven-time All-Star and was regularly amongst the league leaders in many key pitching categories.

Wilbur Wood (1967–78) had an interesting career in that after three years as an effective short reliever, he became a starter and used his knuckleball to post four consecutive 20+-win and 300+-IP seasons. The first of these seasons also saw him compile a 1.91 ERA (compared with a 3.60 league average, but still second to phenom Vida Blue's 1.82). He led the league in wins in 1972 and 1973 with 24 each year.

Mark Buehrle (2000–11) was a workhorse for Chicago. He never had 20 wins in a season, but he did manage 15+ wins five times and started 30+ games in 11 consecutive seasons. Overall, his time in Chicago produced a respectable 161-119 record, a .575 winning percentage.

Next up was **Doc White** (1903–13), a teammate of Walsh who pitched all but his first two seasons for the White Sox. He had seven seasons with 15+ wins and led the league with a 1.52 ERA in 1906. The following year he led the league in wins with a 27-13 record.

I considered several other starting pitcher candidates for this All-Time team, but decided to choose just one more. Although he is now gone from Chicago, **Chris Sale** (2010–16) was a five-time All-Star and ended up in the top six in the AL Cy Young vote in each of those seasons. He posted an impressive 1.065 WHIP and recorded 200+ strikeouts four times, including a league-leading 274 in 2015 (which also set a White Sox franchise record).

You could certainly make a case for others instead of Sale, starting with Gary Peters (1959–69), who pitched seven full seasons for the White Sox, starting with his Rookie of the Year season in 1963, when he had a 19-9 record and led the league with a 2.33 ERA. He led the AL in wins the next season with a 20-8 record, and then in 1966 led the league with a 1.98 ERA. He was solid again in 1967, making the All-Star team and posting a 16-11 record and 2.28 ERA.

Thornton Lee (1937–47) was a reliable starter for several years before having his best season in 1941, when he completed 30 of his 34 starts, posted a 22-11 record, and had a league-leading 2.37 ERA. He missed most of the following three seasons due to injury but came back at age 38 in 1945 to post a 15-12 record and 2.44 ERA.

The other starting pitchers whom I considered and who deserve brief mention include (in chronological order):

- Frank Smith (1904–10) was a teammate of Walsh and White during the early years and posted five seasons with 15+ wins, including 23-10 in 1907 and 25-17 in 1909. He also pitched no-hitters for the Sox in 1905 and 1908.

- Jim Scott (1909–17) pitched his entire short career for Chicago, winning 20+ games twice but ending up with an overall losing record of 107-114.

- Reb Russell (1913–19) also pitched his entire short career for the White Sox, posting a 22-16 record and 1.90 ERA in his rookie season, but never winning more than 18 in a season again.

- Tommy Thomas (1926–32) won between 14 and 19 games in each of his first four seasons, but he ended up with a losing record for the Sox overall (83-92). His real first name, by the way, was not Thomas, but Alphonse.

- Joe Horlen (1961–71) posted seven consecutive double-digit-win seasons in the 1960s for the Sox, with an ERA under 3.00 for five of those years. His best season was easily 1967, when he went 19-7, won the ERA crown with a 2.07 mark, pitched a no-hitter, and was second in the Cy Young Award balloting and fourth in the MVP race.

- Tommy John (1965–71) pitched for Chicago early in his career but never managed more than 14 wins in a season (though to be fair, some of the teams he pitched for were awful).

- Jack McDowell (1987–88, '90–94) was an All-Star three times for the White Sox, including 1992, when he posted a 20-10 record and was second in the Cy Young Award vote, and 1993, when he went 22-10 and took home the award.

Relief Pitching

Name	YR	WAR	W3	SV	W-L	ERA	WHIP	ERA+
Hoyt Wilhelm	6	16.2	9.8	99	41-33	1.92	0.935	171
Keith Foulke	6	14.4	11.1	100	18-19	2.87	0.991	166
Terry Forster	6	13.0	10.4	75	26-42	3.36	1.370	111
Matt Thornton	8	11.2	7.3	23	31-35	3.28	1.196	137
Roberto Hernández	7	11.0	9.4	161	29-24	2.87	1.223	153
Rich Gossage	5	9.8	11.6	30	29-36	3.80	1.406	97
Gerry Staley	6	9.7	7.7	38	38-25	2.61	1.148	147
Bobby Jenks	6	8.9	6.8	173	14-18	3.40	1.206	136
Bobby Thigpen	8	8.6	7.2	201	28-33	3.26	1.340	125

The White Sox have had their share of quality closers. Even with Wilbur Wood making it as a starter, there were still three guys who I thought deserved to make this All-Time team. I started with the first relief pitcher ever elected to the Hall of Fame, **Hoyt Wilhelm** (1963–68), who was enshrined in part because of his years as the Sox's closer. Even though he was already 40 years old, Wilhelm used his knuckleball to earn double-digit save totals in five seasons, and had impressive ERAs, including 2.64, 1.99, 1.81, 1.66, 1.31, and 1.73.

Bobby Thigpen (1986–93) broke the record for saves in a season in 1990, when he recorded 57 along with a 1.83 ERA. He had three other seasons with 30+ saves, and his 201 saves is the most all-time for the White Sox.

Roberto Hernández (1991–97) was generally a good closer for the White Sox after Thigpen's departure, having three seasons of 30+ saves and another with 27 before being dealt two-thirds of the way through 1997 to the Giants. He was an All-Star in 1996, ending the year with 38 saves and a 1.91 ERA, which was way ahead of the AL league average of 4.70.

There were several other White Sox relievers I considered and who deserve brief mention, including (in chronological order):

- Gerry Staley (1956–61) was a short reliever for the Sox in the late 1950s. He led the AL in saves with a modest total of 15 in 1959, and then was an All-Star the following year when he posted a 2.42 ERA with 9 saves and a 13-8 record.

- Terry Forster (1971–76) was occasionally used as a starter, but mostly was a reliever for the Sox in the early 1970s. His best two seasons were 1972, when he had 29 saves and 2.25 ERA, and then 1974, when he led the AL with 24 saves.

- Rich Gossage (1972–76) started his Hall of Fame career with the White Sox, and after struggling for three seasons he used his dominating fastball in 1975 to post one of the best all-time seasons for a relief pitcher: 1.84 ERA, 212 ERA+, 130 strikeouts in 141.2 IP, and a league-leading 26 saves. The Sox tried to convert him to a starter the following year, and while he did have 15 complete games, his ERA ballooned to 3.94 and he had a 9-17 record. After that season he was traded with Forster to the Pirates for slugger Richie Zisk.

- Keith Foulke (1997–2002) was a solid setup man in 1999, posting a 2.22 ERA with 9 saves. He took over the closer duties the next year and had 34 saves in 2000 and 42 in 2001.

- Bobby Jenks (2006–10) held the closer role for the Sox for five years, recording 173 saves during that span.

- Matt Thornton (2006–13) was a capable setup man for Jenks and others for many years, posted 486 strikeouts in 463.1 IP, and was an All-Star in 2010.

Managers

Name	YR	From-To	W-L	PCT	PS	WS
Al López	11	1957–69	840-650	.564	1	0
Ozzie Guillén	8	2004–11	678-617	.524	2	1
Jimmy Dykes	13	1934–46	899-940	.489	0	0
Fielder Jones	5	1904–08	426-293	.592	1	1
Pants Rowland	4	1915–18	339-247	.578	1	1
Jerry Manuel	6	1998–2003	500-471	.515	1	0
Tony LaRussa	8	1979–86	522-510	.506	1	0

You could argue a bit here, depending on what you consider most important: most career wins, best winning percentage, or greatest postseason success. For instance, **Al López** has both more wins and a higher winning percentage than **Ozzie Guillén**, but he only took the Sox to the postseason once compared to Ozzie doing so twice, and actually winning the World Series once. **Fielder Jones** and Pants Rowland (who earned his nickname as a child) had short tenures at the helm but had high winning percentages, and each won a World Series. On the other hand, **Jimmy Dykes** ended up with a winning percentage just below .500, but he managed the White Sox longer than anyone else and so has the most career wins for the franchise.

Starting Lineup

What would mythical starting lineups look like for this All-Time roster?

Against RHP:
Eddie Collins 2B (L)
Joe Jackson DH (L)
Frank Thomas 1B (R)
Harold Baines RF (L)
Robin Ventura 3B (L)
Minnie Miñoso LF (R)
Carlton Fisk C (R)
Luke Appling SS (R)
Fielder Jones CF (L)

Against LHP:
Eddie Collins 2B (L)
Luke Appling SS (R)
Frank Thomas DH (R)
Paul Konerko 1B (R)
Magglio Ordóñez RF (R)
Minnie Miñoso LF (R)
Carlton Fisk C (R)
Willie Kamm 3B (R)
Johnny Mostil CF (R)

These lineups leave out two of the best players on this dream team roster, 2B Nellie Fox and SS Luis Aparicio. The available numbers indicate that Willie Kamm hit significantly better against LHP, so I figured a platoon with Ventura made some sense. But all three catchers on the roster were right-handed batters, so no platoon was available there.

Depth Chart

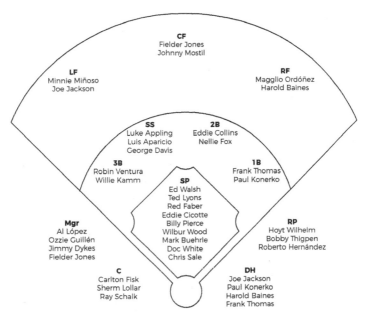

CF
Fielder Jones
Johnny Mostil

LF
Minnie Miñoso
Joe Jackson

RF
Magglio Ordóñez
Harold Baines

SS
Luke Appling
Luis Aparicio
George Davis

2B
Eddie Collins
Nellie Fox

3B
Robin Ventura
Willie Kamm

1B
Frank Thomas
Paul Konerko

SP
Ed Walsh
Ted Lyons
Red Faber
Eddie Cicotte
Billy Pierce
Wilbur Wood
Mark Buehrle
Doc White
Chris Sale

Mgr
Al López
Ozzie Guillén
Jimmy Dykes
Fielder Jones

RP
Hoyt Wilhelm
Bobby Thigpen
Roberto Hernández

C
Carlton Fisk
Sherm Lollar
Ray Schalk

DH
Joe Jackson
Paul Konerko
Harold Baines
Frank Thomas

Prospects for Current Players

What are the prospects of current White Sox players making this All-Time team? As of 2017, the White Sox are clearly in a rebuilding mode. It would take many more seasons for José Abreu to replace Paul Konerko on this roster, but less for him to earn one of the two "extra spots." Avisaíl García has talent, as shown in 2017, when he batted .330 with 18 HR and 80 RBI. And 2B Yoán Moncada does too, but with 217 strikeouts in 2018 he clearly hasn't figured out major league pitching yet. We'll see...

Retired Player Numbers

Nellie Fox (2), Harold Baines (3), Luke Appling (4), Minnie Miñoso (9), Luis Aparicio (11), Ted Lyons (16), Billy Pierce (19), Frank Thomas (35), Carlton Fisk (72)

Selections from Other Authors and Fan Surveys

1949: Fan Survey

A poll of 5,000 fans was conducted in May 1949, the results of which I found in *The White Sox Encyclopedia*, by Richard C. Lindberg: 1B Kuhel, 2B Collins, SS Appling, 3B Jimmie Dykes, C Schalk and Billy Sullivan (tied), LF Simmons, CF Mostil, RF Harry Hooper, and pitchers Lyons, Walsh, Faber, and White. Going with long-time manager Jimmie Dykes at 3B instead of Willie Kamm was a mistake I think. Simmons had only two good seasons for the White Sox, so picking him over Jackson or Falk in LF was a mistake too. Harry Hooper played five seasons at the end of his career and batted .303 for the club, so he wasn't a bad pick in RF. But including extremely light-hitting catcher Billy Sullivan (.207) in a tie was unfair to Schalk.

1957: *Sport* magazine, September issue

As part of a running series, *Sport* magazine reported on all-time all-star teams picked by "big league publicity departments and the writers covering the clubs." Here is what they had to say:

First Base: Joe Kuhel, who played for the Sox from 1938 through 1943, and again in 1946-47. His lifetime average was .277.

Second Base: Eddie Collins, now in baseball's Hall of Fame, who was with the Sox during the years 1915-26. He had a lifetime batting average of .333, and is rated by many as the greatest second-baseman of all time.

Shortstop: Luke Appling, who was there for so long he didn't really give anybody else a chance at the all-time job. He held down the shortstop position in Chicago from 1930 through 1950 and had a life-time average of .310.

Third Base: Willie Kamm, who played with the Sox from 1923 through 1931 and batted .281 as a big-leaguer.

Left Field: Al Simmons, who was honored even though he played only three seasons in Chicago, 1933-35. This famous slugger's average was .334, and he's in the Hall of Fame, too.

Center Field: Johnny Mostil, who spent all of his big-league career in Chicago, beginning with 1918, and then from 1921 through '29. He batted .301.

Right Field: Minnie Miñoso, the flashiest of the current "Go-Go" brigade. Minnie arrived in Chicago in 1951 and has hit at a .307 clip.

Catcher: None listed.

Righthanded Pitcher: Ted Lyons, who spent all of his pro career with the Sox (1923-46) and won 260 games to earn a place in the Hall of Fame. Ted managed Chicago in 1947-48.

Lefthanded Pitcher: Billy Pierce, like Miñoso, one of the two current Sox to be honored. Billy came to Chicago in 1949 and had won 114 American League games before this season.

I'm not sure why no catcher was listed, perhaps just an oversight. Voters I think again erred in preferring Simmons' brief stint to the contributions of Jackson and arguably Falk.

1969: *The Sporting News* Fan Poll

The July 5, 1969, issue reported the results of a fan poll for the long-standing franchises of the day. The results for the White Sox were: 1B Eddie Robinson, 2B Eddie Collins, 3B Willie Kamm, SS Luke Appling, C Ray Schalk, LF Al Simmons, CF Johnny Mostil, RF Harry Hooper, RHP Ted Lyons, and LHP Billy Pierce.

While Eddie Robinson had three good seasons for Chicago from 1950 through '52, I don't think that should have been enough to rank first at 1B. And once again we see Simmons and Hooper in the outfield over the likes of Jackson and Miñoso.

1990: "All-Time All-Star Teams," in *The Baseball Research Journal*

In an interesting article, Robert C. Berlo used Thorn and Palmer's TPR (Total Player Rating) system to choose all-time teams. He selected players based on their best 800 consecutive games for the franchise, with a minimum of five years played. His results: 1B Jiggs Donahue, 2B Collins, SS Appling, 3B Melton, RF Jackson, CF Lemon, LF Miñoso, C Fisk, SP Walsh, SP Lyons, SP Cicotte, SP Pierce, and RP Wood.

Jiggs Donahue played parts of only five seasons for the Sox during their first decade, stealing 25+ bases three times, but hitting only .256 with a total of three home runs.

1992: *The All-Time All-Star Baseball Book*, by Nick Acocella and Donald Dewey

The authors chose a lineup of 1B Allen, 2B Collins, 3B Weaver, SS Appling, OF Jackson, Miñoso, Baines, C Fisk, and P Lyons. Weaver was not a horrible pick at 3B—apparently, they preferred picking him at his secondary position to going with Kamm or Melton. The players given honorable mention included Walsh, Schalk, Felsch, Fox, and Aparicio.

1995: *Baseball Ratings*, by Charles F. Faber

The Faber system as applied in 1995 created a reasonable all-time team. Sheely was the 1B, since Thomas, although already a superstar, was just getting started. Up the middle Fox and Aparicio got the nod over Collins and Appling. Kamm was tops at 3B, and Lollar rated higher than Fisk at C. The three outfielders were Jones, Miñoso, and Baines, and the top five starters didn't include Walsh: Lyons, Faber, Pierce, Wood, and White.

2000: Chicago White Sox "Team of the Century"

A 27-player "Team of the Century" was announced on September 30, 2000, commemorating 100 years of White Sox baseball. More than 200,000 votes were cast on 18,500 in-stadium and online ballots during the month-long voting. As reported on the official White Sox website at mlb.com, the position players included were: 1B Thomas, Allen; 2B Collins, Fox; 3B Ventura, Weaver, Melton; SS Appling, Aparicio, Guillén, Carrasquel; C Fisk, Lollar, Schalk; and OF Jackson, Miñoso, Landis, and Baines.

Not a bad set of players, though it is a little odd that they chose four shortstops but only four outfielders. As for pitchers, I'm not sure what order these came in the vote, but the selections were all fairly reasonable: Cicotte, Faber, Lyons, Peters, Pierce, Walsh, White, and Wilhelm as the only reliever.

2003: *Rob Neyer's Big Book of Baseball Lineups*, by Rob Neyer

Neyer's starting infield of Fisk, Thomas, Collins, Appling, and Ventura was the same as mine. And his backups were the same too, except at 1B where he went with Allen's short but brilliant time in Chicago. For LF he went with Jackson as the starter, and then of course gave Miñoso his due as the backup. His choices of Jones and Lemon in CF and Baines and Ordóñez in RF were solid.

For pitchers, Neyer went with Walsh, Lyons, Pierce, Faber, Cicotte, White, Wood, and Lee. The toughest choice was that last one, and Neyer provided this support: "Won 22 in 1941; only Sox to win 20 between 1937 and 1955, and only ALer that season aside from DiMaggio and Williams to get first-place vote for MVP." His two relief pitcher picks were reasonable in Wilhelm and Hernández.

2016: *101 All-Time Fantasy Baseball Teams*, by Jack Sweeney

Sweeney's lineup was very good with Konerko, Collins, Appling, Aparicio, Jackson, Miñoso, Baines, Schalk, and then of course Thomas listed as the DH. (He cheated a bit by listing both Appling and Aparicio, as Appling played only 88 games at 3B and Aparicio never played any.) His four starting pitcher selections were all reasonable with Lyons, Walsh, Faber, and Buehrle, as was his choice of Wilhelm as the reliever.

Top WAR Single Seasons – Hitters (8+)

Name	Year	WAR	AVG	HR	R	RBI	SB	OPS+
Eddie Collins	1915	9.4	.332	4	118	77	46	165
Dick Allen	1972	8.6	.308	37	90	113	19	199
Minnie Miñoso	1954	8.2	.320	19	119	116	18	154

It is striking there have been only three seasons for White Sox hitters that resulted in a WAR score of 8 or higher. Some of that can be explained by the White Sox calling pitcher-friendly Comiskey Park home for so much of their history. Eddie Collins' top score here was actually his first season for Chicago, after having had several seasons of this caliber for the Athletics to start his amazing career. Dick Allen's 1972 season was not only his best of the three he had for the White Sox, but was also arguably his best season overall. And Miñoso's 1954 campaign was clearly the best of his many fine seasons in Chicago. But the top results of other key stars didn't quite make the 8+ threshold: Nellie Fox (7.9), Luke Appling (7.6), Joe Jackson (7.6), Frank Thomas (7.3), and George Davis (7.2).

Top WAR Single Seasons – Pitchers (8+)

Name	Year	WAR	W-L	ERA	IP	SO	ERA+
Ed Walsh	1912	12.2	27-17	2.15	393.0	254	149
Eddie Cicotte	1917	11.5	28-12	1.53	346.2	150	174
Ed Walsh	1910	11.5	18-20	1.27	369.2	258	187
Red Faber	1921	11.0	25-15	2.48	330.2	124	170
Wilbur Wood	1971	10.9	22-13	1.91	334.0	210	189
Ed Walsh	1908	10.5	40-15	1.42	464.0	269	162
Wilbur Wood	1972	10.3	24-17	2.51	376.2	193	126

Eddie Cicotte	1919	9.5	29-7	1.82	306.2	110	176
Red Faber	1922	9.4	21-17	2.81	352.0	148	143
Thornton Lee	1941	9.2	22-11	2.37	300.1	130	174
Reb Russell	1913	9.1	22-16	1.90	316.2	122	154
Ed Walsh	1911	9.1	27-18	2.22	368.2	255	146
Rich Gossage	1975	8.3	9-8	1.84	141.2	130	212
Ted Lyons	1927	8.1	22-14	2.84	307.2	71	143
Tommy Thomas	1927	8.0	19-16	2.98	307.2	107	136

As noted, Comiskey Park was very much a pitcher's park, hence the reason there are so many more pitcher seasons with 8+ WAR scores than hitters. Walsh not surprisingly appears on this list four times, including two of the top three spots, and three of the top six. That said, it was initially surprising to see what would seem to be his most impressive season of 1908 ranked only sixth. A 40-15 season scores lower than an 18-20 season? That poor record was largely due to the White Sox being a much worse team in 1910 than in 1912, and he had stronger ERA, ERA+, and K/9 numbers that year as well. Also worthy of note is Rich Gossage's 1975 season as a reliever being good enough to make this list. He pitched 141.2 IP in only 62 games, so that works out to over 2 IP per game, something today's closers never do.

Franchise Player

This was a tough choice, because relatively speaking the White Sox haven't had many big boppers or big-name pitchers with a lot of longevity. Eddie Collins, Luke Appling, Nellie Fox, and others played for the club for a long time and each built up numerous accolades. But I decided to give this honor to Frank Thomas, based on his two MVP Awards (and nearly a third in 2000) and because he is the career leader for this franchise in several categories, including HR, doubles, RBI, runs, walks, OBP, SLG, and OPS+.

CHAPTER 12

The Braves Franchise All-Time Dream Team

The Braves franchise has a long history dating all the way back to the late 1860s, when they were the Cincinnati Red Stockings. For the purposes of this book, I considered the franchise only from 1876 forward, the year the National League was born. By that time the team had moved and was the Boston Red Stockings for several years until they became the Boston Beaneaters from 1883 through 1906. They then spent four years as the Boston Doves and one as the Boston Rustlers before finally taking the name Braves in 1912. During the 19th century, the franchise had mixed success but managed to win the NL pennant seven times, and produced several players who you will see on this All-Time team roster.

The Braves' first World Series championship came in four games in 1914, but then they had a long dry spell until 1948, when they finally won the NL pennant, only to lose the Series to the Indians. The franchise moved from Boston to Milwaukee for the 1953 season. Backed by the big bats of Hank Aaron and Eddie Mathews, and the consistent pitching of ace Warren Spahn, the Braves finished well above .500 every year from 1953 to 1960, winning the World Series in seven games in 1957 but losing it in seven games in 1958.

The franchise moved again from Milwaukee to Atlanta for the 1966 season and won the newly created West Division in 1969. They managed winning seasons only five times from 1970 to 1990, but then a stable of good starting pitchers led the Braves to consistent success from 1991 through 2005. During that period the Braves won their division every year except 1994, but unfortunately took home only one World Series ring (1995).

Even with only limited postseason success, with such a long history, you'd expect this All-Time team to be very strong. It certainly had some solid positions (e.g., third base, pitching), but it also had some noticeable weak spots (the middle infield).

1st Base

Name	YR	WAR	W3	W/G	AVG	HR	SB	OPS+
Fred Tenney	15	38.9	14.5	.0224	.300	17	260	111
Freddie Freeman	9	33.1	18.3	.0279	.293	189	37	137
Joe Adcock	10	26.6	12.5	.0220	.285	239	11	131
John Morrill	13	23.0	9.2	.0189	.262	41	NA	113
Earl Torgeson	6	18.6	13.7	.0258	.265	82	80	122
Fred McGriff	5	11.1	9.5	.0175	.293	130	23	128

There were three top candidates I considered at 1B. Current Atlanta Braves 1B **Freddie Freeman** (2010–18) was worthy of one of the two spots on this roster, and arguably deserves the nod as the starter. After two productive seasons, Freeman broke through with 23 HR, 109 RBI, and a .319 average in 2013. He has since increased his HR power with a high of 34 in 2016. A three-time All-Star, Freeman is signed through the 2021 season, so presumably his résumé for this All-Time team will only get stronger in the coming years.

Joe Adcock (1953–62) provided solid power for the Milwaukee Braves, hitting 20+ HR six times and 30+ HR twice. And those numbers looked even better considering that he played 140+ games only twice.

You could make a case for old-timer **Fred Tenney** (1894–1907, '11) over either Adcock or Freeman. He had very little power (even for his era) but was a .300 hitter and provided some speed, with five seasons with 20+ SB. He scored 100+ runs three times, including 125 in 1897. Overall, his accomplishments were enough to earn one of the two "extra spots" on this roster.

An even earlier 1B for this franchise was John Morrill (1876–88). A .262 hitter, he didn't have much power, and we don't have SB numbers for most of his career. In 1883 he hit 16 triples in only 97 games, and in 1887 he managed 12 HR and 19 SB.

I looked at two other 1B who deserve brief mention, starting with Earl Torgeson (1947–52). He hit 20+ HR twice and led the NL in runs with 120 in

1950. And Fred McGriff (1993–97) played for the Braves in the middle of his fine career, was an All-Star for them three times, and hit 20+ HR in all four of his full seasons.

2nd Base

Name	YR	WAR	W3	W/G	AVG	HR	SB	OPS+
Rabbit Maranville	15	29.7	14.8	.0165	.252	23	194	83
Bobby Lowe	12	19.1	7.7	.0135	.286	70	260	91
Glenn Hubbard	10	16.8	9.1	.0140	.245	64	32	85
Marcus Giles	6	16.7	15.0	.0247	.285	72	60	108
Martín Prado	7	16.2	13.5	.0237	.295	52	30	109
Tony Cuccinello	7	16.0	13.6	.0259	.278	30	14	104

Even weaker than 1B, this franchise's history at 2B has not been impressive at all. So, I decided to do something I rarely do in this book and include a player at his secondary position. Hall of Famer **Walter James Vincent "Rabbit" Maranville** (1912–20, '29–33, '35) had two stints with the Boston Braves, at the beginning and end of his long career. Only a .252 hitter, he provided very little power—only 23 HR in 1,795 games played. But he could steal bases, swiping 25+ in four seasons, and he hit double-digit triples five times. Rabbit's biggest strength was his defense, where he remains the all-time leader in SS putouts and fifth all-time in SS assists, while also playing several hundred games at 2B. He came in third in the MVP vote in 1913 and second in 1914, when the Braves won the World Series.

There were five other 2B candidates, and you could make an argument in favor of any of them. In the end, I went with **Marcus Giles** (2001–06), as he played most of his short career for the Braves, scored 100+ runs twice, and was an All-Star in 2003, when he hit .316 with 21 HR, 14 SB, and 49 doubles.

The very versatile Martín Prado (2006–12) started his career for Atlanta and was a .295 hitter while playing 2B, 3B, LF, and a little at 1B and SS too. An All-Star in 2010, he hit .307 that year with 40 doubles and 100 runs. Tony Cuccinello (1936–40, '42–43) played three full seasons and parts of four others for the Boston Braves. He was an All-Star in 1938, but arguably had his best season in 1936, when he batted .308 with 86 RBI.

Two others played for this franchise longer than those three, including old-timer Bobby Lowe (1890–1901). As with most players of that era, he had limited power but some speed, stealing 20+ bases six times. His most impressive numbers came during the high-offense season of 1894, when he hit .346 with 17 HR, 115 RBI, 23 SB, and an impressive 158 runs in only 133 games. And lastly, Glenn Hubbard (1978–87) played in more games at 2B than any other player in franchise history. Only a .245 hitter, his best season was his one All-Star campaign in 1983, when he managed to hit .263 with 12 HR and 70 RBI.

3rd Base

Name	YR	WAR	W3	W/G	AVG	HR	SB	OPS+
Eddie Mathews	15	94.4	24.5	.0425	.273	493	66	145
Chipper Jones	19	85.0	21.9	.0340	.303	468	150	141
Billy Nash	10	28.7	13.2	.0242	.281	51	232	108
Bob Elliott	5	26.4	18.4	.0368	.295	101	13	139
Ezra Sutton	12	24.8	14.0	.0254	.287	20	NA	117
Darrell Evans	9	22.8	20.1	.0263	.246	131	31	118
Bob Horner	9	21.5	10.5	.0224	.278	215	14	128
Jimmy Collins	6	21.1	16.1	.0313	.309	34	71	110
Terry Pendleton	5	12.3	13.5	.0207	.287	71	24	107

While the candidates at 1B and 2B for this All-Time team were relatively weak, the candidates at 3B were amazingly strong. **Eddie Mathews** (1952–66) played all but his final two seasons for the Braves, clubbing 493 HR with 1,388 RBI and 1,452 runs scored. He hit 40+ HR four times and 30+ another six times, including a league-leading 47 in 1953 and 46 in 1959 (earning second place in the MVP vote both years). He had 100+ RBI five times and scored 100+ runs an impressive eight times. A .273 hitter with a .379 OBP, he was an All-Star nine times.

Chipper Jones (1993, 1995–2012) played his entire career for Atlanta, mostly at 3B, with a few seasons patrolling LF. He had 30+ HR six times, 100+ RBI nine times, 100+ runs eight times, and managed to top both 100 RBI and 100 runs in six consecutive seasons (1996–2001). A switch-hitter with a .304 average and an impressive .402 OBP, he led the NL with a .364 average and .470 OBP in 2008. An eight-time All-Star, his best all-around numbers came during his MVP year in 1999, when he hit .319 with 45 HR, 110 RBI, 116 runs, and 25 SB.

Hall of Famer Jimmy Collins (1895–1900) hit .346 in 1897 while providing an amazing 132 RBI even with only six home runs. He then led the league with 15 HR and 111 RBI the next year, and overall hit .309 while providing outstanding defense at the hot corner.

Bob Elliott (1947–51) came to the Braves via a trade with the Pirates and immediately won the NL MVP Award in 1947 after hitting .317 with 22 HR and 113 RBI. He followed that up with 23 HR, 100 RBI, and a league-leading 131 walks in 1948.

There were five other 3B from this franchise's history who deserve mention, including (in chronological order):

- Ezra Sutton (1877–88), the first 3B for this franchise, batted .346 and led the NL with 162 hits in 110 games in 1884.

- Billy Nash (1885–95) scored 100+ runs four times and stole 20+ bases eight times. He had career highs of 123 RBI in 1893 and 132 runs the following year.

- Darrell Evans (1969–76, '89) started and ended his long career with Atlanta, and while only a .246 hitter, he walked a lot and so provided a .368 OBP. His best year was 1973, when he hit .281 with 41 HR, 104 RBI, and 114 runs.

- Bob Horner (1978–86) played all but his final season for the Braves, starting with his Rookie of the Year campaign, when he clubbed 23 HR and 63 RBI in only 89 games. Overall, he had 30+ HR three times and 20+ HR another four times, but never had a 100+-RBI season—in part because he was not very durable and played 140+ games only twice.

- Terry Pendleton (1991–94, '96) led the NL with a .319 average and 187 hits in 1991, and along with 22 HR and his clubhouse leadership he took home the MVP trophy that year in a close vote over Barry Bonds of the Pirates. He again led the league with 199 hits the next season, and won the Gold Glove Award at 3B that year as well, but his numbers slipped the following year.

Shortstop

Name	YR	WAR	W3	W/G	AVG	HR	SB	OPS+
Herman Long	13	35.4	13.4	.0215	.280	88	434	95
Johnny Logan	11	33.0	15.6	.0244	.270	92	19	96
Rabbit Maranville	15	29.7	14.8	.0165	.252	23	194	83
Rafael Furcal	6	21.7	15.3	.0266	.284	57	189	95
Jeff Blauser	11	20.6	12.8	.0174	.268	109	61	106
Andrelton Simmons	4	17.3	14.3	.0347	.256	31	16	85

The candidates at SS were more like those at 1B and 2B than those at 3B—not very impressive. The starter was **Johnny Logan** (1951–61), who played most of his career for the Braves, providing a .270 average with moderate power. He was an All-Star four times and had his best season in 1955, when he batted .297 with 95 runs and a league-leading 37 doubles.

For the backup I went with old-timer **Herman Long** (1890–1902), who was a .280 hitter with ample speed, stealing 30+ bases six times with a high of 60 in 1891. He scored 100+ runs in six consecutive seasons, with highs of 149 in 1893 and 136 the following year.

Three others deserve brief mention, starting with Rafael Furcal (2000–05), who started his career with Atlanta, winning the Rookie of the Year Award in 2000 after batting .295 with 40 SB. He stole 20+ bases in all six of his seasons in Atlanta and had a high of 130 runs scored in his one All-Star campaign for the Braves in 2003. Jeff Blauser (1987–97) played most of his career for the Braves, hitting double-digit HR seven times and having his best all-around year in 1993, when he hit .305 with 15 HR, 16 SB, and 110 runs scored. Lastly, defensive wizard Andrelton Simmons (2012–15) started his career for the Braves and took home Gold Glove Awards in both 2013 and 2014.

Catcher

Name	YR	WAR	W3	W/G	AVG	HR	SB	OPS+
Joe Torre	9	33.3	17.0	.0321	.294	142	10	130
Del Crandall	13	27.3	13.6	.0196	.257	170	25	98
Brian McCann	9	23.5	13.4	.0213	.277	176	23	117
Javy López	12	23.4	13.6	.0202	.287	214	8	114

The Braves had some pretty good catchers over the years, with four in particular who were candidates for this All-Time team. The starter was **Joe Torre** (1960–68), who played the first half of his career for the Braves, playing mostly catcher but keeping his bat in the lineup by logging some time at 1B too. He hit 20+ HR four times, with his best season coming in 1966, when he hit .315 with 36 HR and 101 RBI. A five-time All-Star, his defense behind the plate was pretty solid, as he took home a Gold Glove Award in 1965.

The backup choice was not an easy decision, but I went with **Del Crandall** (1949–50, '53–63). He missed two early seasons due to military service in the Korean War, but still managed to hit 15+ HR in eight seasons. His numbers in the table above don't look impressive, but he was an All-Star eight times and provided excellent defense, taking home four Gold Glove Awards.

You could make a case for Brian McCann (2005–13), who was a consistent power source for the Braves, swatting 18 to 24 HR in each of his eight full seasons in Atlanta. He was an All-Star in seven of those seasons, but he was granted free agency after the 2013 season and signed with the Yankees.

Javy López (1992–2003) also provided the Braves with ample power, hitting 20+ HR five times with highs of 34 in 1998 and 43 in 2003. A .287 hitter, he was chosen as an All-Star three times.

Left Field

Name	YR	WAR	W3	W/G	AVG	HR	SB	OPS+
Rico Carty	8	23.2	15.2	.0280	.317	109	11	143
Sid Gordon	4	19.1	16.1	.0336	.289	100	5	141
Lonnie Smith	5	17.3	15.2	.0334	.291	46	52	131
Ralph Garr	8	12.7	12.0	.0159	.317	49	137	113
Ryan Klesko	8	10.7	8.0	.0135	.281	139	26	127

None of the players who primarily played LF were really deserving of spots on this All-Time team roster (and I was alright with that given that some of the other outfielders did play some LF.) Rico Carty (1963–67, '69–70, '72) came the closest, starting his career with the Braves and coming in second in the Rookie of the Year vote in 1964 after hitting .330 with 22 HR and 88 RBI. A .317 hitter for the franchise, he had his best season in 1970, when he hit 25 HR with 101 RBI and paced the NL with a .366 average and .454 OBP.

Sid Gordon (1950–53) played for the Braves for only four seasons, but they were productive years, as he hit 19 to 29 HR in each and had 100+ RBI twice.

Lonnie Smith (1988–92) came to Atlanta in the second half of his career, but he was still productive and had a particularly good season in 1989, when he batted .315 with 21 HR, 25 SB, and a league-leading .415 OBP.

Ralph Garr (1968–75) played the first half of his career for Atlanta, providing limited power but good speed on the bases (four seasons with 25+ SB). A .317 hitter for the Braves, his best year came in his one All-Star campaign in 1974, when he led the NL with a .353 average, 214 hits, and 17 triples. And lastly, Ryan Klesko (1992–99) also played the first half of his career for Atlanta, and he hit 20+ HR four times, with a high of 34 in 1996.

Center Field

Name	YR	WAR	W3	W/G	AVG	HR	SB	OPS+
Andruw Jones	12	61.0	22.7	.0346	.263	368	138	113
Dale Murphy	15	47.0	21.3	.0244	.268	371	160	125
Wally Berger	8	36.6	18.2	.0346	.304	199	29	141
Hugh Duffy	9	28.6	15.1	.0248	.332	69	331	121
Billy Hamilton	6	23.8	15.2	.0345	.339	14	274	132
Felipe Alou	6	21.9	18.3	.0260	.295	94	40	120
Bill Bruton	8	17.8	9.5	.0169	.276	48	143	95

Andruw Jones (1996–2007) first came up to the Braves at the age of 19. He showed some speed early in his career, stealing 20+ bases in four consecutive seasons. But his main value came from his power and his defense in center field. He hit 25+ in ten consecutive seasons, leading the league with 51 HR (a new franchise record) and 128 RBI in 2005. Defensively he was a one-man highlight film and took home ten consecutive Gold Glove Awards.

Dale Murphy (1976–90) first came up as a catcher but was quickly switched over to 1B and eventually the outfield (primarily CF). He hit 20+ HR 11 times, including an amazing string of consistency when he hit 36 in three straight seasons. He scored 100+ runs four times and had 100+ RBI five times. He was MVP in 1982 and had even better numbers in 1983, when he was again MVP after hitting .302 with 36 HR, 121 RBI, 30 SB, and 131 runs. A seven-time All-Star, like Jones he provided great defense in center field, taking home five consecutive Gold Glove Awards.

Wally Berger (1930–37) was a rookie for the Boston Braves in 1930 and hit .310 with 38 HR and 119 RBI. His power numbers dropped the next two years, but then he had four more years with 25+ HR and 90+ RBI, leading the league with 34 HR and 130 RBI in 1935. He was an All-Star four times and batted .304 for the Braves overall.

Hugh Duffy (1892–1900) joined the franchise after four good years with other teams. He contributed immediately, stealing 51 bases and scoring 125 runs in 1892, and batting .363 with 44 SB, 118 RBI, and 147 runs the following year. In 1894 Sir Hugh led the league with a whopping .440 average (the highest ever in the major leagues), and also led the league with 237 hits, 51 doubles, and 18 HR, while adding 16 triples, 145 RBI, 48 SB, and 160 runs—quite a season! Overall, he had seven seasons for the franchise with 100+ RBI, six with 100+ runs, and five with 40+ SB, all while batting .332.

Another old-timer, **Billy Hamilton** (1896–1901), still had a good batting eye and plenty of speed when he finished his career with the Boston Beaneaters. Although his most impressive statistics came earlier with the Phillies, he still managed to hit .339 with an outstanding .456 OBP for Boston. Sliding Billy stole 50+ bases three times, including a high of 83 in 1896. And he scored 100+ runs four times, including 153 in 1896 and a league-leading 152 the following year. These numbers impressed me enough to give him the other "extra spot" on this roster (over Tenney, McCann, López, and others).

Two other center fielders deserve brief mention, starting with Felipe Alou (1964–69), who played for the Braves in the middle of his career. He was an All-Star for them twice and had his best year in 1966, when he hit .327 with 31 HR and a league-leading 218 hits and 122 runs scored. Bill Bruton (1953–60) led the league in SB in his first three seasons with modest totals of 26, 34, and 25. A .276 hitter, he didn't have much power but did hit double-digit triples four times.

Right Field

Name	YR	WAR	W3	W/G	AVG	HR	SB	OPS+
Hank Aaron	21	142.1	26.2	.0462	.310	733	240	158
Tommy Holmes	10	34.7	16.9	.0269	.303	88	40	123
Jason Heyward	5	24.6	18.4	.0361	.262	84	63	114
David Justice	8	24.2	13.8	.0296	.275	160	33	132
Ron Gant	7	18.9	15.6	.0220	.262	147	157	115

Hank Aaron (1954–74) played all but his final two seasons for the Braves, and his career numbers for the franchise were just staggering: .310 average, 3,600 hits, 733 HR, 600 doubles, 2,107 runs, 2,202 RBI, and 240 SB, to give just a few. He led the NL in batting average twice, HR four times, total bases eight times, RBI four times, doubles three times, hits twice, and runs three times. Hammerin' Hank was an All-Star for the Braves for 20 consecutive seasons, scored 100+ runs 15 times, and had 100+ RBI 11 times. He won three Gold Glove Awards early in his career, and his speed on the bases peaked in the middle of his career, when he had six seasons with 20+ SB. He won the NL MVP Award in 1957 and came in third in the voting six times.

Tommy Holmes (1942–51) played all but his final season for the Braves. He had a fine .303 average but had only one truly outstanding season, in 1945, when he came in second in the MVP vote after batting .352 with 125 runs, 117 RBI, 15 SB, and a league-leading 224 hits, 47 doubles, and 28 HR. Amazingly, he struck out only nine times that year.

David Justice (1989–96) took home Rookie of the Year honors in 1990 after batting .282 with 28 HR, 78 RBI, and 11 SB in only 127 games. He went on to provide 20+ HR four more times for the Braves, with a high of 40 HR and 120 RBI in 1993. His teammate Ron Gant (1987–93) started his career for the Braves and provided them with a good combination of power and speed, hitting 30+ HR three times and stealing 25+ bases four times.

And lastly, recent Braves right fielder Jason Heyward (2010–14) arrived in Atlanta with much anticipation at the age of 20 and was the Rookie of the Year runner-up after hitting .277 with 18 HR, 72 RBI, and a lofty .393 OBP. He regressed the following year and then bounced back with 27 HR and 21 SB in 2012 (though he struck out a career-high 152 times). His value came more from his outstanding defense, as he won Gold Glove Awards for the Braves in both 2012 and 2014, before being traded to the Cardinals.

Starting Pitching

Name	YR	WAR	W3	W-L	ERA	WHIP	ERA+
Kid Nichols	12	108.6	36.0	329-183	3.00	1.234	143
Warren Spahn	20	99.4	26.4	356-229	3.05	1.189	120
Phil Niekro	21	90.0	26.8	268-230	3.20	1.229	119
John Smoltz	20	70.1	19.1	210-147	3.26	1.170	127
Greg Maddux	10	67.3	26.0	194-88	2.63	1.051	163
Tom Glavine	17	64.2	22.7	244-147	3.41	1.296	121
Vic Willis	8	43.7	27.0	151-147	2.82	1.258	120
John Clarkson	5	42.6	35.1	149-82	2.82	1.258	128
Jim Whitney	5	41.1	30.3	133-121	2.49	1.082	114
Tommy Bond	5	40.1	39.0	149-87	2.21	1.120	113
Jack Stivetts	7	28.6	18.2	131-78	4.12	1.445	114
Lew Burdette	13	28.5	12.1	179-120	3.53	1.234	102
Tim Hudson	9	26.0	15.5	113-72	3.56	1.242	115
Dick Rudolph	11	25.3	15.8	121-108	2.62	1.154	106
Charlie Buffinton	5	24.7	26.4	104-70	2.83	1.179	103
Johnny Sain	7	24.1	21.9	104-91	3.49	1.319	108

For the ace of this All-Time team's pitching staff I chose lefty **Warren Spahn** (1942, '46–64), who pitched all but his final season for the Boston and Milwaukee Braves. Extremely durable and consistent, Spahn started between 32 and 39 games in 17 consecutive seasons, winning 20+ games an impressive 13 times. He led the league in victories in eight of those years, and also led the league in complete games nine times, ERA three times, and strikeouts four times. He was an All-Star 14 times and won the Cy Young Award in 1957.

Based on the numbers in the table above, you could argue that old-timer **Kid Nichols** (1890–1901) should be given the honor of ace of this All-Time team. But as I did for all teams in this book, I discounted to some degree the statistics of 19th century pitchers. In some cases, that meant a pitcher didn't merit inclusion on an All-Time team at all; in this case, it just meant I chose a great pitcher second rather than first. A Hall of Famer, Charles Augustus Nichols played most of his career for the Boston Beaneaters. He had a winning record in 11 of his 12 seasons, resulting in 329 wins and 183 losses for a .643 winning percentage. He won 25+ games in nine consecutive seasons (including 30+ seven times) and led the NL in wins for three consecutive seasons from 1896 through '98. In fact, his 297 wins during the 1890s were the most ever for a pitcher in a decade. Although often amongst the leaders in ERA and strikeouts, he never led the league in either category.

Knuckleballer **Phil Niekro** (1964–83, '87) pitched most of his long career for the Braves, winning 20+ games for them three times. He led the league with a 1.87 ERA in his first full season in 1967, but never led the league in that category again. He posted 200+ strikeouts three times, including leading the NL with 262 in 1977. Knucksie led the league in wins with a 20-13 mark in 1974 and again in 1979 with a 21-20 mark. That season was the middle of a stretch of four consecutive years where the Braves provided such meager run support that Niekro led the league in losses each year with records of 16-20, 19-18, 21-20, and 15-18. A four-time All-Star, he also fielded the position well, taking home four Gold Glove Awards.

The next three pitchers were the core of the Braves' successful run in the 1990s and early 2000s. The best peak performances came from **Greg Maddux** (1993–2003), who was signed as a free agent after winning his first Cy Young Award for the Cubs in 1992. He continued his dominance of NL hitters by winning three more consecutive Cy Young Awards, leading the league in ERA each year with phenomenal marks of 2.36, 1.56, and 1.63. Although he won 20 games for the Braves only once, he won 15+ in all 11 of his seasons in Atlanta. The Professor was a six-time All-Star, and like Niekro, he fielded his position very well, earning 10 of his 18 Gold Glove Awards with the Braves.

Tom Glavine (1987–2002, '08) pitched most of his career for Atlanta, ending with a 244-147 record (.624 winning percentage). He led the NL in wins five times, with 20 to 22 wins in each of those seasons. An eight-time All-Star, he took home the Cy Young Award in 1991 and 1998, and finished in the top three in balloting another four times.

John Smoltz (1988–99, 2001–08) pitched for the Braves longer than Maddux or Glavine and was more of a strikeout pitcher than his two teammates. He didn't get more than 15 wins in a season until 1996, when he won the Cy Young Award after posting a 24-8 record with a 2.94 ERA and leading the league with 276 strikeouts. After injury forced Smoltz to miss the entire 2000 season, the Braves brought him back in a relief role. He excelled in this too, leading the league with 55 saves in 2002 and recording 45 and 44 in 2003 and 2004. He then returned to the rotation and saw success again, going 14-7, 16-9, and 14-8 in his final three full seasons. An All-Star eight times, Smoltz made this team as an outstanding mixed starter/reliever.

The seventh pitcher on this roster was **Lew Burdette** (1951–63), who was initially a mixed starter/reliever until he earned a permanent spot in the rotation in 1954. He posted 20+ wins twice, and 15+ wins another six times. An All-Star twice, he led the NL with a 2.70 ERA in 1956 and led the league in wins with a 21-15 record in 1959. Perhaps most importantly, he was outstanding in the World Series in 1957, starting and winning three games, posting a 0.67 ERA, and taking home the series MVP honors.

Johnny Sain (1942, '46–51) pitched mostly in relief during his rookie campaign, and then lost three prime years to World War II. When he rejoined the Braves, he immediately proved his worth as a starting pitcher, going 20-14 with a 2.21 ERA. He went 21-12 the next year and led the league in wins with a 24-15 record in 1948. Overall, he won 20+ games four times and was an All-Star twice. And in 1948 he pitched great in two World Series games, allowing only two earned runs in 17 innings.

For the final two starting pitcher spots I went with two pitchers from the earlier part of the 20th century, starting with **Dick Rudolph** (1913–20, '22–23, '27), who had several good seasons for the Boston Braves, including three consecutive from 1914 through '16, when he posted records of 26-10, 22-19, and 19-12. His ERAs those three seasons were 2.35, 2.37, and 2.16, and in 1914 he helped the team win the World Series by allowing only one earned run in two complete game victories.

Hall of Famer **Vic Willis** (1898–1905) pitched over half his career for Boston and started out strong with records of 25-13 and 27-8 in his first two seasons, while also leading the league in ERA with a 2.50 mark in 1899. He won 20+ two more times before later leading the league in losses in 1904 and 1905 with 18-25 and 12-29 records.

If I were going to include any of the truly old-timers, besides Nichols, then I would have chosen Hall of Famer John Clarkson (1888–92), who pitched four full seasons for Boston, posting 25+ wins each year and a 149-82 (.645) record overall. His 1889 season was simply insane, as he led the league in just about every pitching category, including wins with a 49-19 record, 2.73 ERA, 72 games started, 68 complete games, 8 shutouts, 620 innings pitched, 284 strikeouts, and 208 walks. How his arm didn't just fall off at the end of that season is not clear to me.

Clarkson wasn't the only workhorse pitcher that the franchise had during those early years:

- Tommy Bond (1877–81) pitched 490+ innings four times for Boston, leading the league in wins with a 40-17 record in 1877 and a 40-19 record the next year. He also led the NL in ERA twice, with a 2.11 mark in 1877 and 1.96 in 1879.

- Jim Whitney (1881–85) joined the club just after Bond's time and pitched 400+ innings in four of his five seasons, including 552 innings in his rookie season, when he led the NL in both wins and losses with a 31-33 record. He also played some OF and 1B when he wasn't pitching, as he was a capable hitter with a .271 average.

- Charlie Buffinton (1882–86) was a teammate of Whitney and pitched three full seasons, including an impressive 1884 campaign, when he logged 587 innings to go with a 48-16 record and 2.15 ERA.

- Jack Stivetts (1892–98) threw for Boston between Clarkson and Willis, winning 20+ games four times, including a 35-16 record in 1892. Like Whitney, he also played some OF and 1B when he wasn't pitching, as he provided a .305 batting average.

And lastly, you could certainly make a case for recent Atlanta Braves pitcher Tim Hudson (2005–13), who joined the team in 2005 after several excellent seasons in Oakland. He continued to win games at a high rate (.611) and had four seasons with 16 or 17 wins each.

Relief Pitching

Name	YR	WAR	W3	SV	W-L	ERA	WHIP	ERA+
Craig Kimbrel	5	12.3	9.1	186	15-10	1.43	0.903	266
Rick Camp	9	12.3	8.6	57	56-49	3.37	1.386	115
Steve Bedrosian	8	10.5	8.4	41	40-45	3.26	1.302	119
Gene Garber	10	10.0	8.7	141	53-73	3.34	1.276	117
Cecil Upshaw	7	6.4	4.6	79	30-26	3.01	1.240	116
Mark Wohlers	9	3.3	4.9	112	31-22	3.73	1.385	112

I found only two relievers with résumés strong enough to be included on this All-Time team. **Craig Kimbrel** (2010–14) pitched only four full seasons for the Braves, but he was the best reliever in the game during that stretch. He led the NL in saves each year with totals of 46, 42, 50, and 47, and he posted impressive ERAs of 2.10, 1.01, 1.21, and 1.61. He struck out 476 batters in only 289 IP and had a 0.903 WHIP, including an outstanding 0.654 WHIP in 2012.

Outside of Kimbrel, and Smoltz's three excellent seasons as closer, the Braves have not had much in the way of dominating relief pitching. That said, **Gene Garber** (1978–87) pitched most of the second half of his long career for Atlanta, posting 20+ saves for the team four times. His best season came in 1982, when the sidearmer recorded 30 saves to go with a 2.34 ERA.

I did consider several others, starting with Rick Camp (1976–78, '80–85), who was a relief pitcher early in his career and had fine seasons in 1980 (22 saves, 1.91 ERA) and 1981 (17 saves, 1.78 ERA). He became a mixed starter/reliever for a few seasons, but he was done playing at age 32 in 1985.

Steve Bedrosian (1981–85, '93–95) started his career for the Braves and had three seasons with double-digit saves, before moving on and having his best seasons for the Phillies. After additional stops in San Francisco and Minnesota, he returned to Atlanta and served as a setup man for his final three seasons. Mark Wohlers (1991–99) served as a setup man for several years before taking over the closer duties in 1995. He was a power pitcher and had three solid seasons with save totals of 25, 39, and 33, averaging well over one strikeout per inning pitched. And lastly, Cecil Upshaw (1966–69, '71–73) was the Braves' closer for four seasons and had his best year in 1969, when he posted 27 saves with a 2.91 ERA.

Managers

Name	YR	From-To	W-L	PCT	PS	WS
Bobby Cox	25	1978–2010	2,149-1,709	.557	15	1
Frank Selee	12	1890–1901	1,004-649	.607	5	0
Fred Haney	4	1956–59	341-231	.596	2	1
Harry Wright	6	1876–81	254-187	.576	2	0
George Stallings	8	1913–20	579-597	.492	1	1
Billy Southworth	6	1946–51	424-358	.542	1	0

Few would dispute that Hall of Famer **Bobby Cox** is the top manager in Braves history. He led the team to 15 postseasons in 25 years, though only five NL pennants and one World Series championship. In the late 1800s, **Frank Selee** led this franchise to over 1,000 wins with a .607 winning percentage and five NL championships. In the late 1950s, **Fred Haney** was at the helm of several strong Braves teams that posted a .596 winning percentage, two NL pennants, and one World Series ring. And even earlier than Selee, **Harry Wright** was the first manager for this franchise, dating back to 1871 in fact, and capturing two consecutive NL championships in 1877 and '78.

Starting Lineup

What would mythical starting lineups look like for this All-Time roster?

Against RHP:
Herman Long SS (L)
Freddie Freeman 1D (L)
Chipper Jones DH (S)
Hank Aaron RF (R)

Against LHP:
Rabbit Maranville 2B (R)
Chipper Jones DH (S)
Hank Aaron RF (R)
Andruw Jones CF (R)

Eddie Mathews 3B (L)   Dale Murphy LF (R)
Andruw Jones CF (R)   Eddie Mathews 3B (L)
Dale Murphy LF (R)   Joe Adcock 1B (R)
Joe Torre C (R)   Joe Torre C (R)
Rabbit Maranville 2B (R)   Johnny Logan SS (R)

As I noted earlier, 2B has not been a strong position for the Braves so that is why Rabbit Maranville is listed there, allowing a platoon of Long and Logan at SS. Freeman and Adcock seemed like another obvious platoon, and the switch-hitting Chipper Jones is clearly the top candidate to DH in these lineups. Andruw Jones and Dale Murphy were both great CF, but I shifted Murphy over to LF, where he did play a little during his career. Chipper also played two full seasons in LF, so if you wanted to get another left-handed bat in against righties, you could have Jones play LF and slot lefties Holmes, Hamilton, or Tenney as DH. And it pains me to bat Maranville and his .310 OBP leadoff (against lefties), but he did hit in that spot more than any other in his career, and no one else in that lineup really spent any time leading off (though Chipper and his .401 OBP would be interesting to slot there).

Depth Chart

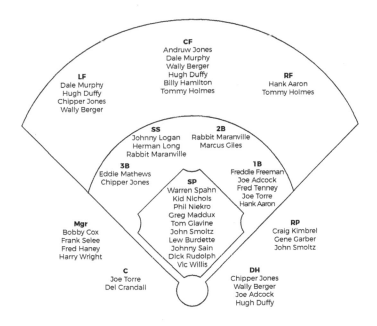

Prospects for Current Players

What are the prospects of current Braves players making this All-Time team? Freddie Freeman is already on the roster at 1B. The Braves have some very promising young players, including Ozzie Albies, Ronald Acuña, Dansby Swanson, Sean Newcomb, and others, but it will take many years of solid play for any of them to make this dream team. We'll see...

Retired Player Numbers

Dale Murphy (3), Bobby Cox (6, manager), Chipper Jones (10), Warren Spahn (21), John Smoltz (29), Greg Maddux (31), Phil Niekro (35), Eddie Mathews (41), Hank Aaron (44), Tom Glavine (47)

Selections from Other Authors and Fan Surveys

1957: *Sport* magazine, November issue

As part of a running series, *Sport* magazine reported on all-time all-star teams picked by "big league publicity departments and the writers covering the clubs." Here is what they had to say:

First Base: Butch Schmidt, who played with the Braves from 1913-15 and batted .272.

Second Base: Rogers Hornsby, the Hall of Famer, who was with the Braves for only one year, 1928 (as a playing manager), but he clouted .387 that season.

Shortstop: Rabbit Maranville, one of the greatest little men who ever played the game. He was with the Braves from 1912 through 1920, and again from 1929 through 1935.

Third Base: Ed Mathews, who, we presume, needs no introduction. He's still making his reputation.

Left Field: Wally Berger, one of the National League's all-time home-run stars, who was with the Braves from 1930 until 1937, when he was traded to the Giants. He had a lifetime batting average of .300 for 11 big-league seasons.

Center Field: Tommy Holmes, who played in Boston from 1942 through 1951, managing the Braves his last year there. He had a .302 lifetime average.

Right Field: Hank Aaron, another young man whose deeds need no elaboration here.

Catcher: Hank Gowdy, who served two terms as Boston catcher, 1911-23 and 1929-30.

Lefthanded Pitcher: Warren Spahn, the ace of today's brilliant Milwaukee staff.

Righthanded Pitcher: Dick Rudolph, the man whose 27 victories brought the Braves their "miracle" pennant in 1914. Dick pitched in Boston from 1913 through 1920, and made return appearances in '22, '23, and '27.

The choices that are pretty easy to understand here were Maranville, Berger, Holmes, and Spahn. And I couldn't really fault the voters for choosing Mathews and Aaron, even though it was very early in their respective careers.

While it was true that Hank Gowdy played for the Boston Braves for parts of 14 seasons, he played 100+ games only three times. When this vote occurred, Del Crandall was in the midst of his career with the Braves, providing good defense, and had already been an All-Star four times—so I thought he would have been the better pick for catcher at that point.

But the choices at 1B and 2B were the most amazing ones to me. Butch Schmidt? In their write-up about him, they said he played three seasons for the Braves, and that is true, except that in the first he had only 78 at-bats. He batted .272 with no power and little speed. Why not go with Fred Tenney, Earl Torgeson, or current 1B Joe Adcock, who had already done more for the Braves franchise than Schmidt ever did? And Rogers Hornsby at 2B, based on one good season? This is a tough call since, as I've noted, 2B has been very weak for this franchise over the years. If they were ignoring 19th century players, then that ruled out Bobby Lowe, so the only other option would have been Bill Sweeney (1907–13), who batted .280 with a high of .344 in 1912 and also had 25+ SB four times.

1969: *The Sporting News* Fan Poll

The July 5, 1969, issue reported the results of a fan poll for the long-standing franchises of the day. The results for the Braves were: 1B: Adcock, 2B: Red Schoendienst, 3B: Mathews, SS: Maranville, C: Crandall, LF: Duffy, CF: Alou, RF: Aaron, RHP: Burdette, LHP: Spahn.

These were generally good choices in my view. It was a little strange that the fans remembered Hugh Duffy well enough to select him for LF, but went with

Lou Burdette over the clearly superior Kid Nichols as the RHP. And I thought Wally Berger would have been a better pick than Felipe Alou for the CF spot. Again the desperation shows at 2B, as Red Schoendienst played parts of only four seasons for the Braves at the end of his career.

1990: "All-Time All-Star Teams," in *The Baseball Research Journal*

In an interesting article, Robert C. Berlo used Thorn and Palmer's TPR (Total Player Rating) system to choose all-time teams. He selected players based on their best 800 consecutive games for the franchise, with a minimum of five years played. His results: 1B Tenney, 2B Hubbard, SS Maranville, 3B Mathews, RF Aaron, CF Murphy, LF Berger, C Torre, SP Nichols, SP Spahn, SP Niekro, SP Whitney, RP Garber.

1992: *The All-Time All-Star Baseball Book*, by Nick Acocella and Donald Dewey

The authors split up their picks for this franchise into three lineups, one for each city. So, starting with Boston, they chose Fred Tenney, Bill Sweeney, Bob Elliott, Rabbit Maranville, Tommy Holmes, Wally Berger, Hugh Duffy, King Kelly, and Kid Nichols. I was glad to see that they included some 19th century guys, notably Duffy and Nichols, but also King Kelly, who played for Boston from 1887 through '89 and returned for a little bit in 1891 and '92. During the first stint he had strong SB totals of 84, 56, and 68, and scored 120 runs twice. For honorable mentions, they listed Vic Willis, Warren Spahn, Johnny Sain, Tommy McCarthy, and Tommy Tucker. McCarthy was an outfielder who played for Boston from 1892–95, stole 40+ bases three times, scored 100+ runs three times, and provided 100+ RBI twice. Tommy Tucker was a teammate of McCarthy and played 1B for Boston from 1890 through '97, scored 100+ runs three times, and provided a little speed.

For the Milwaukee Braves lineup, the authors wrote, "With the exception of Rico Carty, this is the team that won pennants in 1957 and 1958 and lost a season-ending playoff to Los Angeles in 1959." The players were Joe Adcock, Red Schoendienst, Eddie Mathews, Johnny Logan, Hank Aaron, Wes Covington, Rico Carty, Del Crandall, and Warren Spahn. Not a bad lineup given that they had only 13 years to work with. The only player not discussed already was Covington, who was a part-time player for Milwaukee from 1956 through '61. Even though he never played more than 103 games in a season for the Braves, he still had two seasons with 20+ HR. The lone honorable mention given out for this lineup was for Lew Burdette.

For the Atlanta Braves lineup, the authors went with Orlando Cepeda, Félix Millan, Bob Horner, Rafael Ramírez, Hank Aaron, Rico Carty, Dale Murphy, Joe Torre, and Phil Niekro. Honorable mention was given to Felipe Alou and Glenn Hubbard. Cepeda joined Atlanta late in his career, but he did hit 22 HR in 1969 and 34 HR in 1970. Félix Millan played the first half of his career for Atlanta, and between providing a .281 average and outstanding defense (two Gold Glove Awards), he was chosen as an All-Star three times. And lastly, Rafael Ramírez played for Atlanta from 1980 through '87. His highlights included stealing 27 bases in 1982 and being selected as an All-Star in 1984.

1995: *Baseball Ratings*, by Charles F. Faber

Faber also split up the franchise and used his system to generate a separate lineup for Boston, Milwaukee, and Atlanta. For Boston, he had Fred Tenney, Bill Sweeney, Rabbit Maranville, Bob Elliott, Phil Masi, Tommy Holmes, Wally Berger, and Sid Gordon. Catcher Phil Masi played for the Braves from 1939 through 1949, though in only four of those years did he get into 100+ games. A .262 hitter with little power, his good defense led to three All-Star selections.

The Milwaukee lineup included Joe Adcock, Frank Bolling, Johnny Logan, Eddie Mathews, Del Crandall, Hank Aaron, Bill Bruton, and Lee Maye. Bolling played 2B for the Braves from 1961 through '65, and although he was a light hitter, his good defense led to All-Star selections in 1961 and '62. Lee Maye (1959–65) started his career with the Braves, had four seasons with double-digit HR, and led the NL with 44 doubles in 1964.

The Atlanta lineup included Chris Chambliss, Glenn Hubbard, Rafael Ramírez, Bob Horner, Bruce Benedict, Dale Murphy, Hank Aaron, and Ralph Garr. Chambliss played 1B for the Braves from 1980 through '86. He batted .272 and hit 20 HR for them twice. Benedict (1978–89) played his entire career for Atlanta. Although he played 100+ games only three times and was a .242 hitter with no power, his good defense made him an All-Star twice.

For pitching, Faber applied his system to the franchise as a whole, and that resulted in a top five of Warren Spahn, Phil Niekro, Lew Burdette, Tom Glavine, and Vic Willis. I assumed here that the pitchers, like Nichols, who were purely 19th century hurlers were excluded from consideration. The top reliever was of course Gene Garber.

2003: *Rob Neyer's Big Book of Baseball Lineups*, by Rob Neyer

Neyer gave a single lineup for the full franchise, though he too excluded 19th century players from consideration. He went with C Crandall, 1B Adcock, 2B

Hubbard, SS Maranville, 3B Mathews, LF Carty, CF Murphy, RF Aaron. He acknowledged center field as a position of strength, noting that other candidates included Andruw Jones, Wally Berger, and Bill Bruton. For pitchers, he listed Maddux first, apparently preferring his strong peak performances over Spahn's long, consistently good career. The third pitcher was Niekro and the fourth Glavine, with Garber obviously the reliever.

Neyer separately chose both a starting and backup lineup for just the Atlanta era of this franchise. His picks here were solid: C López and Torre, 1B McGriff and Chambliss, 2B Hubbard and Millan, SS Blauser and Ramírez, 3B Jones and Evans, LF Carty and Klesko, CF Murphy and Jones, and RF Aaron and Justice. For pitchers, his first four starters are of course Maddux, Niekro, Glavine, and Smoltz. The next four starters were Pat Jarvis (1966–72), who won 15+ games three times; Kevin Millwood (1997–2002), who started his career for Atlanta and won 17+ games three times for the Braves; Denny Neagle (1996–98), who led the NL in wins with a 20-5 record in 1997 and followed it up with a 16-11 season in 1998; and Carl Morton (1973–76), who won 15+ games for the Braves three times. The two relief choices were Garber and Wohlers.

2010: "The All-Time Atlanta Braves All-Star Team" by Terry W. Sloope, on behalf of the Magnolia Chapter of SABR

This selection of players appeared in the 2010 SABR publication *The National Pastime: Baseball in the Peach State*, edited by Ken Fenster and Wynn Montgomery. The players chosen were (note Atlanta Braves only, not the entire historical franchise): 1B: Fred McGriff, Chris Chambliss; 2B: Glenn Hubbard, Mark Lemke; 3B: Chipper Jones, Bob Horner; SS: Rafael Furcal, Jeff Blauser; C: Javy López, Brian McCann; OF: Hank Aaron, Dale Murphy, Andruw Jones, David Justice, Rico Carty; SP: Greg Maddux, Phil Niekro, Tom Glavine, John Smoltz, Kevin Millwood; Bullpen: Gene Garber, Mark Wohlers, Steve Bedrosian, John Rocker, Rick Camp.

2016: *101 All-Time Fantasy Baseball Teams*, by Jack Sweeney

Sweeney's lineup was interesting with McGriff, Millan, Jones, Maranville, Berger, Murphy, Aaron, and Mathews listed as the DH since Jones was listed at 3B. I think Joe Adcock definitely is more deserving than Fred McGriff at 1B, and it is hard to leave Andruw Jones off. His four starting pitcher selections were all reasonable with Spahn, Maddux, Niekro, and Glavine. He chose Smoltz as the reliever, which I assume is as much about honoring his entire career as it is a reflection of his three strong years as closer.

Top WAR Single Seasons – Hitters (8+)

Name	Year	WAR	AVG	HR	R	RBI	SB	OPS+
Hank Aaron	1961	9.4	.327	34	115	120	21	163
Hank Aaron	1963	9.1	.319	44	121	130	31	179
Darrell Evans	1973	9.0	.281	41	114	104	6	156
Rogers Hornsby	1928	8.8	.387	21	99	94	5	202
Lonnie Smith	1989	8.8	.315	21	89	79	25	168
Hank Aaron	1959	8.6	.355	39	116	123	8	182
Hank Aaron	1967	8.5	.307	39	113	109	17	168
Hank Aaron	1962	8.5	.323	45	127	128	15	170
Eddie Mathews	1953	8.3	.302	47	110	135	1	171
J.D. Drew	2004	8.3	.305	31	118	93	12	157
Eddie Mathews	1959	8.2	.306	46	118	114	2	168
Andruw Jones	2000	8.2	.303	36	122	104	21	126
Hank Aaron	1969	8.0	.300	44	100	97	9	177
Hank Aaron	1957	8.0	.322	44	118	132	1	166
Tommy Holmes	1945	8.0	.352	28	125	117	15	175
Hank Aaron	1960	8.0	.292	40	102	126	16	156
Eddie Mathews	1963	8.0	.263	23	82	84	3	146

Hank Aaron appears on this list an impressive eight times (and had another five seasons with a 7+ WAR.) His top season in 1961 doesn't seem offensively better than others, but he earned significantly higher defensive WAR that year. Eddie Mathews appears three times on the list, but no one else appears more than once. Interestingly, none of the great seasons of Chipper Jones and Dale Murphy made the list: Jones' high was 7.6, and Murphy's high was 7.7.

Lonnie Smith's 1989 season was surprising to see as high as fifth on this list, but when I looked into it I found that he had a much higher defensive WAR score that year than any other in his career. Hall of Fame 2B Rogers Hornsby played for this franchise for only one year, but he took home one of his seven batting titles in 1928 while also pacing the NL in OBP and SLG. Outfielder J.D. Drew played for the Braves for only one year as well, and it happened to be the best season of his career.

Top WAR Single Seasons – Pitchers (8+)

Name	Year	WAR	W-L	ERA	IP	SO	ERA+
Kid Nichols	1897	11.3	31-11	2.64	368.0	127	168
Kid Nichols	1898	11.1	31-12	2.13	388.0	138	174
Phil Niekro	1978	10.4	19-18	2.88	334.1	248	142
Vic Willis	1899	10.2	27-8	2.50	342.2	120	165
Kid Nichols	1895	9.7	26-16	3.41	390.2	148	146
Greg Maddux	1995	9.6	19-2	1.63	209.2	181	260

Warren Spahn	1947	9.3	21-10	2.33	289.2	123	170
Tom Glavine	1991	9.3	20-11	2.55	246.2	192	153
Warren Spahn	1953	9.1	23-7	2.10	265.2	148	188
Vic Willis	1901	8.7	20-17	2.36	305.1	133	154
Greg Maddux	1994	8.7	16-6	1.56	202.0	156	271
Bill James	1914	8.7	26-7	1.90	332.1	156	150
Johnny Sain	1948	8.5	24-15	2.60	314.2	137	149
Phil Niekro	1977	8.4	16-20	4.03	330.1	262	111
Vic Willis	1902	8.1	27-20	2.20	410.0	225	128
Irv Young	1905	8.0	20-21	2.90	378.0	156	106
Warren Spahn	1951	8.0	22-14	2.98	310.2	164	124
Phil Niekro	1974	8.0	20-13	2.38	302.1	195	159
Phil Niekro	1979	8.0	21-20	3.39	342.0	208	119

As I do throughout this book, this list excludes any pitcher's seasons from 1894 and earlier, as they often pitched 400+ innings and could accumulate 8+ WAR without necessarily pitching very well. Phil Niekro appears on this list the most with four seasons, though Kid Nichols appears three times and also had a WAR of 8+ each year from 1890 through '94. Warren Spahn and Vic Willis also appear on this list three times each, and Greg Maddux appears twice (1994 and 1995, both strike-shortened seasons).

Bill James had a very short career, but at age 22 he was a key part of the Boston Braves World Series championship club. He pitched part of 1915, but then served in World War I as an instructor of bomb throwing for the U.S. Army. After the war he continued to pitch, mostly in the minor leagues, until 1925.

Irv Young had the misfortune of pitching for this franchise during some of its very worst seasons. As a rookie in 1905, he posted a 20-21 record after completing 41 of his 42 starts. That is one of only two seasons since 1901 in which a pitcher won 20 games for a team that lost 100 or more (Ned Garver for the 1951 St. Louis Browns is the other).

Franchise Player

This honor clearly had to be given to Mr. Henry Aaron, with honorable mention going to the two third basemen (Mathews and Jones) and the top four hurlers (Spahn, Nichols, Niekro, and Maddux).

CHAPTER 13

The Athletics Franchise All-Time Dream Team

The Philadelphia/Kansas City/Oakland Athletics (A's) franchise was born in 1901 with the beginning of the American League. They played in Philadelphia for 54 seasons, and with some success: nine pennants and five World Series championships. The majority of that success came in the earliest years, and the team certainly had their poor stretches too, such as a seven-year span from 1915 through '21 when they finished over .400 only once, or the 1934–1946 dry spell when they never finished over .500 and were regularly below .400. With plenty of good and bad, what was amazing was that they had just one manager, Connie Mack, for almost all of those years (1901–1950).

The team moved to Kansas City for the 1955 season and stayed there through 1967. That period was a gloomy one for the franchise, as they didn't have a winning season even once. Things improved when, in 1968, the team moved even further west to Oakland. This began a series of nine consecutive winning seasons that included a mini-dynasty from 1971 through '75 when they won the AL West division every year and took the World Series crown from 1972 through '74.

The 12 years that followed were fairly unimpressive ones, but when Tony LaRussa took the helm during the 1986 season, things once again looked up for the A's. During his tenure, they made the playoffs four times and won the World

Series once (1989). After losing seasons from 1993 through '98, the A's were winners again from 1999 through 2006, making the postseason five more times.

As you will see, the All-Time Athletics team was pretty strong overall, with only a couple of positions of relative weakness.

1st Base

Name	YR	WAR	W3	W/G	AVG	HR	SB	OPS+
Jimmie Foxx	11	62.5	28.7	.0498	.339	302	48	175
Mark McGwire	12	42.8	18.5	.0322	.260	363	8	155
Harry Davis	16	36.0	15.3	.0255	.279	69	223	124
Jason Giambi	8	28.8	22.8	.0278	.300	198	9	144
Stuffy McInnis	9	25.9	14.8	.0249	.313	13	127	122
Ferris Fain	6	21.8	13.4	.0259	.297	35	33	124

The clear starter here was slugger **Jimmie Foxx** (1925–35), who played most of his games in Philly at 1B, while putting in some time at both 3B and C. In his first three seasons he didn't play much, but at the still young age of 20 in 1928 he began his dominance of AL hurlers, and from 1929 through '35 he hit 30+ HR with 100+ RBI. In 1929 he hit .354, and in 1930 he smacked 37 HR with 156 RBI. In 1932 he took his first AL MVP Award, hitting .364 with 58 HR and 169 RBI, missing the Triple Crown by just three BA points. But that was rectified in 1933, when he captured that rare honor by leading the AL with a .356 average, 48 HR, and 163 RBI.

After a brief stint with the A's in 1986, **Mark McGwire** (1986–97) burst onto the scene with a .289 BA, 49 HR (led the AL) and 118 RBI to take the 1987 Rookie of the Year Award. His average plummeted for several seasons (bottoming out at .201 in 1991), but his power remained strong, as he hit 30+ HR seven more times for the A's. In 1996 Big Mac hit .312 with 52 HR (again led the AL) and 113 RBI, and was doing much the same in 1997 when he was traded to St. Louis in late July. If you think the steroid issue that is a part of McGwire's legacy started during his time in Oakland, then I could understand keeping him off this All-Time roster. However, I gave him this backup spot on the basis of his nine All-Star appearances and my overall impression of his Oakland résumé.

Old-timer **Harry Davis** (1901–11, '13–17) had an interesting career for the Athletics. Fifth all-time for the franchise in at-bats and first in games played at 1B, he was with them at the beginning, and played as the regular 1B for most seasons through 1911. In 1912 he played a little for the Cleveland Naps (as they were called at the time), and then returned to the Athletics as a player-coach from 1913 through 1917, but he was mostly a coach, as he played in a total of 19 games with 28 at-bats during those years. At first glance, his numbers made me think he had more speed than power, but this conclusion dropped the context of the Deadball Era. He did steal 20 or more bases in 8 of 10 seasons. But his career high of 36 was only good enough for fifth in the league, and he never again was in the top ten. Meanwhile, he was one of only a few players in history (and was the first) to lead the league in HR in four consecutive seasons. He did so from 1904 through '07, with Herculean totals of 10, 8, 12, and 8, respectively. He also led the league in doubles three times and RBI twice. After considering the options at other positions, I decided to give Davis one of the two "extra spots" allotted for position players on each team.

Jason Giambi (1995–2001, '09) also got a good look. While he played for the A's for only seven seasons, several of them were quite impressive. In 1999 he hit .315 with 33 HR and 123 RBI, he took AL MVP honors the next year with a .333 average, 43 HR, and 137 RBI, and then was runner-up in 2001 after hitting .342 with 38 HR and 120 RBI. But that wasn't enough to crack a deep 1B position on this All-Time team.

No one else came close at 1B, but I did look at a couple of others briefly. Stuffy McInnis (1909–17) took over for Davis as the A's regular 1B in 1911 and held that job through 1917. He hit over .300 every year during that span and stole 20+ bases three times. Ferris Fain (1947–52) hit .344 in 1951 and .327 in 1952—both good enough to lead the AL. He also had a very high OBP, as he walked a lot: 100+ walks five times, including 136 in 1949 and 133 in 1950.

2nd Base

Name	YR	WAR	W3	W/G	AVG	HR	SB	OPS+
Eddie Collins	13	57.3	29.3	.0496	.337	16	373	156
Max Bishop	10	35.5	15.4	.0301	.272	39	37	104
Danny Murphy	12	35.4	14.9	.0251	.290	40	185	126
Mark Ellis	9	26.7	13.5	.0253	.265	86	62	95
Dick Green	12	16.0	8.5	.0124	.240	80	26	87

At 2B the starter was also quite clear. Although no 2B in Athletics history played more than 1,200 games at the position, **Eddie Collins** (1906–14, '27–30) played the third most (996) and was by far the most productive. Collins started and ended his Hall of Fame career in Philadelphia, playing six full seasons and several other partial seasons for the club. In those six seasons from 1909 through 1914, he hit between .324 and .365, hit 10+ triples, and stole between 38 and 81 bases. In 1912 he twice stole six bases in a game (during an 11-day stretch in

September). He four times had an OBP over .440, led the league in runs from 1912 through '14, in stolen bases with 81 in 1910, and was voted AL MVP in 1914. Collins was a key member of four Athletics World Series teams (three of which they won) and was arguably the greatest all-around 2B of all time.

Max Bishop (1924–33) played most of his career for the Athletics and was the regular at 2B during those years (though he never played more than 130 games in a season). Although Bishop had a mediocre average (.272), his OBP was outstanding (.423) given his willingness to take a free pass: he walked 100+ times in seven seasons. His top HR total was only 10 in 1930, and he didn't have much speed either, but he scored 100+ runs from 1928 through '31 and was an important part of the 1929–31 AL champions.

You could also make a case for Danny Murphy (1902–13), an early member of the Athletics who played in 1,412 games but split his time between 2B and OF. A significant contributor from 1902 through '13, he hit for average and ran a bit as well. He had 15+ SB in eight seasons and managed 17 triples in 1904 and 18 in 1910.

No one else came close. Mark Ellis (2002–03, '05–11) provided good defense but only moderate power and speed. And Dick Green (1963–74) played 1,158 games at 2B for the Kansas City and Oakland Athletics, spending his entire career with this franchise. A low-average hitter (.240), his best offensive season was in 1969, when he hit .275 with 12 HR and 64 RBI.

3rd Base

Name	YR	WAR	W3	W/G	AVG	HR	SB	OPS+
Sal Bando	11	52.0	21.2	.0354	.255	192	60	127
Frank Baker	7	42.3	24.5	.0471	.321	48	172	153
Eric Chávez	13	34.8	16.8	.0264	.267	230	47	115
Jimmy Dykes	15	29.0	10.6	.0170	.283	86	61	99
Carney Lansford	10	27.2	13.9	.0226	.288	94	146	112

Sal Bando (1966–76) played in the most games at 3B for the Athletics (1,446). After two partial seasons in Kansas City, he moved with the club to Oakland in 1968 and soon became a key slugger during their pennant-winning streak in the 1970s. His best numbers came in 1969, when he hit .281 with 31 HR, 113 RBI, and 106 runs. In 1971 he was the runner-up AL MVP based on a .271 average, 24 HR, and 94 RBI (teammate and pitching phenom Vida Blue took the honors). In 1973 he came in fourth in MVP voting, and in 1974 third. Although in 1976 he hit 27 HR and 84 RBI, and even managed a career-high 20 SB, he sought and was granted free agency after the season and went to the Brewers to finish out his career.

The backup spot went to **Frank "Home Run" Baker** (1908–14). After a brief 1908 campaign, Baker played full-time for the Athletics from 1909 through '14. He was amongst the league leaders in most offensive categories in most of those seasons and garnered some MVP consideration in four of them. He led the league in HR four times during this Deadball Era, with totals of 11, 10, 12, and 9 from 1911 through '14. He also paced the league in RBI in 1912 with 130 and in 1913 with 117. Not a one-dimensional player, he hit for a high average (.321 for the Athletics), hit plenty of doubles and triples, and stole bases as well, with 30+ in three seasons.

For a while, **Eric Chávez** (1998–2010) was a consistent run producer, hitting 20 to 34 HR in his seven full seasons with the club. He also smashed 100+ RBI four times, with 2001 being perhaps his best year with a .288 average, 32 HR, 43 doubles, and 114 RBI. He also provided outstanding defense at the hot corner, capturing the Gold Glove Award every year from 2001 through '06. With such accolades, it was a little strange that he was never named an All-Star during his time in Oakland. That seemed like a snub to me, so lest I snub him further, I gave him the other "extra spot" on this roster.

Jimmy Dykes (1918–32) played for the Athletics for a long time, playing significantly at both 3B and 2B. In fact, he ranked third in both games and at-bats for the franchise. He hit over .300 five times, but displayed limited power and speed. He had a fine 1929 campaign, hitting .327 with 13 HR and 79 RBI, to help Philadelphia to the World Series. And once there, he helped them win it over the Cubs as he went 8-for-19 in the five-game Series.

After five seasons with the Angels and the Red Sox, Carney Lansford (1983–92) came over to the A's before the 1983 season in a trade for slugger Tony Armas. Lansford could hit for a high average: his .336 in 1989 ranked second in the AL. He had a little power, hitting double-digit HR five times, and displayed some ability to steal bases late in his career (25+ bases from 1987 through '89).

Shortstop

Name	YR	WAR	W3	W/G	AVG	HR	SB	OPS+
Bert Campaneris	13	48.9	17.8	.0272	.262	70	566	93
Eddie Joost	8	26.2	16.9	.0286	.249	116	33	114
Jack Barry	8	22.9	13.5	.0253	.250	8	131	93
Miguel Tejada	7	22.0	14.7	.0235	.270	156	49	107

At SS it seemed pretty clear that **Bert Campaneris** (1964–76) deserved the starting spot. A five-time All-Star, he was very good defensively and also a demon on the basepaths: he stole 50+ bases seven times, leading the league six times, and is second all-time for the club in that category. And just imagine how many he would have swiped had he been able to get on base more often: his .314 OBP was definitely a weakness in his game. Not a power hitter, he never had over 10 home runs in a season except in 1970, when he busted out with 22. Although he never came in higher than tenth, he received some MVP consideration in eight seasons. And while he played almost all of his games at SS, he famously displayed the ultimate flexibility by becoming the first player in MLB history to play all nine positions in one game.

The decision for the backup spot came down to three candidates. I went with **Eddie Joost** (1947–54), who was an All-Star twice and garnered some MVP votes five times. Not a high-average hitter (.249), he walked a lot and so had a strong .392 OBP. He also had some power for a middle infielder, hitting between 13 and 23 HR for six consecutive seasons. In 1949 he scored 128 runs, which was second in the AL.

Miguel Tejada (1997–2003) started his major league career as a 19-year-old in 1997 and matured into a major run producer a few years later. From 2000 through 2003 he hit 27 to 34 HR and had 100+ RBI. In 2002 he hit .308 with 34 HR and 131 RBI, which was good enough to garner the AL MVP Award. Highly durable, Tejada started one of the longest contemporary playing streaks (1,152 games) while with Oakland and continued it after signing with Baltimore as a free agent after the 2003 season. You could make a case for him instead of Joost as the backup—I admit it was a tough call.

Lastly, Jack Barry (1908–15) was an early SS for this franchise and was a typical light hitter for that era: he had only 8 HR in 3,072 at-bats and didn't hit many doubles or triples either, leading to a low .315 slugging percentage. A good fielder, his only offensive contribution was providing 20+ SB three times.

Catcher

Name	YR	WAR	W3	W/G	AVG	HR	SB	OPS+
Mickey Cochrane	9	40.7	17.4	.0349	.321	108	50	129
Terry Steinbach	11	24.8	10.9	.0207	.275	132	15	107
Gene Tenace	8	23.5	14.8	.0292	.245	121	18	136
Frankie Hayes	11	15.9	9.9	.0160	.270	101	26	104

Hall of Famer **Mickey Cochrane** (1925–33) played all but his last four seasons for Philadelphia, hitting .321 with a .412 OBP. He had good power for a catcher during his era, hitting 15+ HR in three seasons, and also scored 100+ runs four times. He won one of his two MVP Awards for the Athletics, though it wasn't for one of his most impressive seasons statistically, as he hit .293 with 10 HR and 57 RBI. Compare that with 1932, when he hit 23 HR with 112 RBI and 118 runs, or his 1929–31 seasons, when he hit .331, .357, and .349, respectively.

Gene Tenace (1969–76) played the first half of his career with the A's, splitting his time between C and 1B, and slugging 20+ HRs in his four full seasons with the club. A low-average hitter (.245), he walked a lot, leading to a solid .374 OBP. He was also the 1972 World Series MVP after hitting 4 HR with 9 RBI.

You could also make a case for Terry Steinbach (1986–96), who was a three-time All-Star with moderate power for most of his career until his final season in Oakland, when he busted out with 35 HR and 100 RBI. He became a free agent afterwards and signed with the Twins, where he played for three more years before retiring.

Lastly, Frankie Hayes (1933–34, '36–42, '44–45) was a little-known four-time All-Star, including in 1939, when he hit .283 with 20 HR and 83 RBI, and 1940, when he hit .308 with 16 HR and 70 RBI.

Left Field

Name	YR	WAR	W3	W/G	AVG	HR	SB	OPS+
Rickey Henderson	14	72.5	25.6	.0425	.288	167	867	137
Al Simmons	12	50.8	23.2	.0394	.356	209	65	147
Bob Johnson	10	44.8	16.9	.0307	.298	252	78	137
Topsy Hartsel	10	25.2	12.1	.0220	.266	21	196	125
Joe Rudi	11	21.3	13.8	.0192	.272	116	21	118

While **Rickey Henderson** (1979–84, '89–93, '94–95, '98) is often considered the best leadoff hitter in the history of the game, he was nonetheless traded quite a lot and actually had four stints in Oakland. He was drafted by the A's in 1976 and made it to the major league club in 1979. After the 1984 season he was traded to the Yankees, but he was traded back to the A's in June of 1989. He was traded to the Blue Jays on July 31, 1993, but was granted free agency at the end of the season and re-signed with the A's. After also playing a bit for the Padres and Angels, he returned to the A's for the 1998 season (and then played for five more teams after that).

Rickey sure was a fantastic player, and great fun to watch. He still has the single-season record for SB, swiping an amazing 130 in 1982 (and he ran a lot that year, as he was caught 42 times too). And that was far from a fluke, as he also swiped 100+ in 1980 and 1983 and regularly paced the AL in this category. He sometimes hit over .300, but he always had a high OBP in part because of his unique batting stance that limited the size of his strike zone. He displayed power in some of his seasons, and he was well known for his leadoff HRs to start ballgames (he holds the career record with 81). He scored 100+ runs in seven seasons for the A's, plus twice more when he split time with other clubs. In 1990 he took home AL MVP honors after hitting .325 with 28 HR, 65 SB, and 119 runs. And he did well in several postseason series, including the 1989 World Championship run, when he hit .400 with eight SB and two HR in the ALCS and then hit .474 in the World Series.

Al Simmons (1924–32, '40–42) had some great seasons for the Athletics, and though regularly near the top of the MVP voting, he never took home the prize. Starting as a CF, he switched to LF after his first few seasons. After hitting .308 as a rookie, he broke out in 1925 by hitting .387 with 253 hits, 24 HR, 129 RBI, and 122 runs. In 1927 Aloysius managed a .392 average, and later had one of the best four-year stretches that any hitter ever has. In 1929 he hit .365 with 34 HR, 157 RBI, and 114 runs. In 1930 it was .381, 36 HR, 165 RBI, and 152 runs. In 1931 it was .390, 22 HR, 128 RBI, and 105 runs. And in 1932 it was .322, 35 HR, 151 RBI, and 144 runs. He led the AL in batting average twice and came in second twice more. Amazingly, Simmons had 100+ RBI in his first 11 seasons in the majors, the first 9 of which were with the Athletics. He performed well in the World Series too, as he hit .333 with 6 HR in the 1929–31 Series, helping to lead the A's to championships in the first two of them.

A third left fielder also earned a spot on this All-Time team, **Bob Johnson** (1933–42), who played all but his last three seasons for the Philadelphia Athletics. A five-time All-Star, he hit .298 with a .395 OBP, hit 20+ HR nine times, and had seven consecutive 100+-RBI years.

Two others deserve brief mention, starting with early Athletics star Topsy Hartsel (1902–11). In 1902 Hartsel led the league with 109 runs and 47 SB. He had a good batting eye, leading the league in walks five times. And Joe Rudi (1967–76, '82) was a good fielder (three Gold Glove Awards) with moderate power. 1974 was his best year, as he hit .293 with 39 doubles, 22 HR, and 99 RBI. In both 1972 and 1974, Rudi was amongst the A's getting MVP consideration, and he finished second in the vote each year.

Center Field

Name	YR	WAR	W3	W/G	AVG	HR	SB	OPS+
Dwayne Murphy	10	31.6	17.1	.0261	.247	153	99	115
Amos Strunk	13	23.0	13.8	.0224	.283	11	144	119
Bill North	6	20.0	16.7	.0299	.271	13	232	105
Dave Henderson	6	19.5	16.6	.0278	.263	104	19	117
Sam Chapman	11	18.1	11.0	.0142	.268	174	38	108
Rube Oldring	12	14.7	9.5	.0124	.271	25	187	104

Dwayne Murphy (1978–87) provided a good combination of power and defense. Like Chávez, Murphy was surely one of the best players never chosen as an All-Star. He won six Gold Glove Awards and played in more games as a center fielder than anyone in team history. Murphy hit 20+ HR three times during his time with Oakland, and his 33 HR in 1984 was third-best in the AL. He also could run well, swiping 26 bases in both 1980 and 1982.

None of the other CF candidates did enough to earn a roster spot, including (in chronological order):

- Rube Oldring (1906–16) provided some speed and in 1913 was amongst the AL leaders in both runs (101) and SB (40).

- Amos "Lightning" Strunk (1908–17, '19-20, '24) was a teammate of Oldring, and like many of this era, he could steal bases, nabbing 20 or more three times for Philadelphia.

- Sam Chapman (1938–41, '45-51) played almost all of his career for the Athletics and lost several prime seasons to World War II. He hit 20+ HR five times and had his best season in 1941, when he hit .322 with 35 HR, 106 RBI, and 97 runs.

- Bill North (1973–78) was plenty fast on the bases, stealing 53 bases in his first full season and then leading the league with 54 in 1974 and 75 in 1976.

- Dave Henderson (1988–93) provided the A's with some power in the late '80s and early '90s, hitting 20+ HR four times.

Right Field

Name	YR	WAR	W3	W/G	AVG	HR	SB	OPS+
Reggie Jackson	10	48.0	23.7	.0357	.262	269	145	145
José Canseco	9	27.1	18.0	.0256	.264	254	135	136
Elmer Valo	15	26.3	11.2	.0193	.285	47	103	117
Socks Seybold	8	24.7	12.7	.0253	.296	51	64	133
Bing Miller	12	22.6	11.4	.0166	.311	94	109	108
Wally Moses	10	21.4	12.2	.0184	.307	64	58	113

Hall of Famer **Reggie Jackson** (1967–75, '87) started his career with Oakland and then returned for his final year in 1987 (mostly as a DH). His hitting style meant lots of strikeouts, but it also meant 25+ HR seven times for the A's. In 1973 he garnered the AL MVP Award after hitting .293 with a league leading

32 HR and 117 RBI. But his best power numbers were earlier, in 1969, when he smashed 47 HR with 118 RBI and 123 runs while hitting .275. In these early years he could also run pretty well, swiping 20 or more bases three times.

Although steroid use and other matters have tarnished the way history views **José Canseco** (1985–92, '97), his accomplishments remained impressive to me, enough so that I thought he deserved a spot on this All-Time team roster. He started by winning the Rookie of the Year Award in 1986 after smashing 33 HR with 117 RBI (though striking out 170 times and hitting only .240). In 1988 he had a career year and took home AL MVP honors after becoming the first 40/40 man in history: .307, 42 HR, 40 SB, 120 runs, and 124 RBI. In total, he had five seasons of 30+ HR and 100+ RBI from 1986 to '91. In late 1992 he was traded to the Rangers, and he played for several teams before returning to the A's for one more season.

I considered several other RF candidates, including (in chronological order):

- Socks Seybold (1901–08) was part of the Athletics at the beginning of the franchise, and his best season was 1902, when he hit .316 with 97 RBI and a league-leading 16 HR.

- Bing Miller (1922–26, '28–34) hit a cumulative .311 in his two stints with the Athletics. Mostly a singles and doubles hitter, his best statistical season was arguably 1922, when he hit .335 (fifth-best in the AL) with 21 HR and 90 RBI.

- Wally Moses (1935–41, '49–51) hit over .300 in all of his first seven seasons. His one All-Star season in 1937 was easily his best, as he hit .320 with 208 hits, 45 doubles, 13 triples, 25 HR, 86 RBI, and 113 runs.

- Elmer Valo (1940–43, '46–56) was a teammate of Moses for some years and hit .300+ a few times, but he never had more than 10 HR or 14 SB in a season. He walked a lot, producing an impressive .403 OBP for the Athletics.

Starting Pitching

Name	YR	WAR	W3	W-L	ERA	WHIP	ERA+
Eddie Plank	14	73.7	23.3	284-162	2.39	1.127	120
Lefty Grove	9	61.7	28.0	195-79	2.88	1.250	151
Eddie Rommel	13	50.1	18.7	171-119	3.54	1.350	121
Chief Bender	12	47.5	17.6	193-102	2.32	1.091	117
Rube Waddell	6	44.8	28.7	131-82	1.97	1.062	146

Catfish Hunter	10	31.3	18.1	161-113	3.13	1.126	105
Tim Hudson	6	31.0	18.9	92-39	3.30	1.222	136
Barry Zito	8	30.3	16.8	102-63	3.58	1.256	124
Rube Walberg	11	28.6	14.4	134-114	4.11	1.433	106
Vida Blue	9	28.6	21.0	124-86	2.95	1.165	118
Jack Coombs	9	25.3	17.4	115-67	2.60	1.223	105
Bobby Shantz	8	20.7	15.1	69-65	3.80	1.334	111
Mark Mulder	5	19.5	15.9	81-42	3.92	1.284	114
Dave Stewart	8	19.1	13.9	119-78	3.73	1.318	103
George Earnshaw	6	17.4	15.2	98-58	4.18	1.430	106
Ken Holtzman	4	11.6	10.0	77-55	2.92	1.175	115
Bob Welch	7	10.9	9.3	96-60	3.94	1.362	97

As with the Athletics outfield, this franchise was absolutely loaded with starting pitchers to consider. Interestingly, the top three were all left-handers. **Lefty Grove** (1925–33) pitched the first, and better, half of his career with the Athletics. He had seven straight 20+-win seasons and regularly had an ERA well below 3.00 (even while the league average was well over 4.00). He won the pitching Triple Crown two years in a row, first in 1930 when he posted a 28-5 record with a 2.54 ERA and 209 strikeouts. Then in 1931 he won the AL MVP Award with a ridiculous 31-4 record, 2.06 ERA and 175 strikeouts. While with the A's, he led the AL in ERA five times, wins four times, and strikeouts seven times. He also kept himself busy by pitching one-third of his games out of the bullpen, saving 50 games during his time in Philadelphia, including a league-leading 9 in 1930. And he was also solid in the World Series of 1929–31, going 4-2 with a 1.75 ERA.

By far the club's leader in games started, innings pitched, and wins, Hall of Famer **Eddie Plank** (1901–14) was the clear second choice for this staff. He pitched for the first 14 Athletics teams, which amounted to all but his last three seasons. He managed 20+ wins seven times for this franchise and had 19 twice. League ERAs were low back then, but Plank's mark was always better than the league average, and sometimes significantly so. He was usually amongst the league leaders in the major pitching statistics but rarely paced the AL in anything. In four World Series he went only 2-5 but could not have pitched much better, as he completed six of his seven starts and had a cumulative 1.32 ERA.

Rube Waddell (1902–07) pitched in the first decade of the team's existence. In 1905 he led the AL in the three Triple Crown categories with a 27-10 record, 287 strikeouts, and a 1.48 ERA (though this wasn't yet a standard statistic). Waddell led the AL in strikeouts every year for the Athletics and had 349 in 383 innings in 1904 (a record that held up for more than six decades).

Chief Bender (1903–14) was a good right-hander alongside Plank and Waddell during the early years, so he was the fourth starter on this roster. He won 20+ twice and 17+ another five times. His best season was 1910, when he posted an outstanding 23-5 record with a 1.58 ERA (though again, the league average was 2.37, so his mark ranked only fifth that year).

Eddie Rommel (1920–32) spent his entire career with the Athletics, winning 20+ twice and 18 in two other seasons. His best year was 1922, when he led the AL in wins with a 27-13 mark. He led the league again in 1925 with 21 wins. On this dream team roster, Rommel could serve well as a swingman too, as he started only 249 of the 501 games he appeared in, entering games in relief increasingly more often in the second half of his career.

James "Catfish" Hunter (1965–74) had five mediocre seasons to start his career, but then won 18 games in 1970 and 21 in each of the next three years. In 1972 he posted a 2.04 ERA, but 1974 was his best season with the A's, as he went 25-12 with a 2.49 ERA (led league) and 23 complete games to take the AL Cy Young Award. He was generally excellent in the postseason as well, going 7-2 with a 2.55 ERA.

Another star during that era, **Vida Blue** (1969–77) burst onto the scene in 1971 as a 21-year-old phenom. He went 24-8 with a 1.82 ERA, striking out 301 in 312 innings (with 24 complete games), and took home both the Cy Young and MVP Awards in the American League. Although he never again pitched at that level, he did manage to win 20 games in two more seasons for the A's, and also had seasons of 18 and 17 victories before going across the bay to the Giants in 1978.

Next up were two teammates: **Tim Hudson** (1999–04) and **Barry Zito** (2000–06, '15). Hudson went 20-6 in 2000 and was second in Cy Young Award votes. A consistent winner, he posted a 92-39 record for the Athletics, which translated to an impressive .702 winning percentage. After a fine audition in 2000, Zito became a workhorse for the A's, starting 34 or 35 games each year. His best season was in 2002, when he worked his sweeping curveball well enough to win the AL Cy Young Award after posting a 2.75 ERA and leading the league in wins with a 23-5 record.

After reviewing the candidates for relief pitchers, I decided to choose one more starter for this All-Time team. There were many candidates to consider, and you could make a good case for several of them. But in the end, I decided to go with consistent workhorse and postseason star **Dave Stewart** (1986–92, '95). He had bounced around with several teams before joining the Athletics at age 29 during the 1986 season. He won 20+ games in four consecutive seasons (1987–90) and led the league with 14 complete games in 1988 and 11 in 1990.

He didn't win the Cy Young Award in any of those seasons, though he finished in the top four in the vote in each. He was a key part of four postseasons for the A's, going 8-3 with a 2.31 ERA, taking home the World Series MVP Award in 1989 and the ALCS MVP Award in 1990. And here is some nice trivia: on June 29, 1990, Stewart pitched a no-hitter against his future team, the Blue Jays, at the SkyDome. Only hours later, Dodger Fernando Valenzuela no-hit the St. Louis Cardinals at Dodger Stadium, marking the first time in major league history that no-hitters were thrown in both leagues on the same day.

If I hadn't chosen Stewart, then I would have gone with Jack Coombs (1906–14). After four mediocre seasons, he busted out in 1910 to go 31-9, completing 35 of the 38 games he started. He led the league in wins that year and was second in ERA with a 1.30 mark. To top it off, he went on to pitch three complete games in the World Series. He led the AL in wins the next year, posting a 28-12 record, before illness shortened his promising career.

Rube Walberg (1923–33) pitched for the Athletics for over a decade but managed only one 20-win season. He had four others with 16+ but never led the league in any impressive categories (unless you include "leading" the league in the most HR allowed twice). As with many hurlers of that era, he pitched about a third of his games out of the bullpen.

George Earnshaw (1928–33) was a teammate of Walberg, and he managed three seasons of 20+ wins (plus one with 19). He led the AL in wins in 1929 with a 24-8 record.

Bobby Shantz (1949–56) was an All-Star twice for the Athletics, first in in 1951, when he posted an 18-10 record, and then in 1952 he had a career year, going 24-7 with a 2.48 ERA, completing 27 of his 33 starts. He led the league in both wins and ERA that year, which was enough to earn him the AL MVP Award.

Mark Mulder (2000–04) was a teammate of Hudson and Zito and a key part of their success during those years. In his second season, at age 23, he led the AL in wins with a 21-8 record. He followed that up with solid seasons of 19-7, 15-9, and 17-8 before being traded to the Cardinals after the 2004 season.

Like Mulder, Ken Holtzman (1972–75) was a key part of a championship era for this franchise. He pitched only four seasons for the A's, but he won 18 to 21 games each year and was an All-Star twice. He was fine in the postseason too, going 6-4 with a 2.30 ERA.

And lastly, some readers will remember Bob Welch (1988–94) and his impressive 27-6 record in 1990 en route to the Cy Young Award. Aside from that, he posted two 17-win seasons for the A's but not much else of note.

Relief Pitching

Name	YR	WAR	W3	SV	W-L	ERA	WHIP	ERA+
Dennis Eckersley	9	16.2	9.2	320	41-31	2.74	0.953	145
Rollie Fingers	9	12.8	7.8	136	67-61	2.91	1.135	117
John Wyatt	7	6.2	5.6	72	27-29	3.77	1.442	103
Huston Street	4	5.8	5.1	94	21-12	2.88	1.071	150
Billy Taylor	5	4.8	4.1	100	15-24	3.84	1.333	121
Jack Aker	5	2.8	5.2	59	19-20	3.54	1.232	92

Dennis Eckersley (1987–95) began his career as a starter for the Indians, Red Sox, and Cubs, and had some success in that role. But when he joined the A's in 1987, manager Tony LaRussa used him as a closer when Jay Howell faltered in that role. For the next five seasons he was as unhittable as almost any pitcher has ever been. He racked up save totals of 45, 33, 48, 43, and 51. His pinpoint control led to some insanely good numbers. In 1989 he pitched 57.2 innings and struck out 55 but walked only 3. Then in 1990 he had a microscopic 0.60 ERA over 73.1 innings, while striking out 73 and only walking 4. He regularly earned consideration for both the Cy Young and MVP Awards, and in 1992 finally took home both based on a 7-1 record, 51 SV, and a 1.91 ERA. He had some issues in the postseason—including allowing the famous one-legged HR to Kirk Gibson in 1988. But he clearly did enough to earn the top relief spot on this roster.

This meant that **Rollie Fingers** (1968–76) was bumped to the number two spot. He pitched the first half of his career for Oakland, and the first few years were mixed as a starter and reliever. He took over short-relief duties in 1972 and had five consecutive seasons of 18 to 24 SV and an ERA below 3.00. He was generally solid in the postseason too, saving 8 games with a 2.22 ERA.

No other relievers came close, but I'll briefly mention four, starting with John Wyatt (1961–66, '69), who started his career with the Kansas City Athletics. He was an effective reliever for a few years and saved 20+ games twice, including in 1964 when he was an All-Star. Jack Aker (1964–68) overlapped a little with Wyatt, and he had an outstanding 1966 campaign, when he saved 32 games and posted a 1.99 ERA and 0.965 WHIP.

More recently, Billy Taylor (1994, '96–99) was the closer for Oakland for four seasons. His best season came in 1998, when he posted 33 saves. And Huston Street (2005–08) started his impressive career with the A's, earning the AL Rookie of the Year Award at age 21 in 2005, after posting 23 saves with a 1.72 ERA. He recorded 37 saves the following year, though his ERA grew to 3.31. After two less impressive seasons he was traded to the Rockies (in a deal that included a young Carlos González too).

Managers

Name	YR	From-To	W-L	PCT	PS	WS
Connie Mack	50	1901–50	3,582-3,814	.484	9	5
Tony LaRussa	10	1986–95	798-673	.542	4	1
Dick Williams	3	1971–73	288-190	.603	3	2
Art Howe	7	1996–2002	600-533	.530	3	0
Bob Melvin	8	2011–18	634-599	.514	4	0
Al Dark	4	1966–75	314-291	.519	2	1
Ken Macha	4	2003–06	368-280	.568	2	0

Even with a losing lifetime record, **Connie Mack's** 50 years and 3,500+ wins earn him the top spot here. **Tony LaRussa's** résumé is more than enough for the second spot, and **Dick Williams'** short but strong tenure is deserving of third in the list. After that it becomes debatable, with the choice coming down to the longer tenure of **Art Howe** and Bob Melvin vs. Al Dark's one World Championship.

Starting Lineup

A mythical starting lineup for this squad might look like this:

Against RHP:
Rickey Henderson LF (R)
Eddie Collins 2B (L)
Al Simmons DH (R)
Jimmie Foxx 1B (R)
Reggie Jackson RF (L)
Mickey Cochrane C (L)
Frank Baker 3B (L)
Dwayne Murphy CF (L)
Bert Campaneris SS (R)

Against LHP:
Rickey Henderson LF (R)
Eddie Collins 2B (L)
Al Simmons CF (R)
Jimmie Foxx 1B (R)
Mark McGwire DH (R)
José Canseco RF (R)
Mickey Cochrane C (L)
Sal Bando 3B (R)
Bert Campaneris SS (R)

The only obvious position platoon was at third base, where I had two strong candidates for the starting spot. I chose to split RF between Jackson and Canseco as well, since Reggie hit better against RHP. And it was hard not to get Simmons and McGwire into both of these lineups, so I used the DH spot and leveraged Simmons' experience in CF as well.

Depth Chart

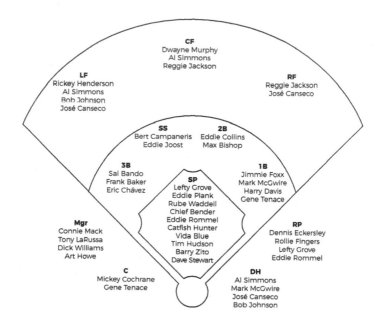

CF
Dwayne Murphy
Al Simmons
Reggie Jackson

LF
Rickey Henderson
Al Simmons
Bob Johnson
José Canseco

RF
Reggie Jackson
José Canseco

SS
Bert Campaneris
Eddie Joost

2B
Eddie Collins
Max Bishop

3B
Sal Bando
Frank Baker
Eric Chávez

1B
Jimmie Foxx
Mark McGwire
Harry Davis
Gene Tenace

SP
Lefty Grove
Eddie Plank
Rube Waddell
Chief Bender
Eddie Rommel
Catfish Hunter
Vida Blue
Tim Hudson
Barry Zito
Dave Stewart

Mgr
Connie Mack
Tony LaRussa
Dick Williams
Art Howe

RP
Dennis Eckersley
Rollie Fingers
Lefty Grove
Eddie Rommel

C
Mickey Cochrane
Gene Tenace

DH
Al Simmons
Mark McGwire
José Canseco
Bob Johnson

Prospects for Current Players

What are the prospects of current A's players making this All-Time team? Not very good, but not due to a lack of talent. Khris Davis hits lots of HR, including a league-leading 48 in 2018. But he strikes out a lot and hits only .247 (in fact, he has somehow hit exactly .247 in each of the past four seasons). Matt Chapman and Matt Olsen are rising stars at 3B and 1B, respectively. And Blake Treinen was outstanding as a closer in 2018, posting a 0.78 ERA to go with 38 saves. We'll see…

Retired Player Numbers

Reggie Jackson (9), Rickey Henderson (24), Catfish Hunter (27), Rollie Fingers (34), Dennis Eckersley (43)

Selections from Other Authors and Fan Surveys

1958: *Sport* magazine, October issue

As part of a running series, *Sport* magazine reported on all-time all-star teams picked by "big league publicity departments and the writers covering the clubs." Here is what they had to say:

First base: Jimmy Foxx played 11 years for Mr. Mack and set slugging records that have still not been equalled. His 58 home runs in 1932 ties him with Hank Greenberg for the best mark since Ruth.

Second base: Eddie Collins, like Foxx a member of the Hall of Fame, started his career at Philadelphia and was one of the greatest hitters, fielders and base-stealers the game has ever known.

Shortstop: Jack Barry, the slickest fielder of the $100,000 infield, never hit .300 or made the Hall of Fame, but has always been considered an integral part of the old Athletics who terrorized the American League in 1910 and 1911.

Third base: Frank "Home Run" Baker, a consistently good hitter and the first of the home-run sluggers, was a key man in Connie Mack's fabulous $100,000 infield, the greatest of its era.

Outfield: Al Simmons never hit under .300 in nine seasons in Philadelphia, with .392 in 1927 and .390 in 1931. He and Foxx are probably the best hitters ever to play for the Athletics.

Outfield: Bing Miller, who played from 1922-26 and 1928 to 1934 for the A's, hit .300 regularly, his best season being .342 in 1924.

Outfield: Wally Moses, of more recent vintage, never won a batting championship but never hit under .300 while playing a fine game in the field from 1935 to 1941.

Catcher: Mickey Cochrane, another Hall of Fame immortal, played from 1925 to 1933 and set the standards for modern catchers.

Righthanded Pitcher: Eddie Plank, whose 14 years with the Athletics produced 284 victories, wins by a narrow margin over fellow Hall of Famer Chief Bender.

Lefthanded Pitcher: Lefty Grove won just under 200 games in nine seasons for the Athletics, an amazing feat that stamps him as the greatest southpaw of any team.

There was at least one obvious error in these selections: Eddie Plank. Why, you ask? Well, he was left-handed, not right-handed. So, the real selection for RHP should have been Rommel or Bender, who they at least acknowledged came close.

1985: *Oakland Athletics Magazine*, Vol. 5, No. 4

Denis Telgemeier wrote an interesting article providing and defending his selections for a 25-man roster spanning the entire Athletics franchise history up to that point. The only rule was that players had to have played for at least three years to qualify, which he noted would mean including only "25 of the more than one thousand men who have played for the White Elephants in the last 85 years." This was his roster:

Catchers: Mickey Cochrane, Buddy Rosar, Gene Tenace

First Base: Jimmie Foxx, Ferris Fain

Second Base: Eddie Collins

Shortstop: Campy Campaneris

Third Base: Frank Baker, Sal Bando

Reserve Infielders: Vic Power, Dick Green

Outfielders: Rickey Henderson, Al Simmons, Reggie Jackson

Designated Hitter: Bob Johnson

Reserve Outfielders: Dwayne Murphy, Danny Murphy, Gus Zernial

Starting Pitchers: Lefty Grove, Eddie Plank, Chief Bender, Rube Waddell, Catfish Hunter, Vida Blue

Stopper: Rollie Fingers

Manager: Connie Mack

Coaches: Jimmy Dykes, Dick Williams, Ty Cobb

Overall, I found this to be a very solid roster. Buddy Rosar (1945–49) played for the Philadelphia Athletics for five seasons, and was an All-Star in three of them. Only a .251 hitter with no power or speed, his value came from his defense, as he led the league in caught stealing percentage at 68% in both 1947 and 1948. As Telgemeier noted, Rosar didn't commit many errors either, including in 1946, when he didn't commit any in 117 games behind the plate.

Vic Power (1954–58) played a mix of 1B, 2B, 3B, and OF for the Athletics during their final year in Philly and their first four years in Kansas City. A two-time All-Star, he was a .290 hitter and had his best season in 1955, when he batted .319 with 10 triples and 19 HR. Gus Zernial (1951–57) also played during the transition from Philadelphia to Kansas City. He hit 25+ HR five times, with a high of 42 in 1953.

1990: "All-Time All-Star Teams," in *The Baseball Research Journal*

In an interesting article, Robert C. Berlo used Thorn and Palmer's TPR (Total Player Rating) system to choose all-time teams. He selected players based on their best 800 consecutive games for the franchise, with a minimum of five years played. His results: 1B Foxx, 2B Collins, SS Joost, 3B Baker, RF Jackson, CF Simmons, LF Henderson, C Cochrane, SP Grove, SP Waddell, SP Bender, SP Plank, RP Rommel.

Grove was far ahead of all the pitchers here, and it was no surprise that Waddell came in second given the method used. And Rommel's mixed career rated him as the top relief pitcher for this franchise.

1992: *The All-Time All-Star Baseball Book*, by Nick Acocella and Donald Dewey

I couldn't really compare my selections with these authors, because they split the Athletics up into three distinct lineups: Philadelphia, Kansas City, and Oakland. For Philly they sensibly had Grove at P, Cochrane at C, Foxx at 1B, Collins at 2B, and Baker at 3B. The outfield was Simmons and Miller plus Mule Haas, who was a pretty good hitter for several years in the late '20s and early '30s. In 1929 he hit .313 with 16 HR, 115 runs, and 82 RBI. But how they chose him over Bob Johnson, or even Hartsel, Chapman, or others I described, is a mystery to me. And at SS they chose Joe Boley, who played for the A's only from 1927 through '32, was a mediocre hitter, and never played more than 132 games in a season. They listed only pitchers as honorable mentions: Waddell, Plank, Bender, and Earnshaw.

For the sad Kansas City incarnation, they had 1B Vic Power, 2B Jerry Lumpe, 3B Ed Charles, SS Dick Howser, OF Gus Zernial, Norm Siebern, and Bob Cerv, C Hal Smith, and P Bud Daley.

The Oakland A's version was only through 1991, and included 1B Mark McGwire, 2B Dick Green, 3B Sal Bando, SS Bert Campaneris, OF Rickey Henderson, José Canseco, and Reggie Jackson, C Gene Tenace, and P Catfish Hunter. Good selections, as were the honorable mentions: Joe Rudi, Dennis Eckersley, and Dave Stewart.

1995: *Baseball Ratings*, by Charles F. Faber

For hitting lineups, Faber applied his system to the Philadelphia, KC, and Oakland eras of this franchise separately. For the first, it produced a reasonable lineup of 1B Foxx, 2B Collins, 3B Baker, SS Joost, C Cochrane, OF Simmons, Johnson, and Strunk. Without comment, the Kansas City version: 1B Norm Siebern, 2B Jerry Lumpe, 3B Ed Charles, SS Wayne Causey, C Hal Smith, OF Bob Cerv, Bill Tuttle, and Roger Maris. And for the Oakland batch, a solid lineup of 1B McGwire, 2B Phillips, 3B Bando, SS Campaneris, C Steinbach, OF Henderson, Jackson, and Rudi. Tony Phillips had little power or speed, but was as versatile as any player in the 1980s, regularly playing SS, 2B, 3B, and OF.

For the pitchers, Faber combined them and reported a solid top five of Plank, Grove, Bender, Hunter, and Rommel, with Eckersley as the top reliever.

2003: *Rob Neyer's Big Book of Baseball Lineups*, by Rob Neyer

Neyer first discussed an all-time roster that was limited to just the Oakland A's (through the 2002 season). But he later gave his selections for an all-time starting lineup for the complete Athletics franchise, so I'll discuss that first. His infield was Cochrane, Foxx, Collins, Joost, and Baker. For SS he wrote, "Tough choice between Joost and Campaneris, but Joost's excellence trumps Campy's longevity." As for preferring Baker at 3B, he wrote, "Good fielder, great hitter, and AL's best third baseman until George Brett and Wade Boggs; famous, of course, for homering in consecutive Series games in 1911."

Neyer rightly listed Henderson in LF, Murphy in CF, and Jackson in RF. Regarding CF he wrote, "A's have never had a great center fielder, but they've enjoyed a number of very good ones, including Dave Henderson, Billy North, Sam Chapman, and Amos Strunk." He did note both Simmons and Hartsel as runners-up to Henderson for the LF spot. He listed four fine starters in Grove, Plank, Waddell, and Hunter, and of course Eckersley as the reliever.

For the Oakland-only roster he listed both starters and backups, per usual for his book. The starting infield was quite reasonable: Steinbach, McGwire, Green, Bando, and Tejada, though choosing Miguel was clearly weighing peak performance heavily over the longevity (and speed) of Campaneris.

The starting OF was the same as before with Henderson, Murphy, and Jackson. The backup hitters were Mike Heath as C, Giambi at 1B, utility man Tony Phillips at 2B, Campaneris at SS, and Lansford at 3B. I didn't like the choice of Heath, who played for Oakland from 1979 through '85, batted .251, and had a top HR total of 13 (twice). Neyer noted, "One could argue for Gene Tenace, but his hitting didn't pick up until he started playing 1B." That was true enough, but in those seasons (1973–76) he still played a lot at catcher, including a majority of the time (125 games) in 1975. The backup OF had Rudi in LF, speedy Bill North in CF, and of course Canseco in RF.

The SP were Hunter, Blue, Stewart, Welch, Hudson, Holtzman, Mike Moore, and Blue Moon Odom. Moore pitched for Oakland for only four years (1989–92), but went 19-11 with a 2.61 ERA in 1989 and also won 17 games for them twice. And Odom (1964–75) was inconsistent for the Athletics but did post three solid seasons of 16-10/2.45, 15-6/2.92, and 15-6/2.50. Neyer noted that Zito and Mulder hadn't pitched enough to qualify yet, so these choices made sense to me. Eck and Fingers were the two relievers, naturally.

2016: *101 All-Time Fantasy Baseball Teams*, by Jack Sweeney

Sweeney's lineup was interesting with McGwire, Ellis, Baker, Campaneris, Henderson, Simmons, Jackson, Cochrane, and Foxx (listed as the DH). The choice of Ellis over Collins at 2B seemed bizarre, until I remembered the author's restriction of listing a player on only one all-time team. Since Collins played more for the White Sox than the Athletics, he was listed there—a shame though, since that lineup could have had Nellie Fox as a strong 2B selection, allowing Collins to appear here for the Athletics. His four starting pitcher selections were all reasonable with Grove, Hunter, Plank, and Bender, and he of course went with Eckersley as the reliever.

Top WAR Single Seasons – Hitters (8+)

Name	Year	WAR	AVG	HR	R	RBI	SB	OPS+
Eddie Collins	1910	10.5	.324	3	81	81	81	152
Jimmie Foxx	1932	10.5	.364	58	151	169	3	207
Rickey Henderson	1990	9.9	.325	28	119	61	65	189
Eddie Collins	1909	9.7	.347	3	104	56	63	170
Frank Baker	1912	9.3	.347	10	116	130	40	174
Reggie Jackson	1969	9.2	.275	47	123	118	13	189
Jimmie Foxx	1933	9.2	.356	48	125	163	2	201
Jason Giambi	2001	9.2	.342	38	109	120	2	199
Eddie Collins	1914	9.1	.344	2	122	85	58	176
Eddie Collins	1913	9.0	.345	3	125	73	55	164
Jimmie Foxx	1934	9.0	.334	44	120	130	11	186
Rickey Henderson	1980	8.8	.303	9	111	53	100	135
Eddie Collins	1912	8.8	.348	0	137	64	63	158
Nap Lajoie	1901	8.4	.426	14	145	125	27	198
Jimmie Foxx	1935	8.3	.346	36	118	115	6	182
Sal Bando	1969	8.3	.281	31	106	113	1	153
Matt Chapman	2018	8.2	.278	24	100	68	1	136

I wasn't surprised to see Eddie Collins appear the most often in this table (five times)—and no, that isn't a typo for his top season in 1910; he really did have 81 runs, 81 RBI, and 81 SB. Jimmie Foxx had the second-highest season overall and appeared on the list four times, while Rickey Henderson had the third-highest season and was the only other player to appear more than once. And impressively, Matt Chapman's combination of offense and outstanding defense at 3B was enough to earn him a spot on this list in his first full season in 2018.

The only player listed who wasn't discussed above was Hall of Famer Nap Lajoie, who played one year for the Athletics during his prime and also returned for his final two seasons much later. His 1901 numbers are some of the most impressive of any player ever: in only 131 games, he led the league with a .426 average, 14 HR, 48 doubles, 232 hits, 145 runs, 125 RBI, and a 198 OPS+.

Top WAR Single Seasons – Pitchers (8+)

Name	Year	WAR	W–L	ERA	IP	SO	ERA+
Rube Waddell	1902	10.3	24-7	2.05	276.1	210	178
Jack Coombs	1910	10.1	31-9	1.30	353.0	224	182
Lefty Grove	1931	9.7	31-4	2.06	288.2	175	217
Rube Waddell	1904	9.7	25-19	1.62	383.0	349	165
Bobby Shantz	1952	9.6	24-7	2.48	279.2	152	159
Lefty Grove	1930	9.4	28-5	2.54	291.0	209	185
Rube Waddell	1905	9.2	27-10	1.48	328.2	287	179
Eddie Plank	1904	9.0	26-17	2.17	357.1	201	124
Lefty Grove	1932	8.8	25-10	2.84	291.2	188	160
Vida Blue	1971	8.6	24-8	1.82	312.0	301	183
Rube Waddell	1903	8.0	21-16	2.44	324.0	302	125

I was a bit surprised that the pitcher who appeared most often on this list was Rube Waddell (four times), and not Lefty Grove (three times) or Eddie Plank (only once, though he had three other seasons with 7+ WAR).

Franchise Player

With so many talented players, and no clear-cut best of the bunch, it was hard to give out this top honor. Grove and Plank were outstanding starters, and for a few years Eck was unhittable. Simmons and Foxx put up some insane numbers. If I were picking a team captain, then Eddie Collins would get strong consideration. But for this particular honor I went with Rickey Henderson because of his value as a leadoff hitter and his all-out dominance on the basepaths.

CHAPTER 14

The Twins Franchise All-Time Dream Team

Most serious baseball fans know that the Minnesota Twins were previously the Washington Senators, the version that dates back all the way to 1901 and the birth of the American League (though baseball in Washington actually goes even further back, with various teams competing as early as 1860). The early years for this franchise were not successful ones, as it took the Senators until 1912 to even have a winning season (and they had five years below .400 during that span). It is somewhat ironic then that the first century of this franchise included arguably the greatest pitcher in the history of the game, Walter Johnson. It wasn't until late in his career that the Senators managed to make it to the World Series: in 1924 they won the championship in seven games over the Giants, and then in 1925 they lost in seven games to the Pirates.

They played fairly well for the following ten seasons, including several where Johnson, after his playing days were over, led the club as manager. In 1933 they took the AL pennant with a 99-53 record but lost the World Series in five games to the Giants. After that season, the franchise suffered a drought of 33 years away from the championship, including a span of 16 years where they posted a .500+ record only twice and six times had a sub-.400 percentage.

After so many poor seasons, the team moved to Minnesota in 1961 and very quickly saw better results. In 1965 they posted a 102-60 record before losing the World Series to the Dodgers in seven games. Over two decades later, led by Kirby Puckett, Kent Hrbek, and others, they won the World Series in both 1987 and 1991.

The nine-year stretch from 2002 through 2010 saw the Twins reach the playoffs six times, but they never made it to the World Series. Since then, the Twins have generally not been a strong club, with a surprise Wild Card appearance finally coming in 2017.

As noted already, Walter Johnson is an all-time great. Aside from him, this All-Time team has some other legitimate stars, but also has several positions of relative weakness.

1st Base

Name	YR	WAR	W3	W/G	AVG	HR	SB	OPS+
Harmon Killebrew	21	60.5	18.6	.0260	.258	559	18	145
Joe Judge	18	47.0	11.9	.0226	.299	71	210	115
Kent Hrbek	14	38.4	13.9	.0220	.282	293	37	128
Mickey Vernon	14	26.6	14.6	.0147	.288	121	125	117
Justin Morneau	11	23.3	13.2	.0182	.278	221	5	121
Joe Kuhel	11	16.5	11.5	.0137	.288	56	79	107

Based on the table above, it would be logical to assume Harmon Killebrew should be the starting 1B. However, after reviewing the candidates at 3B, since Harmon played over a third of his games at the hot corner, I decided to select him as the starter there.

There were several strong candidates for the starting 1B honor, but in the end, I went with **Kent Hrbek** (1981–94). He played his entire career for the Twins, and although only an All-Star in 1982, two years later he was AL MVP runner-up after batting .311 with 27 HR and 107 RBI. He provided very consistent power, slugging 20+ HR an impressive ten times, so I decided to give him the starting spot.

You could make a case for **Joe Judge** (1915–32) as the starter instead, so he pretty clearly deserves at least to make this roster as the backup. He played 18 of his 21 seasons for the Senators and was a solid .299 hitter with a .379 OBP. He had little power but some speed, as he posted 15+ SB six times.

Another solid candidate was **Mickey Vernon** (1939–43, '46–48, '50–55). He lost two playing years to World War II service but came back strong in 1946 to win the AL batting title with a .353 mark and a league-leading 51 doubles. A five-time All-Star, his best season was arguably 1953, when he scored 101 runs, had 115 RBI, and again led the AL with a .337 average and 43 doubles. I think that is a strong enough résumé to deserve one of the two "extra spots" on this All-Time team.

This means there isn't room for another star, Justin Morneau (2003–13). A four-time All-Star for the Twins, Morneau hit 30+ HR three times and posted 100+ RBI four times. He was the AL MVP in 2006 after hitting .321 with 34 HR and 130 RBI, and was runner-up for the award two years later after hitting .300 with 23 HR, 47 doubles, and 129 RBI. Because of these peak performances, you could certainly make a case for him over Judge, Hrbek, or Vernon, not to mention the various candidates for the other "extra spot."

Lastly, Joe Kuhel (1930–37, '44–46) played over half of his long career for the Senators, providing a .288 average but with only moderate power and speed. His two best seasons came in 1933, when he hit .322 with 107 RBI, and 1936, when he hit .321 with 118 RBI.

2nd Base

Name	YR	WAR	W3	W/G	AVG	HR	SB	OPS+
Rod Carew	12	63.7	24.9	.0390	.334	74	271	137
Buddy Myer	16	40.7	15.9	.0248	.303	35	118	109
Chuck Knoblauch	7	37.9	22.0	.0374	.304	43	276	114
Brian Dozier	7	23.9	16.0	.0250	.248	167	98	109

Hall of Famer **Rod Carew** (1967–78) played his best seasons for the Twins, batting an impressive .334 and taking home seven AL batting titles. He was an All-Star in all 12 of his years in Minnesota, and his best season came in 1977, when he led the AL with a .388 average, .449 OBP, 239 hits, 128 runs, and 16 triples.

While Carew was obviously the starter here, the backup spot was a much tougher choice. This was a classic case of longevity vs. peak performance, and in the end, I favored the latter and gave the honor to **Chuck Knoblauch** (1991–97). He took home the AL Rookie of the Year Award in 1991, and then went on to be an All-Star four times. In 1996 he batted .341 and set a franchise record by scoring 140 runs. A .304 hitter for the Twins overall, he posted 25+ SB in all seven of his seasons, including a high of 62 in 1997. Knoblauch also provided good defense, taking home one Gold Glove Award.

Buddy Myer (1925–27, '29–41) played most of his long career for this franchise, scoring 100+ runs four times. He had very little power but was a solid .303 hitter who led the league with a .349 mark in 1935, and he provided a little speed, leading the league with 30 SB in 1928. Although you could argue for various others, I decided to honor Myer's longevity and overall résumé with the other "extra spot" on this roster.

Lastly, recent Twins slugger Brian Dozier (2012–18) had 20+ HR seasons, including a high of 42 in 2016. While only a .248 hitter with a .325 OBP, he most often batted leadoff and so scored 100+ runs four times. He was also a good defender at 2B, taking home his first Gold Glove Award in 2017.

3rd Base

Name	YR	WAR	W3	W/G	AVG	HR	SB	OPS+
Harmon Killebrew	21	60.5	18.6	.0260	.258	559	18	145
Ossie Bluege	18	28.3	10.6	.0152	.272	43	140	85
Gary Gaetti	10	27.1	13.3	.0199	.256	201	74	100
Buddy Lewis	11	26.7	12.9	.0198	.297	71	83	111
Eddie Yost	14	26.3	13.5	.0189	.253	101	58	108
Corey Koskie	7	22.2	14.5	.0272	.280	101	66	116
Eddie Foster	8	20.8	12.0	.0186	.266	6	166	94
John Castino	6	15.1	11.1	.0227	.278	41	22	97
Steve Braun	6	15.0	9.8	.0200	.284	35	32	116

As mentioned earlier, **Harmon Killebrew** (1954–74) played the most at 1B but also logged significant time at both 3B and LF, and so will make this All-Time team as the starting 3B. A fearsome slugger, Killer posted eight seasons with 40+ HR, including six when he led the AL. He posted 100+ RBI an impressive 9 times and was an All-Star 11 times. Only a .256 hitter, he walked a lot and so had a .378 OBP. Killer was in the top five in the AL MVP vote six times and took home the award in 1969 after hitting .276 and leading the AL with 49 HR, 140 RBI, 145 walks, and a .427 OBP.

There were many candidates to consider for the backup spot, but in the end, I gave the honor to **Gary Gaetti** (1981–90), who played the first half of his long career for the Twins. He hit 20+ HR six times for Minnesota and was a great defender at the hot corner, taking home four consecutive Gold Glove Awards.

You could make a case based on longevity for Ossie Bluege (1922–39), who played all of his long career for the Senators. Not an offensive force, he provided a little speed but mostly contributed by being a good defender at 3B: he led the AL in assists four times and was regularly amongst the leaders in fielding percentage at his position.

After only one year in the minors, Buddy Lewis (1935–41, '45-47, '49) was playing in the major leagues at the young age of 18. He scored 100+ runs in four of his first six seasons, including a high of 122 in 1938. A .297 hitter and two-time All-Star, he served in the military for three years during World War II and then retired relatively early at the age of 32.

Eddie Yost (1944, '46–58) started even younger, playing in the majors at age 17 in 1944. He played most of his career for the Senators, including four seasons with 100+ runs. Only a .253 hitter, he was very good at drawing walks: he led the AL four times while with the Senators and so boasted a .394 OBP.

There were several others who deserve brief mention, including (in chronological order):

- Eddie Foster (1912–19) was a typical Deadball Era hitter in that he had very little power (only 6 HR in 4,418 at-bats) but had some speed, with 20+ SB in six seasons.

- Steve Braun (1971–76) started his career in Minnesota and was a very versatile player who split most of his time between 3B and LF, but also played a little 1B, 2B, SS, and RF for the Twins. That was his primary value, because although a .284 hitter he provided very little power or speed.

- John Castino (1979–84) played about two-thirds of his games at 3B and most of the rest at 2B. His rookie season was not outstanding (.285 average, 5 HR, 5 SB) but was good enough to earn a tie (with Alfredo Griffin) in the AL Rookie of the Year Award voting in 1979. His career was cut short by a bad back, and he retired after only six seasons in the majors.

- Corey Koskie (1998–2004) provided the Twins with some power and a little speed too, with his best season coming in 2001, when he hit 26 HR, had 27 SB, and had 100+ runs and RBI.

Shortstop

Name	YR	WAR	W3	W/G	AVG	HR	SB	OPS+
Joe Cronin	7	36.8	22.4	.0391	.304	51	56	118
Cecil Travis	12	29.5	16.2	.0222	.314	27	23	108
George McBride	13	22.8	12.8	.0156	.221	5	116	67
Roy Smalley	10	20.8	13.6	.0181	.262	110	15	104
Greg Gagne	10	17.9	11.2	.0157	.249	69	79	83
Zoilo Versalles	9	14.6	12.3	.0132	.250	87	85	86

The starting SS on this roster was fairly obvious, even though he played for the Senators for only seven years. Hall of Famer **Joe Cronin** (1928–34) was a .304 hitter with a .387 OBP. He didn't hit many home runs but still posted 100+ RBI five times, with his best season arguably being 1930, when he batted .346 with

13 HR, 17 SB, 127 runs, and 126 RBI. He was also outstanding defensively, leading the AL in SS putouts three times, SS assists three times, and SS fielding percentage twice. And finally, he was player-manager his last two seasons in Washington before being traded/sold to the Red Sox, where he continued as a player-manager for many more years.

The choice for backup was also pretty clear: **Cecil Travis** (1933–41, '45–47), who played his entire career for the Senators. A three-time All-Star, he had very little power or speed but batted .314 with highs of .344 in 1937 and .359 in 1941, when he paced the AL with 218 hits. He missed the following three years and part of a fourth due to World War II military service. In 1944 he was sent to Europe, and he suffered a severe case of frostbite during the Battle of the Bulge, necessitating an operation to prevent amputation of his feet. Travis received a Bronze Star for his military service, but when he returned to baseball at the age of 32, he understandably wasn't the same hitter he had been and so retired in 1947.

I considered several other candidates, including (in chronological order):

- George McBride (1908–20) played most of his career with the Senators and was an extremely light hitter: he had a .221 BA with only 5 HR in 4,833 AB. Like many players of this time, he did steal some bases (10 to 17 in eight consecutive seasons), but his main value was providing outstanding defense, leading the AL in SS fielding percentage five times.

- Zoilo Versalles (1959–67) played most of his career for this franchise. Only a .250 hitter, he had a high of 20 HR in 1964 and led the AL in triples three times. He was strong defensively, taking home two Gold Glove Awards. Zoilo's best season was easily 1965, when he was voted the league MVP after batting .273 with 19 HR, 77 RBI, 27 SB, and leading the league with 45 doubles, 12 triples, and 126 runs scored.

- Roy Smalley (1976–82, '85–87) had two stints for the Twins, first primarily as a SS and then to end his career primarily as a DH. He was an All-Star once, in 1979, when he hit .271 with 24 HR and 95 RBI.

- Greg Gagne (1983–92) was drafted by the Yankees, but before he reached the majors was part of a trade for Roy Smalley. He hit only .249 with moderate power and speed, but he was an above-average fielder for the Twins.

Catcher

Name	YR	WAR	W3	W/G	AVG	HR	SB	OPS+
Joe Mauer	15	55.1	19.5	.0297	.306	143	52	124
Earl Battey	8	17.5	10.6	.0177	.277	91	12	109
Muddy Ruel	8	16.0	9.8	.0177	.290	2	44	92
Butch Wynegar	7	15.2	11.6	.0191	.254	37	8	89
Brian Harper	6	13.4	8.0	.0184	.306	48	7	110

Joe Mauer (2004–18) has thus far played his entire career for the Twins, and was the obvious top choice here. A six-time All-Star, Mauer is a career .306 hitter with three AL batting titles. He was good defensively early in his career, taking home three Gold Glove Awards (more recently he has primarily played 1B). He has never hit for much power, with the exception being his MVP season in 2009, when he hit 28 HR with 96 RBI, while leading the AL with a .365 average and .444 OBP.

Choosing the backup was not an easy decision at all, as there were four candidates to consider. **Earl Battey** (1960–67) was a four-time All-Star who provided some power, with a high of 26 HR and 84 RBI in 1963. He also was outstanding defensively, earning three Gold Glove Awards. I gave him the slightest of edges over Muddy Ruel (1923–30), who was a solid .290 hitter with a .382 OBP over his eight seasons for the Senators. He had no power (2 HR in 2,875 AB) and only a little speed, but he was considered one of the best defensive catchers of his era. He didn't hit well in the 1924 World Series against the Giants, but importantly scored the winning run in the 12th inning of Game Seven.

Butch Wynegar (1976–82) started his career in Minnesota and was an All-Star in his first two seasons. He was regularly amongst the league leaders in catching base stealers, but he was only a .254 hitter with little power or speed. Brian Harper (1988–93) was the opposite in that he was more valuable for his bat than his glove, providing the Twins with a .306 average.

Left Field

Name	YR	WAR	W3	W/G	AVG	HR	SB	OPS+
Goose Goslin	12	43.2	20.8	.0317	.323	127	117	131
Heinie Manush	6	19.8	13.9	.0250	.328	47	29	121
Shane Mack	5	19.6	15.4	.0310	.309	67	71	130
Larry Hisle	5	17.2	12.7	.0260	.286	87	92	127
Roy Sievers	6	14.9	10.6	.0174	.267	180	8	134

Hall of Famer **Leon "Goose" Goslin** (1921–30, '33, '38) had three stints for the Senators. Early in his career he had five consecutive 100+-RBI seasons, including leading the AL with 129 RBI in 1924. A .323 hitter, he led the AL with a .379 average in 1928. He had moderate power, sometimes hitting more triples than HR, including leading the AL in triples with 18 in 1923 and 20 in 1925. He also hit well in the postseason, swatting 3 HR in each of the World Series in 1924 and 1925.

I considered several others who were primarily LF for this franchise, but none had a strong enough résumé to earn a spot on this All-Time team. Hall of Famer Heinie Manush (1930–35) played for the Senators in the middle of his career and provided an impressive .328 average. He didn't provide much power or speed, but he did lead the AL with 221 hits and 17 triples in 1933. His best all-around season for the Senators came the year before, when he batted .342 with 214 hits, 41 doubles, 14 triples, 14 HR, 121 runs, and 116 RBI.

Shane Mack (1990–95) played for the Twins for only five seasons, but he was a .309 hitter with a nice combination of power and speed. His best numbers came in 1992, when he hit .315 with 16 HR, 75 RBI, 101 runs, and 26 SB. He was versatile in the field as well, spending significant time at all three OF positions.

Like Manush, Larry Hisle (1973–77) played the middle part of his career for this franchise, and like Mack, he provided a nice combination of power and speed. His best season for the Twins was his last, when he was an All-Star and hit .302 with 28 HR, 21 SB, 95 runs, and a league-leading 119 RBI.

And finally, Roy Sievers (1954–59) played mostly in LF for the Senators, but also many games at 1B. He hit 20+ HR in all six of his seasons in Washington, was an All-Star three times, and had the best season of his career in 1957, when he batted .301 and led the AL with 42 HR and 114 RBI.

Center Field

Name	YR	WAR	W3	W/G	AVG	HR	SB	OPS+
Kirby Puckett	12	50.9	20.5	.0285	.318	207	134	124
Clyde Milan	16	40.1	14.9	.0202	.285	17	495	109
Torii Hunter	12	26.2	12.8	.0191	.268	214	128	103
César Tovar	8	25.9	13.2	.0237	.281	38	186	102
Stan Spence	5	21.7	15.3	.0289	.296	66	19	138
Denard Span	5	17.2	13.1	.0292	.284	23	90	104

Hall of Famer **Kirby Puckett** (1984–95) was a fan favorite throughout his playing career. He was a ten-time All-Star and took home six Gold Glove Awards for his outstanding defense. A career .318 hitter, he hit .356 in 1988 and then led the AL with a .339 average in 1989. He hit 20+ HR six times, had 100+ runs three times, 100+ RBI three times, and led the AL in hits four times, including a high of 234 in 1988. He generally performed well in the postseason as well, with highlights like hitting 10-28 (.357) in the 1987 World Series, and then in 1991 batting .429 with two HR in the ALCS against the Blue Jays (earning him MVP honors), and then hitting another two HR in the Twins' victory over the Braves in the World Series. Sadly, in 1996 he was forced to retire at the age of only 36 due to sudden loss of vision in one eye.

Clyde Milan (1907–22) played his entire career for the Senators. He hit .285 for his career but had little power. That wasn't such an issue though, as he was very fast and provided 30+ SB in seven consecutive seasons, including leading the AL with 88 in 1912 and then 75 in 1913. And Milan's 495 career SB make him the all-time leader for this franchise.

You could make a strong case for Torii Hunter (1997–07, '15) to be included on this All-Time team. Although he batted only .268 with a .321 OBP, he provided both power and speed, including seven seasons for the Twins with 20+ HR. Perhaps his greatest value came from his defense, as he won seven of his nine Gold Glove Awards while playing for Minnesota.

Another interesting candidate was César Tovar (1965–72), who played most of his major league career for the Twins. He didn't hit for power but ran well, including three seasons with 30+ SB. His best offensive numbers came in 1970, when he hit .300 with 30 SB, 120 runs, and a league-leading 36 doubles and 13 triples. But perhaps his most valuable quality was his position versatility. While he played more games in CF than anywhere else, he also spent significant time playing LF, RF, 3B, SS, and 2B. And in 1968 he became only the second player to play all nine positions in one game (Bert Campaneris was the first, in 1965).

Two others deserve brief mention, starting with Stan Spence (1942–44, '46–47), who provided solid offense for the Senators in the 1940s. After playing a little for the Red Sox, he had his first full major league season for Washington and was immediately an All-Star, hitting .323 and leading the AL with 15 triples. By 1944 he was hitting with more power, to the tune of 18 HR and 100 RBI. After one year of military service, he was an All-Star twice more, including in 1946, when he hit a career-high 50 doubles. Lastly, Denard Span (2008–12) started his career for the Twins, providing good defense in CF and stealing 15+ bases four times.

Right Field

Name	YR	WAR	W3	W/G	AVG	HR	SB	OPS+
Sam Rice	19	52.7	13.9	.0228	.323	33	346	113
Tony Oliva	15	43.0	20.2	.0257	.304	220	86	131
Bob Allison	13	33.9	18.4	.0220	.255	256	84	127
George Case	10	16.4	9.7	.0148	.288	20	321	98
Tom Brunansky	7	16.0	11.1	.0175	.250	163	36	109
John Stone	5	14.4	12.3	.0259	.317	32	21	123

Tony Oliva (1962–76) played his entire career (which included only 11 full seasons) for the Twins. A .304 hitter, he won three AL batting titles and led the AL five times in hits and four times in doubles. He had an outstanding Rookie of the Year campaign in 1964, hitting 32 HR with 94 RBI and leading the AL with a .323 average, 109 runs, 217 hits, and 43 doubles. An eight-time All-Star, Oliva was a good fielder early in his career, taking home a Gold Glove Award in 1966, before knee injuries eventually forced him into a DH role.

Hall of Famer **Sam Rice** (1915–33) played all but his final season for the Senators. A career .323 hitter, Rice never had a full season in which he batted below .295. He had very little power, hitting only 33 HR in 8,934 AB. But he was very consistent in hitting 30+ doubles and 10+ triples in ten consecutive seasons. He scored 100+ runs five times, recorded 200+ hits six times, and was a good base runner, with 20+ SB in eight seasons and a high of 63 in 1920.

Bob Allison (1958–70) played his entire career for this franchise, splitting his time between RF and LF, while also getting in some games in CF and at 1B. He won the AL Rookie of the Year Award in 1959 after hitting 30 HR with 85 RBI and leading the league with a modest 9 triples. That was his first of three All-Star seasons, and his first of eight seasons with 20+ HR.

Three others deserve brief mention, including (in chronological order):

- John Stone (1934–38) was acquired when the Senators traded their aging but still productive star Goose Goslin to the Tigers. Stone split his time between RF and LF and batted well over .300 for four seasons, though he provided little power or speed. In 1938 his average fell to .244 and he retired at age 32.

- George Case (1937–45, '47) played all but one of his seasons for the Senators, and split his time mostly between RF and LF, while playing a bit in CF too. A three-time All-Star, he scored 100+ runs four times and led the AL in SB an impressive six times, with a high of 61 SB in 1943.

- Tom Brunansky (1982–88) was an additional power bat alongside Hrbek and Gaetti for the Twins in the 1980s. He hit only .250 but smacked 20+ HR in six seasons for the Twins, with a high of 32 in both 1984 and 1987.

Starting Pitching

Name	YR	WAR	W3	W-L	ERA	WHIP	ERA+
Walter Johnson	21	165.6	43.6	417-279	2.17	1.061	147
Bert Blyleven	11	49.3	23.9	149-138	3.28	1.186	119
Brad Radke	12	45.5	18.0	148-139	4.22	1.269	113
Camilo Pascual	13	36.4	21.7	145-141	3.66	1.295	106
Jim Kaat	15	36.2	15.2	190-159	3.34	1.231	110
Johan Santana	8	35.9	23.4	93-44	3.22	1.094	141
Jim Perry	10	28.7	15.5	128-90	3.15	1.196	113
Frank Viola	8	27.4	20.2	112-93	3.86	1.295	111
Dave Goltz	8	24.6	16.4	96-79	3.48	1.311	112
Dutch Leonard	9	24.2	13.1	118-101	3.27	1.239	116
Tom Zachary	9	21.0	13.3	96-103	3.78	1.436	104
Kevin Tapani	7	19.3	12.6	75-63	4.06	1.266	108
Bump Hadley	7	18.5	14.4	68-71	3.98	1.418	107

As I reviewed the career and accomplishments of **Walter Johnson** (1907–27) I had the same sense of awe that I did when I reviewed those of Babe Ruth. The stats are just mind-boggling, and in Johnson's case he did it all for just one team, the Washington Senators. A 417-279 (.599) lifetime record would have been even better had the Senators fielded better teams during some of his seasons. Even so, he led the league in wins five times, including a career-best record of 36-7 in 1913. His career ERA of 2.17 included 11 seasons where it was sub-2.00 and 5 seasons where he led the AL. The Big Train was an outstanding strikeout pitcher, leading the AL 12 times, including 3 seasons where he earned the pitching Triple Crown. All of this and he was a relatively capable hitter too, batting .235 with 24 HR in his career.

No one else came close to Johnson, but that's not to say this franchise hasn't had plenty of fine hurlers over the years. Hall of Famer **Bert Blyleven** (1970–76, '85–88) started for the Twins at age 19 and returned for several more years late in his long career. He won 20 games for the Twins only once, in 1973, when he started 40 games and completed 25 of them to earn a 20-17 record. Blyleven used his outstanding curveball to strike out 200+ batters six times while with Minnesota. And in 1987, at age 36, he was a key part of the Twins' championship season, including winning two games in the ALCS against the Tigers and one of two starts against the Cardinals in the World Series.

Jim Kaat (1959–73) also started his long career for this franchise, and like Blyleven won 20 or more games for them only once, in 1966, when he posted a 25-13 record after completing 19 of 41 starts. Less of a strikeout pitcher than Blyleven, he topped 200+ only twice. He was outstanding defensively on the mound, though, capturing 11 of 16 Gold Glove Awards while with the Twins.

Johan Santana (2000–2007) didn't pitch for the Twins for nearly as long but arguably had stronger peak seasons than either Blyleven or Kaat. After four seasons working his way into the rotation, in 2004 he went 20-6 and led the league with a 2.61 ERA and 265 strikeouts, earning him the AL Cy Young Award. He led the league in strikeouts again the next season, and then earned the pitching Triple Crown and AL Cy Young Award in 2006 after going 19-6 with a 2.77 ERA and 245 strikeouts. He had 200+ strikeouts again in 2007 but was not quite as dominant, posting only a 15-13 record and 3.33 ERA, and so was traded to the Mets before the 2008 season.

Cuban-born **Camilo Pascual** (1954–66) pitched for both the Senators and the Twins (and interestingly the later Senators too). He won 20+ games twice and 15+ another three times. A five-time All-Star, he used an outstanding curveball to lead the AL in complete games three times and strikeouts three times. Owing to some poor records early in his career, he ended up with a 145-141 record for this franchise, barely above .500.

Jim Perry (1963–72) pitched the majority of his career for the Twins. After several years mixing his time as a starter and reliever, he went 20-6 with a 2.82 ERA in 1969. He then topped that by winning the AL Cy Young Award in 1970 after leading the AL in wins with a 24-12 record.

Based on career WAR, you could make a case for **Brad Radke** (1995–2006) ranking higher in this rotation. He pitched his entire career for the Twins, posting a 20-10 record in 1997 but never winning more than 15 games in any other season. Although his 4.22 ERA might seem high, his ERA+ of 113 indicates it was a relatively good mark for that high-offense time period.

Frank Viola (1982–89) began and pitched just over half of his career for the Twins. He had four seasons of 16 to 18 wins before busting out in 1988 with a 24-7 record and 2.64 ERA, earning him the AL Cy Young Award.

After considering the remaining starting candidates and looking at the relief pitching candidates, I decided to select one more starter here. There were several options, but I went with **Dutch Leonard** (1938–46), who pitched about half of his long career for the Senators. He posted a 20-8 record in 1939 but led the AL in losses with a 14-19 record the following year. A three-time All-Star because of his outstanding knuckleball, Leonard didn't strike out many hitters—only 657 in 1,899.1 IP for Washington.

You could make a case for a few others, including (in chronological order):

- Tom Zachary (1919–25, '27–28) was a teammate of Johnson and had four seasons with 15+ wins.

- Bump Hadley (1926–31, '35) had a promising rookie campaign in 1927, when he posted a 14-6 record and 2.85 ERA. But then he won that many games only once more for the Senators, in 1930, when he went 15-11.

- Dave Goltz (1972–79) led the AL in wins with a 20-11 record in 1977 and had four other seasons with 14 or 15 wins.

- Kevin Tapani (1989–95) had two 16-win seasons for the Twins, including 1991, when he went 16-9 with a career-best 2.99 ERA.

Relief Pitching

Name	YR	WAR	W3	SV	W-L	ERA	WHIP	ERA+
Firpo Marberry	11	25.5	13.5	94	117-71	3.59	1.323	117
Joe Nathan	7	18.5	10.5	260	24-13	2.16	0.956	204
Rick Aguilera	11	15.8	6.9	254	40-47	3.50	1.182	130
Eddie Guardado	12	9.7	5.7	116	37-48	4.53	1.340	105
Al Worthington	6	9.7	6.9	88	37-31	2.62	1.194	134
Glen Perkins	12	8.7	5.5	120	35-25	3.88	1.288	108
Mike Marshall	3	6.9	6.9	54	21-30	2.99	1.281	141
Ron Perranoski	4	4.2	6.8	76	25-29	3.00	1.385	120
Jeff Reardon	3	4.2	4.2	104	15-16	3.70	1.153	116
Ron Davis	5	0.1	3.1	108	19-40	4.51	1.492	95

Joe Nathan (2004–09, '11) is the all-time leader in saves for this franchise, and with a 2.16 ERA he clearly deserves the top spot in this bullpen. A four-time All-Star, Nathan was a dominating closer for six seasons, with save totals ranging from 36 to 47 and an ERA ranging from 1.33 to 2.70. He had 561 strikeouts in only 463.1 IP, a 204 ERA+, and an impressive 0.956 WHIP.

During the 1989 season, **Rick Aguilera** (1989–99) was part of the package of players sent to the Twins for Frank Viola. Although he had been used in a mix of roles previously, Minnesota gave him the closer role, and he excelled for many years, with six seasons of 25+ saves. During that stretch, Aguilera was briefly traded to the Red Sox in July of 1995, but immediately signed back with the Twins as a free agent after that season.

Firpo Marberry (1923–32, '36) was one of the rare relief specialists during the era before relief pitching became a widespread specialty. While he did start 133 games across 11 seasons with the Senators, he appeared in relief in 337 games and finished 251 games. Although the save was not a recognized statistic during his time, if it had been then Marberry would have led the AL six times, with highs of 15 in 1924, 16 in 1925, and 22 in 1926.

You could make a case based on longevity for Eddie Guardado (1993–2003, '08) to have a spot on this roster. It took several years for him to get his ERA below 5.00, but then he had several seasons as an effective setup man before becoming the team's closer. Everyday Eddie was an All-Star in both 2002 and 2003, when he posted a 2.93 ERA and league-leading 45 saves, and then a 2.89 ERA and 41 saves.

Al Worthington (1964–69) had mixed success in various roles for four different clubs before finally becoming a solid short reliever at the end of his career for the Twins. He came over from the Reds during the 1964 season and was immediately successful, posting 14 saves and a 1.37 ERA. Over the next four years he recorded 16 to 21 saves per year, with an ERA between 2.13 and 2.84.

Glen Perkins (2006–17) started his career with the Twins as a starter, but when that didn't work out well he became a solid setup man and ultimately the team's closer for three years. An All-Star from 2013 through '15, he posted save totals between 32 and 36 each year. Unfortunately, a shoulder injury has greatly limited his playing time since, and it appears that his time with the Twins is now over.

This franchise has had a few other solid relievers who deserve brief mention, including (in chronological order):

- Ron Perranoski (1968–71) came to the Twins after many solid years as a reliever for the Dodgers. In 1969 he had a 2.11 ERA and led the AL with 31 saves, and in 1970 he had a 2.43 ERA and led the league with 34 saves.

- Mike Marshall (1978–80) joined the Twins late in his career, posted 21 saves with a 2.45 ERA in 1978, and then led the AL with 32 saves in 1979.

- Ron Davis (1982–86) was the Twins closer for four seasons, posting 20+ saves each year.

- Jeff Reardon (1987–89) joined the Twins after many years as the Expos closer, and posted 31, 42, and 31 saves in his three years in Minnesota.

Managers

Name	YR	From-To	W-L	PCT	PS	WS
Tom Kelly	16	1986–2001	1,140-1,244	.478	2	2
Bucky Harris	18	1924–54	1,336-1,416	.485	2	1
Ron Gardenhire	13	2002–14	1,068-1,039	.507	6	0
Sam Mele	7	1961–67	524-436	.546	1	0
Clark Griffith	9	1912–20	693-646	.518	0	0
Walter Johnson	4	1929–32	350-264	.570	0	0

For the top spot here, you could make a good case for any of the top three longest-serving managers. Although **Tom Kelly** has the lowest winning percentage, his two World Series championships gave him the edge. After **Bucky Harris** and **Ron Gardenhire**, I selected **Sam Mele** to round out a top four.

Starting Lineup

What would mythical starting lineups look like for this All-Time roster?

Against RHP:
Rod Carew 2B (L)
Sam Rice RF (L)
Tony Oliva DH (L)
Goose Goslin LF (L)
Kirby Puckett CF (R)
Harmon Killebrew 3B (R)
J. Judge/K. Hrbek/M. Vernon 1B (L)
Joe Mauer C (L)
Cecil Travis SS (L)

Against LHP:
Rod Carew 2B (L)
Joe Cronin SS (R)
Kirby Puckett CF (R)
Harmon Killebrew 1B (R)
Bob Allison DH (R)
Goose Goslin LF (L)
Gary Gaetti 3B (R)
Tony Oliva RF (L)
Joe Mauer C (L)

Loaded with left-handed batters, the lineup against RHP would be very formidable. There was a natural platoon at SS for Cronin and Travis, and I worked both Rice and Allison into the lineups along with Oliva at the RF and DH spots. All three of the 1B batted from the left side of the plate, so at least against the toughest lefties I thought it would be best to shift Killebrew across the diamond and get Gaetti into the lineup at 3B. And I've listed Mauer as the catcher in both lineups, but as he doesn't hit lefties as well, you could give him a rest against the toughest southpaws and benefit from Battey's superior defense.

Depth Chart

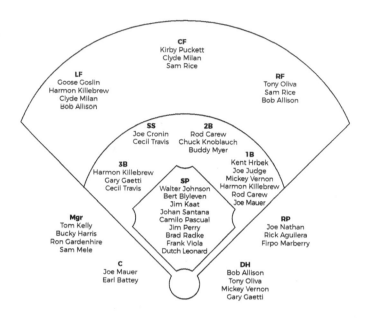

CF
Kirby Puckett
Clyde Milan
Sam Rice

LF
Goose Goslin
Harmon Killebrew
Clyde Milan
Bob Allison

RF
Tony Oliva
Sam Rice
Bob Allison

SS
Joe Cronin
Cecil Travis

2B
Rod Carew
Chuck Knoblauch
Buddy Myer

3B
Harmon Killebrew
Gary Gaetti
Cecil Travis

1B
Kent Hrbek
Joe Judge
Mickey Vernon
Harmon Killebrew
Rod Carew
Joe Mauer

SP
Walter Johnson
Bert Blyleven
Jim Kaat
Johan Santana
Camilo Pascual
Jim Perry
Brad Radke
Frank Viola
Dutch Leonard

Mgr
Tom Kelly
Bucky Harris
Ron Gardenhire
Sam Mele

RP
Joe Nathan
Rick Aguilera
Firpo Marberry

C
Joe Mauer
Earl Battey

DH
Bob Allison
Tony Oliva
Mickey Vernon
Gary Gaetti

Prospects for Current Players

What are the prospects of current Twins making this All-Time team? Joe Mauer is already on the roster. Brian Dozier had a shot to one day join him, but was traded away during the 2018 season. Others on the Twins like Miguel Sanó, Byron Buxton, and José Berríos clearly have talent but are still very young. We'll see...

Retired Player Numbers

Harmon Killebrew (3), Tony Oliva (6), Tom Kelly (10), Kent Hrbek (14), Bert Blyleven (28), Rod Carew (29), Kirby Puckett (34)

Selections from Other Authors and Fan Surveys

1947: *The Washington Senators*, by Morris A. Bealle

This book doesn't just cover the Senators who began with the AL in 1901, but also spans earlier Washington teams going back as early as 1860. The subtitle for the book was "An 87-year History of the World's Oldest Baseball Club and Most Incurable Fandom." On page 182, the author chose two all-time teams for

Washington players, with the first team consisting of a starting batting order of Clyde Milan CF, Sam Rice RF, Joe Judge 1B, Ed Delahanty LF, Joe Cronin SS, Buddy Myer 2B, Ossie Bluege 3B, Muddy Ruel C, and then listed Luke Sewell as a second catcher. Sewell played only two years of his long career for Washington, so that was an odd choice. But the most bizarre was choosing Delahanty as the top LF over Goose Goslin. Delahanty was a great Hall of Famer, but he played only his final one-and-a-half seasons for the Senators.

The top pitchers chosen were Walter Johnson, Win Mercer, Roger Bresnahan, Earl Whitehill, and Stan Coveleski, with Clark Griffith listed as the manager. Win Mercer pitched from 1894 through '99 for the Senators when they were part of the NL, ironically posting a losing 95-116 record, and later joined the Senators for their inaugural 1901 AL campaign. I was completely unaware that Hall of Fame catcher Roger Bresnahan started his career in 1897 at age 18 as a pitcher for the Senators. He went 4-0 in six starts, but that doesn't seem like much of a résumé to be included on an all-time team. Fellow Hall of Famer Stan Coveleski pitched his best seasons for the Indians, joining the Senators in 1925 and posting a solid 20-5 record and league-leading 2.84 ERA. But then he had only one more full season for Washington after that.

The second lineup is as follows: Harry Berthrong CF, Stanley (Bucky) Harris 2B, Bill Coughlin 3B, Goose Goslin LF, Buck Freeman RF, Joe Kuhel 1B, Gene DeMontreville SS, Eddie Ainsmith C, and then listed Jim McGuire as a second catcher. Harris, Goslin, and Kuhel were discussed in this chapter. Coughlin played for the Senators from 1901 through '04 and was a .274 hitter with some speed, stealing 29 bases in 1902 and 30 in 1903. Freeman had one great year for Washington in 1899, hitting .318 with 21 SB, 122 RBI, 25 triples, and a league-leading 25 HR. But his contract was then purchased by Boston and he went on to have several more star seasons there. Ainsmith was a very light-hitting (.207) catcher, and while he played for the Senators from 1910 through '18, he got into 100+ games in a season only one time. James "Deacon" McGuire had a very long career that spanned from 1884 to 1912. This included 1891–99 playing in Washington, where he was a capable .298 hitter with his best season coming in 1895, when he hit .336 with 10 HR, 97 RBI, and 17 SB. Berthrong is no doubt the most interesting in this lineup, as he fought in the Civil War and then later played for the Washington Olympics in 1871, getting into 17 games, mostly as an outfielder, and batting .233 (not sure why the author decided to bat him leadoff in this lineup).

The pitchers chosen for this second team were Hank O'Day, "Long Jim" Whitney, Bill Dinneen, Emil "Dutch" Leonard, and Bob Barr, with the manager being Bucky Harris. All of these pitchers except Leonard pitched for the 19th century Washington teams, and none were very noteworthy. The best season any of them had was Whitney's 1887 season, when he posted a 24-21 record.

1958: *Sport* magazine, September issue

As part of a running series, *Sport* magazine reported on all-time all-star teams picked by "big league publicity departments and the writers covering the clubs." In this case, they noted the following: "Traditionally first in war, first in peace and last in the American League, the Senators have had their share of glory, though, and their all-timers needn't bow their heads. Clark Griffith selected the all-time team shortly before his death and, with a single change, it is still the club's official selection."

First Base: Mickey Vernon, the only Senator ever to win two batting titles, with .353 in 1946 and .337 in 1953, gets the nod over Griffith's selection, Joe Judge, an 18-year infield mainstay.

Second Base: Bucky Harris, a fine player-manager for five years, rates the position by a narrow margin over Buddy Myer, whose .349 in 1935 led the league. Myer was the better hitter but Harris' teams won pennants in 1924 and 1925, two of his best playing years.

Shortstop: Joe Cronin, always a fine hitter, was player-manager of the 1933 champions, Washington's last pennant winners, and wins the position over Roger Peckinpaugh, who turned in five good seasons for the Senators after being turned loose by the Yankees in 1922.

Third Base: Ossie Bluege played his entire major-league career, 18 years, with Washington, during which time he never hit .300 but was never far below that figure. He was picked over a good hitter, Cecil Travis, because Travis was shunted between third and short and had some of his best hitting years as a shortstop.

Left Field: Goose Goslin, one of the Senators' greatest won the batting championship in 1928 with .379 and was a consistent .300 hitter. He was the Senators' all-time home-run slugger until the recent resurgence of Roy Sievers.

Center Field: Clyde Milan, who played from 1907 to 1922, was known as Deerfoot because he was such a terror on the basepaths, but three times he led the club with averages under .300, which shows what kind of help he had.

Right Field: Sam Rice won the club batting championship five times and shared it once during his 18 years as a Senator outfielder (he broke in as a pitcher). Since his worst year was .294, he would have made just about anybody's all-time team.

Catcher: Muddy Ruel, who eventually played for six American League teams, averaged over .300 from 1923 to 1930 with Washington and gets the call over Eddie Ainsmith, a good but light-hitting catcher of earlier vintage.

Righthanded Pitcher: Walter Johnson is easily the greatest player ever to wear a Washington uniform. His 416 victories and seasonal earned-run average of 1.14 are still major-league records.

Lefthanded Pitcher: Earl Whitehill played only four years for the Senators, but won 22 games in 1933 and 14 in each of his next three seasons.

Relief Pitcher: Firpo Marberry, who toiled from 1923 to 1932, often making 50 or more appearances in a season, was a consistent winner. He actually led the staff in 1929 with 19 victories.

Not much to disagree with here, the one exception being the choice of Harris over Myer at 2B. The LHP options were limited, so I wouldn't argue with the choice of Whitehill over the longer tenure of Zachary.

1969: *The Sporting News* Fan Poll

The July 5, 1969, issue reported the results of a fan poll for the long-standing franchises of the day. In this case, two separate lineups were chosen, one for Washington and one for Minnesota, even though they had been the Twins for less than a decade. For the Senators, the lineup included 1B Mickey Vernon, 2B Bucky Harris, 3B Ossie Bluege, SS Joe Cronin, C Muddy Ruel, LF Goose Goslin, CF Clyde Milan, RF Sam Rice, RHP Walter Johnson, LHP Earl Whitehill. It was interesting to see the same choices here of Harris and Whitehill as the 1958 choices.

For the Twins, the lineup included 1B Harmon Killebrew, 2B Rod Carew, 3B Rich Rollins, SS Zoilo Versalles, C Earl Battey, LF Bob Allison, CF Ted Uhlaender, RF Tony Oliva, RHP Camilo Pascual, LHP Jim Kaat. Rollins played for the Twins from 1961 through '68, so he was the obvious choice at 3B. He had a little power, hitting 16 HR with 96 RBI in 1962, and then leading the AL with 10 triples in 1964. There weren't very good options for CF, with Ted Uhlaender hitting .262 from 1965 through '69.

1990: "All-Time All-Star Teams," in *The Baseball Research Journal*

In an interesting article, Robert C. Berlo used Thorn and Palmer's TPR (Total Player Rating) system to choose all-time teams. He selected players based on their best 800 consecutive games for the franchise, with a minimum of five years played. His results didn't really surprise me at all: 1B Killebrew, 2B Carew, SS Cronin, 3B Lewis, RF Allison, CF Puckett, LF Oliva, C Ruel, SP Johnson, SP Blyleven, SP Pascual, SP Kaat, RP Marberry.

1992: *The All-Time All-Star Baseball Book*, by Nick Acocella and Donald Dewey

The authors chose separate All-Time lineups for the Senators and the Twins, with the former including Vernon, Harris, Yost, Cronin, Manush, Goslin, Rice, Ruel, and Johnson. They gave honorable mention to Judge and Bluege, which left Myer, Travis, and Milan unmentioned.

For the Twins lineup they listed Hrbek, Carew, Gaetti, Versalles, Killebrew, Oliva, Puckett, Battey, and Kaat. They listed Killebrew as an OF, thereby allowing both Hrbek and Gaetti to be included. The honorable mentions were Perry and Allison, which left Blyleven and Pascual unmentioned.

1995: *Baseball Ratings*, by Charles F. Faber

Faber applied his system to the Senators and Twins eras separately, with the former producing fairly reasonable All-Time lineup composed of Vernon, Myer, Cronin, Yost, Ruel, Rice, Milan, and Goslin. For the Twins the lineup was solid and included Hrbek, Carew, Smalley, Gaetti, Battey, Puckett, Oliva, and Tovar. He also listed five starting pitchers for the entire franchise's history: Johnson, Kaat, Blyleven, Pascual, and Leonard. For relievers he again chose separately, going with Marberry and Aguilera.

1999: *Minnesota Twins Official Team Yearbook*

This included a two-page feature that was described as: "To bring the two components of franchise history together, here's a 'Team of the Century', the best of those who played for either the Senators or Twins since the franchise was founded in 1901." The selections were all pretty good, with honorable mentions often being noted: 1B Harmon Killebrew (Kent Hrbek), 2B Rod Carew (Buddy Myer), SS Joe Cronin (Zoilo Versalles), 3B Eddie Yost (Gary Gaetti), LF Goose Goslin (Heinie Manush), CF Kirby Puckett (Clyde Milan), RF Tony Oliva (Sam Rice), C Earl Battey (Rick Ferrell), SP Walter Johnson, Jim Kaat,

Bert Blyleven, Camilo Pascual, Frank Viola, RP Rick Aguilera, Jeff Reardon, Al Worthington, Firpo Marberry.

2003: *Rob Neyer's Big Book of Baseball Lineups*, by Rob Neyer

As Neyer did for each franchise that had a significant city relocation, he provided an All-Time starting lineup for the combined Senators/Twins, and also a full All-Time roster for the Twins only. For the combined team, he went with a solid lineup of 1B Killebrew, 2B Carew, SS Cronin, 3B Yost, LF Goslin, CF Puckett, RF Oliva. He noted it was a very close call in RF between Oliva and Rice, and at 3B he wrote, "Perhaps a surprise to see Yost instead of Gaetti, but Gaetti just had too many seasons where he wasn't very good." Neyer picked four good starters in Johnson, Blyleven, Kaat, and Pascual, and Marberry as the top reliever.

For the Twins-only All-Time roster, Neyer made very reasonable infield choices with Battey and Wynegar as the catchers, Killebrew and Hrbek at 1B, Carew and Knoblauch at 2B, Smalley and Versalles at SS, and Gaetti and Koskie at 3B. RF was easy with Oliva and Allison as the picks. For LF he went with Hisle first, and then Gary Ward as the backup, while noting he also considered Dan Gladden, Marty Cordova, and Jacque Jones. The first CF pick was of course Puckett, and for the backup he chose Jimmie Hall, who played for the Twins from 1963 through '66 and about whom he wrote, "Hit 98 homers and made two All-Star teams in his first four seasons, but stopped hitting by 30; nobody forgot his talent, though, and so he played for five other clubs."

The eight starting pitchers he chose were Blyleven, Kaat, Viola, Perry, Pascual, Radke, Tapani, and Eric Milton, who was a starter for the Twins for five years, including his one All-Star season in 2001, when he posted a 15-7 record. Neyer's top two Twins relievers were Aguilera and Reardon.

2016: *101 All-Time Fantasy Baseball Teams*, by Jack Sweeney

Sweeney's picks consisted of 1B Mickey Vernon, 2B Rod Carew, 3B Harmon Killebrew, SS Cecil Travis, OF Heinie Manush, OF Kirby Puckett, OF Goose Goslin, C Joe Mauer, and he chose Sam Rice as the DH. Not bad, though I think Joe Cronin is the better pick at SS. The starting pitchers chosen were Walter Johnson, Bert Blyleven, Jim Kaat, and Johan Santana, with Joe Nathan as the top RP.

Top WAR Single Seasons – Hitters (8+)

Name	Year	WAR	AVG	HR	R	RBI	SB	OPS+
Rod Carew	1977	9.7	.388	14	128	100	23	178
Chuck Knoblauch	1996	8.6	.341	13	140	72	45	143
Joe Cronin	1930	8.4	.346	13	127	126	17	135

Only these three seasons? Wow. It is interesting that none of these three came from power hitters. This can be partially explained by the Senators playing at Griffith Stadium from 1911 through 1960, where the outfield dimensions favored pitchers. Rod Carew had three other seasons with a 7+ WAR, including a 7.9 score in 1975. Kirby Puckett came close with a 7.8 score in 1988, and Joe Mauer did the same in 2009.

Top WAR Single Seasons – Pitchers (8+)

Name	Year	WAR	W-L	ERA	IP	SO	ERA+
Walter Johnson	1913	16.0	36-7	1.14	346.0	243	259
Walter Johnson	1912	14.6	33-12	1.38	369.0	303	243
Walter Johnson	1914	13.0	28-18	1.72	371.2	225	164
Walter Johnson	1915	12.1	27-13	1.55	336.2	203	191
Walter Johnson	1918	11.6	23-13	1.27	326.0	162	214
Walter Johnson	1910	11.4	25-17	1.36	370.0	313	183
Walter Johnson	1919	10.8	20-14	1.49	290.1	147	215
Walter Johnson	1916	10.7	25-20	1.90	369.2	228	147
Bert Blyleven	1973	9.9	20-17	2.52	325.0	258	156
Walter Johnson	1911	8.8	25-13	1.90	322.1	207	173
Johan Santana	2004	8.7	20-6	2.61	228.0	265	182
Camilo Pascual	1959	8.6	17-10	2.64	238.2	185	149
Frank Viola	1987	8.1	17-10	2.90	251.2	197	159
Walter Johnson	1917	8.0	23-16	2.21	326.0	188	120

It appears that Walter Johnson was pretty good during the decade of 1910 through 1919. Indeed, this is the only time a pitcher has ever posted an 8+ WAR every year for a decade. Also of note is that Bert Blyleven's impressive 1973 campaign only earned him a tie for seventh in the AL Cy Young vote that year, presumably because of his large number of losses. And I was surprised to see that Frank Viola's 1987 season rated higher than his AL Cy Young Award season the following year, when he posted a more impressive 24-7 record and 2.64 ERA—that season came close with a 7.7 WAR.

Franchise Player

The clear choice here was Walter Johnson, who played his entire career with the Senators and is arguably the greatest pitcher of all time. Honorable mention goes to Harmon Killebrew, Rod Carew, and Kirby Puckett.

CHAPTER 15

The Orioles Franchise All-Time Dream Team

Most serious baseball fans know that the Baltimore Orioles were previously the St. Louis Browns. But did you know that the franchise began as the Milwaukee Brewers? This team began in 1894 as a member of the minor Western League, which was renamed in 1900 as the American League, and became a competing "major league" in 1901. The league's founder and first president, Ban Johnson, wanted a team in St. Louis, to compete for attention with the National League's Cardinals organization. Due to investors backing out of a deal that would have moved the team right away, they had to play one more season in Milwaukee before becoming the St. Louis Browns for the 1902 season.

The franchise stayed in St. Louis for 52 seasons but rarely was able to field a very competitive team. They had a losing record in 38 of those seasons, and 18 times had a winning percentage below .400. Their only AL pennant came in 1944, when they lost the World Series in six games to their St. Louis Cardinals counterparts.

After a tumultuous several years under colorful owner Bill Veeck, including an attempted move back to Milwaukee, the Browns were sold to a group of investors and moved to Baltimore to become the Orioles for the 1954 season. The team started to see consistent success in the 1960s and eventually won their first World Series in 1966, sweeping the Dodgers in four games. They appeared in three consecutive World Series from 1969 through '71, winning the championship in five games in 1970 over the Reds. They lost the World Series against the Pirates in 1979, but then took the crown in 1983 over the Phillies, led by Cal Ripken's first of two MVP seasons.

Unfortunately, Cal's career included only two other postseason appearances, in 1996 and '97, with the Orioles losing in the ALCS both years. And after that the Orioles posted a losing record for 14 straight seasons, with the streak finally coming to an end during their surprising 2012 campaign.

While there are some bona fide superstars on this franchise's All-Time team, with so many years of failure in their history, there are also some clear weak spots.

1st Base

Name	YR	WAR	W3	W/G	AVG	HR	SB	OPS+
Eddie Murray	13	56.3	19.3	.0299	.294	343	62	139
George Sisler	12	55.0	25.3	.0334	.344	93	351	132
Boog Powell	14	35.4	16.7	.0201	.266	303	18	135
Rafael Palmeiro	7	24.4	16.2	.0244	.284	223	38	127
George McQuinn	8	18.2	9.9	.0160	.283	108	28	113
Chris Davis	8	15.6	15.1	.0151	.235	241	15	115
Jim Gentile	4	14.8	12.5	.0254	.272	124	3	145

First base has definitely been a position of strength for much of this franchise's history. There were three top candidates here for this All-Time team, starting with Hall of Famer **Eddie Murray** (1977–88, '96). Steady Eddie played the first half of his career for the Orioles, starting with his Rookie of the Year campaign in 1977, when he hit .283 with 27 HR and 88 RBI. That was the first of ten seasons in Baltimore with 25+ HR, and he also led the AL with 22 HR and 78 RBI during the strike-shortened 1981 season. A seven-time All-Star for the Orioles, he had five seasons with 100+ RBI and scored 100+ runs three times. One of the most productive switch-hitters of all time, Murray was also great defensively, taking home Gold Glove Awards from 1982 through '84.

Coming in a close second here was another great hitter and Hall of Famer, **George Sisler** (1915–22, '24–27). Gorgeous George played most of his career for the St. Louis Browns and batted an impressive .344 for them. This included leading the AL with a .407 average and 257 hits in 1920, and a .420 average and 246 hits in 1922. He had four seasons with 100+ RBI and 100+ runs and was also a great runner, stealing 25+ bases eight times and leading the league four times, with a high of 51 SB in 1922. His 351 career SB remain the most for this franchise to this day. He was also widely regarded as the best fielding 1B of his generation and would have won numerous Gold Glove Awards had they existed then.

Selecting Sisler as the backup meant that **Boog Powell** (1961–74) could only make this All-Time team via one of the two "extra spots" designated for each franchise. While only a .266 hitter, Powell swatted 30+ HR five times for the Orioles. A four-time All-Star, he batted .304 with 37 HR and 121 RBI in 1969, which was good enough for second place in the MVP Award vote. He took home that trophy the next year after hitting .297 with 35 HR and 114 RBI.

Although Rafael Palmeiro's (1994–98, 2004–05) accomplishments have been tainted by PED accusations, some of his numbers during his two stints in Baltimore were impressive. He batted .290 and hit 38 to 43 HR with 100+ RBI in four consecutive seasons. He was also a great fielder at 1B, winning two Gold Glove Awards for the Orioles in 1997 and '98.

Current Orioles slugger Chris Davis (2011–18) is definitely an all-or-nothing type of hitter. He has hit 25+ home runs in six seasons, including leading the AL with impressive highs of 53 (a new franchise record) in 2013 and 47 in 2015. But Crush has also struck out 190+ times in five seasons, leading the AL with 208 in 2015 and 219 in 2016, and then even batted a horrible .168 in 2018.

George McQuinn (1938–45) played most of his career for the St. Louis Browns. A four-time All-Star, he hit .283, scored 100+ runs twice, and provided double-digit HR in seven consecutive seasons. And lastly, Jim Gentile (1960–63) played for the Orioles for only four seasons, but he hit 20+ HR in each of them, was an All-Star three times, and in 1961 hit .302 with 46 HR and a league-leading 141 RBI (tied with Roger Maris).

2nd Base

Name	YR	WAR	W3	W/G	AVG	HR	SB	OPS+
Bobby Grich	7	36.0	22.9	.0458	.262	70	77	127
Brian Roberts	13	28.9	16.6	.0218	.278	92	278	102
Del Pratt	6	22.7	14.1	.0251	.282	21	174	120
Davey Johnson	8	20.1	11.4	.0202	.259	66	26	104
Marty McManus	7	15.4	11.3	.0180	.298	56	51	103
Roberto Alomar	3	12.5	12.5	.0303	.312	50	44	122

Bobby Grich (1970–76) started out as a shortstop in the early 1970s but switched to 2B, where he earned four consecutive Gold Glove Awards from 1973 through '76. He also provided a consistent combination of power and speed, with 12 to 19 HR and 13 to 17 SB in all of his five full seasons.

A three-time All-Star, he was granted free agency and joined the Angels after the 1976 season.

Brian Roberts (2001–13) was a prolific doubles hitter for the Orioles, with five seasons of 40+, including a league-leading 50 in 2004 and 56 in 2009. A two-time All-Star, he also ran the bases well, with 20+ SB in seven consecutive seasons and a league-leading 50 in 2007. He also scored 100+ runs four times before injuries greatly limited his playing time in his last four seasons with the Orioles.

Del Pratt (1912–17) played the first six years of his career for St. Louis. He provided a .282 average with little power but good speed, stealing 20+ bases five times. Another highlight came in 1916, when he led the league with 103 RBI while hitting only 5 home runs.

Davey Johnson (1965–72) was only a .259 hitter with limited power and speed for the Orioles. But he was very good defensively, earning three consecutive Gold Glove Awards and three All-Star nominations.

Marty McManus (1920–26) was a .298 hitter with moderate power and speed, with his best year coming in 1923, when he hit .309 with 15 HR, 94 RBI, and 14 SB. And lastly, Roberto Alomar (1996–98) played for the Orioles for three seasons in the middle of his Hall of Fame career. He batted .312, was an All-Star all three years, and took home two of his many Gold Glove Awards while playing for Baltimore.

3rd Base

Name	YR	WAR	W3	W/G	AVG	HR	SB	OPS+
Brooks Robinson	23	78.4	24.2	.0271	.267	268	23	104
Harlond Clift	10	37.6	18.1	.0261	.277	170	67	118
Manny Machado	7	30.9	20.7	.0359	.283	162	47	121
Melvin Mora	10	29.0	15.0	.0231	.280	158	82	109
Doug DeCinces	9	22.8	15.1	.0266	.253	107	39	112
Jimmy Austin	16	19.7	9.1	.0150	.251	10	192	92

Brooks Robinson (1955–77) was nicknamed The Human Vacuum Cleaner, and with good reason. His defensive prowess at the hot corner was unparalleled, earning him an amazing 16 consecutive Gold Glove Awards. It wasn't only his defense that made him an All-Star in 15 consecutive seasons, as he also had some pop in his bat, hitting 20+ HR six times and providing 100+ RBI twice. A first-ballot Hall of Famer, his best season was 1964, when he won the MVP Award after hitting .317 with 28 HR and 118 RBI.

Less obvious was who the backup 3B should be on this dream team roster, but I decided on **Harlond Clift** (1934–43), who played all but his final two seasons for the Browns. An All-Star only once, Clift was a .277 hitter with enough power to hit 20+ HR four times, including 29 HR and 118 RBI in 1937, and 34 HR and 118 RBI the following year. He was more of a run scorer, with 90+ runs in his first nine seasons, including a high of 145 in 1936.

Manny Machado (2012–18) was a star for the Orioles in recent seasons, hitting 30+ HR three times. A four-time All-Star, Machado was excellent defensively, earning two Gold Glove Awards so far. But he was traded to the Dodgers during the 2018 season, so it seems his time with Baltimore is over before he could crack this All-Time team.

Melvin Mora (2000–09) played several positions for the Orioles but most often was at 3B. A two-time All-Star, he batted .280, hit 20+ HR three times, and had his best season in 2004, when he hit .340 with 27 HR, 104 RBI, and 111 runs, and led the league with a .419 OBP.

Doug DeCinces (1973–81) started his career with the Orioles, had his best season for them in 1978, when he hit .286 with 28 HR and 80 RBI, and then like Grich went west to join the Angels. And lastly, Jimmy Austin (1911–23, '25–26, '29) played all but his first two seasons for the Browns. As was typical for Deadball-Era hitters, he hit only .251 with very little power, but he was capable running the bases and tallied seven seasons of 15+ SB.

Shortstop

Name	YR	WAR	W3	W/G	AVG	HR	SB	OPS+
Cal Ripken Jr.	21	95.5	29.7	.0318	.276	431	36	112
Bobby Wallace	15	48.2	18.1	.0307	.258	8	138	103
Mark Belanger	16	40.9	16.1	.0208	.227	20	166	68
Vern Stephens	10	25.8	14.9	.0260	.292	121	16	122
Miguel Tejada	5	19.5	17.8	.0272	.305	109	17	119
Luis Aparicio	5	16.4	13.3	.0227	.251	33	166	83

The starting SS on this All-Time dream team was obviously **Cal Ripken Jr.** (1981–2001). A hugely popular player in Baltimore, Ripken played his entire career for the Orioles, and that included of course his record-breaking ironman streak of 2,632 consecutive games played. He won the Rookie of the Year Award in 1982 after batting .264 with 28 HR and 93 RBI. He led the Orioles to a World Series title the following year after he hit .318 with 27 HR, 102 RBI, and a league-leading 47 doubles, 211 hits, and 121 runs. That brought the first of two MVP Awards he would win, with the other coming in 1991, when he hit .323 with 34 HR and 114 RBI and became the first AL shortstop to hit .300+ with 30+ HR and 100+ RBI. Overall, he hit 20+ HR 12 times and had

100+ RBI 4 times. An All-Star for 19 consecutive seasons, he was quite tall for a shortstop (6⊠4⊠) but still fielded the position well, earning Gold Glove Awards in 1991 and 1992.

For the backup spot it came down to two light-hitting, great-defense candidates. **Bobby Wallace** (1902–16) played the majority of his lengthy, Hall of Fame career with the Browns. He was probably the best defensive shortstop during the American League's first decade. But he was only a .258 hitter, with only moderate speed and virtually no power, hitting only 8 HR in 5,529 at-bats.

Mark Belanger (1965–81) won eight Gold Glove Awards and, together with Robinson, made for arguably the greatest defensive left side of the infield ever. Belanger ran fairly well too, stealing 10+ bases nine times, with a high of 27 in his one All-Star season in 1976. What Belanger could not do well was hit the baseball, as his anemic .227 average and 20 HR in 5,734 at-bats for the Orioles make painfully clear. His ghastly 68 OPS+ gave me pause, but in honor of his defense and longevity with the team, I decided to give him one of the two "extra spots" on this roster.

This means that Vern Stephens (1941–47, '53–55) doesn't have a spot on this dream team. He started his career for the Browns and returned to the franchise for a few more years after his outstanding stint for the Red Sox. He was a .290 hitter and three-time All-Star, and had 20+ HR for the Browns three times, leading the league with a modest 109 RBI in 1944 and 24 HR in 1945.

Two others were briefly considered, starting with Miguel Tejada (2004–07, '10), who was a .305 hitter and three-time All-Star for the Orioles, including in 2004, when he batted .311 with 34 HR and a lofty 150 RBI. And Hall of Famer Luis Aparicio (1963–67) played for the Orioles for five years in the middle of his career. Although only a .251 hitter for Baltimore, he led the AL with 40 SB in 1963 and 57 SB (also the franchise record) in 1964, and took home two Gold Glove Awards for his defense.

Catcher

Name	YR	WAR	W3	W/G	AVG	HR	SB	OPS+
Chris Hoiles	10	23.5	13.3	.0263	.262	151	5	119
Rick Dempsey	12	21.3	9.4	.0171	.238	75	16	89
Hank Severeid	11	19.2	8.1	.0162	.290		34	92
Matt Wieters	8	16.3	11.0	.0185	.256	117	7	99
Gus Triandos	8	13.0	8.9	.0136	.249	142	1	107
Rick Ferrell	8	9.1	7.1	.0129	.270	9	13	89

Relatively speaking, catcher has not been a position of strength for this franchise. I considered several candidates here and, in the end, went **Chris Hoiles**

(1989–98) as the starter. Better offensively than defensively, he hit 19 to 29 HR five times, even though he played 100+ games only four times. On August 14, 1998, Hoiles pulled off a rare feat when he hit two grand slams in one game. He played his entire career with the Orioles, and although only a .262 hitter, he provided a .366 OBP.

For the backup spot I chose a player who was in some ways the opposite of Hoiles. **Rick Dempsey** (1976–86, '92) was not a great hitter (.238 average with limited power), but he provided great defense behind the plate, including his strong throwing arm. He also hit above expectations in the 1979 postseason, and even more so in the 1983 World Series, when had five hits—four doubles and a homer—to earn the World Series MVP Award. Dempsey also got points for having a great sense of humor. He was famous for his rain delay performances, in which he would run around the soaked tarp in his stockings, pretending that he'd hit an inside-the-park home run that required a head-first slide into home plate.

Matt Wieters (2009–16) came up to the majors as a highly touted rookie in 2009 and for several years provided the Orioles with some pop, hitting 20+ HR in three consecutive seasons. A four-time All-Star, he was great defensively, earning two Gold Glove Awards. He seemed well on his way to earning a spot on this All-Time team until he signed with the Nationals as a free agent before the 2017 season.

You could make a case for Wieters, as well as three-time All-Star Gus Triandos (1955–62), who was acquired from the Yankees after the 1954 season as part of a big (18 players!) trade. He hit 15+ HR for the Orioles five times, with a high of 30 in 1958. Triandos also played 953 games with the Orioles, and 1,206 total in his career, and was *never* caught stealing. That sounds great, until you realize he only attempted to steal a base once, as he was arguably the slowest runner of his era.

I also considered Hank Severeid (1915–25), who played for over a decade with the Browns. He was a .290 hitter and actually hit over .300 in his last four full seasons with the team. But he had limited power and speed numbers, so in the end didn't do enough to warrant one of the two catcher spots.

Lastly, Hall of Famer Rick Ferrell (1929–33, '41–43) had two stints for the Browns during his long career. A .270 hitter with virtually no power or speed, he at least didn't strike out much and provided a solid .368 OBP. He was a capable defender and was above average at throwing out runners.

Left Field

Name	YR	WAR	W3	W/G	AVG	HR	SB	OPS+
Ken Williams	10	40.4	20.9	.0364	.326	185	144	144
George Stone	6	25.9	19.0	.0306	.301	23	132	144
Don Buford	5	19.2	14.7	.0289	.270	67	85	126

Ken Williams (1918–27) played for a decade for the Browns and was a .326 hitter with a .403 OBP. He also provided a good combination of power and speed, stealing 20+ bases three times and hitting 20+ HR four times. His best overall season came in 1922, when he batted .332 with 128 runs, 37 SB, and a league-leading 39 HR and 155 RBI. This season was the first ever 30-HR/30-SB season, and also set the franchise record for RBI that still stands today.

With several strong CF candidates, no other left fielders were chosen for this All-Time team roster. George Stone (1905–10) came the closest, as he was a good hitter for the Browns, but he had a very short career. He led the league with 187 hits in his rookie season and led the league with a .358 average, .417 OBP, and .501 SLG the following year. He also ran well, stealing 20+ bases in five of his six seasons.

And lastly, Don Buford (1968–72) played the second half of his ten-year career for the Orioles. He was a .270 hitter who provided a decent combination of power and speed, with three seasons of 15+ HR and four seasons of 15+ SB.

Center Field

Name	YR	WAR	W3	W/G	AVG	HR	SB	OPS+
Paul Blair	13	39.7	19.8	.0234	.254	126	167	99
Brady Anderson	14	34.8	18.0	.0198	.257	209	307	110
Adam Jones	11	31.5	13.6	.0195	.279	263	90	109
William Jacobson	10	27.9	14.7	.0225	.317	76	81	115
Al Bumbry	13	24.6	13.1	.0172	.283	53	252	105
Burt Shotton	8	20.7	14.3	.0199	.274	6	247	112

Paul Blair (1964–76) was best known for his great defense in CF, which earned him eight Gold Glove Awards. He was only a .254 hitter, but he did provide a combination of moderate power and speed. He had 15+ SB six times and 15+ HR three times. A two-time All-Star, his best offensive season came in 1969, when he hit .285 with 26 HR, 20 SB, and 102 runs.

Brady Anderson (1988–2001) played almost his entire career for the Orioles, most often covering CF but also playing significant games in LF (where he excelled defensively). He was only a .257 hitter, but he was very athletic and served as the team's leadoff hitter, so he scored 100+ runs four times while providing a good combination of speed and power. He stole 20+ bases seven times, with a high of 53 in 1992. He hit 12 to 24 HR eight times but had one bust-out season in 1996, when he clubbed 50 HR (a new Orioles record) and provided 110 RBI.

Adam Jones (2008–18) has by now accomplished enough to earn a spot on this All-Time team roster. A five-time All-Star, Jones has hit 25+ HR in seven seasons while also providing stellar defense in CF, earning four Gold Glove Awards.

Including Jones means there is no spot for William "Baby Doll" Jacobson (1915, '17, '19–26). A .317 hitter for the Browns, he provided only moderate power and speed. He scored 100+ runs twice and had 100+ RBI twice, including in 1920, when he hit .355 with 14 triples, 9 HR, and 122 RBI. If you can't stomach including Belanger and his poor hitting on this All-Time team, then you could do a lot worse than Jacobson as a replacement on this roster.

Al Bumbry (1972–84) played all but his final season for the Orioles, starting with a fine Rookie of the Year campaign in 1973, when he hit .337 and led the league with 11 triples. A .283 hitter with little power, he could run well, stealing 20+ bases five times, with highs of 42 in 1976 and 44 in 1980, his one All-Star season.

And lastly, **Burt Shotton** (1909, '11–17) was a .274 hitter and was patient at the plate, twice leading the league in walks and posting a .372 OBP for the Browns. Like many in that era, he had virtually no power, but he stole 25+ bases six times, including four years with 40 or more.

Right Field

Name	YR	WAR	W3	W/G	AVG	HR	SB	OPS+
Frank Robinson	6	32.3	20.6	.0391	.300	179	35	169
Ken Singleton	10	29.9	16.0	.0207	.284	182	8	135
Nick Markakis	9	25.5	14.5	.0187	.290	141	61	113
Jack Tobin	9	17.1	10.8	.0151	.318	48	85	111
M. Rettenmund	6	17.0	14.8	.0298	.284	50	52	133

Hall of Famer **Frank Robinson** (1966–71) was an All-Star and hit 25+ HR in five of his six seasons for the Orioles. His best year was his first with the club, when he won the MVP Award after achieving the Triple Crown with 49 HR, 122 RBI, and a .316 average, while also leading the AL with 122 runs and a .410 OBP.

Ken Singleton (1975–84) was a three-time All-Star and had 20+ HR four times, but he didn't provide much speed on the bases. His best season was probably 1979, when he hit .295 with 35 HR and 111 RBI.

Nick Markakis (2006–14) played nine years in Baltimore and was about to make picking these outfielders more complicated before he was signed by the Braves as a free agent before the 2015 season. A good defensive right fielder, Markakis took home two Gold Glove Awards while with the Orioles. A .290 hitter, he also posted 100+ RBI twice early in his career.

Jack Tobin (1916, '18–25) provided the Browns with a .318 average overall, had 200+ hits in four consecutive seasons, and scored 132 runs in 1921 and 122 runs the following year. Along with Williams and Jacobson, Tobin was part of a great outfield trio the Browns had for several years in the early 1920s.

And lastly, Merv Rettenmund (1968–73) played in 110 or more games only once in his career, but he was a capable hitter when on the field, hitting .322 in 1970 and .318 the following year.

Starting Pitching

Name	YR	WAR	W3	W-L	ERA	WHIP	ERA+
Jim Palmer	19	69.4	22.6	268-152	2.86	1.180	125
Mike Mussina	10	47.8	19.8	147-81	3.53	1.175	130
Urban Shocker	7	41.3	22.7	126-80	3.19	1.239	127
Jack Powell	10	33.1	15.6	117-143	2.63	1.152	109
Ned Garver	5	27.1	20.3	59-68	3.64	1.423	124
Dave McNally	13	26.2	14.0	181-113	3.18	1.203	107
Harry Howell	7	25.1	18.2	78-91	2.06	1.085	121
Carl Weilman	8	23.8	17.1	84-93	2.67	1.191	112
Lefty Stewart	6	22.6	16.1	73-74	4.11	1.384	112
Mike Flanagan	15	22.1	9.8	141-116	3.89	1.323	100
Barney Pelty	10	21.1	13.1	91-113	2.62	1.151	100
Nels Potter	6	20.6	17.1	57-43	3.05	1.243	119
Scott McGregor	13	20.4	10.7	138-108	3.99	1.291	98
Milt Pappas	9	19.9	10.7	110-74	3.24	1.206	113
George Blaeholder	10	19.0	10.8	90-111	4.55	1.427	102
Mike Boddicker	9	17.6	12.6	79-73	3.73	1.289	109
Jeremy Guthrie	5	16.4	12.7	47-65	4.12	1.273	107
Steve Barber	8	15.9	10.6	95-75	3.12	1.329	115
Sam Gray	6	15.7	13.7	67-82	4.37	1.446	104
Mike Cuellar	8	15.6	10.6	143-88	3.18	1.188	109

Just as Cal Ripken played his entire career with the Orioles and was the clear top choice at SS, the same was true for **Jim Palmer** (1965–67, '69–84) here. Palmer posted 20+ wins eight times, led the league in wins in three consecutive seasons, and had an impressive 268-152 (.638) overall record. He led the league with a 2.40 ERA in 1973 and a 2.09 ERA in 1975. Those performances earned the first two of his three AL Cy Young Awards, with the third coming in 1976, when he went 22-13 with a 2.51 ERA. He also fielded the position well, taking home Gold Glove Awards from 1976 through '79. A six-time All-Star, Palmer was oddly not selected as an All-Star in two of his three Cy Young Award seasons.

Mike Mussina (1991–2000) pitched a bit more than half of his career for the Orioles before leaving via free agency for the Yankees. While in Baltimore, he posted an impressive 147-81 (.645) record and had four seasons with 18+ wins, leading the AL with 19 wins in strike-shortened 1995. A five-time All-Star, like Palmer he also fielded the position well, taking home Gold Glove Awards from 1996 through '99.

Urban Shocker (1918–24) pitched the middle and best part of his career for the Browns. He won 20+ games in four consecutive seasons, including a 27-12 record in 1921 and 24-17 the following year. The spitball pitcher's overall record for St. Louis was 126-80, which was a .612 percentage.

After those top three in career WAR for this franchise, there were many candidates to consider. For the fourth spot I went with **Dave McNally** (1962–74), who pitched his entire career for the Orioles except for his final season. He had four consecutive seasons with 20+ wins, starting in 1968, when he went 22-10 with an impressive 1.95 ERA. A three-time All-Star, he led the AL in wins in 1970 with a 24-9 record, and had his best winning percentage in 1971 with a 21-5 record. He also earned a 4-2 record and 2.34 ERA in World Series play, including a clinching 1-0 victory in Game Four of the 1966 Series.

Mike Cuellar (1969–76) pitched his best seasons for Baltimore and is fourth on their all-time wins list. He had four seasons with 20+ wins and another two with 18 wins. A three-time All-Star, he shared the Cy Young Award in 1969 with Denny McLain, when he posted a 23-11 record with a 2.38 ERA. The next year, he led the league in wins with a 24-8 record and defeated the Reds in Game Five to bring the World Series title to Baltimore.

Jack Powell (1902–03, '05–12) had his best season for the Browns in 1902, his first year with the club, when he posted a 22-17 record. He had a 2.63 ERA, which looks great but was only a little better than average for that time period. His ability to win games very much depended on his teammates, and so like the Browns overall, he had losing seasons more often than not, ending up with a 117-143 record for the franchise.

After reviewing the relief pitching candidates, I decided to go with just eight starting pitchers for this All-Time team. You could make a case for nearly a dozen candidates, but in the end, I went with two lefty teammates. **Mike Flanagan** (1975–87, '91–92) had 15+ wins five times for the Orioles, and by far his best season came in 1979, when he won the Cy Young Award after posting a 23-9 record with a 3.08 ERA. **Scott McGregor** (1976–88) pitched his entire career for the Orioles and posted 15+ wins four times. He had his best season in 1980, when he went 20-9 with a 3.32 ERA. McGregor also pitched well in the post-season in both 1979 and 1983, with a combined 1.63 ERA in six starts.

The many others I considered included (in chronological order):

- Barney Pelty (1903–12) had a tidy 1.59 ERA to go with a 16-11 record in 1906. The following year, he led the AL in losses with a 12-21 record, and he ended up with a losing 91-113 record for the Browns.

- Harry Howell (1904–10) was a teammate of Pelty and had a 2.06 ERA (good even for his time period), but he posted a losing 78-91 record.

- Carl Weilman (1912–17, '19–20) pitched his entire short career for the Browns and had three seasons of 17+ wins. His 2.67 ERA was better than league average, though he ended up with a losing record.

- George Blaeholder (1925, '27–35) managed 15 wins twice and 14 wins twice, but also ended up with a losing record of 90-111 for St. Louis.

- Lefty Stewart (1927–32) ended up just below .500 for the Browns and had his best season in 1930, when he posted a 20-12 record.

- Sam Gray (1928–33) was a teammate of Blaeholder and Stewart, and was effective in his first two seasons with the Browns, going 20-12 in 1928 and 18-15 in 1929. His ERA climbed in the next two years, leading to abysmal losing records of 4-15 and 11-24.

- Nels Potter (1943–48) was a mixed starter and reliever for the Browns, with two solid seasons of 19-7 in 1944 and 15-11 in 1945.

- Ned Garver (1948–52) pitched for the Browns for his first five seasons and was an All-Star in 1951, when he posted a 20-12 record with a 3.73 ERA for an awful Browns team. In fact, no other hurler had more than six wins for St. Louis that year, so

Garver's efforts were recognized by finishing a close second to Yogi Berra in the AL MVP voting.

- Milt Pappas (1957–65) started his career for the Orioles before playing for three different clubs in the NL. A two-time All-Star for Baltimore, Pappas won 16 games twice and 15 games twice.

- Steve Barber (1960–67) posted an 18-12 record in his second season in 1961, and then went 20-13 in 1963.

- Mike Boddicker (1980–88), in his first full season, was a key member of the 1983 World Champions club. He posted a 16-8 record with a 2.77 ERA that year, and in two postseason starts he allowed 0 ER in 18 IP. In 1984 he was an All-Star and led the AL in wins with a 20-11 record and also in ERA with a 2.79 mark.

- Jeremy Guthrie (2007–11) pitched for some very bad Orioles clubs, so he twice led the AL in losses with a 10-17 record in 2009 and a 9-17 record in 2011.

Relief Pitching

Name	YR	WAR	W3	SV	W-L	ERA	WHIP	ERA+
Hoyt Wilhelm	5	14.1	12.0	40	43-39	2.42	1.107	156
Dick Hall	9	13.3	9.1	60	65-40	2.89	1.005	124
Stu Miller	5	12.1	10.7	99	38-36	2.37	1.120	145
Gregg Olson	6	11.8	8.3	160	17-21	2.26	1.253	176
Zach Britton	8	11.4	9.2	139	30-22	3.22	1.266	130
Darren O'Day	6	11.3	7.7	17	28-12	2.34	0.988	178
Jim Johnson	8	10.5	7.4	122	18-26	3.11	1.233	139
Sammy Stewart	8	9.9	6.7	42	51-45	3.47	1.394	114
Eddie Watt	8	8.5	5.7	74	37-34	2.74	1.133	123
B.J. Ryan	7	8.0	7.4	42	16-19	3.54	1.310	127
Tippy Martinez	11	7.8	6.3	105	52-40	3.46	1.370	112

There were many relief pitching candidates that I needed to consider, and none of them stood out as being the clear number-one selection for this team. In the end, I went with the franchise's all-time saves leader, **Gregg Olson** (1988–93), who started his career, and had his best years, with the Orioles. He won the Rookie of the Year Award in 1989 after posting 27 saves and a 1.69 ERA. That was the first of five seasons in which he had 25+ saves, with highs of 37 in

1990 and 36 in 1992. Olson had a great curveball which helped him to strike out nearly a batter per inning and post a strong 2.26 ERA during his time in Baltimore.

Zach Britton (2011–18) didn't work out as a starter, but in 2014 he took over the closer duties and dominated, locking down 37 saves with a 1.65 ERA. More of the same the next year, when he posted 36 saves with a 1.92 ERA. Then in 2016 he was even more dominating, posting a microscopic 0.54 ERA and a league-leading 47 saves.

Late in his career, **Stu Miller** (1963–67) became the closer for the Orioles, recording a 2.37 ERA and posting 15+ saves four times (although saves were not yet an official stat). Unlike most late-inning relievers, Miller didn't come in and blow people away—quite the opposite, as he used a baffling array of change-ups to retire hitters.

For the last pitching spot on this roster, I decided to go with Hall of Famer **Hoyt Wilhelm** (1958–62), who pitched for Baltimore for a few years in the middle of his career. As a starter, he pitched a no-hitter in 1958 and was an All-Star in 1959, ending that season with a 15-11 record and a league-leading 2.19 ERA. During the next year, Wilhelm and his knuckleball were used in both starting and relief roles, and by 1961 he was the team's primary short reliever, posting 18 saves and a 2.30 ERA, and then 15 saves and a 1.94 ERA the following year.

There were several others I considered, starting with Eddie Watt (1966–73), who pitched most of his career for the Orioles. He had four seasons with double-digit saves, although never more than 16 in a year. Dick Hall (1961–66, '69–71) had two stints in the Orioles bullpen, provided the team with a solid 2.89 ERA, and picked up some of the saves that Miller or Watt didn't record (though never more than 12 in a season).

Two mainstays of the Orioles bullpen from the 1970s and early 1980s also deserve to be mentioned. Tippy Martinez (1976–86) posted double-digit saves in five consecutive seasons and had his best season in 1983, when he notched 21 saves with a 2.35 ERA. Sammy Stewart (1978–85) was capable of pitching long- or short-relief innings, and even working as a spot starter as needed. His top season for saves was only 13 in 1984, but he managed to win the ERA title in the strike-shortened 1981 season with a 2.32 mark while pitching mostly in relief.

Three more recent relievers also deserved a look, starting with B.J. Ryan (1999–2005). He had mixed results as a reliever for several seasons but became a dominating setup man in 2004, when he posted a 2.28 ERA with 122 strike-outs in 87 IP. He took over the closer duties in 2005 and was an All-Star with

36 saves and a 2.43 ERA before signing as a free agent with the Blue Jays for the 2006 season. Jim Johnson (2006–13) was a capable setup man for several years and was given the closer duties in 2012. He responded by posting a 2.49 ERA and a league-leading 51 saves. He nearly equaled that performance in 2013 with a 2.94 ERA and league-leading 50 saves. And lastly, sidearmer Darren O'Day (2012–17) has at times been one of the league's best setup men, with impressive ERAs from 2012 through '15 of 2.28, 2.18, 1.70, and 1.52.

Managers

Name	YR	From-To	W-L	PCT	PS	WS
Earl Weaver	17	1968–86	1,480-1,060	.583	6	1
Hank Bauer	5	1964–68	407-318	.561	1	1
Buck Showalter	9	2010–18	669-684	.494	3	0
Luke Sewell	6	1941–46	432-410	.513	1	0
Paul Richards	7	1955–61	517-539	.490	0	0
Jimmy McAleer	8	1902–09	551-632	.466	0	0

Hall of Famer **Earl Weaver** was the clear top choice here, as he not only managed twice as long as anyone else but amazingly has the highest winning percentage in team history as well. No one else came close, though I went with **Hank Bauer, Buck Showalter, and Luke Sewell** to round out a top four.

Starting Lineup

What would mythical starting lineups look like for this All-Time roster?

Against RHP:
Brady Anderson CF (L)
Brian Roberts 2B (S)
George Sisler 1B (L)
Eddie Murray DH (S)
Frank Robinson RF (R)
Ken Williams LF (L)
Cal Ripken SS (R)
Brooks Robinson 3B (R)
Chris Hoiles/Rick Dempsey C (R)

Against LHP:
George Sisler 1B (L)
Bobby Grich 2B (R)
Cal Ripken SS (R)
Frank Robinson RF (R)
Eddie Murray DH (S)
Brooks Robinson 3B (R)
Ken Williams LF (L)
Paul Blair CF (R)
Chris Hoiles/Rick Dempsey C (R)

Sisler almost always batted third, but against LHP there weren't really any candidates who fit the description of a typical leadoff hitter: high average and/or high OBP, usually with lots of SB potential. Sisler fits that exactly, so I thought he should lead off. And while Murray was a fine gloveman at 1B, I think Sisler might have been even better relative to his peers, so I listed Murray as the DH.

There were natural platoon possibilities at 2B and CF. These aren't weak lineups, of course, but they also aren't as fearsome looking as many of the other All-Time dream teams. I considered listing Singleton as the LF against LHP, but while a switch-hitter, he generally batted better against righties. And although Adam Jones is a right-handed hitter, he actually has inverted splits and generally hits righties better than lefties. As for the catcher spot, the lineup could use either Hoiles or Dempsey, depending on whether offense or defense was preferred.

Depth Chart

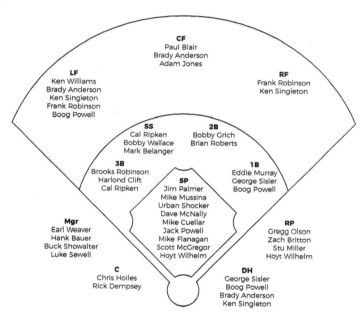

CF
Paul Blair
Brady Anderson
Adam Jones

LF
Ken Williams
Brady Anderson
Ken Singleton
Frank Robinson
Boog Powell

RF
Frank Robinson
Ken Singleton

SS
Cal Ripken
Bobby Wallace
Mark Belanger

2B
Bobby Grich
Brian Roberts

3B
Brooks Robinson
Harlond Clift
Cal Ripken

SP
Jim Palmer
Mike Mussina
Urban Shocker
Dave McNally
Mike Cuellar
Jack Powell
Mike Flanagan
Scott McGregor
Hoyt Wilhelm

1B
Eddie Murray
George Sisler
Boog Powell

Mgr
Earl Weaver
Hank Bauer
Buck Showalter
Luke Sewell

RP
Gregg Olson
Zach Britton
Stu Miller
Hoyt Wilhelm

C
Chris Hoiles
Rick Dempsey

DH
George Sisler
Boog Powell
Brady Anderson
Ken Singleton

Prospects for Current Players

What are the prospects of current Orioles players making this All-Time team? Adam Jones is already on the roster. After trading Manny Machado, I don't see any strong candidates to join Jones as the Orioles are clearly in a rebuilding phase. We'll see...

Orioles Retired Player Numbers

Earl Weaver (4, manager), Brooks Robinson (5), Cal Ripken Jr. (8), Frank Robinson (20), Jim Palmer (22), Eddie Murray (33)

Selections from Other Authors and Fan Surveys

1958: *Sport* magazine, November issue

As part of a running series, *Sport* magazine reported on all-time all-star teams picked by "big league publicity departments and the writers covering the clubs." In this case, they noted the following: "In preparing such a team for the Baltimore Orioles, we certainly had to include the old St. Louis Browns, from whom they are directly descended. But what about the proud Baltimore Orioles of old, one of the greatest teams ever put together? Since modern Baltimoreans are a lot prouder of the ancient Orioles than of the more recent Browns, we felt we had to include some of them. They were wonderful players and they certainly deserve this small honor."

First Base: George Sisler, the greatest Brownie of them all, played from 1915 to 1927 and compiled a lifetime average of .340. He hit .420 in 1922, .407 in 1920, and still holds most of the all-time Browns-Orioles hitting records.

Second Base: Marty McManus played for the Browns from 1920 to 1926 and hit .300 in three of those seasons. His lifetime average was .289.

Third Base: John McGraw, the Little Napoleon of an earlier era, is not often remembered as a hitter, but he was a great one. He played with the old Orioles in the American Association in 1891, in the National League from 1892-1899, and in the American League from 1901 to 1902. He hit over .300 for nine consecutive seasons, had a lifetime average of .334 and stole 444 bases.

Shortstop: Hugh Jennings, who played with the Orioles from 1893 to 1899, is often ranked as second only to Honus Wagner among all-time shortstops. He was equally proficient as a fielder and hitter and made the Hall of Fame with a .314 lifetime average. Jennings hit .386 in 1895 and .398 in 1896. Not bad for a glove man.

Outfielders: Willie Keeler, of "hit-'em-where-they-ain't" fame, played with the Orioles from 1894 to 1898 and never hit under .367. His best was .432 in 1897. In that same year he hit in 44 consecutive games and got 243 hits. Joe Kelley, of the 1892-1898 Orioles, was considered the best all-around player of the championship teams in that era. He hit over .300 every season and played a fine game in left field. His best averages were .391 in 1894 and .389 in 1897. Ken Williams, who played for the Browns from 1918 to 1927, had a lifetime mark of .319 and hit over .300 in eight seasons. He still holds the club record for RBIs, 155, and home runs, 39.

Catcher: Wilbert Robinson, who like McGraw is more remembered as a manager, caught for the Orioles from 1890 to 1902 and three times hit better than .338. He made the Hall of Fame on his fine defensive work as much as hitting and is our close choice over Hank Sevareid [sic], the Browns' backstop from 1915 to 1925 and a .289 lifetime hitter.

Righthanded Pitcher: Urban Shocker, who won 126 games in seven seasons with the Browns, from 1918 to 1924, gets the spot over Joe McGinnity, a Hall of Famer who won 244 games in his career, but only 66 of them in three years with the old Orioles. Shocker holds the present team record of 27 victories in a season.

Lefthanded Pitcher: Matt Kilroy played only four years for the Orioles of 1886 to 1889, but won an amazing 119 games in that time. He holds the old Oriole record of 46 victories in 1887, also the records of 505 strikeouts in a season and 73 games played.

This is an interesting lineup, in part because they avoided weaker selections from the poor Browns years by including so many players from the earlier Baltimore Orioles of the 19th century.

1969: *The Sporting News* Fan Poll

The July 5, 1969, issue reported the results of a fan poll for the long-standing franchises of the day. In this case, Baltimore fans chose only players from the relatively short history (about 15 years) of the Orioles. The results were: 1B Boog Powell, 2B Jerry Adair, 3B Brooks Robinson, SS Luis Aparicio, C Gus Triandos, LF Gene Woodling, CF Paul Blair, RF Frank Robinson, RHP Milt Pappas, LHP Dave McNally.

There were only two players the fans chose that I didn't discuss above. Jerry Adair (1958–66) played five full seasons with the Orioles but was only a .258 hitter with little power or speed. Gene Woodling (1955, '58–60) played for the Orioles for three full seasons near the end of his career and was an All-Star in 1959, when he hit .300 with 14 HR and 77 RBI.

1983: *This Date in Baltimore Orioles & St. Louis Browns History*, by John C. Hawkins

The author chose separate Browns and Orioles All-Time teams, but then also provided a combined All-Time roster as well, so I only considered the latter. He sensibly chose Sisler and Powell at 1B, but then I think erred when he chose Johnson and McManus at 2B (he listed Johnson over Grich on his Orioles-only All-Time team). His 3B picks were obviously Robinson and Clift, and his SS selections of Wallace and Stephens were understandable. His outfield consisted of Williams, Stone, Jacobson, Blair, Robinson, and Singleton, and his catchers were Severeid and Triandos.

I'm not clear on the rationale for the order of the pitchers the author chose (roughly chronological I suppose), but the names given were Powell, Shocker, Bobo Newsom, Satchel Paige, Pappas, Miller, McNally, Cuellar, Watt, and Palmer. Bobo Newsom pitched for nine different teams in his long career and had three stints with the Browns (1934–35, '38–39, 1943). In his rookie season in 1934, he posted a 16-20 record and led the league with 149 walks. He managed to win 20 games for the Browns in 1938, completing 31 of his 40 starts, but also walking an amazing 192 batters and posting a 5.08 ERA (the worst in history for a 20-game winner). And Satchel Paige of course played mostly in the Negro Leagues, joining the Browns late in his career and posting an 18-23 record across three seasons.

1990: "All-Time All-Star Teams," in *The Baseball Research Journal*

In an interesting article, Robert C. Berlo used Thorn and Palmer's TPR (Total Player Rating) system to choose all-time teams. He selected players based on their best 800 consecutive games for the franchise, with a minimum of five years played. His results: 1B George Sisler, 2B Bobby Grich, SS Cal Ripken, 3B Harlond Clift, RF Frank Robinson, CF Paul Blair, LF Ken Williams, C Rick Ferrell, SP Jim Palmer, SP Urban Shocker, SP Harry Howell, SP Ned Garver, RP Dick Hall.

Some of these results were not surprising, but it was interesting to see that Cal Ripken was already the top SS according to this approach in 1990. Even more interesting was Harlond Clift outranking Brooks Robinson—no doubt in part because Robinson's value was spread out so evenly over a long career. And I was surprised to see Dave McNally and Mike Cuellar apparently do worse by this system than Harry Howell and Ned Garver.

1992: *The All-Time All-Star Baseball Book*, by Nick Acocella and Donald Dewey

The authors chose separate All-Time lineups for the Browns and the Orioles, with the former sensibly including Sisler, McManus, Clift, Wallace, Williams, Jacobson, Tobin, Severeid, and Shocker. They listed only two players as honorable mentions—Stephens and Jack Kramer, a pitcher who won more than 13 games for the Browns only once, in 1944, when he went 17-13 with a 2.49 ERA.

For the Orioles, the authors chose a lineup of Murray, Johnson, B. Robinson, Ripken, F. Robinson, Blair, Singleton, Triandos, and Palmer. Again I was confused by the choice of Johnson over Grich at 2B—one of a host of instances of people underrating what Grich did. And they didn't even have him in their list of honorable mentions, which included Dempsey, Belanger, McNally, and Cuellar.

1995: *Baseball Ratings*, by Charles F. Faber

Faber applied his system to the Browns and Orioles eras separately, with the former producing a reasonable All-Time lineup composed of Sisler, Pratt, Wallace, Clift, Severeid, Jacobson, Williams, and Tobin. For the Orioles the lineup was solid and included Murray, Grich, Ripken, B. Robinson, Dempsey, Blair, F. Robinson, and Singleton. He also listed five top starting pitchers for the entire franchise's history, and this included Palmer, McNally, McGregor, Flanagan, and Shocker, with Martinez listed as the top reliever.

2003: *Rob Neyer's Big Book of Baseball Lineups*, by Rob Neyer

As Neyer did for each franchise that had a significant city relocation, he provided an All-Time starting lineup for the combined Browns/Orioles, and also a full All-Time roster for the Orioles only. For the combined team, he went with a solid lineup of Murray, Grich, Ripken, B. Robinson, Dempsey, Williams, Anderson, and F. Robinson. He picked four good starters in Palmer, Shocker, Mussina, and McNally, and then Olson as the top reliever.

For his Orioles-only All-Time roster, Neyer made very reasonable infield choices with Dempsey and Triandos as the catchers, Murray and Powell at 1B, Grich and Alomar at 2B, Ripken and Belanger at SS, and B. Robinson and DeCinces at 3B. His outfield consisted of Anderson, Buford, Blair, Bumbry, F. Robinson, and Singleton. His eight starting pitchers were Palmer, Mussina, McNally, Cuellar, Pappas, Flanagan, McGregor, and Dennis Martinez. About Martinez he wrote, "Had a world of stuff, but struggled badly his last four seasons in Baltimore; career didn't really take off until he was traded to Montreal and stopped drinking." For the two relief spots he of course listed Olson first and went with Hall as the second, writing, "Came to the majors as outfielder with Pirates and became one of the game's greatest control pitchers; with Orioles, went 65-40 with 2.89 ERA and 58 saves."

2016: *101 All-Time Fantasy Baseball Teams*, by Jack Sweeney

Sweeney's picks consisted of Sisler, Johnson, Robinson, Ripken, Powell, Blair, Jones, Ferrell, and he chose Murray as the DH. I again don't understand the choice of Johnson over Grich. The rules of his book didn't allow a player to appear on more than one of these rosters, so that explains why Frank Robinson (Reds) wasn't included here. The four pitchers he chose were Palmer, McNally, Mussina, and Flanagan, and his reliever was Martinez.

Top WAR Single Seasons – Hitters (8+)

Name	Year	WAR	AVG	HR	R	RBI	SB	OPS+
Cal Ripken	1991	11.5	.323	34	99	114	6	162
Cal Ripken	1984	10.0	.304	27	103	86	2	146
George Sisler	1920	9.9	.407	19	137	122	42	182
George Sisler	1922	8.7	.420	8	134	105	51	170
George Stone	1906	8.7	.358	6	91	71	35	193
Brooks Robinson	1968	8.4	.253	17	65	75	1	117
Bobby Grich	1973	8.3	.251	12	82	50	17	116
Cal Ripken	1983	8.2	.318	27	121	102	0	144
Brooks Robinson	1964	8.1	.317	28	82	118	1	145

I was not surprised to see Cal Ripken appear both at the top of this list and the most often on the list. Ditto for George Sisler appearing twice due to his offensive numbers, and Brooks Robinson due to his combined offense and defense. Bobby Grich had a 6+ WAR in five seasons for the Orioles, but in 1973 he got a boost from a higher than usual defensive component to his numbers.

Top WAR Single Seasons – Pitchers (8+)

Name	Year	WAR	W-L	ERA	IP	SO	ERA+
Jim Palmer	1975	8.5	23-11	2.09	323.0	193	169
Urban Shocker	1921	8.5	27-12	3.55	326.2	132	127
Mike Mussina	1992	8.2	18-5	2.54	241.0	130	157
Ned Garver	1950	8.2	13-18	3.39	260.0	85	146

What is there to say: only four seasons make this list, and none higher than 8.5. The one surprise here was Ned Garver's 1950 season, when his ERA was well below average for the league, but he had a losing 13-18 record.

Franchise Player

With apologies and honorable mention to Eddie Murray, George Sisler, Brooks Robinson, and Jim Palmer, I think the choice for this team's franchise player obviously had to be shortstop Cal Ripken. He is their all-time leader in lots of categories, including games played, at-bats, hits, singles, doubles, HR, runs, RBI, and walks.

CHAPTER 16

The Phillies Franchise All-Time Dream Team

The current Philadelphia Phillies franchise dates all the way back to 1883, when the Philadelphia Quakers were an early member of the National League. It was not an auspicious start, as that team produced one of the worst single-season records (17-81, .173) ever for a professional baseball team. The team improved quickly, though, and the Quakers had several winning seasons through 1890, when they changed their name to the Phillies.

The franchise had mixed success for the next couple of decades but didn't win an NL pennant until slugger Gavvy Cravath and ace Pete Alexander led them to first place in 1915 (they then lost to the Boston Red Sox in five games.) After coming in second in the NL the next two seasons, the Phillies had one of the worst stretches in major league baseball history. From 1918 through 1948, a span of 31 seasons, they were over .500 only once—in 1932, when they posted a 78-76 record. And some of their seasons during this time were truly awful, with winning percentages like .283 in 1928, .300 and .298 in 1938–39, and .279 and .278 in 1941–42.

Finally, in 1949, a core group of young players came together that included eventual Hall of Famers Robin Roberts and Richie Ashburn, as well as Curt Simmons, Del Ennis, Granny Hamner, and Willie Jones. This group won the NL pennant in 1950, though they promptly lost the World Series in four games to the powerhouse Yankees.

For the next two decades, the Phillies would post a winning season only five times. Then from 1976 through 1983, led by future Hall of Famers Mike Schmidt and Steve Carlton, the Phillies won their division five times, and finally won their first World Series in 1980.

After some success over the next two decades, including an NL pennant in 1993, the Phillies had their most recent successful period from 2003 to 2011. Led by a core group that included Jimmy Rollins, Chase Utley, Ryan Howard, Shane Victorino, Cole Hamels, and others, Philadelphia won their division every year from 2007 through '11 and took home their second World Series championship in 2008, beating Tampa Bay in five games.

Although ultimate success has been rare for this franchise, they have had some superstars over the past 130+ years. As you will see, some positions are stronger than others, with pitching being a strength and 1B and C being relative weak spots on this All-Time team.

1st Base

Name	YR	WAR	W3	W/G	AVG	HR	SB	OPS+
Dick Allen	9	35.4	22.7	.0331	.290	204	86	153
Fred Luderus	11	19.8	11.4	.0151	.278	83	55	115
John Kruk	6	18.4	13.6	.0247	.309	62	33	138
Ryan Howard	13	14.9	12.1	.0095	.258	382	12	125
Don Hurst	7	13.3	10.0	.0156	.303	112	41	119
Dolph Camilli	4	13.0	12.7	.0241	.295	92	23	132
Jim Thome	4	8.5	8.4	.0217	.260	101	0	139
Pete Rose	5	1.3	4.4	.0017	.291	8	51	101

As 1B was not historically a position of consistent strength for the Phillies, I found it important to consider the candidates in the context of this overall All-Time team roster. As you will see, there are so many good OF candidates that the two "extra spots" on the roster will come from that crop. There are three deserving 3B candidates, and since one of them also played some at 1B, I decided to shift him here. **Dick Allen** (1963–69, '75–76) played most of his early seasons at 3B, but then he played at 1B in 1969, and returned to the Phillies and played 1B in 1975–76. His power was immediately apparent when he hit 29 HR in 1964, which along with a .318 average and league-leading 125 runs and 13 triples, earned him NL Rookie of the Year honors. Two years later, he batted .317 with 110 RBI and a career-high 40 HR.

The rest of the list above presented a challenge in selecting the backup 1B. In short, it amounted to one of the rare times in this book that I chose a player not supported by a strong WAR score. **Ryan Howard** (2004–2016) was a fearsome slugger who played his entire career for the Phillies (although not yet officially retired, he did not play in 2017). After winning the NL Rookie of the Year Award in 2005, Howard became a key part of Philadelphia's success, as he hit 30+ HR each year from 2006 through '11, leading the league with 58 in 2006 and 48 in 2008. Howard also paced the NL with impressive RBI totals of 149 in 2006, 146 in 2008, and 141 in 2009. Only a .258 career hitter, his batting average of .313 along with the HR and RBI titles were enough to earn him NL MVP honors in 2006. All of that power did come at a cost, as he struck out 150 or more times in seven seasons, including a high of 199 in both 2007 and 2008. In fact, he holds the record for the most career "golden sombreros"—games with at least four strikeouts (his 27 top Reggie Jackson's 23).

Howard was also not strong defensively at 1B, leading the NL in errors four times and coming in second another three times. But his early HR prowess was literally record-breaking, as 58 HR is the most ever for a player's second season, and he became the fastest player (in terms of games played) to reach 100 HR (beating Ralph Kiner), 150 HR (beating Eddie Mathews), and both the 200 and 250 HR levels (again beating Ralph Kiner in each case). Howard ended up second all-time in HR for the Phillies, and third all-time in RBI. Lastly, his 15 career grand slams were by far a Phillies record (Mike Schmidt comes in second with 7). So that is my case for choosing Howard as the backup at 1B on this All-Time team, even though his WAR score—decreased significantly due to the defensive component—would not argue in favor of his selection.

Fred Luderus (1910–20) played most of his career for the Phillies. He was a capable hitter, showing some relatively good power for the Deadball Era with highs of 16 HR in 1911 and 18 HR in 1913. He was good defensively at 1B, but unlike many players during that time he didn't steal many bases.

After several years with the Padres, John Kruk (1989–94) joined the Phillies during the 1989 season and hit .331 in 81 games. A .309 hitter overall for Philadelphia, Kruk played mostly 1B but also logged some time at all three OF positions. He was an All-Star three times and had a high of 21 HR and 92 RBI in 1991.

Four others deserve brief mention, starting with Don Hurst (1928–34). In his second season, Hurst batted .304 with 31 HR and 125 RBI, and in 1932 he had his best season with a .339 average, 24 HR, and 143 RBI. He slumped badly the next two seasons and was traded in June of 1934 to the Cubs for another 1B, Dolph Camilli (1934–37). Camilli hit 25+ HR in his three full seasons for the Phillies, and batted .315 in 1936 with a career-high .339 in 1937.

Pete Rose (1979–83) of course played most of his long career for the Reds, but he signed with Philadelphia after the 1978 season and was an All-Star for the Phillies four times. He batted .331 with 208 hits in 1979, led the league with 42 doubles in 1980, and hit .325 with a league-leading 140 hits in the strike-shortened 1981 season. By all accounts his joining the team was a critical factor in their success in 1980, as his hustle and leadership rallied the team to perform at a higher level and ultimately win the World Series.

And lastly, Hall of Famer Jim Thome (2003–05, '12) played only two full seasons for the Phillies, but they were good ones. He posted 131 RBI and led the NL with 47 HR in 2003, and followed that up with 42 HR and 105 RBI the next year.

2nd Base

Name	YR	WAR	W3	W/G	AVG	HR	SB	OPS+
Chase Utley	13	61.5	25.0	.0397	.282	233	142	122
Tony Taylor	15	17.7	9.7	.0106	.261	51	169	88
Nap Lajoie	5	17.6	13.3	.0358	.345	32	87	147
Juan Samuel	7	11.8	9.8	.0138	.263	100	249	105

Chase Utley (2003–15) was the obvious choice as starting 2B for this dream team. A six-time All-Star, Utley provided a good combination of power, speed, and defense. Although not the most durable of players (he played 140+ games only five times), he hit 30+ HR three times and had double-digit SB in eight seasons. He led the NL with 131 runs in 2006 and had a knack for getting hit by pitches, leading the league each year from 2007 through '09.

Choosing the backup at 2B was not nearly as easy, as there were two candidates where the debate comes down steady longevity vs. strong peak performance. **Tony Taylor** (1960–71, '74–76) played most of his long career for the Phillies, mostly at 2B but a little at 3B too. He was a modest .261 hitter with little power, but he provided some speed, stealing 20+ bases four times.

You could make a case for old-timer Nap Lajoie (1896–1900), who started his long, Hall of Fame career with the Phillies. Playing mostly 1B, Lajoie provided a .361 average and 127 RBI in his first full season in 1897, then switched to 2B the following year and led the league with 43 doubles and 127 RBI. Hitting .345 in parts of five seasons for the Phillies is impressive, but in the end, I gave this spot to Taylor.

Only one other second baseman deserves brief mention, Juan Samuel (1983–89), a speedster for the Phillies in the 1980s. Only a .263 hitter with a .310 OBP, Samuel had some power, as he led the league with 19 triples in 1984, and then 15 triples in 1987 to go along with a career-high 28 HR and 100 RBI. He had 30+ SB five times, including a high of 72 in his All-Star rookie campaign in 1984. An interesting accolade is that Samuel was the first player in history to post double-digit doubles, triples, home runs, and stolen bases in each of his first four seasons (he fell short of a fifth consecutive season by just one triple). On the flip side, he also led the league in strikeouts four times and led the NL in errors at 2B three times.

3rd Base

Name	YR	WAR	W3	W/G	AVG	HR	SB	OPS+
Mike Schmidt	18	106.5	27.3	.0443	.267	548	174	147
Dick Allen	9	35.4	22.7	.0331	.290	204	86	153
Scott Rolen	7	29.2	16.8	.0346	.282	150	71	126
Willie Jones	13	24.3	11.2	.0160	.258	180	39	102
Plácido Polanco	7	15.8	10.0	.0230	.289	51	31	96
Pinky Whitney	10	14.5	9.0	.0125	.307	69	34	100

Mike Schmidt (1972–89) is arguably the greatest 3B of all time, so since he played his entire career for the Phillies, he clearly was the top choice here. A 12-time All-Star, Schmidt was best known for his power. He belted 30+ HR in 13 seasons and led the NL an amazing 8 times, with career highs of 48 HR and 121 RBI in 1980. That was his first of three NL MVP seasons, with the others coming in strike-shortened 1981 and, at age 36 in 1986, when he batted .290 and led the NL with 37 HR and 119 RBI. Early in his career, Schmitty had some speed, posting highs of 23 and 29 SB in 1974–75. But besides his great power, his other major value was his defense at the hot corner. He earned ten Gold Glove Awards, the most ever in the NL and second to Brooks Robinson overall.

With Allen already given a spot at 1B on this All-Time team, **Scott Rolen** (1996–2002) seemed the clear backup here at 3B. He earned the NL Rookie of the Year Award in 1997 after hitting .283 with 21 HR, 92 RBI, and 16 SB. He had his best year with the Phillies the following season, when he batted .290 with 45 doubles, 31 HR, 120 runs, and 110 RBI. Like Schmidt, Rolen was also outstanding defensively at 3B, winning three of his eight Gold Glove Awards while with the Phillies.

This meant there was no room on this dream team roster for Willie Jones (1947–59), who played most of his career for the Phillies. Only a .258 hitter with little speed, Jones had some pop in his bat with seven seasons of 15+ HR, including highs of 25 in 1950 and 22 in 1951, his two All-Star seasons. He was also good defensively, leading NL 3B in fielding percentage six times during the 1950s.

Two others deserve brief mention, starting with Plácido Polanco (2002–05, '10–12), who had two stints with the Phillies and played a mix of 3B and 2B. He was a good fielder and a .289 hitter, but he provided only moderate power or speed, with highs of 17 HR and 14 SB, respectively. And lastly, Pinky Whitney (1928–33, '36–39) also had two stints with the Phillies, with time spent with the Boston Braves in between. A solid .307 hitter, Whitney didn't hit many homers but nonetheless had four seasons with 100+ RBI, including a high of 124 in 1932.

Shortstop

Name	YR	WAR	W3	W/G	AVG	HR	SB	OPS+
Jimmy Rollins	15	46.1	16.4	.0221	.267	216	453	97
Larry Bowa	12	21.4	12.1	.0123	.264	13	288	72
Granny Hamner	16	19.4	12.4	.0129	.263	103	35	84
Dave Bancroft	6	14.9	10.8	.0219	.251	14	64	94
Mickey Doolin	9	14.0	8.3	.0108	.236	11	119	75

Just as Chase Utley was the clear top choice at 2B, his long-time double-play partner **Jimmy Rollins** (2000–14) was the number one choice at SS. He had a strong rookie campaign in 2001, scoring 97 runs and leading the NL with 12 triples and 46 stolen bases. That was the first of four seasons he would lead the league in triples, with an impressive high of 20 coming in 2007. That was his NL MVP season, when he batted .296 with 212 hits, 30 HR, 94 RBI, 41 SB, and a league-leading 139 runs scored. In all, J-Roll scored 100+ runs six times and stole 30+ bases ten times. He was also an outstanding defensive SS, taking home four Gold Glove Awards.

The backup SS is not nearly as obvious, but after considering several candidates I settled on **Larry Bowa** (1970–81). A .264 hitter with an anemic .301 OBP and virtually zero power (13 HR in 6,815 AB), Bowa did provide some speed, with nine seasons of 20+ SB. That and his strong defense, which earned him two Gold Glove Awards, led to him being an All-Star five times for the Phillies.

You could make a case for Granny Hamner (1944–59) as the backup instead of Bowa. A three-time All-Star who played almost his entire career for the Phillies, Hamner didn't run much but provided a little pop in his bat, with a high of 21 HR and 92 RBI in 1953.

Dave Bancroft (1915–20) started his career for the Phillies, providing good defense but little power and only some speed on the bases. He had his better seasons later with the Giants and Braves and was even chosen for the Hall of

Fame, though not without controversy, as several of his teammates were on the Veterans Committee who selected him.

And lastly, Mickey Doolin (1905–13) was a very light hitter, with a .236 average and virtually no power. Like many of that era, he stole a few bases, nabbing 10 or more in seven seasons for the Phillies. His main value to the club came from his defense, as he led the NL in assists by a SS and double plays by a SS five times each.

Catcher

Name	YR	WAR	W3	W/G	AVG	HR	SB	OPS+
Jack Clements	14	29.0	13.2	.0290	.289	70	54	118
Darren Daulton	14	22.4	15.8	.0202	.245	134	48	114
Carlos Ruiz	11	21.8	11.8	.0204	.266	68	24	100
Andy Seminick	12	17.4	10.8	.0177	.244	123	20	110
Stan Lopata	11	17.0	9.9	.0207	.257	116	18	117
Spud Davis	8	16.2	11.9	.0199	.321	53	6	111
Mike Lieberthal	13	15.5	9.1	.0132	.275	150	8	102
Clay Dalrymple	9	15.1	10.5	.0150	.234	50	3	84
Bob Boone	10	12.9	9.1	.0115	.259	65	23	90

Catcher has not been a position of consistent strength for the Phillies over the years. They have had several solid or even good catchers, but none that were superstars. In all, I looked at nine candidates in order to come up with a top two for this dream team roster. In the end, I chose **Darren Daulton** (1983, '85–97) to be the starter. He played almost his entire career for the Phillies and was an All-Star three times. By the mid-point of his career, he started to hit for more power and posted highs of 27 HR and 109 RBI in 1992, and 24 HR and 105 RBI the following year. Although only a .245 hitter, he had patience, and so provided a .357 OBP.

Andy Seminick (1943–51, '55–57) got the nod as the backup. Some of his numbers are quite similar to Daulton's, as he hit only .244 but provided a .351 OBP and twice had 20+ HR in a season. An All-Star only once, his overall numbers just came up a little short compared to Daulton's.

Old-timer Jack Clements (1884–1897) played most of his career for Philadelphia. It's a little hard to compare his numbers with more recent players, as many of his seasons were short by modern standards (he only twice played over 100 games). His .289 batting average is also a bit inflated when you see that in the high-offense mid-1890s, he suddenly batted .351, .394, and .359.

Mike Lieberthal (1994–2006) took over as the primary catcher after Daulton, and he hit 15+ HR five times, with his best season coming in 1999, when he hit .300 with 31 HR and 96 RBI. Primarily valuable for his hitting, he did win a Gold Glove in 1999 after leading NL catchers in fielding percentage.

Carlos Ruiz (2006–16) was the most recent regular catcher for the Phillies, and he provided a .266 average and .352 OBP. His career year came in 2012, when he was an All-Star and batted .325 with 16 HR.

Stan Lopata (1948–59) played all but his final two seasons for the Phillies. He had some power, hitting 22 HR in only 303 AB in 1955, and hit 32 HR with 95 RBI in the one season in which he played more than 120 games.

Virgil "Spud" Davis (1928–33, '38–39) had two stints with the Phillies and hit for a high .321 average. He had no speed and only moderate power, connecting for a high of 14 HR in both 1930 and 1932.

Bob Boone (1972–81) played the first half of his long career for the Phillies. He batted .259 and posted 10+ HR only three times. He earned recognition as an NL All-Star three times due more to his outstanding defense, earning two of his eight Gold Glove Awards while playing for Philadelphia.

And lastly, Clay Dalrymple (1960–68) played most of his career for the Phillies. He was not much of a hitter, batting only .234 with a high of 11 HR coming in 1962. His value came more from his defense, including his strong arm, as he twice led the NL in caught-stealing percentage.

Left Field

Name	YR	WAR	W3	W/G	AVG	HR	SB	OPS+
Ed Delahanty	13	60.9	22.2	.0391	.348	87	412	153
Sherry Magee	11	47.8	19.2	.0314	.299	75	387	143
Billy Hamilton	6	36.4	21.0	.0497	.360	23	510	154
Del Ennis	11	33.9	15.1	.0208	.286	259	44	120
Greg Luzinski	11	19.1	12.6	.0148	.281	223	29	133
Pat Burrell	9	16.7	10.5	.0128	.257	251	5	119

Hall of Famer **Ed Delahanty** (1888–89, '91–1901) was one of the game's early stars. He mostly played LF, but he also spent time for the Phillies at CF, 1B, and subbing at other positions when needed. Big Ed hit .348 with a .415 OBP, leading the league in doubles four times, triples once, HR twice, RBI three times, batting average once, and SB once. He posted 25+ SB ten times, scored 100+ runs eight times, and had 100+ RBI seven times. He hit over .400 three times, with a high of .410 in 1899.

Sherry Magee (1904–14) was a hitting star for the Phillies soon after Delahanty's time. He batted .299 and had 40+ SB five times. His two best seasons came in 1910, when had 49 SB and led the NL with a .331 average, .445 OBP, 110 runs, and 123 RBI, and then in 1914, when he batted .314 and led the league with modest totals of 39 doubles, 103 RBI, and 171 hits.

Old-timer **Billy Hamilton** (1890–95) had his best seasons for the Phillies, splitting his time between LF and CF. In those six years, he batted an impressive .360 with a .468 OBP and led the league in runs three times with a mind-boggling high of 198 in the high-offense season of 1894. Sliding Billy also led the NL in steals four times while in Philadelphia, with 97 to 111 SB in each of those seasons.

Having not used either of the two "extra spots" for any of the infield positions, I was able to select eight outfielders for this dream team roster. The problem was that I considered there to be no less than 13 legitimate outfield candidates—players who were deserving and likely would have been chosen for at least some of the other long-standing franchises. Selecting only 8 of these 13 was not easy, and I wouldn't argue if your preferred picks look very different from mine.

That said, after much consideration I decided not to include Del Ennis (1946–56). He spent most of his career in Philadelphia, playing about two-thirds of his games in LF and the rest in RF. During that time, he hit 25+ HR seven times and had 100+ RBI six times. His best numbers came in 1950, when he batted .311 with 31 HR and led the NL with 126 RBI. A three-time All-Star, perhaps the best argument in favor of Ennis would be that he ranks third in HR, fourth in total bases, and fourth in RBI all-time for the Phillies.

Two other LF sluggers deserve brief mention here, starting with Greg "The Bull" Luzinski (1970–80). He played most of his career for the Phillies before finishing as a DH for the White Sox. A four-time All-Star, Luzinski hit 25+ HR four times for Philadelphia, with career highs of 39 HR and 130 RBI coming in 1977. He was NL MVP runner-up that year, as he had been in 1975, when he hit 34 HR and led the league with 120 RBI.

And lastly, Pat Burrell (2000–08) hit 25+ HR six times. His best numbers came in 2002, when he hit .282 with 37 HR and 116 RBI, and in 2005, when he hit .281 with 32 HR and 117 RBI.

Center Field

Name	YR	WAR	W3	W/G	AVG	HR	SB	OPS+
Richie Ashburn	12	57.4	20.7	.0320	.311	22	199	111
Roy Thomas	12	36.6	15.9	.0285	.295	6	228	125
Cy Williams	13	30.3	13.3	.0207	.306	217	77	131
Garry Maddox	12	28.8	16.5	.0217	.284	85	189	99
Von Hayes	9	27.0	14.0	.0224	.272	124	202	118
Lenny Dykstra	8	25.7	18.5	.0350	.289	51	169	122
Tony González	9	24.3	14.4	.0217	.295	77	68	123
Shane Victorino	8	23.5	13.5	.0238	.279	88	179	105

Richie Ashburn (1948–59) played most of his Hall of Fame career for the Phillies. Widely considered one of the best defensive CF ever, his great range helped him lead the NL nine times in CF putouts. A four-time All-Star, Ashburn was also a capable hitter, batting .311 in his 12 years in Philadelphia, including batting titles in 1955 (.338) and 1958 (.350). He led the NL with 32 SB in his rookie season and later led the NL in hits three times, walks three times, and triples twice.

Turn-of-the-century outfielder Roy Thomas (1899–1908, '10–11) was an interesting player, and you could make a case that he deserves a spot on this All-Time team. He was very good defensively in CF, and he ran the bases pretty well, stealing 20+ bases in six seasons. But his strongest attribute was his patience at the plate. He was adept at fouling pitches off and had a very good eye, enabling him to lead the NL in walks seven times. A .295 hitter, he provided a .421 OBP and so scored a lot of runs, including 137 in his rookie season and 132 the following year. What he didn't have was any pop in his bat: he never hit more than 15 doubles in a season and had only a .334 slugging percentage.

Cy Williams (1918–30) led the NL with a modest 15 HR in 1920 and then saw his numbers grow as baseball emerged from the Deadball Era. He led the NL with 41 in 1923 and again with 30 in 1927. He was a feared slugger of his day, and the "Williams Shift," a defensive move most often affiliated with Ted Williams, was actually first employed against Cy Williams in the 1920s.

Garry Maddox (1975–86) began with a few good seasons for the Giants but was traded early in 1975 and played the rest of his career for the Phillies. He was a .284 hitter and stole 20+ bases in six seasons for Philadelphia, but his primary value came from his defense in CF, which earned him seven consecutive Gold Glove Awards and the nickname The Secretary of Defense.

During the 1989 season, the Mets traded Lenny "Nails" Dykstra (1989–96) along with reliever Roger McDowell to the Phillies for Juan Samuel. The Phillies definitely got the better of that deal, as it turned out Samuel's best seasons were behind him, and though Dykstra would often get injured, he was an All-Star three times for the Phillies before retiring early at age 33. His best two seasons in Philadelphia came in 1990, when he batted .325, scored 106 runs, had 33 SB, and led the NL with 192 hits and a .418 OBP, and in 1993, when he was the NL MVP runner-up after batting .305 with a .420 OBP, 19 HR, 37 SB, and a league-leading 194 hits, 129 walks, and 143 runs.

After the 1982 season, the Phillies traded five players to acquire the highly regarded youngster Von Hayes (1983–91). He never blossomed into a superstar, but he did provide a solid mix of power and speed, with a high of 26 HR in 1989 and 48 SB in 1984. His best all-around season was 1986, when he batted .305 with 19 HR, 98 RBI, 24 SB, and a league-leading 107 runs and 46 doubles.

Tony González (1960–68) was a .295 hitter with modest power and speed. His two best seasons were 1962, when he hit .302 with 20 HR and 17 RBI, and 1967, when he hit .339, which came in second to Roberto Clemente's .357.

And lastly, Hawaiian native Shane Victorino (2005–12) played the majority of his career for the Phillies. An outstanding defender, he took home three Gold Glove Awards. He had a little power but excelled more in the running game with three 30+-SB seasons and leading the league in triples with 13 in 2009 and 16 in 2011.

Right Field

Name	YR	WAR	W3	W/G	AVG	HR	SB	OPS+
Bobby Abreu	9	47.0	19.1	.0347	.303	195	254	139
Johnny Callison	10	39.4	20.3	.0275	.271	185	60	122
Chuck Klein	15	34.9	20.6	.0248	.326	243	71	139
Gavvy Cravath	9	30.9	17.0	.0280	.291	117	80	153
Sam Thompson	10	30.8	15.9	.0298	.334	95	192	144
John Titus	10	26.0	12.5	.0213	.278	31	131	126
Elmer Flick	4	21.7	17.4	.0404	.338	29	119	157

As the table above demonstrates, the Phillies have had a good number of quality RF over the years. **Bobby Abreu** (1998–2006) was for many years one of the top power/speed combos in the game. He had seven consecutive 20/20 seasons, with a high of 31 HR in 2001 and 40 SB in 2004. He was a .303 hitter and had a great eye at the plate, leading to an impressive .416 OBP while with Philadelphia.

Chuck Klein (1928–33, '36–44) played most of his career for the Phillies, and technically had three stints with them since he was briefly traded to the Pirates during the 1939 season. During his final five years, he was only a part-time player, and often used as a pinch-hitter only. But his early years were very productive, especially the five-year stretch from 1929 through '33. Some will discount his statistics from these years because of the high-offense nature of the game at that time, and his playing his home games at the Baker Bowl. During his first six seasons, Klein batted a respectable .296 on the road, but hit a ridiculous .420 at home (and his power numbers were just as lopsided). With that noted, Klein led the NL three times in runs, twice in hits, twice in doubles, four times in HR, twice in RBI, once in SB, once in batting average, and four times in total bases. He was the NL MVP once and the runner-up twice. In 1930 he put up impressive raw stats: 158 runs, 250 hits, 59 doubles, 40 HR, 170 RBI, and a .386 average. His numbers in 1933 weren't as big, but it was a more impressive season in that he won the Triple Crown and actually led the league in just about everything: hits, doubles, HR, RBI, average, OBP, SLG, OPS+, and total bases.

Gavvy Cravath (1912–20) might be the most prolific power hitter that most casual baseball fans have never heard of. He had the misfortune of being the top power hitter of the Deadball Era, the time before Babe Ruth came along and changed the game forever. As with Klein, Cravath does pretty well according to the Black Ink Test, as he led the league in HR six times, RBI twice, OBP twice, SLG twice, hits once, and runs once. His HR crowns from 1913 through '15 came with 19, 19, and 24 HR. He then led the NL with 12 HR in 1917, a mere 8 in 1918, and 12 again in 1919—even though he played only 83 games and had 214 at-bats.

With apologies to Del Ennis, Roy Thomas, Cy Williams, and Garry Maddox, I decided to give the final "extra spot" on this roster to **Johnny Callison** (1960–69). A three-time All-Star, Callison hit 20+ HR four times, led the NL in triples twice, and in 1964 was the NL MVP runner-up after hitting .274 with 31 HR, 101 runs, and 104 RBI. He was a good fielder too, leading NL RF in assists four times, putouts five times, and fielding percentage twice.

I also considered old-timer Sam Thompson (1889–98), a Hall of Famer who played the majority of his career for the Phillies. Across various seasons he led the NL two times each in hits, doubles, HR, and RBI, including 149 RBI in only 102 games in 1894 and 165 RBI in 119 games in 1895. A .331 hitter, he had his highest averages during the high-offense mid-1890s, batting .370, .415, and .392 from 1893 through '95.

Elmer Flick (1898–1901) started his Hall of Fame career with the Phillies and was a .338 hitter over four seasons. He posted 20+ SB each season, and his best year was 1900, when he batted .367 with 35 SB and a league-leading 110 RBI.

And lastly, John Titus (1903–12) played all but his final two seasons for the Phillies. An above-average hitter for his era, he had little power but had 20+ SB three times and scored 90+ runs three times.

Starting Pitching

Name	YR	WAR	W3	W-L	ERA	WHIP	ERA+
Robin Roberts	14	71.7	27.0	234-199	3.46	1.171	114
Steve Carlton	15	69.5	29.6	241-161	3.09	1.211	120
Pete Alexander	8	61.3	32.4	190-91	2.18	1.075	140
Cole Hamels	10	44.4	18.9	114-90	3.30	1.145	124
Curt Schilling	9	36.3	18.3	101-78	3.35	1.120	126

Charlie Ferguson	4	32.1	30.1	99-64	2.67	1.117	120
Jim Bunning	6	30.8	25.3	89-73	2.93	1.111	122
Chris Short	14	29.6	18.5	132-127	3.38	1.283	105
Al Orth	7	27.2	16.0	100-72	3.49	1.330	109
Charlie Buffinton	3	27.0	27.0	77-50	2.89	1.203	131
Curt Simmons	13	24.7	12.7	115-110	3.66	1.332	108
Cliff Lee	5	23.5	21.4	48-34	2.94	1.089	132
Kid Gleason	10	20.2	19.3	78-70	3.39	1.380	105
Eppa Rixey	8	16.0	11.9	87-103	2.83	1.245	108
Roy Halladay	4	10.7	12.5	55-29	3.25	1.119	122

Based on the numbers in the above table, it was pretty clear that there are three top starting pitchers in this franchise's long history. How to rank them could be debated, but I decided to give the top honor to lefty **Steve Carlton** (1972–86), who played the majority of his Hall of Fame career for the Phillies. After three seasons as an All-Star with St. Louis, Carlton was traded after the 1971 season to Philadelphia for Rick Wise. The Phillies got the better of that deal right away, as Carlton posted one of the best all-around seasons for any pitcher ever, taking home the Cy Young Award after winning the Triple Crown with a 27-10 record, 1.97 ERA, and 310 strikeouts. He completed 30 of his 41 starts that year, which was a good thing since the Phillies were a pitiful 59-97 that season. Carlton's ERA ballooned to 3.90 and he led the NL in losses with a 13-20 record in 1973, but he got back on track in the years that followed, leading the league in wins three more times and strikeouts four more times. A seven-time All-Star for the Phillies, he took home additional Cy Young Awards in 1977, 1980, and 1982.

As good as those peak seasons were for Carlton, Hall of Famer **Grover Cleveland "Pete" Alexander** (1911–17, '30) had even stronger peak years for the Phillies, so you could make a case for him for the top spot on this All-Time team's staff. In his rookie season in 1911, he led the NL with 7 shutouts, 31 complete games, and wins with a 28-13 record. He would go on to lead the NL in wins, complete games, and shutouts four more times before he was 30, and he led the NL in strikeouts five times and ERA three times, including a low of 1.22 in 1915.

Hall of Famer **Robin Roberts** (1948–61) pitched most of his career for the Phillies, and like Carlton and Alexander he had some very strong peak seasons. A seven-time All-Star, he won 20+ games in six consecutive seasons, including four consecutive seasons from 1952 through '55 when he led the NL in wins with records of 28-7, 23-16, 23-15, and 23-14. A workhorse, he led the NL in games started six times and complete games five times.

After those top three, who should come next was not clear. I considered five candidates and decided that lefty **Cole Hamels** (2006–15) was as deserving as any, and since he had the highest WAR of the group, I gave him the nod. A three-time All-Star, he posted 200+ strikeouts three times but never had more than 17 wins in a season. He was outstanding in the 1998 postseason, winning the MVP Awards in both the NLCS and the World Series.

Curt Schilling (1992–2000) was similar during his time with the Phillies, in that he was an All-Star three times but never posted more than 17 wins in a season. He led the NL in complete games twice, including an impressive high of 15 in 1998, and also had impressive league-leading strikeout totals of 319 in 1997 and 300 in 1998.

You could make a case based on peak performance for Hall of Famer **Jim Bunning** (1964–67, '70–71), who was traded from the Tigers to the Phillies after the 1963 season. From 1964 through '67 he posted 17 to 19 wins, 200+ strikeouts, and had an ERA between 2.29 and 2.63. A key rotation mate during those seasons, **Chris Short** (1959–72), pitched all but his final season for the Phillies. Twice an All-Star, Short had four seasons with 17 to 20 wins, but he never led the NL in any major statistical category. And before those two, **Curt Simmons** (1947–50, '52–60) was a top pitcher for the Phillies, posting 14 to 17 wins five times and being chosen as an All-Star three times.

You could make a case for two recent starting pitchers, starting with Cliff Lee (2009, '11–14). He won the AL Cy Young Award for the Indians in 2008, but they struggled badly in 2009 and so traded Lee to the contending Phillies before the trade deadline. He pitched well the rest of the season and then was dominant in the postseason, starting five games and posting a 4-0 record and 1.57 ERA. He was traded by the Phillies after the season but returned to finish his career and was an All-Star two more times while posting 200+ strikeouts three times. And Roy Halladay (2010–13) won the NL Cy Young Award in 2010 after posting a 21-10 record, 2.44 ERA, and 219 strikeouts. He was runner-up for the award the following year after going 19-6 with a 2.35 ERA and 220 strikeouts.

I also considered Hall of Famer Eppa Rixey (1912–17, '19–20), who started his long career for the Phillies but had most of his best seasons later with the Reds. After four seasons as a mixed starter/reliever, he went 22-10 with a 1.85 ERA in 1916. He had a fine 2.27 ERA the following year but led the league in losses with a 16-21 record. He missed the 1918 season to serve in the Chemical Warfare Division of the United States Army during World War I. Rixey again led the NL in losses with an 11-22 record in 1920 before being traded to the Reds, where he found renewed success and played the rest of his career.

The only others who appeared in the table above were old-timers from the 19th century. Charlie Ferguson (1884–87) was well on his way to a great career but died from typhoid fever at age 25 after only four seasons. His best season came in 1886, when he went 30-9 with a 1.98 ERA and 43 complete games in 45 starts. Charlie Buffinton (1887–89) pitched for this franchise for three seasons, with records of 21-17, 28-17, and 28-16. Al Orth (1895–1901) started his career for the Phillies and won 100 games with a .581 winning percentage, including a high of 20 wins in 1901.

And lastly, Kid Gleason (1888–91, 1903–08) started his very long career in baseball as a pitcher for the Phillies, posting an impressive 38-17 record and 2.63 ERA in 1890. A capable hitter, fielder, and runner, he switched to playing mostly 2B while with the Giants, and later returned to the Phillies as a 2B from 1903 through '08.

Relief Pitching

Name	YR	WAR	W3	SV	W-L	ERA	WHIP	ERA+
Turk Farrell	9	11.2	8.4	65	47-41	3.25	1.310	114
Ron Reed	8	10.7	7.8	90	57-38	3.06	1.151	122
Ryan Madson	9	9.0	5.7	52	47-30	3.59	1.294	122
Tug McGraw	10	8.7	7.8	94	49-37	3.10	1.198	120
Jim Konstanty	7	8.4	7.4	54	51-39	3.64	1.294	110
Jonathan Papelbon	4	7.6	6.0	123	14-11	2.31	1.022	167
Steve Bedrosian	4	4.3	3.7	103	21-18	3.29	1.253	118
Mitch Williams	3	2.9	2.9	102	20-20	3.11	1.517	119
Brad Lidge	4	1.7	4.4	100	3-11	3.73	1.430	113
José Mesa	4	-0.6	1.3	112	13-18	4.05	1.421	102

The many relief pitching candidates were an interesting mix from across several eras, making it hard to compare their accomplishments. **Tug McGraw** (1975–84) pitched the second half of his career for the Phillies and had his best season in 1980, when he posted 20 saves with a 1.46 ERA. After mixed results in the NLCS against the Astros, McGraw was dominant in the World Series, finishing four games with one win, two saves, ten strikeouts, and only one earned run allowed in 7.2 innings pitched.

Jim Konstanty (1948–54) was the closer for the Phillies before that role became a specialty. He had a few good seasons, and one great one in 1950, when he posted a 16-7 record, 2.66 ERA, and 22 saves, which collectively earned him NL MVP honors. And that was in the days when short relievers pitched more than just the last inning: in 1952, Konstanty pitched 152 innings in 74 games.

After those two you could make a case for several others, but in the end, I chose two more, starting with **Turk Farrell** (1956–61, '67–69). He started and ended his career with the Phillies, and posted 10 to 12 saves five times, including his rookie campaign in 1957, when he also had a 10-2 record and 2.38 ERA. And **Ron Reed** (1976–83) was a reliable right-handed complement to lefty Tug McGraw in the Phillies pen for a number of seasons. His best years were the four when he posted a sub-3.00 ERA with between 14 and 17 saves.

Jonathan Papelbon (2012–15) pitched for the Phillies for only three-and-a-half seasons, but his ERA was always sub-3.00 and he notched 38, 29, and 39 saves in his three full seasons. In fact, his modest total of 123 saves is actually the most all-time for this franchise.

Steve Bedrosian (1986–89) also pitched for the Phillies for three-and-a-half years, including his one All-Star campaign in 1987, when he had a 2.83 ERA and led the NL with 40 saves. In a very high-offense season, that was good enough to take home NL Cy Young Award honors in a very close vote over Rick Sutcliffe and Rick Reuschel.

Mitch "Wild Thing" Williams (1991–93) was the closer for the Phillies for three seasons. He went 12-5 with 30 saves and a 2.34 ERA in 1991, and then followed that up with 29 and 43 saves the next two seasons. He pitched very well in the 1993 NLCS but then got hit hard in the World Series against the Blue Jays, surrendering 6 earned runs in 2.2 IP, including the series-winning home run to Joe Carter in Game Six.

Flamethrower Brad Lidge (2008–11) pitched a few seasons for the Phillies and was very effective in 2008, when he posted a 1.95 ERA and was 41-for-41 in save opportunities. As good as he was in 2008, he was equally as bad in 2009, when he had an 0-8 record while saving only 31 of 42 opportunities. His 7.21 ERA set a record as the worst amongst pitchers with 20 or more saves. He was also generally effective in the postseason across all four seasons with the team, posting 12 saves and a 1.79 ERA in 20.1 IP.

José Mesa (2001–03, '07) had impressive totals of 42 and 45 saves in his first two seasons for the Phillies, but then he had an ugly 6.52 ERA and only 24 saves in 2003. And lastly, Ryan Madson (2003–11) pitched many years as an effective setup man for the Phillies and had a short-lived, failed experiment as a starter in 2006. His best season was arguably in 2011, when he was the team's closer and posted 32 saves with a 2.37 ERA.

Managers

Name	YR	From-To	W-L	PCT	PS	WS
Charlie Manuel	9	2005–13	780-636	.551	5	1
Danny Ozark	7	1973–79	594-510	.538	3	0
Dallas Green	3	1979–81	169-130	.565	2	1
Harry Wright	10	1884–93	636-566	.529	0	0
Pat Moran	4	1915–18	323-257	.557	1	0
Jim Fregosi	6	1991–96	431-463	.482	1	0
Eddie Sawyer	8	1948–60	390-423	.480	1	0
Gene Mauch	9	1960–68	646-684	.486	0	0

Bolstered by a loaded lineup and strong pitching, **Charlie Manuel** led the Phillies to five straight division titles and one of their World Series championships, so he seemed like the top choice here. After that I think it is debatable, but I'd rate **Danny Ozark** next (three postseasons), then **Dallas Green** (only three seasons, but one World Series championship), and then perhaps old-timer **Harry Wright**, as he managed the team for ten seasons and had a winning record.

Starting Lineup

What would mythical starting lineups look like for this All-Time roster?

Against RHP:
Richie Ashburn CF (L)
Chase Utley 2B (L)
Ed Delahanty LF (R)
Mike Schmidt 3B (R)
Ryan Howard 1B (L)
Chuck Klein DH (L)
Bobby Abreu RF (L)
Darren Daulton C (L)
Jimmy Rollins SS (S)

Against LHP:
Richie Ashburn CF (L)
Jimmy Rollins SS (S)
Ed Delahanty LF (R)
Mike Schmidt 3B (R)
Dick Allen 1B (R)
Scott Rolen DH (R)
Gavvy Cravath RF (R)
Andy Seminick C (R)
Chase Utley 2B (L)

There was a natural platoon between the two sluggers at 1B, and another with Daulton and Seminick behind the plate. Just as choosing the outfielders for this roster was a challenge, so too was determining the OF and DH spots in these lineups. One issue is that there is an abundance of lefties, e.g., both Ashburn and Hamilton are left-handed CF. Besides Delahanty and Cravath, the only other right-handed options were Magee and Rolen. So in the above, I platooned Abreu and Cravath in RF and Klein and Rolen at DH, but you could mix things up in any number of ways to include more speed from Hamilton or Magee, or have Delahanty play some 1B in place of Howard.

Depth Chart

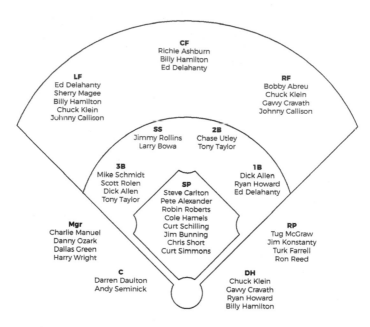

CF
Richie Ashburn
Billy Hamilton
Ed Delahanty

LF
Ed Delahanty
Sherry Magee
Billy Hamilton
Chuck Klein
Johnny Callison

RF
Bobby Abreu
Chuck Klein
Gavvy Cravath
Johnny Callison

SS
Jimmy Rollins
Larry Bowa

2B
Chase Utley
Tony Taylor

3B
Mike Schmidt
Scott Rolen
Dick Allen
Tony Taylor

SP
Steve Carlton
Pete Alexander
Robin Roberts
Cole Hamels
Curt Schilling
Jim Bunning
Chris Short
Curt Simmons

1B
Dick Allen
Ryan Howard
Ed Delahanty

Mgr
Charlie Manuel
Danny Ozark
Dallas Green
Harry Wright

RP
Tug McGraw
Jim Konstanty
Turk Farrell
Ron Reed

C
Darren Daulton
Andy Seminick

DH
Chuck Klein
Gavvy Cravath
Ryan Howard
Billy Hamilton

Prospects for Current Players

What are the prospects of current Phillies players making this All-Time team? Not very good, at least not any time soon. The Phillies are in a rebuilding phase, and while they have some talented young players like Aaron Nola, Rhys Hoskins, Maikel Franco, and others, they also have 130+ years to compete with here. We'll see...

Retired Player Numbers

Richie Ashburn (1), Jim Bunning (14), Mike Schmidt (20), Steve Carlton (32), Robin Roberts (36), Pete Alexander (honored, no number), Chuck Klein (honored, no number)

Selections from Other Authors and Fan Surveys

1958: *Sport* magazine, July issue

As part of a running series, *Sport* magazine reported on all-time all-star teams picked by "big league publicity departments and the writers covering the clubs."

First Base: Dolph Camilli, later of Dodger fame, who played for the Phils from 1934 through 1937.

Second Base: Nap Lajoie, a Hall of Famer, who was a Phillie star from 1896 until 1900.

Third Base: Pinky Whitney, a fixture at third for the Phils from 1928 until early in 1933 when he was traded to the Braves. He returned to Philadelphia in 1936 and finished his career there in 1939.

Shortstop: Dave (Beauty) Bancroft, who began his big-league career with the Phils in 1915 and stayed with them until he was traded to the Giants during the 1920 season.

Left Field: Lefty O'Doul, who played only two seasons with the Phillies, 1929-30, but seems to have left a big impression. The reason for the impression was that he posted batting averages there of .398 and .383.

Center Field: Big Ed Delahanty, who played in Philadelphia from 1888 through 1901 (except for 1890, when he was with Cleveland) and had a lifetime batting average of .346.

Right Field: Chuck Klein, who first came to the Phils in 1928, was traded to Chicago in 1934, but returned to Philadelphia in 1936 and finished his career there in 1944. He is one of seven big leaguers who have walloped four homers in one game.

Catcher: Bill Killefer, the Phillies receiver from 1911 through 1917.

Righthanded Pitcher: Who else but Grover Cleveland Alexander, the Phils' ace from 1911 through 1917 and briefly, in 1930.

Lefthanded Pitcher: Eppa Rixey, one of the best pitchers of his time, who toiled for the Phils from 1912 through 1920.

Not a bad lineup at that time, though several of the selections could have been debated: Camilli over Luderus, Whitney over Jones, Bancroft over Hamner, and Killefer (a .241 hitter with no power) over Clements, Lopata, or Davis. The only one I really object to was choosing O'Doul based on two great seasons over the longer tenure of Sherry Magee or the outstanding numbers of old-timer Billy Hamilton.

1969: *The Sporting News* Fan Poll

The July 5, 1969, issue reported the results of a fan poll for the long-standing franchises of the day. For the Phillies, the results were: 1B Eddie Waitkus, 2B Cookie Rojas, 3B Willie Jones, SS Granny Hamner, C Andy Seminick, LF Del Ennis, CF Richie Ashburn, RF Chuck Klein, RHP Robin Roberts, LHP Chris Short.

Granted 1B is a weak position for this franchise, but Eddie Waitkus, who played six seasons for the Phillies during the 1950s, was only a .281 hitter with no power or speed. He was a good fielder and very difficult to strike out, but I wonder if the vote for Waitkus was influenced by fans' memories of the fact that during his first year with the Phillies a fan shot him at a hotel, a woman obsessed with him from his earlier days with the Cubs. The bullet narrowly missed his heart, so he was able to recover and continue playing.

I also think voters in 1969 were enamored with their current 2B, Cookie Rojas, perhaps thinking he was going to stick in Philadelphia for many years to come. A .262 with no power or speed, he was instead traded to the Cardinals at the end of the season.

1983: "Schmidt Tops Phillies' Fan Voting," *The Sporting News*, August 22, 1983

A small news item noted the following: "Philadelphia fans, voting in a contest to select an all-star team marking the Phillies' 100th anniversary celebration, named Mike Schmidt, slugging third baseman, as the greatest Phillies player of all time. Schmidt totaled 19,767 votes to lefthander Steve Carlton's 14,174. Others named to the team: catcher Bob Boone, first baseman Pete Rose, second baseman Manny Trillo, shortstop Larry Bowa, outfielders Garry Maddox, Richie Ashburn and Del Ennis and pitchers Robin Roberts, Jim Konstanty and Tug McGraw. Dallas Green was selected manager."

Many of these choices demonstrated a clear bias towards current or recent Phillies players. Boone and Maddox were at least debatable, but I really don't think that Rose and Trillo were deserving.

1990: "All-Time All-Star Teams," in *The Baseball Research Journal*

In an interesting article, Robert C. Berlo used Thorn and Palmer's TPR (Total

Player Rating) system to choose all-time teams. He selected players based on their best 800 consecutive games for the franchise, with a minimum of five years played. His results: 1B Allen, 2B Samuel, SS Bancroft, 3B Schmidt, RF Klein, CF Hamilton, LF Delahanty, C Clements, SP Alexander, SP Carlton, SP Roberts, SP Orth, RP Reed.

1992: *The All-Time All-Star Baseball Book*, by Nick Acocella and Donald Dewey

The authors began by noting that, "Given the owners they had in the 1920s and 1930s, when Philadelphia players were considered only as good as the checks they could attract from other teams to buy them, it's a wonder the Phillies are still around at all." They went on to select a lineup composed of 1B Fred Luderus, 2B Bill Hallman, 3B Mike Schmidt, SS Larry Bowa, OF Chuck Klein, Richie Ashburn, and Cy Williams, C Andy Seminick, and P Grover Alexander. For honorable mentions they named Nap Lajoie, Sam Thompson, Elmer Flick, and Robin Roberts, with Danny Ozark as manager.

They dug deep to find old-timer Bill Hallman at 2B. He had three stints for this franchise (1888–89, 1892–97, and 1901–03) and scored 100+ runs three times. He had 20+ SB three times but was only a .278 hitter with an 87 OPS+. Cy Williams was an interesting choice, as was listing Thompson and Flick as OF honorable mentions instead of Delahanty, Ennis, Callison, Cravath, and others. Speaking of which, given who they included, I think Carlton and Allen both should have been listed as honorable mention.

1995: *Baseball Ratings*, by Charles F. Faber

Faber applied his system to the Phillies, and that resulted in a lineup of Luderus, Taylor, Bowa, Schmidt, Boone, Ashburn, Magee, and Thomas. The top five starting pitchers were reasonable with Carlton, Roberts, Alexander, Short, and Simmons, and then Reed was listed as the top reliever.

2003: *Rob Neyer's Big Book of Baseball Lineups*, by Rob Neyer

Neyer noted that 1B "hasn't been a strong position for the Phils" and then selected Kruk and Camilli for the two spots. He sensibly went with Taylor at 2B and chose Dave Cash as the backup, writing, "Only a Phillie for three seasons, but he played virtually every game and was an All-Star all three years, but left after '76 season as one of the first big-name free agents." His SS and 3B picks were solid in Hamner, Bancroft, Schmidt, and Allen.

As Neyer didn't include the 19th century players in the scope of his book, his OF choices were all good ones with Magee and Ennis in LF, Ashburn and Thomas in CF, and Callison and Cravath in RF. That leaves only Chuck Klein and his big 1930s numbers out in the cold.

For starting pitchers, Neyer's top seven selections were all very strong: Carlton, Alexander, Roberts, Simmons, Short, Bunning, and Schilling. For an eighth spot he went with Tully Sparks, who pitched from 1903 through '10, and about whom he wrote, "According to Johnny Evers, Sparks was a master of the 'slow ball,' and in 1907 he went 22-8 with a 2.00 ERA; won only 95 games with Phillies, but 2.48 ERA with Phils ranks fourth all-time." Lastly, for the two relief pitching spots Neyer sensibly went with teammates McGraw and Reed.

2012: *Few and Chosen: Defining Phillies Greatness Across the Eras*, by Gary Matthews with Phil Pepe

As with each book in this fun series, the authors chose a list of the top five players at each position:

C: Boone, Seminick, Daulton, Lieberthal, Ruiz/Smokey Burgess

1B: Howard, Rose, Camilli, Thome, Waitkus

2B: Utley, Lajoie, Samuel, Taylor/Cookie Rojas/Manny Trillo

SS: Rollins, Bowa, Hamner, Bancroft, Dick Bartell

3B: Schmidt, Allen, Rolen, Jones, Whitney

LF: Delahanty, Ennis, Luzinski, Burrell, Magee

CF: Ashburn, Williams, Hamilton, Maddox, González

RF: Klein, Thompson/Flick, Abreu, Cravath, Callison

RHP: Roberts, Alexander, Bunning, Halladay, Schilling

LHP: Carlton, Short, Lee, Simmons, Hamels

RP: Konstanty, Bedrosian, McGraw, Lidge, Mesa

Manager: Manuel, Green, Mauch, Ozark, Sawyer

The authors noted that Burgess played for the Phillies for only three seasons, having been acquired in a trade for Andy Seminick and others, only to be traded back to the Reds for Seminick and others again a few years later. As a platoon catcher he was a good hitter, batting .296, .292, and .368 in his three seasons in Philadelphia.

At 1B I think choosing Rose at number two is a bit high, especially as Kruk and Hurst don't make the list at all. But Matthews makes a good case for including Rose on the list somewhere at least, noting that, "What Pete brought with him to Philadelphia was an impressive résumé: a reputation for fierce, relentless competitiveness; leadership; a winning attitude; a swagger, a cockiness, a passion, and a fire; and an enormous on-the-field ego – all the things a team needs in this game in order to be successful. All of that propelled the Phillies to two division titles, two National League pennants – including their first in 30 years – and the first World Series championship in their history."

2016: *101 All-Time Fantasy Baseball Teams*, by Jack Sweeney

Sweeney's picks consisted of 1B Howard, 2B Utley, 3B Schmidt, SS Bancroft, OF Delahanty, OF Ashburn, OF Klein, C Daulton, and he chose Allen as a DH. All great picks except I think Jimmy Rollins should have been chosen over Bancroft at SS. The starting pitchers chosen were Carlton, Alexander, Roberts, and Schilling, with Konstanty as the top reliever.

Top WAR Single Seasons – Hitters (8+)

Name	Year	WAR	AVG	HR	R	RBI	SB	OPS+
Mike Schmidt	1974	9.7	.282	36	108	116	23	158
Chase Utley	2008	9.0	.292	33	113	104	14	136
Lenny Dykstra	1990	8.9	.325	9	106	60	33	138
Mike Schmidt	1980	8.8	.286	48	104	121	12	171
Mike Schmidt	1977	8.8	274	38	114	101	15	151
Dick Allen	1964	8.8	.318	29	125	91	3	162
Chase Utley	2009	8.2	.282	31	112	93	23	137
Billy Hamilton	1894	8.2	.403	4	198	90	100	157
Johnny Callison	1963	8.1	.284	26	96	78	8	140
Mike Schmidt	1976	8.0	.262	38	112	107	14	151
Ed Delahanty	1899	8.0	.410	9	135	137	30	191

I was not surprised to see Mike Schmidt appear the most often on this list, and in addition to the four above he had another five seasons with a 7+ WAR score. I was, however, surprised that Lenny Dykstra's 1990 season rated as highly as it did, especially as compared to his 1993 MVP runner-up season, when he hit 19 HR, had 37 SB, and led the NL with 143 runs, 194 hits, and 120 walks. Investigation revealed that the 1993 season did have a higher offensive WAR score, but the 1990 season received a much higher defensive WAR score, and that made the difference. And lastly, Hamilton's 198 runs scored looks crazy, but 1894 was an infamously high-offense season—the Phillies batted .350 as a team that year!

Top WAR Single Seasons – Pitchers (8+)

Name	Year	WAR	W-L	ERA	IP	SO	ERA+
Steve Carlton	1972	12.5	27-10	1.97	346.1	310	182
Pete Alexander	1916	11.7	33-12	1.55	389.0	167	172
Pete Alexander	1915	10.8	31-10	1.22	376.1	241	225
Steve Carlton	1980	10.2	24-9	2.34	304.0	286	162
Aaron Nola	2018	10.0	17-6	2.37	212.1	224	175
Pete Alexander	1917	9.9	30-13	1.83	388.0	200	154
Robin Roberts	1953	9.8	23-16	2.75	346.2	198	153
Cliff Lee	2011	9.2	17-8	2.40	232.2	238	160
George McQuillan	1908	9.2	23-17	1.53	359.2	114	157
Pete Alexander	1914	8.9	27-15	2.38	355.0	214	122
Jim Bunning	1966	8.9	19-14	2.41	314.0	252	150
Hal Carlson	1926	8.8	17-12	3.23	267.1	55	132
Roy Halladay	2011	8.7	19-6	2.35	233.2	220	163
Robin Roberts	1954	8.7	23-15	2.97	336.2	185	136
Robin Roberts	1951	8.6	21-15	3.03	315.0	127	127
Robin Roberts	1952	8.5	28-7	2.59	330.0	148	141
Jim Bunning	1965	8.4	19-9	2.60	291.0	268	132
Curt Davis	1934	8.3	19-17	2.95	274.1	99	160
Roy Halladay	1910	8.1	21-10	2.44	250.2	219	167
Pete Alexander	1911	8.0	28-13	2.57	367.0	227	132
Jim Bunning	1967	8.0	17-15	2.29	302.1	253	149

Steve Carlton's 1972 season is truly one of the best ever, especially when you consider his 27-10 record relative to the team's awful 59-97 record. Beyond that, I was interested to see the spans of 8+ WAR excellence from Pete Alexander (1914–17), Robin Roberts (1951–54), and Jim Bunning (1965–67).

There were three seasons on this list from pitchers not described earlier, starting with George McQuillan's 1908 campaign. That was his first full season, and he never achieved that level of success again. Hal Carlson pitched for the Phillies for only three full seasons, and I was surprised to see a 17-12 record, 132 ERA+, and only 55 strikeouts rate an 8.8 WAR. The record was actually more impressive than it looks, as the Phillies that year were a pathetic 58-93 (.384), and so Carlson actually garnered some support for league MVP. And lastly, Curt Davis started his career for the Phillies, and his rookie campaign was his best.

Franchise Player

With apologies to their top pitchers Roberts, Carlton, and Alexander, this honor clearly had to go to Mike Schmidt. Arguably the greatest 3B of all time and a lifelong Phillie his combination of power and defense was truly remarkable.

CHAPTER 17

The Angels Franchise All-Time Dream Team

The Angels joined the AL as an expansion team in 1961. Aside from finishing third in their second season, it took them quite a long time to have much success. In fact, they didn't even finish second in their division until 1978, followed by winning the AL West in 1979. They repeated that again in 1982 and 1986, but in each case lost in the ALCS. It wasn't until 2002 that they finally made it to the World Series, managing to win it in seven games over the Giants. That was Mike Scioscia's third year as the club's manager, and he has continued to lead them well since then, as they won their division five out of six seasons from 2004 through 2009.

While postseason success for the franchise was elusive for a long time, the Angels have had plenty of great players over the years. As you will see, their All-Time team would be quite competitive with other expansion-era clubs.

1st Base

Name	YR	WAR	W3	W/G	AVG	HR	SB	OPS+
Wally Joyner	7	18.9	11.1	.0201	.286	117	29	121
Rod Carew	7	17.3	11.1	.0207	.314	18	82	119
Albert Pujols	7	13.3	11.8	.0135	.260	188	27	112

There were essentially three candidates at 1B. **Wally Joyner** (1986–91, 2001) started with a bang in 1986, his first year in the majors, hitting .290 with 22 HR and 100 RBI, and came in second to Oakland's José Canseco in the AL Rookie of the Year vote. Wally World was even better in 1987, as he hit .285 with 34 HR and 117 RBI. But then his power numbers tailed off over his next four years, and he was granted free agency after the 1991 season, signing with the Royals. He eventually returned for his last season in 2001, but he hit only .243 in 148 at-bats. Although I most associate Joyner with the Angels, he actually played more than half of his career elsewhere.

You could make a case for Hall of Famer **Rod Carew** (1979–85) as the starter instead of Joyner. He was traded to the Angels from the Twins before the 1979 season. At that point in his career, Carew was still a fine singles hitter, as he hit .314 in his seven seasons before retiring after 1985. He no longer stole bases or hit triples at the rate he did playing for Minnesota. And he played over 140 games only once in seven years for the Angels. But he hit .331 in 1980 and .339 in 1983, and he was still selected as an All-Star in six of those seven seasons.

The third candidate is of course Albert Pujols (2012–18), who signed with the Angels as a free agent after an incredible 11-year start to his career with the Cardinals. While he is clearly not the hitter he was during those years, he still has power, hitting between 23 and 40 HR in the five seasons he has played 120 or more games in California.

2nd Base

Name	YR	WAR	W3	W/G	AVG	HR	SB	OPS+
Bobby Grich	10	34.9	14.3	.0286	.269	154	27	124
Howie Kendrick	9	27.5	13.3	.0254	.292	78	95	108
Adam Kennedy	7	18.3	12.1	.0184	.280	51	123	91
Bobby Knoop	6	13.2	8.9	.0164	.240	44	13	90

Bobby Grich (1977–86) started his career as an Oriole, but he had some of his finest seasons as an Angel. Although his Gold Glove Awards all came with Baltimore, he nonetheless provided the Angels with superb defense. He also gave them power at a position that usually lacked it during that era, hitting double-digit HR seven years in a row. A three-time All Star in California, his best offensive season was 1979, when he hit .294 with 30 HR and 101 RBI.

It took **Howie Kendrick** (2006–14) several years to get a full-time role with the Angels, but over nine seasons he posted a respectable .292 average and often had double-digit HR and SB, with highs of 18 HR and 14 SB, both in 2011, his one All-Star campaign.

Two others deserve brief mention, starting with Adam Kennedy (2000–06). He was a steady but unspectacular performer for seven years, providing a decent average (twice .300 or better) and consistent speed (12 to 22 SB each year). And Bobby Knoop (1964–69) played over 800 games at 2B for the Angels in the mid- and late 1960s and hit 17 HR with 72 RBI and a league-leading 11 triples for them in 1966. He was a great defender (three Gold Glove Awards) but struck out a lot and had a low batting average (.240).

3rd Base

Name	YR	WAR	W3	W/G	AVG	HR	SB	OPS+
Troy Glaus	7	22.5	17.3	.0272	.253	182	49	120
Chone Figgins	8	22.3	15.0	.0238	.291	31	280	99
Doug DeCinces	6	18.8	13.4	.0239	.265	130	19	117

The situation at 3B was similar to 1B, as it wasn't obvious whom to select as the starter. I went with slugger **Troy Glaus** (1998–2004), who hit 47 HR in 2000 to lead the league, and then hit 41 the following season. He also had three consecutive 100+-RBI seasons, but as many sluggers do he struck out a lot too: 140+ times in each of his four full seasons. A three-time All-Star, Glaus was outstanding in the 2002 postseason, hitting seven HR, including three in the World Series, garnering him WS MVP honors.

You could also make a case for the versatile and speedy **Chone Figgins** (2002–09). He managed 30+ steals in all of his full seasons for the Angels and led the league with 62 in 2005. Other stat highlights included a .330 average in 2007, 17 triples in 2004, and 113 and 114 runs in 2005 and 2009, respectively. As noted, he also provided valuable versatility for the team, playing 3B, 2B, and various outfield positions, especially early in his career.

Like Grich, Doug DeCinces (1982–87) started his career with the Orioles, only to join the Angels later. Although not quite the power source that Glaus was, he did hit between 16 and 30 HR in each of his six seasons in California. 1982 was his best year for them, when he hit .301 with 30 HR and 97 RBI.

Shortstop

Name	YR	WAR	W3	W/G	AVG	HR	SB	OPS+
Jim Fregosi	11	45.9	21.1	.0321	.268	115	71	116
Erick Aybar	10	23.8	12.4	.0195	.276	48	141	93
Dick Schofield	12	16.3	10.4	.0150	.232	48	99	74

Jim Fregosi (1961–71) began with the team during the inaugural season in 1961 and was the SS for them until after the 1971 season, when he was traded to the Mets for four players, one of whom was named Nolan Ryan. But even aside from his value to the team in leaving it, he provided both good defense (one Gold Glove Award) and some power, hitting 10+ HR five times. He was a six-time All-Star and in 1970 hit .278 with 22 HR and 82 RBI.

Erick Aybar (2006–15) became the everyday SS in 2009, hitting .312 that year. He managed to steal 22 bases the next year and 30 in 2011. He took home a Gold Glove Award in 2011 and was an All-Star in 2014.

Also worthy of mention is Dick Schofield (1983–92, '95–96), who was a slick-fielding, light-hitting (.232) shortstop for the Angels from the mid-1980s through the early 90s. He had some speed, swiping around 20 bases a year from 1986 through '88.

Catcher

Name	YR	WAR	W3	W/G	AVG	HR	SB	OPS+
Bob Boone	7	12.1	8.4	.0125	.245	39	11	71
Mike Napoli	5	11.1	8.0	.0219	.251	92	21	119
Bengie Molina	8	7.4	5.7	.0103	.273	65	2	84
Buck Rodgers	9	3.4	3.8	.0036	.232	31	17	74

Catcher has never been a particularly strong position for the Angels. **Bob Boone** (1982–88) was an outstanding defensive backstop (four Gold Glove Awards) even in the latter half of his career, which is when he played for the Angels. He was a very light hitter (.245), so his value was all in his defense.

Bengie Molina (1998–2005) was also a great defender (two Gold Glove Awards) and had more pop in his bat than Boone did, hitting 10+ HRs four times and batting .295 in 2005. He played in 100+ games in only four seasons for the Angels, and never in more than 130.

You could make a case for Mike Napoli (2006–10) instead of the defensive whiz Molina. He started his career with the Angels and managed to hit 20+ HR in three of his five seasons, even though he played over 115 games in a season only once. But at catcher, I'm giving the nod to Molina based on the value of his defense.

Lastly, light-hitting (.232) Buck Rodgers (1961–69) played his entire career for the Angels before spending many years as a manager for the Expos, Brewers, and eventually the Angels too.

Left Field

Name	YR	WAR	W3	W/G	AVG	HR	SB	OPS+
Brian Downing	13	37.8	15.5	.0228	.271	222	27	126
Garret Anderson	15	28.0	12.4	.0139	.296	272	78	105
Chili Davis	7	12.4	9.5	.0131	.279	156	28	123
Rick Reichardt	7	11.0	9.1	.0195	.261	68	29	118
Leon Wagner	3	6.5	6.5	.0147	.279	91	17	124
Don Baylor	6	6.2	6.7	.0075	.262	141	89	118

Brian Downing (1978–90) came up primarily as a catcher for the White Sox in the early 1970s. After being traded to the Angels in a multiplayer deal (that sent Bobby Bonds to Chicago), he continued to catch for a few more years before switching to the OF, and eventually just to DH. Playing in California for 13 seasons, he hit 20+ HR six times and scored 100+ runs twice. With a strong OBP, Downing was a rare breed, leading off one day and batting cleanup the next.

Garret Anderson (1994–2008) was a good hitter right away, but it took a few years for his run-producing capabilities to mature. In his sixth full season, he belted 35 HR with 117 RBI, and then had three more seasons in a row with HR totals of 28, 29, and 29, and RBI totals of 123, 123, and 116. Also a good doubles hitter, he led the AL with 56 in 2002 and 49 in 2003. A three-time All-Star, he had a low OBP of only .327, as he never walked more than 38 times in a season.

A few others deserve brief mention, including (in chronological order):

- Leon Wagner (1961–63) was not a good fielder but was the first offensive star for the Angels. He played in LA from 1961 through '63, hitting 28, 37, and 26 HR, respectively. Twice an All-Star, his 1962 campaign was good enough for fourth in the AL MVP balloting.

- Rick Reichardt (1964–70) provided moderate power for five seasons during the Angels' first decade. A kidney ailment and operation likely kept him from blossoming into a star.

- Don Baylor (1977–82) was primarily a DH for the Angels, playing only 203 games in LF and 57 in RF. He won the AL MVP Award in 1979 after hitting .296 with 36 HR, 22 SB, 120 runs, and 139 RBI. He had 20+ HR three other times for the Angels, and 20+ SB in two of those seasons.

- Chili Davis (1988–90, '93–96) had two stints with the Angels, playing initially in the outfield and later primarily as DH. He hit 20+ HR in six of his seven seasons, and hit over .300 twice.

Center Field

Name	YR	WAR	W3	W/G	AVG	HR	SB	OPS+
Mike Trout	8	64.3	31.2	.0604	.307	240	189	175
Darin Erstad	11	32.6	18.0	.0247	.286	114	170	96
Torii Hunter	5	21.2	14.7	.0297	.286	105	60	122
Jim Edmonds	7	20.4	15.3	.0288	.290	121	26	119
Devon White	6	15.2	13.0	.0248	.247	59	123	89
Gary Pettis	6	13.2	10.9	.0226	.242	13	186	80
Albie Pearson	6	13.1	11.0	.0190	.275	24	61	108
Fred Lynn	4	10.2	10.1	.0216	.271	71	12	128

During the 2018 season **Mike Trout** (2011–18) turned 27 years old, and few players have accomplished so much by that age. He won the Rookie of the Year Award in 2012 after hitting 30 HR with a .326 average, leading the AL with 129 runs and 49 stolen bases while playing in only 139 games. Through 2017 he has won the AL MVP Award twice and been the runner-up three times. He plays great defense in CF, though he hasn't taken home a Gold Glove Award yet.

Like Anderson, **Darin Erstad** (1996–2006) played the vast majority of his career with the Angels. A different style of player, he provided some power but also some speed, as he five times stole 20+ bases. By far his best season was 2000, when he busted out for a .355 average, 240 hits, 121 runs, 25 HR, 100 RBI, and 28 SB. Defensively he excelled everywhere he played, winning a Gold Glove Award at 1B, CF, and LF.

Torii Hunter (2008–12) came over from the Twins and added two more Gold Gloves to the seven he already had. A two-time All-Star for the Angels, he batted .286 and had 20+ HR in four of his five seasons.

Jim Edmonds (1993–99) started his career with the Angels and, after two partial seasons, had four full and productive ones before a final one shortened by a shoulder injury. Although his most impressive offensive numbers came later with the Cardinals, he did hit 25+ HR and .290+ in his four full seasons as an Angel. Plus he provided highlight-film-quality defense with two Gold Glove Awards in center field. While both Hunter and Edmonds had short tenures for the Angels, they did enough to earn the two "extra spots" on this All-Time team roster.

Four other Angels center fielders deserve mention, starting with Devon White (1985–90), who like Trout, Erstad, Hunter, and Edmonds provided outstanding defense. A two-time Gold Glover, he also swiped 32 bases in 1987 and 44 in 1989. He did not hit for a high average (.247), and he didn't walk much either, leading to an atrocious .295 OBP for the Angels.

Gary Pettis (1982–87) also provided stellar CF defense, taking home two Gold Glove Awards for the Angels (and another three later for other clubs). He had less power than White but even more speed on the bases, as he stole 48 in 1984, 56 in 1985, and 50 in 1986. Although he walked a bit more than White, he similarly hit for a low batting average (.242).

Albie Pearson (1961–66) joined the Angels at their birth, and he led the league with 115 runs in 1962. Pearson was only 5'5" and 140 pounds, but he was a capable leadoff man for the Angels. And lastly, Fred Lynn (1981–84) was a three-time All-Star with the Angels, hitting 20+ HR in each of those seasons.

Right Field

Name	YR	WAR	W3	W/G	AVG	HR	SB	OPS+
Tim Salmon	14	40.5	16.7	.0242	.282	299	48	128
Vladimir Guerrero	6	22.8	15.9	.0270	.319	173	52	141
Reggie Jackson	5	3.5	5.4	.0051	.239	123	14	114

Tim Salmon (1992–2004, '06) played his entire career for the Angels and had five seasons with 30+ HR and another three with 20+. He won the AL Rookie of the Year Award in 1993 after hitting .283 with 31 HR and 95 RBI. His best two seasons were 1995, when he hit .330 with 34 HR and 105 RBI, and 1997, when he hit .296 with 33 HR and 129 RBI. He was surely one of the best players never to appear in an All-Star Game since the institution of that mid-season contest.

Vladimir Guerrero (2004–09) played for the Angels for only six seasons, but he hit 27 to 39 HR in five of them and had 100+ RBI in four. After coming over from the Expos, he immediately provided value by winning the AL MVP Award in 2004, when he hit .337 with 39 HR, 126 RBI, and a league-leading 124 runs.

Lastly, Reggie Jackson (1982–86) was an aging star when he joined the Angels in 1982, but he still managed to lead the league with 39 HR that year. He hit another 84 over the next four seasons, while getting most of his at-bats as the team's DH.

Starting Pitching

Name	YR	WAR	W3	W-L	ERA	WHIP	ERA+
Chuck Finley	14	52.3	21.9	165-140	3.72	1.369	118
Nolan Ryan	8	40.5	21.9	138-121	3.07	1.294	115
Jered Weaver	11	36.0	17.3	150-93	3.55	1.185	113
Frank Tanana	8	34.6	23.2	102-78	3.08	1.166	118
Mark Langston	8	26.3	19.3	88-74	3.97	1.309	109
John Lackey	8	24.7	15.1	102-71	3.81	1.306	116
Mike Witt	10	22.2	14.1	109-107	3.76	1.317	107
Jarrod Washburn	8	20.9	12.7	75-57	3.93	1.275	114
Dean Chance	6	17.9	15.1	74-66	2.83	1.226	122
Andy Messersmith	5	15.7	11.3	59-47	2.78	1.140	118
Kirk McCaskill	7	14.9	11.9	78-74	3.86	1.342	104
Jim Abbott	6	14.4	14.8	54-74	4.07	1.419	101
Kelvim Escobar	5	14.3	12.8	43-36	3.60	1.264	125
Clyde Wright	8	13.4	10.5	87-85	3.28	1.253	100
Ervin Santana	8	12.9	11.0	96-80	4.33	1.300	97

Legendary strikeout pitcher **Nolan Ryan** (1972–79) got the nod as the ace of this staff. In his eight seasons as an Angel, he twice won 20+ games and two other times had 19. He was a workhorse, completing 20 or more games in five seasons and regularly pitching 280 or more innings. But his most impressive statistics were his leading the league in strikeouts in seven of those eight seasons, including five with 300+ and an amazing record of 383 in 1973. Overall, he recorded 2,416 strikeouts in 2,181.1 IP for the Angels. And he did all of that while pitching for mostly losing ballclubs (six out of eight seasons).

Chuck Finley (1986–99) was not as flashy as Ryan, but he was nonetheless the ace of the Angels staff for most of his major league career. He never won more than 18 games in a season, but he did win between 15 and 18 six times. A four-time All-Star for the Angels, he never led the league in any major pitching categories, but he did place second in ERA in both 1989 (2.57) and 1990 (2.40).

Not as famous, **Frank Tanana** (1973–80) was the other good strikeout pitcher for the team in the 1970s. He notched 15+ wins four times and struck out 200+ hitters three times. His 1975–77 seasons sported ERAs of 2.62, 2.43, and 2.54, with the last one leading the league.

Jered Weaver (2006–16) burst onto the scene in 2006, posting an 11-2 record and 2.56 ERA. He posted an impressive .617 winning percentage over his 11 seasons with the Angels. In 2011 he went 18-8 with a 2.41 ERA, and then in 2012 he paced the AL in wins with a 20-5 record and 2.81 ERA.

Mark Langston (1990–97) pitched five full seasons and three partial ones for the Angels during the 1990s. He had 15+ wins three times, going 19-8 in

1991 and 16-11 in 1993 (surprisingly, this produced an 8.7 WAR, the highest single season for an Angels pitcher). Langston also defended his position very well, capturing five Gold Glove Awards while in California.

Dean Chance (1961–66) started out as a mixed starter and reliever but emerged as the first real ace the Angels ever had. He had several fine seasons, but 1964 was by far his best, as he went 20-9 with a 1.65 ERA, 15 complete games, and an impressive 11 shutouts, all of which led the league and earned him AL Cy Young Award honors. He even pitched 11 games in relief that year, saving 4 games.

I decided to go with three more starters for this All-Time roster and three relievers. **John Lackey** (2002–09) started his career with the Angels and had his best season in 2007, when he went 19-9 and led the AL with a modest 3.01 ERA. **Jarrod Washburn** (1998–2005) pitched three partial and five full seasons for the Angels but had only one season of note, his 2002 campaign, when he posted an 18-6 mark with a 3.15 ERA.

And lastly, **Mike Witt** (1981–90) played most of his career with the Angels, starting in 1981 and staying until May of 1990, when he was traded to the Yankees for Dave Winfield. He was a pretty steady performer, notching 15+ wins four times. Witt tossed a perfect game in 1984, a 1-0 victory over the Rangers on the road in Texas. His best year overall was 1986, when he went 18-10 with a 2.84 ERA to help lead the team to the playoffs.

The others I considered included (in chronological order):

- Clyde Wright (1966–73) pitched most of his career for the Angels but was a regular in their rotation only from 1970–73. His best season was in 1970, when he tossed a no-hitter and went 22-12 with a 2.83 ERA.

- Andy Messersmith (1968–72) had a 2.78 ERA in five years for the Angels and posted a 20-13 record in 1971.

- Kirk McCaskill (1985–91) won 15+ games twice but also led the AL in losses in 1991 with a 10-19 record.

- Jim Abbott (1989–92, '95–96), the one-armed wonder, had two stints with the Angels, with his best season coming in 1991, when at age 23 he posted an 18-11 record and a 2.89 ERA. That year he combined with Finley and Langston to be the first trio of left-handed teammates to win 18+ games in the same season. By his late 20s he didn't have much left, as indicated by his horrible 1996 season, when he went 2-18 with a 7.48 ERA.

- Kelvim Escobar (2004–07, '09) pitched only three full seasons for the Angels, with his best being his last in 2007, when he went 18-7 with a 3.40 ERA. A shoulder injury in 2008 required surgery, and then another shoulder injury led to his retirement in 2009 after some time in the minors and just one game back in the majors.

- Ervin Santana (2005–12) was in the Angels' rotation for eight years but with mixed results. He posted good seasons with 16-8, 16-7, and 17-10 records, but also went 7-14 with a 5.76 ERA in 2007, and two other times had ERAs of 5.00+.

Relief Pitching

Name	YR	WAR	W3	SV	W-L	ERA	WHIP	ERA+
Troy Percival	10	17.2	9.0	316	29-38	2.99	1.101	157
Francisco Rodríguez	7	16.2	9.5	208	23-17	2.35	1.114	189
Scot Shields	10	12.4	7.8	21	46-44	3.18	1.244	139
Bob Lee	3	9.5	9.5	58	20-16	1.99	1.089	167
Bryan Harvey	6	8.6	7.1	126	16-20	2.49	1.121	159

Troy Percival (1995–2004) spent only one year as a setup man before taking over as the Angels' closer. From that point, he had 27 or more saves every year for nine straight years, amassing 316 saves for the Angels. A four-time All-Star, his best season was 2002, when he had 40 saves and a 1.92 ERA.

Francisco Rodríguez (2002–08) burst onto the scene late in the 2002 season and earned a prominent role in the postseason, where he pitched brilliantly in all three series. In 18.2 innings, he struck out 28 batters while allowing only 10 hits and 4 earned runs, collecting a 5-1 record in relief. When the 2003 season began, he was still behind Percival on the bullpen depth chart, so he spent two years as a setup man. In 2004 he was again dominant, striking out 123 batters in 84 innings and posting a 1.82 ERA. This allowed the Angels to let Percival go as a free agent and give the closer's job to K-Rod. He didn't disappoint, leading the league in saves with 45 and then 47, and ultimately setting a new MLB record with 62 saves in 2008.

I also decided to include **Bryan Harvey** (1987–92) on this All-Time team, as he used his great splitter to lock down 126 saves with a 2.49 ERA in five full seasons. In 1991 he led the league in saves with 46 and had an impressive 1.60 ERA to go with it.

I considered a couple others, starting with early reliever Bob Lee (1964–66), who recorded 58 saves and a 1.99 ERA in three years for the Angels. And Scot Shields (2001–10) played his entire major league career as a solid setup man for the Angels, collecting a few saves here and there and posting a respectable 3.18 ERA overall.

Managers

Name	YR	From-To	W-L	PCT	PS	WS
Mike Scioscia	19	2000–18	1,650-1,428	.536	7	1
Gene Mauch	5	1981–87	379-332	.533	2	0
Bill Rigney	9	1961–69	625-707	.469	0	0
Jim Fregosi	4	1978–81	237-249	.488	1	0

The clear top of the list here was **Mike Scioscia**. He has managed the team far longer than anyone else and with greater success. Thus far he has led the Angels to the postseason seven times, with his one World Series championship coming in the first of those in 2002. His coaching staff on this All-Time team would be composed of **Gene Mauch**, **Bill Rigney**, and **Jim Fregosi**—mostly based on their longevity at the helm, as they had only three Angels postseason appearances between them.

Starting Lineup

A mythical starting lineup for this squad might look like this:

Against RHP:
Chone Figgins 3B (S)
Mike Trout CF (R)
Wally Joyner 1B (L)
Vladimir Guerrero DH (R)
Garrett Anderson LF (L)
Tim Salmon RF (R)
Bobby Grich 2B (R)
Jim Fregosi SS (R)
Bob Boone C (R)

Against LHP:
Rod Carew 1B (L)
Bobby Grich 2B (R)
Mike Trout CF (R)
Vladimir Guerrero DH (R)
Troy Glaus 3B (R)
Tim Salmon RF (R)
Brian Downing LF (R)
Jim Fregosi SS (R)
Bob Boone C (R)

At 1B I wanted to get both Joyner and Carew into these lineups. They are both lefties, but Joyner had the more pronounced split, so that is why I listed him against RHPs. At 3B there is a more natural platoon: Figgins was a switch-hitter but did better against RHPs, and Glaus definitely hit LHPs better. I listed only three left-handed bats against righties, so if you preferred you could have Carew or Erstad in place of Guerrero at DH, or use Erstad in LF and shift Anderson over to RF (though Salmon actually hit righties slightly better than lefties). And lastly, if you wanted more offense you could have Downing catch some games instead of Boone.

Depth Chart

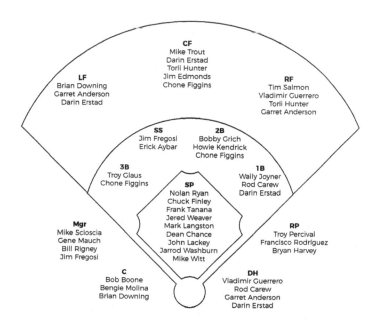

CF
Mike Trout
Darin Erstad
Torii Hunter
Jim Edmonds
Chone Figgins

LF
Brian Downing
Garret Anderson
Darin Erstad

RF
Tim Salmon
Vladimir Guerrero
Torii Hunter
Garret Anderson

SS
Jim Fregosi
Erick Aybar

2B
Bobby Grich
Howie Kendrick
Chone Figgins

3B
Troy Glaus
Chone Figgins

1B
Wally Joyner
Rod Carew
Darin Erstad

SP
Nolan Ryan
Chuck Finley
Frank Tanana
Jered Weaver
Mark Langston
Dean Chance
John Lackey
Jarrod Washburn
Mike Witt

Mgr
Mike Scioscia
Gene Mauch
Bill Rigney
Jim Fregosi

RP
Troy Percival
Francisco Rodríguez
Bryan Harvey

C
Bob Boone
Bengie Molina
Brian Downing

DH
Vladimir Guerrero
Rod Carew
Garret Anderson
Darin Erstad

Prospects for Current Players

What are the prospects of current Angels players making this All-Time team? Mike Trout is already on the roster, of course. Albert Pujols is obviously past his peak, but it wouldn't take much more for him to be in the mix for one of the extra spots or even at 1B. Shortstop Andrelton Simmons is as good as it gets defensively, and if he continues to improve offensively he could one day make this team. And outfielder Kole Calhoun also has a shot if he stays productive for the Angels long enough. We'll see...

Retired Player Numbers

Jim Fregosi (11), Gene Autry (26, owner), Rod Carew (29), Nolan Ryan (30), Jimmie Reese (50, coach)

Selections from Other Authors and Fan Surveys

1969: *The Sporting News* Fan Poll

The July 5, 1969, issue reported the results of a fan poll for most teams, and this included the Angels—even though they had less than a decade in the league at that time. The selections were: 1B Don Mincher, 2B Bobby Knoop, 3B Aurelio Rodríguez, SS Jim Fregosi, C Bob Rodgers, LF Rick Reichardt, CF Albie Pearson, RF Leon Wagner, RHP Dean Chance, LHP George Brunet.

By now, only Fregosi and Chance still make an Angels All-Time team. A few comments on some of these other players, starting with Mincher, who played most of his career for the Twins but joined the Angels for two seasons in 1967–68. He hit 25 HR the first year but only 13 the next. In 1969 I think the stronger selection would have been 1B/OF Lee Thomas, who played three+ seasons at the birth of the franchise and hit 24 HR in 1961 and 26 HR in 1962. Aurelio Rodríguez played 3B for the Angels for parts of the 1967–70 seasons. He was a good gloveman, but even his modest power didn't develop until later. Lastly, George Brunet pitched for the team from 1964 through '69, compiling a respectable 3.13 ERA. With little support, however, he led the AL in losses with 19 in 1967 and 17 in 1968.

1992: *The All-Time All-Star Baseball Book*, by Nick Acocella and Donald Dewey

The authors went with Carew, Grich, DeCinces, Fregosi, Baylor, Jackson, Downing, Boone, and Ryan. All sensible choices, though one could argue the merits of Baylor and Jackson as opposed to the other OF options. They humorously noted that, "The history of the Angels' pitching is still divided into three periods – before Nolan Ryan, Nolan Ryan, and after Nolan Ryan." As for honorable mentions, they listed Leon Wagner and Alex Johnson, an outfielder who played only one full season for the franchise (1970, when he led the AL with a .329 average).

1995: *Baseball Ratings*, by Charles F. Faber

The Faber system in 1995 produced a similar lineup, except that Albie Pearson was chosen instead of Reggie Jackson. The top pitcher was again Nolan Ryan, and the top reliever was Bryan Harvey.

Neyer's starting lineup was nearly the same as mine is today, with Jim Edmonds joining Downing and Salmon in his starting OF. For backups he had Carew, Knoop, Schofield, DeCinces, and Rodgers in the infield, with Anderson, Lynn, and Bobby Bonds in the outfield, and sensibly listed Baylor and Davis as his two DHs.

While Neyer admitted that Bonds didn't even play two full seasons for the Angels (hitting 37 HR with 115 RBI in 1977), he noted that RF has been very unstable for them over the years. He mentioned Lee Stanton as the other RF candidate he considered, but that he "didn't do enough in his four years." I agreed with that—his best season was 1975, when he .261 with 14 HR, 82 RBI, and 18 SB. Reggie Jackson would probably have been my choice here instead of Bonds, as he played a mix of RF and DH, hit 25+ HR three times, and led the AL with 39 HR in his first year with the Angels.

For starting pitchers he listed Finley first, then Ryan, Tanana, and Witt. His next four were solid too: Chance, Langston, Wright, and McCaskill. And Percival and Harvey were the two obvious closers at that time.

Top WAR Single Seasons – Hitters (7+)

Name	Year	WAR	AVG	HR	R	RBI	SB	OPS+
Mike Trout	2012	10.8	.326	30	129	83	49	168
Mike Trout	2016	10.6	.315	29	123	100	30	174
Mike Trout	2018	10.2	.307	39	101	79	24	199
Mike Trout	2015	9.4	.299	41	104	90	11	176
Mike Trout	2013	9.3	.323	27	109	97	33	179
Darin Erstad	2000	8.3	.355	25	121	100	28	137
Jim Fregosi	1964	7.9	.277	18	86	72	8	141
Mike Trout	2014	7.9	.287	36	115	111	16	168
Troy Glaus	2000	7.8	.284	47	120	102	14	150
Jim Fregosi	1970	7.7	.278	22	95	82	0	127
Chone Figgins	2009	7.7	.298	5	114	54	42	110
Doug DeCinces	1982	7.6	.301	30	94	97	7	149
Andrelton Simmons	2017	7.1	.278	14	77	69	19	103

Not surprisingly, Mike Trout dominates this list. Erstad's career year is the only other one to rate 8+. And shortstop Andrelton Simmons has always been a defensive whiz, but in 2017 he did a bit more offensively.

Top WAR Single Seasons – Pitchers (7+)

Name	Year	WAR	W-L	ERA	IP	SO	ERA+
Mark Langston	1993	8.7	16-11	3.20	256.1	196	140
Dean Chance	1964	8.6	20-9	1.65	278.1	207	200
Frank Tanana	1977	8.3	15-9	2.54	241.1	205	154
Nolan Ryan	1977	7.9	19-16	2.77	299.0	341	141
Nolan Ryan	1973	7.8	21-16	2.87	326.0	383	123
Chuck Finley	1990	7.7	18-9	2.40	236.0	177	158
Jim Abbott	1991	7.6	18-11	2.89	243.0	158	142
Frank Tanana	1976	7.6	19-10	2.43	288.1	261	136
Frank Tanana	1975	7.4	16-9	2.62	257.1	269	135
Mark Langston	1991	7.3	19-8	3.00	246.1	183	137
Chuck Finley	1993	7.2	16-14	3.15	251.1	187	142
Chuck Finley	1998	7.2	11-9	3.39	223.1	212	140
Jered Weaver	2011	7.0	18-8	2.41	235.2	198	156

I was surprised to see Langston's 1993 season rate higher than Chance's 1964 campaign—but upon closer inspection I learned that Chance had a 9.3 pitching WAR, only to lose 0.7 for his hitting. I found it interesting also that Ryan only made this list twice, compared to three times each for Tanana and Finley.

Franchise Player

By now Mike Trout has clearly done enough to earn this honor. He already has the highest career WAR for this franchise, and has done so in a relatively short period of time.

CHAPTER 18

The Blue Jays Franchise All-Time Dream Team

The Blue Jays have only been around since 1977, so their All-Time team had a limited history to draw upon. After an understandably miserable start as an expansion team, they had notable success during the nine years from 1985 through 1993, during which time they captured five division titles and two consecutive World Series championships (1992–93). For about 20 years after that, Toronto had mostly seasons slightly above or slightly below .500, until 2015 and 2016, when they finally made the postseason again, losing the ALCS both times.

Toronto's All-Time team roster is fairly well balanced, and boasts at least one star player at most positions, with OF and 1B arguably having the most depth.

1st Base

Name	YR	WAR	W3	W/G	AVG	HR	SB	OPS+
Carlos Delgado	12	36.7	20.0	.0258	.282	336	9	142
Edwin Encarnación	8	24.4	13.7	.0244	.268	239	37	136
John Olerud	8	22.5	14.2	.0245	.293	109	3	130
Fred McGriff	5	19.4	18.0	.0336	.278	125	21	153
Willie Upshaw	9	12.7	9.4	.0114	.265	112	76	104
Lyle Overbay	5	12.3	8.6	.0170	.268	83	9	110
Adam Lind	9	8.1	7.8	.0085	.273	146	6	112

This position was loaded with candidates. That said, **Carlos Delgado** (1993–2004), the all-time HR leader for the Blue Jays, was the obvious choice as 1B starter. After a slow start, he hit 30+ HR every year from 1997 through 2004. He also had six consecutive 100+-RBI seasons and three others with 90+. His best season was 2000, when he hit .344 with 57 doubles (led league), 41 HR, 115 runs, 137 RBI, and a .470 OBP. Later, in 2003, he became the 15th player to hit four homers in a game.

There were three strong candidates for the backup spot at 1B, and after much consideration I decided to go with recent slugger **Edwin Encarnación** (2009–16). He had displayed some power when he came up for the Reds, but it wasn't until his third season in Toronto, at age 29, that he began a streak of five seasons with between 34 and 42 HR. A three-time All-Star, he initially was a 3B before playing most of his games at 1B and DH. Encarnación led the league with 127 RBI in 2016, but he signed as a free agent with the Indians before the 2017 season.

Fred McGriff (1986–90) started his fine career with the Jays, essentially playing four seasons for Toronto. He hit 30+ HR in three of them, including 1989, when he led the AL with 36. McGriff's WAR numbers shown above are impressive, so I decided to give him one of the "extra spots" on this All-Time team roster.

You could make a good case for John Olerud (1989–96), who came directly from Washington State University to the Blue Jays, bypassing the minors entirely. He was their regular 1B from 1990 through '96 and was a fine gloveman (although his Gold Glove Awards came later in his career). He was third in the MVP balloting in 1993, when he led the AL with a .363 average, .473 OBP, and 54 doubles, while also providing 24 HR and 107 RBI.

Three others deserve brief mention, starting with Willie Upshaw (1978, '80–87), who was the starter at 1B for six years, hitting 15+ HR in five of them. He played most of his relatively short career for the Blue Jays, and his best season was 1983, when he hit .306 with 27 HR and 104 RBI. Between Delgado and Encarnación, the Jays had Lyle Overbay (2006–10), who provided moderate power, with his best season being his first in Toronto, when he hit .312 with 46 doubles, 22 HR, and 92 RBI. And lastly, Adam Lind (2006–14) played 394 games at DH, 304 at 1B, and 224 in LF. He posted 20+ HR four times for the Jays, with his best season coming in 2009, when he hit .305 with 46 doubles, 35 HR, and 114 RBI.

2nd Base

Name	YR	WAR	W3	W/G	AVG	HR	SB	OPS+
Roberto Alomar	5	22.2	17.2	.0316	.307	55	206	123
Aaron Hill	7	17.2	14.8	.0197	.265	96	39	92
Orlando Hudson	4	12.6	11.9	.0273	.270	35	19	93
Dámaso García	7	8.5	7.9	.0094	.288	32	194	86

Roberto Alomar (1991–95) played for Toronto for only five years, but he was an All-Star and Gold Glove Award winner every season. During that span he batted .307 and stole 206 bases. His most impressive numbers came in 1993, when he hit .326 with 17 HR, 93 RBI, 109 runs, and 55 SB.

Aaron Hill (2005–11) started his career in Toronto and showed some power in 2007, when he hit 17 HR with 47 doubles. He busted out in 2009 with 36 HR and 108 RBI, and he hit 26 HR the next year though his average slipped badly to .205. That continued in 2011, so he was traded in August in a 2B swap to Arizona for Kelly Johnson.

Two others deserve brief mention, starting with Orlando Hudson (2002–05), who started his career with the Blue Jays. A .270 hitter with little power or speed, Hudson was a great defensive 2B and won the first of his four Gold Glove Awards in Toronto. And Dámaso García (1980–86) provided the team with fine speed, with highs of 54 SB in 1982 and 46 in 1984. A two-time All-Star, he hit for a .288 average but didn't walk much, so he had only a .312 OBP.

3rd Base

Name	YR	WAR	W3	W/G	AVG	HR	SB	OPS+
Josh Donaldson	4	21.4	21.1	.0463	.281	116	17	148
Kelly Gruber	9	16.1	14.3	.0175	.259	114	80	102
Rance Mulliniks	11	15.9	8.5	.0143	.280	68	12	114
Brett Lawrie	4	12.1	10.4	.0351	.265	43	29	104
Eric Hinske	5	7.3	7.0	.0111	.259	78	46	100
Ed Sprague	8	5.8	5.4	.0065	.245	113	2	89

Not traditionally a position of strength for the Blue Jays, the player with the highest WAR is actually **Josh Donaldson** (2015–18). After being acquired from the Athletics for four players, Donaldson won the AL MVP Award after hitting .297 with 41 HR and leading the league with both 122 runs and 123 RBI. He came in fourth in the MVP vote in 2016 after hitting 37 HR with 99 RBI and again scoring 122 runs, and then hit 33 HR in only 113 games in 2017 before being traded to the Indians during the 2018 season.

Before Donaldson came to town, the 3B starter on this roster would have been **Kelly Gruber** (1984–92). He played only six full seasons for the Blue Jays and was a good defender, winning one Gold Glove Award. A two-time All-Star, Gruber also had some pop in his bat, with his best numbers coming in 1990, when he hit 31 HR with 118 RBI, finishing fourth in the MVP voting.

Rance Mulliniks (1982–92) played most of his career with the Blue Jays, often platooned at 3B (most often with Garth Iorg), and also got playing time as a DH. He never was in more than 129 games in a season, but he still managed to hit 10 to 12 HR five times and ended up with a .280 average and .365 OBP for the Blue Jays.

A few others deserve brief mention, starting with Brett Lawrie (2011–14), who started his career with the Blue Jays and provided a little power and speed, though the most games he played in a season was 125 in 2012. Ed Sprague (1991–98) was a low-average (.245) hitter with some power. His best year was 1996, when he hit 36 HR with 101 RBI. And finally, Eric Hinske (2002–06) played for Toronto for the first four-and-a-half years of his career, but his offensive production was only mediocre. After hitting 24 HR and winning the Rookie of the Year Award in 2002, he didn't hit more than 15 HR in a year for the Jays.

Shortstop

Name	YR	WAR	W3	W/G	AVG	HR	SB	OPS+
Tony Fernández	12	37.4	14.4	.0258	.297	60	172	106
Alex Gonzalez	8	9.6	6.3	.0108	.245	83	85	77
Alfredo Griffin	8	-1.3	2.5	-.0013	.249	13	79	64

Tony Fernández (1983–90, '93, '98–99, 2001) was the obvious choice at SS for this All-Time team. He actually had four separate stints with the Blue Jays, and overall hit .297 with 172 SB for the team. He had 20+ SB four times and paced the AL in triples in 1990 with 17. A four-time All-Star, he also was a great fielder, taking home four Gold Glove Awards.

There was no clearly deserving candidate for the backup SS spot, so I went with **Alex Gonzalez** (1994–2001), as he was a good fielder for several years in Toronto. A low-average hitter, he often provided double-digit HR and SB.

Alfredo Griffin (1979–84, '92–93) had a fine rookie season in 1979, hitting .287 with 21 SB and tying for the Rookie of the Year Award with Minnesota 2B John Castino. He then led the league with 15 triples in 1980, and he was a good fielder during his time in Toronto. Griffin had virtually no power, and also didn't run particularly well: he had 79 SB but also 74 CS. He was only a .249 hitter and carried an awful .280 OBP.

Catcher

Name	YR	WAR	W3	W/G	AVG	HR	SB	OPS+
Ernie Whitt	12	19.3	8.9	.0158	.253	131	22	102
Gregg Zaun	5	10.8	8.1	.0202	.255	45	4	98
Russell Martin	4	7.5	6.5	.0168	.225	66	7	99
Darrin Fletcher	5	4.9	5.3	.0091	.276	61	1	92
Pat Borders	8	4.4	4.6	.0059	.256	54	6	83

Like third base, the catcher position has not been a consistently strong one for Toronto over the years. **Ernie Whitt** (1977-78, 80-89) played most of his career as a bluebird, hitting 10 to 19 HR for eight consecutive seasons. Whitt provided reliable defense, but he earned the starting spot on this roster in part simply because of his longevity with the team.

There were a few candidates for the backup spot, and none were very compelling. Journeyman Gregg Zaun (2004–08) played for nine major league teams and spent the longest time (five seasons) in Toronto. He had some power, as he hit 10+ HR three times, even though he only played in more than 110 games in one of those three seasons. Darrin Fletcher (1998–2002) played four full seasons and one last partial one for the Blue Jays at the end of his career. He batted .276 for Toronto and hit 18 HR in 1999 and 20 the next year. Current catcher Russell Martin (2015–18) is solid behind the plate, and though only a .225 batter, he has connected for 20+ HR in two of his four seasons in Toronto.

But in the end, I went with **Pat Borders** (1988–94, '99) who started his long career for Toronto and played for the Jays in parts of eight seasons. He had a high of 15 HR in 1990, even though he had only 346 at-bats that year. What earned him this spot was his performance in the 1992 World Series: he went 9-for-20 with three doubles and a HR, taking home the series MVP Award.

Left Field

Name	YR	WAR	W3	W/G	AVG	HR	SB	OPS+
George Bell	9	21.1	12.8	.0179	.286	202	59	119
Shannon Stewart	10	18.6	12.4	.0205	.298	74	166	108

George Bell (1981, '83–90) had considerable power, hitting 20+ HR in six of his seven full seasons in Toronto. His best season was easily his MVP year in 1987, when he swatted 47 HR, had a league-leading 134 RBI, and batted .308. He didn't have a lot of speed, but he did manage to swipe 21 bases in 1985.

Shannon Stewart (1995–2003, 2008) played five full seasons for the Blue Jays, was traded in July 2003 to the Twins, and returned several years later for a partial final season at age 34. He hit a solid .298 with a little power, but most of his value came from his speed on the bases, as he stole 20+ bases four times, including a high of 51 in 1998. You could make a case for him to make this All-Time team, but there are many other strong OF candidates, and 1B was loaded with good options, so in the end I decided he didn't quite make the cut.

Center Field

Name	YR	WAR	W3	W/G	AVG	HR	SB	OPS+
Vernon Wells	12	28.7	15.2	.0206	.280	223	90	108
Lloyd Moseby	10	25.9	17.2	.0186	.257	149	255	103
Devon White	5	22.2	18.7	.0338	.270	72	126	102
Kevin Pillar	6	14.3	11.4	.0207	.261	55	69	87
José Cruz	6	11.4	7.5	.0163	.250	122	85	102

Vernon Wells (1999–2010) played for the Blue Jays for nine full seasons until after the 2010 season, when he was traded to the Angels. He had 30+ HR and 100+ RBI three times each, while batting a respectable .280. His most impressive numbers came in 2003, when he led the AL with 49 doubles and 215 hits, had 33 HR, 117 RBI, 118 runs, and batted .317. He also provided great defense in CF for the Blue Jays, winning three Gold Glove Awards.

Lloyd Moseby (1980–89) patrolled center field for the 1980s decade in Toronto and provided a nice balance of speed and power. He hit 18 to 26 HR in five consecutive seasons, managed 24 to 39 SB in seven consecutive seasons, and is also the franchise's career leader in SB with 255. His batting average was only .257, and he was an All-Star only once, but he clearly did enough to earn a roster spot on this team.

Devon White (1991–95) hit 10 to 17 HR in each of his five Blue Jays seasons and also stole 30+ bases three times. Most valuable was his defense in center field, which earned him a Gold Glove Award every year he was in Toronto.

I also considered José Cruz Jr. (1997–2002), who hit 30+ HR twice, including a 30/30 season in 2001 when he smacked 34 HR and stole 32 bases. And lastly, Kevin Pillar (2013–18) shines more defensively than offensively as Toronto's current center fielder.

Right Field

Name	YR	WAR	W3	W/G	AVG	HR	SB	OPS+
José Bautista	10	35.9	21.1	.0290	.253	288	56	136
Jesse Barfield	9	29.5	19.1	.0286	.265	179	55	118

Álex Ríos	6	20.4	16.1	.0252	.285	81	112	105
Shawn Green	7	13.1	12.4	.0184	.286	119	76	117
Otto Vélez	6	9.0	6.9	.0172	.257	72	6	127
Joe Carter	7	8.4	9.2	.0081	.257	203	78	104

José Bautista (2008–17) struggled and bounced around with the Orioles, Devil Rays, Royals, and Pirates early in his career. But in his second full season with the Blue Jays, at age 29, he busted out with a league-leading 54 HR to go with 124 RBI and 109 runs. His batting eye and patience continued to improve, and in 2011 he again led the league with 43 HR but now also led the league with 132 walks and posted a .302 average and an impressive .447 OBP. Injuries limited him in 2012–13, but he returned in 2014–15 with 35+ HR, 100+ runs, and 100+ RBI each season. Joey Bats was a six-time All-Star, though his batting average dropped the past two years to a low of .203 in 2017.

Before Bautista came along, **Jesse Barfield** (1981–89) would have been the starter in RF on this dream team. He hit 25+ HR in four Blue Jays seasons, with his best year being 1986, when he drilled 40 HR to go with 108 RBI and a .289 average. In addition to a powerful bat, he had a powerful arm, taking home Gold Glove Awards in 1986 and 1987, before being traded to the Yankees early in 1989 for pitcher Al Leiter.

Álex Ríos (2004–09) started his career in Toronto and for six seasons provided the Jays with a good combination of power (a high of 24 HR) and speed (a high of 32 SB). A good fielder, he was an All-Star in both 2006 and 2007.

Shawn Green (1993–99) also started his solid career with the Blue Jays. The first three of his five full seasons were statistically unimpressive, but in 1998 he exploded with 35 HR, 106 runs, 100 RBI, and 35 SB, and he topped that in 1999, hitting .309 with 45 doubles, 42 HR, 134 runs, 123 RBI, and 20 SB, while also taking home the Gold Glove Award for his improved work in RF.

Otto Vélez (1977–82) played a mix of OF and DH and hit 15+ HR three times, even though he never played more than 120 games in a season. He hit only .257 but walked at a good rate, which resulted in a respectable .372 OBP.

Perhaps the most counterintuitive WAR result I encountered during this entire project was that of **Joe Carter** (1991–97) for the Blue Jays. In his seven seasons playing for Toronto, he hit 20+ HR every year and had 30+ HR four times. He was a very reliable RBI guy, with 100+ RBI in six of those seven seasons, earning him All-Star recognition five times. In 1992 he was third in the MVP balloting after hitting 34 HR with 119 RBI, and he was a key part of the team that won the franchise's two World Series championships. His overall postseason statistics were nothing special really (.252 average, .282 OBP, 6 HR in 119 AB), but it was his Series-winning three-run HR in the sixth game of the 1993 World Series against the Phillies that people most remember.

Carter's postseason heroics don't factor into his WAR score. But a total WAR of 8.4 across seven seasons? What explains this? One factor was his poor defense, which contributed a cumulative dWAR of -7.6. But another factor was Carter's hitting approach, which didn't lead to a lot of walks, and hence a very low .308 OBP and only a 104 OPS+. With apologies to Olerud, Stewart, and Ríos, based on Carter's RBI totals, All-Star selections, and postseason heroics, I decided to give him the second "extra spot" on this dream team roster.

Starting Pitching

Name	YR	WAR	W3	W-L	ERA	WHIP	ERA+
Dave Stieb	15	57.5	22.6	175-134	3.42	1.241	123
Roy Halladay	12	48.3	22.4	148-76	3.44	1.198	133
Jimmy Key	9	30.2	17.4	116-81	3.42	1.196	121
Pat Hentgen	10	26.6	19.6	107-85	4.28	1.391	110
Jim Clancy	12	25.5	15.5	128-140	4.10	1.360	103
Juan Guzmán	8	21.2	15.7	76-62	4.07	1.353	111
Roger Clemens	2	20.2	20.2	41-13	2.33	1.061	196
David Wells	8	15.1	12.2	84-55	4.06	1.275	110
Doyle Alexander	4	13.7	12.4	46-26	3.56	1.232	118
Marcus Stroman	5	10.9	9.6	41-34	3.91	1.287	108
Luis Leal	6	10.8	9.7	51-58	4.14	1.362	103
Kelvim Escobar	7	10.7	7.8	58-55	4.58	1.461	104
Todd Stottlemyre	7	10.3	9.5	69-70	4.39	1.401	95

Dave Stieb (1979–92, '98) was arguably the best overall pitcher in the AL during the 1980s. He was very durable, starting 30 or more games every year from 1980 through 1990 (except strike-shortened 1981, when he started 25), and from 1980 through '84 he had 10+ complete games per year, leading the league with 19 in 1982. In 1985 he led the AL in ERA with a 2.48 mark. A seven-time All-Star, he never won more than 18 games in a season, but six times won between 16 and 18.

Roy Halladay (1998–2009) struggled in his first several seasons but went 19-7 with a 2.93 ERA in 2002 and followed that with a 22-7 record and 3.25 ERA in 2003, which was good enough to win the AL Cy Young Award. He had a bad shoulder in 2004 which limited him to an 8-8 record, and in 2005 he was going strong with a 12-4 record and a 2.41 ERA until a line drive off the bat of Kevin Mench broke his leg and ended his season. His last four years in Toronto were solid, as he posted win totals of 16, 16, 20, and 17, respectively. A six-time All-Star, he was in the top five in AL Cy Young voting five times.

Jimmy Key (1984–92) managed 12 to 17 wins in each of his eight seasons in the Blue Jays rotation. A two-time All-Star while with Toronto, his best season came in 1987, when he was the runner-up for the AL Cy Young Award with a 17-8 record and a league-leading 2.76 ERA.

Pat Hentgen (1991–99, 2004) was a key part of the 1993 World Series team's success, posting a 19-9 record in his first full season as a Blue Jays starter. Three years later he went 20-10 with a 3.22 ERA (second best in the league) and won the AL Cy Young Award.

Jim Clancy (1977–88) had a losing record for the Blue Jays, but that was largely because he was with the team during the weak initial years in the league. He twice won 15 games, once won 16, and completed 15 of his 34 starts in 1980.

Juan Guzmán (1991–98) was in the rotation for the Jays for parts of eight seasons, though he pitched over 200 innings for them only once. His best season was his second, 1992, when he went 16-5 with a 2.64 ERA. Another highlight was winning the ERA crown in 1996 with a 2.93 mark, while compiling an 11-8 record.

David Wells (1987–92, '99–2000) started his illustrious career with Toronto, pitching for them as a reliever for three years, then as a starter for three years, and returned to the club for two seasons in 1999–2000. His second stint provided his two best seasons for the Jays, as he went 17-10 and 20-8, leading the league in complete games in both seasons.

For most any other franchise it would not be possible to make their All-Time team roster with only two seasons on your résumé. But the Blue Jays have a relatively short history, and **Roger Clemens** (1997–98) posted two AL Cy Young Award seasons for them. Few remember that he won the pitching Triple Crown both of those years: in 1997 he went 21-7 with a 2.05 ERA and 292 K, and in 1998 he went 20-6 with a 2.65 ERA and 271 K.

Doyle Alexander (1983–86) had a tenure with the Blue Jays that was almost as short, pitching only two full seasons and two partial seasons for the club, late in his career. But he did manage to go 17-6 and 17-10 for them, including 17 complete games in those two full years.

You could make a case for Kelvim Escobar (1997–2003), who actually pitched 200 games in relief and 101 as a starter. His highest win total for the club was 14 in 1999, and in his one full year as closer he managed to record 38 saves.

Three others deserve brief mention, starting with Todd Stottlemyre (1988–2004), who ended up with a losing (69-70) record for the Blue Jays, with his best season being 1991, when he went 15-8 with a 3.78 ERA. Luis Leal (1980–85) was from Venezuela and pitched his entire, short career for the Blue Jays. He had three seasons of 35+ starts, but only won 12 or 13 games in each. And finally, current Blue Jays starter Marcus Stroman (2014-18) has the talent to one day crack this All-Time team, but he has a way to go. 2017 was his best season so far, with a 13-9 record and 3.09 ERA, and he took home a Gold Glove Award.

Relief Pitching

Name	YR	WAR	W3	SV	W-L	ERA	WHIP	ERA+
Tom Henke	8	17.2	9.7	217	29-29	2.48	1.025	167
Mark Eichhorn	6	11.7	11.6	15	29-19	3.03	1.241	142
Paul Quantrill	6	11.4	8.4	15	30-34	3.67	1.441	134
Duane Ward	9	10.9	8.8	121	32-36	3.18	1.240	128

The Blue Jays did not have a consistent closer until **Tom Henke** (1985–92) took on the role in the mid-1980s. From 1986 through 1992, The Terminator was amongst the league's best, saving 20 to 34 games each year, often with an ERA well below 2.50. He ended up with 217 career saves for the Blue Jays, with a 2.48 ERA.

Duane Ward (1986–93, '95) was Henke's fellow bullpen mate for many of those years, and they shared the save opportunities enough for him to get 10 or more each year from 1988 through 1992. When Henke was granted free agency after the 1992 season, Ward stepped in as the full-time closer, saving 45 games and posting a 2.13 ERA. But this success was short-lived, as injury eliminated his 1994 season and limited him to only four games in an attempted comeback in 1995.

Mark Eichhorn (1982, '86–88, '92–93) had an outstanding 1986 season, going 14-6 with 10 saves and a 1.72 ERA. He pitched two more seasons as a setup man for Henke and later returned in a trade during the 1992 season, posting a 2.72 ERA the following season.

And lastly, another solid setup man for the Blue Jays was Paul Quantrill (1996–2001), who posted a 1.94 ERA in 1997 and was an All-Star in 2001.

Managers

Name	YR	From-To	W-L	PCT	PS	WS
Cito Gaston	12	1989–2010	894-837	.516	4	2
John Gibbons	11	2004–18	793-789	.501	2	0
Bobby Cox	4	1982–85	355-292	.549	1	0
Jimy Williams	4	1986–89	281-241	.538	0	0

I don't think there could be much debate about the top managers in Blue Jays history. **Cito Gaston** managed the team for the most seasons, had the most wins, and took them to the postseason four times, including their two World

Series championships. **John Gibbons** might one day catch up to him in wins, and while he has made the postseason twice, it is unlikely he will match Gaston's championships. Then **Bobby Cox** and **Jimy Williams** were the only two other managers in franchise history to manage the team for four seasons, and they both had winning percentages well over .500 too.

Starting Lineup

What would mythical starting lineups look like for this All-Time roster?

Against RHP:
Tony Fernández SS (S)
Robert Alomar 2B (S)
Josh Donaldson 3B (R)
Carlos Delgado 1B (L)
José Bautista DH (R)
Vernon Wells CF (R)
George Bell LF (R)
Jesse Barfield RF (R)
Ernie Whitt C (L)

Against LHP:
Tony Fernández SS (S)
Robert Alomar 2B (S)
Josh Donaldson 3B (R)
José Bautista DH (R)
Edwin Encarnación 1B (R)
Vernon Wells CF (R)
George Bell LF (R)
Jesse Barfield RF (R)
Pat Borders C (R)

These were fairly potent lineups given that the franchise only dated back to 1977. It is every manager's dream to have two switch-hitters at the top of the order. Then the power bats could be re-arranged in any number of ways, and I slotted Bautista as the DH. There were two righty/lefty platoons, with the sluggers at 1B and the one weak spot in the lineup at C.

Prospects for Current Players

What are the prospects of current Blue Jays players making this All-Time team? Given the relatively weak pool of candidates at C, Russell Martin might soon deserve a spot. And the same could potentially arise for Troy Tulowitzki as backup SS. Starting pitchers Marcus Stroman and Aaron Sanchez are young and talented, so perhaps they too could make this team one day. We'll see…

Retired Player Numbers

Roberto Alomar (12), Roy Halladay (32)

Depth Chart

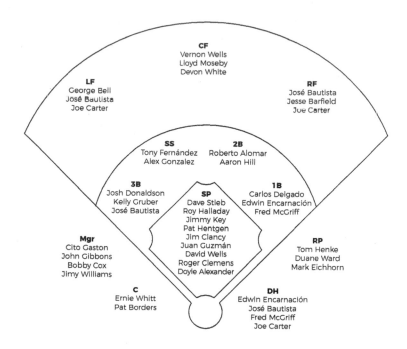

CF
Vernon Wells
Lloyd Moseby
Devon White

LF
George Bell
José Bautista
Joe Carter

RF
José Bautista
Jesse Barfield
Joe Carter

SS
Tony Fernández
Alex Gonzalez

2B
Roberto Alomar
Aaron Hill

3B
Josh Donaldson
Kelly Gruber
José Bautista

SP
Dave Stieb
Roy Halladay
Jimmy Key
Pat Hentgen
Jim Clancy
Juan Guzmán
David Wells
Roger Clemens
Doyle Alexander

1B
Carlos Delgado
Edwin Encarnación
Fred McGriff

Mgr
Cito Gaston
John Gibbons
Bobby Cox
Jimy Williams

RP
Tom Henke
Duane Ward
Mark Eichhorn

C
Ernie Whitt
Pat Borders

DH
Edwin Encarnación
José Bautista
Fred McGriff
Joe Carter

Selections from Other Authors and Fan Surveys

1992: *The All-Time All-Star Baseball Book*, Nick Acocella and Donald Dewey

Their choices were exactly what mine would have been at that time: McGriff, García, Gruber, Fernández, Bell, Moseby, Barfield, Whitt, and Stieb.

1995: *Baseball Ratings*, by Charles F. Faber

The Faber system produced a very credible lineup with no big surprises: Upshaw, Alomar, Fernández, Gruber, Whitt, Moseby, Bell, Barfield, Stieb, and Henke. No complaints from me, except for Upshaw at 1B.

2003: *Rob Neyer's Big Book of Baseball Lineups*, by Rob Neyer

Neyer's starting lineup was solid with Delgado, Alomar, Gruber, Fernández, Whitt, Bell, Moseby, and Barfield. For the infield backups, he chose McGriff over Olerud at 1B, naturally had García at 2B, went with Griffin over Gonzalez at SS, and then Mulliniks at 3B. The outfield was Carter in LF, White in CF, and Green in RF. He also listed Paul Molitor and Cliff Johnson as two designated hitters, both of whom had brief stints in Toronto.

Neyer's top eight starting pitchers were solid with Stieb, Key, Hentgen, Clancy, Wells, Guzmán, Stottlemyre, and Clemens. Henke and Ward were the obvious relief selections.

Top WAR Single Seasons – Hitters (7+)

Name	Year	WAR	AVG	HR	R	RBI	SB	OPS+
Josh Donaldson	2015	8.8	.297	41	122	123	6	151
José Bautista	2011	8.1	.302	43	105	103	9	182
John Olerud	1993	7.7	.363	24	109	107	0	186
Jesse Barfield	1986	7.6	.289	40	107	108	8	146
Josh Donaldson	2016	7.4	.284	37	122	99	7	152
Carlos Delgado	2000	7.3	.344	41	115	137	0	181
Lloyd Moseby	1984	7.3	.280	18	97	92	39	127
José Bautista	2010	7.0	.260	54	109	124	9	164

In terms of WAR, it is interesting to see that Donaldson's first two seasons in Toronto rank first and fifth all-time for the Blue Jays. Bautista's two biggest seasons of course also make this list, as do the career years for Olerud and Barfield (Bell's 1987 MVP season did not). Delgado had several big-number seasons, but only one generated a WAR of 7.0 or higher.

Top WAR Single Seasons – Pitchers (7+)

Name	Year	WAR	W-L	ERA	IP	SO	ERA+
Roger Clemens	1997	12.2	21-7	2.05	264.0	292	222
Pat Hentgen	1996	8.5	20-10	3.22	265.2	177	156
Roger Clemens	1998	8.2	20-6	2.65	234.2	271	174
Roy Halladay	2003	8.1	22-7	3.25	266.0	204	145
Dave Stieb	1984	7.9	16-8	2.83	267.0	198	146
Dave Stieb	1982	7.7	17-14	3.25	288.1	141	138
Mark Eichhorn	1986	7.4	14-6	1.72	157.0	166	246
Jimmy Key	1987	7.4	17-8	2.76	261.0	161	164
Roy Halladay	2002	7.3	19-7	2.93	239.1	168	157
Dave Stieb	1983	7.0	17-12	3.04	278.0	187	142

Clemens' 1997 season was, according to WAR, by far the best any Blue Jays pitcher has ever had. And his other season in Toronto was good enough to rate third in team history. Not surprising was Dave Stieb showing up on this list three times, nor Halladay making it twice. Arguably the second-most impressive season on this list was Eichhorn's outstanding rookie season, as it isn't often that a partial-closer/partial setup man can generate such a high WAR score.

Franchise Player

This wasn't an easy honor to award, but I decided to go with pitcher Dave Stieb. You could make a case for several others, most notably Delgado, Fernández, and Bautista. But Stieb's long tenure and consistency on the mound earned him this top spot.

CHAPTER 19

The Astros Franchise All-Time Dream Team

The Houston Astros began in 1962 as the Colt .45s, winning their first game 11-2 against the Cubs. Unfortunately, they were a consistently bad team for the three years they played with that name (winning only 64 to 66 games per season). A move from Colt Stadium to indoor play at the Astrodome in 1965 didn't improve things immediately, but eventually the team posted its first .500 season in 1969. They didn't win their first division title until 1980, when they were supported by the strong pitching of Nolan Ryan and J.R. Richard. They won another in 1986, this time backed by a career year by pitcher Mike Scott.

In the late 1990s they developed a more balanced club led by Jeff Bagwell and Craig Biggio, came in second in the Central Division from 1994 to 1996, and then won the division from 1997 through '99 and again in 2001. The Astros made it to the NLCS in 2004 and finally the World Series for the first time in 2005—where they lost in four straight games to the White Sox.

From 2009 through 2013 the Astros were miserable, failing to post a winning percentage above .420. During that time, they were pushed to switch leagues from the NL to the AL, ending up in the AL West division starting in 2013. *Sports Illustrated* ran a cover story on June 30, 2014, boldly predicting that the Astros would be the 2017 World Series champions. After a few years of strong player development and a few good acquisitions, in 2017 the Astros posted a 101-61 record and won the World Series over the Dodgers in seven games.

The Astros' All-Time team roster has many positions of strength, with a few weak spots too. They've had many talented players in the more than 50 years of their existence and compare fairly well with the other franchises that sprang up during the expansion period of the 1960s.

1st Base

Name	YR	WAR	W3	W/G	AVG	HR	SB	OPS+
Jeff Bagwell	15	79.6	23.4	.0370	.297	449	202	149
Bob Watson	14	23.5	12.5	.0170	.297	139	21	130
Glenn Davis	7	18.8	13.1	.0227	.262	166	23	129
Lee May	3	6.2	6.2	.0138	.274	81	5	122

Obviously, **Jeff Bagwell** (1991–2005) was the starter here. He was the career leader in HR and RBI for Houston and amongst the club's leaders in most other categories. He had some simply phenomenal seasons, playing his entire 15-year career for the Astros, including eight in which he managed 30/100/100 HR/RBI/R. He also had seven seasons with 100+ walks, leading to a career .408 OBP. He won the Rookie of the Year Award in 1991 and the MVP in the strike-shortened 1994 season (the first Astro to take home the prize). The trade that brought Bagwell to Houston from the Red Sox has to be one of the biggest steals of all time: 37-year-old middle-reliever Larry Andersen for Bagwell, one of the top-ten 1B of all time.

Before Bagwell, there was **Glenn Davis** (1984–90), who played most of his short career for the Astros. A power hitter who six times provided 20+ HR, he enjoyed his finest year in 1986, when his 31 HR and 101 RBI helped the Astros take the Western Division title.

Bob Watson played more of his games at 1B than in the OF, but there is more room for him on this dream team in the OF, so he'll be reconsidered there. Lastly, I'll note that slugger Lee May (1972–74) had three 20+-HR seasons at 1B for the Astros, but that wasn't nearly enough to make this roster.

2nd Base

Name	YR	WAR	W3	W/G	AVG	HR	SB	OPS+
Craig Biggio	20	65.1	22.2	.0228	.281	291	414	112
José Altuve	8	35.1	22.1	.0314	.316	97	248	126
Joe Morgan	10	30.6	16.3	.0297	.261	72	219	120
Bill Doran	9	30.3	14.8	.0260	.267	69	191	107

Just as obvious as Bagwell at 1B, the clear starter at 2B was **Craig Biggio** (1988–2007). As you will see, it would be mighty tempting to ask Biggio to play catcher on this dream team, as he did play 427 games there early in his career. But with 1,989 games at 2B, it only seems right to list him here. He also played 363 games in the outfield, though not because his defense at 2B was lacking (he won four Gold Glove Awards there.) Biggio long provided a great combination of power and speed, especially for a middle infielder: he managed eight 20+-homer seasons, and his 414 stolen bases compare nicely with only 124 times caught stealing. He scored 146 runs in 1997, then had another strong year in 1998 with 210 hits, 123 runs, 51 doubles, 20 home runs, 88 RBI, 50 SB and only 8 CS, a .325 average, and a .403 OBP. Biggio had a knack for getting hit by pitches, leading the league five times and ending his career in second place all-time with 285, only two behind old-timer Hughie Jennings.

Current Astros star **José Altuve** (2011–2018) showed ample speed and potential for greatness early in his career. And sure enough, in 2014 he led the AL with 225 hits, a .341 average, and 56 SB. He led the AL in hits and SB again the next year, but with a bit more power in his bat, and also took home a Gold Glove Award. In 2016 and 2017 he improved again, leading the league in hits and batting average both seasons, but now showing legit power with 24 HR each year. He came in third in the AL MVP vote in 2016, and took home the award in 2017, his fifth All-Star season.

Hall of Famer **Joe Morgan** (1963–71, '80) admittedly had his best seasons with the Reds, but he did have some good early years in Houston, scoring 100+ runs twice and stealing 40+ bases three times. He returned to Houston for the 1980 season, helping them win the Western Division. And **Bill Doran** (1982–90) also had some fine seasons for the Astros, as he regularly stole 20+ bases, with highs of 42 in 1986 and 31 in 1987. I'd argue that Morgan and Doran are as deserving as anyone else for the two "extra spots" on this roster—and with so much quality at 2B, that would allow Biggio to get in some games as a catcher too!

3rd Base

Name	YR	WAR	W3	W/G	AVG	HR	SB	OPS+
Doug Rader	9	18.3	9.8	.0156	.250	128	32	104
Ken Caminiti	10	16.5	12.2	.0152	.264	103	48	102
Morgan Ensberg	7	14.1	14.5	.0210	.266	105	22	116
Denny Walling	13	14.1	7.4	.0132	.277	47	43	112
Art Howe	7	13.8	8.9	.0195	.269	39	9	109
Phil Garner	7	12.3	8.8	.0163	.260	49	68	103
Enos Cabell	8	9.4	8.1	.0088	.281	45	191	99

Not a particularly strong position for the Astros, so defensive standout **Doug Rader** (1967–75) was the starter. The Red Rooster won five Gold Glove Awards and hit 20 or more home runs three times.

I considered several other 3B candidates, but in the end, I went with **Morgan Ensberg** (2000, '02–07), who played most of his short career for the Astros and definitely had some pop in his bat. He hit 20+ HR three times, with his best year coming in 2005, his one year as an All-Star, when he hit .283 with 36 HR and 101 RBI.

You could make a case for Ken Caminiti (1987–94, 1999–2000) as the backup, as he was good with the glove at the hot corner. But his big-number seasons came later with San Diego, with most of his Astros years being of the .265, 30 doubles, 15 HR, 75 RBI variety.

Art Howe (1976–1982) split his time between 3B and 2B for the Astros, playing parts of seven years before later managing the club for five. But he never played in more than 125 games in a season, and he didn't have much power or speed.

Like Howe, Phil Garner (1981–87) also played a mix of 3B and 2B, both throughout his career and during his time in Houston. Also like Howe, he later managed the Astros for several years. As a player, his best two years in Houston were perhaps in 1982, when he had 13 HR and 24 SB, and 1983, when he had 14 HR and 18 SB.

Enos Cabell (1975–80, '84–85) was not a great gloveman at the hot corner, but he provided the Astros with some speed by stealing 30+ bases in four consecutive seasons. And lastly, Denny Walling (1977–88, '92) had a long major league career, 18 years in all with most of them spent playing for the Astros. He played a mix of 3B, 1B, and OF, but played in 100+ games in only 6 of his 13 seasons in Houston.

Shortstop

Name	YR	WAR	W3	W/G	AVG	HR	SB	OPS+
Carlos Correa	4	18.2	16.7	.0386	.277	81	32	129
Dickie Thon	7	16.1	14.7	.0284	.270	33	94	106
Adam Everett	7	12.4	9.6	.0191	.248	35	59	69
Craig Reynolds	11	9.8	7.6	.0084	.252	32	43	79
Denis Menke	5	9.1	8.9	.0144	.266	30	17	109

Like third base, shortstop has not historically been a position of strength for the Astros. At this point, I'm willing to give the starting spot to young superstar **Carlos Correa** (2015–18). Playing at the age of 20 for most of his rookie season, he hit .279 with 22 HR and 14 SB in only 99 games, good enough to take home Rookie of the Year honors. In 2016, his first full season, he hit 36 doubles and 20 HR with 96 RBI and 13 SB. An All-Star in 2017, injury limited him to only 109 games, but he still posted a career-high .315 average, 24 HR, and 82 runs scored. Although injury slowed him in 2018, Correa's future is very bright, and he should be with the Astros at least through 2021, further building his résumé for this dream team roster.

For the backup spot I went with **Dickie Thon** (1981–87), who like Correa seemed well on his way to having a good career for the Astros, as at age 25 he was an All-Star and hit .286 with 20 HR, 79 RBI, and 34 SB. But then he was hit in the eye with a pitch and understandably was never the same again as a player.

A few others deserve mention, starting with Craig Reynolds (1979–89). Only a .252 hitter with little power, he did surprise and lead the NL with 12 triples in strike-shortened 1981. While Reynolds played a long time for the Astros, he managed to play 130+ games in a season only four times.

Adam Everett (2001–07) was very good defensively but had only modest power and speed, and he played 130 or more games for the Astros in only two seasons. And lastly, Denis Menke (1968–71, '74) played only four full seasons for the Astros but was an All-Star in two of them, years in which he had double-digit HR and 90+ RBI.

Catcher

Name	YR	WAR	W3	W/G	AVG	HR	SB	OPS+
Jason Castro	6	9.5	7.6	.0154	.232	62	5	93
Alan Ashby	11	7.9	6.2	.0082	.252	69	3	98
Cliff Johnson	6	5.8	4.9	.0154	.256	52	1	142
Evan Gattis	4	5.4	5.0	.0110	.245	96	3	109
Johnny Edwards	6	5.0	4.1	.0079	.237	25	8	82
Brad Ausmus	10	5.0	4.7	.0040	.246	41	51	69

No offense to the guys listed above, but relatively speaking catcher for the Astros must be one of the weakest positions of any franchise in this book. This is a case where considering the career WAR values is of little help, as the differences in those values are very small.

After considering the six candidates listed above, I decided the two catchers for this roster should be **Brad Ausmus** (1997–98, 2001–08) and **Alan Ashby** (1979–89). Ausmus never had more than 10 homers in a season, though he did have above-average speed for a catcher (twice he had double-digit SB for the

Astros). His strength was less at the plate than behind it, as he provided great defense, taking home three Gold Glove Awards.

Alan Ashby was a good game-caller with a knack for helping hurlers achieve no-hitters, as he caught three of them: Ken Forsch, Nolan Ryan, and Mike Scott. Ashby played parts of 11 seasons for the Astros but never had over 400 AB in a year. He had a little more pop in his bat than Ausmus, but far less speed.

Jason Castro (2010, '12–16) was a recent low-average, moderate-power catcher for the Astros. He was an All-Star in 2013, when he had thus-far career highs of 18 HR and a .276 average. Cliff Johnson (1972–77) also provided some power to the Astros, while splitting his playing time between C, 1B, and OF. He hit 20 HR in only 340 AB in 1975 and had good plate discipline that produced a .370 OBP while with Houston. Johnny Edwards (1969–74) finished his career for the Astros and was a good defender but not much of a hitter. And lastly, Evan Gattis (2015-18) has by now switched to being primarily a DH, but with three seasons of 25+ HR he could one day crack this All-Time team.

Left Field

Name	YR	WAR	W3	W/G	AVG	HR	SB	OPS+
José Cruz	13	51.2	17.8	.0274	.292	138	288	125
Lance Berkman	12	48.0	19.3	.0302	.296	326	82	146
Bob Watson	14	23.5	12.5	.0170	.297	139	21	130
Luis Gonzalez	7	15.1	11.5	.0203	.266	62	63	107
Moises Alou	3	11.7	11.7	.0278	.331	95	19	148
Carlos Lee	6	8.8	9.1	.0108	.286	133	26	117

There were two top candidates in LF, and their career WAR for the Astros was nearly identical. Due to higher peak performances, I gave the top spot to **Lance Berkman** (1999–2010), who actually split his time between 1B and the OF for the Astros. He had ten consecutive seasons of 20+ homers, with highs of 42 in 2002 and 45 in 2006. Arguably his best statistical season came in 2001, when he smashed 55 doubles and 34 HR, had 126 RBI, and batted .331. A five-time All-Star, other highlights include leading the NL in RBI with 128 in 2002, driving in 136 runs in 2006, and posting an impressive .410 OBP for Houston.

After several unimpressive seasons for the Cardinals, **José Cruz** (1975–87) played 13 seasons for the Astros, with a few seasons as their regular RF, but far more spent in LF. He provided ample speed on the bases, a .292 average, and about 10 to 15 HR a year. Only an All-Star twice, he had five seasons of 30+ SB, with a high of 44 in 1977.

As mentioned earlier, **Bob Watson** (1966–79) played more games at 1B (790) than OF (568), but there is more room for him here on this roster. A .297 hitter for the Astros, his best years were in 1976 and 1977, when he managed 102 and 110 RBI, respectively. A two-time All-Star, Watson also sticks in my memory as being the answer to an impossible trivia question: he was supposedly the player who scored Major League Baseball's one millionth run.

Three other Astros LF deserve brief mention, starting with Luis Gonzalez (1990–95). He started his impressive career for the Astros, though his power stroke only developed later in his 30s while playing for Arizona. Moises Alou (1998, 2000–01) had three strong seasons for the Astros, in which he posted 27 to 38 HR, 100+ RBI, and a .310+ average. And Carlos Lee (2007–12) was a solid power source for the Astros and hit between 18 and 32 HR in his five full seasons, including 32 HR and 119 RBI in 2007, his one All-Star year with the club.

Center Field

Name	YR	WAR	W3	W/G	AVG	HR	SB	OPS+
César Cedeño	12	49.6	21.1	.0328	.289	163	487	129
Jim Wynn	11	41.4	20.0	.0290	.255	223	180	131
Steve Finley	4	16.0	13.5	.0287	.281	32	110	107
Michael Bourn	4	12.1	12.7	.0224	.271	11	193	89

As with LF, there are two clear top choices for this dream team in CF, and you could make an argument for either as the starter. I thought four-time All-Star **César Cedeño** (1970–81) was the more deserving of that honor, as he stole 50+ bases in six consecutive seasons, provided some power, and took home five Gold Glove Awards patrolling CF in the Astrodome.

Jimmy "The Toy Cannon" Wynn (1963–73) provided a lot of power to the Astros, with seven seasons of 20+ homers, including a high of 37 in 1967. He also managed 20+ steals three times, with a high of 43 in his first full season in 1965.

Two other Astros CF deserve mention, starting with Steve Finley (1991–94), who played for the Astros in four seasons early in his career and stole 34 bases in 1991 and 44 the following year. He was a great defender, but like Gonzalez his power didn't surface until later with the Padres and Diamondbacks. And Michael Bourn (2008–2011) provided even more speed on the bases, as he had 41 SB in 2008, then led the NL with 61 in 2009, 52 in 2010, and 61 in 2011 (a season he ended with the Braves after being traded at the July deadline). He also provided stellar defense in CF, taking home two Gold Glove Awards.

Right Field

Name	YR	WAR	W3	W/G	AVG	HR	SB	OPS+
Terry Puhl	14	28.4	13.3	.0187	.281	62	217	112
George Springer	5	18.7	14.0	.0300	.265	121	41	127
Richard Hidalgo	8	17.6	14.0	.0216	.278	134	44	115
Kevin Bass	10	16.5	11.2	.0147	.278	87	120	111
Hunter Pence	5	16.0	10.6	.0235	.290	103	61	117
Rusty Staub	6	13.6	11.9	.0163	.273	57	8	117
Derek Bell	5	11.4	10.9	.0167	.284	74	102	104

Historically for the Astros, RF hasn't been nearly as strong as LF and CF. I noted earlier that Berkman and Cruz spent some time in RF, but in terms of players making this roster as primarily a RF, I opted to include only **Terry Puhl** (1977–90). Nearly a lifetime Astro (he played 15 games for Kansas City in his last season in 1991), the Canadian-born player was not flashy, but was a consistent hitter with some speed (six seasons with 20+ steals.)

That said, things are looking better in RF these days, as current Astros star George Springer (2014–18) will likely soon force his way onto this All-Time team. He managed 20 HR in only 78 games in his rookie season, and then two years later played all 162 games and scored 116 runs with 29 HR. Providing a lot of power out of the leadoff spot, he was an All-Star for the first time in 2017 and ended the regular season with 112 runs and a career-high 34 HR. After a mixed performance in the first two rounds of the playoffs, he blew up in the World Series, batting .379 with 5 HR and 3 doubles, taking home the WS MVP Award.

Several others deserved consideration, starting with Kevin Bass (1982–89, '93–94), who had two stints in Houston and provided a good combination of speed and power. His best season statistically was his one All-Star year in 1986, when he batted .311 with 20 HR and 22 SB.

Richard Hidalgo (1997–2004) had a few good campaigns and one outstanding season, as in 2000 he posted 44 HR, 122 RBI, and a .314 average. Hunter Pence (2007–11) started his fine career in Houston and was an All-Star there twice. He provided the Astros with a good combination of power and speed, including 25 HR each year from 2008 through 2010. Rusty Staub (1963–68) started his long career with six seasons in Houston. He was an All-Star there twice, including in 1967, when he hit .333 and led the NL in doubles with 44. And Derek Bell (1995–99) provided both power and speed for the Astros, including two seasons with 100+ RBI and SB highs of 27 and 29.

Starting Pitching

Name	YR	WAR	W3	W-L	ERA	WHIP	ERA+
Roy Oswalt	10	46.0	19.6	143-82	3.24	1.196	133
Larry Dierker	13	32.0	17.1	137-117	3.28	1.214	104
Don Wilson	9	27.9	14.8	104-92	3.15	1.212	109
Mike Scott	9	23.9	18.1	110-81	3.30	1.144	107
Nolan Ryan	9	23.5	13.0	106-94	3.13	1.206	110
Joe Niekro	11	23.2	11.8	144-116	3.22	1.264	105
J.R. Richard	10	22.3	15.2	107-71	3.15	1.243	108
Shane Reynolds	11	19.5	11.7	103-86	3.95	1.292	106
Ken Forsch	11	18.3	9.1	78-81	3.18	1.250	108
Dallas Keuchel	7	18.1	16.1	76-63	3.66	1.250	108
Mike Hampton	7	17.8	13.9	76-50	3.59	1.370	114
Roger Clemens	3	17.2	17.2	38-18	2.40	1.074	180
Turk Farrell	6	16.3	14.6	53-64	3.42	1.142	100
Wade Miller	6	14.1	12.1	58-39	3.87	1.309	117
Mike Cuellar	4	13.2	12.6	37-36	2.74	1.162	119
Bob Knepper	9	9.4	10.1	93-100	3.66	1.306	94
Darryl Kile	7	6.2	7.8	71-65	3.79	1.408	100

Roy Oswalt (2001–10) seemed to be the clear choice for the top spot on this All-Time team's pitching staff. He went 14-3 and 19-9 in his first two seasons, before injuries held him to a 10-5 record in 2003. But he came back strong to post 20-10 and 20-12 seasons and led the NL with a 2.98 ERA in 2006. A three-time All-Star, his .636 winning percentage for the Astros is outstanding, and he twice had 200+ strikeouts.

After Oswalt at the top, the order of the next six starters on this roster could be debated indefinitely. In deference to his highest WAR total, I'll start with **Larry Dierker** (1964–76). He pitched all but his final season for the Astros, with his best year being 1969, when he went 20-13 with a 2.33 ERA and 232 K. A two-time All-Star, he is the franchise's all-time leader in games started, innings pitched, complete games, and shutouts. He was also the club's manager from 1997 through 2001, leading them to the division crown in four of those five seasons, and also had a long tenure as the franchise's broadcaster.

Mike Scott (1983–91) was a three-time All-Star and was the first Astros pitcher to take home the Cy Young Award. Scott earned that during his career year of 1986, when he used his split-fingered fastball to lead Houston to the division title with an 18-10 record, 2.22 ERA, 306 strikeouts, and division-clinching no-hitter on September 25th against the Giants.

J.R. Richard (1971–80) had a relatively short career but was a very intimidating pitcher, especially against right-handed batters, who managed to hit only

.187 against him. Richard won 20 games in 1976 and 18 games a year from 1977 through '79. He led the NL in strikeouts twice, with 303 in 1978 and 313 in 1979. He was doing great in 1980 with a 10-4 record and 1.90 ERA when his career was tragically cut short by a stroke at age 30.

The knuckleballing **Joe Niekro** (1975–85) attained the 20-win plateau twice, going 21-11 in 1979 and 20-12 in 1980. He actually pitched in more games in relief than as a starter in his first three seasons in Houston, having been used that way some on previous teams as well. He nonetheless remains the franchise's all-time leader in wins with a modest total of 144.

Don Wilson (1966–74) pitched his entire, relatively short career for the Astros. He had 15+ wins three times and posted no-hit games in 1967 and 1969. As with Richard, it was tragedy that ended his playing career too soon— in this case, his untimely death at age 29.

Nolan Ryan (1980–88) recorded 1,866 K in 1,855 IP but never won more than 16 games in a year for the Astros. His 1987 season was particularly strange, as he led the NL with a 2.76 ERA and 270 strikeouts, but he posted a horrible 8-16 record due largely to poor run support. Ryan also pitched one of his seven no-hitters while with the Astros, on September 26, 1981, at home against the Dodgers.

After those seven, there were several other candidates to consider for this All-Time team's pitching staff. In the end, I decided to include two more starters, and went with guys with strong peak performances. **Roger Clemens** (2004–06) at age 41 won the NL Cy Young Award after posting an 18-4 record and 2.98 ERA. In 2005, at age 42, he went 13-8 and led the NL with an amazing 1.87 ERA. He saw less action in 2006, his second-to-last season in the majors, but still posted a 2.30 ERA in 19 starts.

Mike Hampton (1994–99, '2009) had one great season for the Astros in 1999, when he was runner-up for the NL Cy Young Award after going 22-4 with a 2.90 ERA. Hampton was also a more capable hitter than most pitchers, taking home the Silver Slugger Award in 1999 and doing the same the four following years with different clubs.

You could also make a case for current Astros hurler Dallas Keuchel (2012– 18). His 2015 campaign was outstanding, earning him the AL Cy Young Award after he posted a 20-8 record, 2.48 ERA, 216 K, and 1.017 WHIP. He had a down year in 2016 but came back in 2017 to post a 2.90 ERA and 14-5 record in only 23 starts. He also fields his position quite well, having already taken home three Gold Glove Awards.

Shane Reynolds (1992–2002) pitched most of his career for the Astros, was selected as an All-Star once, had three seasons with 16+ wins, and had two with 200+ strikeouts. His best year was 1998, when he posted a 19-8 record.

Amongst others, Ken Forsch (1970–80) was an interesting case, as he logged quality time as a starter (no-hitting Atlanta in 1979) but pitched more games as a reliever, notching 50 saves, including 19 with a 2.15 ERA in 1976.

Turk Farrell (1962–1967) toiled for the early Colt .45s and Astros and represented them at the All-Star Game three times, even though his records those years were only 10-20, 11-10, and 11-11. Overlapping some with Farrell was Mike Cuellar, who posted an impressive 2.22 ERA in 1966 and was an All-Star the following year before moving on and having far greater success for the Orioles.

Wade Miller (1999–2004) won between 14 and 16 games for the Astros from 2001 to '03 and had a respectable .598 winning percentage. Bob Knepper (1981–89) was an All-Star twice and posted 14 to 17 wins for the Astros four times. And Darryl Kile (1991–97) was also a two-time All-Star, including in 1997, when he posted a 19-7 record and 2.57 ERA. He also pitched a no-hitter against the Mets in 1993.

Relief Pitching

Name	YR	WAR	W3	SV	W-L	ERA	WHIP	ERA+
Billy Wagner	9	16.2	10.0	225	26-29	2.53	1.039	171
Dave Smith	11	12.8	7.3	199	53-47	2.53	1.189	137
Joe Sambito	8	10.7	7.8	72	33-32	2.42	1.112	140
Octavio Dotel	5	10.5	9.6	42	22-24	3.25	1.169	142
Larry Anderson	5	7.9	6.1	20	22-16	2.57	1.211	141
Brad Lidge	6	7.1	7.0	123	23-20	3.30	1.197	133
Hal Woodeshick	4	7.0	6.2	36	21-38	3.16	1.324	110

Flamethrowing left-hander **Billy Wagner** (1995–2003) had an eye-popping K/IP ratio: 694/504, or 12.4 per 9 innings of work. His 1999 season was one of the most dominating ever recorded: 39 SV, 1.57 ERA, and 124 K in only 74.2 IP. His 2000 season was lost to injury, but he came back strong to post consecutive seasons of 39, 35, and 44 saves.

Dave Smith (1980–1990) pitched all but his final two seasons for the Astros. A two-time All-Star but generally overshadowed by his flashier contemporaries, Smith consistently had an ERA well below 3.00 and managed 20 or more saves for six consecutive seasons.

Like Wagner, **Brad Lidge** (2002–07) struck out batters at an impressive rate (561 K in 401 IP). In 2004 he had 29 saves, a 1.90 ERA, and an insane 157 K in 94.2 IP. He followed that up in 2005 with 42 saves and a 2.29 ERA.

Joe Sambito (1976–82, '84) posted 20 or more saves only once, but his ERA with the Astros was an impressive 2.42. Octavio Dotel (2000–2004) was mostly a setup man for the Astros early in his career, before moving on to pitch for an impressive total of 11 other teams. Larry Andersen was also largely used as a setup man rather than closer for the Astros, posting a respectable 2.57 for Houston. And lastly, Hal Woodeshick was an early reliever in Houston, posting a 1.97 ERA in 1963 and leading the league with 23 saves in 1964.

Managers

Name	YR	From-To	W-L	PCT	PS	WS
Larry Dierker	5	1997–2001	433-348	.556	5	0
AJ Hinch	4	2015–18	374-274	.577	3	1
Bill Virdon	8	1975–82	544-522	.510	2	0
Phil Garner	4	2004–07	277-252	.524	2	0
Bob Lillis	4	1982–85	276-261	.514	0	0
Harry Walker	5	1968–72	355-353	.501	0	0
Art Howe	5	1989–93	392-418	.484	0	0

You could argue how to rank the managers listed above, as it is hard to compare the five postseasons of **Larry Dierker**, **AJ Hinch** leading the team to the franchise's lone World Series championship in 2017, and the longevity of **Bill Virdon**. I went with that order and chose **Phil Garner** to round out a top four.

Starting Lineup

What would mythical starting lineups look like for this All-Time roster?

Against RHP:
Craig Biggio 2B (R)
José Altuve DH (R)
José Cruz LF (L)
Lance Berkman RF (S)
Jeff Bagwell 1B (R)
César Cedeño CF (R)
Carlos Correa SS (R)
Doug Rader 3B (R)
Alan Ashby C (S)

Against LHP:
Craig Biggio 2B (R)
José Altuve DH (R)
César Cedeño CF (R)
Jeff Bagwell 1B (R)
Jim Wynn LF (R)
Carlos Correa SS (R)
Lance Berkman RF (S)
Doug Rader 3B (R)
Brad Ausmus C (R)

The first seven spots in these lineups are strong and could be rearranged in a variety of ways. And this is good because the last two spots are much weaker offensively. Cruz didn't hit lefties very well, so since Wynn did play some LF I have platooned them there. Berkman was a switch-hitter, but he didn't hit lefties nearly as well as righties, so I dropped him in the order. And against some right-handers, if you want to cheat you could ask Biggio to get behind the plate, which would allow Altuve to play 2B and get Wynn's big bat in the lineup as the DH.

Depth Chart

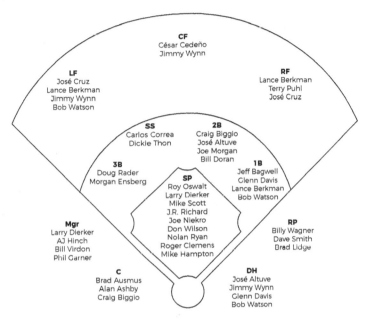

CF
César Cedeño
Jimmy Wynn

LF
José Cruz
Lance Berkman
Jimmy Wynn
Bob Watson

RF
Lance Berkman
Terry Puhl
José Cruz

SS
Carlos Correa
Dickie Thon

2B
Craig Biggio
José Altuve
Joe Morgan
Bill Doran

3B
Doug Rader
Morgan Ensberg

SP
Roy Oswalt
Larry Dierker
Mike Scott
J.R. Richard
Joe Niekro
Don Wilson
Nolan Ryan
Roger Clemens
Mike Hampton

1B
Jeff Bagwell
Glenn Davis
Lance Berkman
Bob Watson

Mgr
Larry Dierker
AJ Hinch
Bill Virdon
Phil Garner

RP
Billy Wagner
Dave Smith
Brad Lidge

C
Brad Ausmus
Alan Ashby
Craig Biggio

DH
José Altuve
Jimmy Wynn
Glenn Davis
Bob Watson

Prospects for Current Players

What are the prospects of current Astros players making this All-Time team? Altuve and Correa are already on this roster. I think it is very likely Springer and Keuchel will join them soon, and others such as Alex Bregman, Evan Gattis, Justin Verlander, or Gerrit Cole could one day too. We'll see...

Retired Player Numbers

Jeff Bagwell (5), Craig Biggio (7), Jimmy Wynn (24), José Cruz (25), Jim Umbricht (32), Mike Scott (33), Nolan Ryan (34), Don Wilson (40), Larry Dierker (49)

Of note here is Jim Umbricht, a reliever who came back after a cancer operation in March of 1963 to post a 4-3 record and a 2.61 ERA, but then died of cancer in April the next year. The team retired his number in 1965.

Selections from Other Authors and Fan Surveys

1992: The All-Time All-Star Baseball Book, by Nick Acocella and Donald Dewey

For the lineup they selected Watson, Morgan, Rader, Metzger, Cedeño, Wynn, Cruz, and Ashby. Not bad, though I would have preferred Thon and even Reynolds over Metzger at SS. They went with J.R. Richard as the pitcher, but wrote: "Yes, Mike Scott and Nolan Ryan were great, but no pitcher in an Astros uniform came so close to dominating the game for a few years as did our selection." The list of honorable mentions included Scott, Ryan, Dierker, Puhl, and Davis.

1995: Baseball Ratings, by Charles F. Faber

The Faber system as applied in 1995 created a reasonable all-time team. Watson beat out Davis at 1B, Doran topped Morgan at 2B, as did Metzger over Reynolds at SS. The others were all the same as my choices would have been in 1995: Rader, Ashby, Cedeño, Wynn, and Cruz.

2003: Rob Neyer's Big Book of Baseball Lineups, by Rob Neyer

Neyer's choices were very similar to mine. He had Ashby and Edwards as the catchers and Reynolds and Thon at SS. His starting OF picks were Cruz, Cedeño, and Puhl, with the backups being Watson, Wynn, and Bass.

The one selection I understand the least is Neyer's choice of Mike Hampton as the first starting pitcher. His 22-4 season in 1999 was impressive, but back in 2003 I would have rated him at best seventh amongst Astros starting pitchers. After Hampton he included Ryan, Richard, Wilson Scott, Niekro, Dierker, and Forsch. His two relief choices of Smith and Wagner were obvious ones, regardless of order.

Top WAR Single Seasons – Hitters (7+)

Name	Year	WAR	AVG	HR	R	RBI	SB	OPS+
Craig Biggio	1997	9.4	.309	22	146	81	47	143
José Altuve	2017	8.3	.346	24	112	81	32	164
Jeff Bagwell	1994	8.2	.368	39	104	116	15	213
César Cedeño	1972	8.0	.320	22	103	82	55	162
Jeff Bagwell	1997	7.7	.286	43	109	135	31	168
José Altuve	2016	7.7	.338	24	108	96	30	155
Jeff Bagwell	1996	7.5	.315	31	111	120	21	178

Jeff Bagwell	1999	7.4	.304	42	143	126	30	164
Jim Wynn	1965	7.4	.275	22	90	73	43	144
Dickie Thon	1983	7.4	.286	20	81	79	34	127
César Cedeño	1973	7.3	.320	25	86	70	56	152
Jim Wynn	1969	7.1	.269	33	113	87	23	166

Biggio is in the top spot but had only one season with a 7+ WAR. Bagwell had four, with his 1994 MVP season coming in third overall—especially impressive as that was a strike-shortened season where the Astros played only 115 games. Nice to see Thon's breakout 1983 campaign on this list too.

Top WAR Single Seasons – Pitchers (7+)

Name	Year	WAR	W-L	ERA	IP	SO	ERA+
Larry Dierker	1969	8.4	20-13	2.33	305.1	232	152
Roger Clemens	2005	8.2	13-8	1.87	211.1	185	226
Mike Scott	1986	8.2	18-10	2.22	275.1	306	161
Mike Hampton	1999	7.8	22-4	2.90	239.0	177	155
Turk Farrell	1962	7.3	10-20	3.02	241.2	203	124
Dallas Keuchel	2015	7.2	20-8	2.48	232.0	216	157

Interesting mix of names here, and Nolan Ryan and J.R. Richard don't appear at all. I wasn't surprised to see Dierker's 1969 season and Mike Scott's 1986 season at or near the top. And I would have guessed that one of Clemens' two full seasons would be on this list as well, but I was initially a bit surprised that it was his 13-8 2005 season rather than his 18-4 2004 season. The difference was in his ERA those two seasons: a league-leading 1.87 in 2005 vs. 2.98 in 2004.

But the biggest head-scratcher on this list has to be Turk Farrell's 1962 season. Admittedly, his 10-20 record is far worse than he deserved given the rest of his stats that year. It was more indicative of the fact that this was the franchise's first season, during which they posted a 64-96 (.400) record. Farrell was asked to do a lot that year: 29 games started, 11 complete games (2 shutouts), plus 14 games pitched in relief, including 4 saves. But still... the fifth- best pitching WAR coming from a 10-20 season is odd to see.

Franchise Player

This honorary choice came down to two guys: Craig Biggio and Jeff Bagwell. Some of Bagwell's seasons provided Houston fans with impressive numbers. But I decided to go with Biggio in part because he was able to stay productive for the team longer and because of his rare up-the-middle position versatility (2B, CF, C). He is also the franchise's all-time leader in games played, at-bats, hits, runs, doubles, and total bases, while ranking second in RBI, walks, and SB, and a respectable third in HR.

CHAPTER 20

The Nationals Franchise All-Time Dream Team

It felt a little strange to consider this the All-Time team for the "Washington Nationals." That franchise was of course the Montreal Expos from its birth in 1969 until 2004. As a small-market team, and one with abysmal attendance for many years north of the border, their economics just seemed to get worse and worse. Several times starting in the 1990s, the Expos would develop fine young players, only to see them leave town when they could command top dollar. Not coincidentally, the Expos never had much success, leading their division only once, in strike-shortened 1994.

Things didn't improve when the team moved to Washington and became the Nationals, as they finished in last place in all but one of their first six seasons in DC. Things changed by 2012, with the arrival of 19-year-old phenom Bryce Harper and 23-year-old hurler Stephen Strasburg. Since then, the Nationals have finished either first or second in the NL East, though they have yet to make it to the World Series.

Even without such ultimate success (yet), this franchise's All-Time team definitely has some bright spots. There are some relatively weak positions too, but overall it would be competitive with many other expansion-era dream teams.

1st Base

Name	YR	WAR	W3	W/G	AVG	HR	SB	OPS+
Ryan Zimmerman	14	38.0	18.1	.0235	.279	264	43	117
Ron Fairly	6	17.6	12.0	.0245	.276	86	19	128
Nick Johnson	5	11.1	9.7	.0228	.280	56	21	129
Andrés Galarraga	8	10.1	9.9	.0106	.269	115	56	109
Mike Jorgensen	6	9.2	8.3	.0137	.254	57	41	110
Al Oliver	2	6.7	6.7	.0211	.315	30	6	131
Tony Pérez	3	6.6	6.6	.0152	.281	46	8	115

First base has not historically been a strong position for this franchise. After reviewing all the options here and at other positions, I decided to go with **Ryan Zimmerman** (2005–18) for the top spot here, even though he only shifted to 1B from 3B in 2015. Although injuries have often reduced his production, Zim has still managed to have seven seasons with 20+ HR so far, including 2009, when he belted 33 HR with 106 RBI and 110 runs, and 2017, when he had a career-high 36 HR. In fact, as of now he is the career leader in HR and RBI for this franchise. A good defender at the hot corner early in his career, he earned the Gold Glove Award in 2009.

If I hadn't shifted Zimmerman over to 1B, then the starter here would have been **Ron Fairly** (1969–74), who after playing a decade with the Dodgers joined the Expos and had double-digit HR in each of his six seasons. He was an All-Star in 1973, when he batted .298 with 17 HR. Fairly was a .276 hitter but had a more impressive .381 OBP.

I did consider a few others briefly, starting with Andrés Galarraga (1985–91, 2002), who started his career in Montreal and then returned in 2002 in a part-time role at the age of 41. In his youth, The Big Cat was a good defender, earning two Gold Glove Awards. He was also productive with the bat, hitting 20+ HR three times and driving in 85+ RBI four times, though his biggest numbers came later for the Rockies and Braves.

Nick Johnson (2004–06, '08–09) was a .280 hitter with a great eye, as he had a .408 OBP in his five partial seasons with the Expos and Nationals. But he played in 130+ games only twice for this franchise, so I couldn't see choosing him for this All-Time team.

Mike Jorgensen (1972–77) had a little pop and was a pretty good fielder, taking home the Gold Glove Award in 1973. Tony Pérez (1977–79) had three fine seasons as an Expo late in his career, and Al Oliver (1982–83) was an All-Star in his two years with the club at the end of his career, including in 1982, when he led the NL with a .331 average, 109 RBI, 43 doubles, and 204 hits.

2nd Base

Name	YR	WAR	W3	W/G	AVG	HR	SB	OPS+
Anthony Rendon	6	21.1	16.8	.0268	.285	102	40	120
José Vidro	10	16.2	13.1	.0137	.310	115	21	111
Ron Hunt	4	12.7	11.2	.0250	.277	5	26	103
Mike Lansing	5	10.7	7.9	.0158	.276	49	96	93
Delino DeShields	4	9.9	8.7	.0184	.277	23	187	106

There were a few different ways I considered 2B and 3B for this team, but as 2B is the weaker position, I decided to select current star **Anthony Rendon** (2013–18) for this spot. He started out playing more 2B than 3B, but when Zimmerman moved to 1B he became the Nationals' everyday 3B. He led the NL with 111 runs in 2014 and had a career-high 25 HR and 100 RBI in 2017, and then a .310 average in 2018.

After poor rookie and sophomore seasons, **José Vidro** (1997–2006) batted over .300 for five consecutive years and was regularly amongst the league leaders in doubles. The three-time All-Star's best season was 2000, when he hit .330 with 24 HR, 97 RBI, 101 runs, 200 hits, and 51 doubles. Not a particularly good fielder, but his hitting was good enough to earn him the backup spot here.

I considered three other candidates, starting with Delino DeShields (1990–93), who played his first four seasons in Montreal. Not a great fielder, he definitely could run, posting SB totals of 42, 56, 46, and 43. Mike Lansing (1993–97) was a pretty good all-around player in his five years in Montreal and was able to play several infield positions. His highest SB total was 27 in 1995, and his highest HR total was 20 in 1997.

And lastly, Ron Hunt (1971–74) had virtually no power and very little speed on the basepaths. What he was good at was getting plunked. He led the NL in hit by pitches seven years in a row, including all four with the Expos. In fact, in 1971 he set the post-1900 major league record by being hit 50 times, far ahead of second place in the NL—teammate Rusty Staub, who had all of 9. The closest anyone has come since is 35 HBP by Don Baylor in 1986. Between all of these free passes, plus his walks, his OBP was an impressive .390 for the Expos.

3rd Base

Name	YR	WAR	W3	W/G	AVG	HR	SB	OPS+
Ryan Zimmerman	14	38.0	18.1	.0235	.279	264	43	117
Tim Wallach	13	36.8	14.8	.0208	.259	204	50	105
Anthony Rendon	6	21.1	16.8	.0268	.285	102	40	120
Bob Bailey	7	18.3	12.7	.0192	.264	118	40	123
Larry Parrish	8	10.8	9.0	.0111	.263	100	17	104

Tim Wallach (1980–92) was a great defensive 3B, taking home three Gold Glove Awards. He also hit 20+ HR in 4 of his 11 full seasons. His biggest numbers came in 1987, when he batted .298 with 26 HR, 123 RBI, and 42 doubles, which was good enough to come in fourth in the NL MVP vote.

Bob Bailey (1969–75) played seven years in Montreal, hitting 20+ HR three times. His defense at 3B wasn't very strong, so he also played a lot of games at LF and 1B.

This leaves out slugger Larry Parrish (1974–81), who had several fine seasons in Montreal in the first half of his career, though his best offensive numbers came later for the Rangers. His standout season for the Expos was 1979, when he hit .307 with 30 HR and 39 doubles.

Shortstop

Name	YR	WAR	W3	W/G	AVG	HR	SB	OPS+
Ian Desmond	7	15.5	10.9	.0167	.264	110	122	99
Trea Turner	4	10.4	10.1	.0289	.289	44	124	109
Orlando Cabrera	8	9.5	8.9	.0105	.267	66	93	84
Chris Speier	8	9.4	5.9	.0105	.245	29	6	83
Hubie Brooks	5	8.7	9.7	.0134	.279	75	27	111
Spike Owen	4	6.4	5.9	.0116	.247	21	22	96
Wil Cordero	7	3.8	4.5	.0059	.274	59	40	99

Like 1B, this franchise did not have very strong SS candidates for this All-Time team. **Ian Desmond** (2009–15) was productive for the Nationals long enough that he earned the top spot, as he provided a good combination of power and speed with three seasons of 20+ HR and four with 20+ SB.

There was no clear choice for the backup spot, but in the end, I went with **Hubie Brooks** (1985–89). His five years in Montreal were split between SS (344) and OF (289), and he wasn't strong defensively at either. A two-time All-Star, he had some pop: he hit 20 HR once and drove in 100 RBI in 1985 (a year when he had only 13 HR). He was having a career year in 1985, batting .340 with 14 HR in 80 games, when injuries struck.

You could make a case for youngster **Trea Turner** (2015-18), who hit .342 with 33 SB during half a season in 2016 and then stole 46 bases in 2017. His best season so far came in 2018, when he scored 103 runs, with 19 HR, and a league-leading 43 SB. With just one more good season Trea will likely deserve at least the backup SS spot on this roster.

Orlando Cabrera (1997–2004) provided good defense, taking home the Gold Glove Award in 2001. He had a little power and also ran pretty well, so you could make a case for him as the backup over Brooks. Chris Speier (1977–84) was a fairly good defensive SS for the Expos for many years, but he was a very light hitter (.245) and didn't steal bases either. Wil Cordero (1992–95, 2002–03) started his career as a good-hitting but poor-fielding shortstop in Montreal, and he returned as an OF/1B several years later. And finally, Spike Owen (1989–92) played SS for the Expos for four years, but like Speier was a light hitter with little power or speed.

Catcher

Name	YR	WAR	W3	W/G	AVG	HR	SB	OPS+
Gary Carter	12	55.6	23.1	.0370	.269	220	34	121
Wilson Ramos	7	9.8	7.5	.0170	.268	83	0	100
Brian Schneider	8	6.7	6.7	.0089	.252	47	4	82
Darrin Fletcher	6	3.4	3.8	.0053	.266	61	1	95
Mike Fitzgerald	7	2.1	4.1	.0033	.238	39	28	93

After a brief rookie season, **Gary Carter** (1974–84, '92) spent his next ten seasons in Montreal, returning eight years later for a final season in 1992. The Kid was an outstanding defensive catcher (three Gold Glove Awards) and was also a great hitter, especially for his position. He had six 20+-HR seasons and two with 100+ RBI. He was runner-up for the 1980 NL MVP Award (Mike Schmidt was the unanimous choice).

Wilson Ramos (2010–16) recently provided the Nationals with good defense and some power, with 2016 being his best season, as he made the All-Star squad and hit .307 with 22 HR and 80 RBI.

Before Ramos, the backup would have been a tough choice, with arguably the top candidate being Brian Schneider (2000–07), who was a good defensive catcher for this franchise for five years. Darrin Fletcher (1992–97) played in 100+ games for the Expos only three times but had double-digit HR four times, with a peak of 17 in 1997. And Mike Fitzgerald (1985–91) played 100+ games for the Expos four times, but he had little power and only a .238 average.

Left Field

Name	YR	WAR	W3	W/G	AVG	HR	SB	OPS+
Tim Raines	13	48.9	20.7	.0337	.301	96	635	131
Warren Cromartie	9	15.5	9.3	.0149	.280	60	49	104
Moises Alou	6	12.3	10.1	.0202	.292	84	53	120
Brad Wilkerson	5	10.7	10.2	.0164	.256	83	43	111

Tim "Rock" Raines (1979–1990, 2001) finally made the Hall of Fame in 2017, and I think deservedly so. He played the first half of his career in Montreal and essentially had all of his best seasons there. He had six consecutive years with 70+ SB from 1981 through '86 (yes, he even had 71 steals in 88 games in the strike-shortened 1981 season). A seven-time All-Star, Raines scored 100+ runs four times and batted .300+ five times, winning the batting title in 1986 with a .334 mark.

No other outfielder for this franchise who primarily played LF did quite enough to earn a spot on this All-Time team roster. Warren Cromartie (1974, '76–83) came closest, as he played nearly his entire career with the Expos and was a consistent if not spectacular hitter of the .280, 10 HR, 35 doubles variety. Moises Alou (1990, '92–96) had most of his best seasons for other teams later in his career, but he was amongst the league leaders in several categories in strike-shortened 1994, finishing third in that year's NL MVP vote. And lastly, Brad Wilkerson (2001–05) provided the Expos with some power, with a peak of 32 HR in 2004.

Center Field

Name	YR	WAR	W3	W/G	AVG	HR	SB	OPS+
Andre Dawson	11	48.1	22.1	.0333	.280	225	253	122
Marquis Grissom	6	19.8	15.7	.0284	.279	54	266	101
Rondell White	8	19.2	12.1	.0259	.293	101	88	113

Predating Raines by a few years, **Andre Dawson** (1976–86) won the Rookie of the Year Award in 1977 after hitting .282 with 19 HR. He went on to provide a good combination of speed and power, hitting 20+ HR seven times and stealing 20+ bases seven times (five times a 20/20 man). He managed 100+ RBI as an Expo only once, but he was an excellent fielder, taking home four Gold Glove Awards as a CF and two more as a RF for the Expos. The Hawk was a three-time All-Star while in Montreal, and was MVP runner-up in both 1981 and 1983.

In the early 1990s, **Marquis Grissom** (1989–94) filled the base-stealing void that Raines' departure had created, as he stole 76, 78, and 53 bases in his three full seasons. He also hit double-digit HR three times, scored 90+ runs three times, and was an excellent center fielder (two Gold Glove Awards for the Expos).

Rondell White (1993–2000) had eight injury-plagued partial seasons in Montreal, but while on the field he did enough to warrant one of the "extra spots" on this All-Time team. He managed two 20+-HR seasons, several with double-digit steals, had a .293 average, and was a good fielder when able-bodied.

Right Field

Name	YR	WAR	W3	W/G	AVG	HR	SB	OPS+
Vladimir Guerrero	8	34.6	20.3	.0345	.323	234	123	148
Bryce Harper	7	27.4	19.9	.0296	.279	184	75	139
Larry Walker	6	21.1	14.5	.0313	.281	99	98	128
Rusty Staub	4	18.5	18.4	.0357	.295	81	24	149
Ellis Valentine	7	16.8	13.3	.0263	.288	95	56	121

Vladimir Guerrero (1996–2003) hit over .300 in all of his full seasons in Montreal, and for five consecutive seasons had 34 to 44 HR, 100+ runs, and 100+ RBI. In 2001–02 he increased his running rate, swiping 37 and 40 bases, respectively. Unfortunately, as with many stars of this franchise, they couldn't afford to keep him forever, and after the 2003 season he signed with the Angels as a free agent. He promptly took home the AL MVP trophy with yet another fine performance.

Bryce Harper (2012–18) was only 25 in 2018 but has already been an All-Star six times. He won the MVP Award in 2015 after posting a .330 average, .460 OBP, 118 runs, 42 HR, and 99 RBI. In 2018 he only batted .249 but hit 34 HR and finally tallied 100 RBI for the first time.

Larry Walker (1989–94) provided fine offensive production (15+ HR and 10+ SB) in his five years as an Expos regular, and he was a star fielder (two Gold Glove Awards), but his best seasons came later in Colorado.

Rusty Staub (1969–71, '79) represented the Expos as an All-Star in their first three years as a franchise. He batted .302 with 29 HR in 1969, and had 30 HR and 94 RBI the next year. Le Grand Orange was the Expos' most popular player in their early years, and his production was just strong enough to warrant the other "extra spot" on this All-Time team roster.

Lastly, you could make a case for yet another RF, as Ellis Valentine (1975–81) was an All-Star in 1977, the first of three solid offensive seasons of 20+ HR, 75+ RBI, and 10+ SB. He also won a Gold Glove Award and was known for his strong throwing arm.

Starting Pitching

Name	YR	WAR	W3	W-L	ERA	WHIP	ERA+
Steve Rogers	13	45.1	19.1	158-152	3.17	1.232	116
Max Scherzer	4	30.7	24.4	68-32	2.71	0.926	156
Dennis Martínez	8	29.7	15.1	100-72	3.06	1.147	122
Stephen Strasburg	9	27.3	14.1	94-52	3.14	1.094	129
Jordan Zimmerman	7	21.0	14.0	70-50	3.32	1.159	118
Liván Hernández	7	20.2	15.7	70-72	3.98	1.349	106

Gio González	7	20.0	13.9	86-65	3.62	1.283	112
Javier Vázquez	6	19.9	17.4	64-68	4.16	1.274	107
Pedro Martínez	4	18.9	16.7	55-33	3.06	1.089	139
Bryn Smith	9	17.4	11.4	81-71	3.28	1.179	111
Tanner Roark	6	17.0	13.6	64-54	3.59	1.209	115
Jeff Fassero	6	15.2	11.8	58-48	3.20	1.242	130
Bill Gullickson	7	12.9	7.6	72-61	3.44	1.211	103
Charlie Lea	6	7.6	7.9	55-41	3.32	1.259	107
Bill Stoneman	5	5.6	8.4	51-72	3.98	1.431	93

The clear ace for this staff was **Steve Rogers** (1973–85), who pitched his entire career for Montreal, was a five-time All-Star, and was often amongst the league leaders in several categories, most notably complete games and shutouts. In 1982 he took the ERA title with a 2.40 mark, and he was a distant second in the Cy Young Award balloting. He won 15+ games five times and excelled in the 1981 Division and League Championship Series, going a combined 3-1 with a 0.97 ERA.

Next up is a pitcher who has had only four seasons for the Nationals so far, but they have been outstanding. **Max Scherzer** (2015–18) signed as a free agent after several great years with the Tigers and promptly posted a 14-12 record with a 2.79 ERA and 276 strikeouts. He pitched not one but two no-hitters that year, first against the Pirates on June 20th, and then against the Mets on October 3rd. In 2016 he took home NL Cy Young Award honors with a 20-7 record, 2.96 ERA, and 284 strikeouts. In many ways he did even better in 2017, as he once again took home the Cy Young Award after posting a 16-6 record, 2.51 ERA, and league-leading 0.902 WHIP and 268 strikeouts. And at age 33 in 2018 he went 18-7 with a 2.53 ERA and 300 strikeouts.

El Presidente, **Dennis Martínez** (1986–93), pitched the first half of his career for the Orioles, but then joined the Expos during the 1986 season. He had four 15+-win seasons and took the ERA crown in 1991 with a 2.39 mark. And most impressively, in 1991 he tossed the first perfect game in franchise history.

Stephen Strasburg (2010–18) was a much-hyped 21-year-old in 2010, and he didn't disappoint in his debut against the Pirates in early June when he pitched seven innings and struck out 14 while walking 0. He then struck out 8 and 10 in his next two games, setting a record of 32 strikeouts in his first three starts. But by late August, injuries required Tommy John surgery. When he returned in late 2011, he posted a promising 1.50 ERA over five starts. Since then, Strasburg has often pitched very well but has continued to suffer injuries.

For the fifth spot I went with **Pedro Martínez** (1994–97), who had his early developmental seasons for Montreal, posting three seasons of increasing

IP and strikeout totals, with records of 11-5, 14-10, and 13-10. Then in 1997 he busted out and won his first Cy Young Award, going 17-8 with a 1.90 ERA, 13 complete games, 305 strikeouts, and only 158 hits allowed in 241.1 IP.

Jordan Zimmerman (2009–15) took a few years to become a regular in the Nationals rotation. He was an All-Star in 2012 with a 19-9 record and then again in 2013 with a 14-5 record.

After two good seasons with Oakland, **Gio González** (2012–18) was traded to the Nationals before the 2012 season and responded by posting a 21-8 record and 2.89 ERA, good enough for third in the NL Cy Young Award voting. His numbers faded for several years after that until 2017 saw a marked improvement, as he posted a 15-9 record and 2.96 ERA.

After looking at the many candidates for relief pitchers, I decided to go with eight starters and four relievers for this All-Time team's pitching staff. I considered several candidates for the eighth and final starting pitcher spot, but in the end went with **Javier Vázquez** (1998–2003). He had four solid years in Montreal, with his best numbers being a 16-11 record in 2001 and 241 strikeouts in 2003. But then he was traded to the Yankees and later went on to have success with other clubs.

You could make a case for Liván Hernández (2003–06, '09–11), who had two stints for this franchise, and particularly during the earlier years was an innings-eating workhorse. A two-time All-Star, he posted a 15-10 record for Montreal in 2003 and did the same again in 2005 for Washington.

Bryn Smith (1981–89) pitched most of his career with the Expos, including six full seasons as a starter. He has a winning record and a respectable 3.28 ERA, but he managed more than 12 wins only once, going 18-5 with a 2.91 ERA in 1985.

Jeff Fassero (1991–96) started his career with the Expos, pitching as a middle reliever for a few years before landing a spot in the rotation. He ended up with a 3.20 ERA and solid 130 ERA+ for the Expos, but he had only one 15-win season for the club. Bill Gullickson (1979–85) had five seasons of 10+ wins, including his rookie year in 1980, when he went 10-5 to come in second in the NL ROY voting, and 1983, when he went 17-12 and had 10 complete games.

Tanner Roark (2013–18) had an effective debut in 2013, going 7-1 with a 1.51 ERA over five games started and nine in relief. That earned him a rotation spot in 2014, and he posted a 15-10 record and a 2.85 ERA. He went back into a mixed role the following year but returned to the rotation in 2016 with almost identical results: 16-10 and a 2.83 ERA.

Two others were not really considered for spots on this team but had notable highlights. Bill Stoneman (1969–72) was the "ace," so to speak, during the first four Expos seasons. He tossed no-hitters in 1969 and 1972, but he walked a lot of batters (twice led the NL) and so ended up with a losing 51-72 record for the franchise. And French-born Charlie Lea (1980–84, '87) had three seasons with 12 to 16 wins, tossed a no-hitter in 1981, and was the NL's starting pitcher in the 1984 All-Star game. Unfortunately, arm and shoulder injuries kept him out of baseball the next two seasons, and a comeback attempt after that didn't really work out.

Relief Pitching

Name	YR	WAR	W3	SV	W-L	ERA	WHIP	ERA+
Tim Burke	7	12.1	9.6	101	43-26	2.61	1.176	142
Tyler Clippard	7	10.4	6.9	34	34-24	2.68	1.047	148
Mel Rojas	8	9.0	7.2	109	29-23	3.11	1.189	129
Jeff Reardon	6	8.2	6.3	152	32-37	2.84	1.173	126
Andy McGaffigan	5	8.2	7.8	21	27-16	2.92	1.264	130
Woodie Fryman	8	8.0	8.4	52	51-52	3.24	1.318	114
Chad Cordero	6	7.6	5.8	128	20-14	2.78	1.198	155
Mike Marshall	4	7.2	7.6	75	36-34	2.94	1.278	126
John Wetteland	3	7.2	7.2	105	17-13	2.32	1.089	170
Ugueth Urbina	7	7.2	6.2	125	31-26	3.52	1.257	124

The all-time saves leader for the Expos, **Jeff Reardon** (1981–86), was my top choice here. The Terminator pitched five full seasons as the Expos' closer. He had 20+ saves each year and led the league with 41 in 1985. Next was **Tim Burke** (1985–91), who spent two years setting up Reardon before taking over the closer's duties and posting save totals of 18, 18, 28, and 20.

Mike Marshall (1970–73) was the star in the Expos' bullpen from 1971 through '73. In 1972 he went 14-8 with 18 saves and a 1.78 ERA, which placed him fourth in the Cy Young Award vote and tenth in the MVP Award vote. In 1973 he was 14-11 with 31 saves and a 2.66 ERA, good enough for second in the Cy Young Award vote and fifth for MVP.

The final relief pitching spot was a very close call, with several candidates to consider. I went with **John Wetteland** (1992–94), who managed 25+ saves in each of his three seasons in Montreal. In 1993 he posted a 9-3 record with 43 saves, a 1.37 ERA, and 113 K in 85.1 IP. His ERA over these three seasons was a tidy 2.32, which was an impressive ERA+ of 170.

You could make a case for several others instead of Wetteland for this spot, starting with Ugueth Urbina (1995–2001), who also spent three years as Montreal's closer. He had 34 saves and a microscopic 1.30 ERA in 1998, and then led the league in saves with 41 in 1999 (a particularly amazing feat, since the team won only 68 games).

Mel Rojas (1990–96, '99) spent five years primarily setting up Wetteland, including 1992, when he posted a 1.43 ERA over 100.2 IP. He then took over closer duties and had two 30+-save seasons. Chad Cordero (2003–08) pitched most of his short career for the Expos and Nationals and had a career year in 2005, when he had a 1.82 ERA with a league-leading 47 saves. He also is second in all-time saves for this franchise.

Tyler Clippard (2008–14) pitched in the Nationals' bullpen for six seasons, most often as an effective setup man. He was a two-time All-Star and had a 2.68 ERA. He was the team's closer in only one season, 2012, when he posted 32 saves but had his worst ERA (3.72).

Andy McGaffigan (1984, '86–89) pitched for the Expos in the 1980s and was sometimes a starter, more often a reliever, and occasionally closed out games (12 saves in 1987). Overall, he had a 27-16 record and a respectable 2.92 ERA.

And finally, Woodie Fryman (1975–76, '78–83) had two stints in Montreal: from 1975 to '76 as a starter, and then from 1978 to '83 as a reliever. In 1980 he posted 17 saves and a 2.25 ERA.

Managers

Name	YR	From-To	W-L	PCT	PS	WS
Felipe Alou	10	1992–2001	691-717	.491	0	0
Buck Rodgers	7	1985–91	520-499	.510	0	0
Dusty Baker	2	2016–17	192-132	.593	2	0
Davey Johnson	3	2011–13	224-183	.550	1	0
Matt Williams	2	2014–15	179-145	.552	1	0
Dick Williams	5	1977–81	380-347	.523	0	0
Frank Robinson	5	2002–06	385-425	.475	0	0

Felipe Alou and **Buck Rodgers** have by far the most career wins at the helm of this franchise, and both had winning percentages around .500. I ranked Alou at the top since he managed the longest and would have had a postseason appearance in 1994 if not for the strike. To round out a top four you could either go with longevity at the helm and choose Dick Williams and Frank Robinson, or go the route I did and favor postseason appearances and choose **Dusty Baker**, and then either **Davey Johnson** or Matt Williams (flip a coin).

Starting Lineup

What would mythical starting lineups look like for this All-Time roster?

Against RHP:
Tim Raines LF (S)
José Vidro 2B (S)
Vladimir Guerrero RF (R)
Bryce Harper DH (L)
Andre Dawson CF (R)
Ryan Zimmerman 1B (R)
Gary Carter C (R)
Tim Wallach 3B (R)
Ian Desmond SS (R)

Against LHP:
Tim Raines LF (S)
Anthony Rendon 2B (R)
Vladimir Guerrero RF (R)
Andre Dawson CF (R)
Bryce Harper DH (L)
Ryan Zimmerman 1B (R)
Gary Carter C (R)
Tim Wallach 3B (R)
Ian Desmond SS (R)

These lineups start at the top with one of the greatest leadoff hitters of all time. And you could arrange sluggers Guerrero, Dawson, Harper, and others in any number of ways in the middle of the order.

Depth Chart

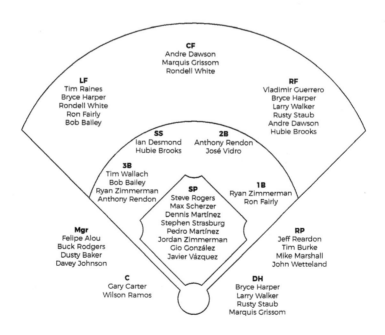

CF
Andre Dawson
Marquis Grissom
Rondell White

LF
Tim Raines
Bryce Harper
Rondell White
Ron Fairly
Bob Bailey

RF
Vladimir Guerrero
Bryce Harper
Larry Walker
Rusty Staub
Andre Dawson
Hubie Brooks

SS
Ian Desmond
Hubie Brooks

2B
Anthony Rendon
José Vidro

3B
Tim Wallach
Bob Bailey
Ryan Zimmerman
Anthony Rendon

SP
Steve Rogers
Max Scherzer
Dennis Martínez
Stephen Strasburg
Pedro Martínez
Jordan Zimmerman
Gio González
Javier Vázquez

1B
Ryan Zimmerman
Ron Fairly

Mgr
Felipe Alou
Buck Rodgers
Dusty Baker
Davey Johnson

RP
Jeff Reardon
Tim Burke
Mike Marshall
John Wetteland

C
Gary Carter
Wilson Ramos

DH
Bryce Harper
Larry Walker
Rusty Staub
Marquis Grissom

Prospects for Current Players

What are the prospects of current Nationals players making this All-Time team? Zimmerman, Rendon, Harper, Scherzer, and Strasburg are already on the roster. As I noted, you could make a case that Trey Turner already deserves a spot too. Young phenoms Juan Soto and Víctor Robles look promising, but it will take time for them to make this team. We'll see...

Expos Retired Player Numbers
(not considered retired by the Nationals)

Gary Carter (8), Andre Dawson (10), Rusty Staub (10), Tim Raines (30)

Selections from Other Authors and Fan Surveys

1992: *The All-Time All-Star Baseball Book*, by Nick Acocella and Donald Dewey

The authors chose a lineup of Galarraga, Hunt, Wallach, Tim Foli, Dawson, Raines, Staub, Carter, and Rogers. I would have gone with Hubie Brooks over light-hitting Foli. They gave honorable mention to Bob Bailey, Ellis Valentine, and Jeff Reardon.

1995: *Baseball Ratings*, by Charles F. Faber

Faber's system resulted in an infield of Galarraga, DeShields, Wallach, and again Foli. The catcher obviously was Carter, with an outfield of Raines, Dawson, and Cromartie. The top pitchers were Rogers and Burke.

2003: *Rob Neyer's Big Book of Baseball Lineups*, by Rob Neyer

Neyer chose Galarraga and Fairly at 1B and Vidro and DeShields at 2B, but then at SS went with Speier and Owen. He gave some praise to their defense—definitely not one of Brooks' strengths. Carter was the obvious starting catcher, and his choice of Fletcher back in 2003 made sense. His starting OF was the same as mine, and his backups were Grissom, Walker, and Alou.

Neyer's first three starting pitcher selections were the same as mine would have been: Rogers, D. Martínez, P. Martínez. Through the 2002 season he had far fewer options for the other pitcher spots, so he went with Smith, Lea, Vázquez, Gullickson, and Steve Renko. About Lea he wrote, "His peak was short but sweet: from 1982 through '84, Lea went 43-31 with 3.07 ERA; relied on throwing his curve at variety of speeds." Neyer finished the staff with Reardon as the top reliever, and then opted for Marshall as the other, writing, "Liberated from Brewers during 1970 season, Marshall brought his screwball out of mothballs and pitched 416 innings, all in relief, from 1971 through '73."

Top WAR Single Seasons – Hitters (7+)

Name	Year	WAR	AVG	HR	R	RBI	SB	OPS+
Bryce Harper	2015	9.9	.330	42	118	99	6	198
Gary Carter	1982	8.6	.293	29	91	97	2	146
Andre Dawson	1982	7.9	.301	23	107	83	39	132
Tim Raines	1985	7.6	.320	11	115	41	70	151
Andre Dawson	1981	7.4	.302	24	71	64	26	157
Gary Carter	1984	7.4	.294	27	75	106	2	143
Vladimir Guerrero	1998	7.4	.324	38	108	109	11	150
Ryan Zimmerman	2009	7.3	.292	33	110	106	2	133
Gary Carter	1983	7.1	.270	17	63	79	1	116
Vladimir Guerrero	2002	7.0	.336	39	106	111	40	160

Bryce Harper's MVP 2015 season rated as the best ever for this franchise. Given that he was only 22 that year, if stays healthy and stays in Washington, presumably he will appear on this list several more times. Some of the early 1980s seasons of Carter, Dawson, and Raines were not surprising to see here, nor Vlad's name appearing twice. Dawson's strike-shortened 1981 season was particularly impressive given that he played only 103 games.

Top WAR Single Seasons – Pitchers (7+)

Name	Year	WAR	W-L	ERA	IP	SO	ERA+
Max Scherzer	2018	9.6	18-7	2.53	220.2	300	168
Pedro Martínez	1997	8.8	17-8	1.90	241.1	305	219
Steve Rogers	1982	7.7	19-8	2.40	277.0	179	152
Max Scherzer	2015	7.6	14-12	2.79	228.2	276	142
Max Scherzer	2017	7.6	16-6	2.51	200.2	268	177

Max Scherzer seems to keep getting better, so it will be interesting to see if he can add more seasons to this list.

Franchise Player

This wasn't an easy honor to give, but I decided to go with Gary Carter, who got bonus points because of the position he played. Honorable mention was deserved by Raines, Dawson, Guerrero, Wallach, Zimmerman, and Rogers.

CHAPTER 21

The Royals Franchise All-Time Dream Team

The Kansas City Royals franchise joined the American League in 1969 and saw quicker success than most other expansion clubs. They played better than .500 ball in three of their first seven seasons and then had a very strong run from 1975 to 1985, making the postseason 7 times in those 11 years, culminating in a World Series win in 1985.

Unfortunately, the economics of being a small-market team with a low budget eventually led to a long dry spell: the Royals had a streak of mostly losing seasons from 1995 through 2012, with only an 83-79 season in 2003 to keep it from being 18 in a row. A core of good young players and a strong bullpen changed things in 2013, and the Royals made two consecutive World Series appearances, losing to the Giants in 2014 and winning over the Mets in 2015.

As with any expansion-era All-Time team, there were some definite weak spots on this roster. However, there were some true stars as well, making for a respectable team overall.

1st Base

Name	YR	WAR	W3	W/G	AVG	HR	SB	OPS+
Mike Sweeney	13	23.2	13.5	.0181	.299	197	50	120
John Mayberry	6	21.2	17.3	.0236	.261	143	16	132
Eric Hosmer	7	14.1	11.1	.0135	.284	127	60	111
Billy Butler	8	12.3	8.6	.0105	.295	127	5	119
Wally Joyner	4	7.6	6.3	.0147	.293	44	22	113
Willie Aikens	4	7.0	5.5	.0137	.282	77	1	129

There were two top candidates at 1B for this All-Time team, and I chose **John Mayberry** (1972–77) as the starter based on his stronger peak performance. He didn't play for the Royals for as long, but he did hit 20+ HR in five of his six seasons, with 100+ RBI three times. A two-time All-Star, he twice led the league in walks, including in 1975, when he batted .291 with a .416 OBP, 34 HR, and 106 RBI, resulting in a second-place finish in the AL MVP vote.

Mike Sweeney (1995–2007) played for the Royals a lot longer, for most of his career in fact. He first came up as a catcher before playing most of his games at 1B and DH. A .299 hitter, Sweeney had enough power to hit 20+ HR six times. A five-time All-Star, Sweeney's best season was in 2000, when he hit .333 with 29 HR and an impressive franchise-record 144 RBI (though in that era such numbers earned him only 11th place in the MVP vote).

Recent star Eric Hosmer (2011–17) was outstanding defensively at 1B, taking home four Gold Glove Awards. What started out as moderate power increased in 2016, when he hit 25 HR, followed by 25 HR again in 2017 to go with a career-high .318 average. But it seems his time with the Royals is over, as he signed with the Padres as a free agent after the 2017 season.

Billy Butler (2007–14) joined the Royals at age 21 and was a fairly consistent hitter for many years, though he spent more time as a DH than at 1B. He was a great doubles hitter, with totals from 2009 through 2011 of 51, 45, and 44, and in 2012 he increased his power output with 29 HR and 107 RBI (his one year as an All-Star). Both his power and his batting average dropped off after that, and he was granted free agency after the 2014 season.

Two other Royals 1B deserve brief mention, starting with Willie Aikens (1980–83), who hit between 17 and 23 HR in each of his four seasons for Kansas City. And Wally Joyner (1992–95) also played four years for the Royals, hitting .293 but never providing more than 15 HR in a season.

2nd Base

Name	YR	WAR	W3	W/G	AVG	HR	SB	OPS+
Frank White	18	34.7	12.1	.0149	.255	160	178	85
Whit Merrifield	3	11.0	11.0	.0286	.293	33	87	109
José Offerman	3	9.7	9.7	.0234	.306	14	78	108
Mark Grudzielanek	3	8.2	8.2	.0244	.300	16	6	96
Cookie Rojas	8	7.2	8.1	.0082	.268	25	46	87

Defensive standout **Frank White** (1973–90) is easily one of the best second basemen not in the Hall of Fame. I'm not endorsing his selection, but he was a star for many years and a key part of several division-winning Royals teams. A fairly good runner early in his career, the Kansas City native developed some power later on—a rarity at the time for second basemen. A five-time All-Star, he took home eight Gold Glove Awards. He also played nearly three times as many games at 2B as any other Royal, so he was clearly the starter here.

For the backup spot I went with longevity and selected **Cookie Rojas** (1970–77), who played the second half of his career for the Royals. Although only a .268 hitter with little power or speed, Rojas was an All-Star four times.

Whit Merrifield (2016–18) has established himself as a new star in Kansas City, playing mostly at 2B but also covering all three OF positions. A capable hitter with some power, his greatest contribution has come on the basepaths where he led the AL with 34 SB in 2017, and again with 45 in 2018.

There were two other talented second basemen who played for the Royals in only three seasons each. José Offerman (1996–98) hit .306 and provided some good speed, hitting 13 triples with 45 SB in 1998. And Mark Grudzielanek (2006–08) was in Kansas City late in his career, and also hit for a good average, though with little power or speed. He was strong defensively, winning the AL Gold Glove Award in 2006.

3rd Base

Name	YR	WAR	W3	W/G	AVG	HR	SB	OPS+
George Brett	21	88.4	26.3	.0327	.305	317	201	135
Kevin Seitzer	6	17.2	12.9	.0232	.294	33	50	115
Joe Randa	8	14.9	8.5	.0146	.288	86	30	95
Mike Moustakas	8	13.5	9.6	.0145	.251	139	14	98
Paul Schaal	6	9.9	8.2	.0163	.263	32	22	107
Gary Gaetti	3	8.4	8.4	.0272	.267	61	3	108

George Brett (1973–93) is clearly the Royals' all-time best player. Inducted into the Hall of Fame in 1999, he batted a phenomenal .390 in 1980 en route to taking the MVP crown and leading the Royals into the World Series for the first time. He also won a batting title earlier in 1976 (.333) and later in 1990 (.329), the only player to have batting titles in three decades. He hit 20+ HR eight times, had 100+ RBI four times, and scored 100+ runs four times. He even led the AL in triples three times, including in 1979, when he hit 20 and became one of only eight players with 20 2B/3B/HR in the same season. Although injury-prone, he was an All-Star 13 times. As if his regular season exploits weren't impressive enough, he also performed well in nine postseason series: a .337 average with 10 HR in 166 AB. He played a good 3B, winning a Gold Glove Award in 1985 and only switching to 1B and DH duties late in his career.

No one came close to Brett at this position for the Royals, but I did need to consider a few candidates for the backup spot. In the end, **Kevin Seitzer** (1986–91) seemed the most deserving, as he played the first half of his career in Kansas City and had a few good seasons, including his first full one in 1987, when he hit .323 with 207 hits, 15 HR, and 83 RBI.

Joe Randa (1995–96, 1999–2004) had two stints with the Royals, with his best season being 2000, when he hit .304 with 15 HR and 106 RBI. Paul Schaal (1969–74) was the Royals' 3B before Brett came along, but he was a .263 hitter and never hit more than 11 HR in a season. Gary Gaetti (1993–95) came to the Royals late in his career and had one good power season in 1995, when he hit 35 HR with 96 RBI.

And lastly, 3B Mike Moustakas (2011–18) was an important, if at times inconsistent, part of the team's recent success. Generally a low-average hitter with some power, his two All-Star seasons came in 2015, when he hit .284 with 22 HR and 82 RBI, and 2017, when he set a new Royals team record with 38 HR.

Shortstop

Name	YR	WAR	W3	W/G	AVG	HR	SB	OPS+
Freddie Patek	9	20.4	10.8	.0164	.241	28	336	78
Alcides Escobar	8	9.2	8.6	.0074	.259	36	160	73
Rey Sánchez	3	9.2	9.2	.0244	.289	3	27	71
U L Washington	8	8.5	6.8	.0112	.254	26	120	84

The options at SS didn't start with a headliner like White or Brett, but the starter was still a fairly obvious choice in **Freddie Patek** (1971–79). He had eight consecutive seasons of 30+ SB, including highs of 49, 51, and 53. Although only a .241 hitter, he was a good fielder and so was named an All-Star three times.

By now **Alcides Escobar** (2011–18) has done enough to warrant the backup spot at SS. A light hitter with some speed (four seasons with 20+

SB), Escobar was an All-Star in 2015 and also took home the AL Gold Glove Award that year.

Before the emergence of Escobar, the backup would likely have been U L Washington (1977–84), who had double-digit steals in six seasons, with a high of 40 in 1983. He also provided a bit of interesting trivia, as that isn't a typo in his name: "U" and "L" are not initials; his name is literally just "U L." And lastly, Rey Sánchez (1999–2001) had a long career, playing for nine teams. He spent parts of three seasons with the Royals, providing strong defense and hitting .289, but with no power and only a little speed on the bases.

Catcher

Name	YR	WAR	W3	W/G	AVG	HR	SB	OPS+
Salvador Pérez	8	22.2	10.9	.0236	.266	141	4	98
Darrell Porter	4	16.7	14.3	.0301	.271	61	5	121
Mike Macfarlane	11	13.0	8.6	.0146	.256	103	9	104
Ed Kirkpatrick	5	9.3	8.5	.0151	.248	56	16	105
John Wathan	10	5.0	5.9	.0058	.262	21	105	83

As with Escobar at SS, **Salvador Pérez** (2011–18) has also by now accomplished enough to warrant inclusion on the Royals All-Time team—and in this case as the starter. An All-Star each year from 2013 through '18, Pérez has provided outstanding defense, taking home four Gold Glove Awards. Salvy's batting average has declined during that time, but his power has inched upwards each year, with a high of 27 HR in 2017 and 2018.

In the middle of his career, **Darrell Porter** (1977–80) played for Kansas City for four years and was an All-Star in three of them. His best season was 1979, when he hit .291 with 20 HR, 10 triples, 101 runs, 112 RBI, and a league-leading 121 walks—only the second time in history that a catcher had 100+ runs, RBI, and walks in the same season (Mickey Cochrane did it in 1932).

I did consider a few other candidates, most notably Mike Macfarlane (1987–94, '96–98). He played many more seasons for the Royals than Porter, but he managed 100+ games only four times. Only a .256 hitter, he had some power, hitting double-digit HR five times. Ed Kirkpatrick (1969–73) split his time between behind the plate and in the outfield over five seasons with Kansas City. Only a .248 hitter, his highest HR total was 18 in 1970. And John Wathan (1976–85) played his entire career for the Royals, hitting .262 with limited power, but interestingly running the bases well—a rarity for catchers. In fact, in 1982, even though he was 32 years old and missed four weeks with a broken ankle, Wathan stole 36 bases to break the MLB record for catchers.

Left Field

Name	YR	WAR	W3	W/G	AVG	HR	SB	OPS+
Alex Gordon	12	35.2	20.1	.0227	.258	173	108	104
Hal McRae	15	27.7	13.6	.0151	.293	169	105	125
Bo Jackson	5	7.0	7.9	.0137	.250	109	81	115

Alex Gordon (2007–18) arrived in the majors as a highly touted 3B prospect and played that position for a few seasons before shifting to left field. He has provided good defense there, taking home five Gold Glove Awards. A three-time All-Star, Gordon has provided a mix of moderate power and speed over the years, with his best season coming in 2011, when he had career highs with a .303 average, 101 runs, 23 HR, 87 RBI, and 17 SB.

Hal McRae (1973–87) also clearly deserves to be on this All-Time team roster, and I'll discuss him here though it must be noted that he played more time as a DH than in the outfield. After four partial seasons for the Reds, McRae played the rest of his long career for the Royals. He had several solid seasons, with his three best being 1976, when he had career highs of 22 SB, a .332 average, and a .407 OBP; 1977, when he hit .298 with 54 doubles, 21 HR, and 92 RBI; and 1982, when he batted .308 with 27 HR and a league-leading 46 doubles and 133 RBI.

Bo Jackson (1986–90) was a physical specimen, a superb multi-sport athlete who eventually suffered a hip injury playing football for the Oakland Raiders in a 1991 playoff game. He played only briefly for the Royals, but he got a lot out of that time, smashing 20+ HR in each of his four full seasons. He hit for a low average (.250) and struck out a lot, but he showed speed on the bases, with highs of 27 and 26 steals in 1988 and 1989. Jackson was an exciting player, but his résumé was not strong enough to make the Royals' All-Time team.

Center Field

Name	YR	WAR	W3	W/G	AVG	HR	SB	OPS+
Amos Otis	14	44.6	17.6	.0236	.280	193	340	118
Willie Wilson	15	42.2	21.0	.0236	.289	40	612	95
Lorenzo Cain	7	25.7	15.5	.0346	.289	56	120	106
Carlos Beltrán	7	24.7	17.6	.0311	.287	123	164	111
David DeJesus	8	18.0	10.0	.0205	.289	61	47	108
Johnny Damon	6	17.3	13.7	.0215	.292	65	156	101

Center field has always been a position of strength for the Royals over the years, so there was no shortage of candidates to consider here. The generally underrated **Amos Otis** (1970–83) played nearly his entire career in KC, providing good power, speed, and defense. No single season was clearly his best overall, as he hit 26 HR in 1973, swiped 52 bases in 1971, and hit over .290 five times. A five-time All-Star, he won three Gold Glove Awards for his work in center field.

Willie Wilson (1976–90) played most of his career for the Royals and is by far their all-time leader in stolen bases. He had 20+ SB steals in all 13 of his full seasons in KC, with his best totals being 83, 79, and two seasons with 59. He hit over .300 five times, including a league-leading .332 in 1982, and led the league in triples five times, with a high of 21 in 1985. His best overall season came in 1980, when he became the first major leaguer to have 700+ at-bats. That year he batted .326, stole 79 bases, and led the league with 230 hits, 133 runs, and 15 triples. An All-Star only twice, he provided strong defense, whether playing LF early in his career (Gold Glove Award in 1980) or CF after Otis departed.

Carlos Beltrán (1998–2004) started his impressive career with the Royals and was a star early, as he took home the 1999 Rookie of the Year Award after hitting .293 with 22 HR, 108 RBI, 112 runs, and 27 SB. He had three other solid seasons in Kansas City from 2001 through 2003, providing 20+ HR, 100+ RBI, and 30+ SB in each.

Next up was **Lorenzo Cain** (2010–17), who has been outstanding defensively in CF and has provided some speed on the bases too, with three seasons of 20+ SB. Perhaps his biggest contribution came in the 2014 ALCS, where he won the series MVP Award after going 8-for-15 (.533) and making several outstanding defensive plays.

Johnny Damon (1995–2000) started his career with the Royals before gaining greater fame with the Red Sox and Yankees. He played all three OF positions, and although he started as a light hitter, that improved during his time in KC. His final season in 2000 provided a .327 average, 16 HR, 10 triples, and a league-leading 136 runs and 46 SB. Given the lack of strong candidates elsewhere, I decided to include Damon and Cain with the two "extra spots."

With so many strong candidates, this means that David DeJesus (2003–2010) doesn't have a spot on this roster. Although not possessing much power or speed, he was a consistent hitter (.289) and scored 101 runs in 2007.

Right Field

Name	YR	WAR	W3	W/G	AVG	HR	SB	OPS+
Danny Tartabull	5	12.7	9.9	.0193	.290	124	28	144
Al Cowens	6	12.1	9.1	.0149	.282	45	80	103
Jermaine Dye	5	8.9	10.1	.0163	.284	85	13	107
Jim Eisenreich	6	4.4	5.0	.0068	.277	23	65	98

Danny Tartabull (1987–91) was not a good fielder for the Royals, and that is one reason his WAR score listed above is not impressive. But he was a .290 hitter and provided the Royals with three seasons of 25+ HR and 100+ RBI. As he was the leading candidate who played mostly RF, I decided to stick to my guidelines and give him a spot on this All-Time team over adding yet another CF.

I also considered Al Cowens (1974–79) here, but he played in 150+ games just twice for the Royals. He provided some speed but only minimal power—except for his career year of 1977, when he took home a Gold Glove Award and hit .312 with 23 HR, 14 triples, and 112 RBI, coming in second to Rod Carew in the AL MVP voting.

Early in his career, Jermaine Dye (1997–2001) played three partial seasons and two full seasons for the Royals, with the latter providing solid numbers: .294, 27 HR, 119 and RBI, and .321, 33 HR, and 118 RBI. And finally, Jim Eisenreich (1987–92) played all three outfield positions in parts of six seasons for the Royals. He hit .277 with little power and only moderate speed, posting a career-high 27 SB in 1989.

Starting Pitching

Name	YR	WAR	W3	W-L	ERA	WHIP	ERA+
Kevin Appier	13	47.3	23.3	115-92	3.49	1.250	130
Bret Saberhagen	8	41.0	25.0	110-78	3.21	1.134	128
Mark Gubicza	13	38.6	19.0	132-135	3.91	1.356	110
Zack Greinke	7	26.3	19.6	60-67	3.82	1.264	116
Dennis Leonard	12	26.3	13.3	144-106	3.70	1.262	107
Paul Splittorff	15	23.5	9.4	166-143	3.81	1.340	101
Charlie Leibrandt	6	23.2	17.9	76-61	3.60	1.315	116
Larry Gura	10	19.0	14.4	111-78	3.72	1.253	107
Steve Busby	8	16.4	15.2	70-54	3.72	1.354	105
Al Fitzmorris	8	16.3	11.9	70-48	3.46	1.306	106
Tom Gordon	8	16.1	10.0	79-71	4.02	1.415	108
David Cone	3	14.0	14.0	27-19	3.29	1.216	144
Bud Black	7	12.9	9.2	56-57	3.73	1.259	111
Dick Drago	5	12.2	8.9	61-70	3.52	1.298	101

There were two top candidates for this All-Time team's pitching staff, but I decided to give the top honor to **Bret Saberhagen** (1984–91), who spent the first, and better, half of his career with the Royals. During that time, he seemed to excel mostly in odd-numbered years. In 1985, in only his second season, Saberhagen went 20-6 with a 2.86 ERA to take home the AL Cy Young Award. He was an All-Star in 1987, when he posted an 18-10 record, and then had his best year in 1989, when he again took home the Cy Young Award after leading the league with a 23-6 mark and 2.16 ERA.

Kevin Appier (1989–99, 2003–04) pitched over half of his career for the Royals, and he had his best two seasons relatively early: in 1992 he went 15-8 with a 2.46 ERA, and then he went 18-8 with a league-leading 2.56 ERA in 1993. He was an All-Star in 1995 and had his only 200+-strikeout season the next year.

Mark Gubicza (1984–96) pitched all but his final two games for the Royals, ending up with a record just slightly below .500 (132-135). A two-time All-Star, his best season was easily 1988, when he went 20-8 with a 2.70 ERA.

Dennis Leonard (1974–83, '85–86) pitched his entire career for the Royals, starting out with records of 15-7 and 17-10 in his first two full seasons. He had his first of three 20+-win seasons in 1977, when he went 20-12 with 244 strikeouts. A workhorse power pitcher, Leonard led the league in games started three times, but strangely was never chosen as an All-Star.

Like Leonard, **Paul Splittorff** (1970–84) pitched his entire career for Kansas City, and is their all-time leader in both wins and losses. A control artist, his highest win totals came in 1973, when he went 20-11, and in 1978, when he went 19-13.

A teammate of Leonard and Splittorff for several years, lefty **Larry Gura** (1976–85) was used out of the bullpen for his first couple of seasons and was transitioned to a starting role in 1978, when he went 16-4 with a 2.72 ERA. Gura was an All-Star in 1980 with an 18-10 mark and 2.95 ERA. He won 18 games again in 1982, but then lost 18 games the next season.

Based on the WAR numbers listed above, you could argue that **Zack Greinke** (2004–10) should be ranked ahead of Leonard, Splittorff, and Gura—but the value he provided came largely from one phenomal season, so I took that into consideration. Greinke joined the Royals as a 20-year-old in 2004 and went 8-11, followed by an awful 5-17 campaign the next year. By 2008 he was much improved, and in 2009 he took home the AL Cy Young Award after going 16-8 with a league-leading 2.16 ERA. But then he pitched only one more year for the Royals before moving on to much success for other teams.

Charlie Leibrandt (1984–89) was in the Royals' rotation for six seasons, with his best year being 1985, when he went 17-9 with a 2.69 ERA. A consistent workhorse for the Royals, he started 33 to 35 games, pitched 230+ IP, and won 13+ games in four consecutive seasons.

After considering the other starting pitchers, and also the many relief pitching candidates, I decided to include only those eight starters on this All-Time dream team. Amongst the others I considered was Tom "Flash" Gordon (1988–

95), whose curveball gave him some success as a mixed reliever and starter for the Royals before later becoming a closer for other teams. He was runner-up for the Rookie of the Year Award in 1989 after posting a 17-9 record (even though he started only 16 games). He had four other seasons with 11 or 12 wins for the Royals before moving on and pitching for seven other teams.

Steve Busby (1972–76, '78–80) pitched all of his abbreviated career for the Royals, but that included only three full seasons as a starter. He posted no-hitters in both 1973 and 1974, and was an All-Star in both 1974 (22-14 record) and 1975 (18-12 record). Unfortunately, a rotator cuff tear derailed his career and after surgery and several seasons trying to come back, he retired at the age of 30. Al Fitzmorris (1969–76) was a teammate of Busby for several years and pitched most of his career for the Royals. His best seasons provided records of 13-6, 16-12, and 15-11.

Dick Drago (1969–73) was a teammate of Fitzmorris in the earliest years of the franchise, and he provided a fine 1971 campaign with a 17-11 record and 2.98 ERA. Bud Black (1982–88) was a starter for parts of five years for Kansas City (and also pitched some in relief), with 1984 being his best season with a 17-12 record and 3.12 ERA. And lastly, David Cone (1986, '93–94) was drafted by the Royals and worked his way to the major league level only to be quickly traded to the Mets. He later returned for two seasons in the middle of his career, and after posting an 11-14 record in 1993, went 16-5 with a 2.94 ERA to take home the AL Cy Young Award in the strike-shortened 1994 season.

Relief Pitching

Name	YR	WAR	W3	SV	W-L	ERA	WHIP	ERA+
Dan Quisenberry	10	26.0	13.4	238	51-44	2.55	1.150	160
Jeff Montgomery	12	21.3	12.0	304	44-50	3.20	1.233	138
Joakim Soria	7	13.2	12.5	162	22-26	2.82	1.130	155
Steve Farr	6	11.7	10.1	49	34-24	3.05	1.315	135
Greg Holland	6	10.0	8.1	145	18-12	2.42	1.123	170
Kelvin Herrera	8	10.0	7.3	57	23-27	2.75	1.131	153
Doug Bird	6	7.9	7.5	58	49-36	3.56	1.245	107
Wade Davis	4	6.8	8.9	47	27-15	2.94	1.226	140
Ted Abernathy	3	4.0	4.0	40	16-13	2.31	1.292	147

Submariner **Dan Quisenberry** (1979–88) once quipped, "I found a delivery in my flaw." Few pitchers had a more unorthodox and yet still effective pitching style than Quiz. He was the best reliever in baseball from 1980 through 1985, led the AL in saves five times, came in the top five in the Cy Young vote in each of those seasons, and posted a 2.55 ERA for the Royals. In fact, his 44 saves in

1984 was the first time anyone had posted 40+ saves in consecutive seasons. (On a personal note, Quisenberry was my favorite pitcher as a kid, and I threw sidearm, and occasionally submarine, from Little League through high school.)

Jeff Montgomery (1988–99) played all but his first season for the Royals, was their primary closer for most of that time, and was an All-Star three times. Not overpowering, he used a variety of pitches to earn 30+ saves five times, including a league-leading 45 in 1993.

In looking over all of the pitching candidates for this All-Time team, I decided to include only eight starting pitchers, thereby leaving four spots for relievers. **Joakim Soria** (2007–11, '16–17) posted an ERA below 2.50 in his first four seasons and was an All-Star twice, first when he posted 42 saves in 2008, and then with 43 in 2010. But he faltered in 2011 with a 4.03 ERA and then required Tommy John surgery, leading him to miss the entire 2012 season. He pitched for three other teams and returned to Kansas City as a setup man in 2016.

Greg Holland (2010–15) did enough with the Royals to also warrant a spot. After one year as a setup man and one as co-closer, Holland was an All-Star in 2013 and 2014 with impressive save totals of 47 and 46, and ERAs of 1.21 and 1.44. Holland seemed to falter a bit the following year, and late in the year it was discovered that, like Soria, he would need Tommy John surgery. He missed all of 2016 and then became a free agent, signing with the Rockies for the 2017 season.

A few other relievers deserve brief mention, starting with Doug Bird (1973–78), who earned 10 to 20 saves four times for the Royals in the 1970s. Steve Farr (1985–90) notched 20 saves with a 2.50 ERA in 1988 and was a mixed starter/reliever in 1990 when he posted a 13-7 record and 1.98 ERA. Ted Abernathy (1970–72) pitched his final three seasons for the Royals, and was still effective, including 23 saves and a 2.56 ERA in 1971.

In addition to Holland, most recently the Royals have had two other strong bullpen arms. After struggling one year as a starter, Wade Davis (2013–16) became a lights-out setup man, posting a 1.00 ERA and 109 K in 72 IP in 2014. He was a setup/closer mix in 2015 with 17 saves and a 0.94 ERA. And then for one year he was the closer in Kansas City, posting 27 saves and a 1.87 ERA in 2016, before being traded to the Cubs after the season. And Kelvin Herrera (2011–18) was a strong setup man for the Royals for five years and finally started to see some save opportunities in 2016, when he notched 12 and then 26 the following year.

Managers

Name	YR	From-To	W-L	PCT	PS	WS
Dick Howser	6	1981–86	404-365	.525	3	1
Ned Yost	9	2010–18	687-736	.483	2	1
Whitey Herzog	5	1975–79	410-304	.574	3	0
Jim Frey	2	1980–81	127-105	.547	2	0
John Wathan	5	1987–91	287-270	.515	0	0
Hal McRae	4	1991–94	286-277	.508	0	0

The top three managers in Royals history would seem to be **Dick Howser**, **Ned Yost**, and **Whitey Herzog**—though one could debate the order. Howser and Herzog both led them to the postseason three times, Yost only twice. Yost and Howser each have a World Series championship with the Royals, but Herzog has the far better winning percentage. If Yost can rack up some additional accomplishments in the coming years, then he'll likely secure the top spot here. As a fourth here I went with **Jim Frey**, who managed the team for only two seasons but made the playoffs in each.

Starting Lineup

What would mythical starting lineups look like for this All-Time roster?

Against RHP:
Willie Wilson CF (S)
Amos Otis RF (R)
George Brett 3B (L)
John Mayberry 1B (L)
Alex Gordon LF (L)
Hal McRae DH (R)
Darrell Porter C (L)
Frank White 2B (R)
Freddie Patek SS (R)

Against LHP:
Willie Wilson LF (S)
Amos Otis CF (R)
George Brett 3B (L)
Hal McRae DH (R)
Danny Tartabull RF (R)
Mike Sweeney 1B (R)
Salvador Pérez C (R)
Frank White 2B (R)
Freddie Patek SS (R)

For these lineups I found a few natural platoons at 1B and C. I also essentially platooned Gordon and Tartabull across LF and RF too.

Depth Chart

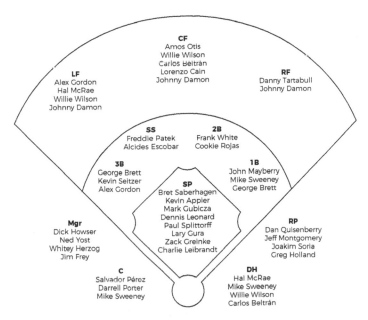

CF
Amos Otis
Willie Wilson
Carlos Beltrán
Lorenzo Cain
Johnny Damon

LF
Alex Gordon
Hal McRae
Willie Wilson
Johnny Damon

RF
Danny Tartabull
Johnny Damon

SS
Freddie Patek
Alcides Escobar

2B
Frank White
Cookie Rojas

3B
George Brett
Kevin Seltzer
Alex Gordon

1B
John Mayberry
Mike Sweeney
George Brett

SP
Bret Saberhagen
Kevin Appier
Mark Gubicza
Dennis Leonard
Paul Splittorff
Lary Gura
Zack Greinke
Charlie Leibrandt

Mgr
Dick Howser
Ned Yost
Whitey Herzog
Jim Frey

RP
Dan Quisenberry
Jeff Montgomery
Joakim Soria
Greg Holland

C
Salvador Pérez
Darrell Porter
Mike Sweeney

DH
Hal McRae
Mike Sweeney
Willie Wilson
Carlos Beltrán

Prospects for Current Players

What are the prospects of current Royals players making this All-Time team? Escobar, Pérez, and Gordon are already on the roster. Kansas City has unloaded some players recently and seem to be in a rebuilding phase, so other than perhaps Merrifield I don't expect many players to join them soon. We'll see...

Retired Player Numbers

George Brett (5), Dick Hoswer (10, manager), Frank White (20)

Selections from Other Authors and Fan Surveys

1992: *The All-Time All-Star Baseball Book*, by Nick Acocella and Donald Dewey

The authors noted that, "Aside from the pitcher, all these players were part of the teams that regularly lost the American League Championship Series to the Yankees in the late 1970s." Their sensible lineup was composed of Mayberry,

White, Brett, Patek, McRae, Otis, Wilson, Porter, and Quisenberry. Honorable mention was given to Leonard and Saberhagen.

1995: *Baseball Ratings*, by Charles F. Faber

A few years later the Faber system produced the exact same All-Time team lineup, with Splittorf as the top starter and Quisenberry of course as the top reliever.

2003: *Rob Neyer's Big Book of Baseball Lineups*, by Rob Neyer

Rob Neyer's starting lineup was the same too, with McRae given as the DH, which allowed Tartabull a starting role in RF. Sweeney was still playing at the time, but he had done enough to be listed as the backup 1B. The rest of the infield backups were the same as my selections, except of course U L Washington was the reserve SS. His backup outfielders were Jackson in LF, Beltrán in CF, and Dye in RF.

His top five starting pitchers were the same as mine, with his order being Saberhagen, Appier, Leonard, Splittorff, and Gubicza. But then he went with David Cone, about whom he wrote, "K.C. native posted a 5.56 ERA in '86; won 27 games and Cy Young Award in his second, two-year stint. Would obviously rank higher if he'd been around a bit longer." In my view, for that very reason he shouldn't have been included at all. Neyer sensibly had Busby as his seventh starter, but then he rounded out his starting pitchers with Jose Rosado, about whom he wrote, "Unimposing 37-45, but got poor support from his mates and pitched in two All-Star Games; not blessed with great stuff, but fearlessly threw inside heat to righties." I could grant the lack of support (leading him to have records of 9-12, 8-11, and 10-14 in his three full seasons). But I wasn't sure why he chose Rosado here and totally omitted Larry Gura. For relief pitchers Neyer of course went with Quisenberry and Montgomery.

Top WAR Single Seasons – Hitters (7+)

Name	Year	WAR	AVG	HR	R	RBI	SB	OPS+
George Brett	1980	9.4	.390	24	87	118	15	203
George Brett	1979	8.6	.329	23	119	107	17	148
Willie Wilson	1980	8.4	.326	3	133	49	79	113
George Brett	1985	8.3	.335	30	108	112	9	179
Darrell Porter	1979	7.6	.291	20	101	112	3	142
George Brett	1977	7.6	.312	22	105	88	14	142
George Brett	1976	7.5	.333	7	94	67	21	144
Amos Otis	1978	7.4	.298	22	74	96	32	151
Alex Gordon	2011	7.2	.303	23	101	87	17	140
Lorenzo Cain	2015	7.2	.307	16	101	72	28	125
John Mayberry	1975	7.2	.291	34	95	106	5	168

It was not at all surprising to see George Brett as the only player to appear on this list multiple times, though impressively he has five of the top seven. His 1980 season ranks number one, even though he played only 117 games that year. And it was interesting to see 1979 and 1980 have two player seasons each in the top five here.

Top WAR Single Seasons – Pitchers (7+)

Name	Year	WAR	W-L	ERA	IP	SO	ERA+
Zack Greinke	2009	10.4	16-8	2.16	229.1	242	205
Bret Saberhagen	1989	9.7	23-6	2.16	262.1	193	180
Kevin Appier	1993	9.3	18-8	2.56	238.2	186	179
Kevin Appier	1992	8.1	15-8	2.46	208.1	150	164
Bret Saberhagen	1987	8.0	18-10	3.36	257.0	163	136
Mark Gubicza	1988	7.8	20-8	2.70	269.2	183	149
Bret Saberhagen	1985	7.3	20-6	2.87	235.1	158	143
David Cone	1993	7.2	11-14	3.33	254.0	191	138

Bret Saberhagen had this thing in the '80s where he would pitch very well in the odd-numbered years, and then struggle in the even-numbered years. The one surprise for me was David Cone's 1993 season, where the numbers don't look that great, especially compared to his 16-5 record and 2.94 ERA the following year, when he won the Cy Young Award. His WAR in 1994 was close (6.9), and the difference is that he pitched nearly 50% more in terms of games started and innings pitched in 1993, since 1994 was a strike-shortened season.

Franchise Player

Few teams have a more clear-cut franchise player than the Royals. George Brett played his entire Hall of Fame career with KC and is their all-time leader in every major offensive category except stolen bases (not known for his base running, he is still fourth on the team).

CHAPTER 22

The Mets Franchise All-Time Dream Team

Oh, the Mets! They must have the toughest little-brother or second-fiddle situation of any professional sports team. They have to compete for dollars, as well as hearts, in the Big Apple with the greatest American sports franchise of all time.

The Mets started in 1962 with a pitiful 40-120 record and didn't have a winning season until their miracle 1969 World Series championship club in 1969. They won the pennant again in 1973 but lost the World Series in seven games to the dynastic Oakland Athletics. They next had postseason success in 1986, culminating in their famous seven-game championship win over the Boston Red Sox. In the past 20 years, the Mets have made the postseason five times, going to the World Series twice, losing in five games in both 2000 and 2015.

Mets fans have a lot they can complain about over the years, but they also have much to be proud of too. This All-Time team wasn't loaded, but it had several bright spots to be sure.

1st Base

Name	YR	WAR	W3	W/G	AVG	HR	SB	OPS+
Keith Hernandez	7	26.5	16.8	.0191	.297	80	17	129
John Olerud	3	17.3	17.3	.0363	.315	63	5	142
Dave Magadan	7	14.0	9.2	.0131	.292	21	5	122

John Milner	7	10.0	6.7	.0090	.245	94	20	113
Lucas Duda	8	7.6	7.7	.0100	.246	125	5	122
Carlos Delgado	4	4.8	4.6	.0103	.267	104	5	121
Ed Kranepool	18	4.4	5.7	.0024	.261	118	15	98
Dave Kingman	6	3.0	4.7	.0045	.219	154	29	108

Keith Hernandez (1983–89) mostly split his career between St. Louis and New York. He regularly provided around 15 HR, 90 RBI, 85 runs, and a .300 average for the Mets. He was an All-Star three times, won five Gold Glove Awards, and managed to come in second in the NL MVP vote in 1984 after hitting .311 with a .409 OBP, 15 HR, and 94 RBI. He was a central part of the 1986 Mets World Championship team, batting .310 with a .413 OBP that year.

John Olerud (1997–99) had three fine seasons for the Mets, including a 1998 campaign when his .354 average was second in the NL. Overall, he batted .315 with a .425 OBP and was also great with the glove. Not a long stay in New York, but enough to be the backup 1B for this All-Time team roster.

There were several others I considered, starting with Dave Magadan (1986–92). He hit .292 for the Mets but played over 130 games only once, and provided little power or speed. And John Milner (1971–77) played both 1B and LF, and while only a .245 hitter, he had some power, hitting 15+ HR four times for the Mets.

I was a bit surprised that three power-hitting Mets 1B didn't manage a cumulative 10 WAR score during their time in New York. Carlos Delgado (2006–09) played his final 3+ seasons for the Mets, including 38 HR and 114 RBI in 2006 and a nearly identical 38 HR and 115 RBI in 2008. But those numbers, along with below-average defense, didn't translate to much of a WAR score. Ditto for Lucas Duda (2010–2017), who hit 30 HR in 2014 and 27 in 2015, but suffered from a low .246 average and wasn't a star defensively. And the most extreme case of this was Dave Kingman (1975–77, '81–83), who split his time on the field in NY between 1B, LF, and RF. Kingman's ridiculously sweeping swing led to monster home runs (including seasons of 36, 37, and 37 for the Mets) but equally extreme strikeout totals and a microscopic batting average (.219 with the Mets).

Lastly, Ed Kranepool (1962–79) first played for the Mets as a 17-year-old in 1962, and went on to play far more games at 1B than anyone else in team history. A lifetime Met, he played a little OF too, but he was a light hitter and played 140+ games in a season only three times in 18 seasons. He had between 10 and 14 HR eight times, but only a .261 average and .316 OBP for his career. Arguably his greatest value came from his ability as a pinch-hitter, especially late in his career. Overall, he had a .277 average while pinch-hitting, but from 1974 through '78, he had five pinch-hit HRs and went 57-for-144, which is an amazing .396 average.

2nd Base

Name	YR	WAR	W3	W/G	AVG	HR	SB	OPS+
Edgardo Alfonzo	8	29.5	18.6	.0272	.292	120	45	113
Daniel Murphy	7	12.5	6.7	.0138	.288	62	57	109
Wally Backman	9	11.6	8.5	.0152	.283	7	106	97
Jeff Kent	5	8.4	7.6	.0169	.279	67	12	107
Ron Hunt	4	8.3	8.3	.0181	.282	20	21	107
Gregg Jefferies	5	6.1	5.4	.0131	.276	42	63	111

Second base has not been a historically strong position for the Mets, in part because they have rarely had the same player as a starter for more than three consecutive seasons. **Edgardo Alfonzo** (1995–2002) spent the majority of his career with the Mets but split his time between 2B (524 games) and 3B (515). He had several solid seasons, including 1999, when he hit .304 with 27 HR and 108 RBI, and 2000, when he was an All-Star and hit .324 with 25 HR and 94 RBI.

The backup 2B for this roster was not an easy choice, but I went with **Daniel Murphy** (2008–09, '11–15), who started his career for the Mets and was an All-Star in 2014. He started to develop a bit more power in 2015, and was the NLCS MVP when he went 9-for-17 with 4 HR. He went only 3-for-20 as the Mets lost the World Series, and then left the club by signing as a free agent with the Nationals.

You could also make a case for the hustling Wally Backman (1980–88), who always seemed to find a way to get dirt on his uniform. He frequently platooned with others and so played in 120 or more games only three times, but he still had 30+ steals twice and with a .320 average was a key part of the 1986 champions.

I briefly considered several other candidates, none of whom achieved a 10 WAR score during their time with the Mets. Gregg Jefferies (1987–91) first played for the Mets at the age of 19 and was a hot prospect early on, but he never lived up to that advanced billing. He had double-digit HR power and stole 20+ bases twice but didn't play very good defense at 2B or 3B. Jeff Kent (1992–96) followed Jefferies at 2B in New York, hitting 20+ HR for the Mets twice before reaching stardom for the Giants and others. And lastly, Ron Hunt (1963–66) started his career with the Mets and hit .282, but with little power or speed. He was an All-Star twice and was the first New York Met to start an All-Star Game.

3rd Base

Name	YR	WAR	W3	W/G	AVG	HR	SB	OPS+
David Wright	14	50.1	22.3	.0318	.296	242	196	133
Howard Johnson	9	21.9	14.8	.0190	.251	192	202	124
Wayne Garrett	8	13.9	9.7	.0157	.237	55	33	95
Robin Ventura	3	11.0	11.0	.0248	.260	77	6	113
Bobby Bonilla	5	8.3	8.3	.0161	.270	95	8	128
Hubie Brooks	6	4.9	5.8	.0075	.267	44	31	94

Amongst non-pitchers, **David Wright** (2004–16, 18) is easily the Mets' all-time WAR leader. Wright hit .300+ with 25+ HR and 100+ RBI in his first four full seasons and even was a 30/30 man in 2007, when he hit 30 HR with 34 SB. He has been an All-Star seven times and earned two Gold Glove Awards for his handiwork at the hot corner. Injuries have in recent years reduced his production, and kept him off the field entirely in 2017 and almost all of 2018, but he is clearly deserving of a starting spot on this All-Time dream team.

Howard Johnson (1985–93) was a two-time All-Star for the Mets, cracking 30+ HRs three times and 20+ twice more. He led the league in 1991 with 38 HR and 117 RBI. What I often forget is that HoJo could run too: in those three 30+-HR seasons, he also swiped 30+ bases, and he stole another 20+ in three other seasons. He had a low batting average (.251), struck out far too often (five times with 100+), and was not a great fielder, but he clearly deserved the backup 3B spot on this roster.

As with 2B, there were several others I considered briefly, starting with Wayne Garrett (1969–76), who hit double-digit HR three times but had a low average (.237) and played 140+ games only twice. Robin Ventura (1999–2001) played three years for the Mets, including an impressive 1999 campaign, when he hit .301 with 32 HR and 120 RBI and took home the Gold Glove Award. But the next two years saw his average plummet into the .230s and his power numbers drop as well. Hubie Brooks (1980–84, '91) started his career with the Mets and returned for one season in 1991. His best offensive seasons were between these two stints while playing for the Expos, and he also didn't provide very good defense at the hot corner. Neither did Bobby Bonilla (1992–95, '99), who also had two trials with the Mets. He hit 34 HR in 1993, and the team tried to hide his good offense at 3B and then the OF, but it just never seemed like he fit in well.

Shortstop

Name	YR	WAR	W3	W/G	AVG	HR	SB	OPS+
José Reyes	12	27.1	15.8	.0199	.282	108	408	104
Bud Harrelson	13	18.6	9.6	.0141	.234	6	115	75
Rey Ordóñez	7	0.9	4.0	.0010	.245	8	28	58

Two switch-hitters were the obvious shortstops for this All-Time team roster. **José Reyes** (2003–11, '16–18) provided the Mets with outstanding speed, leading the NL in SB from 2005 through '07 with totals of 60, 64, and 78. He also paced the NL four times in triples, including 19 in 2008 and two seasons with 17. A four-time All-Star, he led the NL in batting with a .337 average in 2011 before signing as a free agent with the Marlins. He returned to New York in 2016 and now plays a variety of positions, including SS, 3B, 2B, and even a little OF.

Bud Harrelson (1965–77) played most of his career in New York and was a good fielder, capturing the Gold Glove Award in 1971. He had some speed too, stealing 23 and 28 bases during his All-Star campaigns of 1970 and '71. An extremely light hitter, he batted only .234 and had just 6 HR in 4,390 at-bats for the Mets.

Another good-glove, light-hitting Mets SS was Rey Ordóñez (1996–2002). Playing most of his career with NY, Ordonez at times displayed brilliant defense and earned the Gold Glove Award from 1997 through '99. But he batted only .245, had little speed, and hit just 8 HR in 2,937 at-bats for the Mets. Playing in the heavy offense years that he did, Ordóñez's cumulative WAR for the Mets barely registers at 0.9.

Catcher

Name	YR	WAR	W3	W/G	AVG	HR	SB	OPS+
Mike Piazza	8	24.5	14.9	.0252	.296	220	7	136
John Stearns	10	19.5	12.4	.0241	.259	46	91	102
Jerry Grote	12	15.7	8.5	.0127	.256	35	14	85
Gary Carter	5	11.3	11.4	.0188	.249	89	2	104

Coming over in 1998 from the Dodgers (after a few days in Florida), **Mike Piazza** (1998–2005) continued to make the case that he was the best-hitting catcher of all time. Although more of his best years were in LA, he still managed seasons of 40, 38, 36, and 33 HR for the Mets and was an All-Star for them six times. Although often criticized for his poor ability to throw out runners, his batting numbers more than compensated for any deficiency in that aspect of the game.

A good hitter (though in decline with the Mets) and certainly a better defender, **Gary Carter** (1985–89) hit 32 HR with 100 RBI in 1985. He was then a key part of the 1986 championship squad, hitting 24 HR with 105 RBI. Although he played only five seasons in NY, he was an All-Star in four of them.

You could make a case for two other catchers as well, starting with **John Stearns** (1975–84), a four-time All-Star who demonstrated some speed for a catcher with four seasons of double-digit SB, even though he had 400+ at-bats only three times. And Jerry Grote (1966–76) was good behind the plate and was an All-Star twice. But he was a very light hitter and never played more than 126 games in a season. In the end, I decided to give one of the two "extra spots" on the Mets' All-Time roster to Stearns, as it's always wise to carry a third catcher.

Left Field

Name	YR	WAR	W3	W/G	AVG	HR	SB	OPS+
Cleon Jones	12	18.1	15.9	.0151	.281	93	91	111
Kevin McReynolds	6	15.7	11.7	.0199	.272	122	67	120
Bernard Gilkey	3	10.1	10.1	.0266	.273	52	29	117
Steve Henderson	4	9.4	7.8	.0189	.287	35	55	120
Michael Conforto	4	9.1	8.7	.0213	.251	76	7	125
Cliff Floyd	4	7.7	8.1	.0165	.268	81	32	116
George Foster	5	4.7	4.8	.0072	.252	99	5	103

There were two pretty obvious choices here. **Cleon Jones** (1963, '65–75) had a career year in 1969 to help lead the Amazin' Mets to their first championship. That was his one time as an All-Star, as he batted .340 (third in the league) with 12 HR and 16 SB. Jones spent all but his last season playing for New York, often managing double-digit HR or SB, but rarely appearing amongst the league leaders in any category.

After coming over from San Diego, **Kevin McReynolds** (1987–91, '94) hit 20+ HR in his first four seasons in NY. He also showed a little speed, with double-digit steals in three seasons. McReynolds came in third in the MVP vote in 1988, behind outfield mate Strawberry, who came in second.

During the winter of 1996 the Mets made a great trade, shipping Yudith Ozorio, Erik Hiljus, and Eric Ludwick to the Cardinals for the multitalented Bernard Gilkey (1996–98). In his first year in New York, Gilkey produced the third-highest single-season WAR for a Mets non-pitcher when he batted .317 with 44 doubles, 30 HR, 108 runs, 117 RBI, 17 SB and a 155 OPS+. That was easily his career year, though, and the Mets traded him to Arizona during the 1998 season.

Current Mets youngster Michael Conforto (2015-18) has developed into a good player, representing the team as an All-Star in 2017, and hitting 25+ BR both that season and in 2018. He started out primarily as a LF, but now plays quite a bit in CF as well. Another few solid seasons and he'll crack this All-Time team roster.

A few others deserve brief mention, such as Cliff Floyd (2003–06), who played parts of four seasons for the Mets, with his best year being 2005, when he hit 34 HR with 98 RBI. Steve Henderson (1977–80) played his first four seasons for the Mets, batting .287 and providing a moderate combination of power and speed. And George Foster (1982–86) came to NY in the twilight of his career. He provided the Mets with 20+ HR three times, but he was clearly no longer capable of providing the big numbers he had in Cincinnati.

Center Field

Name	YR	WAR	W3	W/G	AVG	HR	SB	OPS+
Carlos Beltrán	7	31.3	20.5	.0373	.280	149	100	129
Mookie Wilson	10	20.7	9.3	.0185	.276	60	281	100
Lenny Dykstra	5	16.5	12.0	.0303	.278	30	116	115
Tommie Agee	5	14.0	14.1	.0212	.262	82	92	110
Lee Mazzilli	10	12.4	11.4	.0123	.264	68	152	112
Ángel Pagán	4	10.9	10.4	.0277	.284	24	87	106

Relatively speaking, the Mets have been strong over the years at center field—enough that I'm going to choose four players here, in place of a second right fielder (some of these guys did in fact play some RF for the Mets too). First up is **Carlos Beltrán** (2005–11), who didn't immediately impress when he joined the Mets, but in his second year smashed 41 HR with 116 RBI and 127 runs scored. He followed that up with 33 and 27 HR with 112 RBI in each of the next two years. A five-time All-Star during his time with the Mets, he also earned three Gold Glove Awards for his defense in center field.

Mookie Wilson (1980–89) provided little power but was a good runner, with three consecutive seasons of 40+ steals and another four with 20+. He was a consistent hitter, batting between .271 and .299 every year from 1981 through 1988. But he almost never walked, so his OBP was a pathetic .318.

Lenny Dykstra (1985–89) started his career with the Mets and was the energetic center fielder for the 1986 championship team. He stole 25+ bases and was a good fielder in each of his three full seasons for the Mets, but he went on to play most of his career, and have his best seasons, with the Phillies.

Tommie Agee (1968–72) played five full seasons for the Mets and was the CF on the 1969 championship team, hitting a career-high 26 HR that year and making two outstanding catches in Game Three of the World Series. He had an even better overall season in 1970, hitting .286 with 24 HR, 31 SB, and 107 runs, and he took home the Gold Glove Award too.

There were two other Mets CF worth mentioning briefly, starting with Lee Mazzilli (1976–81, '86–89). He had three solid seasons of double-digit HR and SB totals of 20, 34, and 41. Primarily a center fielder, he also played a little first base. He returned and played for them again from 1986 to '89, mostly serving as a pinch-hitter. And Ángel Pagán (2008–11) played parts of four seasons for the Mets, and in his two full seasons had 37 and 32 stolen bases.

Right Field

Name	YR	WAR	W3	W/G	AVG	HR	SB	OPS+
Darryl Strawberry	8	36.5	18.1	.0329	.263	252	191	145
Joel Youngblood	6	9.3	8.5	.0152	.274	38	39	108
Ron Swoboda	6	7.0	6.4	.0095	.242	69	20	101
Rusty Staub	9	6.8	6.1	.0072	.276	75	6	119

Darryl Strawberry (1983–90) had many fine power seasons before making poor life decisions that ruined his career. He had 25+ HR in each of his eight seasons with the Mets (with highs of 39, 39, and 37), with 20+ SB in five of those years. He was Rookie of the Year in 1983, and then was an All-Star in his seven other seasons with the Mets. His big swing led to a lot of strikeouts, but he was a very popular player and a key part of their 1986 championship squad.

Interestingly, no one else who primarily played right field for the Mets managed to accumulate a 10+ WAR score. That said, Rusty Staub (1972–75, '81–85) had two stints with the Mets, though during the latter he was mostly used as a pinch-hitter. 1975 was his best season in NY, when he hit .282 with 19 HR and 105 RBI. Ron Swoboda (1965–70) hit 19 HR during his rookie campaign but never again reached that level. He was a low-average hitter (.242), albeit during an era of pitching dominance. And lastly, Joel Youngblood (1977–82) provided useful versatility in that it seemed he could play all over the field, but he was not much of an offensive force.

Starting Pitching

Name	YR	WAR	W3	W-L	ERA	WHIP	ERA+
Tom Seaver	12	79.1	30.1	198-124	2.57	1.076	136
Dwight Gooden	11	46.5	23.2	157-85	3.10	1.175	116
Jerry Koosman	12	36.9	16.2	140-137	3.09	1.219	113

Sid Fernandez	10	29.3	13.6	98-78	3.14	1.113	113
Jon Matlack	7	27.2	19.7	82-81	3.03	1.195	115
Jacob deGrom	5	27.2	20.3	55-41	2.67	1.072	143
Al Leiter	7	26.5	15.8	95-67	3.42	1.300	124
David Cone	7	20.3	14.4	81-51	3.13	1.192	112
Ron Darling	9	17.3	12.5	99-70	3.50	1.288	101
Rick Reed	5	17.2	12.3	59-36	3.66	1.155	117
Tom Glavine	5	17.2	12.0	61-56	3.97	1.373	107
Johan Santana	4	15.6	15.6	46-34	3.18	1.201	127
R.A. Dickey	3	13.5	13.5	39-28	2.95	1.150	129

The ace of this Mets staff was clearly nine-time All-Star **Tom Seaver** (1967–77, '83), who more than any other player lifted the Mets from perennial cellar-dweller to regular contender. After winning the Rookie of the Year Award in 1967 with a 16-13 record and 2.76 ERA, he followed it up with a 16-12 mark and 2.20 ERA. He performed at a truly higher level in 1969, leading the team to the World Series with a 25-7 mark and a 2.21 ERA. Continuing his mastery of the league, he led in ERA in 1970 (2.82), 1971 (1.76), and 1973 (2.08). He had 200+ strikeouts every year from 1968 through 1976 and took home three Cy Young Awards (1969, '73, and '75.) Sporting an appropriate nickname, Tom truly was "terrific."

Equally as impressive early on in his career, perhaps even more so, was **Dwight Gooden** (1984–94). Bursting onto the scene at age 19 in 1984, he went 17-9 with a 2.60 ERA to capture Rookie of the Year honors. His 276 strikeouts that year shattered the long-standing rookie record of 245 held by Herb Score. Gooden didn't suffer a sophomore slump, as he took home the NL Cy Young Award in 1985 after posting a Triple Crown season: 24-4 with a 1.53 ERA and 268 strikeouts. Though not as dominant, he pitched well for the 1986 champions (17-6, 2.84). Dr. K. managed three other 15+-win seasons, but due to a shoulder injury and his admitted drug usage, his career went steadily downhill. His last star season was 1990—at age 25.

The rest of this staff was good but lacked the shockingly awesome peak performances of Seaver and Gooden. In 1968 **Jerry Koosman** (1967–78) was an All-Star and runner-up for the Rookie of the Year Award after posting an impressive 19-12 record and 2.08 ERA. He quickly became a solid lefty complement to Seaver, going 17-9 with a 2.28 ERA for the 1969 Amazin' Mets, and later posting a 21-10 record in 1976. An All-Star in his first two full seasons, he never was chosen again. Kooz revived his career briefly in the AL after suffering through the Mets' abysmal 1977 and 1978 campaigns (which saw Koosman, as their ace, go 8-20 and 3-15, even while maintaining a respectable ERA).

I decided to select four relievers for this All-Time team, so that left five more spots for starting pitchers. I went with three more left-handers next, starting with **Jon Matlack** (1971–77), who was voted the 1972 Rookie of the Year after going 15-10 with a 2.32 ERA. A three-time All-Star for the Mets, he earned the most victories in his final year in New York, posting a 17-10 record and 2.95 ERA.

In his first year with the Mets, at age 32, **Al Leiter** (1998–2004) went 17-6 with a 2.47 ERA—not bad for 1998, the year that saw McGwire and Sosa breaking records. He later added seasons with records of 16-8 and 15-9.

Sid Fernandez (1984–93) pitched for the Mets for a decade and was a key part of the 1986 champions, going 16-6 with 200 strikeouts. He was an All-Star that year and the next, though he never again won more than 14 games in a season. Although not exactly built like your typical athlete, Fernandez held opposing batters to a .197 batting average and was usually amongst the leaders in strikeouts.

After only five seasons, **Jacob deGrom** (2014–18) has earned a spot on this All-Time team's pitching staff. He won the Rookie of the Year Award in 2014 after a partial season with a 9-6 record and 2.69 ERA. Since then he has posted three seasons with 200+ strikeouts, including his phenomenal 2018 campaign where a lack of run support led to a 10-9 record while he led the league with a 1.70 ERA.

You could argue who should get the last two spots. **David Cone** (1987–92, 2003) dominated the NL in his first full season, posting a 20-3 record, 2.22 ERA, and 213 strikeouts. He later led the NL in strikeouts with 233 in 1990 and 241 in 1991, though he won only 14 games each year. And Hawaiian-born **Ron Darling** (1983–91) went 16-6 with a 2.90 ERA in 1985, and essentially did the same for the 1986 championship club by going 15-6 with a 2.81 ERA. He played an important role for the Mets during the World Series, as he was the starter in Games One, Four, and Seven, posting a 1.53 ERA in 17.2 IP. Then in 1988 he went 17-9, and in 1989 he took home a Gold Glove Award.

You could make a case for Johan Santana (2008–10, '12), who came over to the Mets in 2008 from Minnesota, where he had won two Cy Young Awards. He immediately had an impact, going 16-7 and leading the NL with a 2.53 ERA. Injuries struck, and in particular he missed the entire 2011 major league season due to shoulder surgery. He returned in 2012 and pitched the first no-hitter in Mets history, albeit one aided by a controversial call.

Tom Glavine (2003–07) joined the Mets late in his career, and although named an All-Star twice, he clearly wasn't the pitcher he used to be. His best season in NY resulted in a 15-7 record and 3.82 ERA. Rick Reed (1997–

2001) had a winning record each year he pitched for the Mets, with his most victories coming in 1998, when he went 16-11. R.A. Dickey pitched for the Mets for three years, and at age 37 used his knuckleball to take home the NL Cy Young Award in 2012 with a 20-6 record, 2.73 ERA, and league-leading 230 strikeouts.

Relief Pitching

Name	YR	WAR	W3	SV	W-L	ERA	WHIP	ERA+
Tug McGraw	9	13.6	11.3	86	47-55	3.17	1.306	114
Jesse Orosco	8	12.8	8.9	107	47-47	2.73	1.209	133
John Franco	14	11.4	4.6	276	48-56	3.10	1.365	132
Armando Benítez	5	9.9	7.6	160	18-14	2.70	1.133	159
Skip Lockwood	5	8.2	5.4	65	24-36	2.80	1.114	126
Roger McDowell	5	4.9	5.0	84	33-29	3.13	1.234	112
Billy Wagner	4	5.0	4.9	101	5-5	2.37	1.054	183

There was no shortage of talent to choose from for the bullpen. The top three were all lefties, starting with **John Franco** (1990–2001, '03–04). Although his WAR results were not as impressive as some others, he was the closer for the Mets for most of his career. He posted seven seasons of 25+ saves and led the NL with 33 in 1990 and 30 in strike-shortened 1994. Although an All-Star three times early in his career for the Reds, he was selected only once (his first season) in all his years with the Mets.

Tug McGraw (1965–67, '69–74) pitched roughly the first half of his career for the Mets, and then the second half for the Phillies. He toiled before the closer role became the specialty it is today, but his numbers didn't lie. He had five strong seasons, two with 25+ saves, and three with earned run averages of 2.24, 1.70, and 1.70 again.

Jesse Orosco (1979, 1981–87) started his ridiculously long career for the Mets, providing them with five good seasons as a combined setup man and co-closer. He was key to the 1986 champions, posting 21 saves and a 2.33 ERA. Also deserving mention were his All-Star campaigns of 1983 (13-7, 1.47, 17 saves) and 1984 (10-6, 2.59, 31 saves).

Armando Benítez (1999–2003) is second in all-time saves for the Mets, so you could make a case for him over Cone or Darling on this All-Time team. Before taking over the closer role in 2000 and posting consecutive 40+-save seasons, he was co-closer with Franco and was just dominating: a 1.85 ERA with 128 strikeouts in only 78 innings.

There have been a few other Mets relievers of note, starting with Roger McDowell (1985–89), who was co-closer with Orosco for several years but didn't stay with the team as long. He posted 16 to 25 saves in his four full seasons with the Mets and was an important part of the bullpen for their 1986 championship team. Skip Lockwood (1975–79) had three fine years as closer (1976–78), and two other partial seasons with a 1.49 ERA in each. And lastly, Billy Wagner (2006–09) was at times just as dominating as Benítez had been, pitching three years as the Mets closer from 2006 through '08 and posting save totals of 40, 34, and 27.

Managers

Name	YR	From-To	W-L	PCT	PS	WS
Davey Johnson	7	1984–90	595-417	.588	2	1
Gil Hodges	4	1968–71	339-309	.523	1	1
Bobby Valentine	7	1996–2002	536-467	.534	2	0
Terry Collins	7	2011–17	551-583	.486	2	0
Willie Randolph	4	2005–08	302-253	.544	1	0
Yogi Berra	4	1972–75	292-296	.497	1	0

Two managers, **Davey Johnson** and **Gil Hodges**, have led the Mets to World Series championships. But Johnson managed the team longer and had a far higher overall winning percentage, so he deserved the top honors here. To round out a top four I went with **Bobby Valentine** and **Terry Collins**. While Collins' winning percentage is significantly lower than Randolph's, he managed the team longer, got a lot out of the players he had, and when more talent arrived he led them to the postseason twice, including the World Series in 2015.

Starting Lineup

What would mythical starting lineups look like for this All-Time roster?

Against RHP:
José Reyes SS (S)
Carlos Beltrán CF (S)
Keith Hernandez 1B (L)
Mike Piazza C (R)
Darryl Strawberry RF (L)
David Wright 3B (R)
Howard Johnson DH (S)
Edgardo Alfonzo 2B (R)
Mookie Wilson LF (S)

Against LHP:
José Reyes SS (S)
Carlos Beltrán CF (S)
David Wright 3B (R)
Mike Piazza DH (R)
Darryl Strawberry RF (L)
Gary Carter C (R)
Keith Hernandez 1B (L)
Edgardo Alfonzo 2B (R)
Cleon Jones LF (R)

For DH I would suggest Howard Johnson, at least against righties (although a switch-hitter, he hit better against righties than lefties). Against lefties the lineup could include Carter's better defense behind the plate by shifting Piazza to DH, or I suppose McReynolds would be a good DH candidate too. Wilson played over 100 games in LF, so he is a good platoon partner with Jones. And Alfonzo hit both righties and lefties equally well, but you could use the left-handed hitting Murphy against some right-handers.

Depth Chart

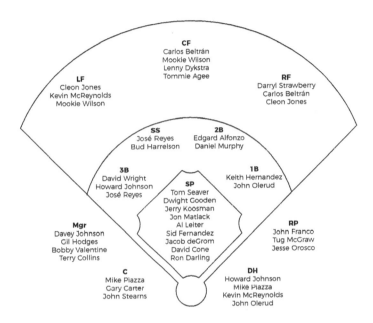

CF
Carlos Beltrán
Mookie Wilson
Lenny Dykstra
Tommie Agee

LF
Cleon Jones
Kevin McReynolds
Mookie Wilson

RF
Darryl Strawberry
Carlos Beltrán
Cleon Jones

SS
José Reyes
Bud Harrelson

2B
Edgard Alfonzo
Daniel Murphy

3B
David Wright
Howard Johnson
José Reyes

1B
Keith Hernandez
John Olerud

SP
Tom Seaver
Dwight Gooden
Jerry Koosman
Jon Matlack
Al Leiter
Sid Fernandez
Jacob deGrom
David Cone
Ron Darling

Mgr
Davey Johnson
Gil Hodges
Bobby Valentine
Terry Collins

RP
John Franco
Tug McGraw
Jesse Orosco

C
Mike Piazza
Gary Carter
John Stearns

DH
Howard Johnson
Mike Piazza
Kevin McReynolds
John Olerud

Prospects for Current Players

David Wright and Jacob deGrom are already on this roster, but what are the prospects of other current Mets players making this All-Time team? With a bit more time I could see outfielders Yoenis Céspedes and Michael Conforto, or some of the young pitchers, forcing some changes to this roster. We'll see...

Retired Player Numbers

Gil Hodges (14, manager), Mike Piazza (31), Casey Stengel (37, manager), Tom Seaver (41)

Selections from Other Authors and Fan Surveys

1981: *This Date in NY Mets History*, by Dennis D'Agostino

This is the earliest Mets all-time team that my research uncovered. Since the Mets began as a franchise in 1962, this roster pulled names from only a 20-year period. The author gave a paragraph or two per position, describing the player's highlights and his reasons for the selection.

At first base was Ed Kranepool, and D'Agostino noted that Steady Eddie was an important pinch-hitter for the Mets when he wasn't the starter. He gave honorable mention to John Milner and Donn Clendenon. At second base he chose Ron Hunt, with Ken Boswell, Félix Millan, and Doug Flynn mentioned.

The obvious choice at short was Bud Harrelson, though I thought the author exaggerated Harrelson's good defense a bit when he said that Bud "had no peer as a defensive shortstop during his Met tenure." For me, Mark Belanger, Luis Aparicio, and Dave Concepción all come to mind as defensive "peers" during the years 1965 to 1977. The author also mentioned Mets shortstops Roy McMillan, Ed Bressoud, and Frank Taveras.

In this pre-HoJo era, the third base selection had to be Wayne Garrett. The author noted that through 1981, this position had been a "revolving door at times," and then mentioned the various others who had occupied it. For catcher, the author chose Jerry Grote, noting that Grote was "one of baseball's top defensive catchers for over a decade" and adding the interesting tidbit that he was "especially adept at gunning down Lou Brock"—an important ability for that era.

For the outfield he chose Cleon Jones in LF, Tommie Agee in CF, and Rusty Staub in RF—all fine selections through 1981. He of course mentioned Mazzilli as another outfielder who had enjoyed success as a Met, alongside Dave Kingman, Frank Thomas, Willie Mays, Art Shamsky, Ron Swoboda, and Steve Henderson.

Seaver and Koosman were obvious top starting pitcher selections, though the author did mention Jon Matlack, Craig Swan, and others. And for relievers, he rightly chose Skip Lockwood as RHP and Tug McGraw as LHP.

1991: Louisville Slugger Presents: The New York Mets, by Bill Shannon

In the Mets installment of this series of books in 1991, the author chose an All-Time all-star team that consisted of Kranepool, Millan, Harrelson, and Johnson in the infield, Jones in LF, Agee in CF, and Strawberry in RF. In choosing Millan at 2B, the author noted that he batted .290 and played a superb second base in 1973, and then said "Indeed, it was probably the acquisition of Millan in an off-season deal with Atlanta that helped move the Mets from third to first in the standings." Koosman as the top LHP, Seaver as the top RHP, and McGraw as the top reliever were all solid choices.

1992: *The All-Time All-Star Baseball Book*, by Nick Acocella and Donald Dewey

A decade later, some players for an All-Time Mets lineup had changed. The authors went with 1B Hernandez, 2B Millan, 3B Johnson, SS Harrelson, C Grote, OF Jones, Strawberry, and Staub, with Seaver of course as the top pitcher. The choice of Millan at 2B was a close call, though the authors rightly gave honorable mention to Hunt, along with Koosman, Agee, McGraw, Mazzilli, Gooden, and Darling.

1995: *Baseball Ratings*, by Charles F. Faber

The Faber system as applied in 1995 created a reasonable all-time team with an infield of Kranepool, Millan, Harrelson, and Johnson and an outfield of Strawberry, Wilson, and Jones. His system seems to weight longevity more, which would explain the choice of Kranepool over Hernandez, and also the choice of Grote over Carter as catcher. He naturally had Seaver as the pitcher and added Orosco as the reliever.

2003: *Rob Neyer's Big Book of Baseball Lineups*, by Rob Neyer

There were not many differences between Neyer's choices and my own. The starting infield was Piazza, Hernandez, Alfonzo, Johnson, and Harrelson. And he included Carter, Olerud, Hunt, Kevin Elster, and Ventura as his backups, though regarding Hunt at 2B he noted that what made him (in)famous—being hit by pitches a lot—didn't really start until he left NY.

Neyer's Mets OF was solid with McReynolds and Jones in LF, Mazzilli and Agee in CF, and Strawberry and Staub in RF. In defense of Mazzilli, one value to the Mets came in what they got in return for trading him to the Rangers before the 1982 season: Ron Darling and Walt Terrell (who ultimately was traded for Howard Johnson).

Neyer's pitching staff was, in order: Seaver, Gooden, Koosman, Leiter, Cone, Matlack, Fernandez, and Reed. He went with Franco and Orosco as his two relief pitching selections, and his top five managers were Johnson, Valentine, Hodges, Berra, and Harrelson.

2009: *Few and Chosen: Defining Mets Greatness Across the Eras*, by
Rusty Staub with Phil Pepe

As with each book in this series, a top-five list was given for each position.

1B: Hernandez, Kranepool, Kingman, Olerud, Milner/Delgado (tie)

2B: Kent, Jefferies, Millan, Backman, Tim Teufel

3B: Wright, Johnson, Alfonzo, Brooks, Garrett

SS: Harrelson, Reyes, Ordóñez, Elster, Rafael Santana

C: Piazza, Carter, Grote, Hundley/Stearns (tie)

LF: Jones, McReynolds, Floyd, Foster, Gilkey

CF: Beltrán, Wilson, Mazzilli, Agee, Dykstra

RF: Strawberry, Bonilla, Swoboda, Shamsky, Youngblood

RHP: Seaver, Gooden, Darling, Cone, Bobby Jones

LHP: Koosman, Leiter, Matlack, Fernandez, Bob Ojeda

RP: Franco, McGraw, Orosco, Wagner, McDowell

I mostly liked Rusty's lists. I would argue Backman deserved to be higher: the
authors said many great things about him, but tied him together with his platoon partner Teufel for those last two spots.

Top WAR Single Seasons – Hitters (7+)

Name	Year	WAR	AVG	HR	R	RBI	SB	OPS+
David Wright	2007	8.3	.325	30	113	107	34	149
Carlos Beltrán	2006	8.2	.275	41	127	116	18	150
Bernard Gilkey	1996	8.0	.317	30	108	117	17	155
John Olerud	1998	7.6	.354	22	91	93	2	163
Lance Johnson	1996	7.2	.333	9	117	69	50	125
Cleon Jones	1969	7.0	.340	12	92	75	16	151
David Wright	2012	7.0	.306	21	91	93	15	144

Not surprising that David Wright is the only player to appear on this list twice.
And Lance Johnson played only one full year for the Mets, but it was his one and
only All-Star campaign, as he hit .333 with 50 SB and 117 runs scored, while
pacing the NL with 682 at-bats, 227 hits, and a very impressive 21 triples.

Top WAR Single Seasons – Pitchers (7+)

Name	Year	WAR	W-L	ERA	IP	SO	ERA+
Dwight Gooden	1985	13.3	24-4	1.53	276.2	268	229
Tom Seaver	1973	11.0	19-10	2.08	290.0	251	175
Tom Seaver	1971	10.9	20-10	1.76	286.1	289	194
Jacob deGrom	2018	10.1	10-9	1.70	217.0	269	216
Jon Matlack	1974	8.7	13-15	2.41	265.1	195	149
Tom Seaver	1975	8.2	22-9	2.38	280.1	243	146
Tom Seaver	1969	7.2	25-7	2.21	273.1	208	165
Johan Santana	2008	7.1	16-7	2.53	234.1	206	166
Tom Seaver	1968	7.0	16-12	2.20	278.0	205	137

Tom Seaver naturally dominates this list, though Dwight Gooden's 1985 campaign not surprisingly tops the list, and by a healthy margin. And Matlack's 1974 season was obviously far better than his record indicates. The Mets were 71-91 that year, and averaged only two runs per game in Matlack's 15 losses.

Franchise Player

The obvious choice here was Tom Seaver—a player who was literally nicknamed The Franchise. He was consistently great, arguably the best pitcher of his era, and a class act. In fact, he is a perfect example of a franchise player in that in some ways he encapsulates the history and the nature of this franchise.

CHAPTER 23

The Rangers Franchise All-Time Dream Team

The Rangers franchise actually started out as the second version of the Washington Senators, the season the original Senators moved to Minnesota to become the Twins. The second Senators franchise joined the American League as an expansion team in 1961 and stayed in DC through 1971, posting only one winning season during that stretch. Before the 1972 season began, the team moved to Arlington, Texas, and became the Rangers. They didn't start out well in their new home, but they improved a bit by the late '70s. Making the postseason didn't happen until 1996, when they won the AL West division. They did so again in 1998 and 1999, but in all three cases lost in the League Division Series.

The Rangers have often had a lineup full of sluggers, while historically their pitching has been weak. More recently they have managed to field both a powerful lineup and a strong rotation, and that led them to consecutive World Series appearances in 2010 and 2011, although they lost to the Giants and Cardinals, respectively. Given this history, the All-Time team for the Rangers was not surprisingly populated with several power hitters, but was relatively weak in speed and pitching.

1st Base

Name	YR	WAR	W3	W/G	AVG	HR	SB	OPS+
Rafael Palmeiro	10	44.4	17.8	.0282	.290	321	44	137
Mark Teixeira	5	21.5	16.2	.0310	.283	153	11	128
Pete O'Brien	7	18.1	10.9	.0191	.273	114	19	112
Mike Hargrove	5	17.1	12.5	.0236	.293	47	10	130
Will Clark	5	15.1	10.1	.0248	.308	77	8	124
Mike Epstein	6	6.0	6.8	.0111	.248	74	7	131

I think that regardless of what you think of his steroid situation, **Rafael Palmeiro** (1989–93, '99–2003) deserves the starting 1B spot on this roster. I say that because even if you reduce his numbers a bit, he still was more productive than any other candidate. Palmeiro had two stints with the Rangers, providing good defense and ample power with three 40+-HR seasons, three more with 30+, and six seasons with 100+ RBI. His best numbers came in 1999, when he hit .324 with 47 HR and 148 RBI.

There were several candidates for the backup spot, but in the end, I decided to go with **Mark Teixeira** (2003–07). He started his career for the Rangers, playing four-and-a-half seasons before being traded to the Braves in a deal that brought them Elvis Andrus, Neftalí Feliz, Matt Harrison, and Jarrod Saltalamacchia. Teixeira hit 26 HR during his rookie season and smashed 33 to 43 HR with 110+ RBI in each of his next three years. Tex also provided great defense, winning the AL Gold Glove Award in both 2005 and 2006.

Like Teixeira, Mike Hargrove (1974–78) started his fine career with the Rangers, batting .323 and winning the Rookie of the Year Award in 1974. He was a .290 hitter during his five seasons in Texas and had a good eye at the plate: he led the league in walks twice and provided a .399 OBP. He had only moderate power, though, with his high HR season being 1977 with only 18.

Another candidate was Pete O'Brien (1982–88), who similarly started his career for Texas and hit 16 to 23 HR in five consecutive seasons. While a good defender at 1B, he was not a very good base runner (31 CS vs. only 19 SB). Will Clark (1994–98) played five seasons for the Rangers during the second half of his career. He hit .308 overall and had a high of 23 HR and 102 RBI in 1998 (the only year he played in more than 125 games for Texas). And finally, Mike Epstein (1967–71 '73) played for the Senators and Rangers for parts of six seasons and smacked 30 HR with 85 RBI in 1969.

2nd Base

Name	YR	WAR	W3	W/G	AVG	HR	SB	OPS+
Ian Kinsler	8	35.1	18.1	.0329	.273	156	172	111
Julio Franco	5	20.2	18.3	.0320	.307	55	98	129
Bump Wills	5	15.6	12.2	.0222	.265	30	161	93
Mark McLemore	5	10.3	8.5	.0162	.268	22	83	83
Lenny Randle	6	5.3	6.8	.0087	.253	11	77	83

Ian Kinsler (2006–13) was the clear top choice at 2B for this All-Time team. Although at times prone to injury, Kinsler was an All-Star three times and provided the Rangers with a good combination of power and speed, including two 30/30 seasons in 2009 and 2011. He also scored 100+ runs four times, with a high of 121 in 2011.

As was the case at 1B, there were a few candidates for the 2B backup. After many good seasons in Cleveland, **Julio Franco** (1989–93) brought his wacky batting stance to Texas and slashed his way to a .297 average that included a league-leading .341 in 1991. He was an All-Star in his first three seasons in Texas, seasons in which he stole 21 to 36 bases and had 11 to 15 HR.

Bump Wills (1977–81) played most of his short career with the Rangers, stealing 161 bases, including 52 in 1978 (still the franchise record). Mark McLemore (1995–99) provided a little speed, stealing 20+ bases twice for the Rangers. And finally, Lenny Randle (1971–76) had three partial seasons, then three full seasons with this franchise, including 1974, when he hit .302 with 26 SB.

3rd Base

Name	YR	WAR	W3	W/G	AVG	HR	SB	OPS+
Adrián Beltré	8	43.4	20.4	.0395	.304	199	8	128
Buddy Bell	8	36.2	19.6	.0378	.293	87	24	117
Ken McMullen	6	21.2	15.2	.0276	.251	86	15	107
Hank Blalock	8	13.4	12.3	.0147	.269	152	13	102
Steve Buechele	8	11.0	9.2	.0124	.240	94	14	92
Dean Palmer	8	8.6	7.4	.0111	.247	154	28	107

Adrián Beltré (2011–18) by now has earned the top spot at 3B on this dream team. A three-time All-Star for the Rangers, he has hit 30+ HR four times to go with a .304 average. And on defense, he continues to shine, having earned three of his five Gold Glove Awards while with Texas.

Until Beltré came along, the clear top 3B for this franchise had been **Buddy Bell** (1979–85, '89). He also provided great defense at the hot corner, taking home six consecutive Gold Glove Awards. A four-time All-Star, he also was a good hitter (.293) with some pop, with 1979 being his best year, as he played every game and hit .299 with 200 hits, 18 HR, and 101 RBI.

Ken McMullen (1965–70) was a good-fielding 3B for the Senators for several years, providing 13 to 20 HR in each of his five full seasons (during an era of strong pitching). You could make a case for him as deserving one of the two "extra spots" on this roster, but there are some solid candidates at other positions too.

Three other players deserve mention here, starting with Hank Blalock (2002–09), who had a relatively short career and played all but his final season for the Rangers. He was an All-Star in his first full year, when he hit .300 with 29 HR and 90 RBI in 2003. He was an All-Star again the next year, when he smacked 32 HR with 110 RBI.

Although not the best fielder and only a .247 hitter, Dean Palmer (1989, '91–97) was another power bat at the hot corner for the Rangers. He provided three seasons with 25+ HR, including 1996, when he clubbed 38 HR with 107 RBI. And immediately prior to Palmer, the Rangers had another low-average (.240) hitter at 3B, Steve Buechele (1985–91, '95). He provided only moderate power for the Rangers, hitting double-digit HR regularly but with a high of only 22, in 1991, when he was traded late in the season to the Pirates.

Shortstop

Name	YR	WAR	W3	W/G	AVG	HR	SB	OPS+
Toby Harrah	11	32.2	17.0	.0238	.257	124	153	112
Elvis Andrus	10	30.0	13.2	.0203	.275	61	271	88
Álex Rodríguez	3	25.5	25.5	.0526	.305	156	44	155
Michael Young	13	25.5	10.1	.0140	.301	177	89	104
Scott Fletcher	4	12.3	11.9	.0234	.280	8	34	94
Ed Brinkman	11	10.1	12.2	.0088	.226	31	27	66

The situation at SS was an interesting one, as it was a case of needing to compare solid, longer careers vs. shorter, peak production. I started at the top of the list above, with **Toby Harrah** (1969, '71–78, '85–86), who spent significant time at 3B and 2B in addition to SS. He provided a combination of power and speed, hitting 20+ HR three times and stealing 20+ bases three times. A three-time All-Star, his best numbers came in 1975, when he hit .293 with 20 HR, 93 RBI, and 23 SB, and in 1977, when he batted just .263 but had 27 HR and 27 SB, while leading the AL with 109 walks.

Current Rangers shortstop **Elvis Andrus** (2009–18) was runner-up for the 2009 Rookie of the Year Award after hitting 8 triples and stealing 33 bases. He was an All-Star the next year and again in 2012, and stole between 21 and 42 bases every year between 2009-17. His best all-around season came in 2017, when like many players he had a power surge leading to career highs of 20 HR, 88 RBI, 44 doubles, and 100 runs, to go with 25 SB and a .297 average.

Michael Young (2000–12) was very versatile but played more games at SS than either 2B or 3B. A fairly consistent hit machine, Young had six seasons with 200+ hits and four with 100+ runs. He also had some power, posting four seasons with 20+ HR and six with 90+ RBI. A seven-time All-Star, he was also a good fielder, taking home the Gold Glove Award at SS in 2008. Overall, Young is the all-time franchise leader in games played, at-bats, hits, runs, doubles, triples, and total bases, and is third in RBI.

What about A-Rod, you ask? Yes, **Álex Rodríguez** (2001–03) had incredible numbers in his three seasons in Texas—in fact, they are three of the four all-time best seasons for the franchise according to WAR. In 2001 he hit .318 with 51 HR, 133 runs, and 135 RBI; in 2002 he hit .300 with 57 HR, 125 runs, and 142 RBI; and finally, in 2003 he hit .298 with 47 HR, 124 runs, and 118 RBI. He led the league in HR every year and in RBI in 2002, won the MVP Award in 2003, and won two Gold Glove Awards for the Rangers as well.

In my view, all four of these players deserve to make this All-Time roster. Who should be considered the starter and backup, and who should make it via the two "extra spots" is what is debatable. In the end, I decided to list Harrah as the starter and Andrus as the backup, but I would listen to arguments for Young and A-Rod too.

I'll close this discussion by noting two others who deserve brief mention, starting with Scott Fletcher (1986–89), who was both a capable fielder and hitter (.280) but provided little power or speed. And lastly, longtime Senators shortstop Ed Brinkman (1961–70, '75) was a very good fielder but also a very light hitter. In fact, he failed to reach the Mendoza Line in several of those years and overall provided only a .226 average.

Catcher

Name	YR	WAR	W3	W/G	AVG	HR	SB	OPS+
Iván Rodríguez	13	49.9	19.3	.0331	.304	217	81	112
Jim Sundberg	12	34.7	14.3	.0229	.252	60	18	91

Obviously, the starter here was one of the greatest combinations of offense and defense that the catcher position has ever seen, Hall of Famer **Iván Rodríguez** (1991–2002, '09). He was an All-Star and Gold Glove Award winner for ten consecutive seasons, hit 20+ HR five times, and regularly hit over .300. Pudge had his best season in 1999, when he took home AL MVP honors after hitting .332 with 35 HR, 113 RBI, 116 runs, and even 25 SB.

The backup was just as obvious, as **Jim Sundberg** (1974–83, '88–89) would have been a respectable starting catcher for an expansion-era All-Time team. Sundberg was not the offensive force that Rodríguez was, as he hit only .252 with little power or speed. But like Rodríguez he was an outstanding glove-man, capturing six consecutive Gold Glove Awards. With two such long-time, dominant selections at this position, no one else even deserved to be considered.

Left Field

Name	YR	WAR	W3	W/G	AVG	HR	SB	OPS+
Frank Howard	8	26.8	14.9	.0229	.277	246	5	153
Rusty Greer	9	22.3	13.7	.0217	.305	119	31	119
Al Oliver	4	11.6	10.1	.0217	.319	49	20	131
David Murphy	7	11.1	7.9	.0134	.275	85	52	104
Chuck Hinton	4	9.6	8.4	.0176	.280	49	92	113
Billy Sample	7	9.5	8.4	.0141	.270	39	92	98
Pete Incaviglia	5	7.3	5.8	.0105	.248	124	26	109

Senators slugger and four-time All-Star **Frank Howard** (1965–72) was the top choice here. The Capital Punisher hit 36 HR in 1967, led the league with 44 in 1968, smacked 48 the next year, and led the AL again in 1970 with 44 HR, 126 RBI, and 132 walks. Because he did all of this during a pitching-dominant era, his OPS+ during his time with the franchise was an impressive 153.

Rusty Greer (1994–2002) played his entire nine-year career for the Rangers. He had double-digit HR in his first six seasons and provided 100+ RBI three times. A .305 hitter, his high was a .332 mark in 1996. Solid numbers, but given the era he played in, he was never an All-Star. His aggressive style of play took a toll on his body, leading to multiple surgeries before a failed comeback attempt led to his retirement at a relatively young age.

After a decade with the Pirates, **Al Oliver** (1978–81) was part of a four-team trade that sent him to Texas. He batted .319 for the Rangers, and in 1980 he posted 19 HR and 117 RBI. He played all three outfield positions and also served as a DH at times. Given the shortage of strong CF candidates, I decided to include him on this All-Time team as the sixth outfielder.

I also considered a few others, starting with David Murphy (2007–13), who played most of his career for the Rangers. He played all three OF positions and provided double-digit capability for both HR and SB. Chuck Hinton (1961–64) played in the OF for the Senators' first four seasons. He provided a combination of power and speed, and had his best year in 1962, when he batted .310 with 17 HR and 28 SB. Billy Sample (1978–84) played in 100+ games for the Rangers only three times, providing generally moderate power and speed. His best season was 1983, when he busted out with 44 SB. And lastly, Pete Incaviglia (1986–90) always seemed to swing for the fences, and this resulted in 20+ HR in each of his five seasons with Texas. It also meant a .248 average and 130+ strikeouts every year, including a whopping 185 during his rookie campaign.

Center Field

Name	YR	WAR	W3	W/G	AVG	HR	SB	OPS+
Josh Hamilton	6	22.7	18.0	.0326	.302	150	40	134
Don Lock	5	10.4	9.1	.0159	.240	99	18	113
Gary Matthews	3	10.1	10.1	.0277	.285	47	24	108
Oddibe McDowell	5	9.3	7.4	.0163	.251	57	129	96

Josh Hamilton (2008–12, '15) has accomplished enough to earn the top CF spot on this All-Time team roster (though like others he has spent time at all three OF positions). After resurrecting his career at age 26 with the Reds, Hamilton was traded to the Rangers and went on to be an All-Star in five seasons. He hit .304 with 32 HR and a league-leading 130 RBI in 2008, then took home MVP honors in 2010, when he led the AL with a .359 average while hitting 32 HR with 100 RBI in only 133 games.

Three others deserve brief mention, starting with Don Lock (1962–66), who was the CF for the early Senators teams. He hit double-digit HR for five seasons, with highs of 27 in 1963 and 28 the following year. Oddibe McDowell (1985–88, '94) had 24 to 33 SB in each of his four full seasons for the Rangers, and also provided 18 HR in each of his first two seasons. And lastly, Gary Matthews Jr. (2004–06) played three seasons in Texas, including his only All-Star campaign in 2006, when he hit .313 with 19 HR, 79 RBI, and 102 runs scored.

Right Field

Name	YR	WAR	W3	W/G	AVG	HR	SB	OPS+
Juan González	13	31.8	15.3	.0227	.293	372	24	133
Rubén Sierra	10	20.1	13.3	.0169	.280	180	90	116
Nelson Cruz	8	11.8	8.5	.0148	.268	157	65	114
Jeff Burroughs	7	9.2	8.7	.0131	.255	108	7	122
Larry Parrish	7	5.1	5.6	.0058	.264	149	13	111

Juan González (1989–99, 2002–03) was a key power source for the Rangers, as he had five seasons with 40+ HR, including leading the league with 43 in 1992 and 46 in 1993. Juan Gone also provided 100+ RBI seven times, including highs of 144 and 157 in his two AL MVP seasons in 1996 and 1998.

Rubén Sierra (1986–92, 2000–01, '03) had three stints with the Rangers and had 20+ HR five times and 100+ RBI three times. A three-time All-Star, in 1989 he hit .306 with 29 HR, 119 RBI, and 14 triples, and in 1991 he hit .307 with 25 HR, 116 RBI, and 44 doubles.

You could make a case for including Nelson Cruz (2006–13) instead of Al Oliver as the sixth outfielder on this All-Time team (even though Cruz played only RF and LF). He was an All-Star twice and hit 22 to 33 HR in each of his five full seasons in Texas. But his 40+-HR seasons came later in Baltimore and Seattle, and his WAR total of only 11.8 across parts of eight seasons in Texas is not very impressive.

You could also make a case for Jeff Burroughs (1970–76), who after a slow start in the majors played four full seasons with the Rangers before being traded to Atlanta after the 1976 season. He had 30 HR in 1973, then captured the AL MVP Award in 1974 with a .301 average, 25 HR, and 118 RBI.

Also worth a brief mention was slugger Larry Parrish (1982–88). Formerly a 3B in Montreal, he played mostly RF and DH in Texas. He hit 17 to 32 HR in his six full seasons there and had 100+ RBI twice.

Starting Pitching

Name	YR	WAR	W3	W-L	ERA	WHIP	ERA+
Charlie Hough	11	33.3	15.6	139-123	3.68	1.282	111
Kenny Rogers	12	32.2	15.8	133-96	4.16	1.405	111
Fergie Jenkins	6	22.1	16.8	93-72	3.56	1.173	106
Yu Darvish	5	18.9	12.9	52-39	3.42	1.181	126
Kevin Brown	8	17.9	12.4	78-64	3.81	1.369	108
Gaylord Perry	4	15.7	13.1	48-43	3.26	1.181	118
Nolan Ryan	5	15.4	13.9	51-39	3.43	1.126	116
José Guzmán	6	14.0	10.2	66-62	3.90	1.359	106

Rick Helling	8	13.8	11.2	68-51	4.86	1.424	101
Jon Matlack	6	12.5	12.8	43-45	3.41	1.293	112
C.J. Wilson	7	11.2	11.0	43-35	3.60	1.291	125
Bert Blyleven	2	11.1	11.1	23-23	2.74	1.094	142
Danny Darwin	8	10.8	8.5	55-52	3.72	1.297	107
Roger Pavlik	7	10.6	9.5	47-39	4.58	1.472	103
Dick Bosman	8	10.4	10.2	59-64	3.35	1.249	98
Derek Holland	9	10.4	7.7	62-50	4.35	1.328	100
Bobby Witt	11	9.8	7.8	104-104	4.85	1.577	90

The all-time leader in games started, innings pitched, wins, losses, and strike-outs for this franchise is knuckleballer **Charlie Hough** (1980–90). He came over from the Dodgers during the 1980 season and was a workhorse for the entire decade. He posted 14 to 18 wins in seven consecutive seasons, with marks of 17-10 and 18-13 being his best. Although not flashy, he got the top spot on this pitching staff.

Kenny Rogers (1989–95, 2000–02, '04–05) had a better winning percent-age than Hough, but he started 61 fewer games for the Rangers. After mostly coming out of the bullpen in his first four years, he later pitched a perfect game for the Rangers in 1994 and compiled solid win-loss records, including 16-10, 17-7, 16-8, and 18-9. Rogers also defended his position well, taking home four Gold Glove Awards.

Hall of Famer **Fergie Jenkins** (1974–75, '78–81) had two brief stints with the Rangers. His first season with the club was by far his best, as he went 25-12 with a 2.82 ERA and 225 strikeouts, narrowly losing the AL Cy Young Award to Catfish Hunter. In 1978 he went 18-8 with a 3.04 ERA, but his other seasons in Texas were mediocre.

Yu Darvish (2012–14, '16–17) started his professional career at age 18 in Japan and after seven seasons there had established himself as arguably the best pitcher in the league. He joined the Rangers at age 25 in 2012 and was an All-Star immediately, posting a 16-9 record with 221 strikeouts in his rookie season. In 2013 he led the AL with 277 strikeouts in only 209.2 IP. Injuries arose, and Darvish had Tommy John surgery and so missed the entire 2015 season and part of 2016. Still not back to his former dominance, he was traded to the Dodg-ers during the 2017 season.

Kevin Brown (1986, '88–94) started his fine career with the Rangers, al-though it took a little while for him to become a star. After several mediocre seasons, in 1992 he paced the AL with a 21-11 record, and he went 15-12 the next year, with a combined 23 complete games.

Nolan Ryan (1989–93) pitched with the Rangers for the final five years of his nearly unbelievable career. At age 42 he went 16-10 with a 3.20 ERA, and amazingly led the AL with 301 strikeouts in only 239.1 IP. The Ryan Express continued in 1990 and 1991, as he posted records of 13-9 and 12-6, while still striking out 200+ and tossing a no-hitter each year.

As with others discussed above, Hall of Famer **Gaylord Perry** (1975–77, '80) joined the Rangers late in his career. He had three full seasons plus a partial one for Texas, twice winning 15 games.

The Rangers tried to use **C.J. Wilson** (2005–11) out of their bullpen for five years, but with very mixed results, including in 2008, when he managed 24 saves even with a 6.02 ERA. Finally moved to the rotation in 2010, he responded with a 15-8 record and 3.35 ERA, and followed that with a 16-7, 2.94 ERA season. Unfortunately for the Rangers, he left for the Angels via free agency, but I included him on this All-Time team based on his full résumé as a reliever and starter.

I decided to go with four relievers for this All-Time team, though you could make a case based on longevity for starter Bobby Witt (1986–92, '95–98). Very wild early on, he led the league in walks in three of his first four seasons. He was a pretty good strikeout pitcher, with 221 being his high mark in 1990, when he posted a 17-10 record. Even with a high ERA (4.85) and WHIP (1.577), Witt still ended up with an even 104-104 record during his time with the Rangers.

There were many others that I considered, starting with José Guzmán (1985–88, '91–92), who pitched six of his eight seasons for the Rangers and managed 11 to 16 wins in four of them. Rick Helling (1994–96, '97–2001) had two stints for the Rangers but pitched only four full seasons as a starter. 1998 was by far his best, as he went 20-7 (one of only three 20-win seasons for this franchise), leading the AL in wins. But his high ERA of 4.86 and a WHIP of 1.424 failed to impress me.

Jon Matlack (1978–83) finished his career with the Rangers, and after going 15-13 with a 2.27 ERA in 1978, he won only another 26 games spread over five seasons. Dick Bosman (1966–73), in his first full season as a starter, posted a 14-5 record and led the league with a 2.19 ERA. The next year he posted a 16-12 mark with a 3.00 ERA, but his other seasons were less impressive. Danny Darwin (1978–84, '95) started his long career with the Rangers and was both a reliever and starter for them, with mixed results. Roger Pavlik (1992–98) pitched all of his relatively short career with the Rangers, making the All-Star team in 1996, when he posted a 15-8 record (though with a 5.19 ERA). Hall of Famer Bert Blyleven's long career included two seasons in Texas, where he posted ERAs of 2.76 and 2.72, but his W-L records were only 9-11 and 14-12.

And lastly, Derek Holland (2009–16) was well on his way to one day making this All-Time team after posting a 16-5 record in 2011 and quality seasons the following two years. But then multiple injuries struck that limited his effectiveness and playing time in 2014–16, and he was granted free agency after the 2016 season.

Relief Pitching

Name	YR	WAR	W3	SV	W-L	ERA	WHIP	ERA+
Jeff Russell	10	11.0	7.8	134	42-40	3.73	1.368	114
Francisco Cordero	7	9.9	7.6	117	21-20	3.45	1.365	142
Darold Knowles	6	9.5	7.2	64	25-29	2.46	1.300	140
Neftalí Feliz	7	8.4	5.2	93	13-10	2.69	1.056	164
John Wetteland	4	8.1	7.2	150	20-12	2.95	1.194	167
Jeff Zimmerman	3	7.7	7.7	32	17-12	3.27	1.098	151
Ron Kline	4	7.4	5.8	83	26-25	2.54	1.237	142
Greg Harris	3	6.8	6.8	31	20-22	3.50	1.301	125
Jim Kern	3	6.2	6.2	37	17-18	2.59	1.329	155

I decided to include four relievers on this All-Time team, starting with **John Wetteland** (1997–2000), who had four solid seasons, two as an All-Star, for the Rangers at the end of his career. His save totals were 31, 42, 43, and 34, and he had impressive ERAs of 1.94 and 2.03 in his first two Texas seasons.

Jeff Russell (1985–92, '95–96) pitched for Texas for ten years but was the closer for only parts of six of them. He started as a setup man and was unimpressive in one year as a starter, but in 1989 he posted a 1.98 ERA and led the AL in saves with 38. He was having an equally good season in 1992 when he was traded with Rubén Sierra and Bobby Witt in an ill-fated deal for José Canseco. He signed back with the Rangers for the 1995 and 1996 seasons before retiring at the end of that year.

Francisco Cordero (2000–06) was co-closer in 2002 and 2003 before posting a 2.13 ERA with 49 saves in 2004 (the all-time franchise record). He added another 37 saves in 2005, but he was traded with Kevin Mench and Laynce Nix in 2006 to Milwaukee for Nelson Cruz and Carlos Lee.

Neftalí Feliz (2009–15) started his career with the Rangers, earning Rookie of the Year honors in his first full season in 2010 after recording 40 saves and a 2.73 ERA. He came back and notched 32 saves in 2011, but in 2012 he was shifted to the rotation, where he did fairly well until an injury took him out of action. He missed almost all of 2013, and then in 2014 he returned to the bullpen, where he notched 13 saves with a 1.99 ERA. In 2010 and 2011, Feliz pitched well in the postseason, compiling a 1.93 ERA in 18.2 IP while locking down 7 saves.

There were a few other relievers I considered, starting with Ron Kline (1963–66), who after pitching as a starter for the Pirates and other teams became the Senators' short reliever in 1963. He led the league in saves with 29 in 1965 and had an ERA below 3.00 in each of his four seasons for Washington. Darold Knowles (1967–71, '77) pitched for the Senators right after Kline. He was an All-Star in 1969, when he posted a 9-2 record with 13 saves and a 2.24 ERA. In 1970 he had 27 saves and a 2.04 ERA, though with an unfortunate 2-14 record.

Jeff Zimmerman (1999–2001) was an interesting case, as he pitched two seasons as a setup man before becoming the Rangers' closer in 2001 and posting 28 saves and a 2.40 ERA. Unfortunately, several injuries and two Tommy John surgeries led him to eventually have to retire without ever pitching in the majors again.

Greg Harris (1985–87) had a long career, including three mixed seasons in Texas: one as a setup man, one as a closer (20 saves and a 2.83 ERA in 1986), and one as a combined starter and reliever. Lastly, Jim Kern also pitched for the Rangers for only three seasons, with one of them being truly impressive: in 1979 he was an All-Star and posted a 13-5 record in relief to go with 29 saves, 136 K in 143 IP, and a fourth-place finish in the AL Cy Young Award voting.

Managers

Name	YR	From-To	W-L	PCT	PS	WS
Ron Washington	8	2007–14	664-611	.521	3	0
Johnny Oates	7	1995–2001	506-476	.515	3	0
Bobby Valentine	8	1985–92	581-605	.490	0	0
Jeff Banister	4	2015–18	325-313	.509	2	0
Buck Showalter	4	2003–06	319-329	.492	0	0

The top two managers for the Rangers have clearly been **Ron Washington** and **Johnny Oates**. They both made the playoffs three times, with Washington going the farthest with two World Series appearances (losses in 2010 and 2011). **Bobby Valentine** managed the Rangers for about the same amount of time but never made the postseason. And current skipper **Jeff Banister** has posted a .509 winning percentage and led Texas to the postseason in two of his four seasons. Lastly, I'll note the Senators were managed by some mighty fine hitters, including Mickey Vernon, Gil Hodges, and most notably Ted Williams.

Starting Lineup

What would mythical starting lineups look like for this All-Time roster?

Against RHP:
Ian Kinsler 2B (R)
Iván Rodríguez C (R)
Josh Hamilton CF (L)
Rafael Palmeiro 1B (L)
Álex Rodríguez DH (R)
Juan González RF (R)
Rusty Greer LF (L)
Adrián Beltré 3B (R)
Toby Harrah SS (R)

Against LHP:
Ian Kinsler 2B (R)
Iván Rodríguez C (R)
Frank Howard LF (R)
Álex Rodríguez DH (R)
Juan González RF (R)
Mark Teixeira 1B (S)
Adrián Beltré 3B (R)
Josh Hamilton CF (L)
Toby Harrah SS (R)

This All-Time team is loaded with power, so you could configure these lineups in any number of ways. In looking this over, I found only two natural platoon options: Howard and Greer for LF, and Palmeiro and Teixeira at 1B. Both Beltré and Bell were righties, and ditto for Harrah, Andrus, and Young. And if you don't like Rodríguez being on this dream team roster, then your options for DH include Teixeira/Palmeiro, Young, Sierra, Franco, and others.

Depth Chart

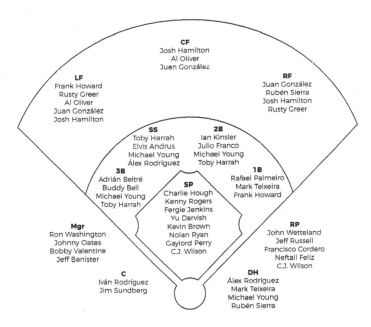

CF
Josh Hamilton
Al Oliver
Juan González

LF
Frank Howard
Rusty Greer
Al Oliver
Juan González
Josh Hamilton

RF
Juan González
Rubén Sierra
Josh Hamilton
Rusty Greer

SS
Toby Harrah
Elvis Andrus
Michael Young
Álex Rodríguez

2B
Ian Kinsler
Julio Franco
Michael Young
Toby Harrah

3B
Adrián Beltré
Buddy Bell
Michael Young
Toby Harrah

SP
Charlie Hough
Kenny Rogers
Fergie Jenkins
Yu Darvish
Kevin Brown
Nolan Ryan
Gaylord Perry
C.J. Wilson

1B
Rafael Palmeiro
Mark Teixeira
Frank Howard

Mgr
Ron Washington
Johnny Oates
Bobby Valentine
Jeff Banister

RP
John Wetteland
Jeff Russell
Francisco Cordero
Neftalí Feliz
C.J. Wilson

C
Iván Rodríguez
Jim Sundberg

DH
Álex Rodríguez
Mark Teixeira
Michael Young
Rubén Sierra

Prospects for Current Players

What are the prospects of current Rangers players making this All-Time team? Beltré and Andrus are already included. 2B Rougned Odor is perhaps most likely to join them, as at age 25 he has already proven he can hit for power in the big leagues, and he only needs to surpass Julio Franco's accomplishments to make this roster. We'll see...

Retired Player Numbers

Iván Rodríguez (7), Johnny Oates (26, manager), Nolan Ryan (34)

Selections from Other Authors and Fan Surveys

1992: *The All-Time All-Star Baseball Book*, by Nick Acocella and Donald Dewey

The authors separated the short-lived Washington Senators years from the Texas Rangers. For the former they provided a lineup of Mike Epstein, Bernie Allen, Ken McMullen, Ed Brinkman, Frank Howard, Del Unser, Chuck Hinton, Paul Casanova, and Dick Bosman. For the latter they chose a lineup of Hargrove, Franco, Bell, Harrah, Oliver, Burroughs, Sierra, Sundberg, and Jenkins. The only complaint I have was the choice of Jenkins over Hough, whom they don't even list as an honorable mention, indicating only Bump Wills and Larry Parrish. Why no love for the knuckleballer?

1995: *Baseball Ratings*, by Charles F. Faber

This author also split up the Washington years from those in Texas. For the former he came up with the same lineup as Acocella and Dewey did, with the exception of Don Lock getting the third OF spot instead of Del Unser. For the Rangers, his system resulted in an infield of Sundberg, Palmeiro, Wills, Bell, and Fletcher, which meant Harrah was strangely left out. The outfield was Sierra, Burroughs, and Parrish, with Hough as the top starter.

2003: *Rob Neyer's Big Book of Baseball Lineups*, by Rob Neyer

Neyer's starting lineup was very reasonable, though he gave the starting SS spot to A-Rod after only two seasons with the Rangers, noting a lack of competition for the job. He named Pudge as the catcher, Palmeiro at 1B, Franco at 2B, and Bell at 3B. He chose Howard, Lock, and González as his outfield, and then

Parrish as the DH. About Lock he noted that he was "known for making spectacular catches in CF." The backup infielders were Sundberg, Hargrove, Wills, Harrah, and McMullen. He sensibly had Greer, McDowell, and Sierra as the second-tier OF, and Downing at DH, even though he played in Texas for only his last two seasons.

For pitching he listed Hough, Jenkins, Brown, Ryan, Rogers, Helling, Matlack, and Bosman, and the two closers he selected were Russell and Wetteland.

Top WAR Single Seasons – Hitters (7+)

Name	Year	WAR	AVG	HR	R	RBI	SB	OPS+
Álex Rodríguez	2002	8.8	.300	57	125	142	9	158
Josh Hamilton	2010	8.7	.359	32	95	100	8	170
Álex Rodríguez	2003	8.4	.298	47	124	118	17	147
Álex Rodríguez	2001	8.3	.318	52	133	135	18	160
Adrián Beltré	2012	7.3	.321	36	95	102	1	139
Mark Teixeira	2005	7.2	.301	43	112	144	4	144
Ian Kinsler	2011	7.1	.255	32	121	77	30	118
Toby Harrah	1975	7.1	.293	20	81	93	23	145
Adrián Beltré	2014	7.0	.324	19	79	77	1	144

Interestingly, Álex Rodríguez's three seasons make up three of the top four all-time seasons for this franchise. Beltré appears on the list twice in part because he gets added points from strong defense. His 2014 season didn't have as impressive counting stats as some of his others, but it rated well in part because he boosted his OBP to a career-high .388 that year.

Top WAR Single Seasons – Pitchers (7+)

Name	Year	WAR	W-L	ERA	IP	SO	ERA+
Fergie Jenkins	1974	7.8	25-12	2.82	328.1	225	126

This franchise historically has not had a wealth of strong pitching—only this one season ever had a WAR of 7 or higher.

Franchise Player

With apologies to hitters Palmeiro, Howard, and González, this honor had to go to Iván Rodríguez given his numerous All-Star appearances, Gold Glove Awards, and overall accomplishments.

CHAPTER 24

The Brewers Franchise All-Time Dream Team

The Brewers franchise actually started out in 1969 as the Seattle Pilots, an expansion club in what was then the west coast's third-largest metro area. They won their first game on the road and their first home game, but ended up having a horrible season, going 64-98 and finishing last in the AL West. After much dispute, a last-minute bankruptcy decision led to the team relocating to Milwaukee to become the Brewers for the 1970 season.

Unfortunately, their results didn't improve any time soon, as they won fewer than 70 games in each of the next three seasons, and then three more times from 1975 through '77. They came to life in 1978–79, winning 93 and 95 games, respectively, and made the postseason for the first time in strike-shortened 1981. In 1982, the powerful brew crew known as Harvey's Wallbangers (a play on the drink and the team's manager, Harvey Kuenn) made it to the World Series before falling to the defense, speed, and pitching of the St. Louis Cardinals in seven games.

Since then the Brewers have not had a lot of success. They were up and down from 1983 through '92, with six seasons of .500 or better ball. But then the economics of being a small-market team really began to have an effect, and they played sub-.500 every year from 1993 through 2004, managing to climb to an 81-81 record finally in 2005. During that time, they also had to adjust first to changing divisions within the American League (1994), and then switching leagues to the National League (1998), where they remain today.

As with any expansion-era club, their All-Time team had some definite weak spots. But they also had some long-time players who were legit Hall of Famers, so their team overall wasn't too shabby.

1st Base

Name	YR	WAR	W3	W/G	AVG	HR	SB	OPS+
Cecil Cooper	11	30.5	16.6	.0205	.302	201	77	123
George Scott	5	22.4	15.7	.0188	.257	154	27	103
Prince Fielder	7	16.8	14.5	.0168	.282	230	16	143
Richie Sexson	4	11.2	9.1	.0210	.276	133	5	133
John Jaha	7	8.7	8.2	.0136	.268	105	33	113

Cecil Cooper (1977–87) started his career in Boston but played 10+ seasons as the Brewers' 1B. He provided good defense (two Gold Glove Awards) and hit for both power and average, with five seasons of 20+ HR, and seven hitting .300+. His best years were 1980, when he hit .352 with 25 HR, 122 RBI, and a career-high 17 SB, and then 1982 and 1983, when he hit 30+ HR and 120+ RBI. In all three of those seasons, he came in fifth in the league MVP voting.

Like Cooper, **George Scott** (1972–76) also started his career with the Red Sox before joining the Brewers. While in Milwaukee for only five years, he provided respectable numbers every year, including a league-leading 36 HR and 109 RBI in 1975. And like Cooper, Scott provided outstanding defense at 1B, as he took home the Gold Glove Award each year he toiled in Wisconsin.

Not nearly as good a fielder as Scott or Cooper, **Prince Fielder** (2005–11) was a powerful hitter who started his career with the Brewers, hitting 28 or more HR in all six of his full seasons there. He led the NL with 50 HR in 2007 and hit 46 with a league-leading 141 RBI in 2009. Although he struck out quite a bit, he also walked a lot, resulting in a .390 OBP for Milwaukee. Based on his power, you could make a case for him as the starter or backup 1B on this All-Time team, but I decided to at least include him with one of the two "extra spots."

Two other power-hitting 1B deserve brief mention, starting with Richie Sexson (2000–03), who was acquired via a trade from the Indians as part of a multiplayer deal for closer Bob Wickman. He hit a total of 119 HR from 2001 through 2003, with over 100 RBI every year. He struck out a lot but hit in the .270s each season. And John Jaha (1992–98) also provided some power but played only two full seasons for the Brewers. His best year was easily 1996, when he hit .300 with 34 HR and 118 RBI.

2nd Base

Name	YR	WAR	W3	W/G	AVG	HR	SB	OPS+
Jim Gantner	17	22.3	9.2	.0124	.274	47	137	88
Rickie Weeks	11	12.3	8.7	.0108	.249	148	126	105
Fernando Vina	5	6.0	5.9	.0114	.286	22	57	90

In compiling this All-Time roster, 2B was not a strong position for the Brewers. **Jim Gantner** (1976–92) played his entire career with the Brewers and was a steady though not spectacular performer. He was never an All-Star, and indeed managed 50+ RBI only twice, including his 1983 campaign, which was the only season in which he hit double-digit HR. He also had only moderate speed, stealing 10+ bases six times. But with a pretty good glove and such a long career, he clearly deserves to be the starter at 2B on this dream team roster.

The best of the other candidates was clearly **Rickie Weeks** (2003, '05–14), who had his best year in 2010, when he hit 29 HR with 83 RBI and 112 runs. He led the NL that year with 25 hit-by-pitches, but he also managed to strike out a whopping 184 times. Weeks regularly had double-digit HR and SB, but his lifetime .249 batting average was a weakness, as was the fact that he played 130 or more games in a season only twice.

I did briefly consider Fernando Vina (1995–99), who played parts of five seasons for the Brewers, but only twice played 140+ games. 1998 was his best year, as he hit .311 with 39 doubles, 101 runs, and 22 SB (though he was caught 16 times).

3rd Base

Name	YR	WAR	W3	W/G	AVG	HR	SB	OPS+
Paul Molitor	15	59.6	17.9	.0321	.303	160	412	125
Don Money	11	28.2	14.9	.0236	.270	134	66	114
Jeff Cirillo	8	26.2	16.0	.0268	.307	73	37	113
Kevin Seitzer	5	10.4	6.4	.0193	.300	34	26	109
Sal Bando	5	9.4	9.9	.0171	.250	50	15	98
Tommy Harper	3	8.7	8.7	.0191	.264	54	136	115

Paul Molitor (1978–92) played most of his Hall of Fame career in Milwaukee, but at various positions (791 3B, 400 2B, 418 DH, 131 1B, 57 SS). He led the league in runs scored three times and was regularly amongst the leaders in batting average. He had some power, but he never hit more than 20 HR for the Brewers. More impressive was his speed, as he swiped 30+ bases eight times (and is the franchise's all-time leader in SB). A five-time All-Star for the

Brewers, Molitor had a 39-game hitting streak in 1987, the same year he had a career-high 45 SB and .353 average, and managed to lead the AL with 114 runs and 41 doubles even though he played in only 118 games.

Don Money (1973–83) also played many different positions for the Brewers and was a four-time All-Star. He had 10+ HR in eight seasons, including two years when he had fewer than 300 at-bats. His best year was 1977, when he hit 25 HR with 83 RBI.

I considered several other candidates, starting with **Jeff Cirillo** (1994–99, 2005–06), who was a two-time All-Star for the Brewers. A .307 hitter for the Brewers, he had only moderate power, but with good defense his overall résumé was arguably enough to earn the second "extra spot" on this roster.

Tommy Harper (1969–71) was with the team during their inaugural season in Seattle and led the AL with 73 SB that year. He followed with an outstanding 1970 season, hitting .296 with 31 HR, 104 runs, 82 RBI, and 38 SB (a 30/30 year, the only time in his career that he came close). After a disappointing 1971 campaign, he was traded to the Red Sox as part of a massive multiplayer deal that brought over George Scott and others. Kevin Seitzer (1992–96) was a .300 hitter for the Brewers and an All-Star for them in 1995. And Sal Bando (1977–81) finished his fine career with the Brewers, though he hit double-digit HR for them only twice.

Shortstop

Name	YR	WAR	W3	W/G	AVG	HR	SB	OPS+
Robin Yount	20	77.0	24.8	.0270	.285	.251	.271	115
José Valentín	8	11.4	8.4	.0150	.240	90	78	90
J.J. Hardy	5	10.9	9.7	.0191	.262	75	5	95
Bill Hall	8	9.4	10.1	.0113	.253	102	49	95
Mark Loretta	8	5.9	5.4	.0074	.289	29	22	92

The most obvious top-spot selection for this entire team was **Robin Yount** (1974–1993) as the starting SS. Having played his entire Hall of Fame career for Milwaukee, Yount is by far the all-time Brewers leader in games, at-bats, hits, doubles, triples, runs, RBI, and walks, and he also ranks second all-time in HR and SB. He started out as a SS and played 1,469 games there before switching to CF, where he played 1,150 games. Amazingly, he managed to win an MVP Award while playing at each position: first in 1982, when he hit .331 with 210 hits, 46 doubles, 29 HR, 129 runs, and 114 RBI, then again in 1989, when he hit .318 with 21 HR, 101 runs, and 103 RBI. He had consistently good power and speed, hitting 15+ HR eight times and stealing 15 bases nine times. For all his accomplishments and awards, it is worth pondering why he was selected as an All-Star only three times—including exactly zero times as a center fielder (even in his 1989 MVP season).

The backup was **José Valentín** (1992–99), who played the first half of his career for the Brewers. A switch-hitter with a low average (.240) but moderate power and speed, he had 10+ HR six times and 10+ SB five times for the Brewers, before hitting 25+ I IR in five seasons for the White Sox.

Three others deserve brief mention, starting with J.J. Hardy (2005–09), who had 26 HR in 2007 and 24 the next year, but played only four full seasons for the Brewers. Bill Hall (2002–09) played many positions for the Brewers, hit 10+ HR four times, and busted out in 2006 with 35 HR, 39 doubles, 101 runs, and 95 RBI. And similarly, Mark Loretta (1995–2002) played all around the infield for Milwaukee for several years. He batted .289 but displayed little power or speed.

Catcher

Name	YR	WAR	W3	W/G	AVG	HR	SB	OPS+
Jonathan Lucroy	7	18.1	13.4	.0225	.284	79	29	111
B.J. Surhoff	9	15.4	7.9	.0140	.274	57	102	92
Darrell Porter	6	11.0	10.6	.0205	.229	54	19	105
Charlie Moore	14	10.5	5.2	.0082	.262	35	51	89
Dave Nilsson	8	10.5	7.5	.0125	.284	105	15	110
Ted Simmons	5	6.1	8.4	.0092	.262	66	8	100

Even though he was traded to the Texas Rangers during the 2016 season, **Jonathan Lucroy** (2010–16) had by that time accomplished enough in Milwaukee to merit the top spot at C on this All-Time team. A two-time All-Star, Lucroy was both strong defensively and a capable hitter, notably leading the NL with 53 doubles in 2014.

Before Lucroy came along, **B.J. Surhoff** (1987–95) would have been the top pick here. He started his long career with the Brewers and batted .274 for them and stole 10+ bases six times. He caught 704 games but also spent time at other positions, and during his last two seasons in Milwaukee played mostly at 3B, OF, and 1B.

I also considered Australian Dave Nilsson (1992–99), who was a lifetime Brewer, though his career spanned only eight seasons (he retired from MLB relatively young but went on to play for Australia in the Olympics and focus on further developing baseball in his native country). Like many others I've discussed, he played all over the field: 309 games at C, 178 in the OF, 166 at 1B, and

163 as the DH. He twice hit 20+ HR, and he batted .331 in 453 AB in 1996.

Charlie Moore (1973–86) played all but his last season in Milwaukee. During that span he played 100+ games in a season six times but played 130+ only three times. A .262 hitter with little speed or power, the case for Moore to make this roster would be based mostly on his longevity with the club.

Finally, two others deserve brief mention here. Darrell Porter (1971–76) started his fine career with the Brewers, hitting 10+ HR three times, but he also hit for a rather low average (.229). Conversely, Ted Simmons (1981–85) joined the Brewers for five seasons late in his career. Twice an All-Star during that time, in 1983 he hit .308 with 13 HR and 108 RBI, but he played nearly as many games as the DH as he did behind the plate.

Left Field

Name	YR	WAR	W3	W/G	AVG	HR	SB	OPS+
Ryan Braun	12	46.4	20.8	.0293	.299	322	204	137
Geoff Jenkins	10	22.0	13.6	.0178	.277	212	31	116
Ben Oglivie	9	21.4	13.9	.0191	.277	176	44	124
Greg Vaughn	8	15.3	12.2	.0169	.246	169	62	111
John Briggs	5	14.3	10.5	.0245	.258	80	26	131

As a third baseman in 2007, **Ryan Braun** (2007–18) batted .324 with 34 HR, 97 RBI, and 15 SB, taking home Rookie of the Year honors. Since then he has mostly played LF and has been an All-Star six times. So far, he has hit 25+ HR eight times, and by now is the franchise's all-time HR leader. He has scored 100+ runs four times, and had 100+ RBI five times. 2011 was arguably his best year, as he hit .332 with 33 HR, 111 RBI, and 33 SB, which was good enough to capture the NL MVP Award. His highest HR total came the following year, when he led the NL with 41, although it was during those years that Braun came under scrutiny for failing a testosterone test and then served a suspension in 2013 for violating the league's drug policy. While these issues taint his résumé, I think his numbers have clearly earned him the starting LF spot on this roster.

Ben Oglivie (1978–86) had several mediocre, partial seasons with Boston and Detroit before playing out his career and having his best years with Milwaukee. A three-time All-Star, in 1980 he led the AL in HR with 41 and was second in RBI with 118. And he was a key part of the 1982 pennant-winning team, as he hit 34 HR with 102 RBI.

Geoff Jenkins (1998–07) spent all but his final season in Milwaukee, playing mostly in LF but also some in RF. He hit 20+ HR seven times but never topped the 100-RBI mark. Jenkins had arguably his best season in 2000, when he hit .303 with 34 HR and 94 RBI.

I considered slugger Greg Vaughn (1989–96), who started his career with Milwaukee before taking his bat to several other teams. He was an All-Star in 1993, when he hit 30 HR with 97 RBI, and again in 1996, when he hit 31 HR with 95 RBI for the Brewers before being traded to San Diego, where he tacked on another 10 HR and 22 RBI that year. Lastly, John Briggs (1971–75) was a .258 hitter with moderate power, with his top HR totals for the Brewers being 21 in both 1971 and 1972.

Center Field

Name	YR	WAR	W3	W/G	AVG	HR	SB	OPS+
Carlos Gómez	6	20.0	15.6	.0287	.267	87	152	110
Gorman Thomas	11	18.4	13.0	.0167	.230	208	38	119
Dave May	6	11.3	10.3	.0158	.259	69	44	103
Darryl Hamilton	7	11.0	8.9	.0165	.290	23	109	100

Carlos Gómez (2010–15) struggled a bit early in the majors with the Mets, Twins, and Brewers. By 2012 his combination of power and speed had matured, as he hit 19 HR to go with 37 SB. He was an All-Star the next two years, when he provided Milwaukee with 24 HR and 40 SB, and then 23 HR and 34 SB. A great defender in CF, he took home a Gold Glove Award in 2013.

You could make a case for all-or-nothing slugger **Gorman Thomas** (1973–76, '78–83, '86) as the starter instead of Gómez. Playing most of his career with Milwaukee, he had some impressive HR totals, including 45 to lead the league in 1979 and 39 to lead the league in 1982. Stormin' Gorman had 100+ RBI three times but was an All-Star only once, owing to his high strikeout rate and low batting average (.230).

I considered two others, starting with Dave May (1970–74, '78), who batted .259 for Milwaukee and had some power. He had a career year in 1973, when he was an All-Star and batted .303 with 25 HR and 93 RBI. And lastly, Darryl Hamilton (1988, '90–95) was a .290 hitter with very little power, but good speed, enough to steal 41 bases in 1992.

Right Field

Name	YR	WAR	W3	W/G	AVG	HR	SB	OPS+
Sixto Lezcano	7	19.0	13.3	.0242	.275	102	34	125
Corey Hart	9	15.7	12.0	.0166	.276	154	83	116
Jeromy Burnitz	6	15.6	11.6	.0199	.258	165	42	123
Rob Deer	5	6.9	5.6	.0103	.229	137	32	112

There were three main candidates here in RF, but I decided to select only one for this All-Time dream team roster. **Sixto Lezcano** (1974–80) started his career with the Brewers and was a good fielder, winning the Gold Glove Award in 1979. He had moderate power, hitting 15+ HR four times, with his best year being 1979, when he hit .321 with 28 HR and 101 RBI.

You could make a case for two others, starting with Jeromy Burnitz (1996–2001), as he provided the Brewers with consistent power for five full seasons, hitting 27 to 38 HR each year with 100+ RBI three times. His biggest numbers came in 1998, when he clubbed 38 HR with 125 RBI. And Corey Hart (2004–12) played most of his career in Milwaukee, including six full seasons. A two-time All-Star, he hit 20+ HR five times and stole 20+ bases in two of those years. His biggest power output came in 2010, when he hit 31 HR with 102 RBI.

Lastly, like Thomas before him, Rob Deer (1986–90) was a major power provider and a major strikeout risk. He hit 23 to 33 HR in each of his five Milwaukee seasons, but he also struck out between 147 and 186 times per year.

Starting Pitching

Name	YR	WAR	W3	W-L	ERA	WHIP	ERA+
Teddy Higuera	9	30.7	23.3	94-64	3.61	1.236	117
Ben Sheets	8	22.8	15.0	86-83	3.72	1.201	115
Yovani Gallardo	8	18.8	8.9	89-64	3.69	1.303	109
Chris Bosio	7	18.8	13.9	67-62	3.76	1.238	107
Bill Wegman	11	18.1	13.8	81-90	4.16	1.294	102
Mike Caldwell	8	17.5	15.0	102-80	3.74	1.284	103
Moose Haas	10	16.0	10.9	91-79	4.03	1.304	97
Jim Slaton	12	15.4	9.9	117-121	3.86	1.389	97
Cal Eldred	9	13.0	11.5	64-65	4.51	1.395	101
Lary Sorensen	4	12.3	10.6	52-46	3.72	1.275	107
Jim Colborn	5	12.2	9.5	57-60	3.65	1.268	98

The Brewers franchise has never had particularly strong pitching. As the ace of this staff, I went with southpaw **Teddy Higuera** (1985–91, '93–94), who pitched his entire career with the Brewers. He ended up with a solid 94-64 record (a .595 winning percentage), though most of his value came from his first four seasons, starting with his 15-8 rookie campaign. The following year he was runner-up for the Cy Young Award after posting a 20-11 record with a 2.79 ERA and 207 strikeouts. He went 18-10 in 1987 with 240 strikeouts, and then 16-9 with a 2.45 ERA in 1988.

Ben Sheets (2001–08) never won more than 13 games in a season for the Brewers, but he consistently won 10 to 13 games every year except one. Even with a 12-14 record, his best year was 2004, because he posted a 2.70 ERA, 0.983 WHIP, and 264 K in 237 IP (the most strikeouts in franchise history).

Yovani Gallardo (2007–14) showed great promise at age 21, when he posted a 9-5 record with 101 K in 110 IP in his rookie campaign. He lost most of 2008 to a knee injury but came back strong to post four consecutive 200+-strikeout seasons. Gallardo was also a relatively good hitter, batting .195 with 12 HR in 416 AB.

Mike Caldwell (1977–84) was traded from the Reds during the 1977 season, and he quickly paid dividends. In 1978 he was runner-up for the NL Cy Young Award, going 22-9 with a 2.36 ERA and leading the league with 23 complete games. He never pitched that well again but did manage to go 16-6 in 1979 and 17-13 in 1982.

For the fifth spot I went with **Chris Bosio** (1986–92), who pitched the majority of his big-league career for Milwaukee. He had three solid seasons, with records of 15-10, 14-10, and 16-6.

Next up was the all-time Brewers wins leader (117), **Jim Slaton** (1971–77, '79–83), who won 10+ games for Milwaukee nine times. His best season came in 1979, when he went 15-9. It might sound a little rude, but I'd say one of the best things Slaton did for the team was to get traded away for one year. He and Rich Folkers were sent to Detroit for Ben Oglivie, and then Slaton re-signed with the Brewers as a free agent after the 1978 season.

Bill Wegman (1985–95) was a lifetime Brewer but won 10+ games only four times. His best year was 1991, when he went 15-7 with a 2.84 ERA. **Moose Haas** (1976–85) played most of his career for the Brewers and was a long-time teammate of Caldwell. He won 10 or more games six times but only once pitched 200 or more innings, in 1980, when he went 16-15 with a 3.10 ERA.

I decided to go with one more starting pitcher on this dream team roster, and that was **Cal Eldred** (1991–99), who was phenomenal in 14 games as a rookie in 1992, going 11-2 with a 1.79 ERA. He led the league in games started and IP the next year, but posted an even 16-16 record. He went on to win 10 or more games for the Brewers only two more times after that.

Two others deserve brief mention, starting with Jim Colborn (1972–76), who had an outstanding 1973 season, his only year as an All-Star. He went 20-12 (one of only three 20-win seasons in franchise history) with a 3.18 ERA, completing 22 games and pitching 314 innings. But his other four Milwaukee seasons were mediocre at best. And Lary Sorensen (1977–80) pitched his first four years for the Brewers, with his best being 1978, when he was an All-Star and went 18-12 with a 3.21 ERA (even though he had only 78 K in 280.2 IP).

Relief Pitching

Name	YR	WAR	W3	SV	W-L	ERA	WHIP	ERA+
Dan Plesac	7	12.3	8.3	133	29-37	3.21	1.232	128
Ken Sanders	3	8.8	8.8	61	14-23	2.21	1.100	154
Rollie Fingers	4	8.0	8.2	97	13-17	2.54	1.081	150
Chuck Crim	5	8.0	7.1	42	33-31	3.47	1.314	118
Mike Fetters	6	7.5	5.2	79	13-19	2.92	1.367	155
Bob McClure	10	7.1	4.7	34	45-43	3.97	1.423	99
Bill Castro	7	6.6	4.9	44	25-23	2.96	1.273	131
Bob Wickman	5	6.0	5.0	79	21-25	3.20	1.397	143
Francisco Rodríguez	5	5.2	4.3	95	13-16	2.91	1.081	136
John Axford	5	2.3	4.0	106	21-19	3.35	1.325	120

Hall of Famer **Rollie Fingers** (1981–82, '84–85) only pitched his final four seasons for the Brewers, but three of them were outstanding. In strike-shortened 1981, he had 28 saves and an insane 1.04 ERA, capturing both the AL Cy Young and MVP Awards. He followed that up with 29 saves and a 2.60 ERA in 1982, and then 23 saves and a 1.96 ERA in 1984 (after being out with an injury the entire 1983 season).

Dan Plesac (1986–92) is the all-time leader in saves for the Brewers, so that is a strong reason to give him the next spot. The lefty was the closer for the club from 1986 through 1990, and twice posted save totals of 30 or more.

Francisco Rodríguez (2011–15) pitched parts of five seasons for Milwaukee, first joining in 2011 after being traded by the Mets. After having been a closer for many years for the Angels and Mets, he stepped into a setup role that year for the Brewers and posted a 1.86 ERA. He continued in that role in 2012, and then started saving games in 2013, when he had 10 saves and 1.09 ERA before he was traded to the Orioles in July. He re-signed with the Brewers and was again an All-Star closer, with 44 saves in 2014 and 38 in 2015.

There were several other relievers I considered, starting with John Axford (2009–13), who was the Brewers closer for three full seasons. His best season came in 2011, when he posted a 1.95 ERA and led the league with 46 saves (a new franchise record). Mike Fetters (1992–97) had save totals of 17, 22, and 32 from 1994 through '96. He had a 2.99 ERA for the Brewers, including a 1.87 ERA over 50 games of middle relief in 1992. Bob Wickman (1996–2000) had similar overall numbers, and like Fetters had a long career but was the closer for the Brewers for only a short while. He posted 25 saves in 1998, 37 in 1999, and 16 in 2000 before being traded to the Indians.

Ken Sanders (1970–72) was a short reliever for the Brewers for three years. He provided a 1.75 ERA in 1970 and a 1.91 ERA in 1971 to go with a league-leading 31 saves in 136 innings of work. Chuck Crim (1987–91) pitched most of his career for Milwaukee, spending time as a setup man and occasional closer but never topping 12 saves in a season. Bill Castro (1974–80) similarly pitched most of his career for the Brewers, posting a 2.96 ERA with impressive low ERAs of 1.81 in 1978 and 2.03 the following year. Lastly, Bob McClure (1977–86) pitched over half of his long career for the Brewers, first as a reliever and then three seasons as a starter. The most saves he had was 10 in 1980, and his best record as a starter was 12-7.

Managers

Name	YR	From-To	W-L	PCT	PS	WS
Harvey Kuenn	2	1982–83	160-118	.576	1	0
Buck Rodgers	3	1980–82	124-102	.549	1	0
Ron Roenicke	5	2011–15	342-331	.508	1	0
Phil Garner	8	1992–99	563-617	.477	0	0
Ned Yost	6	2003–08	457-502	.477	0	0
Tom Trebelhorn	6	1986–91	422-397	.515	0	0
George Bamberger	5	1978–86	377-351	.518	0	0
Craig Counsell	4	2015–18	316-308	.506	1	0

There were a couple of ways to consider the managers here, but I decided to rank **Harvey Kuenn** at the top of the list because of what he did in the 1982 season. That year the Brewers were considered heavy favorites to win the AL East, but by June, the team was only 23-24 under Buck Rodgers. So, the club replaced Rodgers with their hitting coach, Kuenn. His low-key style led to results, and the team went 72-43 the rest of the way and made it to the World Series, losing to the Cardinals in seven games. That said, I'd still rank **Buck Rodgers** next, followed by **Ron Roenicke** and **Phil Garner**. And current manager Craig Counsell could earn a spot soon, as he has led the Brewers to a better record in each of his first four seasons.

Starting Lineup

What would mythical starting lineups look like for this All-Time roster?

Against RHP:
Paul Molitor 3B (R)
Robin Yount SS (R)
Cecil Cooper 1B (L)
Prince Fielder DH (L)

Against LHP:
Paul Molitor 3B (R)
Robin Yount SS (R)
Ryan Braun LF (R)
Gorman Thomas DH (R)

Ben Oglivie RF (L)
Ryan Braun LF (R)
B.J. Surhoff C (L)
Carlos Gómez CF (R)
Jim Gantner 2B (L)

George Scott 1B (R)
Carlos Gómez CF (R)
Jonathan Lucroy C (R)
Sixto Lezcano RF (R)
Rickie Weeks 2B (R)

I decided to go with Molitor and Yount at the top, because I'd want to have those two great hitters see the most at-bats. There were several platoon possibilities on this roster, such as Cooper/Scott at 1B, Gantner/Weeks at 2B, and Lucroy/Surhoff at C—though Surhoff hit both lefties and righties about equally well. In the outfield, you could platoon Braun with either Oglivie or Jenkins in LF, but I'd rather play Braun all the time and use Oglivie or Jenkins in a platoon with Lezcano in RF. There is no lack of power options for a DH, including Fielder, Thomas, Oglivie, and Jenkins.

Depth Chart

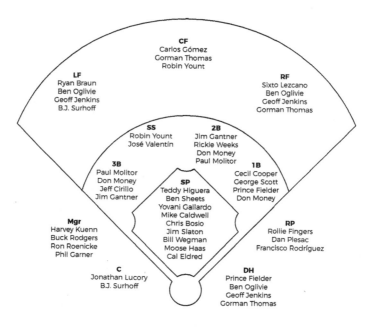

CF
Carlos Gómez
Gorman Thomas
Robin Yount

LF
Ryan Braun
Ben Oglivie
Geoff Jenkins
B.J. Surhoff

RF
Sixto Lezcano
Ben Oglivie
Geoff Jenkins
Gorman Thomas

SS
Robin Yount
José Valentin

2B
Jim Gantner
Rickie Weeks
Don Money
Paul Molitor

3B
Paul Molitor
Don Money
Jeff Cirillo
Jim Gantner

SP
Teddy Higuera
Ben Sheets
Yovani Gallardo
Mike Caldwell
Chris Bosio
Jim Slaton
Bill Wegman
Moose Haas
Cal Eldred

1B
Cecil Cooper
George Scott
Prince Fielder
Don Money

Mgr
Harvey Kuenn
Buck Rodgers
Ron Roenicke
Phil Garner

RP
Rollie Fingers
Dan Plesac
Francisco Rodríguez

C
Jonathan Lucory
B.J. Surhoff

DH
Prince Fielder
Ben Oglivie
Geoff Jenkins
Gorman Thomas

Prospects for Current Players

What are the prospects of current Brewers players making this All-Time team? Ryan Braun is already on this roster. The Brewers loaded up their offense in 2018, so if Christian Yelich, Lorenzo Cain, Travis Shaw, or others stay with the team long enough they could join Braun. Corey Knebel had an outstanding 2017 campaign with 39 saves, a 1.78 ERA, and 126 strikeouts in only 76 innings pitched. He was then part of a strong bullpen in 2018 that also included Josh Hader and Jeremy Jeffress. We'll see...

Retired Player Numbers

Bud Selig (1, team owner), Paul Molitor (4), Robin Yount (19), Rollie Fingers (34), Hank Aaron (44), Bob Uecker (50, broadcaster)

Selections from Other Authors and Fan Surveys

1992: *The All-Time All-Star Baseball Book*, by Nick Acocella and Donald Dewey

Possibly for humor value, the authors created an "all-time" team for the one-year Seattle Pilots, separate from the Milwaukee Brewers that they became. Ignoring that, the Brewers roster was mostly composed of players who were on the team for their 1982 pennant-winning club: Cooper, Gantner, Molitor, Yount, Surhoff, Oglivie, Thomas, Hisle, and Higuera. I liked these selections, except perhaps for Larry Hisle (1978–82), who played for Milwaukee at the very end of his career, and in fact had only one full season for them, 1978, when he hit .290 with 34 HR and 115 RBI. The honorable mentions they named went to George Scott, Ted Simmons, Rollie Fingers, and Don Money.

1995: *Baseball Ratings*, by Charles F. Faber

Written in 1995, the Faber system produced a very credible lineup with no surprises: Cooper, Gantner, Yount, Molitor, Surhoff, Oglivie, Thomas, and Lezcano. Slaton was the top starter, and Plesac the reliever.

2003: *Rob Neyer's Big Book of Baseball Lineups*, by Rob Neyer

Neyer bit the bullet and went with Charlie Moore as the starting catcher, writing, "He spent 14-plus years in the majors, and was generally a good-hitting catcher except for three mid-career seasons in which he was a poor-hitting right fielder." Looking at his career, I thought it was a stretch to describe Moore as "good-hitting" (not to mention that he was often just a platoon player). He also chose Porter as the backup catcher, so I wasn't clear on why Surhoff and Nilsson were bypassed.

The starting infield was Cooper, Gantner, Molitor, and Yount, and the back-ups were Scott, Vina, Cirillo, and Valentín. Neyer listed Molitor as starting DH as well, and also doubled up Yount in the OF. The other two starting OF were Oglivie in LF and Burnitz in RF, with the OF backups being Thomas in CF, Lezcano in RF, and Johnny Briggs in LF. Regarding the latter, Neyer wrote, "Greg Vaughn's the obvious choice because of his long tenure, but Briggs, now mostly forgotten, posted the highest adjusted OPS for a career in franchise history."

His top four starters were Higuera, Caldwell, Slaton, and Wegman. About Higuera he correctly wrote, "The closest thing to a superstar pitcher in franchise history, Higuera went 69-38 in his first four seasons before injuries over-whelmed his career." The next four starters were Bosio, Sorensen, Haas, and Marty Pattin, who pitched for the Brewers for only two years but was solid in each and an All-Star in 1971. Plesac and Fingers were the two obvious relievers, with Neyer opting to give the top spot to Plesac.

Top WAR Single Seasons – Hitters (7+)

Name	Year	WAR	AVG	HR	R	RBI	SB	OPS+
Robin Yount	1982	10.5	.331	29	129	114	14	166
Carlos Gómez	2013	8.5	.284	24	80	73	40	128
Ryan Braun	2011	7.8	.332	33	109	111	33	166
Christian Yelich	2018	7.6	.326	36	118	110	22	164
Tommy Harper	1970	7.4	.296	31	104	82	38	146
Robin Yount	1983	7.2	.308	17	102	80	12	150
Robin Yount	1980	7.1	.293	23	121	87	20	130
Ryan Braun	2012	7.0	.319	41	108	112	30	158

I was not surprised to see Robin Yount appear the most often on this list, with his 1982 MVP season being by far the top rated here. His other MVP season of 1989 didn't rate as highly as his 1983 and 1980 seasons, in part because of the defensive boost for his play at SS those seasons compared to CF in his later years. Carlos Gómez's two All-Star seasons don't initially look very different, but when I looked into why 2013 had such a higher WAR score than 2014 (8.5 vs. 4.8), I learned that some of his defensive numbers were higher in 2013, and that led to a significant defensive WAR contribution. Ryan Braun's two 30/30 seasons were not surprising to see make this list, nor was Tommy Harper's career year in 1970, which was also a 30/30 campaign (his only season with more than 18 HR and the only time he was an All-Star).

Top WAR Single Seasons – Pitchers (7+)

Name	Year	WAR	W–L	ERA	IP	SO	ERA+
Teddy Higuera	1986	9.4	20-11	2.79	248.1	207	156
Mike Caldwell	1978	8.1	22-6	2.39	293.1	131	160
Teddy Higuera	1988	7.4	16-9	2.45	227.1	192	162
Ben Sheets	2004	7.3	12-14	2.70	237.0	264	162

As with Yount above, I wasn't surprised to see Higuera as the only pitcher to appear on this list twice. Caldwell's 1978 season was by far his best, and ditto for Sheets' 2004 campaign, even though he only had a 12-14 record.

Franchise Player

For this club, this was an easy honor to bestow: Robin Yount, hands down. As noted earlier, he is the franchise's all-time leader in lots of categories, and is second in HR and SB.

CHAPTER 25

The Mariners Franchise All-Time Dream Team

The Mariners started out as one of two expansion clubs in the AL in 1977. They did not have a winning season until 1991. Since then they have had good seasons and bad, but they have at least managed to make the playoffs four times, winning their division three times. Their 2001 season was by far their best, as they finished with an incredible 116-46 record, though they were defeated by the Yankees in the ALCS.

With only these relatively few good or great seasons during their history, it would be reasonable not to have high expectations for the quality of their All-Time team. And as you'll see, it did have some weak spots. There were some superstars, though, making it a respectable roster in the end.

1st Base

Name	YR	WAR	W3	W/G	AVG	HR	SB	OPS+
Alvin Davis	8	19.9	12.9	.0171	.281	160	7	128
John Olerud	5	17.0	13.9	.0242	.285	72	3	121
Bruce Bochte	5	10.1	8.4	.0148	.290	58	16	119
Ken Phelps	6	9.6	7.1	.0181	.249	105	8	145
Richie Sexson	4	5.5	5.5	.0108	.244	105	4	114
Tino Martinez	6	7.7	7.8	.0142	.265	88	3	112

There were two clear choices here, but one could debate who deserves to be listed as the starter. I decided to go with **Alvin Davis** (1984–91), who was a consistently good hitter for the Mariners, as he had between 17 and 29 HR and hit between .271 and .305 each season. Even so, his only All-Star appearance was his Rookie of the Year 1984 season, when he hit 27 HR and had 116 RBI.

You could also make a case for **John Olerud** (2000–04) as the starter, as he joined the Mariners late in his career and had 95+ RBI in his first three seasons with the team. He was an All-Star once and provided great defense, taking home three Gold Glove Awards.

I did consider a few others briefly, starting with Bruce Bochte (1978–82), who played a bit more at 1B than LF, and was an All-Star in 1979, when he hit .316 with 16 HR and 100 RBI. Ken Phelps (1983–88) was primarily a DH but played some 1B as well. Only a .249 hitter, he was a strong power source from the left side of the plate, hitting 24 to 27 HR three times for the Mariners, even though he never had more than 344 at-bats in a season. He was doing more of the same in 1988, when he was traded to the Yankees for Jay Buhner (a deal that would later become a comedic point in a *Seinfeld* episode).

Richie Sexson (2005–08) came to Seattle late in his career and immediately provided the Mariners with 39 HR and 121 RBI in 2005, and 34 HR and 107 RBI in 2006. Conversely, Tino Martinez (1990–95) began his career in Seattle and after several mediocre seasons started to blossom in the strike-shortened 1994–95 seasons, hitting .293 with 31 HR and 111 RBI as an All-Star in 1995.

2nd Base

Name	YR	WAR	W3	W/G	AVG	HR	SB	OPS+
Robinson Canó	5	23.6	17.1	.0335	.296	107	13	129
Bret Boone	7	19.0	18.9	.0237	.277	143	50	116
Harold Reynolds	10	14.9	11.7	.0129	.260	17	228	85
Julio Cruz	7	12.7	7.8	.0171	.243	17	290	76
José López	7	10.2	8.6	.0117	.266	80	23	86

Robinson Canó (2014–18) has already done enough after five seasons to warrant selection as the starter at 2B for this dream team roster. His first two seasons in Seattle were relatively weak compared to what he had been doing for the Yankees, but in 2016 he returned to his former greatness, as he hit .298 with 39 HR, 103 RBI, and 107 runs scored. Signed through 2023, assuming he isn't traded, Canó will only add to his résumé for this All-Time team.

You could make a case for **Bret Boone** (1992–93, 2001–05) as the starter over Canó. He started out in Seattle but really became a star when he returned to the Mariners in 2001. That year he hit .331 with 37 HR and a league-leading 141 RBI—very impressive numbers for a middle infielder (although there was suspicion of steroid use at this point in his career). He had a less impressive 24-HR, 107-RBI campaign in 2002, but he batted .294 with 35 HR and 117 RBI the following season. He was also great defensively, taking home three Gold Glove Awards while with the Mariners.

Beyond those two, I decided that **Harold Reynolds** (1983–92) deserved one of the two "extra spots" on this roster. A two-time All-Star, he took home Gold Glove Awards from 1988 through '90. In 1987 he led the league with 60 SB (still the franchise record), and he had five other 25+-SB seasons, even though his OBP wasn't that high (.326).

I also considered an even more prolific base stealer, Julio Cruz (1977–83). Not only did he have five consecutive 40+-SB seasons, but he was also very efficient (290 SB vs. only 59 CS). His batting average was pretty low, though (.243), including a .209 mark in 1980. And finally, José López (2004–10) started his career with the Mariners, playing two partial and five full seasons in Seattle. He had double-digit HR power, with his best year being 2009, when he hit .272 with 25 HR, 96 RBI, and 42 doubles.

3rd Base

Name	YR	WAR	W3	W/G	AVG	HR	SB	OPS+
Edgar Martínez	18	68.3	20.0	.0332	.312	309	49	147
Kyle Seager	8	27.9	17.0	.0242	.258	175	45	114
Adrián Beltré	5	21.2	14.8	.0297	.266	103	49	101
Jim Presley	6	3.3	5.1	.0041	.250	115	8	93

Since I didn't select designated hitters as such for these All-Time teams, players like **Edgar Martínez** (1987–2004) were considered at their primary fielding position (he played 563 games at 3B compared with 1,412 as DH). Martínez played his entire career as a Mariner, ramping up slowly before busting out in 1992 to lead the AL with a .343 average and 46 doubles. His power stroke developed further, and in 1995 he hit 29 HR with 113 RBI, while leading the AL with a .356 average, 52 doubles, 121 runs, and a .479 OBP. His power peaked in 2000, when he smacked 37 HR and led the AL with 145 RBI. Overall, he had six 100+-RBI seasons, batted an impressive .312, was an All-Star seven times, and is the franchise's all-time leader in games played, runs, RBI, doubles, and walks.

There were two other strong candidates at 3B, so I'm including them both. By now **Kyle Seager** (2011–18) has done enough to earn a spot on this All-

Time team, having hit 20+ HR in seven consecutive seasons, with an increase each of the first five years to a high of 30 in 2016. He also provides good defense at the hot corner, taking home a Gold Glove Award in 2014.

At age 25, **Adrián Beltré** (2005–09) had a breakout campaign for the Dodgers, hitting .334 with 121 RBI and leading the NL with 48 HR. He tested free agency after that season and signed with the Mariners. His numbers in Seattle were respectable—but never approached his 2004 MVP runner-up levels. He hit 19 to 26 HR in each of four full seasons but never batted higher than .276. He provided good defense at 3B, winning two Gold Glove Awards, so overall his résumé was strong enough to merit the other "extra spot" on this roster.

The only other candidate that I considered was Jim Presley (1984–89), who played most of his short career with the Mariners and hit 20+ HR three times. His best year was his one All-Star campaign in 1986, when he hit 27 HR with 107 RBI. On the downside, Presley had an abysmal OBP of .293 and struck out a lot (172 in 1986 and 157 in 1987).

Shortstop

Name	YR	WAR	W3	W/G	AVG	HR	SB	OPS+
Álex Rodríguez	7	38.0	28.3	.0481	.309	189	133	138
Omar Vizquel	5	10.3	8.2	.0156	.252	6	39	70
Carlos Guillén	6	9.1	8.0	.0186	.264	29	15	93

Álex Rodríguez (1994–2000) joined the Mariners at the young age of 18 and understandably struggled a bit at first until his first full season in 1996, when he smashed 36 HR with 123 RBI, leading the AL with a .358 average, 54 doubles, and 141 runs (coming in second place in the MVP vote). Two years later, in 1998, he joined the 40/40 club with 42 HR and 46 SB. He was an All-Star four times for the Mariners before leaving Seattle for Texas and eventually New York.

The backup was a closer call, but I went with **Omar Vizquel** (1989–93), who started his outstanding career for the Mariners, winning the first of his many Gold Glove Awards in his final season in Seattle. His offensive numbers were weak at this point in his career: he batted .252, with a .309 OBP, a grand total of 6 HR in 2,111 at-bats, and few SB relative to later in his career. But I still gave him the edge over Carlos Guillén (1998–2003), who was a mediocre hitter early in his career, with his increased power coming only later for the Tigers.

Catcher

Name	YR	WAR	W3	W/G	AVG	HR	SB	OPS+
Dan Wilson	12	13.6	9.6	.0109	.262	88	23	80
Dave Valle	10	9.5	7.0	.0113	.235	72	4	87
Mike Zunino	6	6.9	7.0	.0118	.207	95	2	89
Kenji Johjima	4	5.3	5.0	.0115	.268	48	7	91

Catcher has never been a strong offensive position for the Mariners. The starter was **Dan Wilson** (1994–2005), who played almost all of his career with the Mariners, hitting 10+ HR three times. Very strong defensively, his one All-Star year came in 1996, when he hit .285 with 18 HR and 83 RBI.

Light-hitting **Dave Valle** (1984–93) preceded Wilson as the primary backstop for the Mariners. He topped 400 at-bats in a season only once, often splitting time with other catchers, but his longevity with the club was enough to give him the backup spot on this roster.

You could make a case for Kenji Johjima (2006–09) instead of Valle. He came over from Japan at age 30 and promptly hit .291 with 18 HR and 76 RBI. Unfortunately, he never matched any of those numbers in his three other seasons in the major leagues, and returned to Japan where he hit 25+ HR five times through his career.

And lastly, current backstop Mike Zunino (2013-18) has played in 100+ games for the Mariners four times, and provides some power having hit 20+ HR three times. But with a .207 average and .276 OBP, it is hard to make a case for him for this All-Time team.

Left Field

Name	YR	WAR	W3	W/G	AVG	HR	SB	OPS+
Raúl Ibañez	11	14.5	10.4	.0131	.279	156	21	115
Phil Bradley	5	12.7	11.4	.0209	.301	52	107	124

Raúl Ibañez (1996–2000, 2004–08, '13) had three stints with the Mariners. He struggled during his first five partial seasons, but then he found his power stroke during three years with the Royals. He returned to the Mariners and ramped up his power further, leading to 33 HR and 123 RBI in 2006, and two more 20+-HR and 100+-RBI seasons before he left for Philadelphia via free agency. At age 41 he came back to Seattle for one year in 2013, slugging 29 HR in only 454 at-bats.

You could make a case for Phil Bradley (1983–87) to make this dream team roster, as he was a .301 hitter, stole between 21 to 40 bases in his four full seasons, and managed 26 HR and 88 RBI in his 1985 All-Star season. But some other outfielders are stronger candidates so there just isn't a spot for him.

Center Field

Name	YR	WAR	W3	W/G	AVG	HR	SB	OPS+
Ken Griffey Jr.	13	70.4	27.5	.0418	.292	417	167	144
Mike Cameron	4	18.3	14.7	.0300	.256	87	106	112
Franklin Gutierrez	7	12.9	11.9	.0203	.257	74	61	100
Ruppert Jones	3	8.0	8.0	.0177	.257	51	68	105
Dave Henderson	6	7.7	6.3	.0118	.257	79	25	104

Bursting his way onto the scene in 1989 at age 19, **Ken Griffey Jr.** (1989–99, 2009–10) became the best player in baseball in the 1990s—in fact, he was an All-Star and Gold Glove Award winner every year of that decade. From 1996 through '99, Junior had 48 or more homers and 134 or more RBI, and his 1997 season of 56 HR and 147 earned him MVP honors. He played most of the second half of his career for the Reds but did return to Seattle at age 39 for a couple of partial seasons to close out his Hall of Fame career.

The CF backup was **Mike Cameron** (2000–03), who played only four seasons in Seattle but provided 18 to 25 HR and 17 to 34 SB in each. He struck out a lot and batted only .256, but he was a great center fielder, taking home two Gold Glove Awards for the Mariners.

There were three other Mariners CF worth a brief mention, starting with Ruppert Jones (1977–79). He played his first three full seasons for the Mariners, hitting 20+ HR and stealing 20+ bases twice each. Franklin Gutierrez (2009–13,'15–16) played parts of seven seasons for the Mariners but was only a full-timer in two of them: in 2009, when he hit 18 HR and stole 16 bases, and in 2010, when he hit 12 HR, stole 25 bases, and won a Gold Glove Award. And lastly, Dave Henderson (1981–86) started his career with the Mariners and provided them with double-digit HR five times. And no, that isn't a typo, all three of these guys really did have a .257 batting average while playing in Seattle (and Cameron hit .256!).

Right Field

Name	YR	WAR	W3	W/G	AVG	HR	SB	OPS+
Ichiro Suzuki	13	56.3	22.6	.0303	.322	99	438	113
Jay Buhner	14	23.0	9.6	.0160	.255	307	6	125
Nelson Cruz	4	16.8	13.9	.0277	.284	163	7	148
Leon Roberts	3	9.6	9.6	.0244	.276	47	17	120

Ichiro Suzuki (2001–12, 18) came over from Japan at age 27 and immediately led the AL with a .350 average, 242 hits, and 56 SB—taking home the AL MVP Award, a Gold Glove Award, and Rookie of the Year honors. He went on to win another batting title in 2004, when he hit .372 and set the major league record with 262 hits. Ichiro paced the AL in hits seven times, scored 100+ runs in his first eight seasons in the major leagues, and almost always had 30+ SB a year. Like Griffey, he also managed to be an All-Star and win the Gold Glove Award in ten consecutive seasons.

The Mariners certainly came out ahead in the 1988 trade in which they sent DH Ken Phelps to the Yankees for **Jay Buhner** (1988–2001). Although it took a few years, by 1991 Buhner had matured into a big power threat. He always struck out a lot, but his big swing also produced four 20+-HR seasons followed by three with 40 or more. A good right fielder with a strong arm, he won a Gold Glove Award in 1996, the same year he smashed 44 HR with 138 RBI.

Even with only four seasons in Seattle, slugger **Nelson Cruz** (2015–18) has done enough to make this All-Time team. His power has been pretty consistent with 44, 43, 39, and 37 HR, to go with solid RBI numbers including a league-leading 119 in 2017.

Lastly, deserving of brief mention was Leon Roberts (1978–80), who provided the Mariners with some power in their early years, including 22 HR, 92 RBI, and a .301 average in 1978.

Starting Pitching

Name	YR	WAR	W3	W-L	ERA	WHIP	ERA+
Félix Hernández	14	50.9	19.9	168-128	3.34	1.197	120
Randy Johnson	10	39.5	23.4	130-74	3.42	1.250	128
Jamie Moyer	11	34.9	18.0	145-87	3.97	1.254	112
Mark Langston	6	19.5	16.0	74-67	4.01	1.372	107
Freddy García	6	19.1	12.7	76-50	3.89	1.299	114
Mike Moore	7	18.1	14.6	66-96	4.38	1.395	97
Erik Hanson	6	17.0	12.7	56-54	3.69	1.276	111
Hisashi Iwakuma	6	16.7	12.1	63-39	3.42	1.143	112
Floyd Bannister	4	13.5	12.1	40-50	3.75	1.286	112

You could argue about who deserves the top spot on this pitching staff, but at this point I think **Félix Hernández** (2005–18) has earned it. King Felix came up to the majors at the young age of 19, and for many years was a very durable, high-strikeout pitcher. He hasn't won 20 games in a season yet, but he does own a lifetime .584 winning percentage. His best years have been 2009, when he led the league in wins with a 19-5 record, and the following year, when he led the league with a 2.27 ERA, taking home the AL Cy Young Award even with a 13-12 record. In 2014 he led the AL in ERA with a 2.14 mark, and he's so far had six 200+-strikeout seasons.

Randy Johnson (1989–98) was the other top candidate, having compiled a .637 winning percentage in Seattle. Although he became even more dominant later in his career, The Big Unit was plenty good starting in 1993, when he went 19-8 with 308 strikeouts. He had even better seasons during strike-shortened 1995 (18-2, 2.48, 294 K), when he won the Cy Young Award, and 1997 (20-4, 2.28, 291 K), when he came in second in the vote. He was an All-Star five times and led the AL in strikeouts each year from 1992 through '95.

Depending on your edition, if you looked up "late bloomer" in the dictionary you might see a picture of **Jamie Moyer** (1996–2006). After generally struggling for ten years in the majors, Jamie came to Seattle in 1996 and turned his career around. He went 20-6 in 2001 and 21-7 in 2003 (two of only three 20-win seasons ever for this franchise), and he posted a .625 winning percentage overall for the Mariners.

The third southpaw starter on this team, **Mark Langston** (1984–89) started his career with the Mariners and was the team's somewhat wild, high-strikeout ace for several years. He had four 200+-K seasons in Seattle, but he also had over 100 walks in each of those years. He was the runner-up for the 1984 Rookie of the Year Award, losing out to teammate Alvin Davis.

Freddy García (1999-2004) pitched five-and-a-half years for the Mariners, posting seasons of 17-8, 18-6, and 16-10. During this era of massive run scoring, his 3.05 ERA in 2001 was actually good enough to lead the AL.

Hisashi Iwakuma (2012–17) played for a decade in the Japanese league and then joined the Mariners at age 31 and has posted a strong .618 winning percentage, with three seasons of 14 to 16 wins. His best year was 2013 when he went 14-6 with a 2.66 ERA and came in third in the AL Cy Young Award voting.

Erik Hanson (1988–93) had one standout season for Seattle, in 1990, when he went 18-9 with 211 K and a 3.24 ERA. His four-plus other seasons were mediocre at best, but that was enough to make this All-Time team.

You could make a case for two others, starting with Mike Moore (1982–88) who pitched the first half of his career for Seattle and went 17-10 with a 3.46 ERA in 1985. While he had several fine seasons later for the Oakland A's, he was more of a workhorse for the Mariners, posting poor records like 7-14, 7-17, 9-19, and 9-15. And Floyd Bannister (1979–82) was an All-Star in 1982, when he led the AL with 209 strikeouts. But he won only 9 to 12 games in each of his four seasons in Seattle, so I opted to go with five relief pitchers instead.

Relief Pitching

Name	YR	WAR	W3	SV	W-L	ERA	WHIP	ERA+
Jeff Nelson	8	8.6	5.7	23	24-23	3.26	1.308	134
J.J. Putz	6	8.5	7.5	101	22-15	3.07	1.158	143
Arthur Rhodes	5	6.9	5.8	9	28-16	3.05	1.049	142
Michael Jackson	5	6.1	5.6	34	23-26	3.38	1.244	125
Edwin Díaz	3	5.5	5.5	109	4-14	2.64	1.016	156
Mike Schooler	5	4.3	3.9	98	12-29	3.30	1.294	123
Kazuhiro Sasaki	4	3.7	3.6	129	7-16	3.14	1.084	138
Norm Charlton	5	2.2	4.0	67	14-21	4.03	1.335	115

As I noted, given the lack of strong starting pitcher candidates, I decided to select four relief pitchers for this roster. **J.J. Putz** (2003–08) played the first half of his career for Seattle and was their closer for three seasons. His best two years came in 2006, when he locked down 36 saves with a 2.30 ERA, and then his one All-Star campaign in 2007, when he had 40 saves and a microscopic 1.38 ERA.

Next up I decided to include **Kazuhiro Sasaki** (2000–03), as he is the Mariners' all-time saves leader with 123 and has three of their top eight seasons for saves. He came over from Japan in 2000 at age 32 and won Rookie of the Year honors after tallying 37 saves. He was an All-Star the next two years, recording 45 and 37 saves, respectively.

Edwin Díaz (2016–18) had already established himself as the Mariners closer in this first two seasons, but in 2018 he became an All-Star and broke the team's all-time record by posting 57 saves. His dominant season also included an impressive 1.96 ERA and 124 strikeouts in 73.1 IP.

Mike Schooler (1988–92) pitched out of the Mariners bullpen for five of his six seasons in the big leagues. He had 33 saves and a 2.81 ERA in 1989, and 30 saves and a 2.25 ERA the next year. And **Norm Charlton** (1993, '95–97, 2001) had three stints in Seattle, first providing 18 saves and a 2.34 ERA in 1993, and then returning with 14 saves and a 1.51 ERA in 1995. He became more and more hittable the next two years, and after bouncing around for a few years, he returned for one last season as a capable setup man in 2001.

Other closers typically pitched for the Mariners for only a couple of seasons, such as Bill Caudill (1982–83), Bobby Ayala (1994–98), Eddie Guardado (2004–06), David Aardsma (2009–10), and Fernando Rodney (2014–15).

While the Mariners have lacked consistent closers, they have had some quality setup men, so I decided to include two of them on this All-Time team. **Jeff Nelson** (1992–95, 2001–03, '05) had three stints with the Mariners, always as a short reliever but never a closer. His best season in Seattle came in 1995, when he posted a 7-3 record and 2.17 ERA, striking out 96 batters in 78.2 IP.

Arthur Rhodes (2000–2003, '08) had a very long career that included two stints in Seattle. His best season was 2001, when like Nelson he was an important part of the historic Mariners team that won 116 games. He posted a perfect 8-0 record in relief and a 1.72 ERA. The next year he went 10-4 in relief with a 2.33 ERA.

And lastly, Michael Jackson (1988–91, '96) had a long career that also included two stints for the Mariners. His best season for Seattle was arguably 1988, when he posted a 2.63 ERA.

Managers

Name	YR	From-To	W-L	PCT	PS	WS
Lou Piniella	10	1993–2002	840-711	.542	4	0
Jim Lefebvre	3	1989–91	233-253	.479	0	0
Mike Hargrove	3	2005–07	192-210	.478	0	0
Darrell Johnson	4	1977–80	226-362	.384	0	0

Lou Piniella had by far the longest tenure as manager of the Mariners, and also by far the most success—as measured by both winning percentage and post-season appearances. This included the record-setting season of 2001, when he guided the powerhouse Mariners to a 116-46 (.716) record, only to lose to the Yankees in the ALCS, 4 games to 1.

After Piniella, there aren't any obvious candidates who would serve as his lieutenants on this All-Time dream team. I listed **Jim Lefebvre** and **Mike Hargrove** as the two who had the best results amongst those who managed the club for three years, and then **Darrell Johnson**, who managed them for four—a tough job, as it was their first several years in the league as an expansion team. But you could make a case for several others who managed the team for one to three years each, and I wouldn't argue with you.

Starting Lineup

What would mythical starting lineups look like for this All-Time roster?

Against RHP:
Ichiro Suzuki RF (L)
Edgar Martínez DH (R)
Ken Griffey Jr. CF (L)
Álex Rodríguez SS (R)
Raúl Ibañez LF (L)
Robinson Canó 2B (L)
Alvin Davis/John Olerud 1B (L)
Kyle Seager 3B (L)
Dan Wilson C (R)

Against LHP:
Ichiro Suzuki RF (L)
Edgar Martínez DH (R)
Álex Rodríguez SS (R)
Ken Griffey Jr. CF (L)
Adrián Beltré 3B (R)
Bret Boone 2B (R)
Alvin Davis/John Olerud 1B (L)
Phil Bradley LF (R)
Dan Wilson C (R)

The first four hitters in these lineups compared well with many other All-Time teams, even those with far longer histories. At LF, 2B, and 3B there are natural platoons that could be used. And at 1B it was a close call between Davis and Olerud, so I listed them both. Nelson Crus is a powerful bat off the bench.

Depth Chart

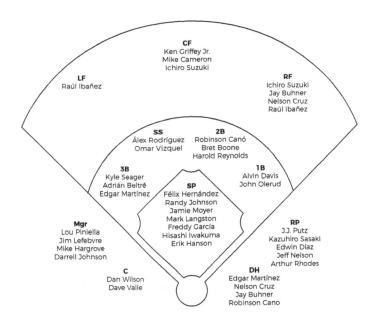

Prospects for Current Players

What are the prospects of current Mariners players making this All-Time team? There are already several current Mariners on this roster, including Hernández, Seager, Canó, Cruz, and Díaz. Starting pitcher James Paxton has had moments of brilliance, so he could soon join them. We'll see...

Retired Player Numbers

Edgar Martínez (11), Ken Griffey Jr (24)

Selections from Other Authors and Fan Surveys

1992: *The All-Time All-Star Baseball Book*, by Nick Acocella and Donald Dewey

With only about 15 years of franchise history to work with, the authors chose a reasonable lineup of Alvin Davis, Harold Reynolds, Jim Presley, Craig Reynolds, Phil Bradley, Tom Paciorek, Ken Griffey Jr., Dave Valle, and Mark Langston. Craig Reynolds (1977–78) played for Seattle for only two years, though he was an All-Star in 1978, when he batted .292. Tom Paciorek (1978–81) played for Seattle for parts of four seasons, making the All-Star squad in strike-shortened 1981, when he hit .326 with 14 HR and 13 SB. The authors gave honorable mentions to pitcher Floyd Bannister and DH Richie Zisk.

1995: *Baseball Ratings*, by Charles F. Faber

The Faber system as applied in 1995 created a reasonable all-time team. The infield was Alvin Davis, Harold Reynolds, Spike Owen, Jim Presley, and Dave Valle, and the outfield was Ken Griffey Jr., Phil Bradley, and Dave Henderson. The top pitcher was Randy Johnson, presumably just eclipsing Mark Langston at that time.

2003: *Rob Neyer's Big Book of Baseball Lineups*, by Rob Neyer

Neyer's selections for his starting lineup were quite solid in my opinion. He listed Martínez at both DH and 3B, and of course had Reynolds at 2B and Bradley in the outfield instead of Ichiro. His backup selections were sensible too: DH Phelps, C Valle, 1B Olerud, 2B Cruz, 3B Presley, SS Vizquel, LF Greg Briley, CF Cameron, and RF Al Cowens. I didn't consider Briley, who played a few seasons but never had more than 400 at-bats in a year. Neyer described him as "the winner by default," but I think there were several candidates stronger than Briley, especially if you allowed Bruce Bochte or Dan Meyer to be considered as outfielders.

As for pitching, Neyer rightly chose Johnson, Moyer, Langston, and García as the top four, followed by Hanson, Bannister, Brian Holman, and Aaron Sele. The last two didn't pitch for the Mariners for long, and while Sele was effective, Holman was nothing special. Even given his poor winning percentage, I preferred Moore's longevity with the club. His selections of Sasaki and Schooler in relief were good choices.

Top WAR Single Seasons – Hitters (7+)

Name	Year	WAR	AVG	HR	R	RBI	SB	OPS+
Álex Rodríguez	2000	10.4	.316	41	134	132	15	163
Ken Griffey Jr.	1996	9.7	.303	49	125	140	16	154
Álex Rodríguez	1996	9.4	.358	36	141	123	15	161
Ichiro Suzuki	2004	9.1	.372	8	101	60	36	130
Ken Griffey Jr.	1997	9.1	.304	56	125	147	15	165
Bret Boone	2001	8.8	.331	37	118	141	5	153
Ken Griffey Jr.	1993	8.7	.309	45	113	109	17	171
Álex Rodríguez	1998	8.5	.310	42	123	124	46	136
Ichiro Suzuki	2001	7.7	.350	8	127	69	56	126
Robinson Canó	2016	7.3	.298	39	107	103	0	138
Ken Griffey Jr.	1991	7.1	.327	22	76	100	18	155
Edgar Martínez	1995	7.0	.356	29	121	113	4	185

This is an impressive list for a franchise with such a short history. Griffey and Rodríguez account for seven of the entries, not surprisingly, with Ichiro showing up twice. A-Rod's 1998 was a 40/40 season but rates lower because of a lower .310 average and .360 OBP, compared to 1996, when he had a .358 average, and 2000, when he had over twice as many walks for a .420 OBP. Martínez's 1995 season has the highest OPS+ on this list, but he ranks last here because he was a DH for almost the entire season and so doesn't get a positive boost to his WAR from defense.

Top WAR Single Seasons – Pitchers (7+)

Name	Year	WAR	W-L	ERA	IP	SO	ERA+
Randy Johnson	1995	8.7	18-2	2.48	214.1	294	193
Randy Johnson	1997	8.0	20-4	2.28	213.0	291	197
Félix Hernández	2010	7.1	13-12	2.27	249.2	232	174
Hisashi Iwakuma	2013	7.0	14-6	2.66	219.2	185	138

Some great seasons here. Hernández's 2010 is an interesting one, since his record was 13-12, but that was the year he took home the Cy Young Award. He's had two other seasons with an ERA+ of 170 or higher: 2009, when he went 19-5 with a 2.49 ERA (6.0 WAR), and 2014, when he went 15-6 with a 2.14 ERA (6.8 WAR). It is interesting that those two don't rate higher than Iwakuma's season with a 138 ERA+.

Franchise Player

I had to go with Griffey Jr. here, because he had the highest WAR total, edging out Martínez while doing so in fewer seasons. Additional honorable mentions go to Suzuki, Rodríguez, Hernández, and Johnson.

CHAPTER 26

The Padres Franchise All-Time Dream Team

The Padres joined the National League as an expansion club in 1969. As one would expect, they were awful for many years early on; they didn't reach even a .400 winning percentage until 1975. Nothing particularly good happened for them until 1984, when they won the NL pennant before losing to the powerful Detroit Tigers in the World Series. But that success was short-lived, and they didn't return to the postseason until 1996, their second season under manager Bruce Bochy. Two years later, they had their best season ever, going 98-64 and again making it to the championship, this time losing to the powerhouse Yankees. Their next postseason appearances came in 2005 and 2006, but in both cases, they lost in the first series.

With such limited success over the years, you'd expect there to be some relative weak spots in their All-Time team. And there were. But there were many great star players too.

1st Base

Name	YR	WAR	W3	W/G	AVG	HR	SB	OPS+
Adrián González	5	20.3	14.7	.0254	.288	161	1	141
Nate Colbert	6	17.3	11.9	.0200	.253	163	48	127
Ryan Klesko	7	15.9	12.0	.0192	.279	133	60	134

Name								
Fred McGriff	3	9.5	9.5	.0245	.281	84	16	149
Wally Joyner	4	9.0	8.5	.0181	.291	38	9	117
Steve Garvey	5	1.4	3.5	.0023	.275	61	6	100

Adrián González (2006–10) was productive in all five of his seasons for the Padres, starting with a .304 average, 24 HR, and 82 RBI in his first full year in the majors. He managed 30 to 40 HR and 99 to 119 RBI in his other four years. Not a fast runner (a grand total of 1 SB during his time in San Diego), he was a three-time All-Star and great defender (two Gold Glove Awards).

The backup was another slugger, **Nate Colbert** (1969–74), who was the 1B for the Padres' first six seasons. He was essentially their first star hitter, belting 20+ HR in five seasons, including 38 in 1970 and 38 again in 1972, when he also added 111 RBI and even 15 SB. He did strike out a lot (100+ every season), but he was a good fielder and an All-Star for the team three times.

Several other candidates were considered, starting with Ryan Klesko (2000–05), who played more games for San Diego at 1B than OF, but I'll discuss him more at the latter position, where there was room for him to make this roster. Fred McGriff (1991–93) played for only two-and-a-half seasons with the Padres, but they were productive: in 1991 he had 31 HR with 106 RBI, and in 1992 he had 35 HR and 104 RBI. Wally Joyner (1996–99) spent four years near the end of his career in San Diego and actually managed a .327 average for them in 1997.

And Steve Garvey (1983–87) wrapped up his fine career with the Padres, although by then his offensive production was a shadow of its former self, as he never hit over .300 or more than 21 HR. He did, however, provide San Diego with one of their greatest baseball moments. In Game Four of the NLCS against the Cubs, he had four hits, including a two-run, walk-off HR in the ninth inning.

2nd Base

Name	YR	WAR	W3	W/G	AVG	HR	SB	OPS+
Bip Roberts	7	12.4	10.8	.0186	.298	20	148	106
Roberto Alomar	3	12.1	12.1	.0270	.283	22	90	103
Mark Loretta	3	11.3	11.3	.0274	.314	32	18	121
Tim Flannery	11	9.1	5.9	.0094	.255	9	22	85
Alan Wiggins	5	7.8	8.3	.0195	.260	4	171	85
Quilvio Veras	3	5.7	5.7	.0137	.270	15	87	95

This has historically been a very weak position for San Diego. **Bip Roberts** (1986–91, '94–95) split his time at several positions, including (in order): 2B,

LF, 3B, CF, SS, and RF. He got on base a lot (.298 average and .361 OBP), and then once there ran a lot too, stealing 46 bases in 1990 and 20+ in four other seasons. If you don't like Roberts as the starter here at 2B, then I think he still deserves to make this All-Time team as a utility player.

Roberto Alomar (1988–90) started his Hall of Fame career in San Diego but had his best seasons elsewhere. An All-Star in 1990, he was a good fielder and ran well (90 SB in three seasons), but he hit for a higher average and more power later in his career.

You could make a case for Mark Loretta (2003–05) instead of Alomar, as he was an All-Star in 2004, with a .335 average (fourth best in the NL), 16 HR, 108 runs, and 47 doubles. Like Alomar, two other speedy, switch-hitting Padres 2B were Quilvio Veras (1997–99), who had 87 SB in three seasons, and Alan Wiggins (1981–85), who had impressive totals of 33, 66, and 70 (still the franchise record).

And finally, lifetime Padres infielder Tim Flannery (1979–89) played parts of 11 seasons for San Diego but appeared in 100 or more games only four times and had a total of 9 HR in his career. A .255 hitter, his hard work and versatility kept him on the roster for a long time.

3rd Base

Name	YR	WAR	W3	W/G	AVG	HR	SB	OPS+
Chase Headley	9	18.6	13.6	.0199	.263	87	73	111
Phil Nevin	7	17.7	13.2	.0220	.288	156	14	129
Ken Caminiti	4	17.5	14.8	.0314	.295	121	40	147
Luis Salazar	7	6.7	5.1	.0095	.267	40	93	90
Gary Sheffield	2	5.8	5.8	.0271	.319	43	10	151

Chase Headley (2007–14, 18) is the all-time leader in games played at 3B for the Padres. He generally displayed only moderate power or speed for San Diego, with the exception being his outstanding 2012 campaign, when he came in fifth in the MVP vote after batting .286 with 17 SB, 31 HR, and 115 RBI, while also taking home a Gold Glove Award.

Ken Caminiti (1995–98) had four fine seasons for the Padres, hitting 25+ HR each year and playing great defense, taking home three Gold Glove Awards. His 1996 season was one of the best statistical years anyone has ever had in San Diego, as he took home the NL MVP Award after hitting .326 with 40 HR, 130 RBI, and 11 SB (though these numbers are tainted, as he later admitted to steroid use in 1996 and for several years following).

Phil Nevin (1999–2005) played 6+ years in San Diego, hitting 20+ HR four times and accumulating 100+ RBI three times. In his one All-Star season in 2001, he hit .306 with 41 HR and 126 RBI. He split his time, playing mostly 3B and 1B, but also got in a few games at C, LF, and RF. His power and his versatility were enough to earn him the one of the two "extra spots" on this All-Time team.

Two other players deserve brief mention, starting with Luis Salazar (1980–84, '87, '89), who had three stints in San Diego. Not an impressive hitter (.267), he provided some speed, including 32 SB in 1982 and 24 in 1983, and some versatility in the field.

And lastly, some readers will remember Gary Sheffield's (1992–93) fine 1992 season, when he led the league with a .330 average and hit 33 HR with 100 RBI. But that was his only full season in San Diego, as he was traded to the Marlins before the All-Star break the next year. Not that Padres fans complained for long, since that deal was how they acquired star closer Trevor Hoffman.

Shortstop

Name	YR	WAR	W3	W/G	AVG	HR	SB	OPS+
Ozzie Smith	4	10.8	9.8	.0168	.231	1	147	66
Garry Templeton	10	10.0	7.6	.0059	.252	43	101	77
Khalil Greene	6	9.3	9.3	.0141	.248	84	23	96

The career WAR scores for the candidates at SS were extremely low, and they leave open room for debate as to who should be selected. Interestingly, Hall of Famer **Ozzie Smith** (1978–81) scores highest. He spent the first four years of his career with the Padres. His hitting was weak (.231 average and just one HR), but he still posted solid SB totals of 40, 28, 57, and 22. His defense was of course superb, earning him the first 2 of his 13 consecutive Gold Glove Awards.

Garry Templeton (1982–91) came to San Diego in a trade for Ozzie Smith, supposedly an exchange of defense for offense. Unfortunately, Templeton never hit for the Padres the way he had for St. Louis, batting .252 with only 36 triples and 43 HR over ten seasons (compared to leading the league in triples, with seasons of 18, 13, and 19 from 1977 through '79). His speed on the bases also deteriorated, as he stole 27 bases in 1982 but never topped 16 again.

The other candidate I considered here was Khalil Greene (2003–08), who had a short career, playing all but his final year in San Diego. He batted .248 and had a low .304 OBP, but he did provide some power, with 2007 being his best year: 27 HR, 97 RBI, and 44 doubles.

Catcher

Name	YR	WAR	W3	W/G	AVG	HR	SB	OPS+
Gene Tenace	4	19.7	15.8	.0344	.237	68	17	136
Terry Kennedy	6	16.9	11.6	.0202	.274	76	3	105
Benito Santiago	7	14.1	8.8	.0179	.264	85	62	95

Gene Tenace (1977–1980) played for the Padres for only four years, but he hit 15 to 20 HR in each of them and has the highest WAR of any candidate here. Although only a .237 hitter for San Diego, he walked so much that he compiled an impressive .403 OBP.

Terry Kennedy (1981–86) played the best years of his career for the Padres, hitting 10+ HR five times. A three-time All-Star for San Diego, his best year was 1982, when he hit .295 with 21 HR and 97 RBI.

Benito Santiago (1986–92) started his long career with the Padres, earning Rookie of the Year honors in 1987 after hitting .300 with 18 HR, 79 RBI, and 21 SB. A four-time All-Star, he provided moderate power and speed, but his arm behind the plate was his most valuable attribute, earning him three Gold Glove Awards. Based on that you could make a case for him as the starter here, but I think he at least deserves the second "extra spot" on this All-Time dream team roster. Interestingly, his 7 years in San Diego were his only extended stay, as he went on to play for nine other teams in 13 seasons.

Left Field

Name	YR	WAR	W3	W/G	AVG	HR	SB	OPS+
Gene Richards	7	18.8	10.5	.0200	.291	26	242	113
Ryan Klesko	7	15.9	12.0	.0192	.279	133	60	134
Carmelo Martínez	6	9.7	9.8	.0124	.248	82	8	109

I briefly mentioned **Ryan Klesko** (2000–06) earlier, as he played more games at 1B than LF for the Padres, but there was more room for him to make this roster here. He played most of the second half of his career for San Diego, providing four seasons with 20+ HR. His best year was his one All-Star season in 2001, when he hit 30 HR with 113 RBI.

You could make a case for **Gene Richards** (1977–83) to be the starter in LF over Klesko, as he played most of his short career with the Padres and hit for a good average (.291). He also provided plenty of speed, swiping 30+ bases four times, including 56 in his rookie season and 61 in 1980.

Also worth a brief mention was Carmelo Martínez (1984–89), who split time between LF and 1B for six seasons, but he was only a .248 hitter with highs of 21 HR and 72 RBI.

Center Field

Name	YR	WAR	W3	W/G	AVG	HR	SB	OPS+
Kevin McReynolds	4	12.4	12.0	.0250	.263	65	17	110
Darrin Jackson	4	9.1	9.1	.0253	.250	44	22	95
Steve Finley	4	8.6	8.7	.0143	.276	82	85	112

The Padres have not had many outfielders who primarily played CF and excelled for the team for very long. **Kevin McReynolds** (1983–86) played his first four years with the Padres, provided good defense, and hit .288 with 26 HR and 96 RBI in 1986.

Two others deserve mention, but given the stronger candidates at RF, I'm not selecting either to make this All-Time roster. Darrin Jackson (1989–92) played parts of four seasons for the Padres but played in 125+ games only once, in 1992, when he hit 17 HR with 70 RBI and 14 SB. And Steve Finley (1995–98) had 25+ HR and 90+ RBI in two of his four seasons with the Padres, and excelled defensively, taking home two Gold Glove Awards.

Right Field

Name	YR	WAR	W3	W/G	AVG	HR	SB	OPS+
Tony Gwynn	20	68.8	21.4	.0282	.338	135	319	132
Dave Winfield	8	31.9	18.7	.0286	.284	154	133	134
Brian Giles	7	17.3	13.3	.0208	.279	83	43	122
Will Venable	8	13.2	8.2	.0144	.252	81	130	105

As far as these All-Time teams have gone, this one was relatively weak so far. But here we finally got a true superstar who played a long time for the Padres, **Tony Gwynn** (1982–2001). He was even nicknamed Mr. Padre, and rightly so, since he played his entire career for San Diego. Gwynn led the league in hits seven times and took home eight batting titles. He sometimes showed double-digit HR power, and early in his career provided speed as well, stealing 30+ bases four times. Amazingly, he hit .300+ in 19 of his 20 seasons, all but his partial rookie season. His best averages were .370 in 1987, .372 in 1997, and .394 during the strike-shortened 1994. A 15-time All-Star, he provided good defense early in his career, taking home five Gold Glove Awards.

Although far behind Gwynn's accomplishments as a Padre, at least **Dave Winfield** (1973–80) provided an additional big-name player on this roster. He started his Hall of Fame career in San Diego and hit 20+ HR five times for them. In 1979 he hit .308 with 34 HR and a league-leading 118 RBI—good enough to earn him third place in the MVP vote. He stole 15+ bases in six seasons and also provided a strong arm and solid defense, taking home two Gold Glove Awards.

Brian Giles (2003–09) finished his fine career for the Padres, although he never provided for them the 35+-HR, 100+-RBI seasons he had given the Pirates. He did hit 23 HR with 94 RBI in 2004, and the next year led the NL in walks (119), which generated a lofty .423 OBP.

One other Padres outfielder deserves mention, Will Venable (2008–15), who played mostly in RF but also at times patrolled CF. He provided moderate power and speed, including four consecutive seasons with 20+ SB.

Starting Pitching

Name	YR	WAR	W3	W-L	ERA	WHIP	ERA+
Jake Peavy	8	26.9	17.0	92-68	3.29	1.186	119
Andy Ashby	8	22.9	13.6	70-62	3.59	1.246	112
Andy Benes	7	20.2	12.4	69-75	3.57	1.239	109
Randy Jones	8	20.1	14.6	92-105	3.30	1.208	104
Eric Show	10	16.7	9.9	100-87	3.59	1.283	101
Ed Whitson	8	16.2	15.9	77-72	3.69	1.229	99
Greg Harris	6	15.5	12.4	41-39	2.95	1.182	128
Bruce Hurst	5	14.9	14.1	55-38	3.27	1.181	113
Joey Hamilton	5	14.8	10.3	55-44	3.83	1.343	104
Dave Dravecky	6	12.2	8.4	53-50	3.12	1.202	115

Jake Peavy (2002–09) is the all-time WAR leader for Padres starting pitchers, and I think he is the clear top choice for their dream team pitching staff. At age 23 in 2004, he went 15-6 and led the NL in ERA with a 2.27 mark. Then in 2007 he took home the pitching Triple Crown, leading the NL with a 19-6 record, 2.54 ERA, and 240 strikeouts, en route to winning the NL Cy Young Award.

The other top candidate was lefty **Randy Jones** (1973–80), who had a poor start in his first full season in 1974, posting an abysmal 8-22 record. But he quickly turned things around, using his sinker to induce countless groundouts and leading the NL in 1975 with a 2.24 ERA. That year he went 20-12 and came in second in the NL Cy Young Award voting. The next year he led the NL in wins with a 22-14 record, good enough to take the award home for himself. He never again posted a winning record for the Padres, but in light of his two stellar All-Star seasons, I gave him the second spot on this staff.

Andy Ashby (1993–99, 2004) took a while to get established in the majors but finally had his first of two All-Star seasons in 1998, when he went 17-9 with a 3.34 ERA. **Andy Benes** (1989–95) was the first pick in the 1988 amateur draft and made it to the Padres during his first professional season. A highly touted strikeout pitcher, Benes never became the star some thought he would be. He twice won 15 games in San Diego, but also had a 6-14 season.

Who has the most wins all-time for the Padres? Would you believe the answer is **Eric Show** (1981–90) with a modest 100? He won 16 games once and 15 games twice, but he was never an All-Star.

Ed Whitson (1983–84, '86–91) had two stints in San Diego and managed double-digit wins five times, with his best two seasons being 1989 with a 16-11 record and 2.66 ERA, and 1990 with a 14-9 record and 2.60 ERA.

Left-hander **Bruce Hurst** (1989–93) pitched four strong seasons in San Diego in the second half of his career, posting a winning record each year and winning 15 games twice.

In part because of the many (relatively) strong relief pitching candidates, I didn't select any other starting pitchers for this All-Time team. That said, a few deserve brief mention, starting with Joey Hamilton (1994–98), who started his career with five seasons for the Padres, collecting 12 to 15 wins in three of them.

Dave Dravecky (1982–87) split his time as a starter and reliever for the Padres, three times posting a sub-3.00 ERA, but never posting more than 14 victories. Greg Harris (1988–93) also split his time as a reliever and starter, generally providing a good ERA but never winning more than 10 games in a season for San Diego.

Relief Pitching

Name	YR	WAR	W3	SV	W-L	ERA	WHIP	ERA+
Trevor Hoffman	16	26.3	11.1	552	54-64	2.76	1.043	146
Heath Bell	5	8.6	6.9	134	27-19	2.53	1.118	150
Mark Davis	5	8.6	8.8	78	14-20	2.75	1.260	135
Scott Linebrink	5	7.5	6.1	4	27-12	2.73	1.147	145
Mike Adams	4	6.4	5.2	1	9-5	1.66	0.903	224
Craig Lefferts	7	6.2	6.8	64	42-40	3.24	1.249	114
Lance McCullers	4	5.6	5.6	36	21-28	2.96	1.273	125
Rollie Fingers	4	5.3	6.6	108	34-40	3.12	1.250	111
Goose Gossage	4	4.3	5.3	83	25-20	2.99	1.164	123

The relief pitching candidates were relatively strong compared with the starting pitchers just discussed. Up first of course is **Trevor Hoffman** (1993–2008), who if not for Tony Gwynn would be the star of this entire roster. He was the Padres' closer every year from 1994 through 2008, with the exception of 2003, when he was injured. His ERA was below 3.00 all but three of those seasons, and he had 40+ saves nine times, and 30+ four other times. A six-time All-Star,

1998 was his best year, when he posted a 1.48 ERA, led the league with 53 saves, and came in second in the NL Cy Young voting.

Heath Bell (2007–11) had big shoes to fill when he took over the closer duties for the Padres, but he didn't disappoint, as he immediately led the league with 42 saves. And that was only the first of three consecutive All-Star, 40+-save seasons Bell provided San Diego.

Mark Davis (1987–89, '93–94) was acquired by trade from the Giants in July of 1987. He had been used as both a starter and a reliever previously, but the Padres saw his potential as a closer. He was excellent in 1988, saving 28 games with a 2.01 ERA. In 1989 he saved 44 games with a 1.85 ERA and earned the NL Cy Young Award. He opted for free agency, and the Padres decided not to sign him, which turned out to be a good move. He was never the same again, even when he returned to the Padres for parts of the 1993 and 1994 seasons.

After signing with the Padres as a free agent from the Oakland Athletics, future Hall of Famer **Rollie Fingers** (1977–80) led the NL with 35 saves in 1977 and 37 saves in 1978. **Rich "Goose" Gossage** (1984–87) also came aboard via free agency and was the closer in San Diego for four seasons, getting 20+ saves three times. He was an All-Star twice and was an important part of the 1984 NL championship team.

A few others deserve mention, starting with Craig Lefferts (1984–87, '90–92), who had two stints with the Padres. From 1984 through '87 he was primarily a setup man, though in their 1984 NL championship season he shared closer duties with Goose Gossage, posting 10 saves and a 2.13 ERA. After pitching for the Giants for a few seasons, he returned in 1990 and recorded 23 saves both that year and the next.

Then there were two non-closers in recent years who posted some impressive ERAs. Scott Linebrink (2003–07) pitched in 73 games in both 2004 and 2005, with ERAs of 2.14 and 1.83. Mike Adams (2008–11) posted an impressive 0.73 ERA in 37 games in 2009, then a 1.76 ERA in 70 games in 2010. He had a 1.13 ERA across 48 games in 2011 when he was traded to the Rangers at the July 31st deadline. And lastly, Lance McCullers (1985–88) did a bit of everything as a pitcher for the Padres, ending up with a 2.96 ERA for San Diego.

Managers

Name	YR	From-To	W-L	PCT	PS	WS
Bruce Bochy	12	1995–06	951-975	.494	4	0
Dick Williams	4	1982–85	337-311	.520	1	0
Bud Black	9	2007–15	649-713	.477	0	0
Jack McKeon	3	1988–90	193-164	.541	0	0
Greg Riddoch	3	1990–92	200-194	.508	0	0
John McNamara	4	1974–77	224-310	.419	0	0

Only two managers have led the Padres to the postseason, **Bruce Bochy** and **Dick Williams**. Bochy managed the club for three times as long and is by far the leader in all-time wins for San Diego, so he deserves the top spot here. How you rank the managers after these two could be argued, especially between **Bud Black**, who led for nine years but had only a .477 winning percentage, and **Jack McKeon**'s three years but .541 winning percentage.

Starting Lineup

What would mythical starting lineups look like for this All-Time roster?

Against RHP:
Tony Gwynn CF (L)
Bip Roberts 2B (S)
Dave Winfield RF (R)
Adrián González 1B (L)
Chase Headley 3B (S)
Ryan Klesko LF (L)
Brian Giles DH (L)
Terry Kennedy C (L)
Ozzie Smith SS (S)

Against LHP:
Tony Gwynn DH (L)
Robert Alomar 2B (S)
Dave Winfield RF (R)
Nate Colbert 1B (R)
Ken Caminiti 3B (S)
Kevin McReynolds CF (R)
Bip Roberts LF (S)
Gene Tenace/Benito Santiago C (R)
Ozzie Smith SS (S)

With both Gwynn and Winfield as primarily right fielders, one of them needed to play out of position. So, I decided to shift Gwynn to CF (where he did play a little) against right-handers and have him DH against left-handers. This allowed McReynolds, the only primary CF on the roster, to get in the lineup against lefties at least.

Bip Roberts provides great flexibility of course, so I elected to include Alomar in the lineup against lefties and Klesko in the lineup against righties (against whom he hit significantly better). González and Colbert form a natural platoon, and you could also rotate catchers based on the opposing pitcher too. At 3B, both Headley and Caminiti are switch-hitters, but Caminiti hit better against lefties than he did righties, so I thought I'd include him in that lineup. Not in these lineups are some valuable guys like Nevin for power and Richards for speed.

Depth Chart

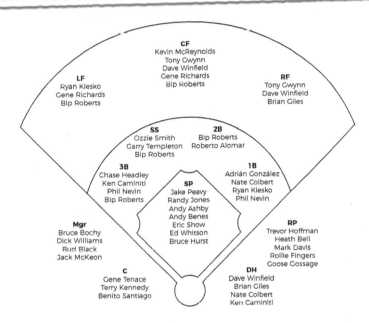

CF
Kevin McReynolds
Tony Gwynn
Dave Winfield
Gene Richards
Bip Roberts

LF
Ryan Klesko
Gene Richards
Bip Roberts

RF
Tony Gwynn
Dave Winfield
Brian Giles

SS
Ozzie Smith
Garry Templeton
Bip Roberts

2B
Bip Roberts
Roberto Alomar

3B
Chase Headley
Ken Caminiti
Phil Nevin
Bip Roberts

1B
Adrián González
Nate Colbert
Ryan Klesko
Phil Nevin

SP
Jake Peavy
Randy Jones
Andy Ashby
Andy Benes
Eric Show
Ed Whitson
Bruce Hurst

RP
Trevor Hoffman
Heath Bell
Mark Davis
Rollie Fingers
Goose Gossage

Mgr
Bruce Bochy
Dick Williams
Bud Black
Jack McKeon

C
Gene Tenace
Terry Kennedy
Benito Santiago

DH
Dave Winfield
Brian Giles
Nate Colbert
Ken Caminiti

Prospects for Current Players

What are the prospects for current Padres players making this All-Time team? Not very good, but mostly because the current Padres roster does not have any star players who have been with the team very long. Wil Myers has displayed some power, and Eric Hosmer joined the team in 2018, but the rest are all very young and unproven. It wouldn't take a lot at positions like 2B, SS, LF, CF, and others—but it will take a while to see any changes here. We'll see...

Retired Player Numbers

Steve Garvey (6), Tony Gwynn (19), Dave Winfield (31), Randy Jones (35), Trevor Hoffman (51)

Selections from Other Authors and Fan Surveys

1992: *The All-Time All-Star Baseball Book*, by Nick Acocella and Donald Dewey

The authors in 1992 made sensible choices of Colbert, Alomar, Smith, Winfield, Gwynn, Kennedy, and Jones. At third base they chose Graig Nettles, who played for the Padres in the twilight of his career. He did provide the 1984 championship club with 20 HR, but he batted only .228 that year. I couldn't agree with their selection of Cito Gaston as the other outfielder—what about Gene Richards, who wasn't even given honorable mention? The other players who were mentioned included Rollie Fingers, Garry Templeton, Eric Show, Steve Garvey, and Benito Santiago.

1995: *Baseball Ratings*, by Charles F. Faber

Written in 1995, the Faber system produced a pretty good lineup: Colbert, Alomar, Smith, Salazar, Kennedy, Gwynn, Winfield, and Richards. No starting pitcher was listed, and Craig Lefferts was the top reliever.

2002: *The San Diego Padres Encyclopedia*, by David Porter and Joe Naiman

In chapter 18 of this book, the authors selected an All-Time All-Star team through the 2001 season, "designating one player for each of the starting positions, one utility infielder and outfielder, three starting pitchers, two relief pitchers, one manager, and one executive. The general criteria for selections included the on-field accomplishments and impact made by the team member." They described each selection at length, making for an interesting read.

They went with Colbert at 1B, Alomar at 2B, and Caminiti at 3B. They chose Smith as the SS, though they noted that "Garry Templeton received some recognition." For the reserve infielder spot, they went with Tim Flannery over Bip Roberts, touting the former's "all out style of play and hustle." They of course chose Gwynn and Winfield for the top two OF spots, but picked Steve Finley as the "unanimous" third outfielder. For the reserve outfielder they went with Kevin McReynolds, saying that Richards was "close behind."

For catcher they went with Santiago and had Kennedy "finishing close behind." For starting pitchers they selected Ashby, Jones, and Show, stating that Clay Kirby was close behind. Strangely, they discussed Fingers as the first relief pitcher, and only after that went on at some length about Hoffman as the other (giving honorable mention to Gossage). I thought that even through only 2001, Hoffman had done far more for the Padres than Fingers did. They selected Bruce Bochy as top manager, with Dick Williams as runner-up, and Ray Kroc as top Padres executive.

2003: *Rob Neyer's Big Book of Baseball Lineups*, by Rob Neyer

Neyer started McGriff at 1B, which I thought did a disservice to Colbert, whom he listed on his second team. He also chose Alomar, and listed Veras as the backup (claiming that he beat out Jody Reed for this spot). Nowhere on either of his teams did he include Roberts, so I figured he just missed him because Bip's games played were spread around to so many positions. He sensibly selected Templeton and Smith as the two SS, Caminiti and Nevin at 3B, and Kennedy and Santiago at C.

His outfield had Richards in LF, Finley in CF, and Gwynn in RF. This meant Winfield was relegated to the second squad (RF), along with Kevin McReynolds (CF), and surprisingly Greg Vaughn in LF. Vaughn basically had one great season for the Padres, 1998, when he hit 50 HR. Neyer noted that "left field has been the franchise's position of instability over the years," so his choice of Vaughn made some sense.

For pitching his first four starters were solid: Jones, Show, Benes, and Ashby. Whitson dropped down to sixth, followed by Hurst and Andy Hawkins (1982–88), whose best year was 1985, when he went 18-8 with a 3.15 ERA. His fifth pitcher was an interesting pick: Gaylord Perry, who pitched only two seasons with the Padres. In 1978 he went 21-6 with a 2.73 ERA, winning the NL Cy Young Award in what was one of the best San Diego pitching seasons ever. However, his 1979 season was far less impressive (12-11), so Neyer was clearly weighing that one season heavily. He rounded out his picks with Hoffman and Fingers as the top relievers.

Top WAR Single Seasons – Hitters (7+)

Name	Year	WAR	AVG	HR	R	RBI	SB	OPS+
Tony Gwynn	1987	8.5	.370	7	119	54	56	158
Dave Winfield	1979	8.3	.308	34	97	118	15	166
Ken Caminiti	1996	7.6	.326	40	109	130	11	174

I was surprised that only one of Gwynn's many impressive seasons produced a WAR of 7 or higher. I was not surprised that Winfield's 1979 and Caminiti's 1996 seasons made this short list.

Top WAR Single Seasons – Pitchers (7+)

Name	Year	WAR	W–L	ERA	IP	SO	ERA+
Kevin Brown	1998	9.1	18-7	2.38	257.0	257	164
Dave Roberts	1971	7.7	14-17	2.10	269.2	135	157
Randy Jones	1975	7.6	20-12	2.24	285.0	103	156
Ed Whitson	1990	7.1	14-9	2.60	228.2	127	148

The top season here was from a pitcher who threw for the Padres for only one season. Kevin Brown was an All-Star for San Diego in 1998 and ended up placing third in the Cy Young Award vote. Also of note here is Dave Roberts, who was a rookie for the original Padres in 1969. He was both a starter and reliever in 1970, and then was arguably the ace of the staff in 1971 (his last year in San Diego), when he went 14-17 with an impressive 2.10 ERA and 14 complete games in 34 starts.

Franchise Player

This honor had to go to Tony Gwynn, no doubt about it. He leads this franchise in games played, at-bats, hits, batting average, runs, RBI, doubles, triples, SB, and walks. Honorable mention goes to Trevor Hoffman who, if not for Gwynn, would have been the only relief pitcher to be given the franchise player honor in this book.

CHAPTER 27

The Diamondbacks Franchise All-Time Dream Team

In terms of overall winning percentage, the Arizona Diamondbacks have been the most successful of the four newest expansion franchises. Over their first 20 seasons, they have won 49.3% of their games and have made the playoffs six times. They impressively won a World Series championship in 2001, in only their fourth season in the league, and made the playoffs in three of their first five seasons. Other postseason appearances have been more spread out, but their current roster seems strong enough to lead to more success in the years to come.

As with other recent expansion teams, there are some superstars on this All-Time team, but also some relatively weak positions, especially when it comes to looking for backup selections at some positions and the last few pitcher picks.

1st Base

Name	YR	WAR	W3	W/G	AVG	HR	SB	OPS+
Paul Goldschmidt	8	40.1	21.6	.0367	.297	209	124	145
Chad Tracy	6	5.9	7.0	.0084	.280	78	11	100
Greg Colbrunn	5	3.6	3.8	.0108	.310	34	1	126
Conor Jackson	6	2.2	3.9	.0042	.277	46	22	98
Travis Lee	3	0.7	0.7	.0021	.252	39	30	89

Paul Goldschmidt (2011–18) quickly established himself as one of the best 1B in the game, and in his third season he led the NL with 36 HR and 125 RBI. Already a six-time All-Star, Goldy has had six seasons with 20+ HR, four seasons with 100+ runs, and three seasons with 100+ RBI. He runs well for a 1B, with a career-high 32 SB in 2016. And he is outstanding defensively, having already taken home three Gold Glove Awards.

Before Goldschmidt, the history of 1B for the Diamondbacks was not a pretty sight. After looking at several options, I went with **Chad Tracy** (2004–09), who split his time fairly evenly between 1B and 3B. A .280 hitter, he had some power, with 27 HR in 2005 and then 20 HR in 2006.

Greg Colbrunn (1999–2002, '04) had a .310 batting average but was more of a pinch-hitting specialist than a regular 1B. As a result, he topped 200 at-bats only once for Arizona, though he still managed to hit 10+ HR twice.

Conor Jackson (2005–10) was the primary 1B for two seasons, and in other years played a mix of 1B and LF. He was a .277 hitter with limited power, hitting 10+ HR three times. And lastly, Travis Lee (1998–2000) was a rookie 1B for the Diamondbacks in their inaugural season and hit 22 HR with 72 RBI, appearing to be a solid player for them to build around. His average and power declined the next two seasons, so he provided his greatest value to the franchise by being part of a trade package that brought Curt Schilling to Arizona from the Phillies.

2nd Base

Name	YR	WAR	W3	W/G	AVG	HR	SB	OPS+
Orlando Hudson	3	10.5	10.5	.0261	.294	33	23	105
Jay Bell	5	9.7	9.6	.0157	.263	91	17	104
Aaron Hill	5	6.2	7.8	.0118	.273	55	31	108

After four seasons in Toronto, **Orlando Hudson** (2006–08) was traded to the Diamondbacks and over three years provided a .294 average with moderate power and speed. An All-Star in 2007, his greatest value was his defense, where his great range led him to win two of his four Gold Glove Awards while with Arizona.

Late in his career, after many seasons as the Pirates' starting shortstop, **Jay Bell** (1998–2002) joined the Diamondbacks and after one year switched over to 2B. Generally not a power hitter throughout his career, Bell had an outstanding 1999 season, when he hit .289 with 38 HR, 112 RBI, and 132 runs.

You could make a case for Aaron Hill (2011–15), as he also provided the Diamondbacks some power from the 2B position, with a high of 26 HR and 85 RBI in 2012.

3rd Base

Name	YR	WAR	W3	W/G	AVG	HR	SB	OPS+
Matt Williams	6	8.3	7.8	.0139	.278	99	12	100
Jake Lamb	5	6.4	5.7	.0128	.247	75	17	101
Mark Reynolds	4	5.6	5.1	.0099	.242	121	42	108

Matt Williams (1998–2003) finished his fine career with Arizona, providing both power and good defense at the hot corner. In 1999 he came in third in the NL MVP vote after hitting .303 with 35 HR and 142 RBI.

I considered two candidates for the backup here, and decided that current 3B **Jake Lamb** (2014–18) has by now done enough to deserve the honor. His power blossomed in his first full season in 2016, when he hit 29 HR with 91 RBI, and he followed that up as an All-Star in 2017, when he hit 30 HR with 105 RBI.

You could certainly make a case for **Mark Reynolds** (2007–10), who started his career with the Diamondbacks and hit 28+ HR three times, including a high of 44 in 2009 (when he also had a career high of 24 SB). Reynolds was an all-or-nothing type of hitter, as he provided only a .242 average and led the NL in strikeouts with embarrassing totals of 204 in 2008, 223 in 2009, and 211 in 2010. Based on his big HR numbers, I decided to give Reynolds one of the two "extra spots" on this All-Time team.

Shortstop

Name	YR	WAR	W3	W/G	AVG	HR	SB	OPS+
Stephen Drew	7	13.2	9.9	.0171	.266	72	33	96
Craig Counsell	6	12.7	9.8	.0191	.266	24	68	80
Chris Owings	5	4.1	4.0	.0086	.257	27	59	79
Tony Womack	5	1.4	2.5	.0022	.269	21	182	70

Stephen Drew (2006–12) was the starting SS for Arizona longer than any other player, and he provided 10+ HR four times. His best season came in 2008, when he batted .291 with 91 runs, 21 HR, and 44 doubles.

After playing for two of the other recent expansion clubs (Rockies and Marlins), **Craig Counsell** (2000–03, '05–06) found his way to the Diamondbacks. A scrappy, versatile player, Counsell split his time in Arizona almost evenly between 2B, 3B, and SS. Only a .266 hitter with little power, he could run a little and provided 10+ SB four times, with a high of 26 in 2005. I thought he deserved a spot on this All-Time team roster, and SS was the position where I could get him in.

Tony Womack (1999–2003) was also versatile in the field, starting his career mostly as a 2B for the Pirates, but then playing RF in his first season for the Diamondbacks and then switching to mostly SS. Offensively, his strongest attribute was his speed, and in 1999 he led the NL with a career-high 72 SB. He swiped 45, 28, and 29 the next three years, and led the NL with 14 triples in 2000.

Current Diamondbacks player Chris Owings (2013–17) is also quite versatile, having played a significant number of games at SS, 2B, CF, and RF. He has nabbed 10+ SB three times, with his high being 21 in 2016.

Catcher

Name	YR	WAR	W3	W/G	AVG	HR	SB	OPS+
Miguel Montero	9	13.3	12.1	.0147	.264	97	2	103
Damian Miller	5	6.0	4.6	.0128	.269	48	3	93
Chris Snyder	7	4.6	4.3	.0083	.233	62	0	88

Miguel Montero (2006–14) was the clear top choice at catcher. A two-time All-Star, he hit 10+ HR six times. His best numbers came in 2011, when he hit .282 with 18 HR and 86 RBI.

The backup selection was a closer call, but I went with **Damian Miller** (1998–2002), who hit 10+ HR four times. Chris Snyder (2004–10) followed Miller as a catcher for the Diamondbacks, but he was only a .233 hitter with moderate power.

Left Field

Name	YR	WAR	W3	W/G	AVG	HR	SB	OPS+
Luis Gonzalez	8	30.1	18.5	.0252	.298	224	32	130
David Peralta	5	12.2	10.0	.0214	.293	73	29	115
Gerardo Parra	6	11.5	10.7	.0146	.274	39	51	94
Eric Byrnes	4	4.2	5.5	.0096	.261	61	88	91

For the first nine years of his career, **Luis Gonzalez** (1999–2006) was a .270 hitter and had managed 20+ HR only once. Then he joined the D-backs in 1999 at age 31 and his numbers took off: .336 average, 26 HR, 112 runs, 111 RBI, 45 doubles, and a league-leading 206 hits. The following year he batted .311 with 31 HR and 114 RBI, and then in 2001 he hit .325 and exploded with 57 HR, 142 RBI, and 128 runs, coming in third in the NL MVP voting. A five-time All-Star, he had five consecutive seasons with 100+ RBI and six seasons with 20+ HR for Arizona.

David Peralta (2014–18) has played his first five seasons for the Diamondbacks, splitting his time mostly between LF and RF. He led the league with 10 triples in 2015 and then increased his power with 30 HR in 2018.

Gerardo Parra (2009–14) started his career with the Diamondbacks and was very good defensively, winning a Gold Glove Award while playing mostly LF in 2011, then another while playing mostly RF in 2013. He didn't star as much offensively, hitting .274 with highs of only 10 HR and 15 SB, but his résumé is strong enough to secure the second "extra spot" on this All-Time team roster.

Lastly, Eric Byrnes (2006–09) played two full seasons for Arizona, hitting 26 HR with 25 SB in 2006, and 21 HR with 50 SB and 103 runs in 2007. He played in fewer than 100 games in each of his last two seasons with the Diamondbacks, and his average slumped badly to .218.

Center Field

Name	YR	WAR	W3	W/G	AVG	HR	SB	OPS+
A.J. Pollock	7	20.0	14.0	.0314	.281	74	103	112
Steve Finley	6	18.1	12.2	.0213	.278	153	70	111
Chris Young	7	14.3	11.9	.0162	.239	132	112	95
Ender Inciarte	2	8.6	8.6	.0344	.292	10	40	95

At this point you can make the case that **A.J. Pollock** (2012–18) deserves the starting spot here. Although he has missed some time due to injury, when on the field Pollack provides the Diamondbacks with a good combination of speed and power, with his best numbers coming in 2015, when he hit .315 with 111 runs, 20 HR, and 39 SB. He is also an outstanding defensive CF, taking home one Gold Glove Award so far.

The backup is **Steve Finley** (1999–2004) who hit 20+ HR for the Diamondbacks five times, including 34 HR in 1999 and 35 the following year. An outstanding defensive CF, he earned two of his five Gold Glove Awards while with Arizona.

Another Diamondbacks CF who provided both power and speed was **Chris Young** (2006–12), who had 20+ HR four times and 20+ SB three times. He didn't hit for a high average (.239) and struck out a lot (five consecutive seasons with 130 or more). But he was an All-Star in 2010, ending that year with 27 HR, 91 RBI, and 28 SB.

Lastly, **Ender Inciarte** (2014–15) played only his first two seasons for Arizona, providing some versatility by playing all three outfield positions. He was a .292 hitter and had 19 and 21 SB in those two years.

Right Field

Name	YR	WAR	W3	W/G	AVG	HR	SB	OPS+
Justin Upton	6	13.7	11.9	.0187	.278	108	80	118

Justin Upton (2007–12) first joined the Diamondbacks as a 19-year-old in 2007, and by 2009 he was an All-Star. He provided a good combination of power and speed, hitting 25+ HR twice and stealing 20+ bases twice while in Arizona.

Two other Diamondbacks RF deserve brief mention, even though they didn't play for the club long enough to warrant real consideration. In the second half of his career, Reggie Sanders (2001) played for seven teams in nine years, and one of those was Arizona, where he hit 33 HR with 90 RBI and 14 SB. And more recently, J.D. Martinez (2017) was traded by the Tigers to the Diamondbacks before the 2017 trade deadline, and he proceeded to put on a power display like few before, hitting 29 HR with 65 RBI in only 62 games and 232 at-bats. Apparently not a part of Arizona's long-term plans, he was granted free agency after the season and eventually signed with the Red Sox.

Starting Pitching

Name	YR	WAR	W3	W-L	ERA	WHIP	ERA+
Randy Johnson	8	50.8	28.5	118-62	2.83	1.068	164
Brandon Webb	7	31.0	18.7	87-62	3.27	1.239	142
Curt Schilling	4	25.3	22.7	58-28	3.14	1.036	148
Dan Haren	3	15.2	15.2	37-26	3.56	1.132	125
Zack Greinke	3	13.7	13.7	45-25	3.53	1.131	127
Patrick Corbin	6	12.3	10.8	56-54	3.91	1.285	109
Miguel Batista	4	10.5	8.5	40-34	3.99	1.364	117
Robbie Ray	4	9.0	7.9	34-34	3.84	1.327	115
Ian Kennedy	4	8.9	10.4	48-34	3.82	1.231	106
Josh Collmenter	6	7.4	5.3	36-33	3.54	1.180	112

Hall of Famer **Randy Johnson** (1999–2004, '07–08) had many outstanding seasons for the Mariners, but he had his best string of consecutive seasons for the Diamondbacks. He was dominant from 1999 through 2002, winning the NL Cy Young Award every year. Johnson won three ERA titles and led the NL in strikeouts every season, with eye-popping totals of 364, 347, 372, and 334. His W-L record improved each year, and in 2002 he took home the NL pitching Triple Crown, when he led the league in wins with a 24-5 record. The Big Unit struggled in the NLDS in 1999 and 2002, but he was outstanding throughout the postseason in 2001: he started five games, posted a 1.52 ERA, had 47 strikeouts in 41.1 IP, and was particularly strong in the World Series, winning both of his starts and winning a game in relief, sharing the World Series MVP Award with fellow starter Curt Schilling.

Brandon Webb (2003–09) pitched his entire, relatively short career for the Diamondbacks. He had a strong rookie season, posting a 2.84 ERA over 28 starts. He didn't do nearly as well in his sophomore campaign, leading the NL in walks with 119 and losses with a 7-16 record, though still posting a solid 3.59 ERA. But by 2006 he was one of the best pitchers in the league, leading the NL in wins with a 16-8 record and taking home the NL Cy Young Award. This was his first of three consecutive All-Star seasons, as he posted an 18-10 record in 2007 and led the league in wins again with a 22-7 record in 2008, placing second in the Cy Young vote both years. Unfortunately, a series of shoulder injuries cut his career short at that point, and he didn't pitch in the majors past age 30.

Curt Schilling (2000–03) was acquired in a trade with the Phillies before the deadline in 2000. In his two full seasons, he was an outstanding right-handed complement to the lefty Johnson. In 2001 he led the NL in wins with a 22-6 record, and he had a 2.98 ERA with 293 strikeouts in 256.2 IP. Then in 2002 he went 23-7 with a 3.23 ERA and 316 strikeouts in 259.1 IP. He was runner-up to Johnson in the Cy Young Award voting both seasons, and as noted earlier also shared with him the 2001 World Series MVP Award. His postseason numbers that year were simply amazing: a 4-0 record in six starts, 1.12 ERA, and 56 strikeouts in 48.1 IP.

After several good seasons with the Athletics, **Dan Haren** (2008–10) was traded to the Diamondbacks following the 2007 season. He was an All-Star in two seasons for Arizona, going 16-8 and 14-10 and posting 200+ strikeouts both years. He was then traded to the Angels before the deadline during the 2010 season in a deal that landed Arizona a group of players that included Patrick Corbin.

Zack Greinke (2016–18) had three great seasons for the Dodgers, including a 19-3 record and 1.66 ERA in 2015, before signing a massive, six-year contract with the Diamondbacks. He struggled to start the 2016 season, spent some time on the DL, and ended the year with a disappointing 4.37 ERA, though he did manage a 13-7 record. He bounced back in 2017 with a 17-7 record, 3.20 ERA, and 215 strikeouts. A very good fielder on the mound, Greinke has won two of his four Gold Glove Awards while with the Diamondbacks.

Another current Diamondbacks starter also deserves a spot on this All-Time team roster, **Patrick Corbin** (2012–13, '15–18). He was an All-Star in his first full season in 2013 and ended that year with a 14-8 record and 3.41 ERA. He underwent Tommy John surgery and missed the entire 2014 season and half of 2015. While he had a very disappointing 2016 season, posting a 5-13 record and 5.15 ERA, he improved in 2017 with a 14-13 record and 4.03 ERA, and then 3.15 ERA and 246 strikeouts in 2018.

Ian Kennedy (2010–13) was acquired from the Yankees after the 2009 season as part of a three-team trade (which included the Diamondbacks sending a young Max Scherzer to the Tigers). Kennedy was only 9-10 in his first season with Arizona but had his career year in 2011, leading the NL in wins with a 21-4 record, while posting a 2.88 ERA and 198 strikeouts. His ERA climbed to 4.02 the next year, when he recorded a 15-12 mark. He struggled further in 2013 and was dealt just before the deadline to the Padres.

After considering the remaining starting and relief pitching candidates, I decided to include **Miguel Batista** (2001–03, '06), who was a mixed starter and reliever for the Diamondbacks. He had two stints with Arizona and posted 10 or 11 wins for the club three times.

Josh Collmenter (2011–16) was also a mixed pitcher for the Diamondbacks, starting 75 games and coming in as a reliever in 125 games. His best two seasons as a starter came as a rookie in 2011, when he went 10-10 with a 3.38 ERA, and 2014, when he posted an 11-9 record and 3.46 ERA.

And **Robbie Ray** (2015–18) could one day earn a spot on this roster, because after two losing seasons he was an All-Star in 2017 and ended the season with a 15-5 record, 2.89 ERA, and 218 strikeouts in only 162 IP.

Relief Pitching

Name	YR	WAR	W3	SV	W-L	ERA	WHIP	ERA+
Byung-Hyun Kim	6	8.3	8.5	70	21-23	3.43	1.204	136
Brad Ziegler	6	7.1	5.4	62	21-11	2.49	1.144	161
José Valverde	5	5.7	5.9	98	9-14	3.29	1.173	141
J.J. Putz	4	3.4	3.7	83	7-9	2.81	1.091	142
Matt Mantei	6	2.7	3.3	74	8-11	4.04	1.342	116

José Valverde (2003–07) was an impressive rookie in 2003, when he had a 2.15 ERA, 10 saves, and 71 strikeouts in 50.1 IP. He had mixed results the next three seasons, at times closing games and posting a 2.44 ERA in 2005 but a 5.84 ERA in 2006. In 2007 he took over full-time closer duties and responded very well, making the All-Star team and leading the league with 47 saves with a 2.66 ERA. He was traded after the season to the Astros, where he led the NL again in saves with 44.

Sidearmer **Byung-Hyun Kim** (1999–2003, '07) was signed as a 20-year-old phenom out of Korea and shared the Diamondbacks' closer duties in 2000, when he had 111 strikeouts in 70.2 IP. He became their primary closer in 2001 and had 19 saves with a 2.94 ERA. He was an All-Star in 2002 and ended the season with 36 saves, an 8-3 record, and a 2.04 ERA. After being switched to a starting role, in late May 2003 he was traded to the Red Sox for Shea Hillenbrand.

Another sidearmer, **Brad Ziegler** (2011–16) was traded at the deadline by the Athletics to the Diamondbacks in 2011. He was an effective reliever for several years and took over closer duties in 2015, ending the year with 30 saves and a 1.85 ERA. In 2016, he had 18 saves and a 2.82 ERA when he was traded in early July to the Red Sox.

J.J. Putz (2011–14) finished his career with the Diamondbacks and served as their closer for two seasons, posting 45 saves and a 2.17 ERA in 2011, and 32 saves and a 2.82 ERA in 2012.

You could make a case for Matt Mantei (1999–2004), as he was the team's closer for three seasons, interrupted by the need for Tommy John surgery. His best two seasons for Arizona came in 1999, when he posted 22 saves with a 2.79 ERA, and 2003, when he posted 29 saves with a 2.62 ERA.

Managers

Name	YR	From-To	W-L	PCT	PS	WS
Bob Brenly	4	2001–04	303-262	.536	2	1
Buck Showalter	3	1998–2000	250-236	.514	1	0
Bob Melvin	5	2005–09	337-340	.498	1	0
Kirk Gibson	5	2010–14	353-375	.485	1	0
Torey Lovullo	2	2017-18	175-149	.540	1	0

Bob Brenly led the Diamondbacks to their only World Series championship and had a solid .536 winning percentage over four seasons, so he clearly gets the nod for the top spot here. How to rank the candidates after that is debatable, so I went with winning percentage as the deciding factor, since Buck **Showalter**, **Bob Melvin**, and **Kirk Gibson** each led Arizona to one postseason. Current manager Torey Lovullo could make this list more interesting if he can continue the success he had with the team in 2017 and 2018.

Starting Lineup

What would mythical starting lineups look like for this All-Time roster?

Against RHP:
A.J. Pollock CF (R)
Justin Upton RF (R)
Luis Gonzalez LF (L)
Paul Goldschmidt 1B (R)
Steve Finley DH (L)
Matt Williams 3B (R)
Stephen Drew SS (L)
Orlando Hudson 2B (S)
Miguel Montero C (L)

Against LHP:
A.J. Pollock CF (R)
Justin Upton RF (R)
Paul Goldschmidt 1B (R)
Matt Williams 3B (R)
Luis Gonzalez LF (L)
Chris Young DH (R)
Jay Bell 2B (R)
Stephen Drew SS (L)
Damian Miller C (R)

The two platoons I thought were reasonable were at 2B and C. You can't go wrong with either Finley or Pollock roaming in CF, with the other making for a fine DH, along with Young who hits lefties pretty well.

Depth Chart

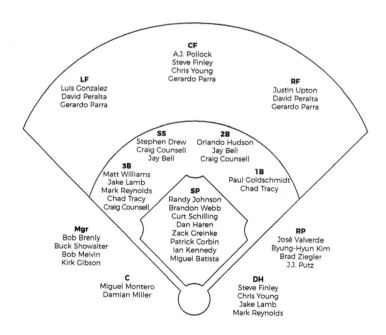

Prospects for Current Players

What are the prospects for current Diamondbacks making this All-Time team? Goldschmidt, Pollock, Lamb, Peralta, Greinke, and Corbin are already on the roster, but I'm not seeing many candidates to join them soon. We'll see...

Retired Player Numbers

Luis Gonzalez (20), Randy Johnson (51)

Top WAR Single Seasons – Hitters (7+)

Name	Year	WAR	AVG	HR	R	RBI	SB	OPS+
Paul Goldschmidt	2015	8.7	.321	33	103	110	21	168
Luis Gonzalez	2001	7.9	.325	57	128	142	1	174
A.J. Pollock	2015	7.2	.315	20	111	76	39	130
Paul Goldschmidt	2013	7.1	.302	36	103	125	15	160

Only one season with a WAR of 8+, with even Gonzalez's impressive 2001 numbers coming up just short.

Top WAR Single Seasons – Pitchers (7+)

Name	Year	WAR	W-L	ERA	IP	SO	ERA+
Randy Johnson	2002	10.5	24-5	2.32	260.0	334	195
Randy Johnson	2001	9.4	21-6	2.49	249.2	372	188
Randy Johnson	1999	8.6	17-9	2.48	271.2	364	184
Curt Schilling	2001	8.5	22-6	2.98	256.2	293	157
Curt Schilling	2002	8.5	23-7	3.23	259.1	316	140
Randy Johnson	2004	8.2	16-14	2.60	245.2	290	176
Randy Johnson	2000	8.1	19-7	2.64	248.2	347	181
Dan Haren	2009	7.0	14-10	3.14	229.1	223	142
Brandon Webb	2006	7.0	16-8	3.10	235.0	178	152

Far more pitcher seasons than hitter seasons, largely due to Randy Johnson, who dominates the list with some eye-popping numbers. Pairing him with Schilling in those 2001 and 2002 seasons was almost unfair to the competition.

Franchise Player

Honorable mentions go to Paul Goldschmidt, Luis Gonzalez, and Brandon Webb, but the clear choice here was Randy Johnson. Four consecutive Cy Young Awards plus his strong performance in the 2001 postseason were plenty enough to earn this honor.

CHAPTER 28

The Marlins Franchise All-Time Dream Team

The Marlins were one of two expansion teams in 1993, the first new major league franchises since 1977. Known as the Florida Marlins, they barely managed to top .400 in their first two seasons, and were around .500 in their next two. Before the 1997 season, the Marlins brought in Jim Leyland as a new manager and signed several free agents that raised expectations for the young club. They earned a Wild Card berth and managed to go all the way, winning the World Series against the Indians in seven games.

Even with a World Series championship, owner Wayne Huizenga claimed financial losses and disappointed fans by holding a fire sale and trading away many of the team's best players. As a result, the 1998 Marlins posted a 54-108 (.333) record, the first of five consecutive losing seasons. In 2003 the Marlins started very poorly, but after making a change in manager and calling up some key prospects, the team played well and again earned an NL Wild Card berth. As with 1997, the Marlins were underdogs but managed to get through the playoffs and win the World Series, this time in six games against the Yankees.

For the next eight seasons the Marlins had mixed success but never made the playoffs. In 2012, after 19 years as the Florida Marlins and playing home games at Sun Life Stadium, the club unveiled new uniforms, changed the name to the Miami Marlins, and switched to playing home games at Marlins Park.

The changes haven't yet made a difference in terms of winning, as the franchise has not had a winning season since 2009.

Through 2018 the Marlins have had only a 26-year history from which to select players for this All-Time team roster, so obviously there are some weak spots, especially when it comes to choosing backups and the last few pitchers.

1st Base

Name	YR	WAR	W3	W/G	AVG	HR	SB	OPS+
Derrek Lee	6	9.9	8.0	.0117	.264	129	51	115
Justin Bour	5	4.8	4.3	.0100	.262	83	2	125

Derrek Lee (1998–2003) joined the Marlins as one of three young players traded by the Padres for Marlins ace Kevin Brown, as part of the fire sale that followed Florida's surprising 1997 world championship. His power was apparent immediately, but he struggled to hit for average until 2000, when he batted .281 with 28 HR. That was his first of four seasons with 20+ HR for the Marlins, and he later provided some speed on the bases, swiping 19 bases in 2002 and 21 in 2003. A good defender at 1B, he took home one of his three Gold Glove Awards while with the Marlins in 2003.

There simply weren't many other candidates at 1B, so that meant recent Marlins slugger **Justin Bour** (2014–18) gets this backup spot. Although he never played more than 129 games in a season for the Marlins, Bour has had HR totals of 23, 15, 25, and 19 from 2015 through '18, when he was traded away in the second half of the season.

2nd Base

Name	YR	WAR	W3	W/G	AVG	HR	SB	OPS+
Luis Castillo	10	22.5	12.8	.0199	.293	20	281	94
Dan Uggla	5	15.7	11.8	.0202	.263	154	19	117
Dee Gordon	3	8.9	8.9	.0233	.309	7	148	98

Luis Castillo (1996–2005) started and played the majority of his career for the Marlins. He hit .300+ five times, including a high of .334 in 2000. He stole a lot of bases, including 50 in 1999, and an NL league-leading 62 in 2000 and 48 in 2002. A three-time All-Star, Castillo was also good defensively at 2B, taking home three Gold Glove Awards. For now, Castillo is the franchise's all-time leader in games played, at-bats, hits, runs, triples, walks, and stolen bases.

Dan Uggla (2006–10) also started his career for the Marlins and took over 2B duties from Castillo in 2006. That is where the similarities end, though, as

Uggla was a power hitter with very consistent HR production, belting 27 to 33 in each of five seasons. He was an All-Star as a rookie in 2006 and ended that season with a .282 average, 27 HR, 105 runs, and 90 RBI. His best numbers came in his final season in Florida, when he batted .287 with 33 HR, 100 runs, and 105 RBI.

Dee Gordon (2015–17) started his career with the Dodgers and in 2014 led the league with 64 SB before being traded to the Marlins in the off-season. In 2015 he led the NL with a .333 average, 205 hits, and again in SB with 58. Injured for part of 2016, he still managed to swipe 30 bases in only 79 games, and then returned strong in 2017 to hit .308, score 114 runs, and pace the NL with 60 SB. Gordon was also a good defender at 2B, and so I decided to give him one of the two "extra spots" on this roster.

3rd Base

Name	YR	WAR	W3	W/G	AVG	HR	SB	OPS+
Miguel Cabrera	5	18.3	14.5	.0254	.313	138	17	143
Mike Lowell	7	14.2	10.1	.0144	.272	143	21	109

Miguel Cabrera (2003–07) was one of the key rookies on the Marlins' 2003 World Series championship club, but his performance that year at age 20 was only a glimpse of what was to come. An All-Star in each of his next four seasons, Cabrera hit 26 to 34 HR, posted 112 to 119 RBI, and batted over .290 with a high of .339 in 2006. Sadly for Marlins fans, he was traded along with pitcher Dontrelle Willis to the Tigers after the 2007 season, and has gone on to even greater success for Detroit.

Mike Lowell (1999–2005) was the other pretty clear choice at 3B, as he hit 20+ HR four times and posted 100+ RBI twice. A three-time All-Star, Lowell worked hard and developed into a solid defensive 3B, taking home a Gold Glove Award in 2005.

Shortstop

Name	YR	WAR	W3	W/G	AVG	HR	SB	OPS+
Hanley Ramírez	7	26.9	19.0	.0285	.300	148	230	129
Edgar Rentería	3	5.0	5.0	.0127	.288	12	89	89
Álex González	8	1.6	3.0	.0018	.245	81	23	78

Hanley Ramírez (2006–12) was a young prospect when he was part of a big trade that involved Mike Lowell and Josh Beckett going from the Marlins to the Red Sox. He made an immediate impact for Florida, winning the NL Rookie of the Year Award after hitting .292 with 46 doubles, 11 triples, 17 HR, 119 runs, and 51 SB. He stole 51 bases again in 2007 while seeing most of his other numbers increase to a .332 average, 48 doubles, 29 HR, and 125 runs. The following year he had a career-high 33 HR to go along with 35 SB and a league-leading 125 runs. Then in 2009 he hit 24 HR with 106 RBI and led the NL with a .342 average. A three-time All-Star, Ramírez saw his production drop in 2011, and after being forced to change positions to 3B when the Marlins acquired José Reyes, he was traded to the Dodgers in July of 2012.

Edgar Rentería (1996–98) was only 19 when he started his fine career with the Marlins. He played for Florida for only three seasons, but he stole 32 bases in 1997 and was an All-Star the following year, when he stole 41 bases.

Based mostly on longevity, you could make a case for Álex González (1998–2005) instead of Rentería, as he played for the Marlins for eight seasons and was the starting shortstop in six of them. He was an All-Star in his first full season in 1999, showing promise with a .277 average, 14 HR, and 81 runs. While he did hit 18 HR in 2003 and 23 in 2004, his average was only .245 overall and his OBP was an anemic .291.

Catcher

Name	YR	WAR	W3	W/G	AVG	HR	SB	OPS+
J.T. Realmuto	5	13.0	10.5	.0241	.279	59	31	111
Charles Johnson	7	11.7	9.9	.0199	.241	75	1	96

Charles Johnson (1994–98, 2001–02) had two stints with the Marlins and posted 10+ HR four times, with a high of 19 in their 1997 championship season. A two-time All-Star, Johnson was outstanding defensively, taking home three Gold Glove Awards while with Florida.

Current Marlins backstop **J.T. Realmuto** (2014–18) was the other obvious selection here. He is an above-average defender, has some pop with a high of 21 HR in 2018, and even has shown some speed with 8-12 SB in three seasons.

Hall of Famer Iván Rodríguez (2003) was a key part of the Marlins' championship season in 2003, as he hit .297 with 16 HR, 85 RBI, and 10 SB, while providing his typical outstanding defense. And he was MVP of the NLCS against the Cubs after going 9-for-28 with 2 doubles, 2 HR, and 10 RBI. But he was granted free agency after that one season in Florida and signed with the Tigers.

Left Field

Name	YR	WAR	W3	W/G	AVG	HR	SB	OPS+
Christian Yelich	5	18.6	13.3	.0289	.290	59	72	120
Cliff Floyd	6	16.9	12.4	.0265	.294	110	90	135
Jeff Conine	8	13.7	9.1	.0135	.290	120	15	114
Kevin Millar	5	7.7	7.1	.0154	.296	59	1	127
Josh Willingham	5	6.4	6.6	.0154	.266	63	13	117

Three LF were deserving of making this Marlins All-Time team, so the only decision was how to rank them. **Christian Yelich** (2013–17) provided the Marlins with a nice combination of power and speed, with a high of 21 HR in 2016 and 21 SB in 2014. And he was good defensively, winning a Gold Glove Award in 2014 and later shifting to CF for the 2017 season. But he was traded to the Brewers after that year, so it seems his time with the Marlins is now over.

Based on offensive counting stats, you could make a case for **Cliff Floyd** (1997–2002), as he hit 20+ HR three times for the Marlins with a high of 31 in 2001, and he also had 20+ SB twice with a high of 27 in 1998. But he wasn't nearly as good as Yelich defensively, so I gave him the backup spot.

Jeff Conine (1993–97, 2003–05) was a key player during the early years of the Marlins franchise and rejoined the team in his late 30s for parts of three more seasons. He played mostly in LF but also spent some time at 1B, where he was better defensively due in part to agility developed from being an outstanding racquetball player. A .290 hitter, he had some pop in his bat, hitting 25 HR with 105 RBI in 1995 and 26 HR with 95 RBI the next season. Conine's longevity with the team and his overall accomplishments were enough to earn him one of the two "extra spots" on this roster.

Two others deserve brief mention, starting with the versatile Kevin Millar (1998–2002), who played many games in LF, RF, and at 1B, plus a few at 3B too. A .296 hitter, he had a little power too, with a high for the Marlins of 20 HR and 85 RBI in 2001. And Josh Willingham (2004–08) started his career in Florida and hit 26 HR in 2006 and 21 HR the following season.

Center Field

Name	YR	WAR	W3	W/G	AVG	HR	SB	OPS+
Marcell Ozuna	5	14.1	12.8	.0216	.277	96	11	114
Cody Ross	5	9.4	8.6	.0164	.265	80	22	104
Juan Pierre	4	7.6	7.8	.0127	.295	7	190	91
Preston Wilson	5	6.2	6.2	.0105	.262	104	87	109

Marcell Ozuna (2013–17) showed a lot of promise, and after making the All-Star team in 2016 he really blossomed the following year, when he hit .312 with 37 HR and 124 RBI. He switched spots in the field with Yelich, played mostly LF in 2017, and did very well, taking home the Gold Glove Award. Unfortunately, while only beginning his prime years at age 27, Ozuna was traded to the Cardinals after the 2017 season as part of the Marlins' massive team restructuring.

There were three candidates for the backup CF spot on this roster, and after some consideration I went with **Juan Pierre** (2003–05, '13). For three consecutive seasons in Florida, he played every game—literally, 162 games each year. A .295 hitter for this franchise, his biggest asset was his speed, as he led the NL with 65 SB in 2003 and swiped 45 and 57 bags the next two seasons. He led the NL with 221 hits and 12 triples in 2004, though he also paced the NL in times caught stealing in all three of those seasons.

You could make a case for Preston Wilson (1998–2002) based on his combination of power and speed. He hit 20+ HR in all four of his full seasons for the Marlins and also had 20+ SB three times, including a high of 36 in 2000. But he also struck out a lot, including a league-leading 187 in 2000, and was only average defensively.

The other candidate here was Cody Ross (2006–10), who mostly played CF but also spent some time in RF for the Marlins. He hit 20+ HR twice but had little speed and provided only a .322 OBP.

Right Field

Name	YR	WAR	W3	W/G	AVG	HR	SB	OPS+
Giancarlo Stanton	8	35.2	19.5	.0357	.268	267	36	146
Gary Sheffield	6	13.2	10.7	.0237	.288	122	74	156

Giancarlo Stanton's (2010–17) power potential was clear from the beginning, as he hit 22 HR in 359 at-bats as a 20-year-old rookie in 2010. He hit between 24 and 37 HR each year from 2011 through 2016, even while injuries at times limited his availability on the field. A four-time All-Star, it all came together for him in 2017, when he led the league with 59 HR and 132 RBI, earning him the NL MVP Award. Sadly for Miami fans, Stanton's huge contract didn't suit the Marlins' desire to rebuild, so he was traded in the off-season to be part of a new Yankees Murderers' Row.

Gary Sheffield (1993–98) played for many teams during his 22-year career, and that included parts of six seasons with the Marlins. By far his best season in Florida came in 1996, when he batted .324, had 42 HR, 16 SB, 118 runs, and 120 RBI, and led the NL with an impressive .465 OBP.

Starting Pitching

Name	YR	WAR	W3	W-L	ERA	WHIP	ERA+
Josh Johnson	8	25.8	13.4	56-37	3.15	1.233	133
Dontrelle Willis	5	20.8	17.4	68-54	3.78	1.359	111
Kevin Brown	2	14.7	14.7	33 19	2.30	1.063	176
José Fernández	4	13.9	13.0	38-17	2.58	1.054	150
Aníbal Sánchez	7	13.1	10.0	44-45	3.75	1.352	111
A.J. Burnett	7	12.2	9.4	49-50	3.73	1.284	111
Ricky Nolasco	8	11.0	8.2	81-72	4.44	1.295	94
Josh Beckett	5	10.9	9.7	41-34	3.46	1.235	118
Alex Fernandez	3	8.2	8.2	28-24	3.59	1.239	117
Carl Pavano	3	8.1	8.1	33-23	3.64	1.245	114
Brad Penny	6	7.6	7.8	50-43	4.12	1.332	101

After dominating in the minors to the tune of a 27-5 record, **Dontrelle Willis** (2003–07) was called up early in the 2003 season and posted a 14-6 record and 3.30 ERA en route to winning the NL Rookie of the Year Award. He had a sophomore slump in 2004 but rebounded in 2005, using his high-leg-kick motion to come in second in the NL Cy Young Award vote after posting a 2.63 ERA and leading the NL in wins with a 22-10 record (the only 20-win season for this franchise so far). D-Train was a relatively capable hitter too, as he batted .234 with 8 HR in 351 at-bats during his time in Florida. After his strong 2005 season, his pitching numbers declined, and he was dealt along with Miguel Cabrera to the Tigers after the 2007 season.

In part due to injuries, **Josh Johnson** (2005–12) never quite lived up to the hype he had as a rookie. A two-time All-Star, he did lead the NL with a 2.30 ERA in 2010. But he never won more than 15 games in a season, and he was done in the majors before he turned 30.

Kevin Brown (1996–97) pitched for the Marlins for two years during the middle of his long career. An All-Star both seasons, he went 17-11 with a league-leading 1.89 ERA in 1996, and 16-8 with a 2.69 ERA and 205 strikeouts in 1997. One highlight that season was the no-hitter he threw on June 10th against the Giants at Candlestick Park.

Cuban-born **José Fernández** (2013–16) was an All-Star and Rookie of the Year in 2013, finishing with a 12-6 record, 2.19 ERA, and 187 strikeouts in 172.2 IP. He got off to a great start in 2014 before being shut down for Tommy John surgery. He came back strong at the end of 2015 with a 6-1 record and 2.92

ERA. He was then an All-Star in 2016 and was having a great year with a 16-8 record, 2.86 ERA, and 253 strikeouts in 182.1 IP, when he died in a boating accident off the coast of Miami Beach on September 25th. He was 24 years old.

Josh Beckett (2001–05) was an outstanding high school pitcher and was selected by the Marlins in the 1999 draft second overall (the Devil Rays chose Josh Hamilton with the first pick). He dominated A and AA baseball in 2001 and then had 24 strikeouts in 24 IP in four starts with the Marlins. He struggled a bit in his rookie season in 2002 but was a critical part of the Marlins' 2003 championship. Although injuries limited him to 23 starts during the regular season, he came through big in the postseason. After pitching generally well in three starts in the NLDS and NLCS, he was named World Series MVP after posting a 1.10 ERA in two starts. He went 15-8 in 2005, and after that season provided the Marlins with one additional value by being part of a package sent to the Red Sox for prospects that included Hanley Ramírez and Aníbal Sánchez.

Speaking of whom, **Aníbal Sánchez** (2006–12) was called up in June of 2006 and had an impressive rookie campaign, pitching a no-hitter against the Diamondbacks on September 6th and finishing the year with a 10-3 record and 2.83 ERA. After three injury-plagued seasons, Sánchez stabilized in the rotation and had a career-high 202 strikeouts in 2011.

A.J. Burnett (1999–2005) pitched parts of seven seasons for the Marlins, missing most of 2003 and part of 2004 due to Tommy John surgery. He never posted more than 12 wins in a season, but he did throw a no-hitter against the Padres on May 12th, 2001, and he had 203 strikeouts in 2002.

After looking over the relief pitching candidates, I decided to select only eight starting pitchers. **Ricky Nolasco** (2006–13) makes this All-Time team roster in part due to longevity with the club, as he is the franchise's all-time leader in wins (and losses). He won 10+ games in all six of his full seasons with the Marlins, with 2008 being his best season, as he posted a 15-8 record and 3.52 ERA.

There were a few others I considered, starting with Carl Pavano (2002–04), who joined the Marlins during the 2002 season in a trade that sent Cliff Floyd to the Expos. He was only 12-13 in 2003, but he pitched well as both a starter and reliever in the postseason, allowing only 3 earned runs in 19.1 IP. In 2004 he was an All-Star and ended the season with an 18-8 record and 3.00 ERA before leaving via free agency.

Brad Penny (2000–04, '14) started his career with the Marlins and had a high of 14 wins in 2003. After pitching poorly in the NLDS and NLCS, he won two games to help the Marlins win the 2003 World Series. He was traded to the

Dodgers just before the deadline in 2004, only to return to the Marlins briefly ten years later for his final major league games as part of a failed, multi-team attempt at a comeback from injuries.

And lastly, after many fine seasons with the White Sox, Alex Fernandez (1997, '99–2000) signed as a free agent with the Marlins. He went 17-12 with a 3.59 ERA in 1997 but missed the entire 1998 season due to injury. He came back and pitched in parts of 1999 and 2000, but he had to retire early at age 30 due to nagging shoulder woes.

Relief Pitching

Name	YR	WAR	W3	SV	W-L	ERA	WHIP	ERA+
AJ Ramos	6	6.5	5.2	99	15-16	2.78	1.228	140
Robb Nen	5	5.0	5.0	108	20-16	3.41	1.283	122
Steve Cishek	6	4.9	4.6	94	17-20	2.86	1.222	137
Antonio Alfonseca	6	2.5	2.9	102	19-25	3.86	1.483	109
Bryan Harvey	3	4.0	4.0	51	1-5	2.50	0.971	173
Todd Jones	1	2.9	2.9	40	1-5	2.10	1.027	191
Armando Benítez	2	2.5	2.5	47	4-7	2.72	1.062	155
Juan Carlos Oviedo	3	2.4	2.4	92	9-13	3.86	1.247	107

Robb Nen (1993–97) had three seasons of 20+ saves for the Marlins, including 35 in both 1996 and 1997. His ERA fluctuated from year to year, with his best coming in 1996, when he posted a 1.95 mark.

Recent Marlins reliever **AJ Ramos** (2012–17) is also deserving of a spot on this All-Time team. He was a quality setup man for two years, including a 7-0 record and 2.11 ERA in 2014. Then he took over the closer duties and saved 32 games with a 2.30 ERA in 2015, and was an All-Star in 2016, with 40 saves and a 2.81 ERA.

Steve Cishek (2010–15) also was a quality reliever for two years before taking over full time as the Marlins' closer. In 2013 he posted 34 saves with a 2.33 ERA and managed 39 saves the following year.

I decided to include **Antonio Alfonseca** (1997–2001, '05) as a fourth reliever on this All-Time team in part because he is second on their all-time saves list. He was the Marlins' closer from 1999 through 2001 and led the NL with 45 saves in 2000 even though he had a rather lofty 4.24 ERA.

I considered several other candidates, starting with Juan Carlos Oviedo (2009–11), who was the team's closer for three seasons and posted saves totals of 26, 30, and 36, though he carried a 3.86 ERA. Armando Benítez (2004, '07) signed as a free agent for the 2004 season and had an outstanding year, posting a 1.29 ERA and leading the NL with 47 saves (also the Marlins team record).

He left as a free agent after that year, only to return briefly in 2007 as part of his final full season. Todd Jones (2005) also pitched for Florida for only one great year, saving 40 games with a 2.10 ERA at age 37.

Lastly, after many fine seasons with the Angels, Bryan Harvey (1993–95) was selected by the Marlins as part of their expansion team draft. He had an outstanding 1993 All-Star campaign, with 45 saves and a 1.70 ERA. But the recurrence of an elbow injury early in 1994 was more than he could come back from, and he retired soon after.

Managers

Name	YR	From-To	W-L	PCT	PS	WS
Jack McKeon	4	2003–11	281-257	.522	1	1
Jim Leyland	2	1997–98	146-178	.451	1	1
Fredi González	4	2007–10	276-279	.497	0	0
Don Mattingly	3	2016–18	219-265	.452	0	0
John Boles	4	1996–2001	205-241	.460	0	0

Only two managers have led the Marlins to the postseason, and both took them all the way: **Jim Leyland** in 1997 and **Jack McKeon** in 2003. I rate McKeon higher in the above list since he led the team for a longer period and had a higher winning percentage, though Leyland can hardly be blamed for the team's pitiful 1998 campaign. To round out a top four, based on winning percentage I'd then rate **Fredi González** and **Don Mattingly** ahead of John Boles.

Starting Lineup

What would mythical starting lineups look like for this All-Time roster?

Against RHP:
Luis Castillo 2B (S)
Hanley Ramírez SS (R)
Miguel Cabrera 3B (R)
Giancarlo Stanton RF (R)
Cliff Floyd DH (L)
Christian Yelich LF (L)
Marcell Ozuna CF (R)
Justin Bour 1B (L)
Charles Johnson C (R)

Against LHP:
Luis Castillo 2B (S)
Hanley Ramírez SS (R)
Miguel Cabrera 3B (R)
Giancarlo Stanton RF (R)
Gary Sheffield DH (R)
Marcell Ozuna CF (R)
Derrek Lee 1B (R)
Jeff Conine LF (R)
Charles Johnson C (R)

Platoons made sense for 1B, LF, and DH. These lineups have some power in Uggla and Lowell, and speed in Pierre and Gordon, on the bench.

Depth Chart

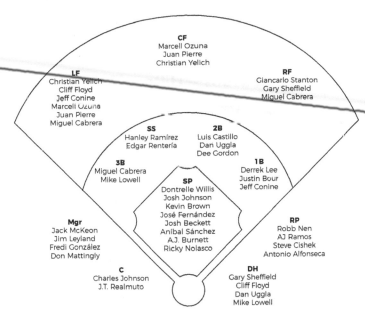

CF
Marcell Ozuna
Juan Pierre
Christian Yelich

LF
Christian Yelich
Cliff Floyd
Jeff Conine
Marcell Ozuna
Juan Pierre
Miguel Cabrera

RF
Giancarlo Stanton
Gary Sheffield
Miguel Cabrera

SS
Hanley Ramírez
Edgar Rentería

2B
Luis Castillo
Dan Uggla
Dee Gordon

3B
Miguel Cabrera
Mike Lowell

1B
Derrek Lee
Justin Bour
Jeff Conine

SP
Dontrelle Willis
Josh Johnson
Kevin Brown
José Fernández
Josh Beckett
Aníbal Sánchez
A.J. Burnett
Ricky Nolasco

Mgr
Jack McKeon
Jim Leyland
Fredi González
Don Mattingly

RP
Robb Nen
AJ Ramos
Steve Cishek
Antonio Alfonseca

C
Charles Johnson
J.T. Realmuto

DH
Gary Sheffield
Cliff Floyd
Dan Uggla
Mike Lowell

Prospects for Current Players

What are the prospects for current Marlins players making this All-Time team? Realmuto is already on this roster. Given the latest fire sale following the 2017 season, it will take a long time for any of the young players on the Marlins to build credentials worthy of consideration. We'll see...

Retired Player Numbers

None

Selections from Other Authors and Fan Surveys

2003: *Rob Neyer's Big Book of Baseball Lineups*, by Rob Neyer

With only ten years of history in the books in 2003, there wasn't much to evaluate in making selections for an all-time Marlins team. Interestingly, all of the position players Neyer chose remain on my roster, at least as backups: Lee, Castillo, Lowell, Rentería, Johnson, Conine, Wilson, and Sheffield. There was less depth at pitching, so Neyer's selections were Kevin Brown, Ryan Dempster, Pat Rapp, and Alex Fernandez, with Robb Nen as the obvious reliever. Dempster had been an All-Star for the Marlins once and at that time was their career leader in wins, while Rapp had a couple of good seasons in 1994 and '95.

Top WAR Single Seasons – Hitters (7+)

Name	Year	WAR	AVG	HR	R	RBI	SB	OPS+
Giancarlo Stanton	2017	7.6	.281	59	123	132	2	165
Hanley Ramírez	2009	7.3	.342	24	101	106	27	148

Only two seasons with a 7+ WAR so far, and I wasn't surprised to see either: Stanton's huge 2017 MVP season and Ramírez's 2009, when he won the NL batting title and was MVP runner-up.

Top WAR Single Seasons – Pitchers (7+)

Name	Year	WAR	W-L	ERA	IP	SO	ERA+
Dontrelle Willis	2005	8.4	22-10	2.63	236.1	170	152
Kevin Brown	1996	7.9	17-11	1.89	233.0	159	215
Josh Johnson	2009	7.4	15-5	3.23	209.0	191	133

Willis led the NL in wins in 2005 and came in second in the Cy Young Award voting, while also being a relatively capable .261 hitter. Similarly, a decade earlier Brown led the NL in ERA in 1996 and also came in second in the Cy Young vote.

Franchise Player

With apologies to Hanley Ramírez, I think this honor had to go to slugger Giancarlo Stanton. A four-time All-Star, his huge 2017 season, along with leading the league in HR and being MVP runner-up in 2014, made him the clear choice.

CHAPTER 29

The Rockies Franchise All-Time Dream Team

Like the Florida Marlins, the Colorado Rockies were one of two teams who joined the National League as expansion teams in 1993. Unlike the Marlins, the Rockies have never won a World Series (let alone two), though they did make it to the Fall Classic in 2007, losing in four games to the Boston Red Sox. They have made the postseason a total of four times in their relatively brief history, but they have had winning seasons in only 9 of their 25 years of existence.

Arguably the most well-known characteristic of the Rockies is derived from where they play, Coors Field in Denver, which due to the altitude of the location leads to lighter air and far more offense than any other stadium in the major leagues today. As a result, the hitting statistics of the players on this All-Time team are relatively strong, while the pitching statistics are almost laughable.

1st Base

Name	YR	WAR	W3	W/G	AVG	HR	SB	OPS+
Todd Helton	17	61.2	25.0	.0272	.316	369	37	133
Andrés Galarraga	5	14.5	11.5	.0214	.316	172	55	126

Todd Helton (1997–2013) played his entire career for the Rockies and is currently the franchise's all-time leader in games played, at-bats, hits, runs, singles, doubles, HR, RBI, walks, strikeouts, and countless less-well-known statistics. Admittedly, like most Rockies sluggers, his offensive numbers were aided by playing in Colorado: he was a .345/.441/.607 hitter at home and a .287/.386/.469 hitter on the road. But he was a five-time All-Star, scoring 100+ runs six times and posting 100+ RBI five times, including a league-leading high of 147 in 2000. The Toddfather belted 25+ HR in seven consecutive seasons, with a high of 49 in 2001. He was a career .316 hitter with a league-leading high of .372 in 2000, and he also provided a .414 OBP over his career. It wasn't all offense either, as he was outstanding defensively at 1B, taking home three Gold Glove Awards.

Before Helton, there was **Andrés "Big Cat" Galarraga** (1993–97), who had five very productive seasons in Colorado. He hit 20+ HR each year, including a league-leading 47 in 1996. He led the NL in RBI that year as well with 150, and again the following year with 140. Like Helton, Galarraga was a .316 hitter for the Rockies, and he also won an NL batting title when he hit .370 in 1993.

2nd Base

Name	YR	WAR	W3	W/G	AVG	HR	SB	OPS+
DJ LeMahieu	7	17.7	11.2	.0193	.299	49	75	93
Eric Young	5	9.5	7.2	.0155	.295	30	180	93

Current Rockies' second baseman **DJ LeMahieu** (2011–18) has by now earned this top spot. A two-time All-Star, LeMahieu has been a .299 hitter and was the NL batting average leader with a .348 mark in 2016. He doesn't provide much power and has only moderate speed, with a high of 23 SB in 2015. But he is outstanding defensively at 2B, so far taking home two Gold Glove Awards.

Eric Young (1993–97) was a speedster for the early Rockies, swiping 30+ bags four times, and leading the NL with 53 SB in 1996. He was an All-Star that year and ended the season with a career-high .324 average and 113 runs. Young played a bit of LF early in his career, as his defense at 2B improved over time. And he definitely benefitted from Coors Field, as he was a .352 hitter there over his entire career.

3rd Base

Name	YR	WAR	W3	W/G	AVG	HR	SB	OPS+
Nolan Arenado	6	33.1	19.6	.0378	.291	186	13	121
Vinny Castilla	9	17.5	11.9	.0159	.294	239	22	106
Jeff Cirillo	2	7.9	7.9	.0268	.320	28	15	99
Garrett Atkins	7	5.3	7.7	.0069	.289	98	8	102

Nolan Arenado (2013–18) has already earned five NL Gold Glove Awards for his outstanding defense at 3B. His power took a little while to develop, but in 2015 he led the league with 42 HR and 130 RBI, did the same in 2016 with 41 HR and 133 RBI, and took home a third NL HR crown with 38 in 2018. An All-Star from 2015-18, he has hit 35+ HR with 110+ RBI in each of those seasons.

Vinny Castilla (1993–99, 2004, '06) was the primary shortstop for the Rockies in their inaugural season, before switching to 3B for the rest of his career. He played good defense at the hot corner, but his main value came from his ability to hit long balls, as he slugged 30+ HR in five consecutive seasons. He posted 100+ RBI in four of those seasons, including a high of 144 in 1998. After playing for three other teams, he came back to Colorado as a 36-year-old and hit 35 HR with an NL league-leading 131 RBI. A two-time All-Star, he was a .294 hitter for the Rockies, though all of these numbers were aided by Coors Field, where he hit .333 with a .609 slugging percentage over his career.

Garrett Atkins (2003–09) had three seasons with 20+ HR, including 2006, when he hit .329 with 29 HR and 120 RBI, and 2007, when he hit .301 with 25 HR and 111 RBI. And lastly, Jeff Cirillo (2000–01) had two strong seasons as the Rockies' 3B, including 2000, when he batted .326 with 53 doubles, 111 runs, and 115 RBI even though he hit only 11 HR.

Shortstop

Name	YR	WAR	W3	W/G	AVG	HR	SB	OPS+
Troy Tulowitzki	10	39.4	20.0	.0376	.299	188	55	123
Trevor Story	3	11.4	11.4	.0286	.268	88	42	111
Clint Barmes	8	9.3	7.2	.0140	.254	61	39	75

Troy Tulowitzki (2006–15) was often injured but was a fan favorite in Colorado for a number of years, hitting 20+ HR six times and providing a .299 average. A five-time All-Star, Tulo also had great range at SS and took home Gold Glove Awards in 2010 and '11.

Trevor Story (2016–18) hit 27 HR in only 97 games during his rookie season and 24 HR the following year. But it was the addition of his 2018 All-Star season that earned him the backup spot on this roster, as he raised his production to a new level with a .291 average, 37 HR, 108 RBI, and even added 27 SB.

Until Story's 2018 season, the backup here would have been Clint Barmes (2003–10) who played parts of eight seasons with the Rockies, splitting his time between 2B and SS. Only a .254 hitter with a .300 OBP, he had some pop in his bat, with a high of 23 HR in 2009.

Catcher

Name	YR	WAR	W3	W/G	AVG	HR	SB	OPS+
Chris Iannetta	7	7.7	8.0	.0136	.233	74	7	97
Jeff Reed	4	4.2	4.6	.0115	.286	36	4	99
Wilin Rosario	5	1.8	3.5	.0040	.273	71	11	98

Chris Iannetta (2006–11, 18) essentially wins the top spot here by default, as catcher has never been a strong position for the Rockies. Iannetta played for the Rockies for several seasons, and then served for the Angels, Mariners, and Diamondbacks before returning to Colorado in 2018. Only a .233 hitter he did manage to hit 14 to 18 HR three times.

A backup catcher? Relatively slim pickings, so I went with the Coors-inflated offensive numbers of **Wilin Rosario** (2011–15), who batted .309 at home and .235 on the road. But he gets my vote because he hit 28 HR in 2012 and 21 HR the following year. Plus, you never know, he could come back to the majors some day: in 2016 he batted .321 with 33 HR and 120 RBI in 127 games in the Korean League, and he did even better in 2017, when he hit .339 with 37 HR and 111 RBI in 119 games.

You could make a case for journeyman catcher Jeff Reed (1996–99), who played parts of four seasons for the Rockies late in his career and batted .297 with 17 HR in only 256 AB in 1997.

Left Field

Name	YR	WAR	W3	W/G	AVG	HR	SB	OPS+
Matt Holliday	6	18.6	15.3	.0257	.319	130	66	131
Dante Bichette	7	4.8	5.2	.0047	.316	201	105	112
Jay Payton	3	4.7	4.7	.0210	.311	36	10	117
Corey Dickerson	3	4.6	4.6	.0174	.299	39	10	125

Matt Holliday (2004–08, 18) started his career for the Rockies and was an All-Star three times. In 2006 he batted .326 with 119 runs, 34 HR, and 114 RBI, and he was the NL MVP runner-up in 2007 after hitting 36 HR with 120 runs and leading the league with a .340 average, 216 hits, 50 doubles, and 137 RBI. Holliday definitely liked hitting in the Denver light air, batting .361 with a .656 slugging percentage.

Dante Bichette (1993–99) was one of the original Rockies, starting out primarily as a RF before later switching to mostly LF. A four-time All-Star, in strike-shortened 1995 he batted .340 and paced the NL with 40 HR, 128 RBI, and 197 hits. The following year he posted career highs with 141 RBI and 31

SB. His WAR numbers shown above seem bizarrely low to me. I don't understand it fully, though surely two factors that counted against him were the ballpark factor—he batted .358 with a .641 slugging percentage in Colorado over his career—and also his generally below-average defense (e.g., he led the NL in errors for his specific outfield position three times).

Two others deserve brief mention, starting with Jay Payton (2002–03, '10), who played parts of three seasons for the Rockies, and in his one full season in 2003 hit .302 with 28 HR and 89 RBI. And Corey Dickerson (2013–15) also played parts of three seasons for the Rockies, with 2014 being his best, when he hit .312 with 24 HR and 76 RBI in 436 at-bats.

Center Field

Name	YR	WAR	W3	W/G	AVG	HR	SB	OPS+
Charlie Blackmon	8	16.1	13.0	.0175	.302	140	127	115
Ellis Burks	5	12.0	11.3	.0231	.306	115	52	128
Dexter Fowler	6	9.4	6.8	.0141	.270	40	83	101
Juan Pierre	3	4.1	4.1	.0114	.308	3	100	76

Charlie Blackmon (2011–18) has by now earned the top CF spot on this All-Time team roster. A three-time All-Star so far, Blackmon stole 28 bases in 2014 and 43 in 2015. He stole fewer bases the next two years, but his power surged to 29 HR in 2016 and then 37 HR in 2017. That year he also led the NL with a .331 average, 14 triples, 137 runs, and 213 hits.

Ellis Burks (1994–98) essentially played the middle part of his career in Colorado. This period, not surprisingly, provided his best statistical season, as in 1996 he came in third in the MVP voting after batting .344 with 40 HR, 128 RBI, 32 SB, and a league-leading 142 runs. While he was solid on the road that year (.291/.367/.535) his slash line at Coors was off the charts (.390/.443/.728).

Dexter Fowler (2008–13) started his career for the Rockies and was a capable hitter with speed for five full seasons. His high in SB was 27 in 2009, and he hit 14 triples in 2010 and 15 the following year. For now, that is good enough to earn Fowler one of the two "extra spots" on this roster.

Lastly, Juan Pierre (2000–02) also started his career for the Rockies, playing a partial rookie season and then two full seasons. He batted .327 and led the NL with 46 SB in 2001, and swiped another 47 bases the following year.

Right Field

Name	YR	WAR	W3	W/G	AVG	HR	SB	OPS+
Larry Walker	10	48.3	23.7	.0413	.334	258	126	147
Carlos González	10	23.6	15.3	.0189	.290	227	118	116
Brad Hawpe	7	5.1	5.8	.0063	.280	118	13	116

After having some success with the Expos, **Larry Walker** (1995–2004) signed with the Rockies as a free agent after the 1994 season. In Colorado, his numbers exploded, as he hit 20+ HR six times, had 100+ RBI five times, and scored 100+ runs four times. His best season came in 1997, when he was named NL MVP after batting .366 with 143 runs, 130 RBI, 33 SB, and leading the league with 49 HR, a .452 OBP, and a .720 slugging percentage. He went on to win three NL batting titles with averages of .363 in 1998, .379 in 1999, and .350 in 2001. A four-time All-Star for the Rockies, he was also an outstanding defender, taking home five of his seven Gold Glove Awards while in Colorado. As I've noted for a few others, Walker's traditional statistics did benefit greatly from playing his home games in Colorado, where he had an unearthly slash line of .381/.462/.710, and in 1999 he hit 26 HR in 232 at-bats with an insane slash line of .461/.531/.879.

Carlos González (2009–18) was born in Venezuela and by age 17 was playing professional baseball in the United States. After working his way up through the minors in the Diamondbacks and Athletics organizations, he was traded along with two others in the deal that sent Matt Holliday to Oakland. Since then Cargo has been a consistent power threat, providing 20+ HR six times, including a high of 40 in 2015. A three-time All-Star, he led the NL in batting average with a .336 mark in 2010 and had 20+ SB in four consecutive seasons. González has also earned three Gold Glove Awards while playing a mix of RF and LF.

Brad Hawpe (2004–10) hit 20+ HR in four consecutive seasons, with his most impressive numbers coming in 2007, when he hit .291 with 29 HR and 116 RBI. His below-average defense reduced his WAR totals, but Hawpe's offensive numbers (which were not boosted by Coors Field nearly as much as some others) were enough for me to give him the second "extra spot" on the Rockies All-Time team.

Starting Pitching

Name	YR	WAR	W3	W-L	ERA	WHIP	ERA+
Ubaldo Jiménez	6	18.1	16.4	56-45	3.66	1.284	128
Aaron Cook	10	17.1	11.1	72-68	4.53	1.468	106
Jhoulys Chacín	6	14.5	12.7	38-48	3.78	1.338	120
Jorge De La Rosa	9	13.8	8.4	86-61	4.35	1.381	105
Jason Jennings	6	12.2	10.2	58-56	4.74	1.548	103
Tyler Chatwood	5	10.4	9.3	34-35	4.18	1.434	113
Pedro Astacio	5	9.8	10.4	53-48	5.43	1.463	102
Jeff Francis	8	9.8	8.7	64-62	4.96	1.446	96
Armando Reynoso	4	8.2	7.5	30-31	4.65	1.473	109
John Thomson	5	7.9	7.7	27-43	5.01	1.408	104
Kevin Ritz	5	7.4	7.7	39-38	5.20	1.574	100

As any knowledgeable baseball fan would expect, the pitching staff for this All-Time team is the weakest of all 30 franchises. The top spot goes to **Ubaldo Jiménez** (2006–11), who started his career for the Rockies and was an All-Star in 2010, ending that year with a 2.88 ERA, 214 strikeouts, and a 19-8 record (the closest anyone on this franchise has gotten to 20 wins in a season).

While I went with Jiménez for the top spot, you could make a case for **Jorge De La Rosa** (2008–16), the all-time leader in wins for the Rockies franchise. He won 10+ games four times, including a 16-9 record in 2009 and 16-6 in 2013, and he ended with a .585 winning percentage for Colorado.

Aaron Cook (2002–11) pitched all but his final season for the Rockies—which was certainly a difficult task—but his ERA was only slightly higher pitching at Coors Field (4.65) than on the road. This was due in part to Cook being a sinkerball pitcher who induced a lot of ground balls as opposed to going for a lot of strikeouts (in fact, he never had more than 100 strikeouts in a season). His best year was his one All-Star season in 2008, when he posted a 16-9 record.

Jeff Francis (2004–08, '10, '12–13) won 10+ games for the Rockies three times, including in 2007, when he was the ace of the staff and posted a 17-9 record to lead the team to the postseason. **Pedro Astacio** (1997–2001) pitched for Colorado for parts of five seasons, also winning 10+ games three times. His best season came in 1999, when despite a 5.04 ERA he posted a 17-11 record with 210 strikeouts.

Jason Jennings (2001–06) started his career with the Rockies and won 10+ games three times, including a 16-8 record in 2002, which was good enough to earn him NL Rookie of the Year honors. **Jhoulys Chacín** (2009–14) also started his career for the Rockies and had his best season in 2013, when he had a 14-10 record and 3.47 ERA. Though he ended up with a losing record overall for Colorado, his relatively low ERA and long tenure with the club were enough to earn him a spot here.

After considering the relief pitching candidates, I decided to select one more starting pitcher, and that ended up being **Tyler Chatwood** (2012–14, '16–17). He seemed well on his way to being a solid starter for the Rockies after the 2013 season, when he posted an 8-5 record and relatively good 3.15 ERA over 20 starts. But he needed Tommy John surgery and so missed most of 2014 and all of 2015. He came back solid in 2016 with a 12-9 record and 3.87 ERA, but then he led the NL in losses with an 8-15 record in 2017 and was granted free agency.

I did consider a few others, starting with Kevin Ritz (1994–98), who pitched parts of five seasons for Colorado and had his best season in 1996, when he posted a 17-11 record despite a 5.28 ERA. Armando Reynoso (1993–96) pitched parts of four seasons for the early Rockies, with their inaugural season being his best, when he went 12-11 with a 4.00 ERA. And lastly, John Thomson (1997–99, 2001–02) started his career for Colorado but never had a winning season there.

Relief Pitching

Name	YR	WAR	W3	SV	W-L	ERA	WHIP	ERA+
Steve Reed	7	11.8	7.1	15	33-29	3.63	1.267	140
Brian Fuentes	7	9.9	6.9	115	16-26	3.38	1.238	144
Curt Leskanic	7	7.2	6.9	20	31-20	4.92	1.474	108
José Jiménez	4	4.9	4.8	102	15-23	4.13	1.414	126
Huston Street	3	3.1	3.1	84	9-9	3.50	1.058	133

Brian Fuentes (2002–08) had mixed results as a reliever for three seasons before taking over as the Rockies' closer in 2005. That would be his first of three consecutive All-Star seasons, and the first of four with 20+ saves. A left-handed sidearmer, he was particularly hard on left-handed batters and ended his career with the Rockies as their all-time saves leader.

Next on that list is **José Jiménez** (2000–03), who was the Rockies' closer for four seasons, posting 20+ saves three times, with a high of 41 in 2002. **Huston Street** (2009–11) was the Rockies' closer for three years and had a high of 35 saves in 2009.

I decided to include a fourth reliever, **Steve Reed** (1993–97, 2003–04), who was one of the original Rockies and returned for two more years near the end of his career. A sidearm specialist, Reed provided a relatively good 3.63 ERA over 461 games. I also considered Curt Leskanic (1993–99), who like Reed pitched for the Rockies for seven seasons but was never their closer. Unlike Reed, however, his ERA was a lofty 4.92 and his WHIP was 1.474.

Lastly, after several outstanding seasons for the Royals, Greg Holland (2017) had Tommy John surgery in 2016 and then signed as a free agent with the Rockies. He had a great comeback season in 2017, posting a relatively good 3.61 ERA and leading the NL with 41 saves (which tied Jiménez's 41 in 2002 for the club record). He left as a free agent, and Wade Davis (2018) was brought in as the new closer. His ERA was 4.13, but he did set a new franchise record with a league-leading 43 saves.

Managers

Name	YR	From-To	W-L	PCT	PS	WS
Clint Hurdle	8	2002–09	534-625	.461	2	0
Don Baylor	6	1993–98	440-469	.484	1	0
Jim Tracy	4	2009–12	294-308	.488	1	0
Bud Black	2	2017–18	178-147	.548	2	0
Buddy Bell	3	2000–02	161-185	.465	0	0
Walt Weiss	4	2013–16	283-365	.437	0	0

I didn't see a clear-cut top choice here, so I went with **Clint Hurdle**, the manager with the longest tenure and the only one to lead the Rockies to an NL pennant. For the next three on this list, I went with the other three managers who have at least led the Rockies to the postseason: **Don Baylor, Jim Tracy,** and **Bud Black**.

Starting Lineup

What would mythical starting lineups look like for this All-Time roster?

Against RHP:
Charlie Blackmon CF (L)
Larry Walker RF (L)
Todd Helton 1B (L)
Nolan Arenado 3B (R)
Carlos González DH (L)
Matt Holliday LF (R)
Troy Tulowitzki SS (R)
DJ LeMahieu 2B (R)
Chris Iannetta C (R)

Against LHP:
Charlie Blackmon CF (L)
Troy Tulowitzki SS (R)
Nolan Arenado 3B (R)
Matt Holliday LF (R)
Vinny Castilla DH (R)
Todd Helton 1B (L)
Larry Walker RF (L)
DJ LeMahieu 2B (R)
Chris Iannetta C (R)

I listed Castilla as the platoon DH with González, with the thinking that Galarraga could spell Helton, Bichette could spell Walker, and Burks could spell Blackmon against the toughest lefty hurlers.

Depth Chart

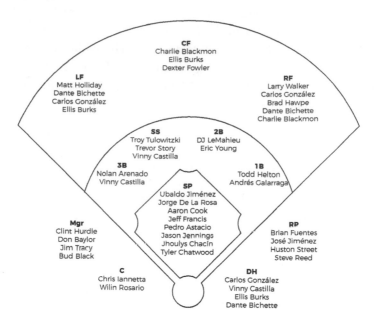

CF
Charlie Blackmon
Ellis Burks
Dexter Fowler

LF
Matt Holliday
Dante Bichette
Carlos González
Ellis Burks

RF
Larry Walker
Carlos González
Brad Hawpe
Dante Bichette
Charlie Blackmon

SS
Troy Tulowitzki
Trevor Story
Vinny Castilla

2B
DJ LeMahieu
Eric Young

3B
Nolan Arenado
Vinny Castilla

1B
Todd Helton
Andrés Galarraga

SP
Ubaldo Jiménez
Jorge De La Rosa
Aaron Cook
Jeff Francis
Pedro Astacio
Jason Jennings
Jhoulys Chacín
Tyler Chatwood

Mgr
Clint Hurdle
Don Baylor
Jim Tracy
Bud Black

RP
Brian Fuentes
José Jiménez
Huston Street
Steve Reed

C
Chris Iannetta
Wilin Rosario

DH
Carlos González
Vinny Castilla
Ellis Burks
Dante Bichette

Prospects for Current Players

What are the prospects for current Rockies players making this All-Time team? LeMahieu, Arenado, Story, Iannetta, Holliday, Blackmon, and González are on the roster already. For this franchise, it wouldn't take much for some pitchers to grab spots too. We'll see...

Retired Player Numbers

Todd Helton (17)

Selections from Other Authors and Fan Surveys

2003: *Rob Neyer's Big Book of Baseball Lineups*, by Rob Neyer

Back in 2003 Neyer's lineup made sense I think: Todd Helton, Eric Young, Neifi Pérez, Vinny Castilla, Jeff Reed, Dante Bichette, Ellis Burks, and Larry Walker, with Pérez being chosen at SS due to his good defense. And ditto for the pitchers, where he was forced to go with Pedro Astacio, Armando Reynoso, Kevin Ritz, John Thomson, and Steve Reed as the reliever.

Top WAR Single Seasons – Hitters (7+)

Name	Year	WAR	AVG	HR	R	RBI	SB	OPS+
Larry Walker	1997	9.8	.366	49	143	130	33	178
Todd Helton	2000	8.8	.372	42	138	147	5	163
Todd Helton	2004	8.3	347	32	115	96	3	165
Ellis Burks	1996	7.9	.344	40	142	128	32	149
Larry Walker	2001	7.8	.350	38	107	123	14	160
Todd Helton	2001	7.8	.336	49	132	146	7	160
Nolan Arenado	2017	7.2	.309	37	100	130	3	132

No real surprises here. Coors Field has helped produce some big numbers, though only three seasons rated above an 8 WAR score.

Top WAR Single Seasons – Pitchers (7+)

Name	Year	WAR	W-L	ERA	IP	SO	ERA+
Kyle Freeland	2018	8.2	17-7	2.85	202.1	173	164
Ubaldo Jiménez	2010	7.4	19-8	2.88	221.2	214	161

Given Colorado's home field, it was not at all surprising that only two seasons have produced a WAR score of 7 or higher.

Franchise Player

With honorable mention going to Larry Walker and Troy Tulowitzki, and Nolan Arenado coming on strong, this honor had to go Todd Helton. Few players dominate their franchise's all-time record books the way Helton does, at least for now.

CHAPTER 30

The Rays Franchise All-Time Dream Team

In the 21 years of their existence so far, the Rays have had a winning record only seven times, with most of those coming consecutively from 2008 through 2013. During that six-year period they reached the postseason four times, going all the way to the World Series in 2008 but losing in five games to the Phillies.

Due to both their short history and relative lack of success thus far, the Rays' All-Time team definitely has some weak spots. But like each franchise, there are some legit stars dotting the roster too, with hopefully more to join them in the years to come.

1st Base

Name	YR	WAR	W3	W/G	AVG	HR	SB	OPS+
Carlos Peña	5	18.1	15.4	.0249	.230	163	12	126
Fred McGriff	5	9.0	9.4	.0156	.291	99	11	122
Travis Lee	3	4.5	4.5	.0116	.261	42	18	101
Logan Morrison	2	4.1	4.1	.0160	.243	52	6	121
James Loney	3	3.6	3.6	.0086	.291	26	9	107

Carlos Peña (2007–10, '12) was a key slugger in some of Tampa Bay's most successful seasons. He signed as a free agent before the 2007 season and immediately paid dividends to the club by hitting .282 with 46 HR and 121 RBI. Although he wouldn't match those numbers for the Rays again, he did hit 30+ HR with 100+ RBI two more times, leading the AL with 39 HR in 2009. He was also an asset defensively at 1B, winning a Gold Glove Award in 2008.

Another slugger, **Fred McGriff** (1998–2001, '04), played for the Devil Rays twice during his long career. After many fine seasons with the Blue Jays, Padres, and Braves, McGriff signed as a 34-year-old free agent for the Devil Rays' inaugural season. A .291 hitter for Tampa Bay, in 1999 and 2000 he provided 25+ HR and 100+ RBI.

A few others deserve brief mention, starting with Travis Lee (2003, '05–06), who had two short stints with Tampa Bay late in his career. His best numbers came in 2003, when he batted .275 with 37 doubles and 19 HR. James Loney (2013–15) played 1B for the Rays for three seasons and was a .291 hitter but didn't provide much power. And most recently, Logan Morrison (2016–17) provided some power for the Rays, including 38 HR in 2017.

2nd Base

Name	YR	WAR	W3	W/G	AVG	HR	SB	OPS+
Ben Zobrist	9	36.0	22.0	.0338	.264	114	102	117
Logan Forsythe	3	9.4	9.4	.0241	.262	43	17	110
Sean Rodríguez	5	7.7	7.1	.0139	.228	40	32	90
Akinori Iwamura	3	6.6	6.6	.0192	.281	14	29	98

Ben Zobrist (2006–14) played the first nine years of his career for Tampa Bay, starting out as a shortstop but earning fame in part through his versatility, playing 547 games at 2B, 331 at RF, 229 at SS, 66 at LF, 34 at CF, 20 at DH, 17 at 1B, and 4 at 3B. A two-time All-Star, he provided a good combination of power and speed, hit 20+ HR three times, and had 15+ SB three times. His best season came in 2009, when he hit .297 with a .405 OBP, 27 HR, 91 RBI, and 17 SB.

There wasn't a clear choice for backup 2B, but I went with **Logan Forsythe** (2014–16), who at least hit 15+ HR twice for the Rays. He mostly played at 2B, but he also got in some games at 3B and 1B. Sean Rodríguez (2010–14) played for the team longer and was versatile defensively, playing 2B, 3B, SS, 1B, and LF, but he was a .228 hitter with minimal power or speed. And lastly, Akinori Iwamura (2007–09) joined the Rays in 2007 after many years as a slugger in Japan. His big power numbers didn't translate, as he never hit more than 7 HR in a major league season.

3rd Base

Name	YR	WAR	W3	W/G	AVG	HR	SB	OPS+
Evan Longoria	10	50.0	22.4	.0348	.270	261	51	125
Aubrey Huff	7	11.8	10.9	.0148	.287	128	20	116

Like Zobrist, **Evan Longoria** (2008–17) has played most of his career for the Rays, only leaving via a trade to the Giants after the 2017 season. Unlike Zobrist, Longoria played just one position for the Rays and for good reason, as his outstanding defense at the hot corner earned him three Gold Glove Awards. An All-Star in his first three seasons, Longo took home the AL Rookie of the Year Award in 2008 after hitting 27 HR with 85 RBI. He hit 20+ HR in all nine of his seasons in which he played 100 or more games, with a high of 36 HR in 2016.

Before Longoria, **Aubrey Huff** (2000–06) provided the Rays with some solid power, connecting for 20+ HR four times, with his best numbers coming in 2003, when he hit .311 with 47 doubles, 34 HR, and 107 RBI. He got into the lineup via three positions, playing 282 games at 3B, 200 at RF, and 149 at 1B.

Shortstop

Name	YR	WAR	W3	W/G	AVG	HR	SB	OPS+
Julio Lugo	4	13.5	11.5	.0267	.287	40	88	105
Jason Bartlett	3	10.4	10.4	.0260	.288	19	61	102

Not a position of strength for Tampa Bay so far, there were really only two candidates here. **Julio Lugo** (2003–06) was a .287 hitter with some speed, including 21 SB in 2004 and 39 in 2005. **Jason Bartlett** (2008–10) followed Lugo a couple of years later and was an All-Star in 2009, hitting .320 with 90 runs, 14 HR, and 30 SB.

Catcher

Name	YR	WAR	W3	W/G	AVG	HR	SB	OPS+
Toby Hall	7	5.7	5.4	.0097	.262	44	2	81
Dioner Navarro	5	1.9	2.2	.0041	.243	29	9	73
John Flaherty	5	0.3	1.9	.0001	.252	35	3	69

Like shortstop, catcher has not been a position of strength for the Rays thus far. There were three candidates with similar résumés, so I wouldn't argue if you preferred any two of them. **Toby Hall** (2000–06) played in 100+ games for the Rays in three of his seven seasons. He was only a .262 hitter with a low .298 OBP, but he was a good defender and had a little power, with a high of 12 HR in 2003. **Dioner Navarro** (2006–10) came after Hall and also played in 100+ games three times for the Rays. His best season came in 2008, when he was chosen as an All-Star and ended the season with a .295 average. The third candidate was the franchise's first regular catcher, John Flaherty (1998–2002). He played for Tampa Bay for five seasons but played in 100+ games just twice. Only a .252 hitter with a very low .289 OBP, he had a little pop in his bat, as he hit 10+ HR twice.

Left Field

Name	YR	WAR	W3	W/G	AVG	HR	SB	OPS+
Carl Crawford	9	35.6	16.9	.0288	.296	104	409	107
Greg Vaughn	3	5.3	5.3	.0160	.226	60	22	101
Corey Dickerson	2	4.2	4.2	.0141	.265	51	4	113

Carl Crawford (2002–10) was a star for Tampa Bay for many years, leading the NL in SB and triples four times each. He had 40+ SB seven times, with a high of 60 in 2009, and 10+ triples five times, with a high of 19 in 2004. A four-time All-Star, Crawford hit .296 and was a good fielder as well, taking home a Gold Glove Award in his final season with the Rays.

Two others deserve brief mention, starting with Greg Vaughn (2000–02), who played a mix of LF and DH for Tampa Bay late in his career, hit 28 HR in 2000, and was an All-Star in 2001, ending the season with 24 HR though only a .233 average. More recently, Corey Dickerson (2016–17) hit 24 HR in 2016 and 27 in 2017, when he represented Tampa Bay as an All-Star.

Center Field

Name	YR	WAR	W3	W/G	AVG	HR	SB	OPS+
Kevin Kiermaier	6	24.0	18.1	.0436	.254	54	70	102
Melvin Upton	8	15.6	10.9	.0161	.255	118	232	105
Desmond Jennings	7	13.4	9.6	.0236	.245	55	95	101
Rocco Baldelli	6	9.6	9.1	.0210	.280	53	59	102
Randy Winn	5	7.4	6.7	.0143	.279	24	80	95

There were far more candidates to consider in CF than LF, and in the end, I decided to give them all spots on this All-Time team roster. Current defensive standout **Kevin Kiermaier** (2013–18) has thus far played in over 110 games for the Rays only once. Providing moderate power and speed, he is outstanding in

CF, taking home Gold Glove Awards in both 2015 and 2016.

Melvin Upton (2004, '06–12) was known as B.J. Upton throughout his years playing for the Rays. He provided a good combination of power and speed, hitting 20+ HR three times and posting 30+ SB five times. **Desmond Jennings** (2010–16) provided a bit less power, but he was also fast on the bases, posting 20+ SB three times, with his best season being 2012, when he had 31 SB while getting caught only twice.

Rocco Baldelli (2003–04, '06–08, '10) was a promising youngster when he batted .289 with 27 SB in his rookie season, and he followed that up with a .280 average, 16 HR, and 17 SB. Sadly, in 2005 Baldelli's career began to suffer from a rare disorder that caused frequent soft tissue injuries, fatigue, and other physical ailments. He missed the entire 2005 season, and although he managed to hit .302 with 16 HR in 92 games in 2006, difficulties in treating his condition would limit his playing time after that.

Lastly, **Randy Winn** (1998–2002) was a rookie for the inaugural Devil Rays team, stealing 26 bases in only 109 games. He had his best season in 2002, his last with Tampa Bay, when he was an All-Star and ended with a .298 average, 39 doubles, 14 HR, and 27 SB.

Right Field

Name	YR	WAR	W3	W/G	AVG	HR	SB	OPS+
Matthew Joyce	6	9.8	7.4	.0155	.250	76	29	118
Steven Souza	3	6.3	6.3	.0167	.238	63	35	107
Ben Grieve	3	3.2	3.2	.0093	.254	34	15	106
Delmon Young	3	2.1	2.1	.0977	.291	19	12	96

Matthew Joyce (2009–14) played significant time in both RF and LF for the Rays and provided a little power, hitting 15+ HR three times. His best season came in 2011, when he represented Tampa Bay at the All-Star Game and hit .277 with 19 HR and 13 SB.

Though you could make a case for a few others, I decided to give the final roster spot to **Steven Souza** (2015–17), as he hit 15+ HR for the Rays three times, with his best season coming in 2017, when he hit 30 HR with 16 SB.

After several fine seasons with Oakland, Ben Grieve (2001–03) was traded to Tampa Bay, where he played two full seasons and one partial season, with a high of 19 HR in 2002. And lastly, Delmon Young (2006–07, '13) was runner-up for the AL Rookie of the Year Award in 2007, when he batted .288 with 38 doubles, 13 HR, 93 RBI, and 10 SB. But he was traded to Minnesota after that season, in a deal that brought Jason Bartlett to Tampa.

Starting Pitching

Name	YR	WAR	W3	W-L	ERA	WHIP	ERA+
David Price	7	21.1	14.6	82-47	3.18	1.142	122
James Shields	7	20.0	15.4	87-73	3.89	1.223	107
Scott Kazmir	6	16.5	14.0	55-44	3.92	1.390	114
Chris Archer	7	12.2	8.4	54-68	3.69	1.230	107
Alex Cobb	6	10.7	10.2	48-35	3.50	1.217	111
Matt Garza	3	8.4	8.4	34-31	3.86	1.251	109
Jake Odorizzi	5	8.0	7.8	40-37	3.82	1.215	103
Jeremy Hellickson	5	7.1	8.0	40-36	3.78	1.261	101
Matt Moore	6	5.4	5.1	39-28	3.88	1.339	100

David Price (2008–14) was a star pitcher for three years at Vanderbilt University before signing his first professional contract in August 2007. He pitched at various levels of the minors in 2008, tallying a 12-1 record and 2.30 ERA before being called up in September. He started one game for Tampa Bay and pitched four in relief, and then he played an important role as a reliever in the postseason, recording the last four outs and getting a save in Game Seven of the ALCS. After struggling a bit in 2009, he broke through in 2010 with a 19-6 record and 2.72 ERA, coming in second in the AL Cy Young Award voting. In 2012 he took home that award after leading the league in ERA at 2.56 and wins with a 20-5 record (the only 20-win season for this franchise so far).

James Shields (2006–12) was a teammate of Price for several seasons and posted 10+ wins six times. He was a workhorse who started 31 to 33 games and pitched 200+ innings in all six of his full seasons in Tampa. Shields was an All-Star in 2011 and ended that season with a 16-12 record, 2.82 ERA, 225 strikeouts, and a league-leading 11 complete games.

After blowing through the minors as an 18- and 19-year-old, **Scott Kazmir** (2004–09) found himself pitching for the Devil Rays as a 20-year-old in 2004. Beginning the following year, he had four seasons with 10+ wins each, was an All-Star twice, and had his best year in 2007, when he went 13-9 and led the league with 239 strikeouts in only 206.2 IP.

Recent Rays hurler **Chris Archer** (2012–18) pitched 32 to 34 games in his four full seasons for the Rays, with high strikeout totals in 2015–2017 of 252, 233, and 249. An All-Star in 2015 and 2017, he had bad luck in 2016, when a mediocre 4.02 ERA and 1.242 WHIP went along with an ugly 9-19 record.

Two teammates of Archer also did enough to earn spots on this roster, starting with **Alex Cobb** (2011–14, '16–17), even though he never pitched more than 180 innings in a season. He won 10 to 12 games in each of his four full seasons, interrupted by the need for Tommy John surgery in 2015. He signed with the Orioles as a free agent after the 2017 season, so it seems his time with the Rays is over.

Similarly, **Jake Odorizzi** (2013–17) had four full seasons as a starter for the Rays, posting 9 to 11 wins each year, but he never pitched more than 190 innings in a season. Like Cobb, it seems 2017 was Odorizzi's last year in Tampa Bay, as he was traded after the season to the Twins.

Jeremy Hellickson (2010–14) pitched three full seasons as a starter for Tampa Bay. He was Rookie of the Year in 2011 after going 13-10 with a 2.95 ERA, and the following season took home the Gold Glove Award for his solid defense on the mound.

After reviewing the relief pitching candidates, I decided to go with nine starting pitchers for this All-Time team. **Matt Garza** (2008–10) pitched three full seasons for the Rays early in his career and had a high of 15 wins in 2010. He had mixed results across five postseason starts in 2008 and 2010, with a highlight being named the ALCS MVP in 2008 after winning two games with a 1.38 ERA and 14 strikeouts in 13 IP.

And lastly, **Matt Moore** (2011–16) dominated several levels of the minors, consistently striking out batters at a high rate, including in 2011, when he posted a 12-3 record and 1.92 ERA with 210 strikeouts in 155 IP before being called up and striking out 15 batters in 9.1 IP, and then posting a 0.90 ERA in 10 IP in the 2011 ALDS against the Rangers. His first full season was mediocre with an 11-11 record and 3.81 ERA, but then he was an All-Star in 2013 and ended the year with a 17-4 record and 3.29 ERA. Unfortunately, an injury early in 2014 led to Tommy John surgery, so he missed the rest of that year and the first half of 2015. Not as effective as he had been previously, the Rays traded him to the Giants in early August 2016.

Relief Pitching

Name	YR	WAR	W3	SV	W-L	ERA	WHIP	ERA+
Roberto Hernández	3	4.9	4.9	101	8-16	3.43	1.358	143
Alex Colomé	6	4.3	3.9	95	17-18	3.21	1.240	125
Fernando Rodney	2	4.3	4.3	85	7-6	1.91	1.040	202
Danys Báez	2	2.9	2.9	71	9-8	3.21	1.318	139
Brad Boxberger	4	2.3	2.4	43	17-19	3.33	1.191	118

Roberto Hernández (1998–2000) had a very long career, including three seasons as the Devil Rays' first closer. He recorded 26, 43, and 32 saves in those seasons and was an All-Star in 1999.

Fernando Rodney (2012–13) was another relief pitcher who has had a long career that included a brief stint as the closer for Tampa Bay. In 2012 he was an All-Star and had a phenomenal season, posting 48 saves (a franchise record) with a 0.777 WHIP and a microscopic 0.60 ERA. While his ERA rose to 3.38 the following season, he still managed a solid 37 saves.

Recent Rays closer **Alex Colomé** (2013-18) also did enough to earn a spot on this All-Time team. After pursuing the possibility of Colomé being a starter, in 2016 he was an All-Star reliever, posting 37 saves and a 1.91 ERA. His ERA rose to 3.24 in 2017, but he led the AL with 47 saves.

Danys Báez (2004–05) comes close to earning a spot on this pitching staff, as he posted 30 saves in 2004 and was an All-Star in 2005, ending the year with 41 saves. You could also make a case for recent Rays reliever Brad Boxberger (2014–17), who was a very effective setup man in 2014, when he posted a 2.37 ERA and struck out 104 batters in only 64.2 IP. He was the team's closer the following year, and although his ERA rose to 3.71, he managed to lead the league with 41 saves.

Lastly, Rafael Soriano (2010) deserves brief mention, as he was an All-Star for Tampa Bay in 2010, when he posted an impressive 1.73 ERA and led the league with 45 saves (WAR score of 2.1).

Managers

Name	YR	From-To	W-L	PCT	PS	WS
Joe Maddon	9	2006–14	754-705	.517	5	0
Kevin Cash	4	2015–18	317-330	.490	0	0
Lou Piniella	3	2003–05	200-285	.412	0	0
Larry Rothschild	4	1998–2001	205-294	.411	0	0
Hal McRae	2	2001–02	113-196	.366	0	0

There have been only five managers for this franchise to date. **Joe Maddon** has both been at the helm the longest and had the most success, both in terms of overall winning percentage and postseason appearances. After Maddon, I'd rank the managers based largely on winning percentage: **Kevin Cash, Lou Piniella, Larry Rothschild.**

Starting Lineup

What would mythical starting lineups look like for this All-Time roster?

Against RHP:
Carl Crawford LF (L)
Ben Zobrist 2B (S)
Evan Longoria 3B (R)
Carlos Peña 1B (L)
Fred McGriff DH (L)
Aubrey Huff RF (L)
Kevin Kiermaier CF (L)
Dioner Navarro C (S)
Julio Lugo SS (R)

Against LHP:
Carl Crawford LF (L)
Melvin Upton CF (R)
Ben Zobrist 2B (S)
Evan Longoria 3B (R)
Carlos Peña 1B (L)
Rocco Baldelli DH (R)
Steven Souza RF (R)
Toby Hall C (R)
Jason Bartlett SS (R)

The most obvious platoon options were at CF and at C. Peña and McGriff are both left-handed batters, but I was able to include McGriff as DH against RHPs. Bartlett and Lugo were both right-handed batters, but Bartlett hit significantly better against lefties while Lugo's numbers were more even, so I decided to platoon them at SS. And for RF, I decided to get Huff's offense into the lineup against RHP, and then use Souza as the platoon partner against LHP.

Depth Chart

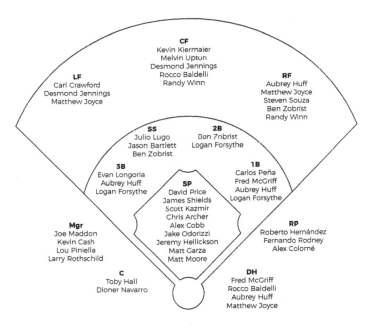

CF
Kevin Kiermaier
Melvin Upton
Desmond Jennings
Rocco Baldelli
Randy Winn

LF
Carl Crawford
Desmond Jennings
Matthew Joyce

RF
Aubrey Huff
Matthew Joyce
Steven Souza
Ben Zobrist
Randy Winn

SS
Julio Lugo
Jason Bartlett
Ben Zobrist

2B
Ben Zobrist
Logan Forsythe

3B
Evan Longoria
Aubrey Huff
Logan Forsythe

1B
Carlos Peña
Fred McGriff
Aubrey Huff
Logan Forsythe

SP
David Price
James Shields
Scott Kazmir
Chris Archer
Alex Cobb
Jake Odorizzi
Jeremy Hellickson
Matt Garza
Matt Moore

Mgr
Joe Maddon
Kevin Cash
Lou Piniella
Larry Rothschild

RP
Roberto Hernández
Fernando Rodney
Alex Colomé

C
Toby Hall
Dioner Navarro

DH
Fred McGriff
Rocco Baldelli
Aubrey Huff
Matthew Joyce

Prospects for Current Players

What are the prospects for current Rays players making this All-Time team? Kiermaier is already on the roster. You could already make a case for Blake Snell, who after two partial seasons broke out with an All-Star campaign in 2018. With such a short history, it won't be too long before others deserve consideration too. We'll see...

Retired Player Numbers

Wade Boggs (12), Don Zimmer (66, coach)

Wade Boggs finished his Hall of Fame career with two seasons on the Devil Rays and then served the team as a hitting coach for a few more seasons.

Top WAR Single Seasons – Hitters (7+)

Name	Year	WAR	AVG	HR	R	RBI	SB	OPS+
Ben Zobrist	2009	8.6	.297	27	91	91	17	149
Evan Longoria	2010	8.2	.294	22	96	104	15	143
Ben Zobrist	2011	7.6	.269	20	99	91	19	131
Kevin Kiermaier	2015	7.5	.263	10	62	40	18	99
Evan Longoria	2011	7.2	.244	31	78	99	3	138
Carlos Peña	2007	7.2	.282	46	99	121	1	172
Evan Longoria	2009	7.0	.281	33	100	113	9	133
Carl Crawford	2010	7.0	.307	19	110	90	47	135

I was not surprised to see Longoria appear the most often on this list. The only surprise to me was Kevin Kiermaier's 2015 score, which was boosted by a very high defensive component.

Top WAR Single Seasons – Pitchers (7+)

Name	Year	WAR	W-L	ERA	IP	SO	ERA+
Blake Snell	2018	9.3	21-5	1.89	180.2	221	219

The Rays franchise never had a pitcher with a 7+ WAR score until 2018 when Blake Snell matured into an ace. With the current Rays not having much pitching depth, and even experimenting with using relievers as "openers," Snell might be the only hurler on this list for a while.

Franchise Player

With honorable mention going to Ben Zobrist and Carl Crawford, this honor had to go to Evan Longoria. He consistently provided a strong power bat to their lineup and superior defense at the hot corner. It seems his tenure in Tampa is over, but for now at least he is their franchise player.

About the Author

For the past ten years, Tom Stone has written on a variety of baseball topics at Seamheads.com. At a very early age Tom started to develop a keen interest in baseball's rich history and statistics, including how to compare players across time. *Now Taking the Field* is the result of nearly twenty years of research, and is the first of several baseball books he plans to write.

Tom is a senior research analyst at i4cp, the Institute for Corporate Productivity, a human capital research firm. He has twenty years of experience in corporate learning and development and the broader human resources industry. He is a popular conference speaker and has spoken at over 150 regional, national, and international conferences on a wide range of topics. He is also co-author of the book *Interact and Engage! 50+ Activities for Virtual Training, Meetings, and Webinars* (ATD Press, 2015).

Tom is married to Kassy LaBorie and lives in Rochester, NY with their son Wyatt and two cats Speedy and Luna.

Bibliography

This bibliography lists the books, articles, fan surveys, etc. referenced in this book in chronological order. I chose this approach rather than alphabetical order by author so that you can more easily track the development of All-Time teams over time (at least the ones I found and was able to include in this book).

1946: *The Chicago Cubs*, by Warren Brown (New York: Putnam, 1946).

1947: *The Washington Senators*, by Morris A. Bealle (Washington: Columbia Publishing Company, 1947).

1949: *The Yankees: A Pictorial History of Baseball's Greatest Club*, by John Durant (New York: Hastings House, 1949).

1949: Fan Survey, as reported in *The White Sox Encyclopedia*, by Richard C. Lindberg (Philadelphia: Temple University Press, 1997).

1953: "50th Yankee Anniversary All-Time Yankee Team," as provided in *The Yankee Encyclopedia*, 4th edition, by Mark Gallagher and Walter LeConte (Champagne: Sports Publishing, 2000).

1957–59: *Sport* magazine series:

- September 1957 – White Sox
- October 1957 – Cardinals
- November 1957 – Braves
- December 1957 – Tigers
- January 1958 – Reds
- February 1958 – Red Sox
- March 1958 – Pirates
- May 1958 – Cubs

- July 1958 – Phillies
- August 1958 – Indians
- September 1958 – Senators
- October 1958 – Athletics
- November 1958 – Orioles
- December 1958 – Dodgers
- January 1959 – Giants
- February 1959 – Yankees

1963: "The All-Yankee Team: The First 60 Years: 1903–1963," as provided in *The New York Yankees 1982 Official Yearbook*, David Szen, ed. (New York Yankee Baseball Co., 1982).

1969: *The Sporting News* Fan Poll, as reported in the July 5 issue.

1980: "Roger Kahn's All-Time Dodger Team," by Roger Kahn, *Sport* magazine, June 1980.

1981: Fan Poll, as reported in *The Giants Encyclopedia*, by Tom Schott and Nick Peters (Champagne: Sports Publishing, 1999).

1981: *The "995" Tigers*, by Fred Smith ([Lathrup Village?]: F.T. Smith, 1981).

1981: *This Date in NY Mets History*, by Dennis D'Agostino (A Scarborough Book, New York: Stein and Day, 1981).

1982: Fan Vote, as reported in *The Boston Red Sox Fan Book*, by David S. Neft, Michael L. Neft, Bob Carroll, and Richard M. Cohen (New York: St. Martin's Griffin, 2002).

1983: *This Date in Baltimore Orioles and St. Louis Browns History*, by John C. Hawkins (A Scarborough Book, New York: Stein and Day, 1983).

1983: "Schmidt Tops Phillies' Fan Voting," *The Sporting News*, August 22, 1983.

1985: "The All-Time A's All-Star Team," by Denis Telgemeier, *Oakland Athletics Magazine*, Vol. 5, No. 4, 1985.

1987: Fan Survey, as reported in the 1995 Pittsburgh Pirates Media Guide.

1990: "All-Time All-Star Teams," by Robert C. Berlo, *The Baseball Research Journal* (Society for American Baseball Research, 1990).

1991: Louisville Slugger collector's edition books, published by Bonanza Books:

- Boston Red Sox, by Dick Lally
- Chicago Cubs, by Dick Lally
- Los Angeles Dodgers, by Bill Shannon
- New York Mets, by Bill Shannon
- New York Yankees, by Dick Lally
- San Francisco Giants, by Bill Shannon

1992: *The All-Time All-Star Baseball Book*, by Nick Acocella and Donald Dewey (Dubuque: Brown & Benchmark, 1992).

1992: Fan Survey, as reported in *The Cardinals Encyclopedia*, by Mike Eisenbath (Philadelphia: Temple University Press, 1999).

1995: *Baseball Ratings*, by Charles F. Faber (Jefferson: McFarland and Company, 1995).

1999: Fan Poll, as reported in *The Giants Encyclopedia*, by Tom Schott and Nick Peters (Champagne: Sports Publishing, 1999).

1999: Fan Survey, as reported in *They Earned Their Stripes: The Detroit Tigers All-Time Team*, Alan Whitt, ed. (Champagne: Sports Publishing, 2000).

1999: Fan Vote for the Pirates Team of the Century, through the Pittsburgh Pirates and the *Pittsburgh Post-Gazette*, as reported in the *Pittsburgh Post-Gazette*, September 19, 1999.

1999: "Team of the Century," as described in the *Minnesota Twins Official Team Yearbook* (1999).

2000: *Red Sox Century: One Hundred Years of Red Sox Baseball*, by Glenn Stout and Richard A. Johnson (Boston: Houghton Mifflin, 2000).

2000: Fan Vote for Chicago White Sox "Team of the Century," with results announced on September 30, 2000. Results provided by the White Sox website.

2001: Fan Ballots in *Boston Globe* Vote, as reported in *The Boston Red Sox Fan Book*, by David S. Neft, Michael L. Neft, Bob Carroll, and Richard M. Cohen (New York: St. Martin's Griffin, 2002).

2001: *Few and Chosen: Defining Yankee Greatness Across the Eras*, by Whitey Ford with Phil Pepe (Chicago: Triumph Books, 2001).

2002: *Yankees Century: 100 Years of New York Yankees Baseball*, by Glenn Stout (Boston: Houghton Mifflin, 2002).

2002: *The Padres Encyclopedia*, by David Porter and Joe Naiman (Champagne: Sports Publishing, 2002).

2003: *Rob Neyer's Big Book of Baseball Lineups*, by Rob Neyer (New York: Simon and Schuster, 2003).

2003: *Few and Chosen: Defining Cardinal Greatness Across the Eras*, by Tim McCarver with Phil Pepe (Chicago: Triumph Books, 2003).

2004: *The Red Sox Century*, by Alan Ross (Nashville: Cumberland House Publishing, 2004).

2004: *Few and Chosen: Defining Red Sox Greatness Across the Eras*, by Johnny Pesky with Phil Pepe (Chicago: Triumph Books, 2004).

2005: *Few and Chosen: Defining Cubs Greatness Across the Eras*, by Ron Santo with Phil Pepe (Chicago: Triumph Books, 2005).

2006: *Few and Chosen: Defining Dodgers Greatness Across the Eras*, by Duke Snider with Phil Pepe (Chicago: Triumph Books, 2006).

2007: *Few and Chosen: Defining Giants Greatness Across the Eras*, by Bobby Thomson with Phil Pepe (Chicago: Triumph Books, 2007).

2009: *Jerry Remy's Red Sox Heroes*, by Jerry Remy with Corey Sandler (Guilford: The Lyons Press, 2009).

2009: *Few and Chosen: Defining Mets Greatness Across the Eras*, by Rusty Staub with Phil Pepe (Chicago: Triumph Books, 2009).

2010: *Few and Chosen: Defining Tigers Greatness Across the Eras*, by Lance Parrish with Phil Pepe (Chicago: Triumph Books, 2010).

2010: "The All-Time Atlanta Braves All-Star Team," by Terry W. Sloope, published in *The National Pastime: Baseball in the Peach State*, Ken Fenster and Wynn Montgomery, eds. (Cleveland: Society for American Baseball Research, 2010).

2012: *Few and Chosen: Defining Phillies Greatness Across the Eras*, by Gary Matthews with Phil Pepe (Chicago: Triumph Books, 2012).

2016: *101 All-Time Fantasy Baseball Teams*, by Jack Sweeney (Wrightsville Beach: Simply Francis Publishing Company, 2016).